ALSO BY TOM CHAFFIN

*Fatal Glory: Narciso López and
the First Clandestine U.S. War Against Cuba*

PATHFINDER

PATHFINDER

JOHN CHARLES FRÉMONT AND

THE COURSE OF AMERICAN EMPIRE

TOM CHAFFIN

 HILL AND WANG

A DIVISION OF FARRAR, STRAUS AND GIROUX

NEW YORK

Hill and Wang
A division of Farrar, Straus and Giroux
19 Union Square West, New York 10003

Copyright © 2002 by Tom Chaffin
Distributed in Canada by Douglas & McIntyre Ltd.
Printed in the United States of America
Published in 2002 by Hill and Wang
First paperback edition, 2004

The Library of Congress has cataloged the hardcover edition as follows:
Chaffin, Tom.
    Pathfinder : John Charles Frémont and the course of American empire /
Tom Chaffin.
        p. cm.
    Includes bibliographical references and index.
    ISBN 0-8090-7557-1 (hc : alk. paper)
    1. Frémont, John Charles, 1813–1890. 2. Explorers—United States—
Biography. 3. Explorers—West (U.S.)—Biography. 4. West (U.S.)—
Discovery and exploration. 5. United States—Territorial expansion.
6. Generals—United States—Biography. 7. Presidential candidates—
United States—Biography. I. Title.

E415.9.F8 C48 2002
973.6′092—dc21
[B]   2002023306

Paperback ISBN: 0-8090-7556-3
EAN: 978-0-8090-7556-0

Designed by Jonathan D. Lippincott

www.fsgbooks.com

1 3 5 7 9 10 8 6 4 2

Frontispiece: John Frémont in a circa 1850s engraving. (Author's collection)

To Meta and Zoie, good traveling companions

Westward the course of empire takes its way;
The four first acts already past,
A fifth shall close the drama with the day:
Time's noblest offspring is the last.
                              —George Berkeley

Fremont, the pathfinder of empire. . . . To his hands was committed
the magnificent task of opening the golden gates of our Pacific empire.
                              —*U.S. Magazine and Democratic Review*

If one could seize America
Or at least a fine forgetfulness
That seeps into our outline
Defining our volumes with a stain
That is fleeting too

But commemorates
Because it does define . . .
                              —John Ashbery

CONTENTS

ACKNOWLEDGMENTS

In writing this book, I've drawn on the work of many fine scholars of John and Jessie Frémont—including Frederick Dellenbaugh, Patricia Richmond, Ferol Egan, Pamela Herr, Donald Jackson, Allan Nevins, Andrew Rolle, and Vernon Volpe. Other historians whose works proved particularly helpful include Fred Anderson, Hubert Howe Bancroft, Martha Coleman Bray, William Nesbit Chambers, William Goetzmann, Neal Harlow, Frederick Merk, Peter Onuf, James Hart, Richard Koebner, D. W. Meinig, Francis Prucha, Henry Nash Smith, Kevin Starr, Robert Utley, and Richard Van Alstyne.

The geographical and thematic breadth of John's Frémont's life led me to call more directly on the help of many other historians. During that process, I was repeatedly touched by their generosity in sharing knowledge. These hearty souls include Michael Bellesiles, Louis Gerteis, Michael Holt, Steven K. Madsen, John Parker, Malcolm J. Rohrbough, and David Weber. Patricia Richmond, chronicler of Frémont's railroad surveys, displayed astounding generosity in sharing her vast knowledge of her beloved San Juan Mountains, and I was particularly touched by the kindness of John Logan Allen, Pam Herr, Jere Krakow and Bob Graham, who read and graciously commented upon the entire manuscript. Bob, who has generously fielded scores of Frémont-related questions over the past few years, also maintains a fine Web site—www.longcamp.com—devoted to Frémont and exploration of the American West.

Deep gratitude also goes out to Frémont scholar ne plus ultra Mary Lee Spence for her early encouragement of this book, for her own published works on the subject, and for her patient fielding of questions along the way. Thanks, too, to librarians and archivists at the following institutions: the Bancroft Library, at the University of California at Berkeley; the California Historical Society; the Society of California Pioneers, in San Francisco; the California State Library, in Sacramento; the College of Charleston's College Archives; the Colorado Historical Society, in Denver; the Copley Library, in La Jolla, California; the Denver Public Library's Western History Department; the Georgia Historical Society; the University of Kentucky; the Library of Congress; the Long Distance Trails Office of the National Park Service, in Salt Lake City; the Minnesota Historical Society; the Missouri Botanical Garden Library; the Missouri Historical Society, in St. Louis; the State Historical Society of Missouri, in Columbia; the National Archives, in Washington; the New York Botanical Garden Library; the New-York Historical Society; the New York Public Library; the Park-McCullough House, in North Bennington, Vermont; University Library's Department of Special Collections at Princeton University; the Rockefeller Archives Center, Sleepy Hollow, New York; the South Carolina Historical Society, in Charleston; the Southwest Museum, in Los Angeles; the Department of Special Collections at the University of California at Los Angeles; the Utah Historical Society, in Salt Lake City; the Department of Special Collections at the University of Vermont; and the Library of the Henry Francis du Pont Winterthur Museum, Winterthur, Delaware. For research help in Washington, thanks to Barbara Kraft. And at Emory University, I'm grateful to the staff of the Robert W. Woodruff Library, most particularly my friends and colleagues Marie Nitschke and Marie Hansen, as well as the staffs of the Reference and Interlibrary Loan Departments. Gratitude is also due Ceja Cooper for his help with photo reproductions and to Barb Moore for her amazing computer expertise.

While writing this book, I had the good fortune to spend nine months as a visiting postdoctoral fellow at the Huntington Library, in San Marino, California. For assistance during my time there, I owe deep gratitude to that wonderful library's entire staff and associated scholars—especially Roy Ritchie, Carolyn Powell, Martin Ridge, Peter Blodgett, Jennifer Martinez, Andrew Rolle, Alan Jutzi, Susi Krasnoo, Jean-Robert Durbin, and Mona Noureldin. Thanks as well to fellow visiting Huntington scholars Ed Gray, Johann Sommerville, and Alan Trachtenberg. Conversations with Alan during Sunday morning bird-watching walks in Pasadena's Arroyo Seco were a true pleasure. For funding the fellowship, I'm deeply grateful to the Andrew W. Mellon Foundation. Besides providing a wonderful research opportunity, my stint at the Huntington allowed me to rekindle my long-standing love affair with the place that John Frémont so aptly christened the Golden State, to discover the splendors of hiking in the brittle but verdant San Gabriels—and to joyfully vanquish all those venal anti–Southern California prejudices gathered during earlier residences north of Santa Barbara.

For their gracious Western hospitality, I thank my friends Jack and Julie Haynes, Steve Rubenstein and Caroline Grannan, Rick and Linda Allen, Dennis and Helen Darling, and Michael and Edith Robertson. And for their kindnesses in New York City, thanks to Steve and Linda Johnson. At Hill and Wang, I thank my talented editors Lauren Osborne, Catherine Newman, and Thomas LeBien for their support and hard work on the book. Gratitude is also due to editorial assistant Kristy McGowan, and to Margaret Ritchie for her astute copyediting. For their friendship and good cheer, I'm grateful to my friends Steve Oney, Ernie Freeberg, Tim Ralston, and Steve Enniss, and to the gang down at Manuel's Tavern. Thanks, too, to faithful canine friend Zoie for her joyous presence on walks, on trips down Frémont's routes, and at home, where, curled on her blanket beneath my desk, she softened the countless hours of writing. And, finally, once again, *tack så mycket* to my wife Meta Larsson—for her abiding love, wisdom, and friendship. Never could I have imagined how a chance encounter, almost two decades ago, on a bridge in Stockholm, outside the Riksdagshuset—Sweden's parliament building—could turn out so well.

CHRONOLOGY

1843   First Expedition *Report* and map published

1843–44   Frémont's Second Expedition

1845   Combined First and Second Expedition *Reports* published, with new map

1845–46   Frémont's Third Expedition

1846   Buchanan-Pakenham Treaty ends U.S.-British joint occupation of Oregon

1846   California Bear Flag Republic

1846–48   Mexican War

1847   Treaty of Cahuenga ends Mexican War in California

1847   Preuss's seven-section map series of Oregon Trail published

1847   Frémont is military governor of California Territory

1847   Frémont court-martialed

1848   Treaty of Guadalupe Hidalgo ends Mexican War

1848   Gold discovered in California

1848–49   Frémont's first San Juan Mountains railroad survey

1849   Gold strike on Frémont Las Mariposas estate in California

1850   Compromise of 1850

1850   California statehood and Frémont's brief term in the U.S. Senate

1853–54   Second San Juan Mountains railroad survey

1854   Kansas-Nebraska Act

1856   Frémont-Buchanan presidential race

1861–65   Civil War

1861   Frémont commands U.S. Army Department of the West

1862   Frémont commands U.S. Army Mountain Department

1869   U.S. transcontinental railroad and Suez Canal both completed

1871   Frémont's conviction in France of fraud in sale of railroad bonds

1878–81   Frémont is governor of Arizona Territory

1887   Frémont's *Memoirs* published

1890   Frémont dies in New York City

1898   Spanish-American War

1902   Jessie Frémont dies in Los Angeles

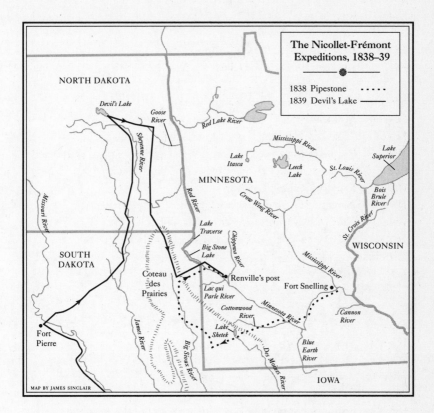

The Nicollet-Frémont Expeditions, 1838–39

1838 Pipestone · · · · ·
1839 Devil's Lake ———

NORTH DAKOTA

Devil's Lake

Goose River

Sheyenne River

Red Lake River

Missouri River

Mississippi River

Lake Itasca

Leech Lake

St. Louis River

Lake Superior

MINNESOTA

Crow Wing River

Bois Brule River

Red River

Lake Traverse

Chippewa River

St. Croix River

WISCONSIN

SOUTH DAKOTA

Big Stone Lake

Coteau des Prairies

Renville's post

Mississippi River

Lac qui Parle River

Fort Snelling

Cottonwood River

Minnesota River

Cannon River

James River

Lake Shetek

Big Sioux River

Blue Earth River

Fort Pierre

Des Moines River

IOWA

MAP BY JAMES SINCLAIR

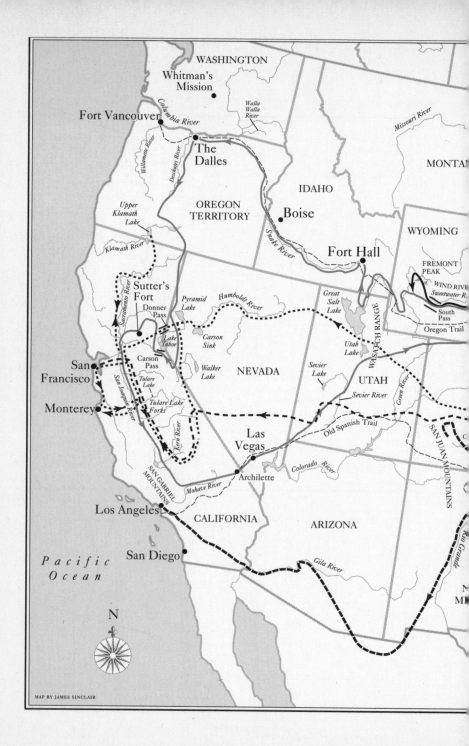

WASHINGTON

Whitman's
Mission

Fort Vancouver

Columbia River

Walla
Walla
River

The
Dalles

Willamette River

Deschutes River

OREGON
TERRITORY

IDAHO

Boise

MONTA

Missouri River

WYOMING

FREMONT
PEAK

WIND RIVE

Sweetwater R.

Upper
Klamath
Lake

Klamath River

Snake River

Fort Hall

South
Pass

Oregon Trail

Sutter's
Fort

Donner
Pass

Sacramento River

Pyramid
Lake

Humboldt River

Great
Salt
Lake

WASATCH RANGE

Lake
Tahoe

*Carson
Sink*

Utah
Lake

San
Francisco

Carson
Pass

*Tulare
Lake*

Walker
Lake

NEVADA

Sevier
Lake

UTAH

Green River

Monterey

San Joaquin River

Tulare Lake
Forks

Kern River

Sevier River

SAN JUAN MOUNTAINS

Las
Vegas

Old Spanish Trail

Archilette

Colorado River

SAN GABRIEL
MOUNTAINS

Mohave River

Los Angeles

CALIFORNIA

ARIZONA

San Diego

Gila River

N
MI

Rio Grande

*Pacific
Ocean*

N

MAP BY JAMES SINCLAIR

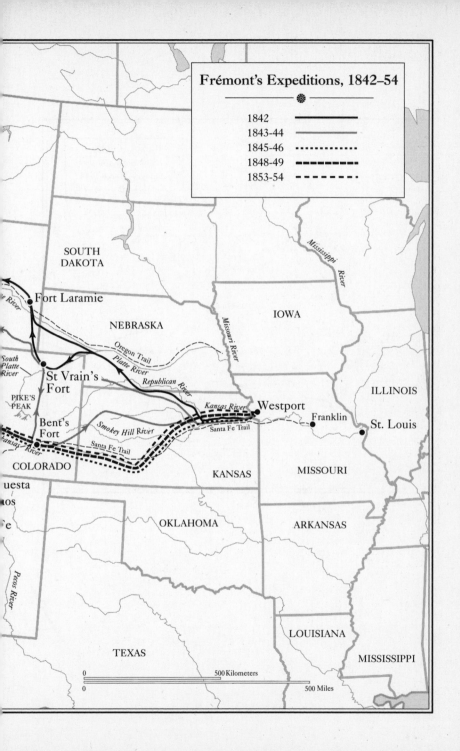

Frémont's Expeditions, 1842–54

1842	
1843-44	
1845-46	
1848-49	
1853-54	

SOUTH DAKOTA

Mississippi River

Fort Laramie

NEBRASKA

IOWA

Oregon Trail

Missouri River

South Platte River

St Vrain's Fort

Platte River

Republican River

ILLINOIS

PIKE'S PEAK

Kansas River

Westport

Franklin

St. Louis

Bent's Fort

Smokey Hill River

Santa Fe Trail

Arkansas River

Santa Fe Trail

COLORADO

uesta

os

KANSAS

MISSOURI

e

OKLAHOMA

ARKANSAS

Pecos River

LOUISIANA

MISSISSIPPI

TEXAS

0   500 Kilometers

0   500 Miles

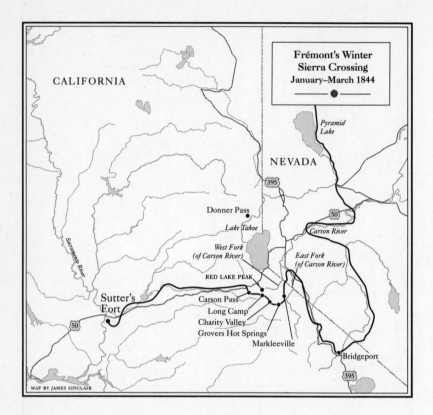

CALIFORNIA

**Frémont's Winter
Sierra Crossing**
January–March 1844

Pyramid
Lake

NEVADA

395

50

Donner Pass

Lake Tahoe

Carson River

West Fork
(of Carson River)

East Fork
(of Carson River)

Sacramento River

RED LAKE PEAK

Sutter's
Fort

Carson Pass

50

Long Camp

Charity Valley

Grovers Hot Springs

Markleeville

Bridgeport

395

MAP BY JAMES SINCLAIR

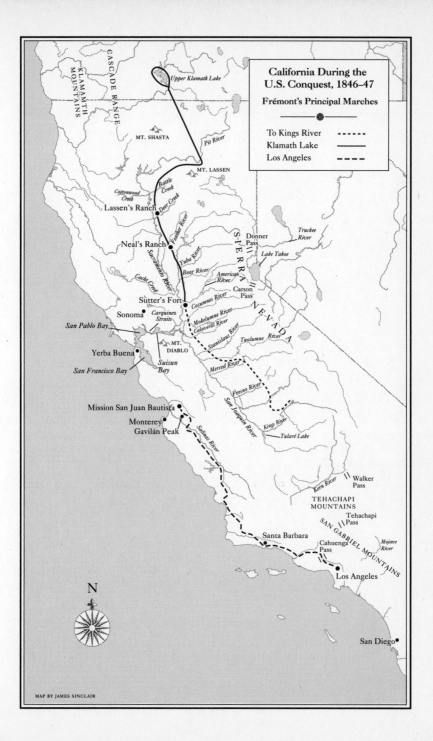

California During the U.S. Conquest, 1846–47

Frémont's Principal Marches

To Kings River
Klamath Lake
Los Angeles

CASCADE RANGE

KLAMAMTH MOUNTAINS

Upper Klamath Lake

MT. SHASTA

Pit River

MT. LASSEN

Battle Creek

Cottonwood Creek

Lassen's Ranch

Deer Creek

Feather River

Neal's Ranch

Sacramento River

Yuba River

Bear River

SIERRA

Donner Pass

Truckee River

Lake Tahoe

American River

NEVADA

Carson Pass

Cache Creek

Sutter's Fort

Cosumnes River

Sonoma

Carquinez Straits

Mokelumne River

Calaveras River

San Pablo Bay

Stanislaus River

Tuolumne River

MT. DIABLO

Yerba Buena

Suisun Bay

Merced River

San Francisco Bay

Fresno River

San Joaquin River

Mission San Juan Bautista

Monterey

Gavilán Peak

Salinas River

Kings River

Tularé Lake

Kern River

Walker Pass

TEHACHAPI MOUNTAINS

Tehachapi Pass

Santa Barbara

Cahuenga Pass

SAN GABRIEL MOUNTAINS

Mojave River

Los Angeles

San Diego

N

MAP BY JAMES SINCLAIR

PREFACE:
HOW THE WEST WAS LOST

THERE ARE PLACES in the American West—a mountaintop, say, or a parking lot—where you can stand and know that John Charles Frémont stopped there and wrote down what he saw. One of the more controversial figures of his era, Frémont was, variously, a leader in the U.S. conquest of California, a gold and railroad speculator, a U.S. senator, the first presidential candidate of the Republican Party, and a Union general in the Civil War. But it is Frémont "the Pathfinder" who is best remembered. During the 1840s, on three successive exploring expeditions for the United States Army Corps of Topographical Engineers, he surveyed and mapped the Missouri-to-Oregon emigrant corridor soon known as the Oregon Trail, as well as substantial portions of California and today's Utah, Nevada, and Colorado.

While writing this book, I tried to retrace Frémont's routes by car, and occasionally on foot. Using the explorer's own journals and maps, along with modern topographical and highway maps, I sought critical river junctures, mountain passes, campsites, and scenes of key incidents. Did I find my topographical quarry? In some cases, yes; in others, no. Frémont's maps and exploration narratives are often too imprecise to inspire certainty of place. I'm also sure that I made my own share of directional errors. I found no physical artifacts, nor did I expect to. Even so, I'm confident I did find some of his campsites. On one particularly splendid spring morning, up at the Sierra Nevada's Carson Pass, I strapped on snowshoes and, led by mountaineer Bob Graham, hiked up to Frémont's "Long Camp," which the explorer established during his epic 1844 winter crossing of that range. Graham, a retired farmer from Sacramento—using Frémont's writings, modern topographical maps, and GPS technology—had discovered the site during his own rambles through the Sierras.

In relative terms, of course, the 1840s are not that distant. But a century and a half does allow ample opportunity for rivers to wander, for riparian islands to sink and new ones to arise. It's also time enough for arid plains to be churned into lush farmlands, for entire valleys that once boasted sublime waterfalls and rock formations to disappear under vast, monotonous reservoirs. And as recent ecological and historical research has reminded us, long before Europeans came to North America, human and nonhuman forces were already shaping and reshaping our wildernesses.

Many topographical changes in the West have played out on a grand scale—including the disappearance and introduction of entire species. Some are well-known: the vast buffalo herds are gone, and the great grassland prairies have given way to today's Midwestern corn- and wheatfields. Other changes are less obvious: the Russian olive, manzanita, and blue-gum eucalyptus, for instance—plants that by now appear to have always belonged in the West—are introduced species. Count "virgin land," then, among the most seductive of the mirages conjured by the continent's first white settlers.

But some, even then, saw through the mirage. Frémont, during an 1839 expedition up the Missouri River, could not help but notice how the surrounding landscape's silence was continually punctured by the "incessant crumbling away of the banks and bars, which the river was steadily undermining and destroying at one place to build up at another." Still later, while working their way across today's Kansas, he and his survey party found themselves almost overcome by one of the typical prairie wildfires that—before mass agriculture and irrigation— once continually reshaped the West's vast wildernesses.

John Frémont's wife, Jessie Benton Frémont, during the couple's twilight years wrote, "All your campfires have become cities." Had she lived another century, she might well have added, "and all your rivers have become industrial and agricultural channels." "So many of these Western rivers by now are really just a series of lakes divided by dams," Ed Sperry, a Montana state court judge I met while camping, mused one night as we gazed into a pristinely clear, starry night in the Rockies. "They're turned on and off just like a spigot."

All the Western rivers along which Frémont traveled in the 1840s—the Missouri, the Platte, the Sweetwater, the Snake, the Columbia—have been rerouted, dammed, and drowned by the forces of mass transportation, urbanization, and mechanized irrigation and agriculture that his explorations helped nurture. So many place-names along Frémont's trail—from the Snake River's "Thousand Springs" to the Columbia River's "Cascades"—bear witness to sublime displays of nature long ago vanquished by hydrological engineering. Frémont envisioned the West's great rivers as conduits for future continental transportation and communication. But few travel on these rivers anymore, and no one uses them for communication.

✸

I began where Frémont began, about twenty miles north of St. Louis, on the Mississippi's eastern (Illinois) side. My wife, Meta Larsson, our dog, Zoie, and I drove up State Highway 3 to catch a view of the Missouri where it joins the Mississippi on the opposite bank. At the litter-strewn point from which we gazed across the Mississippi and saw its union with the Missouri, there stands a fading, weed-choked colonnade dedicated to Lewis and Clark. The two explorers had wintered in the area in 1804, before beginning their own epic trip up the Missouri River and over the Continental Divide to the Pacific Coast. Strange, it occurred to me, that this place—once the point of departure for so much Western exploration and settlement—should be, today, so forlorn, so bleak.

Farther west, in North Platte, Nebraska, good fortune introduced us to rancher Larry Golden, whose spread takes in the point where the Platte splits into its north and south forks. Golden welcomed us, proudly showed us around his water-fringed ranch. But when asked to show us the spot on his property where Frémont camped—at the point formed by the forks' split—he quickly answered that it would not be possible. The Platte River's channels there, he said, have been, over the years, so reconfigured by nature and the U.S. Army Corps of Engineers that they bear little relation to what they looked like—or where they flowed—even 50, much less 150, years ago.

In still other places along Frémont's trail, the landscape remains relatively undisturbed, but the historical record nonetheless lies hope-

xxvi ❋ PREFACE: HOW THE WEST WAS LOST

lessly entangled in myth and lore. North of Monterey, California, in Fremont Peak State Park, for instance, park officials are quick to say that few historians believe any longer what the park's historical markers still commemorate—the explorer's camping atop the park's namesake peak and there becoming the first person to raise Old Glory on California soil. Likewise, in Wyoming's Wind River Range, where Frémont famously climbed what he thought, erroneously, to be the Rockies' highest peak. There, historians and mountaineers can't even agree on which mountain he ascended: Was it Fremont Peak, as was once assumed? Or neighboring Woodrow Wilson or Gannett Peak?

Legal and political boundaries posed still other problems. In southern Idaho, our inability to obtain a "trespass permit" from the Shoshone Indians thwarted plans to inspect the ruins of Fort Hall, a Hudson's Bay Company fort that Frémont's party called on during his Second Expedition, in 1843.

The division and subdivision of once open lands into an infinity of privately held or otherwise restricted parcels yielded similar problems. Just outside tiny Plattsmouth, Nebraska, we found the confluence of the Platte and Missouri Rivers. Might we visit the now-fenced-in forested point where the two rivers meet, and where Frémont camped? It's owned by the PCS Nitrogen chemical company, we were warned; and they forbid visitors.

We encountered a similar story in Wyoming's Sweetwater River valley, along a stretch Frémont recalled "as exceedingly picturesque." There, he recalled, "Everywhere its deep verdure and profusion of beautiful flowers are in pleasant contrast with the sterile grandeur of the rock and the barrenness of the sandy plain." But in the 1950s, this riparian enclave became the site of a uranium mine. The mine went bust in the 1980s; and today the place lies strictly off-limits. The groundwater is polluted with acid, heavy metals, and uranium. Weed-tracked gravel roads run from semideserted mining towns to poetically named oil and gas fields (Crooks Gap, Jade, Antelope, Sheep Creek) scattered among hills with names like Oil Field Mountain and Telephone Line Ridge.

❋

Of course, most of the research for this book was conducted on the indoor paper geography of archives, libraries, books, memoirs, newspapers, letters, and maps. The mosquitoes aren't as bad there, but there, too, Frémont proved an elusive quarry. Was he hero or scoundrel? A poseur or the real thing? Skeptics asked such questions during his lifetime; and those questions persist to this day—among both historians and popular artists. In recent years, the Frémont enigma has provided fodder for such novelists as Irving Stone (*Immortal Wife*, 1944), David Nevin (*Dream West*, 1983), and Cecelia Holland (*Bear Flag*, 1990). Indeed, in a 1986 adaptation of *Dream West*, actor Richard Chamberlain saddled up for a star turn as the Pathfinder in a seven-hour CBS television miniseries.

While traditionalists venerate Frémont as a hero carrying liberty's light into the West, revisionists dismiss him as an advance scout for U.S. imperialism and anti-Indian genocidal policies. Still other critics consider Frémont one of the great hollow men of American history—a blowhard as an explorer, a con man as a businessman, a cipher as a politician, an abject failure as a military commander. Some even question his authorship of the government-published exploration narratives by which he achieved his first fame. By now, I've reached the conclusion that both views—those of the traditionalists and of the revisionists—enjoy a certain factual validity, but that, in the end, the Pathfinder was a far more complex figure than either have imagined him to be.

How did a man who, by the mid-1840s, enjoyed such wide acclaim come to be, in some circles, so widely despised by the time of his death in 1890? At the outset, let us stipulate that there is no way to disentangle Frémont from the federal government's ongoing Indian removal policies of the nineteenth century. On the subject of Indians, the explorer—regardless of whatever else he accomplished—was very much of his day. Beyond their purely scientific achievements, his government-sponsored expeditions advanced U.S. militarization, fortification, conquest, and settlement in the American West.

Beyond that—for reasons ranging from arrogance to sheer bad luck—Frémont during his lifetime accumulated, in addition to his many friends and admirers, a host of formidable enemies, including General Stephen Watts Kearny, the philosopher Josiah Royce, and

Frank Blair of Washington's powerful Blair family. More than any other relationship, however, it was Frémont's Civil War clashes with President Lincoln that diminished his reputation. For, in the years after Lincoln's death, as the fallen President rose in stature, so did Frémont inversely shrink.

Still other, uniquely personal circumstances explain the demise of Frémont's reputation. He won international acclaim through something he was very good at, leading scientific exploring expeditions, only to, through that success, be lifted into other positions—military general, politician, and mining and railroad magnate—for which he lacked equivalent gifts. In the last role particularly, Frémont compounded his problems by a lifelong inattention to financial details that, in time, bordered on outright fraud.

Ironically, too, John and Jessie's own strident efforts, through public statements and writings, to burnish John's reputation probably also had the effect of diminishing it. By overstating John's achievements, they managed to distract contemporaries, as well as later historians, from his very real accomplishments.

Among other acts given short shrift was Frémont's principled opposition to slavery. Long before he ran for public office, he held firm political convictions as a Unionist and an opponent of slavery. And, in 1856, as the Republican Party's first presidential nominee, Frémont was actively involved in that campaign much more than historians have realized. Furthermore, by drawing abolitionists, pacifists, women's rights advocates, and other reformers into the nation's political life, the Frémont campaign brought a sense of inclusion to numerous groups previously alienated from American politics. As poet and Frémont supporter William Cullen Bryant put it at the time, "A very large class of persons who never took any interest in elections are zealous Frémonters now—among these are clergymen and Quakers and [past] indifferents of all sorts."

Frémont lost that election to Buchanan, but his opposition to slavery remained undiminished. Indeed, his emancipation proclamation of 1861, liberating slaves owned by rebel sympathizers in Missouri —which led President Lincoln to fire him as major general—also arguably paved the way for Lincoln's own broader Emancipation Proclamation two years later.

Frémont's performance as major general in the Department of the West has similarly been underrated. In 1861 Missouri, he inherited a dire military situation: outside St. Louis, guerrilla warfare flared throughout the state; and just outside Missouri, Confederates were amassing for an invasion. Though lacking adequate troops and matériel, Frémont managed to hold St. Louis and Missouri for the Union. Before his dismissal by President Lincoln, he also devised the strategy, began the construction of the armada, and installed the general— Ulysses S. Grant—that made possible the later run of victories which won the Union control over the Mississippi, thus fatally dividing the Confederacy into two weakened eastern and western sections.

But it was Frémont's explorations that stamped the most enduring imprint upon the nation's life. A born geographer, the Pathfinder possessed a jeweler's eye for assaying landscapes and ascertaining how mountains, river drainages, valleys, and lakes link up into a continental whole. He placed mapmaking of the American West on a scientific foundation. Equally important, his federal expeditions and his writings revealed the American West to be far more topographically and ecologically variegated—and more amenable to human settlement and agriculture—than previously imagined.

During his expeditions, Frémont and the men of his exploring parties walked thousands of miles, surviving on paltry rations and whatever game they could find. They endured extremes of cold, heat, wind and rain, as well as dangers incomprehensible to modern sensibilities. In most cases, Frémont enjoyed the adulation of the men he commanded. And in an era before specialists came to dominate scientific exploration, he functioned as a one-man-band scientist—expedition geologist, meteorologist, astronomer, and botanist. To meet those tasks, he worked day and night, displaying a peerlessly dogged determination.

✱

By forcing Americans—even those who would never visit the region— to reimagine the American West, he also compelled them to reimagine America itself—to conceive of their nation, for the first time, as a sea-to-sea empire. Walt Whitman—one of many Frémont admirers who never set foot in the Far West—celebrating the breadth of the American continent, would soon proclaim:

> My ties and ballasts leave me, my elbows rest in sea-gaps,
> I skirt sierras, my palms cover continents,
> I am afoot with my vision.

The Good Grey Poet was traveling on his own itinerary, but he got his maps from the Pathfinder.

PATHFINDER

PROLOGUE

AMID A WINDY SNOWSTORM in December of 1887, an elderly couple climbed aboard a train about to leave Manhattan's Grand Central Depot for Los Angeles. As they settled into their seats in a first-class car, the elderly man began coughing violently. His bronchitis had been aggravated by the blustery winds that buffeted their ferry crossing of the Hudson River, earlier in the day.

Though hardly tall, the man bore a stately dignity. A neatly clipped gray beard framed his long face. He was older than his wife by a decade. But she, a corpulent woman with stooped shoulders, looked the frailer. Both were well-dressed, and from the quiet stares and whispered comments of the other passengers, it was apparent that the couple was famous. But they were far from wealthy. The tickets for this trip, as well as the money they carried, had been donated by the man who owned the railroad. They were too poor to buy the tickets, and this white-haired gentleman was too old to cross the continent the way he had so many times as a young man—on foot, on mule- and horseback, and by canoe, leading caravans of scientists, soldiers, and mountain men across wild, then unnamed, mountains and deserts. But at the age of seventy-four, that was all long ago.

Not many years back, he would have refused the charity of Collis P. Huntington, the sixty-five-year-old president of the Central and Southern Pacific railroads. From the old man's perspective, his acute bronchitis and his doctor's order that he move to a warmer climate altered nothing. Personal dignity dictated that the tickets be refused. But like other men who had won fortunes in the construction of the nation's growing matrix of transcontinental rail lines, Huntington had profited from the geographical information gathered by John Charles Frémont's expeditions. So when the old explorer expressed his reservations about accepting the tickets, the rail magnate had a ready rejoinder. "You forget," Huntington said, "our road goes over your buried campfires and climbs many a grade you jogged over on a mule; I think we rather owe you this."[1]

PART I

APPRENTICESHIPS

1813–41

Shut in to narrow limits, the mind is driven in upon it-self.   —John Frémont

THE RISING EMPIRE 1

JOHN CHARLES FRÉMONT lived a life whose epic breadth, romantic aura, and dramatic bends and curves resembled that of a character invented by, say, Theodore Dreiser, Joseph Conrad—or, better yet, James Fenimore Cooper. It was Cooper, after all, who conjured the original "Pathfinder." In his 1840 novel of that title, Cooper hung the sobriquet on his plucky frontier protagonist, Natty Bumppo.

Two years later, when Frémont caught the eye of the American public, the editors of that era's penny press simply transferred the title to the dashingly handsome twenty-nine-year-old explorer. But Frémont was seldom a true pathfinder in that word's literal sense, and—except during his 1856 presidential campaign, in which his political handlers incessantly invoked the term—he never called himself one. He tended to survey already-established paths. Even so, in the explorer's widely read tales of his Western adventures, the public found enough Natty Bumppo to make the title seem apt. By compelling U.S. citizens to reimagine the geographic breadth and diversity of their nation, John Frémont more than earned the Pathfinder title.

❀

As a leader of scientific expeditions, Frémont was often brilliant but also impulsive, vainglorious, and given to quixotic behavior. As a military leader, his actions were often even more inscrutable: he was impetuous and, throughout his life, displayed a career-crippling disdain for authority. Though rumors of libertinism and suggestions of financial improbity followed him through his life, he was otherwise rigorously self-disciplined, and austere in his personal habits. He avoided sharing a tent with anyone who smoked, he limited his drinking to the occasional splash of claret in a glass of water, and chess was his rowdiest indulgence.

The explorer's name endures in the names of over a hundred U.S. places—ranging from counties and towns to mountains and rivers. His legacy endures, too, in California's state flag, patterned after the Bear Flag Revolt to which he lent his name, and in the scores of Western places that he named—from the Great Basin to the Humboldt River to the Golden Gate.

Frémont's career transpired before Americans parsed travel distances with automobile odometers and frequent flier points. Though he lived long enough to take trains across the country, his glory years belonged to an era when travelers seldom moved faster than the speed of a galloping horse. And no one of that era saw more of the North American continent than John C. Frémont, not even Lewis and Clark. They, after all, made but one transcontinental expedition. Frémont participated in ten exploring expeditions—four of them transcontinental crossings.

Even a cursory survey of the nineteenth century's most significant writers—including Whittier, Greeley, Emerson, and Whitman—reveals that Frémont held a central position in U.S. public life. That, after all, is why the Republicans twice called him to run for the presidency. And why President Lincoln appointed him, to command the Union's forces in the Department of the West. This explorer, mapper, naturalist, Indian fighter, soldier, politician, and railroad speculator embodied U.S. expansionism. As the nominal leader of the U.S. conquest of California, Frémont stood at the end of the nation's long push to the Pacific coast. Equally important were his ties, direct and indirect, to earlier expansionists. Frémont was, after all, the son-in-law and protégé of Thomas Hart Benton, the U.S. Senate's chief advocate and architect of U.S. expansion into the Trans-Missouri West,* and

---

*Senator Thomas Hart Benton (1782–1858) was a great-uncle of fellow Missourian and famed American painter Thomas Hart Benton (1889–1975).

history had linked Benton to Thomas Jefferson, the Louisiana Purchase, and Lewis and Clark.

❋

A thoroughly Byronic figure, Frémont was born in Savannah, Georgia, and grew up in Charleston, South Carolina, where he received his formal education at the College of Charleston. During the 1830s, he assisted government surveys of the Cherokee country of Georgia, North Carolina, and Tennessee, and of the broad plateau between the Upper Mississippi and the Missouri Rivers. During the 1840s, he led three federally funded exploring expeditions of the West that captured the public's imagination and inspired thousands of Easterners—often with Frémont's expedition reports in hand—to move west.

Frémont's expedition writings, published initially by the U.S. Senate and widely reissued by private publishers, made him the mid-nineteenth century's chief popularizer of the American West. "Until the late explorations conducted by Col. Frémont [sic], very erroneous ideas have prevailed in regard to the character of the country to the westward of the Rocky Mountains," DeBow's Review noted in 1849. "It was customary to denounce it a hopeless, sterile waste, where the arts of civilized men could never prevail."[1]

The scientific knowledge Frémont collected advanced the West's fortification, settlement, agriculture, and mining—as well as the federal government's ongoing subjugation of Indian peoples. Moreover, his explorations vanquished centuries of cartographic errors from the maps—everything from continent-shrinking distortions to mythical rivers and lakes. As Arctic explorer Adolphus Greely assessed the explorer's legacy in 1893, "In few instances did it fall to Frémont's lot to first explore any section of the country, but it was his good fortune, as it was his intent, to first contribute systematic, extended, and reliable data as to climate, elevation, physical conditions, and geographical positions."[2] Equally important—perhaps more important—Frémont, though never a political philosopher—indeed, by all accounts, never much given to abstract thoughts—nevertheless compelled Americans to rethink the literal, political, and metaphysical contours of what citizens of that day were not embarrassed to call the American empire.

Writing to President James K. Polk in the summer of 1846, U.S. Navy commodore Robert Stockton concluded, praising the U.S. forces who had placed California under Old Glory's dominion, "They deserve it, they did the work; and have secured by their toil and daring this beautiful Empire."[3] Evoking the same spirit, journalist Bayard Taylor entitled his collection of dispatches from mid-nineteenth-century California *Eldorado, or Adventures in the Path of Empire*. And *Littell's Living Age*, in 1850, noting John Frémont's role in pushing America's westward expansion, lauded "his controlling energy in the extension of our empire."

For Franklin, Washington, Jefferson, and other Founding Fathers, such approving talk of American empire would have occasioned no embarrassment. From the nation's infancy, they had envisioned nothing less for the independent nation-state. The *means* by and the *form* in which those aspirations eventually came to fruition, however, would have surprised them. At least initially, when the Founders and their generational peers thought about such matters, they took Great Britain as their model—that is, a nation-state of limited size, but possessed of a far-flung maritime empire, or, in the case of Jefferson, a dispersed collection of sister republics.

By the early 1850s, when Frémont had concluded his major explorations, Americans understood that their empire would be different. To understand Frémont's legacy, then, one must first understand how early Americans thought about their country—and how they embraced their vision of American empire.

In the year 2000, the American urban theorist Jane Jacobs, by way of explaining an earlier decision to move to Canada, told the *New York Times*, "I'm glad I was brought up an American, but I'm not cut out to be a citizen of an empire."[4] By the end of the second millennium, the word *empire* had become, for most Americans, distasteful. Redolent of images of garish thrones, belligerent seafaring armies crashing on foreign shores, and pocket-lining colonial officials.

This was not always the case. Through much of the nation's history, the word *empire* enjoyed a positive connotation. Indeed, not until the 1870s did its less rosy derivative, *imperialism*, firmly entrench itself in the language. George Washington, for instance, referred optimistically to the United States as "a rising empire." Thomas Jefferson spoke of the nation as an expanding "empire for liberty." And in 1856, Abraham Lincoln, then an ambitious former congressman, speaking to a rally in Kalamazoo, Michigan, assured his audience, "We are a great empire," then linked that domain's continued prosperity to the election of the presidential candidate on whose behalf he was orating that day—John Frémont.

Empire—the word derives from the Roman word *imperium* and, in its original usage, referred to the power exercised by that city-state's emperors. But during the Middle Ages, the term was applied to the vast territories and their inhabitants ruled by any conquering power. By the early eighteenth century, as European nation-states established far-flung colonies, the term more commonly referred to the naval might and regulatory machinery by which they enforced trade monopolies with their dispersed colonies and enriched their national coffers.

Within such mercantilist empires, colonies functioned less as areas to be settled, more as opportunities for enriching the home country, the metropolis. Colonies existed mainly as suppliers of raw materials for manufacturing industries in the metropolis, and as a captive market for the goods produced by those industries. Among the British, to the extent the term *empire* referred to physical geography, it referred not to conquered lands but to the oceanic waters prowled by the British Navy. Britain's poet James Thomson captured the essence of the new concept when, in "Britannia, A Poem," he praised his nation's "well earned Empire of the deep" and exhorted his compatriots to "extend your reign from shore to shore." Mercantilists, after all, tended to limit their attention to ports; thriving settlements in the interior might encourage too much autonomy and industry.[5]

But even as the eighteenth-century English celebrated their oceanic empire, their North American colonists, scattered along the Eastern Seaboard, were turning their gaze increasingly westward, toward the rich valleys of the Mississippi and Ohio Rivers. From their infancy, there had been in the colonies a tendency toward territorial expansion. As the colonies prospered in wealth and population, colonial governments, landowners, fur trappers, and speculators became increasingly covetous of the French-held frontier that lay to the north and west. By 1750, a string of French settlements, which had grown from fur-trade posts, stretched from the mouth of the St. Lawrence

River up to the Great Lakes. From there, they reached south of Lake Champlain and down the Mississippi valley to St. Louis and New Orleans. As early as 1613, when a Jamestown, Virginia, ship captain attacked the French settlement of Port Royal on the Bay of Fundy, individual colonists, colonial companies, and even colonial governments had clashed militarily with the French. In response, the French erected a series of forts, garrisoned with professional soldiers, across their North American empire. To provide still more security, they strengthened ties with their Indian allies.

As early as 1609, the colonists had asked for British military assistance to quell threats from Indians and the French. By the mid-eighteenth century—observing what they perceived as a new surge of French militarization of the frontier—the American colonists began asking for a heretofore unprecedented level of assistance from the British military. In making their case for military aid, the colonists increasingly presented their cause as one with the British empire. Indeed, in 1751, Benjamin Franklin imagined North America as the future center of Britain's empire:

There are supp'd to be now upwards of One Million *English* souls in *North-America*. . . . This Million doubling, suppose but once in 25 Years, will in another Century be more than the People of *England*, and the greatest Number of *Englishmen* will be on this Side [of] the Water. What an Accession of Power to the *British* Empire by Sea as well as Land! What Increase of Trade and Navigation! What numbers of Ships and Seamen![6]

During the first half of the eighteenth century, such rhetorical flourishes, along with the colonists' appeals for British military assistance, fell on deaf ears. Britain's decision in 1754, however, for its own European geopolitical reasons, to challenge the French empire in North America eventually led English leaders to accept, as a political convenience, the American concept of empire. In 1758, Prime Minister William Pitt, upon taking office in the wake of a series of British defeats, concluded that any final victory would require assistance from the American colonials. To entice them into providing volunteers for the war effort, he offered the colonies more autonomy, economic subsidies, and arms—all incentives designed to make the Americans feel less like colonials, more like full-fledged citizens of the British Empire. Most colonists were eager to comply—here, at least, was an opportunity to open new lands for speculation and settlement. Moreover, New Englanders, swayed by their anti-French and antipapist heritages, were further motivated by fresh memories of support lent by French Catholics to Indian raids against frontier Anglo settlements.

Known as the French and Indian War in its North American theater (1754–63) and the Seven Years' War in its European theater (1756–63), the conflict transfigured political life in British North America. After the British victory, the colonists took pride in being "members" of the newly enlarged British empire. Subsequent polices from London, however, soon chastened that pride. In order to protect his new Indian subjects west of the Appalachians—and manifesting the usual mercantilist wariness about the development of colonial hinterlands—King George III issued the Proclamation of 1763, banning white settlement beyond the crest of that range. And, to defray the war debt, the mother country levied increasingly harsh taxes on the colonies. As the colonists' resistance to British policies gathered, many of their protests—right up to 1776—took the form of appeals for their rights as members of the British empire.

Early resistance sought not to remove the American colonies from the British empire, but to create a firm foundation for a stronger, more stable British empire. Protests sought to extinguish the assumed role of Parliament in governing the colonies. But they also sought to enhance the status of the king as the chief protector of the rights of North American residents of the British empire. In 1774, no less a patriot than Thomas Jefferson argued that King George III should

> no longer persevere in sacrificing the rights of one part of the empire to the inordinate desires of another: but deal out to all equal and impartial right. Let no act be passed by any one legislature which may infringe on the rights and liberties of another. This is the important post in which fortune has placed you, holding the balance of a great, if a well poised empire.[7]

In their arguments, colonists adopted an increasingly idealized view of the British empire. Not surprisingly, then, after the Americans won their independence in 1783, they inherited, but continued to modify, the British thrust toward empire. Jefferson and the other Founders hoped that America's successor empire would prove republican in its governance and, compared to its British predecessor, more benign in spirit. In the years before and after the adoption of the Articles of Confederation, Thomas Jefferson developed the most comprehensive and influential vision of American empire. This new empire, Jefferson believed, would be continental rather than maritime in scope, and be built around North America's rivers instead of its oceans and seaports. True to this new empire's republican credo, membership would be entirely voluntary. America's empire would be built on "federal" relationships among independent governments. Toward that end, Congress, in 1787, passed the Northwest Ordinance, which established an orderly means by which Americans moving ever westward might create self-government and petition for status as territories and, in time, as states. In a territory's initial phase, a governor selected by Congress directed governmental affairs. Once the territory's population included 5,000 free male adults, it would choose an assembly, from which Congress, in turn, would select a governing council for the territory. Congress and the appointed governor retained a veto over the council's action, but once the territory's population reached 60,000, it could petition Congress for statehood and all the attendant rights of self-government that status conferred.

In a caveat that weighed heavily on America's Founding Fathers, the philosopher Montesquieu had warned of the dangers that attend empires dispersed over too large a geographical territory. And so in framing the Articles of Confederation and the Northwest Ordinance, the Americans addressed such concerns: so long as the "united States" took the form of the loose association of sovereign states mandated by those two documents, such dangers of overextension seemed to be held at bay. Characteristically, Jefferson took that cautionary note one step further: in his regard for decentralization and independence, he was even willing to accept the creation of other confederacies—other empires—west of the Mississippi River. California, say, might eventually be settled by Americans, but it need not become part of the United States:

> Whether we remain in one confederacy, or form into Atlantic and Mississippi confederacies, I believe not very important to

the happiness of either part. Those of the western confederacy will be as much our children & descendants as those of the eastern, and I feel myself as much identified with that country, in future time, as with this; and did I now foresee a separation at some future day, yet I should feel the duty & the desire to promote the western interests as zealously as the eastern, doing all the good for both portions of our future family which should fall within my power.[8]

To guarantee independence and autonomy for the empire's constituent parts, Congress, in framing the Constitution, sought to ensure that—at least for men of European ancestry—there would be no second-class citizens, no "colonials," in America's empire. Indians, blacks, and women, of course, occupied a less privileged berth in the empire. Indeed, the Americans' attitude toward Indians would become a defining—highly problematic—aspect of this new empire: departing from the usual strategy of empire-building, the United States wanted the lands it conquered, but not the indigenous people who inhabited them. As for the African peoples and their descendants bound into the human-chattel system of American slavery, no amount of rhetorical legerdemain, extending over two centuries, could adequately justify their continued exclusion from the guarantees of liberty promulgated by the U.S. Constitution and myriad other documents. For its failure to embrace Indians and African-Americans in its dreams of republican empire, the United States would, in the end, pay a very stiff price—countless Indian wars, one single and bloody Civil War, and generations of social turmoil.

Among the enfranchised white males accorded the full blessings of participation in America's envisioned empire, it was assumed that a republican spirit of free trade would animate their economic relationships. That same republican spirit would also infuse economic relationships among the empire's constituent states. This free trade, Jefferson believed, would at once discourage the sort of hierarchical metropolis-colonial relationships that had bedeviled Britain's empire and encourage a binding reciprocity among the empire's citizens.

However eloquent on paper, Jefferson's vision of empire collapsed before the onslaught of actual nation-building. As the new nation's ruling elites grew increasingly frustrated by the limited powers accorded the national government by the Articles of Confederation, they began agitating for a stronger, centralized government. Toward that end, during the 1780s, they drafted and urged the ratification of a new "federal" Constitution. In response, "Antifederalists" argued against the proposed Constitution and its vision of a single consolidated state.

Alexander Hamilton and James Madison, arguing the virtues of a geographically expanded state, turned Montesquieu's caveat about the dangers of overexpansion on its head. In *Federalist Papers* 9, 10, and 51, they borrowed from a less-read section of Montesquieu's work to argue that it was precisely in the very largeness of the new proposed state that Americans would find their greatest protection from tyrannical abuses. A single central government, Hamilton argued, would be able to quell abuses of powers in individual states.[9]

The U.S. Constitution was ratified in 1787. By international standards, the central government it created remained weak until Civil War–era reforms increased its powers. Even so, the new government had the effect of extinguishing the autonomy once enjoyed by individual states.

Beyond the U.S. Constitution's role as a centralizing force in American political life, the continued growth of Eastern Seaboard cities and industrial centers further preempted the decentralized distribution of power that Jefferson had imagined. In fact, Jefferson himself, during his eight years as chief executive (1801–09), did as much as anyone else to undermine his own earlier vision of empire. He did continue to support free trade and the exploration of the Western rivers that he had always believed would become the nation's main watercourses. But the hallmark of his presidency—and the defining gesture of his quest for American empire—came in 1803, when he purchased from France the sprawling and vaguely defined Louisiana Territory, west of the Mississippi River.

Arguing from historical precedents—past treaties, records of exploration, and the like—Jefferson asserted that the Louisiana Purchase contained the entire Mississippi River and all of its tributaries, westward to their sources in the "Stony Mountains." Eager to learn the content and extent of this huge new domain, he dispatched a series of scientific-military expeditions into the West, including those led by William Dunbar and Dr. George Hunter to the Ozark Plateau (1804);

by Meriwether Lewis and William Clark to the headwaters of the Missouri River and over the Rockies to Oregon (1804–06); and by Zebulon Pike to the Upper Mississippi valley (1805–06) and the Arkansas River valley up to its headwaters in the Rocky Mountains (1806–07).

Though exploration and diplomacy would establish that Jefferson's Louisiana Purchase had, on paper, doubled the nation's size, the transaction violated the benign spirit of his earlier vision of republican empire. The Louisiana Purchase was extraconstitutional, coercive, and hardly republican in spirit. Far from having volunteered to join the American empire, French and Spanish subjects and various Indian tribes simply discovered that their lands had been transferred, in exchange for cold cash, to the United States. So much for the Northwest Ordinance and Jefferson's own notion of empires populated by voluntary members! Moreover, Jefferson's soon enunciated intention of using the new territory as a place to relocate Indians from their traditional homelands east of the Mississippi laid the foundation for policies by successor presidents that, in their brutality, would be still more difficult to reconcile with any humane vision of empire.

By the early nineteenth century, the nation's growing white population was pushing westward, beyond the Appalachians, into the Mississippi valley. The 1814 Treaty of Ghent, formally concluding the War of 1812, ended lingering British military intrigue in the Mississippi valley, thus clearing the way for more white U.S. settlement. Within the same decade, Britain and the United States concluded negotiations that, at least on paper, further clarified the extent of U.S. dominion in North America. Ending disputes about the Louisiana Purchase's northern boundary, the Convention of 1818 extended the existing British–U.S. border along the forty-ninth parallel westward, from Lake of the Woods to the crest of the Rocky Mountains.

The 1818 pact with England also eased—though it did not end—long-standing U.S.-British tensions over the timber-dense Oregon country. That vast realm of North America's Pacific Northwest stretched westward from the Rockies to the Pacific Ocean, and southward from Canada to the northern border of today's California and Nevada, then under Spanish title. By 1818, however, only Britain and the United States asserted claims on the territory.

Neither country had encouraged settlement in Oregon. Their rivalry there, occasionally punctuated by military and diplomatic outbursts, turned on economics, mainly hunting rights. First British and then American trappers had developed a profitable trade in the pelts of otter, beaver, and other furbearing animals. As the trade flourished, trappers and traders from both countries, seeking new hunting grounds, fanned out eastward beyond their original coastal posts, through the Columbia River basin and into the Rockies. To ease increasing conflicts in the region, the United States and Britain, in the Convention of 1818, agreed to hold the Oregon country under "joint occupation."

A year later, the United States and Spain concluded a treaty that helped clarify America's southern border. Madrid, in 1819, weakened by military and diplomatic reversals, ceded to Washington all claims to Florida and accepted a new northern boundary for its remaining North American holdings. Ending long-standing disputes over the extent of the expansive Louisiana country purchased by the United States in 1803, Spain agreed to a transcontinental line, running from the Gulf of Mexico northward up the Sabine River, and, in stair-step fashion, westward, along the Red, then the Arkansas Rivers. From the Arkansas River's headwaters on the eastern slope of the Rockies, the new line reached north to the forty-second parallel, thence westward to the Pacific.

By the 1830s, America's vast holdings in the West were being matched by commensurately expansive visions of the nation's territorial destiny. Various constituencies—national and regional, political and economic, intellectual and cultural—were urging a more aggressive role for the central government in the promotion of American settlement and business west of the Appalachians. A growing population of American settlers streaming into the Mississippi valley, meanwhile, clamored for protection from Indians, and for federal support for roads and for river and harbor improvements. And from both the east and the west, there were growing calls for federal support for American settlement still farther to the west—in Oregon, still under joint U.S.–British occupation. It was amid the heady optimism of that season of U.S. empire at surge tide that John Charles Frémont would take his first steps into America's vast Western frontier.

CHARLES FREMON *FILS*

2

EVEN BEFORE HIS BIRTH, upheavals large and small, domestic and public, had conspired to put John Charles Frémont on a restless course. His father, Charles Fremon, helped to set that course.

✳

As the owner of the fashionable Greene Street Academy in Richmond, Virginia, Louis H. Giradin made a good living providing a respectable education to generations of boys and girls. Over the years, scions of the Jeffersons, the Randolphs, and other prominent Virginia families had passed through the school's doors. And Giradin and his assistant, David Doyle, prided themselves on the quality of the academy's instruction. They were thus delighted one afternoon in 1808, when a thin, darkly handsome Frenchman possessed of genteel manners showed up at the school to inquire if there might be work there for a teacher of French.

Though the Frenchman, Charles Fremon, spoke fluent, if heavily accented, English and had an easy charm, he had no local references to offer. He had only recently arrived in America. Even so, Giradin had a good feeling about the newcomer and offered him a job. Over the next few months, Fremon proved a capable addition to the school's faculty, and, slowly, too, Giradin and Doyle came to know more about Fremon's past: he had been born, he said, near Lyon and, during the French Revolution, had fought for the Royalists. After the war, he had left France for Santo Domingo. En route, an English man-of-war captured the French ship on which he sailed, and he was imprisoned for several years in the British West Indies. A man of many talents, during his captivity Fremon had earned his prison allowance by making baskets, and by painting frescoes for the homes of the islands' wealthier residents. When he gained his release, he had come straight to America.

Giradin and Doyle liked Fremon but noticed that he rarely spoke of personal matters. A year later, Doyle began to hear disturbing rumors alleging libertinism in Fremon's personal life. One report had him living with a woman reputed to be "a common prostitute." Doyle confronted Fremon, but instead of denying the stories, Fremon became angry, defiantly answering, "I will do as I please."

Giradin dismissed Fremon the next morning, but within months, he had returned to the teaching profession, as a tutor in private homes. Presumably leaving the alleged woman of ill repute who had inspired Doyle's inquiry, Fremon took out a lease on a small house owned by Major John Pryor, an elderly and socially prominent Revolutionary War veteran. Fatefully, for all concerned, the deal also called for Fremon to teach French to Anne Beverly Whiting Pryor, the elderly veteran's vibrant and attractive young wife.[1]

Anne, the youngest daughter among the twelve children of Colonel Thomas Whiting, belonged to a distinguished Virginia family. A wealthy landowner in Gloucester County, Colonel Whiting had been, prior to the American Revolution, a respected member of the House of Burgesses but died when Anne was only six months old. Her mother soon remarried. The new husband, Samuel Cary, however, quickly squandered most of the widow's estate. For Anne, her mother's death, followed by her stepfather's carelessness with the family's money left the child, as Jessie Frémont later put it, "most defenseless in the hands of Mr. Cary." To remove Anne from Cary and a household tormented by the "the vexations of law suits," her older, married sister, Catherine, took her in.

When Anne was seventeen, Catherine arranged for her to be married to Major John Pryor. In his early sixties when the couple wed, Pryor was by then best known around Richmond as the owner of Haymarket Gardens, a local amusement park alongside the James River. In a later memoir, Jessie Frémont, blaming Catherine for pushing

Anne's youthful marriage, dismissed Pryor as "a man of wealth, but of not equally high social position," possessing "no refinement of character."

Anne, however, in a later statement, refusing to "exculpate" herself, blamed her own youthful naïveté for the union. "I was married too young to be sensible of the importance of the state in which I was about to enter, and found when too late that I had acted with too much precipitancy, and could never feel that love for him to whom I was united, without which the marriage state of all others is the most wretched."[2]

After marrying, the couple remained in Richmond, where the major enjoyed a reputation as a popular wit, a shrewd judge of horses and a tireless organizer of equestrian events. Unfortunately for Major Pryor, however, while he was busy with his horse races, his young wife and her French teacher were developing a mutual infatuation that soon ripened into an affair. The two planned to wait until Pryor died and then marry. But through Fremon's indiscretions, Pryor learned of the relationship and, in July 1811, confronted the two. In an exchange in Pryor's home, he raged at his wife and threatened to kill her. Uncowed, she reputedly answered, "You may spare yourself the crime. I shall leave your house to-morrow morning forever!" Fremon, according to one source, vowed, after the incident, to kill Pryor, or anyone else who interfered with his relationship with Anne. The next morning, July 10, Anne and Charles left Richmond.[3]

The scandal rocked Richmond's elite society. In a divorce petition published that month in the Virginia *Patriot*, Pryor charged that his wife had "totally alienated her affections from me by the vile and invidious machinations of an execrable monster of baseness and depravity, with whom I have recently discovered she has for some time past indulged in criminal intercourse."[4]

Traveling by stagecoach to Williamsburg, then Norfolk, the couple stayed in each town only long enough for her to gather what property she claimed in each. The previous year, Anne, after years of litigation, had inherited slaves valued at $1,930. According to family legend, with the money from Anne's inheritance the couple, fulfilling a long-cherished dream of Charles's, set out for the South on a freewheeling ethnographic expedition, touring its Indian regions with their own horses and carriage.[5]

Whether or not the Indian-tour story is apocryphal, by October the couple had landed in Savannah, Georgia, with most, if not all, of their funds by then apparently depleted. There they settled into a now-long-gone two-story brick building at 563–65 West Bay Street in what was then the city's Yamacraw neighborhood. Over the next year, while Anne took in boarders, Fremon, vainly attempting to put the couple on a solid financial footing, taught French, worked in a dancing academy, opened his own dance school, opened a livery stable, and organized cotillion parties. Making life still more difficult for the couple, Virginia's House of Delegates had declined a divorce petition filed by Major Pryor, so that they could not marry. It was into that unstable milieu, in Savannah, Georgia, on January 21, 1813, that their first son, John Charles Fremon was born.[6]

✻

For whatever reason—lack of work and money, the summer heat, recurring whispers of scandal—the family left Savannah later that year for another round of wandering in the South. If they, as family tradition claims, truly did travel the South, observing Indian life, then among John Charles's earliest sensations were the sights, sounds and smells of aboriginal camps.

Family legend also had it that, during this sojourn, the infant John Charles had a glancing—though nearly fatal—encounter with his future father-in-law Thomas Hart Benton. In Nashville, on the evening of September 14, 1814, the family was staying at Clayton Talbot's tavern, when a bullet, penetrating a wall, suddenly shot into the room where the infant was sleeping. The shot had been fired by Benton (then a mercurial frontier colonel, lawyer, and member of the Tennessee legislature) at General Andrew Jackson, a future U.S. President, and, at that moment, a frontier hero just returned from his successful campaign against the Creek Indians. The gunplay arose from residual tensions resulting from Jackson's having served as a second to an adversary of Thomas's brother Jesse in a duel. Though Jackson nearly bled to death from his shoulder wound, years later he and Thomas would become steadfast political allies.[7]

Charles and Anne lingered in Nashville long enough for her to give birth, a year later, to a second child, Elizabeth. From Nashville, the family moved back to Norfolk, where Anne, in 1817, gave birth to their second son, Horation Francis, called Frank by the family. Charles Fremon died later that same year, leaving Anne in poverty with three young children. Anne had friends and relatives in Norfolk—including Francis Fremon, a brother of Charles. With Charles dead, Francis tried to persuade Anne to take their young children and return with him to France. Instead, she and the children remained for a while in Virginia, where young John Charles received his first schooling, but, by 1823, they had moved to Charleston, South Carolina.[8]

❋

In Charleston, Mrs. Anne Pryor faced the daunting task of raising two sons and a daughter. John Charles possessed Gallic good looks and, brimming with enthusiasm, a healthy outdoor bent. Beyond that, the boy had a gift for attracting the admiration of elite Charlestonians. In 1826, he began working as a clerk for John W. Mitchell, a prominent attorney. Though only thirteen, Frémont—Fremon, as he then still spelled his name—so impressed Mitchell with the passion, depth, and breadth of his growing interests in science and nature that Mitchell volunteered to pay the boy's tuition to study at John Roberton's local preparatory school. There, he quickly excelled in Greek, Latin, and mathematics. "I very gladly received him," Roberton later recalled, "for I immediately perceived he was no common youth, as intelligence beamed in his dark eye, and shone brightly on his countenance, indicating great ability, and an assurance of his future progress."

Pondering the trajectory of John Frémont's life, past biographers have surmised that the circumstances of his youth—his illegitimate birth and fatherlessness—gave him a lifelong contempt for authority figures. But those same conditions also bequeathed to the young man an equally formidable attraction to a series of strong male mentors who played major roles in shaping the course of his life.

Placed in the academy's most advanced class during his first year, Frémont devoured myriad Greek and Latin texts—including works by Caesar, Homer, Nepos, Sallust, Virgil, Horace, and Livy. "Whatever he read, he retained," Roberton later remembered. "It seemed to me, in fact, as if he learned by mere intuition."[9]

In Charleston, Anne joined St. Philip's Episcopal Church, where, at the age of sixteen, John Charles was confirmed. From the time he was fourteen, many had assumed that young Frémont would eventually enter the ministry—as Roberton recalled, "He was always the very pattern of virtue and modesty." But Roberton also soon noticed Frémont's growing fascination with matters of war. After reading Herodotus' account of the battle of Marathon for instance, Frémont, unbidden by any teacher, had written a poem on the subject that he subsequently published in a local newspaper. "When I contemplated," Roberton recalled, "his bold, fearless, disposition, his powerful inventive genius, his admiration of warlike exploits, and his love of heroic and adventurous deeds, I did not think it likely he would be a minister of the Gospel."

In the spring of 1829, Frémont was advanced enough in his studies to enter the College of Charleston as a member of its junior class. The college's curriculum emphasized the classics, mathematics, the sciences, and religion; and though Frémont, at the outset, had to exert extra efforts to keep abreast in mathematics and the sciences, he performed well in all his courses over the first nine months. Then, in early 1830—probably to help out with family expenses—he asked for and was granted a leave of absence to go to the country and work as a tutor, in all likelihood in the home of some wealthy planter.[10]

Frémont returned to college that April. But he had somehow changed. Dimmed was the earlier passion for books and book learning. His attendance in classes began to falter. "While present at class I worked hard," he later recalled, "but frequently absented myself for days together." Distracting Frémont was a growing interest in the outdoors and an infatuation with a local girl named Cecilia, the daughter of French refugees from the Santo Domingo uprising of three decades earlier. With Cecilia and other friends, he spent much of his time exploring the woods around Charleston and sailing to nearby barrier islands.

"The days went by on wings," he recalled. "In the summer we ranged about in the woods, or on the now historic islands, gunning or picnicking, the girls sometimes with us; sometimes in a sailboat on the bay, oftener going over the bar to seaward and not infrequently when the breeze failed us getting dangerously near the breakers on the bar." In February 1831, three months before Frémont's graduation, the College of Charleston, after several warnings, citing "habitual irregularity and incorrigible negligence," expelled him from classes.[11]

✸

The expulsion marked the first of several setbacks that, over the years, would result from Frémont's ambivalence toward rules and figures of authority. At the time, however, he welcomed the dismissal: "To me this came like summer wind, that breathed over something sweeter than the 'bank whereon the wild thyme blows.' I smiled to myself while I listened to words about the disappointment of friends—and the broken career. I was living in a charmed atmosphere and their edict only gave me complete freedom."[12]

He still had to earn money, however, and toward that end, he found work as a teacher at John A. Wooten's private school and in an instructional program offered by Charleston's privately run "Apprentices Library." He also found time to continue his readings; and it was during this period, he later recalled, that he came upon two volumes that would have a lasting impact.

The first—its title is now lost to us—was a collection of tales of men "who had made themselves famous by brave and noble deeds, or infamous by cruel and base acts." "With a schoolboy's enthusiasm," he later recalled, "I read these stories over and over again, with alternate pleasure or indignation. I please myself in thinking they have sometimes exercised a restraining or inspiring influence." The other book—its title is also lost to us—was a work on astronomy in Dutch, a language Frémont could not read. "The language made it a closed book," he recalled, "but for the beautifully clear maps of the stars and many examples of astronomical calculations. By its aid I became well acquainted with the night skies and familiarized myself with the ordinary observations necessary to determine latitude and longitude. This was the beginning of the astronomical knowledge afterwards so essential to me."[13]

✸

Now in his early twenties and yearning for wider fields of experience, Frémont in 1830 met a man who, over the next few years, would help channel his restlessness into more respectable enterprises. Now Joel Poinsett is best remembered for introducing the Mexican plant later named for him, the poinsettia, into the United States. But in the early nineteenth century, the diplomat, physician, and politician ranked as one of America's most refined and well-traveled savants.

When the two first met, Poinsett, fifty-one years old, had just returned to Charleston after having served as the first U.S. minister to the Republic of Mexico. A College of Charleston trustee and a member of St. Philip's Church, to which Frémont belonged, Poinsett took an active interest in Charleston's cultural and intellectual life. Though physically not a striking man, and in ill health by the time he met Frémont, Poinsett nonetheless retained his gifts as a gracious host, a good listener, and a talented raconteur. Through him, Frémont was inducted into an older, more sophisticated orbit of acquaintances.

For years, Poinsett's Sunday breakfasts, held at his two-story, becolumned frame house in Charleston's suburbs, had been a staple of the social life of the city's elite. Each week, he gathered about his table Charleston's brightest, well-read citizens. Distinguished visitors were also frequent guests, such as President James Monroe, in 1819, and General Lafayette, in 1825.[14]

Leaving a lasting imprint on Frémont's worldview, Poinsett helped nudge the young man toward political opinions that, over the years, would become articles of faith—including his dim view of slavery and his beliefs in westward U.S. expansion and Unionism. Poinsett's distaste for slavery had grown out of his observation of Russian serfdom during his travels as a young man; to his mnd, serfdom, like American slavery, hampered both efficiency and innovation.

At the time of Poinsett's return to Charleston, however, it was the issue of Unionism, more than slavery, that burned white-hot in South Carolina politics. During his ministerial turn in Mexico, Poinsett, in urging reforms on that country, had often cited U.S. prosperity as a positive result of democratic government. Even so, when he returned to Charleston, he found South Carolina's economic progress increasingly lagging behind that of the rest of the country. Newly cultivated lands to the west were cutting into the state's agricultural markets; and many South Carolinians were also blaming the state's woes on a protective tariff enacted in 1828, designed to bolster Northern manufacturing interests.

Poinsett opposed the tariff. But he refused to join prominent South Carolinians such as John C. Calhoun and Robert Hayne, who were arguing that the state government enjoyed a constitutional right to "nullify" the tariff. To Poinsett, this "doctrine of nullification" threatened national union. And he had promised President Andrew Jackson that, upon returning to Charleston, he would do everything in his power to thwart "the strange and pernicious doctrines advanced by some of the leading men of our state."

President Jackson, for his part, warning that any armed interference with federal authority constituted treason, dispatched the sloop of war *Natchez* to Charleston, to enforce the tariff. He also threatened, if necessary, to send as many as fifteen thousand troops to South Carolina. For almost four months, the specter of civil war hung over Charleston's harbor. The stalemate ended in March 1833, when congressional leaders, guided by Kentucky senator Henry Clay, struck a compromise by which the offending tariff was reduced, and South Carolina rescinded its recently enacted antitariff legislation. Though barely twenty years old, Frémont, as Poinsett's protégé, had been afforded an intimate view of the confrontation. The experience helped to shape what would become, for him, a lifelong devotion to the cause of Unionism. And—given Frémont's own future of stormy relations with governmental superiors—it likely also taught him a thing or two about the difficulties faced by federal officials in trying to enforce orders over expanses of time and distance.

❀

In May 1833, the *Natchez* departed on an extended cruise to South America. Aboard the vessel was twenty-year-old John Charles Frémont. With Poinsett's grudging assistance—though not his approval—Frémont had won a civilian appointment from the U.S. Navy to serve as a mathematics teacher aboard the ship. Because no naval academy then existed, the Navy relied on onboard teachers to instruct midshipmen in navigational mathematics.

Frémont's naval appointment marked his inevitable break with the bonds of familial domesticity. After his dismissal from the College of Charleston, the restless young man had watched his brother, Frank, leave Charleston at age fifteen to pursue a career in the theater and his sister, Elizabeth, die at the age of seventeen. Now, on the eve of going to sea, he worried about his aging mother. With her paramour, Charles, long dead and two of her three children gone, John hated, he later recalled, to leave her alone:

> Circumstances had more than usually endeared us to each other and I knew that her life would be solitary without me. I was accustomed to be much at home and our separations had been slight. But now it was likely to be for long and the hard part would be for the one left alone. For me it was very different. Going out in the excitement of strange scenes and occurrences I would be forced out of myself and for long intervals could forget what I left behind. For her in the sameness of daily life there would be a blank not easily filled.[15]

Frémont soon glimpsed for the first time the world that lay beyond America's borders. "I saw more of the principal cities and people than a traveller usually does on passing through a country, though nothing of the interior," he later recalled. He also got to know War of 1812 naval hero and future Civil War–era admiral David Farragut, then in his early thirties and a lieutenant aboard the *Natchez*. Even so, Frémont minimized the experience as a shaper of his destiny: "The time spent was long and had no future bearing." Indeed, he later claimed that his most memorable experience during the cruise came when, while acting as seconds for an onshore duel between two fellow sailors, he and a friend averted two possible deaths. Unbeknownst to the combatants, Frémont and the other second had disarmed the duelists' weapons by putting only gunpowder, and no lead, in their pistols. Afterward, "both looked sincerely surprised that they remained standing upright as before. Going up each to his man, we declared the affair over; the cause of quarrel in our opinion not justifying a second shot." They all returned to the ship—"nobody hurt and nobody wiser."

Lackluster memories notwithstanding, Frémont, upon returning to

Charleston, remained sufficiently enticed by the prospects of life at sea to pursue another U.S. Navy appointment. In early 1835, Congress authorized several at-sea professorships in mathematics, with an annual salary of $1,200. In April 1836, Frémont learned that he had one month to prepare for a qualifying exam, to be administered in Norfolk. Though the young man had been a fickle college student, he relished a return to the world of books: "All day long I was at my books, and the earliest dawn found me at an upper window against which stood a tall poplar, where the rustling of the glossy leaves made a soothing accompaniment."

Frémont passed the exam, but not until April 1837 did the long-awaited appointment finally arrive—which he promptly declined. By then, he had other plans.

✸

During the fall of 1836, as twenty-three-year-old Frémont awaited the results from his Navy exam, he had no way of knowing how his career was about to be propelled into a new and unexpected trajectory by the presidential election victory, that November, of New York Democrat Martin Van Buren.

The new president, who had served as Vice-President during Andrew Jackson's administration, intended to retain most of his predecessor's cabinet. One opening, however, did exist—that of Secretary of War. Moving quickly to find a permanent appointee for the job, Van Buren called on Frémont's mentor, Joel Poinsett. The South Carolinian, with his background in military and diplomatic matters, seemed ideal for the post. No doubt the new president also recalled Poinsett's defense of the Jackson administration during South Carolina's nullification crisis.

The appointment gave Frémont's mentor new prestige on the national stage. More to the point, in the War Department, Poinsett would also oversee the U.S. Army's Bureau of Topographical Engineers, the chief federal agency devoted to exploring the nation's various frontiers. And Poinsett, with his long-standing passion for both science and exploration, was bound to prove a friend to those who sought more knowledge of North America's West. Poinsett's interest in Western matters also stemmed from his support of the long-standing policy of opening new territory to white settlers by moving Eastern Indians to designated reserves west of the Mississippi River. Though the Indian Removal Act of 1830 had been passed during Andrew Jackson's administration, much, perhaps most, of its implementation fell to his successor, Van Buren, and Van Buren's Secretary of War, Poinsett.

Poinsett's job also required him to address difficulties *among* Indians west of the Mississippi—difficulties, in many cases, caused by policies originating in Washington. In the forests and on the vast plains that lay between the Mississippi River and the Rocky Mountains, Eastern Indians forcibly removed by the government to areas west of the river were increasingly clashing with the region's established tribes. To ease tensions—both among warring Indian tribes and between Indians and white settlers—Poinsett joined those calling for the construction of more U.S. Army forts in the region.

In 1838, Poinsett would call on Congress to create two north-to-south cordons of forts: one line, consisting of five posts, would be established at advanced positions inside Indian country and would zigzag from Fort Snelling on the Upper Mississippi River to Fort Towson, on the Red River of the South. Another cordon, an "interior" line consisting of at least eight posts, would be constructed near white settlements along the Mississippi River, the nominal boundary separating Indians from white settlers. The forts would give the American government a greater show of force in the West and would help to prevent intertribal and Indian-settler conflicts. The posts would also provide shelter for imperiled settlers and serve as garrisons from which U.S. Army troops could be dispatched to far-flung American frontier settlements in times of trouble. To connect the new forts with one another, and with the Ohio River and other critical waterways, plans also called for the construction of a series of Western roads.[16]

As War Secretary, Poinsett also dealt with policies concerning Oregon. Privately, like many U.S. policymakers of that day, he believed that, in the long run, emigrants from the United States would dominate Oregon. That eventuality, they believed, would lead to the inevitable demise of the U.S.–British joint-occupation arrangement, and to a formal U.S. acquisition of part of—possibly, most of—the territory. In the meantime, like most federal officials, Poinsett had no desire to stir up the Oregon issue. For now, he believed, America's long-term Western interests were best served by ongoing exploration and surveys of those Western territories already under U.S. title. Toward that end, he would prove an energetic supporter of federal reconnaissances of the Northwest—today's "Midwest."

❀

During the spring of 1837, not long after Poinsett became War Secretary, he offered his protégé Frémont an invitation to participate in a survey for a planned railway to run between Charleston and Cincinnati, to be led by Captain W. G. Williams of the U.S. Army's Bureau of Topographical Engineers. Frémont accepted the offer.

Beyond his War Secretary duties, Poinsett was also a principal advocate of the proposed Louisville, Cincinnati, and Charleston Railroad. Like other South Carolinians, he believed the railway would allow Charleston's port to become an outlet for the growing commerce of the Ohio and Mississippi valleys—commerce otherwise bound, in most cases, for New Orleans. As a Unionist, he also saw the line as strengthening South Carolina's links to the national economy. And, as an opponent of slavery, he envisioned it as a conduit by which more free, white laborers might migrate into the South, thus eroding the financial foundation of the region's slavery.[17]

The railroad reconnaissance consisted of several survey parties, and the one to which Frémont was attached was led by Lieutenant Richard M. White, a South Carolina native and West Point graduate who had recently returned to civilian life. In the densely forested Appalachians, the team worked long hours—often to midnight, when moonlight permitted—plotting out various alternative routes for the proposed rail line. White, nonetheless, Frémont later recalled, managed to keep the labor agreeable: "It was cheery, wholesome work. The summer weather in the mountains was fine, the cool water abundant, and the streams lined with azaleas."

The party frequently slept at village inns, but most of the time subsisted on hospitality proffered by farmers, deep in the frontier wilderness. In those sylvan retreats, Frémont later recalled, "milk and honey and many good things were welcome to an appetite shaped by all day labor on foot and a tramp of several miles backward and forward, morning and evening."

If, however, a later accusation can be believed, the "good things" savored during Frémont's village idylls reached beyond culinary pleasures; in 1856, a critic charged that Frémont, while staying at The Mansion boardinghouse, in Greenville, South Carolina, "became acquainted with a very pretty girl, in moderate circumstances," and after promising to marry her, "deserted her without a cause." According to the same critic, a Greenville resident at the time, Frémont's mother soon thereafter spent a summer in Greenville and, aware of the alleged dalliance, made frequent inquiries as to the young woman's welfare. Recalled the critic, "Her mind seemed to be disturbed, at the manner, she [the young lady] had been treated by her son."[18]

❀

No sooner had Frémont returned to Charleston from the railroad project than Captain Williams invited him to participate in another survey—a military reconnaissance, conducted during the winter of 1837–38, of a mountainous strip of land through Tennessee, North Carolina, and Georgia occupied by Cherokee Indians. The survey sought to lay the groundwork for the federal government's planned removal of the Indians to Western reservations.

In a sense, Frémont's turn, during the early nineteenth century, from naval to landlocked activities reflected the evolving course of America's own aspirations for empire. By the mid-1820s, most of the tribes east of the Mississippi had been vanquished by war or diseases, or dispatched to the West—the Cherokees, clinging to a strip of land granted them by the state of Georgia in 1783, being a conspicuous exception. In 1828, however, the discovery of gold in the Cherokees' homelands—triggering the nation's first gold rush—doomed whatever chances the tribe had of hanging onto their lands. As prospectors, soon followed by settlers, poured into Georgia's northern hinterlands, the state's political leaders grew more eager to rid themselves of the Cherokees. By the mid-1830s, war threatened between the tribe and

Georgia. Whether for purposes of warfare or merely to assist the ultimate distribution of the lands to settlers, the state of Georgia needed a survey of the contested region.

With possible war looming, the 1837–38 winter survey of the Cherokee country was, by necessity, conducted in a rush. As Frémont recalled, "The first day's work of twenty miles on foot made me so stiff next morning that I moved like a foundered horse." He began the survey, working with two other men, along with their guide—a white settler in the area named Laudermilk. But for the most part, it was solitary work—with each man working his way up a stream or mountain valley. Sometimes, alone or together, they stopped at night to sleep in some Indian cabin. At other times, they slept in three-sided tents in the glow of huge hickory fires, on which they cooked, feasting on wild pigs. Its physical rigors notwithstanding, Frémont later recalled the experience as joyously formative. "Here I found the path which I was 'destined to walk,' " he later wrote. "There were to be no more years wasted in tentative efforts to find a way for myself. The work was laid out and it began here with a remarkable continuity of purpose."

Like his father, Frémont found Indians ceaselessly fascinating, and he took every opportunity to observe their ways. "As it sometimes chanced, I was present at Indian feasts, where all would get wild with excitement and some furious with drink," he later wrote. "Bloody frays were a certain accompaniment, slashing with knives, hands badly cut from clutching the blades and ugly body wounds. Their exhibition of brute courage and indifference to pain compelled admiration." But those displays, he noted, were "exceptional occasions." "In their villages and in their ordinary farming life they lived peaceably and comfortably. Many of their farms were much the same as those that are to be met with everywhere on our remote frontier. The depreciating and hurtful influence was the proximity of the whites."

Over the years, Frémont would develop a pyramidal hierarchy of Indians—one that began with the Cherokees at its apex and sank to the tribes of the West's Great Basin—"humanity . . . in its lowest form"—at its base. But though Frémont admired certain tribes and viewed Indians as misunderstood souls, often abused by whites, never did he, in any fundamental way, question the Indian removal policies framed by Presidents Monroe and Jackson and continued by subsequent nineteenth-century federal officials. While the explorer occasionally faulted the government for inconsistent policies, he remained convinced throughout his life that the Indians' best hopes lay in their removal to the West and their conversion to a settled life of agriculture and, in time, to Christianity.[19]

By early 1838, Frémont's work in the Appalachians had drawn to an end. But he was about to take the lessons and the evolving worldview culled from those experiences—along with his growing self-confidence as a surveyor and frontiersman—into a new theater, one far larger than he could have then imagined.

BOUNDARIES WHERE
NONE ARE MARKED

W ITH A LETTER of support from Captain William G.
Williams, under whom John Frémont had worked on the
two Appalachian survey expeditions, the budding frontiersman, in December 1837, had applied to his friend War Secretary
Poinsett for a commission to work on another federal survey. Two
months later, in February 1838, Poinsett ordered Captain Williams
to come to Washington to prepare for a new assignment; he asked
Williams to bring Frémont with him.

By the end of March 1838, Frémont was in Washington, awaiting
formal orders from the U.S. Army's Bureau of Topographical Engineers. Although the prospects of another wilderness foray excited
twenty-five-year-old Frémont, he found Washington a lonely, confining place. "Instead of many broad, well-paved, and leafy avenues,
Pennsylvania Avenue about represented the town," he recalled. Indeed, the anticipation of going, once again, into America's vast wilderness only made the city seem that much more confining: "Shut in to
narrow limits, the mind is driven in upon itself and loses its elasticity."

Knowing only Poinsett and his immediate family, Frémont missed
South Carolina: "There was no such attractive spot as the Battery by
the sea at Charleston, where a stranger could go and feel the freedom
of both eye and thought." His spirits rose, when, on April 16, he
learned that he was to participate—at pay of four dollars per day—in a
survey of the wilderness between the Upper Mississippi and the Missouri Rivers. He particularly welcomed the news that, on his next
assignment, rather than working again with Captain Williams, he

would serve as second in command to the expedition's leader, the renowned scientist and explorer Joseph N. Nicollet, who for the past few years had conducted an ambitious survey of the length of the Mississippi River valley: "Field work in a strange region, in association with a man so distinguished, was truly an unexpected good fortune, and I went off from Washington full of agreeable anticipation."[1]

❖

John Frémont was not the only explorer whose career won an unexpected boon from Joel Poinsett's appointment to the War Department. Since 1832—for six often lonely years—the French savant Joseph N. Nicollet, driven by a rare purity of intellectual purpose and using his own money and occasional contributions from kindred spirits, had traveled the United States conducting scientific observations designed to advance geographical knowledge and mapmaking in his adopted nation.

Born in 1786, Nicollet began his career as an astronomer in Paris, at the Bureau of Longitudes in the Royal Observatory. He impressed the observatory's aging director, famed astronomer Pierre-Simon de Laplace, but failed to win the ultimate validation of success in France's scientific establishment—appointment to the Academy of Sciences. That disappointment, among other professional and personal reversals, prompted Nicollet, at the age of forty-five, to set sail for the United States.

Arriving in Washington in March 1832, Nicollet found a scientific milieu more closely attuned to his interests than the one he had left behind in Europe. Unlike in France, where more and more research took place in laboratories, much of American science retained an outdoor setting. Observational sciences, including botany, astronomy, geodesy, and geology—all huddled under the broad rubric of *geography*—remained vital. The surveying and mapping of vast unexplored wildernesses had been a major preoccupation from the nation's infancy. It was not for nothing that philosopher Auguste Comte once remarked that, had the eighteenth-century French mathematician-astronomer Joseph-Louis Lagrange come to the United States, he would have been forced to make his living as a surveyor. Indeed, even George Washington—"father of his country"—had been a surveyor.[2]

❋

In Washington, Nicollet befriended Ferdinand Hassler, the sixty-two-year-old Swiss-born director of the U.S. Coast Survey. Though Hassler's agency, established in 1807, was devoted exclusively to studying America's coastline, its director possessed a breadth of interests that reached far beyond his official mandate. Appointed by President Jefferson as the Coast Survey's first director, Hassler had been, for three often frustrating decades, a combative proponent of federal support for various scientific projects. His intellectual passions, however, remained undiminished. And, as it happened, Nicollet reached Washington just when Hassler had decided that, though still lacking a proper observatory, he would nonetheless go ahead and begin conducting observations on his own. Thus, Hassler encouraged Nicollet's ambitions to travel the United States in pursuit of his scientific objectives. Through Hassler, Nicollet also came to know other prominent Washingtonians with a passion for the geographical sciences, including Bureau of Topographical Engineers chief John Abert, Secretary of the Navy Levi Woodbury, Chief of Army Engineers Charles Gratiot, and U.S. Army Commander-in-Chief General Alexander M. Macomb. In Hassler, a fellow French-speaking émigré, Nicollet thus found both a kindred spirit and a fervent supporter.

❋

Nicollet saw himself working in the tradition of his idol, the German naturalist and explorer Alexander von Humboldt, whose rigorous attention to detail and breadth of interests—ranging from geology to politics, meteorology to languages—had breathed new élan into the geographical sciences. Of particular import for Nicollet, Humboldt, during his explorations of Central and South America, had championed the use of the barometer in measuring the height of land above sea level, and of celestial observations in determining location.

When Nicollet reached Washington, the barometer had yet to be used in American exploration. But to him, the instrument represented the key to unlocking a much broader portrait—a three-dimensional calibration—of the nation's landscapes. By monitoring the barometer's column of mercury, one could measure topographical variances. Nicollet maintained that a map with data drawn from this method would bring a new precision to the nation's understanding of watersheds and other topographical phenomena. That information could help determine an area's suitability for irrigation and agriculture, canal construction, and human settlement.

❉

By the time Nicollet left Washington that April, he had embraced an ambitious project to survey the entire Mississippi River valley. In his baggage were his own sextant and chronometer, plus a lunette and barometer provided by the federal government. He also carried a letter of introduction from the War Department, to be presented to the commander of any U.S. Army post that he might encounter. Prior to heading west, however, he stopped in Baltimore, where he spent the next eight months at St. Mary's College visiting a coterie of French scholars at the school.

During the visit Nicollet also found time to complete a promised revision of a U.S. Army field manual on meteorology. Though not published by the Army until 1839, the revision, issued as "An Essay on Meteorology," impressed Chief of Army Engineers Gratiot, helped secure Nicollet's reputation in Washington, and paved the way for later work for the U.S. military.

Nicollet left Baltimore in December 1832, but news that a cholera outbreak had contaminated the key river valleys to the west led him to delay his journey to the Mississippi River. So he spent the next twelve months traveling through the South, conducting observations and taking copious notes on the region's topography and weather. In January 1834, he reached the Mississippi River and spent the next eighteen months traveling between New Orleans and the Gulf of Mexico, compiling data on the river's lower reaches.[3]

❉

Turning his attention to the Mississippi's upper stretches, in July 1835, Nicollet arrived in St. Louis, where he immediately sought out Henry Chouteau, a member of the famous St. Louis fur-trading family. Nicollet well knew that the Chouteaus and their firm, Pratte, Chouteau and Company—often called the American Fur Company—had a long-standing interest in furthering geographical knowledge of the West.

Henry's father, Auguste Chouteau—patriarch of St Louis in the late eighteenth century—had inaugurated the city's involvement in the Trans-Mississippi fur trade. Beyond its dealings with fur traders and trappers, the family's company frequently helped other Western sojourners such as explorers, painters and scientists—outfitting them, and transporting them on its steamboats—and, drawing on ties to various Indian tribes with which it traded, helping to win the travelers safe passage through otherwise hostile tribal lands. The Chouteau name, as Nicollet put it, "commands safety and hospitality among all the Indian nations of the United States north and south."[4]

❋

In August 1835, a month after he reached St. Louis, Nicollet contracted malaria while ascending the Missouri River on the fur company's steamer, *Diana*. While recuperating in St. Louis, and later in Natchez, Mississippi, he accumulated a diverse coterie of admirers—among them, the painter George Catlin and English geologist George W. Featherstonhaugh. Catlin had just returned from his latest portrait-painting tour of the Upper Missouri River country. Featherstonhaugh had just returned from the Mississippi River's headwaters, on his second federally funded government expedition.

Feathersonhaugh had just completed an ambitious survey of the Coteau des Prairies, the sprawling triangular plateau that separates the three major watersheds of the northern prairies—the Mississippi and the Missouri Rivers, which flow south to the Gulf of Mexico, and the Red River of the North, which flows north into Hudson Bay. Featherstonhaugh's stories about the Mississippi's headwaters intrigued Nicollet; and the Englishman made a point of emphasizing to Nicollet the need for accurate maps of the region.

Once he was healthy enough to travel, Nicollet set out, in June

1836, to make his own survey of the Mississippi's headwaters. Departing St. Louis aboard the *St. Peter's*, another fur company steamer, he spent most of July at Fort Snelling, a U.S. Army fort established in 1819, at the confluence of the Mississippi and the St. Peter's (today's Minnesota) Rivers. There, he befriended Lawrence Taliaferro, the fort's Indian agent, and Henry Sibley, the fur company's representative in the region. On July 29, outfitted by Sibley and Taliaferro with supplies and equipment, Nicollet, along with two guides recruited at the fort, departed for the headwaters of the Mississippi River.

Their subsequent seven-week expedition included a three-day visit to Lake Itasca, identified earlier by Schoolcraft as the source of the river. There, Nicollet conducted astronomical observations and, going beyond Schoolcraft's earlier survey, located the actual streams that fed the lake. The northern tour also included extensive dealings, mostly amiable, with the Chippewa Indians, on whose language and place-names Nicollet made copious notes.

When his survey party returned to Fort Snelling in September 1836, Nicollet had completed his reconnaissance of the Mississippi River. In three years of fieldwork, he had surveyed the river valley's entire length—from the Gulf of Mexico to Lake Itasca. He had established ten observation stations, at which he had determined the mean annual temperature and barometric pressure ratings. Beyond that, he had measured the height above sea level of sixty-five tributary rivers. Nicollet spent the winter of 1836–37 completing a map of the Coteau des Prairies. The resultant work, based on nearly two thousand astronomical and barometric observations, showed "more than 300 rivers and new lakes with their relations, the routes of winter and summer, opening all parts of the region to civilization which will soon be knocking at the door."[5]

In June 1837, a letter from Indian agent Taliaferro to his boss, Carey A. Harris, the Commissioner of Indian Affairs, made Nicollet's work known to Secretary of War Poinsett. In the letter, Taliaferro wrote, "We want information where to locate our Indians west of the Mississippi—as no man is better calculated than Mr. N. to answer this, or any other object of a Scientific nature desired by the Government."[6]

Poinsett—impressed with what he had heard about Nicollet's work and learning that the scientist was expected in Baltimore to visit his friends at St. Mary's College—asked Topographical Bureau chief Abert to summon him to Washington. After meeting with Nicollet, Abert wrote to Poinsett on January 17, 1838, noting that the explorer's work seemed "peculiarly adapted for the basis of a system of military defenses." The War Secretary instructed Abert to offer Nicollet three thousand dollars for the explorer's notes and maps. To hasten the transaction—and to keep it quiet and avoid a Congressional rebuke—Poinsett suggested that the funds be drawn from an existing military appropriation for surveys related to frontier forts.[7]

❋

Throughout its history, the federal government had occasionally found it necessary to employ topographical engineers—a Protean job description that, in those days, summoned everyone from mapmakers to surveyors, explorers to landscape artists. In most cases, these professionals, even if civilians, had some affiliation with the U.S. Army. Their numbers, however, had been few, their service sporadic. During the American Revolution, for instance, the Continental Army's official geographer had conducted surveys of various battle theaters. After the war, when the Continental Army was disbanded, another team, implementing the Land Ordinance of 1785, conducted surveys of the first seven "ranges" of the nation's public lands. And, of course, the federally financed explorations of Zebulon Pike, William Dunbar and George Hunter, Meriwether Lewis, William Clark, and Stephen Long all included observational work similar to that conducted during formal surveys.

Still later, during the War of 1812, the revived U.S. Army organized a topographical engineers corps to assist in logistical planning and intelligence gathering, but its activities, not surprisingly, waned after the war. Not until the 1820s—as settlers pushed increasingly westward, into the Mississippi and Ohio River valleys—did federally sponsored exploration revive. The U.S. Army's Bureau of Topographical Engineers, created in 1818, conducted surveys for a national road from Washington to New Orleans, assisted in the construction of the Chesapeake and Ohio Canal, removed snags from the Ohio and Mississippi

Rivers, and supervised work on the Cumberland Road. Though Army topographical engineers did supervise a survey of the Santa Fe Trail, linking Missouri and New Mexico, most U.S. government surveys of the era stayed east of the Mississippi. When federal policymakers sought geographical information on the West, therefore, they generally turned to sources outside the government.

❋

Since the late 1790s, American trappers, competing with their British rivals of the Hudson's Bay and North West Companies, had been entering the North American fur trade south of Canada. Some of the Americans began on the Pacific and moved eastward. Most, however, started in the Mississippi valley, then fanned out westwardly into the Missouri River valley, the Rockies, and the Oregon Territory.

While both Canadian and American trappers contributed to Western exploration, the Canadians more often published their findings. Typifying the American approach, when Robert Stuart of John Jacob Astor's fur company, in 1812, "discovered" the South Pass—what would later become the key immigrant route through the Rockies— his find stayed within the company. Not until 1830 would the U.S. government learn about South Pass—after trapper Jedediah Smith stumbled upon the route, in what is today southwest Wyoming, and disclosed it in a letter to War Secretary John Eaton. American fur magnates such as Astor, the Chouteaus, and Manuel Lisa tended to tightly control geographical information garnered by their traders and trappers.

By the mid-1820s, American trappers—including the so-called mountain men of the Rockies—dominated the U.S. fur trade; unlike their predecessors, this new breed of trappers signed no contracts for fixed periods of service, working instead in independent fur-trapping "brigades" and selling their pelts each summer at the rollicking, liquor-sodden, fur-company-sponsored "rendezvous," typically held on the Green River in the Rockies.

For those seeking knowledge of the West, however, these boisterous free spirits often proved frustrating. For starters, mountain men were reluctant to draw attention to what, in the eyes of Spanish—and, after 1821, Mexican—officials, was illegal poaching on foreign soil. But even mountain men trapping on U.S. soil posed problems for the government. Resourceful trappers like Etienne Provôt, Kit Carson, Jedediah Smith, and Jim Bridger made excellent guides, but their knowledge of the region—unsystematic, and focused on locating beavers—provided no coherent view of topographical or hydrological systems. And because their knowledge was rarely committed to the printed page, it could not be readily disseminated. The mountain man's physical presence was required for an expedition to fully exploit his expertise; and knowledge accumulated over decades could vanish with a single tomahawk blow. And when a mountain man's experiences did find their way to the printed page, they often merely repeated, or even introduced, geographical inaccuracies.

By January 1837, then, when War Secretary Poinsett sat down with Nicollet, he had grown increasingly aware of the dangers of the government's reliance on mountain men for geographical information. He also sensed growing national support for greater U.S. influence in the West.[8]

❋

Finally meeting in January 1837, Nicollet and Poinsett agreed that Nicollet would embark on a broad mapmaking survey of the Upper Mississippi basin. Earlier explorers like Lewis and Clark had ventured into the sprawling Upper Mississippi and Missouri valleys, but those outings had produced no comprehensive map of the Coteau des Prairies, the broad, fan-shaped plateau that divides the Mississippi, Missouri, and Red River drainage basins. Nicollet, it was decided, would divide his government-funded survey into two expeditions: the first would ascend the Mississippi, link up with his earlier surveys of that river's sources, then go westward into the Missouri River basin; the second would more fully ascend the Missouri River, then move northeast across the prairies, toward the U.S.–Canada border.

Discussing Indians and the growing population of whites in the West, Nicollet and Poinsett agreed that the "unconstrained" life of the region's tribes must give way to the "constraints of civilization." To help facilitate federal Indian policies, Nicollet agreed, during his exploration, to take copious notes on the West's various tribal cultures. He also agreed to report on abuses committed by the federal government's Indian agents and to scout out possible sites for new military forts.

Four months later, Nicollet received his official orders from Bureau of Topographical Engineers Corps head Abert: "As the views of the Secretary [of War] have been fully explained to you in frequent conversations you have had with him on the subject, and as the utmost confidence is reposed in your abilities and industry, further instructions are considered unnecessary." The federal government agreed to provide up to two thousand dollars for the expedition. Nicollet would be paid eight dollars a day while in the field and ten cents a mile to and from his survey route. The federal government also agreed to provide Nicollet with an assistant—"Mr. Freemont [*sic*]" a 25-year-old civilian employee of the Bureau of Topographical Engineers. His pay would be four dollars a day.[9]

❀

Arriving in May 1838, in St. Louis a bustling river city of about five thousand residents, Frémont met Nicollet for the first time. The seasoned explorer, Frémont's senior by almost three decades, and the young South Carolinian quickly developed a convivial mentor-protégé relationship. "Delighted" to be working with this "Pilgrim of Science," Frémont wrote to Poinsett, "Every day—almost every hour I feel myself sensibly advancing in professional knowledge & the confused ideas of Science & Philosophy wh [*sic*] my mind has been occupied are momently [*sic*] arranging themselves into order & clearness." Frémont also fell easily into his gregarious commanding officer's social realm: "His acquaintances he made mine, and I had the pleasure and advantage to share in the amiable intercourse and profuse hospitality which in those days characterized the society of the place."[10]

Nicollet's and Frémont's shared orbit of St. Louis friends came to include various soldiers and scientists, such as English geologist George S. Featherstonhaugh, German-born botanist George Engelmann, the aged explorer and Indian agent William Clark, and young Robert E. Lee, then a captain in the Army Corps of Engineers. Lee, especially, impressed Frémont: "His agreeable, friendly manner to me as a younger officer when I was introduced to him, left a more enduring impression than usually goes with casual introductions."

Frémont also won entree into Nicollet's circle of local French-speaking residents. Years later, basking in the glow of warm memories of Nicollet, John Charles would recall with satisfaction the pride that St. Louis's Francophones took in the French explorer's accomplishments: "They were proud of him as a distinguished countryman, and were gratified by his employment by the American Government, which in this way recognized his distinction and capacity."

Indeed, Nicollet, a stickler for French authenticity, began spelling his assistant's name as *Frémont* months before John Charles Fremon did himself. For Frémont, the "illegitimate" son of a poor wayfaring Frenchman, the matter of his ancestry had always been a painful subject. But through Nicollet's contagious pride in all things French, the budding explorer discovered a newfound confidence in his personal heritage, a satisfaction that, bypassing the circumstances of his own birth, suddenly connected him with an array of stellar Gallic lights—from Molière to Laplace, from La Salle to Nicollet.

In St. Louis, Frémont, along with Nicollet, became a frequent guest of local French Roman Catholic clergy: "The pleasure of these [meals] grew in remembrance afterward, when hard and scanty fare and sometimes starvation and bodily weakness made visions in the mind, and hunger made memory dwell upon them by day and dream of them by night."[11]

Still more interaction with French society came through Frémont's dealings with St. Louis's Chouteau family. Earlier that year, Nicollet had gone to New York and met with Pierre Chouteau, Jr., and Ramsay Crooks, officers of the American Fur Company. The three developed a rough budget for the expedition and agreed that the American Fur Company, from its posts in St. Louis and Fort Snelling, would provide Nicollet with both men and supplies; the federal government would later reimburse the company. Frémont would act as dispersing agent for the arrangement. According to Frémont, the "kindly and efficient aid of the Fur company's officers" transcended mere logistical convenience. Nicollet's party also benefited from the company's decades of experience in assembling wilderness expeditions: "Their personal experience made them know exactly what was needed on the proposed voyage, and both stores and men were selected by them; the men out of those in their own employ. These were principally practiced *voyageurs*, accustomed to the experiences and incidental privations of travel in the Indian country."[12]

✴

On May 18, 1838, Frémont, Nicollet, and Charles Geyer, a German botanist hired by Nicollet at his own expense, departed St. Louis aboard the *Burlington*, a fur company steamer. On May 25, the three arrived at Fort Snelling, the jumping-off point for their wilderness sojourn. Fort Snelling occupied a stunning spot atop a white bluff, on the west bank of the Mississippi at its confluence with the Minnesota River. The redoubt constituted a lonely enclave in a dense wilderness—the only U.S. fort north of a line stretching from today's Prairie du Chien, Wisconsin, to the Pacific Ocean.

Across the Minnesota River from the fort stood the home of Henry Sibley, commander of the American Fur Company's far-flung operations throughout the Upper Mississippi and Missouri River valleys. The tall, handsome, and audacious Sibley already enjoyed a formidable reputation at the age of twenty-seven. The son of a prominent Michigan political figure, he had abandoned legal studies at the age of eighteen and, within a year, was working for the American Fur Company. His savvy as a fur trader and his broad knowledge of the Old Northwest—today's upper Midwest—won widespread admiration.

Sibley's reward came in 1834, when John Jacob Astor retired from the American Fur Company and sold the firm's Western Department to St. Louis's Pratte, Chouteau and Company. Sibley moved to Fort Snelling, built his legendary stone house there, and began overseeing the activities of all the company's posts scattered between the Missouri and Mississippi Rivers, and north to—in some cases, beyond—the U.S.–Canada border. Voyageurs hired in Montreal for three-year stints and outfitted by the company ranged across Sibley's domain, visited Indians, and traded for pelts. Traders, clerks, voyageurs spread across thousands of miles of wilderness. Ultimately, they all answered to Sibley.

For four weeks, as fur company agents completed their provision of men and supplies for the expedition, Nicollet, Frémont, and Geyer stayed as guests in Sibley's rustic bachelor home. To Poinsett, Frémont wrote, "Every instant of our time . . . has been occupied in astronomical & Geological observations." To his mother, however, Frémont offered a softer portrait of his new mentor, telling her, "He is a real Frenchman in this & you know exactly what they are. He has provided a nice little store of Coffee, Chocolate, Tea, prepared Soup &c in addition to the more substantial articles of food. He has got a store of medicine too & makes me take some pills occasionally. As far as regards Science I am improving under him daily & my health under the influence of this delicious climate has become excellent."[13]

Frémont liked Sibley and the house's frontier ambiance, "on the border line of civilization. . . . The house had much the character of a hunting-lodge." He also delighted in Sibley's dogs, who had free run of the place, as well as the "men who love dogs and horses": "Cut off from the usual resources, Mr. Sibley had naturally to find his in the surroundings. The prominent feature of Indian life entered into his, and hunting became rather an occupation than an amusement."

Frémont also savored his first encounters with Western Indians: a Sioux village lay close to Sibley's house, and Indians often lingered on its grounds: "Among these I saw the most beautiful Indian girl I have ever met, and it is a tribute to her singular beauty that after so many years I remember still the name of 'Ampetu-washtoy'—'the Beautiful day.' " Nicollet, by contrast, remained aloof from the charms of Sibley's citadel; in his memoirs, Frémont would recall that Nicollet, while at Sibley's, showed no interest, "in all this stir of frontier life"—"horse and dog were nothing to him."[14]

❋

For all the light-hearted pleasures Frémont took in the company of local Indians at Fort Snelling, he and Nicollet understood the dangers tribesmen posed to them in the wilderness country they were about to enter. No doubt, Sibley told them of his own recent Indian troubles—about how, after the death of one frontier agent and the wounding of another, he had been compelled to close several of the fur company's posts.

Despite the assorted treaties that had nominally secured U.S. dominion over the Upper Mississippi valley, no one with firsthand experience in the area truly believed, in 1838, that Washington controlled the sprawling domain that stretched north and west from Fort Snelling. Indians far outnumbered whites in this country largely devoid of permanent settlements. Once they left Sibley's home and the high citadels of Fort Snelling, Nicollet and his companions would enter a complex world of hostilities—some directed against whites, others fermented by tribal rivalries.

Once residents of the Ohio valley, the Sioux, also known as the Dakota, had, by the eighteenth century, been driven by the Chippewa into the Upper Mississippi valley. Of the Sioux's seven main tribes, the Teton, Yankton, and Yanktonai roamed the plains west of today's Minnesota. Immediately west and south of Fort Snelling lived the four other major Sioux tribes, those under Sibley's jurisdiction—the Wahpekute, Mdewakantonwan, Wahpetonwan, and Sisitonwan.

By 1838, all the major Sioux tribes felt growing pressures from encroaching whites. They also faced persecution by roving bands of Algonquian Indians—the Sac, Fox, and Potawatomi tribes—whose lands, east of the Mississippi, had been ceded to the United States after the Black Hawk War of 1832. The Sac and Fox, though related but not always friendly, were living in today's Iowa and, in ongoing skirmishes, were driving the Sioux northward and westward.

In such a vexed tangle of rivalries, an explorer might be killed for being a white interloper in Indian country or might become a target merely for having been seen in the company of the wrong tribe. On the eve of the party's departure into the north woods, Frémont, in a letter to Poinsett masking any fears he might have felt, boasted, "Our party, tho' small, is well armed, at least sufficiently so to secure us in the event of an accidental rencontrè [sic]. & Mr. Nicollet's knowledge of the the Indians justifies us in believing that we shall meet with no serious difficulty."[15]

❁

On June 9, the party, traveling in two groups, departed Sibley's American Fur Company post. Nine men rowed up the Minnesota River in a boat laden with expedition supplies, while the seven others traveled overland in carts. Within a week, the men had reassembled into a single division. Snaking through the Minnesota River country of marshes, streams, prairies, and meadows, the long, caravan made a motley sight. At its head, in a barouche, rode Joseph Laframboise, then in his early thirties, an able American Fur Company agent, hired by Sibley as the expedition's chief scout. Riding beside Laframboise in the wagon was Eugene Flandin—about eighteen years old, the son of a French merchant in New York. Young Flandin had come along at the behest of that city's French consul. Flandin's father, eager for the boy to experience the West, compensated Nicollet with a hunting dog, who ended up being left behind. Two more Frenchmen would later join the party—Viscount de Montmort, an attaché from the French legation in Washington, and Gaspard de Belligny, a tourist out for a glimpse of Indian country. Following Laframboise and Flandin in the caravan came eight horse-drawn wagons, each led by one of the voyageurs hired by Sibley. In the wagon at the rear, supervising the column, rode Nicollet, Frémont, the botanist Geyer, and Joseph Renville, Jr., the son of famous fur trader and scout Joseph Renville, Sr., and who himself had long experience among the Sioux. In return for taking his son along, the senior Renville had given Nicollet a horse and a double-barreled rifle.

As the party, traveling southwest, moved up the Minnesota River, Geyer, Nicollet, and Frémont tended to their respective scientific tasks. As Geyer collected botanical and geological samples, Nicollet and Frémont conducted astronomical observations. When the weather was clear, Nicollet and his young assistant were obligated to stop at midday and to get up at odd hours of the night to fidget with sextants, chronometers, barometers, telescopes, and books of astronomical tables in order to record latitude, longitude, and altitude.

The Coteau's topographical blandness only reinforced the need for rigorous attention to geodesic observations. Wooded throughout, pocked with lakes, and threaded with streams large and small, the rolling hills of the Coteau des Prairies offered the traveler no grand vistas, no dramatic landscapes, no recognizable natural landmarks except for lakes and rivers. At its highest point, the plateau reaches no more than eight hundred feet above the surrounding flat country. Indeed, only from outside does the Coteau visually cohere as a discrete province. To early French voyageurs traveling across the treeless prairies, the plateau with its dense forests appeared to be nothing less than the coast of the prairie.

✸

Typical of the measurements recorded by explorers using the land navigation tools of that day, the latitudes taken by Nicollet and Frémont are generally accurate, the longitudes less so. To find latitude, one used a sextant to "shoot" the sun at noon—or, at night, Polaris, the North Star—to measure its height in degrees above the horizon, then consulted an astronomical table. Finding longitude, a more complicated process, required knowing the time in Greenwich, England (Longitude 0°), which required a chronometer—a delicate pocket-size timepiece often rattled by the rigors of frontier travel. Knowing the time at Greenwich, one could measure with a sextant the height that a particular star reached at a preappointed time and, from that, using a body of astronomical tables, could deduce one's longitudinal position. If the chronometer stopped, as it often did, one could consult an ephemeris, a book compiling predictable astronomical movements for a given period—say, the eclipse on a given day of one of Jupiter's moons—and then wait with a telescope to observe that night's particular phenomenon. Because such movements appear at the same time the world over, explorers used them to retrieve Greenwich time. To determine sea level, Nicollet and Frémont used a barometer and a series of complex mathematical formulae; and, if the barometer wasn't working, heated water, noting the temperature at which it boiled, and then worked a series of mathematical equations to calculate height above sea level.

The Dutch book on astronomy that Frémont had stumbled upon in Charleston had sparked his passion for observing the night sky, and his naval tour and two Appalachian surveys had provided a solid foundation in geodesy. And now, as the party surveyed the Coteau, Nicollet nurtured in Frémont a discipline that approached that of a religious ritual. Frémont marveled at how, for Nicollet, "an astronomical observation was a solemnity, and required such decorous preparations as an Indian makes when he goes where he thinks there are supernatural beings." Reciprocating the admiration, Nicollet soon assigned Frémont the exacting task of using compass, pen, and paper to render each day's "bird's-eye view" of the terrain covered."[16]

❉

Between June 14 and 17, the party camped at Traverse des Sioux, a favored crossing point on the Minnesota, and met with Sleepy Eyes, chief of the Swan Lake band of Sisitonwan Indians. "We were occupied quietly among the Indians," Frémont noted,—"Mr. Nicollet, as usual, surrounded by them, with the aid of the interpreter getting them to lay out the form of the lake and the course of the streams entering the river near by, and, after repeated pronunciations, entering their names in his note-book." Laframboise was especially helpful: he was married to Sleepy Eyes's daughter. The old chief was so taken with Nicollet that he offered to join the expedition. "Where you go our enemies throng," Frémont recalled him saying. "I must go with you." Nicollet—citing a recent unhealed wound afflicting the chief and the "great jealousy of his wife who would be left behind"—declined the offer.

"I give you then my Son," the chief responded; "—he is to me the dearest thing on earth, but my heart will be rejoiced if he dies fighting for the whites." This offer, Nicollet accepted: "I will answer for his life with mine." Frémont later recalled that all the party's members resolved, then and there, that they would bring the chief's son back alive, "or remain on the prairie" with him.

Before leaving Traverse des Sioux, Nicollet gave the Sisitonwan salutations from the Great Father in Washington and some gunpowder, but warned them to use it for hunting, not killing other Indians. Otherwise, "Your scalp will hang in your enemy's lodge if you carry it with you to war."[17]

❉

During his government-financed expeditions of the late 1830s, Nicollet dutifully executed his role as an emissary of the "Great Father" in Washington to the Indians. His kindness, however, was always accompanied by the same message: The United States now holds dominion over the lands and waters of the region; your best hopes lie in submitting to that authority. Nicollet also kept an eye out for potential sites for the new cordon of U.S. Army forts. In an 1839 journal entry, for instance, on growing intertribal Indian wars along the Missouri River, he noted that Fort Leavenworth lay too far from "these bloody events, which are only too frequently brought about by these quarreling nations." Recommending the construction of a new fort atop Council Bluffs overlooking the river, he noted that while the site offered no timber for construction, "The necessary supplies can be obtained within a range of a very few miles." In the new system of frontier defenses contemplated by the federal government, he added, any alternative site on the Missouri south of Council Bluffs "would be of no use for the purpose intended."[18]

On a personal level, however, Nicollet had little passion for politics—still less for military matters and the government's Indian removal policies. In early 1838, after affiliating with the U.S. Army's Bureau of Topographical Engineers, Nicollet had warned Henry Sibley, "I need not tell you that I want to organize my expedition in the simplest and most economical manner, and not be troubled with taking along a military force."[19] Throughout his life, Nicollet resisted being swept into military or political causes. When politics arose in conversations, he often switched the subject to scientific or philosophical matters, and once complained that talk of politics left him "melancholy" and "distressed." Though Nicollet accepted federal Indian policies, he believed their day-to-day implementation teemed with hypocrisy. U.S. treaties with Indians, he complained, always guaranteed tribes protection, friendship, and hunting rights; "but the people of the United States pay little attention to federal laws and treaties when it is to their advantage to nullify them."

Federal Indian policies were both benign and brutal—in some instances, merely seeking to gather ethnographic information, and to determine how best to protect Indian peoples from other tribes and white interlopers. In other cases, policies advanced coercive actions that left Indians dead, landless, or both. Perhaps Nicollet felt some ambivalence—even hypocrisy—in his role as an agent for such policies. Certainly, in his own dealings with Indians, he showed more concern with ethnographic interests and whatever small kindnesses he might bestow, than with any grand geopolitical visions promulgated by the War Department.[20]

Beyond politics and Indians, it was the land itself that most stirred Nicollet. Most policymakers in Washington, when it came to Western matters, had more explicitly geopolitical concerns. Indeed, many in Washington nourished visions of extending the nation's dominion to lands far west of the Mississippi River. But for Nicollet, such east-west concerns paled beside his desire, however prosaic, to comprehend the continent's various drainage systems.

Nicollet's passions lay in uniformity of measurements, not geopolitics—in natural systems, not man-made boundaries. "Boundaries! On land where there are none marked!" he complained of a Missouri law banning Indians from crossing the state. "A native breathing the air of natural liberty placed against a nation with civil and republican liberties!!!" Anticipating John Wesley Powell's later suggestion that political boundaries trace riparian drainage basins, Nicollet, in 1843, recommended that boundaries for the new state of Iowa and all other contemplated Western states be drawn in such a way that they—eschewing the tyranny of straight lines and other geometric constructs —would provide an equitable distribution of the region's watersheds and other natural resources.[21] If an urgency propelled his work, it answered to natural—not political—sirens. "It is necessary," he noted in his journal, "to make haste in order to take nature by surprise while it is still in a quasi-virgin state and while the consequences of its laws are still open to us."

❋

Such was the vision of nature and the world that Nicollet passed along to his young protégé Frémont. In a letter to War Secretary Poinsett at the conclusion of the Coteau des Prairies expedition, Nicollet described, with evident pride, the intellectual breadth of the tutelage conferred upon his young assistant: "In all the course of our campaign, it is not only in science that I have tried to develop the ideas of Mr. Frémont." Throughout it all, Nicollet wrote, he had strived to give his student, "the large view of politics, commerce, farming, and so on which the regions we have explored may offer in the future to the government and the people of the United States. At the least opportunity, I have made him a part of my long studies and the results of my experience."[22] In the end, Nicollet conferred a spatial and scientific dimension on the nationalist ideology that Frémont had learned from Poinsett. He passed along a sort of protoecological ethos: a way of comprehending landscapes and borders that would help ease Frémont's later transition from scientific explorer to freewheeling transgressor of national borders.[23]

❋

Through mid- to late June, the survey party moved through the forested valleys of the Minnesota, then the Cottonwood River, eventually ascending the eastern slope of the Coteau des Prairies. "The plateau that opens here presents neither hills nor woods," Nicollet recalled. "It is a high, grand, and beautiful prairie (1,000 to 1,100 feet). The view to the south seems limitless, the verdure losing itself far away in the azure of the sky." On the morning of June 26, Nicollet dispatched Laframboise and Frémont to make a reconnaissance and produce a sketch of some nearby lakes. By nightfall, when the two failed to return, Nicollet had grown worried. His fears, as it turned out, were justified. When, at 9 p.m. that evening, Laframboise and Frémont returned, exhausted, they told a harrowing story: That day, while crossing the Des Moines River—in today's southwestern Minnesota—their wagon had become mired in mud on the river's bottom. As Nicollet recorded their tale, the men, in chest-deep water, "attempted to push the wheels, but Mr. Frémont who had just eaten had a cramp because of the water. He lost consciousness and just missed drowning." While the incident must have been traumatic, Frémont—perhaps out of lingering embarrassment—made no reference to it in his memoirs nor in any surviving letters.

Although the exploring party traveled under the imprimatur of the U.S. Army's Bureau of Topographical Engineers, all of its members were civilians. In commanding such an entourage, Nicollet reasoned, prudent solicitousness went further than an iron fist: "They seem to understand, after all, that they have more to gain with me by being honest, obedient, and gay than by thieving, rioting, or anger. Harmony reigns among us. Mr. Laframboise leaves them alone, and they have only to deal with me."[24]

Nicollet's journal's reference to Laframboise—his "State-Major"— underscored his high regard for the scout, as well as the limitations on Frémont's role as Nicollet's official "assistant." Despite his title of second-in-command officer, Frémont was largely confined to scientific matters. In conducting celestial observations and similar tasks, Frémont proved an able collaborator. In the presence of Laframboise and other seasoned scouts, voyageurs, and trappers, however, Nicollet would not entrust the expedition's safety in often hostile country to a twenty-five-year-old with scant experience in the wilds, and none in the West.

✳

Toward 1:30 p.m. on June 29, the party reached Pipestone Quarry, a striking display of ocher-tinged rock outcrops in today's southwestern Minnesota. Renowned then as a peaceful meeting place for rival tribes, its name derived from a layer of red stone in the formation, coveted by Indians for the making of pipes. A Sioux legend told of how the Great Spirit of thunder had first quarried the red stone, and how that deity always greets visitors with bursts of thunder and lightning.

As it turned out, about a half mile from the site, a violent thunderstorm burst upon the exploring party. "The confirmation of the legend," Frémont recalled, "was pleasing to young Renville and the Sioux who had accompanied us." Moments later, "As we came into the valley the storm broke away in a flow of sunshine on the line of red bluff which extended for about three miles." As for the site, "It was in itself a lovely place, made interesting by the mysterious character given to it by Indian tradition, and because of the fact that the existence of such a rock is not known anywhere else."

During six days at Pipestone Quarry, Frémont and Nicollet conducted their usual observations. The entire party shared repasts with visiting Sioux. On one occasion, the explorers, to win favor among the Indians, detonated an explosion to assist some tribesmen quarrying the area's famous red stone. On the Fourth of July, Nicollet gave Frémont the task of planting the Stars and Stripes atop a twenty-five-foot-high column of rock, a job which required a perilous jump from a neighboring bluff. The young explorer—perhaps already with an eye on posterity and, as later critics would charge, a penchant for self-dramatization—recalled the incident: "It was quite a feat to spring to this from the bluff, as the top was barely a foot square and uneven, and it required a sure foot not to go further." Afterward, Frémont and others in the party commemorated the moment: "This was a famous place of the country, and nearly all of us, as is the custom in famous places the world over, carved our names in the stone. It speaks for the enduring quality of this rock that the names remain distinct to this day."[25] Indeed, one of the few surviving archeological vestiges of Frémont's explorations, the carved initials remain at today's Pipestone National Monument, in Pipestone, Minnesota.

❋

From Pipestone Quarry, the expedition marched toward Joseph Renville's trading post and mission, on Lac qui Parle, in today's Chippewa County, Minnesota, which it reached on July 15. There, they enjoyed, for the next four days, Renville's generous hospitality. "We had abundance of milk and vegetables," remembered Frémont, "all seasoned with a traveler's appetite and a hearty welcome."

Indeed, the elder Joseph Renville, a Métis—a halfbreed—born in the region, had worked as a guide for both Zebulon Pike and Stephen Long. Métis—the offspring of French-speaking boatmen and Indian women—made ideal guides for whites passing through Indian country. Renville understood the land, Indian languages, and the intertribal politics of Indian country. In 1835, after years of working for the Hudson's Bay Company and the Columbia Fur Company, Renville moved to Laq qui Parle. There he built his trading post; and, under his protection, soon rose two Protestant missions, which ministered to local Indians. By Lac qui Parle's loquacious waters, Renville—almost sixty years old when Nicollet and Frémont passed through—lived in what another visitor called "barbaric splendor quite like an African king." While Nicollet praised Renville's American patriotism, others took a more skeptical view of this Métis trader who was married to a Sioux woman, and who had fought for the British during the War of 1812. Some suspected him of having no loyalty beyond his own personal interests.

Considered in another light, however, Renville's life and life story only recapitulated three centuries of frontier history, for in the tangle of the wily old trader's American, French, Sioux, and British genetic, political, and economic bloodlines, he embodied nothing less than a multicultural microcosm of life on the Trans-Mississippi frontier.[26]

❀

While at Lac qui Parle, Nicollet, reflecting his growing confidence in his young assistant, decided to double the ground covered by the expedition in its remaining days by dividing the force into two parties—one that he would lead, the other to be led by Frémont. "His rapid progress," Nicollet recalled, "convinced me that I could trust him without misgivings."[27]

On July 19, the party left Lac qui Parle for the return trip down the Minnesota River to its junction with the Cottonwood River. As Nicollet and his party descended the river by canoe, Frémont led the other band on an overland route. After the entire party regrouped at the confluence, Geyer joined Nicollet for a six-day overland survey of the region between the Des Moines and Blue Earth Rivers. Frémont, meanwhile, surveyed by canoe the lower reaches of the Blue Earth, a tributary of the Minnesota River. The entire party reunited and returned to Fort Snelling on August 26.

From Fort Snelling, from late August through mid September, Nicollet and Frémont again conducted separate surveys. Traveling southwest, Nicollet explored the Cannon River watershed, Spirit Lake, and the headwaters of the Des Moines River. Frémont, meanwhile, made a reconnaissance of the area near the junction of the Waki-Oju River—today's Zumbro—with the Mississippi, the site of a proposed U.S. Army fort. By prior arrangement, the two explorers reunited, in late October, at Augustin Rocque's trading post three miles below Lake Pepin, a wide stretch of the river along today's Minnesota-Wisconsin border.

By November 3, Frémont and Nicollet had reached the settlement of Prairie du Chien, just north of the Mississippi's junction with the Wisconsin River. When, three days later, the river froze, blocking navigation from the north, the men began what became a vain monthlong wait for a steamship from the south. In December, they embarked on a wearying overland trip to St. Louis. From Nicollet, Frémont heard the sad news that all of Geyer's boxes of geological and botanical specimens, placed on a steamship for shipment to St. Louis, had failed to arrive. In early January 1839, while a weary Nicollet stayed behind in St. Louis—still hoping for the arrival of Geyer's boxes—Frémont left for Washington. Before leaving, he penned a letter, dated January 1, to John James Abert, accepting an appointment at the rank of second lieutenant in the newly created U.S. Army Corps of Topographical Engineers.[28]

THERE'S GEOGRAPHY FOR YOU!

U PON REACHING WASHINGTON in January 1839, John Frémont learned, to his delight, that War Secretary Joel Poinsett
remained enthusiastic about Nicollet's project. Indeed, in his
annual report to Congress the previous November, Poinsett had
praised the Pipestone expedition, called for more Western surveys,
and linked the need for them to his ongoing advocacy of a line of
Western forts.

From Nicollet, Frémont brought for Poinsett a letter and some
manuscripts, and for Mrs. Poinsett a bedspread, "made by the Indians
of magnificent black bear skins." In the letter to Poinsett, Nicollet
praised Frémont's work: "My satisfaction is without reserve or
shadow." Nicollet reported that although he was disappointed that
Geyer's botanical and geological specimens were still missing, the expedition had proven fruitful. Beyond gathering substantial information related to scientific and military concerns, they had visited
numerous Indian tribes and "have made them friendly to the United
States." Nicollet also noted that "one campaign more, like the last
one, would be a great and lovely affair."[1]

❊

In their hopes for another expedition, Frémont and Nicollet's timing
could not have been better. The previous July, while they were recon-
noitering the Coteau des Prairies, Congress had fulfilled a request
made by Poinsett eight months earlier for a greater federal commit-

ment to Western exploration by creating the U.S. Army Corps of Topographical Engineers, a unit that soon boasted thirty-six officers, twenty-eight of them West Point graduates. Equally advantageous to Nicollet and Frémont, the reorganized corps was directed by John James Abert, an ally who reported directly to their friend Poinsett.[2]

In Abert, Nicollet and Frémont found an ally every bit Poinsett's equal in his zeal for promoting Western exploration. A blunt-speaking soldier and part-time lawyer, well-versed in the sciences, with a passion for horse racing and frontier travel, Abert had become chief of the Army's old Bureau of Topographical Engineers in 1829. Almost immediately, he had begun lobbying for a larger, more autonomous corps, with an expanded mandate—displaying in the process an acute level of political savvy that sustained him for the duration of his Army tenure.

As a unit of the War Department, Abert's Corps of Topographical Engineers lay under the President's nominal direction but looked to Congress to fund its various activities. On a day-to-day basis, however, the Corps tended to elude rigorous scrutiny, both by the White House and by most members of Congress. Abert's immediate superior was the Secretary of War; and so long as Poinsett held that position, Abert had a simpatico boss.

Jealously guarding his prerogatives as the Corps' chief and a devotee of the geographical sciences, Abert over the years proved a loyal friend to many scientists and naturalists—particularly foreign ones such as John James Audubon and Joseph Nicollet. Even so, Abert tended to be a proponent of what one historian called that era's "stowaway sciences" at each turn in his dealings with Washington's political and military bureaucracy. He tended to conceal many of the scientific objectives of his various expeditions within the larger vessel of military purpose. Through such discretion and strategic alliances, Abert's Corps benefited from the nation's broader policies in the West— including the region's militarization, Indian removal, mineral and agricultural exploitation, and promotion of white settlement.[3]

✤

On March 2, 1839, Abert wrote to Frémont, ordering him to "repair to St. Louis as soon as practicable, & there joining Mr. Nicollet, . . . aid him in his geograpl. operations." This second government-funded expedition would more fully ascend the Missouri River, then move northeast across the prairies, toward the U.S.–Canada border.

Once again, funds for the trip would come from Abert's departmental budget—two thousand dollars advanced, five thousand in credit. The American Fur Company would outfit the party again and be reimbursed by the Corps of Topographical Engineers. This time, however, the government would compensate even botanist Geyer—an obligation previously borne by Nicollet from his own pocket. In the same March 2 letter—foreshadowing later, more serious troubles arising from the explorer's carelessness with money—Abert chastised Frémont to keep better accounts of expedition finances. Earlier complaints from War Department accountants had castigated Frémont for his neglect of the agency's rigorous bookkeeping methods, especially his frequent failure to obtain receipts for goods and services obtained in wilderness settings—such as the assistance of Indian scouts and horses purchased from voyageurs: "The experience which you have had with your accts., will, I hope, prevent the encountering of similar difficulties hereafter, & impress upon your mind the necessity of bills in detail and receipts."[4]

Nicollet assumed that this would be the final—and the most important—of his Mississippi valley surveys. He had thoroughly studied the sources of the river; he had seen and measured great expanses of the Old Northwest. But he had yet to penetrate thoroughly the Coteau des Prairies, and to survey the headwaters of the Red River of the North. And until those two feats were accomplished, he did not believe he could produce his promised map.

❋

On April 4, 1839, Nicollet, Frémont, and Geyer left St. Louis, chugging up the Missouri River aboard the *Antelope*, a fur company steamer. Accompanying the party's principal members were five new men hired for the expedition—including mountain man Etienne Provôt and Prussian-born trapper and trader Louis Zindel, known for his expertise with artillery. Provôt, almost sixty when he joined Nicollet's party, ranked as one of the most well-known mountain men of his day. An early participant in the house of Chouteau's Rocky Mountain fur trade, he is often credited with being the first white man to visit the Great Salt Lake. For Frémont, his first encounter with a mountain man marked a signal moment. But over the next ten years Frémont, along with other scientifically trained explorers cast in his image, would supplant mountain men as the nation's chief scouts.

❋

In 1839, with the Missouri River swollen by the Rockies' spring thaw, the *Antelope* made fitful upstream progress. Determined not to squander any mapping opportunity, Nicollet, at the voyage's outset, established shifts for making deckside astronomical observations and periodic "bird's-eye view" sketches of the country that the boat passed through on its upstream voyage: Nicollet handled daybreak to nine in the morning, Frémont nine to two; botanist Charles Geyer took the final shift.

"For nearly two months and a half," Frémont recalled, "we were struggling against the turbid river, which in that season of high waters was so swift and strong that sometimes the boat would for moments stand quite still, seeming to pause to gather strength, until the power of steam asserted itself and she would fight her way into a smooth reach." Logs and branches obstructed navigation; and the ship often dropped anchor for the night, while passengers cut wood for the next day's arduous passage. Indeed, at Council Bluffs, north of the Missouri's junction with the Platte River, the survey party passed the wreckage of the *Pirate*, a ship that had sailed from St. Louis ahead of the *Antelope*, but that had sunk on a snag. Even more disconcerting to Nicollet and his men, the *Pirate* had been carrying six bags of flour for their expedition. "We can only see the top of the roof and the portholes of the state cabins," Nicollet recorded in his journal. "A few Indians, prowling around the wreckage to pull a few pieces off it, cast a shadow of sadness over our thoughts."[5]

Days later, a similar poignancy fell over the party when the men spotted the ruins of a once-flourishing fur company settlement. Four years earlier, Nicollet recalled—on his first, eventually malaria-aborted, trip up the Missouri River—he had sat inside one of the now crumbling buildings and enjoyed a café au lait with the post's manager. Now, as Frémont noted, fallen houses haunted the lonesome spot—a "ruin in the midst of a primitive region still unknown to the history of the world."[6]

But not all thoughts veered toward the melancholy. Frémont also savored the solitude of the Missouri's upper reaches: "Once above the settlements of the lower Missouri, there were no sounds to disturb the stillness but the echoes of the high-pressure steam-pipe, which traveled far along and around the shores, and the incessant crumbling away of the banks and bars, which the river was steadily undermining and destroying at one place to build up at another."[7]

❋

In early June, Nicollet, Frémont, and company—now some thirteen hundred miles from St. Louis—debarked at the American Fur Company's Fort Pierre. Here and throughout their Western travels, Nicollet and Frémont remained ever mindful of past explorers and how they had described local conditions. A particular obsession for both men was explorer Stephen Long's—as it turned out, erroneous—characterization of the region between the Mississippi and the Rockies as the "Great American Desert." Pondering the high plains stretching west from Port Pierre, for instance, Nicollet noticed that rainwater draining into the Missouri transformed the soil of the river's banks into damp clay, but that within two days it was again dry, rough, and brittle:

The soil of the high prairies to the west is of approximately the same sort, and so it is understandable that these vast regions, reputed to reach all the way to the mountains, are so sterile that they are referred to as "the Great American Desert" and that some travelers have compared them to the deserts of Africa. But the fact that the ground is sterile because it is too clayey does not necessarily mean that it cannot be fertilized and improved.[8]

Fertilizer, Nicollet believed, could improve the soil; but, then again, so would the Indian removal policies already in place—or, at the least, the weaning of tribesmen from their traditional nomadic lives and their conversion to a life of settled agriculture. For unlike many whites confronting the West, Nicollet labored under no illusions that he was gazing upon a fixed tableau. In an insight passed along to Frémont, Nicollet, far ahead of most thinkers of his day, discounted all notions of "virgin lands." He understood that, long before the white man's arrival, the West's landscape was already being shaped and reshaped by human occupants: "All the prairies watered by the Mississippi and the Missouri are the work of the Indians who destroy by fire the rich vegetation to assure themselves of animal food. Let the vast and shorn prairies that we cross remain untouched and the forest, with time, will reappear."[9]

✻

As early as the late seventeenth century, French explorers in the Upper Missouri and Upper Mississippi valleys tended to view the region as something of a garden—watered by ample rivers, bountiful in vegetation. In 1763, at the conclusion of the Seven Years' War, British explorers displayed a renewed interest in North America and were preoccupied with finding a Northwest Passage across the continent. For that reason, the British, neglecting more southerly climes, tended to focus their explorations on developing a canoe-and-portage route across Canada and down British Columbia's Pacific slope.

Thus, British explorers and trappers rarely ventured into the Upper Missouri and Mississippi basins. To the extent they did, they tended to characterize the region as desertlike—lacking the soil, vegetation, and climate needed to sustain European-style settlement. What the French and British views shared was a generalization that tended to obscure dramatic ecological, meteorological, and topographical variances within the two riparian basins.

Among Americans of the early nineteenth century, Lewis and Clark's transcontinental expedition of 1804–06—and President Jefferson's subsequent endorsement of their view—had helped to fix among American scientists and travelers an image of the Pacific Northwest as a sublimely bountiful region teeming with splendid forests; rushing, salmon-rich rivers; and soil as rich as any east of the Mississippi. But Lewis and Clark gave short shrift to what they regarded as the West's desert—a zone they confined to a twenty-mile stretch of badlands along the Upper Missouri.[10]

By the 1830s, however, the American view of the sprawling Western plains east of the Rockies had grown complicated. Those in the West and the Southeast who enjoyed firsthand knowledge of the region tended to recognize its broad diversity. But many other Americans—particularly in the Northeast—embraced the English view of the region as a vast desert. That perception had been reinforced by Zebulon Pike and Stephen Long. Pike, in 1806, comparing the plains east of the Rockies to Africa's Sahara, had dismissed them as the "Great Sandy Desert." Fourteen years later, Long, on the map generated by his 1819–20 Western expedition, labeled the same area the "Great American Desert." Of that area, Long's colleague Edwin James, in his official account of the expedition, wrote:

> In regard to this extensive section of country, we do not hesitate in giving the opinion, that it is almost wholly unfit for cultivation, and of course uninhabitable by a people depending upon agriculture for their subsistence. Although tracts of fertile land, considerably extensive, are occasionally to be met with, yet the scarcity of wood and water, almost uniformly prevalent, will prove an insuperable obstacle in the way of settling the country . . . The whole of this country seems peculiarly adapted as a range for buffaloes, wild goats, and other wild game, incalculable multitudes of which find ample pasturage and subsistence upon it.

Moreover, true to the territorially conservative bent of many early American empire-builders, Long and Pike both celebrated what they viewed as the immutable sterility of the northern plains as a barrier to the republic's enlargement. As Pike, sounding like some buckskin Montesquieu, put it:

> From these immense prairies may arise one great advantage to the United States, viz: the restriction of our population to some certain limits, and thereby a continuation of our union. Our citizens being so prone to rambling, and extending themselves, on

the frontiers, will, through necessity, be constrained to limit their extent on the west, to the borders of the Missouri and Mississippi, while they leave the prairies, incapable of cultivation, to the wandering and uncivilized Aborigines of the country.

In 1839, Pike's and Long's view of the northern plains, with its sterile, unvaried topography, still cast a long shadow among the nation's explorers and scientific elite. U.S. maps displayed Long's Great American Desert; and, indeed, decades after his expedition, Western explorers raised in the densely forested East—and confronting for the first time the region's odd (to them) flora and landscapes—found only depressing confirmation of Long's conclusions. And, as it turned out, Nicollet—and Frémont—would spend much of their careers modifying those very conclusions.[11]

❋

At Fort Pierre that June, Nicollet's entourage spent several weeks making celestial observations, updating journals, and preparing for their further travels. While there, Nicollet also found time to hire ten additional men for the expedition, among them William Dixon and Louison Frenière—both Métis, both "well known as fine horsemen and famous hunters," and both hired as scouts and interpreters.

Plans called for the survey party to cross the Missouri, then head northeast across the prairie toward the Red River of the North. "Here we were in the heart of the Indian country," Frémont recalled. "Here the Indians were sovereign." In hopes of securing safe passage across the prairie, the party, laden with gifts, rode toward a nearby Yankton Sioux village. As the explorers neared the settlement, they spotted "thirty of the principal chiefs," mounted and advancing in a procession toward the explorers—as Frémont recalled, "a noble-looking set of men showing to the best advantage, their fine shoulders and breasts being partly uncovered."

Escorted by the chiefs into the settlement, the explorers soon found themselves enjoying the village's hospitality inside a lodge constructed of animal skins stretched across wooden poles: "These were the best formed and best looking Indians of the plains, having the free bearing belonging with their unrestrained life in sunshine and open air." The women of the Yankton tribe—"wearing finely dressed skins nearly white, much embroidered with beads and porcupine quills dyed many colors" and "stuffs from the trading post"—particularly impressed young Frémont. A few days after the visit to the Sioux village, one of its chiefs arrived at Fort Pierre with an interpreter and "a pretty girl of about eighteen" in tow. Standing in a room that opened onto a courtyard in which Nicollet and Frémont were poring over sketchbooks and maps, the chief, through the interpreter, offered the girl to Nicollet as a wife.

Recovering from momentary embarrassment, Nicollet answered that he already had a wife, but that his younger colleague did not. "This put me in a worse situation," Frémont recalled. "But being at bay, I promptly replied that I was going far away and not coming back, and did not like to take the girl away from her people." Pronouncing himself nonetheless flattered by the offer, Frémont, before the visitors departed, gathered a package of gifts for the girl—"scarlet and blue cloths, beads, a mirror, and other trifles." During the entire exchange, as Frémont recalled with characteristic immodesty, the girl leaned against the door, not uttering a word, and "apparently not ill-pleased with the matrimonial possibility."[12]

❋

The party, now comprising nineteen men, thirty-three horses, and ten carts, began its northeasterly, overland march across the prairie to the Red River on July 1. The morning of July 3, moments after the party had completed its climb out of the Missouri's five-hundred-foot-deep channel, a cry of "la vache! la vache!" rang across the prairie. An advance party of returning mounted scouts had spotted a herd of buffalo moving toward the river. The survey party burst into frenetic activity; horses were saddled and mounted, rifles raised. For Frémont, still a plains neophyte, the rush marked an auspicious moment: "Now I was to see the buffalo. This was an event on which my imagination had been dwelling."

The hunting party purposefully stayed downwind of the herd.

"Riding silently up a short slope, we came directly upon them," Frémont recalled. "Not a hundred yards below us was the great, compact mass of animals, moving slowly along, feeding as they went, and making the loud incessant grunting noise peculiar to them." As the men crested the hill and the herd spotted them, chaos erupted: "There was a sudden halt, a confused wavering movement, and then a headlong rout; the hunters in their midst." The hunters separated as they rode into the herd, the exploring party's scattered members now barely visible through rising clouds of dust. Surrounded by buffalo, dust, and chaos, Frémont recalled, "I made repeated ineffectual attempts to steady myself for a shot at a cow after a hard struggle to get up with her, and each time barely escaped a fall."

With the hunters in pursuit, the buffalo scattered toward the horizon, disappearing in increasingly smaller bands. As the last buffalo dropped from sight, Frémont, exhausted and alone, dismounted. Sitting in the grass, he reloaded his rifle. "I could nowhere see any of my companions, and, except that it lay somewhere to the south of where I was, I had no idea where to look for the camp." He decided to ride west, back toward the Missouri River and Fort Pierre: "In this way I could not miss the camp, but for the time being I was lost."

Later that night, Frémont stumbled upon a buffalo trail and began following it back to the Missouri River. Around midnight, he had just reached a stand of woods close to the river when he was suddenly startled by the sight of a rocket—in all likelihood, a beacon from the exploring party sent up by the Prussian-born party member and artillerist Louis Zindel—streaking across the starry sky. "This was the Fourth of July," Frémont later recalled; "I doubt if any boy in the country found more joy in his fireworks than I did in my midnight rocket with its silent message."[13]

But with both horseman and horse in need of rest, food, and water, Frémont stopped and set up camp by the river for a few hours of sleep. At break of dawn, he began riding toward the apparent origin of the rocket: "I had laid my gun by my side in the direction where I had seen the rocket." It was still early morning when, to his relief, he met three scouts dispatched by Nicollet.

How did the experience of being lost affect Frémont? And what, if any, sort of reprimand did the twenty-six-year-old Western greenhorn receive? Certainly, it would not be the last time he would lose his way. But it was the first—and, as he later recalled in his memoirs, he understood its gravity, and how it jeopardized the safety of both him and others in his party: "To be lost on the prairie in an Indian country is a serious accident, involving many chances, and no one was disposed to treat it lightly."

❋

Leaving the Missouri River basin, the party moved on a northwesterly line toward the Coteau du Missouri, the plateau country lying between the Missouri and the Jacques—today's James—Rivers. As the party traveled over and around the Coteau du Missouri, the usual tasks of astronomical observations filled Frémont's days. But there were also stolen moments of carefree bliss, such as when he rode out ahead of the party with the hunter Louison Frenière in search of buffalo: "Sometimes when we had gotten too far ahead of our caravan it was an enjoyment to lie in careless ease on the grass by a pond and be refreshed by the breeze which carried with it the fragrance of the prairie."

In Frémont, the old prairie hand Frenière found a willing student. "With him my prairie education was continued under a master," the explorer recalled. While Nicollet had stressed the virtues of quiet, methodical discipline, Frenière demonstrated a bolder way to exist in the wilds: "He was a reckless rider. Never troubling himself about impediments, if the shortest way after his buffalo led through a pond[,] through it he plunged." Possessed of a painter's eye and a poet's heart, Frenière also instructed Frémont in the "peculiar beauty" of the prairies ("the uniformity is never sameness"), and in the art of savoring the inevitable dramas that played out upon them. For instance, he taught Frémont about the mystery that always attends an approaching figure: "Whatever the object may be—whether horseman, or antelope, or buffalo—that breaks the distant outline of the prairies," it always offers "special interest." "The horseman may prove to be enemy or friend, but the always existing uncertainty has its charm of excitement in the one case, and the joy of the chase in the other. There is always the suspense of the interval needed to verify the strange object; and long before the common man decides anything, the practiced eye has reached certainty. This was the kind of lore in which Frenière was skilled."[14] The mountain man epitomized the sort of rough-hewn eccentric—typical among whites who, during those decades, ventured into the West—with whom the explorer would, over the coming years, cast his lot.

Years later, a Frémont admirer would ponder why a young man would solicit such work—take on "these hardships and dangers in preference to the work of the frontier or the city." Certainly part of the answer lies in the simple fact that Frémont felt comfortable among the men he found in the West. Given the risks and discomforts that characterized Western travel in that age, a certain personal eccentricity was almost a prerequisite for venturing into the region. Frémont, burdened with all the insecurities that attended his austere origins in class-bound Charleston, thus found a level of social comfort among the West's mountain men, soldiers, Indians, traders, miners, and voyageurs that, years after he had attained fame and wealth, would continue to elude him in the drawing rooms of Washington, New York, San Francisco, Paris, and London.[15]

✳

Led by the scout William Dixon, the men of Nicollet's expedition, on July 6, suddenly found themselves gazing out on a stunning view of the James River basin. "Dixon, in truth, had been managing a surprise for us," Nicollet recalled. Their guide had been here before and, without breathing a word about what he had in store for them, had spent the afternoon leading them toward this favorite spot. Once there—savoring the men's stunned reaction to the sublime panorama—Dixon exclaimed, "Well, come now, you want geography: *look*! there's geography for you." For Frémont, after three years of tromping about the leafy forests of the southern Appalachians and the Upper Mississippi, the view offered a tantalizing glimpse of the sort of thirsty, tangled, wind- and water-sculpted, tectonically shattered topography that spreads across much of the West. It was only one view, only one canyon, but the James River basin sufficed to whet the young man's appetite for more, even grander, Western vistas.

❋

The next day, as the line of men and horse-drawn carts descended toward the James River, a cluster of Yankton lodges came into view. But any anxieties Nicollet's party felt upon approaching the Indian settlement evaporated after its elders talked with the interpreters Dixon and Frenière, who knew the band through their work for the American Fur Company. "After an exchange of friendly greetings our camp was pitched nearby," Frémont recalled. "Such a rare meeting is an exciting break in the uneventful Indian life; and the making of presents gave a lively expression to the good feeling with which they received us, and was followed by the usual Indian rejoicing." Later, after the interpreters disclosed the party's destination, the settlement's chief even offered Nicollet a guide. But fearful of being drawn into intertribal wars, Nicollet declined the offer; as Frémont recalled, the presence of Indians from this band "might only prove the occasion for an attack in the event of meeting an unfriendly band."

❋

On July 10, the party struck the James River at a grove of oaks in today's Brown County, South Dakota. This rare cluster of greenery on the otherwise treeless plains—a celebrated spot where Sioux peoples gathered for an annual trading fair—was also, by prior arrangement, the party's point of rendezvous with an expected column of reinforcements that Joseph Renville had promised to dispatch. But after camping under the oaks for three days with no sign of the reinforcements, the party resumed its northerly march along the James's western bank.

The next week, bending to a northeasterly course, the party began ascending the prairie plateau that lies between the James and Cheyenne Rivers, the latter a tributary of the north-flowing Red River of the North. "Here we regained the great prairie plains," Frémont recalled, "and here we saw in their magnificent multitudes the grand buffalo herds on their chief range." Indeed, the buffalo, moving southwest toward the Upper Missouri basin, came so close that the men, on one occasion, felt obliged to hobble and picket their own horses, lest they follow the herd. "For three days we were in their midst," Frémont recalled, "travelling through them by day and surrounded by them at night. We could not avoid them. Evidently some disturbing cause had set them in motion from the north." Frustrated, Nicollet elected to camp by one of the Cheyenne's tributaries, Tampa Creek—now called Spring Creek—and wait for the buffalo to pass through the area.[16]

On July 28, after crossing the Cheyenne on their northern march and entering a country of greenish salt lakes, the party discerned in the misty distance a line of hills that it recognized as marking the eastern shore of their northernmost destination, Mini Waken—today's Devil's Lake—in northeastern North Dakota. The next day, Nicollet dispatched Frémont and several other men to circle its waters on horseback, to conduct observations, and to ascertain the lake's sources.

Frémont found the lake delightful: "It is a beautiful sheet of water, the shores being broken into pleasing irregularity by promontories and many islands." But constrained by time and failing to reach the northern shore, he could not complete a circle of the lake. Two days later, when he returned to the main party, Frémont reported that the lake had no obvious connections with any major river systems; rather, it seemed to function as a cistern, gathering water collected by small streams along its edges. Beyond that, "no outlet was found, but at the southern end there are low grounds by which at the season of high waters the lake may discharge into the Shayen [Cheyenne] River."[17]

❋

After nine days near Devil's Lake, the party, on August 6, marched southward, along the Cheyenne River's eastern bank. Before leaving the region, however, Nicollet insisted upon detouring to the east, to locate the divide separating the Red River drainage from that of the Cheyenne, whose drainage basin ultimately connected to the larger Mississippi watershed. Departing from their southerly course, they marched east until they stood at an altitude of about fifteen hundred feet on the brow of the slope that divides the two drainage systems. A few miles farther east, the party "came in view of the wide-spread valley of the Red River, its green wooded line extending far away to the north on its way to British America."[18]

Hydrologically, Nicollet had now come full circle: his surveys of the Coteau des Prairies had determined the boundary between the Mississippi and Missouri River drainages. And by locating the boundary between the Red River and the Cheyenne watersheds, the old explorer had linked up his 1838 and 1839 observations with his survey, three years earlier, of the sources of the Mississippi.

The party spent the next three days surveying various Red River tributaries and, on August 13, recrossed the Cheyenne River. Three days later, the men were encamped at the northern head of the Coteau des Prairies. There, of the nine men who, along with their horses, had joined the expedition at Fort Pierre, all but scout William Dixon departed to return home. The party's departing members, however, were quickly replaced, when Chief Wahanantan, along with a dozen warriors, "exhausted with hunger and fatigue," arrived at the camp. Uncertain of their directions, the Indians had spent the past three days looking for Nicollet's party.

Wahanantan, whom Nicollet had met during the previous summer's Pipestone expedition, was something of a legend: in 1823, he had served as a scout to Stephen Long and Joseph Renville, Sr., on their explorations of the Red River valley and the Great Plains. Weeks earlier, during the passage through the Cheyenne River country, Nicollet had encountered Wahanantan again and, with regret, had declined the old chief's request to accompany the party to Devil's Lake. While Nicollet remained fond of Wahanantan, he feared his presence would prove a liability as they passed through Assiniboin and Chippewa country. Glad now to see these "brave and intelligent Indians," Nicollet welcomed them, and the expanded party, "marching to the sound of Indian chants with the flag at the head of the procession," continued its march. At the southern end of the Coteau des Prairies, the Indians departed, leaving one scout behind to guide the white men to Renville's post at Lac qui Parle, which they reached by the end of August.

❀

At Renville's post, while Nicollet made repairs on his surviving barometer—one had been destroyed during the trip—the rest of the party spent the next nine days again enjoying the old fur trader's hospitality. On September 5, they descended the Minnesota River, toward Fort

Snelling. There, Henry Sibley again welcomed Nicollet and Frémont into his home, where they remained for several weeks. During their stay, Frémont joined Sibley and the residents of the nearby Sioux village—men, women, and children—for an extended hunt into the Iowa Territory. The rigors of the expedition, as he recalled, had done nothing to dampen Frémont's zeal for the outdoor life. "The day's tramp gave a lively interest to the principal feature which the camp presented; along the woods bright fires, where fat venison was roasting on sticks before them, or stewing with corn or wild rice in pots hanging from tripods; squaws busy over the cooking and children rolling about over the ground. No sleep is better or more restoring than follows such a dinner, earned by such a day."[19]

Upon returning to Fort Snelling from their hunt, Frémont and Sibley learned that Nicollet—along with expedition members Charles Geyer, Louis Zindel, Etienne Provôt, Joseph Fournaise, and Joseph Chartran—were already descending the Mississippi, toward Prairie du Chien. A few days later, hoping to catch up, Frémont, Sibley, and several others set off downriver. They arrived at Prairie du Chien on November 1, but Nicollet, who had reached the post two weeks earlier, had already come and gone; haunted by memories of last year's river freeze, he had already departed for St. Louis by canoe.

With Nicollet gone, Frémont and Sibley concluded that they now had no reason to rush downriver: "A steamboat at the landing was firing up and just about starting for St. Louis, but we thought it would be pleasant to rest a day or two and enjoy comfortable quarters while waiting for the next boat." That next boat, as it turned out, would not arrive until the spring; that night, as Frémont recalled, a snowstorm caused the river to freeze "from bank to bank": "I had time enough while there to learn two things: one, how to skate; the other, the value of a day."

A wagon journey, "in a severe winter," through Illinois returned Frémont to St. Louis—but once again, no Nicollet. By December 10, the Frenchman, along with fur company president Ramsay Crooks, had already departed for Washington. In St. Louis, Frémont wrapped up the expedition accounts. Then he, too, left for Washington, "to assist Mr. Nicollet in working up the material collected in the expeditions."[20]

WASHINGTON AND THE BENTONS

W
HEN JOHN FRÉMONT, in late December of 1839, returned to Washington, Joseph Nicollet was nowhere to be
found. To War Secretary Poinsett, Frémont, recalling the
aging explorer's declining health when he last saw him, suggested that
Nicollet "may be sick at some little roadside inn." Poinsett, for his
part, was eager to meet with Nicollet—even more eager to receive the
explorer's official report and promised map of the Mississippi valley.
Democrats, anticipating a tough presidential race against the newly
formed Whig Party, were already making political hay of Nicollet's
work. For years, Democrats had been promoting a more active U.S.
role in the Trans-Mississippi West. Most recently, Senator Thomas
Hart Benton of Missouri, one of Congress's leading "Western men,"
campaigning against the national bank, had championed the twin
panaceas of hard money and cheap Western farmland as curatives for
the region's woes.

Consistent with such appeals to the yeomanry, Poinsett, in his
annual message to Congress—publicly linking, for the first time, Nicollet's work with national expansion—celebrated the agricultural
richness of the lands Nicollet had surveyed. Paying particular attention to the Coteau des Prairies, the War Secretary—challenging
Stephen Long's notion of the Great American Desert—predicted,
"The soil of this table land is very rich, and will support a numerous
population, that would enjoy the advantage of inhabiting one of the
most beautiful and healthy regions of the far northwest." He even
suggested that Nicollet's methods could be extended to more ambi-

tious surveys, reaching across the Rockies, perhaps even to the Pacific's shore.[1]

On December 27, Frémont left Washington for Baltimore, expecting to find Nicollet recuperating among his friends at St. Mary's College. In Baltimore, Frémont found no Nicollet but decided to linger at St. Mary's. To Poinsett, he wrote, "I can do nothing in the way of work without him and therefore I think I am excusable in remaining here until his arrival." Lamenting a holiday gift's tardy arrival, he added, "I was hoping that Mrs. Poinsett's Buffalo tongues would have been in time for the New Year Dinner, but the state of the roads, I suppose, prevented their arrival."[2]

When Nicollet finally turned up in Washington on January 12, 1840, his appearance confirmed his friends' worst fears. He was haggard, ghostly in demeanor—"a wreck of what he had been"—and it was apparent that, to complete his work, he would need special care. Ferdinand Hassler's daughter Rosalie found an elderly man to assist the Frenchman. Initially, Frémont and Nicollet took rooms at a Washington boardinghouse. By spring, however, as friends feared the effects of the increasing humidity on Nicollet's health, it was arranged for them to live in a series of "large, sparsely furnished rooms" on Capitol Hill, occupied by Hassler and the Coast Survey.

To speed up their work, Hassler arranged for yet another young Topographical Corps officer, Lieutenant Eliakim Scammon, to join their abode. "I had here with me a congenial companion of my own age, and the same corps," Frémont recalled. "Both of us had unusual facility in figures. Like myself, he was a lover of chess, and this engrossed much of our leisure time." In time, their menagerie even included a resident French chef, who had been passed over by President Martin Van Buren because of his high salary demands. "For Nicollet," Frémont remembered, "delicate food had become a necessity. His health had been impaired by the discomforts and exposures in his expeditions, seriously so in that to the sources of the Mississippi."

Nicollet's health continued to decline, but for Frémont, now twenty-seven years old, these were heady days. He now carried the gravitas that attended anyone who had ventured into the then vaguely known Western frontier. As if to mark his new life, he began the new year by adding a *t*—soon followed by an *accent aigu*—to his name. And soon after returning to Washington, he accompanied Joseph Nicollet to the White House, for a meeting with President Van Buren and Secretary of War Poinsett. The President, Frémont recalled, greeting his guests warmly, spoke of his "great satisfaction" with the survey: "It had brought back valuable knowledge concerning a region of great agricultural capacities, little known to the people at large, and which opened to them a new field to occupy."

Through Nicollet, Poinsett, Topographical Corps chief John Abert, and Coast Survey director Ferdinand Hassler, Frémont widened his intellectual circles. Although Nicollet's health continued to falter, the Capitol Hill flat with its resident French chef became an evening salon for the motley milieu of scientists and politicians that congregated around the Coast Survey. By 1840, the West and Western exploration had become a preoccupation of many American intellectuals—a passion that had, in turn, begun to influence politicians and shape national policy. Expansionist politicians were thus frequent guests—including Senators Henry Dodge of Wisconsin and Lewis F. Linn and Thomas Hart Benton of Missouri. Of all the visiting politicians, however, it was Benton who was destined to cast the longest shadow over Frémont's life.[3]

❀

A tall, blue-eyed, Tennessee-born man with a long face crowned by a mane of swept-back hair, Thomas Hart Benton was already sixty-eight years old when Frémont first met him. Benton sparkled with a passion for books. He read English, Spanish, Greek, Latin, and French and had an insatiable intellectual curiosity. Like Frémont, Thomas Hart Benton had been something of a rascal during his youth. The scion of Up-Country—as opposed to Tidewater—Virginia gentry, his own father, Jesse Benton had been a prominent lawyer, land speculator, and planter in the Tennessee Piedmont; a man of reserve and erudition, he owned a personal library reputed to be one of the finest in the region.

Born in 1782, young Thomas, however, had had only a few years to know his father, who died of tuberculosis when the boy was only eight years old. His wife, Nancy, was left alone and debt-ridden to care for eight children. But by aggressively reordering the family's businesses and finances, she managed to hang on to their plantation and raise the children. A headstrong Episcopalian woman determined to shape Thomas into a man of cultivation, Nancy took him into the family library as soon as he was ready and put him on a rigorous reading regimen that ranged from history to folio editions of the *British State Trails*, from Plutarch's *Parallel Lives* to the Bible.

Thomas studied during his teens at a private school in Hillsborough, Tennessee, and at sixteen left for the University of North Carolina at Chapel Hill. Three months later, however, he was expelled from the university after being accused of stealing cash from several students while they were away from their dormitories. The episode produced no legal charges, but the resulting shame instilled in Thomas an exaggerated and lasting sense of personal probity.

From Chapel Hill, he returned to his family in Hillsborough, where he helped run the family farm for the next two years. In 1800—or perhaps 1801, the year is uncertain—Nancy Benton, taking her children and their few slaves, joined the migration of settlers out of the mountains into the new state of Tennessee's Cumberland Valley. There, twenty-five miles south of Nashville, the family acquired a 2,560-acre homestead, where they cultivated cotton and corn.

As the family's oldest son, Thomas played a key role in building and running the Bentons' farm. And, as he matured into a strapping six-foot-tall man, he reveled in frontier recreations such as hunting and fishing, target shooting and wrestling. His enthusiasm for farming, however, waned before the vagaries of crop failures and market forces. Much of Tennessee's agricultural economy, after all, depended on the ability of local farmers to sell their crops through the growing port of New Orleans. And Benton was particularly crestfallen when, in autumn of 1802, he took the family farm's first harvest to Nashville to sell—only to discover that Louisiana's Spanish officials had arbitrarily closed New Orleans to American goods. The Louisiana Purchase the following year ensured that there could be no recurrence of the closure, but the experience left a lasting impression on Benton, who, in the coming years, became a tireless crusader for unfettered international trade.[4]

While in Nashville handling crop sales, Thomas became fascinated with the workings of the local Superior Court. At the age of nineteen, while observing the court, he got his initial firsthand experience with the legal system when that day's presiding judge, future president Andrew Jackson, called the young man for jury duty. By 1804, as his young siblings assumed his farm responsibilities, Thomas—by then smitten with the idea of becoming a lawyer—had gone away to teach school and to teach himself the law. By 1806, his legal education complete, he began traveling the state, handling both criminal and civil cases. During his travels, Benton, observing the problems of farmers on the state's hardscrabble frontier, became increasingly drawn to the Democratic Party and soon began writing newspaper articles espousing what he came to see as a panacea for those problems—the ready availability of cheap land for settlers.

In 1809, Benton won a seat in Tennessee's State Senate. But his stint there lasted a mere sixty-seven days because, for some reason, he decided not to stand for reelection. During that same period, he suffered from a hacking cough, fever, and other symptoms of tuberculosis, a disease that had stalked the Benton family for several generations. We also know that, with the approach of the War of 1812, Benton sent a letter, volunteering for military service, to his friend Andrew Jackson, by then the major general of the Tennessee Militia. Though Benton eventually served as an aide-de-camp to General Jackson, the young man, to his disappointment, saw no military action during the conflict.

In the spring of 1815, after the war's end, Benton made a stop in Virginia that would change his life. Visiting an acquaintance, Colonel James Preston, scion of a distinguished Virginia clan, Benton came to know a Colonel James McDowell and became smitten with McDowell's smart, attractive twenty-one-year-old daughter Elizabeth. Later that year, Thomas made the first of what would be, over the next five years, a series of rejected marriage proposals to her. Thomas had accomplished much in his young years, but his family pedigree could hardly compete with that of the McDowells. Even so—convinced that Elizabeth would make a splendid wife, one committed to every ideal of domestic and social duty—he was resolved to make her his spouse. Not until the autumn of 1820, however, did she agree to marry

Thomas. The couple wed in March 1821 and, during their years together, had six children—four daughters and two sons.[5]

✦

When, during the fall of 1820, Elizabeth McDowell agreed to marry
him, Thomas Hart Benton was passing through Virginia en route to
Washington to begin his service as one of the new state of Missouri's
first two U.S. senators. In 1815, he had emigrated to St. Louis, where,
for five years, he practiced law and edited a Democratic Party newspaper, the Missouri *Inquirer*. Benton's editorials won him a fierce reputation as a proponent of Western interests, and his election to the U.S.
Senate only increased his influence.

Drawing on his considerable learning, Benton held that the
vaguely defined boundaries of Jefferson's Louisiana Purchase reached
all the way across the Rockies to take in Oregon and its Pacific coast.
He maintained that the U.S. title to Oregon had been established
twice: by New England merchant Robert Gray's arrival off the Oregon
coast in 1791, and by the Louisiana Purchase of 1803. From that perspective, Benton and his allies viewed the Convention of 1818, which
established Britain and America's shared "joint occupation" of Oregon, as an abject betrayal of national interests.[6]

In his advocacy of such views, Benton won renown as an eloquent,
if prolix, orator and writer—one who, according to a biographer, "all
too often literally smothered listeners with the volume of his research
and erudition." Along the way, he developed an elaborate theory concerning the nature of historical empires. Empires, he believed, rise
and fall—one supplanting the other, in a westward procession, "a
course of empire," that stretched from Phoenicia across Europe to
England and, in time, he believed, to the United States.[7] In each successive empire, Benton believed, commerce—not agriculture or settlement—created wealth and power. More specifically, according to
his theory, empires were created by trade with Asia. City-states and
nations grew into empires when they developed the means—whether
via camel caravans or oceangoing navies—to monopolize trade with
the East. Toward that end, Benton, by the 1820s, had become preoccupied with developing for the United States a better route to the

East—a "Road to India"—a link, free from the interference of competing nations, that would vanquish Britain's imperial status and hasten America's rise to empire. "Happily," he believed, putting his faith in the development of a transcontinental route across North America, "NATURE has created for us such a route—one which lies through the heart and centre of our dominions—and which may with justice be called *'The American road to India.'* "[8]

Once Americans surveyed and secured this transcontinental corridor, Benton believed, they must establish a port at the mouth of the Columbia River to capture the Orient's trade, at which point the United States would control the mercantilist heart of a vast global trade route, bathing the entire globe in its benign light:

> Upon the people of Eastern Asia the establishment of a civilized power on the opposite coast of America, could not fail to produce great and wonderful benefits. Science, liberal principles in government, and the true religion, might cast their lights across the intervening sea. The valley of the Columbia might become the granary of China and Japan, and an outlet to their imprisoned and exuberant population. The inhabitants of the oldest and the newest, the most despotic and the freest governments, would become the neighbors, and the friends of each other.

Emigration by Americans to Oregon, not military occupation, Benton believed, offered the best means of guaranteeing U.S. control over the region; as "Aeneas entered upon the Tiber, and as our forefathers came upon the Potomac, the Delaware and the Hudson," so American settlers—"mere adventurers"—must advance toward Oregon and the Pacific coast, and there "renew the phenomenon of individuals laying the foundation of a future empire."

✸

"Mr. Benton," Frémont later wrote, echoing the senator's own oft-repeated self-characterization, "was a disciple of Jefferson." Throughout his career, Benton identified himself with Thomas Jefferson and

Jefferson's vision of American empire—and, at first glance, the analogy seems apt: in December 1824, as a young, first-term senator, Benton had even traveled to Virginia to meet the aged, great man. Still later, Benton's memory apotheosized the encounter into a sort of ceremony by which the burden of winning America's destined empire passed from one generation to another.

When Benton recalled his sole encounter with Jefferson, he—ignoring the agrarian and continental cast of Jefferson's vision of empire—made it sound as if Jefferson shared his preoccupation with Asian trade. "Mr. Jefferson," Benton claimed, "was the first to propose the North American road to India, and the introduction of Asiatic trade on that road; and all that I myself have either said or written on that subject from the year 1819, when I first took it up, down to the present day . . . is nothing but the fruit of the seed planted in my mind by the philosophical hand of Mr. Jefferson."

In the Senate, three months after meeting Jefferson, Benton, while calling for nullification of the U.S.–British joint-occupation arrangement and for the promotion of U.S. emigration to Oregon, famously asserted that the Rocky Mountains should mark the nation's western boundary: "Along the back of this ridge, the western limit of this republic should be drawn, and the statute of the fabled god, Terminus, should be raised upon its highest peak, never to be thrown down."[9] Echoing Jefferson's Montesquieu-style warnings about the dangers faced by empires dispersed over great distances, the oration helped to fix Benton's image as a latter-day Jefferson—an image that persists to this day among historians.

But though often quoted, Benton's Rockies-as-Terminus injunction played no subsequent role in the senator's career. Indeed, no recorded instance can be located of his ever mentioning the matter again; and even when Benton quoted the speech in his memoirs, he left out the Terminus caveat. For Benton, borders and territorial domains held no particular interest. When he speculated about future U.S. borders, Benton spoke with an inconsistency that was, literally, all over the map—favoring U.S. acquisition of the entirety of Oregon in some years; none of it in others; and, finally, in 1845, splitting the difference with Britain.

Senator Benton indulged an almost mystical fascination with the West's geography, supported its exploration—and read copiously about its rivers, mountains, and valleys. Among his correspondents was the Western explorer and scholar Henry Rowe Schoolcraft, with whom the senator exchanged speculative letters addressing the region's geology.[10] But for all that, Benton had little interest in the United States acquiring territory for its own sake. He envisioned the West less as a place for settlement or agriculture than as a realm through which American traders could pass with goods to and from distant Asian ports. In Benton's vision of empire, after all, gold and silver—not territorial dominion—constituted the coin of the realm. Not for nothing, after all, did he earn the sobriquet "Old Bullion Benton."

❋

The Panic of 1821 had played a large role in shaping Benton's worldview. In the wake of a regional boom nourished by land speculation and paper money, he had watched as a national depression ground immigration into Missouri to a halt. Crops went unsold, banks foreclosed on farms, and banks suspended payments. The Bank of Missouri, of which Benton was a depositor, stockholder, and director, found itself unable to meet a payment of $152,342 to the U.S. government. In subsequent litigation, the federal government won a seven-thousand-dollar personal judgment against Benton—a court verdict that political enemies quickly used against him. The panic left Benton and other Missourians deeply skeptical of wealth built on land speculation and paper money. Later in the decade, a resurgence of the local farm economy and a renewed vigor among the state's lead mines helped restore Missouri's prosperity. But more than anything else, Missouri owed its revival to the newly opened Santa Fe Trail, a trade conduit that furnished a ready market for goods produced in Missouri and that pumped hard currency into a state starved for specie.[11]

❋

As the Panic of 1821 ravaged Missouri, a revolution south of the border was ending Spain's four-hundred-year rule over Mexico—thus ending a long-standing ban on Yankee traders in Mexico and its northern province of New Mexico. That summer, Missouri entrepreneur William Becknell, becoming the first American to take advantage of the new opening, led a trade caravan to Santa Fe and back, thus becoming known as the father of the Santa Fe Trail—though the route he took was essentially the same one used by various Indians over the centuries, and by Santa Fe's founder Juan de Oñate, in 1601.

Within months after the Mexican Revolution of 1821, hundreds of Americans—their wagons and saddlebags bursting with trade goods—began streaming down the Missouri–to–New Mexico Santa Fe Trail. Months later, after selling their wares in Santa Fe, they returned to St. Louis, carrying bags bulging with Spanish silver.

The exodus of New Mexican silver into Missouri soon left the Mexican province starved for specie. In their own quest for silver, many ambitious American traders, upon reaching Santa Fe, simply continued south, down the older Chihuahua Trail, toward the more prosperous Mexican silver-mining states. In short order, then, American traders along the Santa Fe Trail had captured what had been a north-south trade within Mexico and redirected it into an east-west Mexico–U.S. trade.[12]

❋

Benton spent his first term in the Senate solidifying support among such key state constituencies as landowners, newly arrived settlers, lead miners, and fur company magnates. But it was in January 1825 that Benton sponsored the legislation that most established his future senatorial course. Responding to a constituents' petition, Benton asked Congress to enact measures to help bolster the growing commerce along the Santa Fe Trail. The eventually passed legislation required the federal government to negotiate with Indians along the trail to gain safe passage for Santa Fe traders and required the government to negotiate with Mexico to obtain permission to survey and mark its entire six-hundred-mile length over U.S. as well as Mexican soil. Benton's early sponsorship of the Santa Fe Trail bill established a precedent for the sort of priorities that would engage most of his attention during his second and subsequent Senate terms.

❋

Newspapers in his day, and historians to this day, tended to lump Benton among the Senate's Western expansionists. But his emphasis on trade and currency, as opposed to territorial acquisitions, gave him a curiously conservative bent that often exasperated more conventional Western expansionists. When, for instance, President Tyler, in 1845, proposed legislation to annex the Republic of Texas, Benton opposed it. By his lights, the bill insulted Mexico, and he feared it might disrupt the West's access to Mexican hard currency. Moreover, though Benton represented a slave state and himself owned slaves, he had, by the mid-1840s, developed a growing aversion to the institution of slavery, opposing its extension into areas such as Texas where it did not already exist. "I am Southern by my birth; Southern in my affections, interests, and connections," he vowed, but, "I will not engage in schemes for . . . [slavery's] extension into regions where . . . a slave's face was never seen." And, in May 1846, on the eve of the Mexican War, Benton told President Polk that he had a "decided aversion to war with Mexico if it could be avoided consistently with the honour of the country."[13]

In its preoccupation with hard currency and international trade, Benton's vision of American empire smacked of anachronism. Years after his death, Jessie Frémont recalled that, though her father's ancestry was exclusively English, he had come to view England, as a nation and as an influence in America, as a force to be resisted. Only the West, he believed, could counterbalance America's ossified Eastern "English seaboard" of hidebound tradition. But ironically, though he was a lifelong Anglophobe, Benton's thinking owed much to Britain's eighteenth-century notion of empire. Unlike Jefferson's inward-looking, continental conception of empire, Benton's, like Britain's, was outward-looking and maritime—focused more on trade and ports and gold and silver than on agriculture, territory, and settlement.[14]

However long-pondered and devoutly believed, Thomas Hart Benton's vision of American empire would, over the next few years, be shaken—ultimately transformed—by events that he could not have imagined that spring of 1840. Even less could the senator have imagined the role that the young explorer from South Carolina would play in that transformation.

❋

On his first visit to Nicollet's and Frémont's Capitol Hill quarters, Thomas Hart Benton discovered to his disappointment that no maps had yet been produced from the Mississippi valley expeditions that he had heard so much about. But as his two hosts showed him the astronomical tables and other recorded observations that would have to be calculated to make the promised map—and as Benton curiously handled the sextants, barometers, and other mapping tools lying around the offices—disappointment gave way to fascination. The senator had not traveled west of Missouri, but his vast knowledge of the frontier West, acquired from years of reading and conversation, dazzled Frémont and his colleagues. And Benton, in turn, listened in rapt attention as Frémont and Nicollet shared their tales of Western adventures. Much of their exchange concerned a Benton obsession—the sprawling country west of the Missouri River. "The results of our journeys between the two great rivers had suggested to him the same work for the broader field beyond the Missouri," recalled Frémont, who himself was already indulging similar aspirations: "The thought of penetrating into the recesses of that wilderness region filled me with enthusiasm—I saw visions."[15]

❋

In March 1841, William Henry Harrison, a Virginia-born Whig and a U.S. senator from Ohio, a celebrated Indian fighter, became America's ninth president. After twelve years of Democratic rule, American voters—many shouting "Van Van, he's a used-up man"—denied Martin Van Buren a second term. And so, by April of 1841, Van Buren and his entire cabinet—including Secretary of War Poinsett—were gone from the government. Even so, John Abert, an old hand at riding out such upheavals, managed to keep his job; and the work of his Army Corps of Topographical Engineers continued apace. As the months dragged by and the work on Nicollet's map progressed, however, the old explorer's health continued to deteriorate. To Frémont's frustration, Nicollet, attempting to recuperate, often departed on extended visits to see his friends at St. Mary's College.

In Nicollet's absence, Senator Benton and Frémont, drawn together by their shared fascination with the West, developed a close rapport; and the young lieutenant became a frequent guest in the senator's C Street home: "Congress was in session, and at his house I often met western members; all, at that time, being 'west' which lay beyond Pennsylvania." The visits deepened—and provided a geopolitical framework and sense of history for—Frémont's growing enthusiasm for Western exploration. From Poinsett, Frémont had acquired an ideology of U.S. nationalism, and, from Nicollet, he had gained a scientific and spatial comprehension of the continent, one in which domains defined by river basins and mountains transcended those etched on maps by distant politicians and their hireling mapmakers: "Boundaries! On land where there are none marked!"

Now, from Benton, the young man's worldview gained yet another dimension: Frémont embraced a historical and temporal view of America and its politics—learned to view America as a force moving through history and, equally important, as belonging to a long procession of world empires. Of these early, formative conversations with Benton, Frémont later recalled, "These gave shape and solidity to my own crude ideas." As the relationship and his interest in exploration grew, the young man abandoned the last vestiges of his long-pondered but never seriously pursued aspirations of becoming an engineer: "Strict engineering had lost its inspiration in the charm of the new field into which I had entered during the last few years."[16]

❋

One evening, during that same period, John Frémont found himself escorting Eliza, the eldest of Senator's Benton's four daughters, to a concert at Miss English's boarding school in Georgetown, which she and a younger sister both attended. Frémont enjoyed Eliza's company, but it was sixteen-year-old Jessie Ann, the younger sister at the school, who arrested his attention that evening. The second of the four Benton daughters, Jessie had been named by her father—in his disappointment at her birth that she was not a boy—for his own father, Jesse. She had an oval face, dark brown eyes, still darker auburn hair, and a girlish litheness. Though hardly pretty in a conventional sense, she possessed, by Victorian standards, a refreshing outgoingness, charm, and wit—as well as a convivial poise far beyond her years, which men found hard to resist. "She was," Frémont later recalled, "then just in the bloom of her girlish beauty, and perfect health effervesced in bright talk."

The attraction was mutual, but it would be months before Jessie returned home for summer vacation and the two saw one another again. The Bentons' three-story house on C Street, which the family had rented since 1839, stood "between 3d and 4½ Streets," at the southeastern foot of Capitol Hill. It was a comfortable domicile with generous rooms, thick walls, and a handsome enclosed garden in the rear; and it teemed with bustle. When the senator wasn't in his third-floor study working, he generally joined the rest of the family at a large table in the house's drawing room for meals and conversations. For the lonely John Frémont—weary of both life in the wild and bachelors' quarters in the city—Jessie's appeal was enhanced by the joy he took in seeing her amid the Bentons' commodious family circle: "Insensibly and imperceptibly, in these frequent meetings, there came a glow into my heart which changed the current and color of daily life and gave beauty to common things."[17]

The two came from different worlds: John—born out of wedlock into unstable financial circumstances to star-crossed parents—carried all the self-doubts that attend such origins. Jessie sprang from a familial milieu of privilege and illustrious social ties. Her father was a powerful senator, her mother a scion of Virginia gentry. And while John was often shy, brooding, even morose, Jessie tended to be open, optimistic, and exuberant. What they shared, as John later immodestly recalled, was "a rare union of intelligence." His hardscrabble pluck and her privileged life conferred upon each a shared taste for unconventional—albeit often impulsive and pigheaded—behavior.

While John had come by those qualities as a social outcast, Jessie's rebellious nature sprang from precisely opposite circumstances: as a child of privilege, she had resisted many of the genteel trappings of her family and Washington society. To counter those tendencies, Jessie's parents enrolled her when she was thirteen in Miss English's Female Seminary, the fashionable boarding school in Washington's Georgetown. But to Thomas and Elizabeth Benton's frustration, her experiences at the school only seemed to reinforce Jessie's rebellious instincts. "It was a favorite place for the daughters of Senators and members of congress and army and navy people," she later recalled—a bastion of "class distinction." "I rashly made friends with girls I liked, regardless of their parents' social standing. Really I learned nothing there." In short, the experience nourished the very sort of instincts that made a young man such as John Charles Frémont all the more appealing.[18]

John and Jessie also shared a love of books—and a fascination with the American West. While Jessie had resisted her boarding-school curriculum, she adored her father and, under his tutelage, developed a keen erudition. Like her father, Jessie had never traveled in the Far West. But her earliest memories included listening to her father's verandah conversations, at the family's St. Louis mansion, with the explorer William Clark, the Chouteaus, and other seasoned Western travelers. As she grew older, she heard similar conversations in Washington between her father and various presidents, senators, and congressmen.[19]

❋

Jessie's parents attempted to limit the budding relationship between Jessie and John. While Thomas Hart Benton admired John's talents, the senator likely found in the young man's profile unwelcome reminders of his own wild years and modest origins, as well as his own urge to marry above his social station. In short, Benton regarded the young man, with his unsavory family history and army salary, ill-suited to be the husband of a senator's daughter. Jessie's mother, Elizabeth, for her part, also worried about introducing her daughter to "the unsettled life of an army officer." Jessie, however, characteristically headstrong, continued to see Frémont.

The couple's relationship ripened that April during an encounter occasioned, oddly enough, by the funeral of President Harrison. To the nation's great dismay, its new Whig president died of pneumonia on April 4, 1841, only a month after taking office. After arrangements for the president's interment were announced, John—because his Topographical Corps quarters were on the route of the state funeral procession—invited the entire Benton family to view the spectacle from his workroom. He arranged to be off that day and, before the

Bentons arrived, spent the morning hauling the worktables up to another floor and decorating the room with flowers. As Jessie later recalled:

> A cheerful woodfire made a good contrast to the chill gray day, and there was a pretty tea-table with cakes and ices and bonbons. It was for my grandmother's special pleasure we were there, and only a few of our friends had been added. These wise elders were troubled that their young host should have made such graceful preparations for them—expensive to "a poor army man"—but this was one of the unforeseen chances for meeting which parental wisdom had decreed must be seldom, and so who can blame the happy extravagance of the lucky Lieutenant.

As Jessie's parents and relatives solemnly talked and watched the procession go by, Jessie and John—decked out for the occasion in his dress uniform—quietly vowed their love to one another. The next day, when John arranged to have the roses and geraniums he had purchased for the day sent to the Benton household, Elizabeth Benton's worst fears returned. What happened next remains uncertain, but years later, Jessie conjectured that her mother took drastic action to end the relationship: "The [recently retired] Secretary of War, Mr. Poinsett, was friendly with my mother and Mrs. Poinsett was even more so. To her went my mother and frankly stated the case—my extreme youth, only sixteen—and the need for gaining time to dispel the impression" that John had made on Jessie. Elizabeth enlisted the Poinsetts in her scheme; and, soon thereafter, John was "astonished" by an order from Topographical Engineering Corps chief John Abert "detaching him from his duty on the map, and directing him to proceed without delay to make a survey of the Des Moines River in Iowa." Although Frémont's immediate superior, Nicollet, also suspected a plot, Abert outranked him; and, soon enough, the young lieutenant was, once again, packing to go west.[20]

While John prepared for the expedition, Jessie's parents, eager to find her new distractions, rushed her off to Virginia to attend the wedding of a female cousin who was marrying a proper, middle-aged congressman. But whatever lesson Jessie was expected to find in her cousin's genteel wedding was apparently lost on her: during her visit, she scandalized the family by showing up at a social affair dressed in her cousin Preston's cadet uniform.

✸

By mid-July Jessie was back in Washington. Nicollet, meanwhile, writing to Frémont, was offering thinly veiled assurances that all would turn out well for the couple: "Come as promptly as possible, everyone here and in Baltimore asks for you, even at Mr. B . . . 's, each time I go there," he wrote. "*Everything is fine, you are happily and impatiently awaited.*" For John, the Iowa River survey passed quickly. "It did not take long to get through with it," he recalled. "I returned to Washington and set about reducing to shape the new material just collected, in order to add the results to Mr. Nicollet's map." The infatuation with Jessie, however, remained in full force—the expedition having failed "to cure the special complaint for which I had been sent there." Indeed, Jessie, commencing a lifelong collaboration with John, even helped him to write his brief report on the expedition, the finished draft of which was in her hand.[21]

Upon John's return, the couple had agreed, at Senator Benton's insistence, to "a probation of a year" before making any marriage plans. Impatience, however, soon overtook them, and they decided to elope. The problem lay in finding a minister to perform the rite. The senator's objections to the marriage were well-known. After the couple failed to find a Protestant minister for the ceremony, Mrs. John J. Crittenden, wife of the Kentucky senator, who had watched the couple's relationship blossom, agreed to help. She found a Catholic priest willing to perform the ceremony; and, on October 19, 1841, at either the parlor of Gadsby's Hotel or the Crittendens' home—accounts differ—the couple became husband and wife.

Initially, the couple kept their marriage a secret. Seventeen-year old Jessie returned to her parents' house to live, while John returned to his Coast Survey quarters.

One can only speculate how this arrangement weighed on Frémont over the next few months. A friend's letter of advice the following November suggests it weighed heavily. "The possibility of an accidental discovery is very strong—Why don't you go, manly and open as you are, forward and put things by a single step to right," he wrote. "Only act now and you will soon get over little disturbances which might arise at first. Nothing very serious can happen now more to you—the prize is secured and the rest will soon be smoothed by help of time and mutual affection and love."[22]

Later that month, while John was visiting Nicollet in Baltimore, his old mentor urged him to reveal the marriage to the senator and Mrs. Benton. While Frémont agreed that the disclosure was overdue, he left it to Jessie to set a date. "We will explain together," she replied. "Come to the house tomorrow morning before ten o'clock. I shall ask for an early interview." The next morning, the two appeared together before the senator in his library. As Frémont—nervous and stammering—told the senator of their marriage, Jessie conspicuously placed her hand in her husband's hand. Benton was furious. "Get out of the house and never cross my door again!" he shouted. "Jessie shall stay here!"

According to family lore, Jessie, unfazed—clutching John's arm but looking at her father—defiantly quoted the words of the Biblical Ruth, "Whither thou goest, I will go; and where thou lodgest, I will lodge."

Benton demanded that both leave the house.

The couple found temporary lodging at a hotel, Frémont's quarters—or perhaps a boardinghouse—but the senator's ire remained undiminished. He even turned down his wife's proposal that they find a proper Protestant minister and repeat the ceremony. And when the senator placed a statement in the Washington *Globe* announcing the marriage, he reversed the usual practice of placing the groom's name first:

Of the 19th ult. In this city, by the Rev. Mr. VAN HORSEIGH, MISS JESSIE ANN BENTON, second daughter of Col. BENTON, to Mr. J. C. FRÉMONT, of the United States army.

When a *Globe* editor questioned the senator's departure from typographic protocol, Benton, aware of his daughter's impetuousness, reputedly shouted, "Damn it, sir! It will go in that way or not at all! John C. Frémont did not marry my daughter; she married him."[23]

PART II

THE FIRST EXPEDITION

SPRING 1842–FALL 1842

Frémont has particularly touched my imagination. What a wild life, and what a fresh kind of existence! But, ah, the discomforts!　　—Henry Wadsworth Longfellow

TO SOUTH PASS

I N T I M E, Senator Benton's love for his daughter overcame lingering ill feelings about her marriage to Lieutenant Frémont, and,
soon enough, the couple had moved into the Bentons' C Street
house. And, as Jessie became more drawn into John's world, she came
to share her husband's affection for his old mentor, the ailing Joseph
Nicollet, who, when the two visited him in Baltimore, called them
"mes enfants."[1]

Meanwhile, as John and Jessie settled into their new life, political
developments in Washington continued apace. By 1841, other pressures beyond Nicollet's growing indisposition weighed on Benton and
others in Congress who sought a more vigorous U.S. presence in
the Trans-Missouri West. And with Whigs now occupying the White
House—first Harrison and now his successor, John Tyler—they had
grown increasingly anxious about the fate of various key projects.
Most critically, they worried about White House interference in their
quest to promote the value of Oregon to U.S. domestic and foreign
policy—and to encourage growth of the American emigration that had
just begun to trickle into that distant province, still under joint
U.S.–British title.

By sponsoring an expedition to survey and map the main emigrant
route to Oregon, Senator Benton and his supporters hoped to do for
the Pacific Northwest what Nicollet's expeditions had done for the
Upper Mississippi valley—to heighten public interest in the region
and bolster the case for assisting emigrants and providing government
fortification of the emigrant corridor. And because Congress's Western
men hoped that Nicollet would lead this exploration, they had grown

impatient with the delays that, by hindering the completion of his Upper Mississippi map, also delayed his availability for another expedition.

Frémont, too, felt the pressure: "I was now busily occupied in office-work every day while the light lasted, hurrying in good order what remained for me to do in connection with Mr. Nicollet's surveys." Compounding the pressures, the Western congressmen began talking about an even more ambitious expedition, into the Trans-Missouri country: "With this knowledge, and the hope of having [a] part in such an expedition, I worked unremittingly to have the way cleared of previous work; leaving only the brief evening hours for the new home just begun for me."[2]

By late 1841, however, as Nicollet's health continued to falter, even his staunchest supporters were wondering whether he was fit to lead another expedition. Although Washington gossip often mentioned Frémont as a possible substitute leader, as a non–West Point graduate in an elite corps composed exclusively of officers—most of whom were West Point graduates—he had no assurance of winning the commission.

Prospects, however, seemed to brighten for both John and Jessie over the 1841 Christmas season. Jessie's parents' initial grudging acceptance of the marriage had ripened into genuine pleasure in their new son-in-law. Beyond that, *le tout* Washington was talking about these two smart, attractive, well-connected young people. Gaudy public confirmation of that new status came on New Year's Day, 1842, when the couple arrived for an afternoon reception at the White House in a splendid carriage, known as "The Ark" and loaned to them for the occasion by its owner—Frémont's friend, the eccentric Coast Survey head, Ferdinand Hassler. "It took some nerve," Frémont recalled, "to drive up in the ark among the holiday crowd, who were familiar enough with its Noah, but looked and smiled on the young lady in full dress and officer in uniform."[3]

The gloom that had hovered over the White House since President Harrison's death a year earlier had lifted; and, as the U.S. Marine Band played, the new President, John Tyler, buoyantly greeted the Frémonts and a crush of others—including Senator Benton, Secretary of State Daniel Webster, and Senator John C. Calhoun. Later that day, after a holiday dinner at the Bentons' house, Frémont, Senators Benton and Linn, and other Western congressmen talked long into the night about Oregon and other Western matters. When conversation turned to the next Corps of Topographical Engineers expedition, Benton finally asserted what others had been quietly speculating about for months—that Nicollet seemed too frail for any more frontier travels. Frémont, Benton announced, must lead the next expedition.

This was a splendid development for twenty-nine-year-old Frémont, but one occasioned by the declining health of a dear friend and mentor. Moreover, the precise nature and destination of the expedition remained far from settled. All at the table hoped that it would advance emigration to Oregon. But, to accomplish that, the journey needed political support from the highest levels of the federal government.[4] On that latter point, Benton and his friends, having watched a succession of allies leave the White House, were only cautiously optimistic.

President Tyler, with his War Secretary, John Spencer—John Abert's new boss—opposed encouragement of American emigration into Oregon or, for that matter, any provocative actions that might antagonize Britain. Given those new political realities, Benton and his friends concluded that they would have to work discreetly—avoiding White House interference—to ensure that the next Corps of Topographical Engineers expedition, for which Benton and his congressional friends had already allocated thirty thousand dollars, was directed toward ends that advanced their specific Western objectives. "These," Frémont recalled, "were the altered circumstances which required prudence and reserve in avoiding any check to the projected movement to settle the Oregon question by emigration."[5]

A historian of the West, with good cause, has suggested that, upon associating himself with Senator Benton, Frémont had, for all practical purposes, "cut himself loose, in spirit at least, from the restraints of the Corps."[6] He had become, for the time being, a political surrogate for the geopolitical objectives of Benton, Linn, and other men of the West. But only the coming months would reveal the young surrogate's degree of fealty to those objectives.

❀

For two decades, Benton, Linn, and their friends had maintained a steady chorus for abrogating the joint occupation treaty of 1818. By the late 1830s, weary of rebuffs from Presidents and Congress, the senators had increasingly turned their energies toward shaping the policies of a relatively obscure division of the Executive Branch, the U.S. Army Corps of Topographical Engineers, and its long-term chief, John James Abert. To be sure, the passions of Benton and his friends lay more in geopolitics than in the sciences; and Abert's more in the sciences than in politics. But between the two factions there had grown a reciprocity of interests that allowed each to pursue its respective interests with minimal interference from the White House.

The senators—who could grant or withhold operating funds for the Corps of Topographical Engineers—enjoyed the superior position in this political symbiosis. And Benton in particular was ever ready to exploit that advantage. Of the expedition conceived during that winter of 1841–42, he later boasted that it was, "upon its outside view[,] the conception of the government, but [it was] in fact conceived without its knowledge, and executed upon solicited orders, of which the design was unknown."

❋

Following Benton's lead, Abert put Frémont in charge of the next Corps of Topographical Engineers expedition. Abert's original orders called for Frémont to survey the portion of the emigrant route, east of the Rockies, that parallels the Missouri, Platte, and North Platte Rivers. But Benton later claimed that the headstrong Frémont, upon receiving Abert's original letter containing those orders—deciding that they "did not come up to his views"—"carried it back, and got it altered, and the Rocky Mountains inserted as an object of his exploration, and the South Pass in those mountains named as a particular point to be examined, and its position fixed by him." Recently unearthed letters, however, reveal that it was Benton—not Frémont—who instigated the change in Abert's orders.

Benton envisioned the expedition primarily as a means of focusing public attention on Oregon. More particularly, he hoped to draw attention to the Rockies and South Pass, the then still largely unknown mountain route over the northern Rockies through which Oregon-bound emigrants were beginning to trickle. That spring, soon after Frémont received his original orders, Benton thus wrote Abert:

I think it would be well for you to name, in the instructions for Mr. Frémont, the great pass through the Rocky Mountains, called the South West Pass. It is the gate through the mountains from the valley of the Mppi: . . . [It] will be a through fare for nations to the end of time. In the mean time we only know it from the reports of hunters & traders, its lon. and lat. unknown, its distance & bearings from navigable water equally unknown.

Abert, on April 28, declined the senator's request: "I have received your letter & shall call Lieut. Frémont's attention to it," he wrote, "but I fear to make it a part of his instructions, lest I would overload him. We are extremely anxious to have the survey of the two Rivers named in his instructions & I doubt if he will be able to do more this season. The country to the west of the Missouri is a vast unexplored field, which will require the labor of several seasons."

However, later that day—aware of Benton's powers over the Corps' purse strings—Abert reconsidered the matter. Abert's trust in Frémont fell far short of the "utmost confidence" he had placed in Nicollet, and he had no intention of giving Frémont the sort of wide-open discretion in planning his travels that he had afforded Nicollet. Even so, Abert understood politics and understood Senator Benton's powers in shaping the Corps' budget. In the end, then—bowing to the senator's request, but officially declining to put South Pass in any official orders—Abert found a way to accommodate the senator but also to preserve a fig leaf of his own official authority. To Frémont, the Corps of Topographical Engineers commander wrote, "If you can do what he [Benton] desires this season, without hazarding the work committed to you it is extremely desirable that it be done, but, from my answer to Col. B. you will see why I have not made his wish an instruction to you."[7]

✼

As early as March 1842—when Frémont went to New York to purchase an "experimental" rubber raft—he was already preparing for the expedition. Before leaving for the West, however, Frémont hired only one expedition member—Charles Preuss, a young German-born cartographer, who had shown up at the Bentons' house the previous Christmas Eve, carrying a letter from Coast Survey director Ferdinand Hassler. That night, Preuss was nervous, red-faced, and stammering, and Frémont initially thought him drunk. But he soon learned that Preuss's demeanor was attributable to cold weather and hard times. In his letter, Hassler asked Frémont to find work for Preuss, who had been thrown out of work by a cut in the Coast Survey's budget. Frémont arranged a Christmas dinner for Preuss's family, then found work for Preuss with the Corps of Topographical Engineers.

Preuss's new job was to "reduce" astronomical observations—mathematically distill the raw numbers gathered in notebooks during the Nicollet expeditions into the geographical data needed to complete the official expedition report and their promised great map of the Mississippi basin. As Frémont suspected, Preuss knew absolutely nothing about such work; to keep him on the payroll, Frémont himself went in nights and did the work that Preuss purportedly did. Later, when Frémont got his commission for the exploring expedition, he hired Preuss—a talented renderer of landscapes—as the party's chief cartographer and artist. Under Frémont's tutelage, Preuss would learn in the field the other tasks required of his job.

In April, Preuss joined Frémont on a three-day buying trip to New York. Their expedition purchases, amounting to over $500, ranged from a chronometer for $300, the rubber boat for $150, and a mountain barometer for $35 to six pounds of "Dresden chocolate" for $4.50. And—wishing to be among the first to lead a photographically documented exploring expedition—Frémont also spent $78.25 on daguerreotype equipment.

On May 2, after returning from New York, Frémont finally left Washington, reaching St. Louis twenty days later. There, he stayed at the lavish mansion of Mrs. Sarah Benton Brant, a niece of Senator Benton. Through Sarah and her husband, Joshua, a recently retired U.S. Army lieutenant, Frémont extended his ties to St. Louis society. This time, after all, he had arrived not as the unknown, boyish assistant to an aging explorer—but as Senator Thomas Hart Benton's young, handsome, accomplished son-in-law, now leading his own expedition.[8]

In St. Louis, Frémont enlisted two relatives into the expedition—Henry Brant, his hosts' nineteen-year-old son, and Randolph Benton, Jessie's twelve-year-old brother; both "accompanied me, for the development of mind and body, which such an expedition would give." Frémont also hired, as an expedition hunter, Lucien B. Maxwell, the son-in-law of a wealthy New Mexican trader. The other nineteen men recruited in St. Louis were, for the most part, Creole and Canadian voyageurs already familiar with the frontier through work for fur-trading companies—among them, Basil Lajeunesse, a seasoned traveler of the West, who, over the years, would prove to be one of Frémont's most steadfast loyalists. For most, the work was far from lucrative, but wages varied—from 62½ cents per day for the least experienced voyageur to $100 a month for the party's chief scout.[9]

❋

After several days in St. Louis, Frémont and several other party members ascended the Missouri River via steamboat to Chouteau's Landing, near the site of today's Kansas City; the others straggled to the expedition's staging point via the overland route. As Frémont planned his expedition, he had been pondering who would serve as the party's chief scout. American Fur Company officer Pierre Chouteau, Jr., had written Major Andrew Drips, a seasoned mountain man who had worked for the company, about the job. But somehow Frémont had failed to hire Drips. And mountain man and explorer Joseph Walker later claimed that he had declined the job.

En route up the Missouri River, however, Frémont met another mountain man—a trail-hard young friend of Lucien Maxwell named Kit Carson. Recently widowed, Carson had been in St. Louis arranging for a relative to provide a home and a Catholic education for his half-Indian–half-white daughter. The thirty-three-year-old frontiersman made an instant impression upon the young explorer. "He was," Frémont recalled, "a man of medium height, broad-shouldered and deep-chested, with a clear steady blue eye and frank speech and address; quiet and unassuming." Frémont knew he had found his scout.[10]

❈

Christopher "Kit" Carson possessed only a semblance of schooling and could neither read nor write. But measured by the two men's respective experiences in the West, Carson clearly outranked Frémont. He had been born in Kentucky in 1809. At fourteen, his parents apprenticed him to a saddle maker in Missouri, and, shortly afterward, he ran away with a New Mexico–bound trade caravan. In Santa Fe, then Taos, Carson came to know fur trappers and traders. Between 1828 and 1831, he worked with famed trapper Ewing Young on his rounds through southern Arizona and California. After the two men parted ways, Carson—expanding still more his knowledge of the West—increasingly trapped up and down the length of the Rockies.

Beyond his command of the West's lore and life, Carson possessed a serviceable knowledge of French, Spanish, and several Indian tongues; when he didn't know an Indian language, he knew how to communicate in signs. It would be years before Carson became a celebrated figure—indeed, it would be through his association with Frémont that he eventually became famous. When, in 1842, Carson met Frémont, he had just concluded a one-year stint working as a hunter at Bent's Fort, at the foot of the Rockies' eastern slope. By then, the Rockies fur trade had endured a decade of decline. There were myriad reasons—the Panic of 1837, frenzied economic competition that resulted in overhunting the beaver, and changing fashions. Paris's fashion industry—in a telling trend indicating the growing importance of Benton's coveted Asian trade—increasingly preferred hats made of silk or nutria over beaver. So, like so many mountain men of that day, Carson was looking for other work that would draw on his broad knowledge of the West.[11]

Though in many ways cut from different cloth, Carson and Frémont struck up a natural rapport. "I told him," Carson later recalled, "that I had been some time in the mountains and thought I could guide him to any point he wished to go." The young lieutenant made some quick inquiries about Carson, probably talking to Maxwell, then hired him on at one hundred dollars a month.[12]

❧

From Chouteau's Landing, the party traveled six miles up the Kansas River to the trading post of Cyprian Chouteau. The post had been established in 1828 for the purpose of trade with the Delaware and Shawnee, who lived in the area. And, over the next twenty days, Cyprian, true to his family's tradition of assisting Western explorers, helped out with final preparations—"fitting men and animals, arms and equipment, into place and good order." At the time, Frémont was still awaiting funds promised by the federal government. But rather than delay their start, as he later recalled, "I had recourse to the house of Chouteau & Co. who advanced me money, transacted my business & charged a commission." Frémont's tab with the Chouteaus that month exceeded a thousand dollars—a princely sum for that day— and, as a reimbursement voucher later submitted to the War Department on the Chouteaus' behalf makes clear, from bacon (310 lbs., $12.40) to tobacco (148 lbs., $14.80), from sugar (100 lbs., $7.75) to wagons (8 French carts, $280.00), the family's warehouse stood well-prepared to meet the expedition's material needs.[13]

Bad weather delayed the expedition's start. The lost time, Frémont recalled, "was regained in the strength of the animals, as the spring grass was improving every day. This was now to be their only food; and in a measure regulated the travel, which depended on their condition." The delay also gave Frémont the opportunity, once the skies had cleared, to take the expedition's first astronomical observations.[14] On June 10, when the men finally departed, "we were all well armed; and mounted, with the exception of eight men, who conducted as many carts, in which were packed our stores, with the baggage and instruments, and which were each drawn by two mules." Several loose horses and oxen also followed. Chouteau accompanied the exploring party for several miles, until they met the Indian guide he had hired to guide them over the first thirty or forty miles, to where the prairies began.[15]

Riding west through the forests that trace the Kansas River, the party—passing, along the way, several well-tended Indian farms— soon struck the Santa Fe Trail. The Oregon Trail actually began at a junction along the Santa Fe Trail, about twelve miles southwest of Chouteau's Landing, near today's Olathe, Kansas. From there, as the

Santa Fe Trail continued on to New Mexico, the Oregon Trail lunged northwest, across the Great Plains, toward the Platte River. Recognizing the more dominantly commercial purposes of the older Santa Fe Trail, Frémont and his contemporaries of the early 1840s tended to use the phrase "the Emigrant Road" to refer to what later became better known as the Oregon Trail.

On their first day out, the party covered about ten miles before striking the Santa Fe Trail, down which they traveled another three miles before setting up camp for the night beside a small stream. By noon the next day—June 11—the party, bending northwest toward the Platte River valley, had left the Santa Fe Road and was now traveling on the Emigrant Road.

As the party passed into the prairie county, Frémont settled into his new role as expedition leader. For him—entering, for the first time, the Western wilderness without his old friend Nicollet—the prairie's appearance created a poignant moment. The caravan's passage into the prairie, he wrote, "was like a ship leaving the shore for a long voyage, and carrying with her provision against all needs in her isolation on the ocean."[16]

Though Frémont's boyish impetuousness persisted, he was determined to rebut the Washington skeptics who had questioned the qualifications of this senator's son-in-law and non–West Point graduate to lead such a venture. Frémont literally worked day and night.

Though often solicitous of the men's needs and opinions, he brooked no interference with his command. Adopting the regimen, if not the informality of the command style that he had learned from Nicollet, Frémont routinely ordered the party to set up camp an hour or two before sundown. Carts were unloaded and arranged in a circle about eighty feet in diameter. As the party's four cooks prepared supper, tents were pitched, and horses hobbled and allowed to graze. During the night, the horses were picketed—their halters secured at the other end by a picket, a steel stake, driven into the ground. Meanwhile, Frémont and Preuss continued their regimen of scientific observations. They took altitudinal measurements with their barometer. And, to determine their latitude, they "shot" the sun with their sextant at high noon. Weather permitting, they also conducted astronomical observations at various odd hours of the night to determine both their latitude and longitude.[17]

On June 14, when the party reached the bank where Frémont planned to ford the Kansas River, the men found the stream broader and swifter than anticipated. Even so, undaunted, he ordered the fording process to commence: several men rode across on horseback; the other animals were then driven across. As the carts were unloaded and dismantled for the crossing, Frémont's attention fell on the India rubber boat, brought along, he later claimed, to assist their survey of the Platte River.

The boat was five feet wide and stretched twenty feet. And Frémont believed that it could get the dismantled carts over the swollen river. So the vessel was inflated and a rope attached to its bow, and Basil Lajeunesse, one of the party's strongest swimmers, swam across the river with the rope's other end in his mouth. After the boat was secured with the rope, the ferrying operation commenced. With three men paddling, the craft crossed the river six times.

On the seventh crossing, however, with darkness falling over the prairie, something went awry—the boat's helmsman, for some reason, panicked, capsizing the vessel. "Carts, barrels, boxes, and bales, were in a moment floating down the current," Frémont recalled. Most of the party, by then, had already crossed over the river. Now, seeing many of their provisions floating downstream, most of the party immediately jumped into the water. Though two who could not swim nearly drowned, all made it back to shore safely—and somehow most of the provisions were recovered. Though the party lost most of its sugar rations, the most regretted loss was a fifty-pound bag of coffee—nearly all that they had. As Frémont recalled, "It was a loss which none but a traveller in a strange and inhospitable country can appreciate; and often afterward, when excessive toil and long marching had overcome us with fatigue and weariness, we remembered and mourned over our loss in the Kansas."[18]

With several men—including Maxwell and Carson—ill from their time in the water, the party remained the next day, June 16, at its riverside camp. During the day, several Kansas Indians visited the camp to trade. Frémont exchanged a yoke of oxen for a cow and calf, as well as some butter, pumpkins, beans, onions, lettuce, and—most important—thirty pounds of coffee.

As the party moved deeper into the high plains, the soil became sandier, and the ubiquitous sagebrush soon dominated the local flora.

On June 23, the men spotted cacti for the first time. Game, however—elk, antelope, and deer—became more abundant. That evening—aware that they were now passing into Pawnee Indian country—Frémont, for the first time, ordered sentries posted for the night.

On June 28, as the men ascended the Platte valley, they were startled by the sudden appearance of a party of fifteen white men on foot. The men, as it turned out, were trappers, returning from a star-crossed hunt. A severe drought plagued the Platte River valley that year, and the men had abandoned their barges farther up the river, after discovering that the Platte's currents were too shallow to carry them downstream. As Frémont recalled:

> They started with the annual flood, and, drawing but nine inches [of] water, hoped to make a speedy and prosperous voyage to St. Louis; but, after a lapse of forty days, found themselves only one hundred and thirty miles from their point of departure. . . . Sometimes, they came upon places where the water was spread over a great extent, and here they toiled from morning until night, endeavoring to drag their boat through the sands, making only two or three miles in as many days. Sometimes they would enter an arm of the river, where there appeared a fine channel, and, after descending prosperously for eight or ten miles, would come suddenly upon dry sands, and be compelled to return, dragging their boat for days against the rapid current; and at others, they came upon places where the water lay in holes, and, getting out to float off their boat, would fall into water up to their necks, and the next moment tumble over against a sandbar.

The party's leader had "cached"—hidden for a later recovery—most of their furs at a spot near the river and had left several men behind to guard them. Even with the lighter load, however, the next few weeks proved no easier; and, at length, the party had sunk its barges and cached its remaining goods in trees along the river. "We laughed," Frémont recalled, "at their forlorn and vagabond appearance, and, in our turn, a month or two afterwards, furnished the same occasion for merriment to others."

But beyond their cautionary tales of the rigors of Platte River travel, the trappers also shared good news and good food: "They gave us welcome intelligence that the Buffalo were abundant some two days' march, and made us a present of some choice pieces, which were a very acceptable change from our salt pork." Frémont's men, for their part, refreshed their visitors' by then exhausted supply of tobacco—what Frémont called, "that *sine qua non* of a *voyageur*, without which the night fire is gloomy."

Before the exploring party and the eastbound trappers parted ways, Frémont noticed a familiar face—a man he recalled from travels with Nicollet. Frémont called the man "La Tulipe"—"His real name I never knew." He was a "hardened" man, "hacked and scarred" from years of frontier living; and Frémont was glad to see him: "Finding that he was going to the States only because his company was bound in that direction, and that he was rather more willing to return with me, I took him again into my service."

✳

That night, three mounted Cheyenne tribesmen—actually two men and a thirteen-year-old boy—rode into the party's midst. And—like other white trappers and explorers, who during their Western sojourns often drew on Native American geographical expertise—Frémont that evening availed himself of the Cheyennes' knowledge of the surrounding terrain: "After supper, we sat down on the grass, and I placed a sheet of paper between us, on which they traced rudely, but with a certain degree of relative truth, the watercourses of the country which lay between us and their villages, and of which I desired to have some information."[19] And because Frémont's party was going west, toward the tribesmen's home, the Indians decided to accompany them up the Platte to where the river splits; at that point, the Indians would proceed up what Frémont called the Platte's Lower Fork, known today as the South Platte River; while the exploring party headed up what Frémont called the Upper Fork, today's North Platte River.

✳

Though Frémont called his explorations "surveys," that term, for modern readers, may be misleading, for the men in his parties carried no surveying chains and took no finely tuned measurements of the country they were passing through. The word *reconnaissance* perhaps more aptly describes the work of Frémont's exploring parties. His expeditions, after all, were information-gathering trips, conducted hurriedly, often under difficult circumstances, and designed to yield a very general depiction of the landscapes being crossed. Throughout each day, Preuss would stop and check his compass for bearings, then, typically from some elevation with a view, make a rushed sketch to lay down the course of their route or a local river and its tributaries, or to show the contour of the area's primary range of mountains, or simply to mark the location of that night's campsite. Not until after the completion of the reconnaissance—the survey—would Preuss's sketches and the various astronomical and barometric measurements be distilled into a formal map. Along the way, Frémont also collected, for later study, geological and botanical specimens.

Indeed, throughout his expedition travels, Frémont, as expedition astronomer, geodesic expert, botanist, geologist, ethnologist, and topographer, displayed a plucky resourcefulness in juggling his various tasks—even when equipment failed. On one occasion, upon encountering a gurgling hot spring but lacking a working thermometer, Frémont improvised a novel, if painful, standard for measuring heat: "We had no thermometer to ascertain the temperature, but I could hold my hand in the water just long enough to count to two seconds." Preuss followed suit, but with slightly different results. "The water," *he* concluded, "was so hot that I could hold my finger in it for only three seconds."[20]

Alas, the era of one-man-band scientist-explorers would be short-lived. By the end of the 1850s, Frémont's kind of explorer would give way to a new generation of more specialized explorer-scientists in the West—more often than not, civilian ones at that. Recognizing that transition, Congress, in 1863, would abolish the Corps of Topographical Engineers.

❀

No explorer was needed to find the route that Frémont planned to take that spring of 1842. His task was not to find a route to South Pass, but to map and survey an existing route, one that had been in use for at least seventeen years. In fact, Frémont's party, along the way, stumbled upon campsites and artifacts left behind by others. At Independence Rock that August, for example, the men would find a bloodstained pair of trousers with a pipe still in its pocket, the artifact, the men assumed, of a "straggler" from an emigrant party recently ambushed by Indians.[21]

Other artifacts evoked clearer—but equally troubling—stories. Because troubles—ranging from sudden storms to droughts, from diseases to violent ambushes—dogged both travelers and inhabitants, most of the debris and abandoned campsites seemed to belong to some sort of sustained cautionary tale. Evidence often suggested intertribal violence. On June 18, for instance, near the mouth of Vermilion Creek, the party came upon a large, abandoned Kansas Indian village, which Frémont deduced had been attacked by rival Pawnees in the early spring: "Some of the houses were burnt, and others blackened with smoke, and weeds were already getting possession of the cleared places." On July 2, the party would come on still more evidence of hardships—an assortment of household goods scattered about on the route; Frémont surmised that a party of emigrants "had probably disburdened themselves here of many things not absolutely necessary."[22]

✼

As the party ascended the Platte on June 29, "a few miles brought us into the midst of the buffalo, swarming in immense numbers over the plains, where they had left scarcely a blade of grass." Once encamped each evening, feasts now became de rigueur, the men seated by their campfires, roasting buffalo pieces *en appolas*—on sticks—through the night into daybreak. The party could consume two buffalo each day: "With pleasant weather and no enemy to fear, an abundance of the most excellent meat, and no scarcity of bread or tobacco, they were enjoying the oasis of a voyageur's life."

On July 2, the party approached the juncture of the Platte's north and south forks. Determined now to avoid a recurrence of the sort of accident that had befallen them during their crossing of the Kansas River, Frémont sent several men that afternoon to find a safe spot to ford the South Platte. Though the ford was still difficult—stretches of quicksand lurked beneath the river's shallow waters—they managed to get across without loss of men, animals, or provisions.

They camped that night on the point of land that divides the two forks, on a grassy spot leafy with cottonwoods and willows. There, anticipating the return trip, the party made its first cache—burying a barrel of pork close to the Emigrant Road. On July 4, after the party had covered 25 miles, Frémont ordered an early halt, and the men set up camp along the South Platte. Anticipating the Independence Day celebration, the Chouteaus had packed, among the party's provisions, several specialty items. So, that night, along with the usual buffalo meat, the party also dined on various preserves, macaroni soup, and fruitcake. "We sat," Frémont recalled, "in barbaric luxury around our smoking supper on the grass, a greater sensation of enjoyment than the Roman epicure at his perfumed feast."[23]

❀

Before the men decamped the next morning, Frémont split the party into two groups: a small band, under Frémont, was to head up the South Platte with the Cheyennes; the rest of the men, under Clément Lambert, were to march up the North Platte to Fort Laramie. "The North fork," Frémont recalled, "was the principal object of my survey; but I was desirous to ascend the South branch, with a view of obtaining some astronomical positions, and determining the mouths of its tributaries as far as St. Vrain's fort."

Situated along the South Platte—just east of Long's Peak in the Rockies' northeastern foothills—St. Vrain's Fort had been, since its establishment in 1837, a key way station for trappers and traders in the region. Once behind St. Vrain's gleaming white adobe wall, Frémont hoped to obtain some mules to relieve his horses. But he also had military matters on his mind—more specifically, his orders to find strategic locations for future U.S. Army forts: "I was desirous to form some opinion of the country relative to the establishment of posts on a line connecting the settlements with the South Pass of the Rocky mountains, by way of the Arkansas and the South and Laramie Forks of the Platte."[24]

Frémont's small party covered thirty-six miles on July 5. Toward sunset, unable to find a buffalo, the men settled on a bull, whose meat, once roasted, was barely edible. Making matters worse, they discovered that no one had packed the coffee, salt, sugar, and flour they expected to find among their bales. With fresh memories of yesterday's feast compounding their disappointment, the "very disconsolate party" consumed their "miserable fare" in silence. Afterward, "each man took his blanket, and laid himself down silently; for the worst part of these mishaps is, that they make people ill-humored." So irate was the inveterate complainer Preuss that Frémont, the next morning, sent him back, accompanied by Baptiste Bernier, to rejoin the main party.

After Preuss's and Bernier's departure, Frémont's reduced party, getting by on hares and antelopes for food, continued up the South Platte. On July 8, an attack on them by a large party of Arapahos was barely averted when Lucien Maxwell, recognizing the band's leader, shouted at him in the Indian's native language. As it turned out, the Indians belonged to a larger body of tribesmen participating in a buffalo surround (hunt) not far away. By day's end, Frémont and his men were feasting with the Indians at a nearby village.[25]

On July 9, continuing westward, Frémont got his first glimpse of the Rockies, barely discerning Long's Peak in the distance. Soaring 14,255 feet into the azure Colorado skies, Long's Peak was named for himself by explorer Stephen Long, who, in 1818, upon approaching the Front Range, wrongly assumed the first significant mountain that he spotted to be the Rockies' highest peak. Zebulon Pike had made a similar error in 1806. But Pike at least had the modesty to pass on naming the mountain he had spotted for himself, calling it on his map simply "Highest Peak." Only later was the name Pike's Peak attached to the 14,110-foot-high mountain. John Frémont's resistance to such vanities, as will soon be clear, was far less certain.

The party reached St. Vrain's Fort on July 10, and during its two-day stay there obtained two horses and three mules, and hired a Mexican to help with the new livestock. Three days later, at dusk, they reached Fort Laramie, situated near the conjunction of the Laramie and North Platte Rivers. Built in 1834 and owned by the American Fur Company, Fort Laramie served as both oasis and crossroads for

High Plains and Rocky Mountain travelers. Sprawling across a low bluff above the Laramie River, the wooden stockade made quite an impression—"Its lofty walls, whitewashed and picketed, with the large bastions at the angles gave it an imposing appearance in the uncertain light of evening."[26]

Indians, trading with the fort's proprietors and its guests, frequently camped outside the post. Frémont found a cluster of Sioux teepees, and not far away—also encamped beyond the redoubt's walls—he also found Preuss, Carson, and the rest of his party. After ten days, the men were glad to be reunited with their commander. But as Frémont soon learned, they were hardly relaxed: since reaching the fort several days earlier, they had grown increasingly unnerved by rumors of Indian troubles along the western route they had planned to travel. The stories circulating told of attacks against whites by marauding war parties born of a recent alliance among Sioux, Cheyenne, and Gros Ventre tribesmen.

Observing how the stories of unfriendly Indians discomfited the men, Frémont knew he faced a problem. "Division and misunderstandings had grown up among them," he recalled. "They were already somewhat disheartened by the fatigue of their long and wearisome journey." The party had also heard troubling stories about the conditions of the country to the west—that drought had destroyed all the grass along the route west of the fort, and that few or no buffalo would be found there. Under such conditions, they asked, how, with their already weakened animals, would they ever move their heavy wagons over the mountains? Several party members asked to be discharged at Fort Laramie. Even Carson took the precaution of dictating a will.

Frémont, on July 19, responded to the crisis by urging the men to remain focused on their mission: "I gathered them around me in the evening, and told them that, 'I had determined to proceed the next day . . .'" In addressing the men, Frémont made no effort to empathize with their fears—whether true or not, he said, such rumors came with the job. Beyond that, he reminded them, "They had heard of the unsettled condition of the country before leaving St. Louis, and therefore could not make it a reason for breaking their engagements." Even so—having no desire to go any farther with those who wished to leave—he offered to allow those who wished to leave to do so, with the full pay due them at the time of discharge. To Frémont's surprise, only one man stepped forward: "I asked him some few questions, in order to expose him to the ridicule of the men, and let him go." Frémont also discharged young Henry Brant and Randolph Benton: "I did not think that the situation of the country justified me in taking our young companions." The two would remain at Fort Laramie until the party returned to the post and picked them up on its homeward-bound segment.[27]

Fears aside, the men were rested and well-armed. To assist their safe passage through Indian country, Frémont enlisted Joseph Bissonette, a trader whom the exploring party had met at the fort. Bissonette, who spoke fluent Sioux as well as several other Rocky Mountain Indian tongues, had offered to accompany the party to the Red Buttes, in exchange for being allowed to rejoin the party on its return to the East. It was 135 miles from Fort Laramie to the Red Buttes, Frémont recalled, "and, though only on the threshold of danger, it seemed better to secure the services of an interpreter for the partial distance, than to have none at all."

❀

Rested—though still uneasy about the country they were entering—the men, on July 21, saddled up for the final stretch of their outward trip. Lest troubles bedevil them farther down the trail, Frémont took the precaution of leaving behind some field notes at the fort, as well as a barometer—charging the fort's clerk Charles Galpin to conduct readings on it; and to Randolph Benton, he entrusted the winding of two chronometers. Before leaving, Frémont and several others went inside one of the fort's adobe chambers for a farewell toast with the fort's agents. As they were downing their drinks—"an excellent home-brewed preparation"—several Indian chiefs forced their way into the room and handed Frémont a letter, imploring him to delay his departure at least until the return of a band of youthful warriors bent on killing whites.

In the end, Frémont rebuffed the warning. But he did ask the chiefs if they might spare two or three of their tribesmen to accompany the party. After some hesitation, the chiefs answered that if Frémont would tell them where he planned to camp that night, they would send a young man out to join him: In return, Frémont must agree to provide a horse for the young man. After agreeing to the bargain, recalled Frémont, "I described to him the place where I intended to encamp, and, shaking hands, in a few minutes we were among the hills, and this last habitation of whites shut our from our view."[28]

Continuing up the North Platte, they covered about twelve miles that day. When they retired that night, they slept in a "lodge"—a teepee: "Our tents having been found too thin to protect ourselves and the instruments from the rains, which in this elevated country are attended with cold and unpleasant weather, I had procured from the Indians at Laramie a tolerably large lodge, about eighteen feet in diameter, and twenty feet in height." Such lodges would become an indispensable component of Frémont's expedition gear, a mosquito-free place he could repair to, after sundown, for the laborious task of recording that day's geodesic observations.[29]

The next morning, July 22, the expedition's new guide and interpreter Joseph Bissonette, along with the young Indian guide and his wife, reached the party's camp. And after breakfast, Frémont and Basil Lajeunesse—"my favorite man"—found their way to a spot several miles away, from which they gained a stunning view of the North Platte as it gushed out of the Black Hills, onto the plains:

> Like the whole country, the scenery of the river had undergone an entire change, and was in this place the most beautiful I have ever seen. The breadth of the stream, generally near that of its valley, was from two to three hundred feet, with a swift current, occasionally broken by rapids, and the water perfectly clear. On either side rose the red precipices, vertical, and sometimes overhanging, two and four hundred feet in height, crowned with green summits, on which were scattered a few pines.[30]

Mindful of the military dimension of his orders, Frémont noticed a small but open parcel of prairie nearby that would, he surmised, be ideal for an army post. A fort there, he believed, would help keep

South Pass open and "operate effectually to prevent any such coalitions as are now formed among the Gros Ventre, Sioux, Cheyennes [*sic*], and other Indians." Beyond that, the site offered more general advantages to both whites and Indians: "It is connected with the mouth of the Platte and the Upper Missouri by excellent roads . . . and would not in any way interfere with the range of the buffalo, on which the neighboring Indians depend mainly for support."[31]

Shortly after fording the North Platte to its north bank, Frémont, spotting a group of Indians, dispatched an advance party to ascertain their identity. The scouts soon returned with a party of friendly Oglala Sioux, who had belonged to a village to the west composed of Arapaho, Cheyenne, and Oglala. The settlement had recently broken up, and its members were in the process of fleeing to their former tribal villages. As Bissonette translated, the Indians told Frémont that the drought had rendered the area uninhabitable—no grass, no grasshoppers, no buffalo. Bissonette, who had now reached the point to which he had promised to take Frémont, was already planning to return to Fort Laramie. Upon hearing this latest news, he suggested that Frémont do likewise.

Once again, Frémont asked if anyone wished to turn back: "We had still ten days' provisions; and, should no game be found, when this stock was expended, we had our horses and mules, which we could eat when other means of subsistence failed. But not a man flinched from the undertaking."

"We'll eat the mules," said Basil Lajeunesse.

With that, Frémont shook hands with his interpreter Bissonette— as well as with the Indian guide and his wife, who by now had also decided that they had gone far enough—and bid them all farewell.

❋

It was now time to reduce the party's load. Frémont ordered the men to break down and cache their carts, barrels, and carriage frames. After the items were buried in a six-by-ten-foot hole beneath a stand of willows, the provisions needed for the trip to South Pass were put into packsaddles.[32]

The party was now in country that Kit Carson knew well from his trapping days, and Frémont increasingly relied on him to guide the

expedition's final lunge into the Rockies.[33] On July 31, the party abandoned the North Platte and began following its tributary, the Sweetwater River. Frémont found the country "exceedingly picturesque."
Even so, "there was no timber of any kind on the river, but good fires
were made of drift wood, aided by the *bois de vache*"—"the dry excre-
ment of the buffalo, which like that of the camel in the Arabian
deserts, furnishes to the traveller a very good substitute for wood,
burning like turf." What timber they did see seemed to lie far south of
the river; and, in the evening, they watched it burn—fires, Frémont
presumed, set by Indians passing through the valley.[34]

On August 3, the party spotted their sole grizzly bear of the entire
trip and had their first glimpse of the spectacular Wind River Range to
the north—though, at that distance, the range failed to meet Frémont's expectations: "The view dissipated in a moment the pictures
which had been created in our minds, by many descriptions of travellers, who have compared these mountains to the Alps in Switzer-
land."

By August 8, the party had reached South Pass. The final climb,
however, was so gentle—so anticlimactic—that even Carson wasn't at
first sure they had reached the place. "The ascent," as Frémont recalled in his published report, shrewdly touting the West's accessi-
bility to settlers, "had been so gradual, that, with all the intimate
knowledge possessed by Carson, who had made this country his home
for seventeen years, we were obliged to watch very closely to find the
place at which we had reached the culminating point." The pass
sprawled across a broad, almost flat saddle, bounded by low-lying hills
perhaps 160 feet high to the north and south: "From the impression
on my mind at this time, and subsequently on our return, I should
compare the elevation which we surmounted immediately at the Pass,
to the ascent of the Capitol hill from the avenue, at Washington."[35]
But having reached the Continental Divide, the western limits of his
official orders, Frémont now wondered whether there might be one
more triumph to be wrung from this expedition.

FREMONT PEAK AND BACK

UP TO NOW, twenty-nine-year-old John Frémont had been operating by the book, conducting his expedition according to the orders, however amended, given him by John Abert. Those instructions called on him to survey the Emigrant Road as far as South Pass, and then return. Period. But having reached South Pass, Frémont now began to improvise. After reaching the pass on August 7, Frémont, over the next three days, bent toward a northwesterly course—up the Green River valley, along the Wind River Range's western slope. Along their march, gazing at the high snowcapped peaks to the northeast, he grew increasingly enchanted with the Wind River Range's sublime pinnacles: "The whole valley is glowing and bright, and all the mountain peaks are gleaming like silver. Though these snow mountains are not the Alps, they have their own character of grandeur and magnificence, and will doubtless find pens and pencils to do them justice."

In his later official *Report* on the expedition, Frémont, attempting to justify his improvised course, claimed that, in ascending into the Wind River Mountains, he initially planned a broad hydrographic survey of the range. Attempting to tie it to scientific objectives, he asserted that "on this short mountain chain are the head waters of four great rivers of the continent; namely, the Colorado, Columbia, Missouri, and Platte rivers." He then described an ambitious circuit by which the entire party would march north along the range's western slope, then cross the mountains, then drop south, along the ridge's eastern slope, and eventually regain the line of their earlier, east-to-west march along the Sweetwater River.

In the end, however, Frémont decided against making such a circuit. "I was desirous to keep strictly within the scope of my instructions," he wrote, "and it would have required ten or fifteen additional days for the accomplishment of this object; our animals had become very much worn out with the length of the journey; game was very scarce; and . . . the spirits of the men had been much exhausted by the hardships and privations to which they had been subject." Had Frémont, at that point, turned around and headed back to St. Louis, that explanation would pass any reasonable scrutiny. It's what he did next that raises questions. For, instead of heading back, he continued into the Wind River Range on an improvised trek that—while putting his men, animals, provisions, and scientific specimens at risk—had little if anything to do with his expedition's stated purposes. Indeed, it would prove to be a diversion that evoked more the romantic spirit of a fate-tempting, recreational outing than that of a scientific exploring party.

But why did Frémont take the party on such a sojourn? If he was truly concerned with keeping "strictly within the scope of my instructions," the Wind River detour violated orders just as seriously as his original idea of a broader survey of the range would have. Beyond that, his excursion into the mountains left his men exposed to the same woes that, he claimed, had led him to abandon his earlier plan.

At first blush, neither of Frémont's Wind River itineraries had anything to do with Senator Benton's objective of establishing a trade corridor through the Rockies. Even Frémont never suggested that he might find a practical pass in the Wind River Range. The abandoned idea of the Wind River hydrological survey, however, could claim a certain scientific legitimacy. Had he truly tried to untangle the complex hydrology of the Wind River Range, Frémont would have been taking on exactly the sort of study that, as a man of science, Abert might conceivably endorse—that is, if Frémont had not already violated Abert's orders in the first place.

Frémont, in his *Report*, beyond noting his admiration for the mountains' scenery, offered no particular justification for straying into the range: in his August 10 entry, he blandly recounted, "We were now approaching the loftiest part of the Wind river chain; and I left the valley a few miles from our encampment, intending to penetrate the mountains as far as possible with the entire party." A few passages later, he implied that the Wind River leg had been part of his plans all along: "A great part of the interest of the journey for me was in the exploration of these mountains." Buttressing that claim of prior intention, Frémont's expedition purchases in New York had included— though, inexplicably, he apparently never used them—two pairs of crampons and "ice shoes."

Only five years before Frémont had set off for South Pass, after all, Washington Irving, in his account of Captain Benjamin Bonneville's early-1830s exploration of the Rockies, had praised the Wind River Range as "the most remarkable of the whole Rocky chain." More to the point, Irving—in this work, which Frémont, in all likelihood, knew well—recounted how Bonneville had climbed to what he considered "the loftiest point of the North American continent," only to abandon the summit in frustration, unable to confirm that superlative because he "had no instrument with him with which to ascertain the altitude of this peak." So now, almost a decade later, Frémont found himself in the same lofty country that Bonneville had explored—except that Frémont had working instruments to measure these pinnacles, about whose stature Bonneville could only conjecture.[1]

In the end, one can only assume that having reached South Pass and finding it wanting, Frémont simply gave in to his growing appetite for glory and sheer adventure. As it turned out, however, the Wind River side trip would have far-reaching consequences—politically if not scientifically—for both the nation and Frémont's career.

❋

On August 10, having climbed through increasingly broken ground, up granite-strewn ridges and ravines, the party came upon a tranquil body of water, "set like a gem in the mountains," that Frémont named Mountain Lake—now called Boulder Lake, in western Wyoming: "I was so much pleased with the beauty of the place, that I determined to make the main camp here, where our animals would find good pasturage, and explore the mountains with a small party of men."

That same day, leaving the others behind, Frémont and a small climbing party set off, bound for higher elevations. But they were barely out of sight of the camp when, while fording the swift stream that drained the lake, Frémont broke the party's sole remaining barometer: "We had brought this barometer in safety a thousand miles, and broke it almost along the snow of the mountains. The loss was felt by the whole camp—all had seen my anxiety, and aided me in preserving it." For days, Frémont later recalled, as they ascended into the mountains, the men had been repeating what trappers had said about this area—that it contained the highest peaks of the Rockies. And all, Frémont recalled, eagerly awaited their chance to reach the Wind River's highest peaks—and, with the barometer, to verify the range's rumored superlatives.[2]

Encamped at Boulder Lake, Frémont, that day and the next, labored to repair the barometer's shattered cistern. Initially, he tried to replace it with glass vials found among his baggage, but, one by one, they broke as he tried cutting them to the correct length. Eventually, finding the most transparent powder horn among his gear, he boiled it, stretched it to the right diameter on a piece of wood, then scraped it to increase its transparency:

I then secured it firmly in its place on the instrument, with strong glue made from a buffalo, and filled it with mercury, properly heated. A piece of skin, which had covered one of the vials, furnished a good pocket, which was well secured with strong thread and glue, and the brass cover was screwed to its place. The instrument was left some time to dry; and when I reversed it, a few hours after, I had the satisfaction to find it in perfect order; its indications being about the same as on the other side of the lake before it had been broken.[3]

Frémont's ingenuity restored the barometer to working order, but other worries now weighed on the exploring party. Provisions by now were low—the supply of bread had long been exhausted, and the men were down to less than three pounds of coffee and a small quantity of macaroni. Game was scarce and Frémont had no expectations of acquiring fresh buffalo meat anytime soon: "Our daily meal consisted of dry buffalo meat, cooked in tallow; and, as we had not dried this with Indian skill, part of it was spoiled; and what remained of good, was as hard as wood, having much the taste and appearance of so many pieces of bark." Such paltry fare only further lowered the men's already flagging spirits.

Weighed against those woes, Frémont concluded, his idea of crossing eastwardly across the far northern Rockies seemed overly ambitious. Besides, by now he had another idea: at Boulder Lake, the party now lay within striking distance of several peaks reputed to be among the highest in all the Rockies. Why not find the highest peak and ascend it? Like those characters who "made themselves famous by brave and noble deeds," who had enthralled him as an adolescent reader, Frémont, after all, liked showy gestures. He had already demonstrated his affection for attention-drawing deeds. Besides—who could say what effect his climbing the Rockies' highest peak might have on publicizing the Western causes of Senator Benton and his friends? Or, for that matter, on Frémont's own reputation?

❀

His spirits rejuvenated, Frémont ordered preparations for the climb to commence immediately. Because most of the men, livestock, and provisions would remain behind at Boulder Lake, to protect them from possible attack from Blackfoot Indians, he ordered the construction of a timbered breastwork, five feet high and forty feet in diameter, amid the wind-shivered leaves of a nearby grove of beeches.

The climbing party left Boulder Lake before daybreak on August 12. Fifteen men comprised the ascent party—each rode a mule, with a blanket strapped across his saddle. An extra mule carried provisions for two days—dried meat, a small stock of coffee, a coffee pot, and three or four cups. The men would take turns carrying on their backs the observational instruments—the barometer and a sextant, compass, and spy glass. The ascent party members rode up to the ridge of the first range of mountains, where they gazed into a deep valley containing three lakes. Then, carefully, they began descending toward the valley.

While exploring the valley's floor, the men spotted what appeared to be a promising route up the next ridge, rising above one of the lakes. Ascending toward that next ridgeline, the men camped that night in a defile, in a narrow, grassy spot surrounded by high, pine-covered granite rocks. While supper was being prepared, Frémont, accompanied by his trail-hardened friend from the Nicollet expeditions, botanist Charles Geyer, set off among the surrounding crags and ravines to collect rock and plant specimens. They returned at dusk to a supper that was, though spartan, nonetheless satisfying:

> Our table service was rather scant; and we held the meat in our hands, and clean rocks made good plates, on which we spread our maccaroni [sic]. Among all the strange places on which we had occasion to encamp during our long journey, none have left so vivid an impression on my mind as the camp of this evening. The disorder of the masses which surrounded us; the little hole through which we saw the stars overhead; the dark pines where we slept; and the rocks lit up with the glow of our fires, made a night picture of very wild beauty.

The next morning arrived cool and sunny. The party began the day's ride by ascending a narrow defile that Frémont had spotted the day before while collecting specimens. Although a carpet of grass marked most of the passage, at other times the cleft narrowed so much that the men had to dismount and lead their mules over sheer, rocky ledges. After several miles, they reached the source of the creek, a small lake surrounded by a meadow abloom in asters. From there, in the meadow where they turned the mules loose to graze, the men could see the Wind River Range's towering peaks spread across the horizon like an answered prayer. As he grabbed his spyglass, Frémont's gaze fell upon what appeared to be the highest of the summits—a pinnacle he called Snow Peak. Then and there, he decided to climb the mountain: "The peak appeared so near, that there was no doubt of our returning before night." To lighten their load, Frémont decided to leave all of the mules and most of the provisions by the lake; to guard them, he left behind three men.[4]

After an early meal—leaving what Frémont called the Camp of the Mules—the climbing party, now consisting of twelve men, set off for the peak. "We took with us nothing but our arms and instruments, and, as the day had become warm, the greater part left our coats." Kit Carson led the way. But his scouting talents soon proved no match for the disorienting jumble of summits, false peaks, precipices, waterfalls, and ubiquitous alpine lakes that hindered their progress. In fact, it was Frémont who had underestimated the distance to the peak he sought to climb. Even so, increasingly irritable—fatigued and now beginning to feel the first nauseous turns of altitude sickness—he accused Carson of setting too brisk a pace for the rest of the party.

"We clambered on," Frémont recalled, "always expecting, with every ridge that we crossed, to reach the foot of the peaks, and always disappointed." Around 4:00, "exceedingly fatigued," the men reached the shore of a small lake with an island in its middle. After a brief stop to rest, they pushed on to the lake's other side, where they set up camp for the evening. "The spot we had chosen was a broad flat rock, in some measure protected from the winds by the surrounding crags." A fire that evening built from fallen timbers illuminated their campsite at what Frémont named Island Lake, which lies about eighteen miles northeast of today's Pinedale, Wyoming. But from here on up, Frémont knew that there would be no more fires: "We had reached the upper limit of the piney region; as, above this point, no tree was to be seen, and patches of snow lay every where around us on the cold sides of the rocks."[5]

The fire that night helped stave off the cold but, as Preuss complained to his journal, they lacked food and blankets as well as the coats they had imprudently left behind at the lake: "There was nothing with which to cover oneself, and I can truthfully say that I did not sleep a single minute." Frémont, now suffering a severe headache and still riding out altitude sickness, began vomiting, his ailments aggravated by the frigid winds that soon swept across their rocky berth. "The night was cold," he recalled, "as a violent gale from the north had sprung up at sunset, which entirely blew away the heat of the fires. The cold, and our granite beds, had not been favorable to sleep, and we were glad to see the face of the sun in the morning."[6]

The next morning, August 14, the men set out at daybreak. All on foot now, they followed a ridge up to a partially frozen lake, about a mile in length. From there, they soon found themselves ascending a broken field of ice, amid a disorienting maze of crags and precipices. Attempting to find a route to the chain's main ridge, the men dispersed into groups, each seeking to find a way to the base of

Frémont's Snow Peak. Somehow, amid the activity, Preuss became separated from the others. Like the others, Preuss, over the past few days, had learned to avoid slipping on ice by keeping to the mountains' sunnier and less sloping areas. Because such places were less exposed to freezing winds, snow rather than ice tended to cover them, and it was possible to stamp out relatively safe paths across them.

The only problem, as Preuss learned that afternoon when he felt his legs go out from underneath him, was that these snowy slopes also concealed patches of ice. Suddenly on his backside, careering down a long slope, he somersaulted into a field of rocks. He bruised his rear and an elbow, but somehow managed not to break any bones.[7]

After taking a few minutes to regain his composure, Preuss got back on his feet, recovered the expedition's logbook and once again began climbing. A half hour later—now high enough to survey the lower peaks—he spotted, somewhere below him, Frémont and several other exploring-party members. Preuss yelled—they called back. Though comfortably ahead of the others, Preuss was still about a thousand feet below Snow Peak. Satisfied that the others could see him, he once again began climbing—confident that they would follow, and that he would have the satisfaction of being first to reach the peak.

After climbing another fifty feet, however, Preuss looked down, only to discover that the others had not moved. He waited for a few minutes, then looked back again; this time, he saw two figures moving—the others had vanished from sight. Though puzzled, he resumed his climb—but several hundred feet below the top, he found his ascent blocked by a wall of sheer vertical rocks. Disconsolate, Preuss once again called out for the others. Receiving no response, he began backtracking, away from the vertical wall blocking his path.

Frémont, at that moment, Preuss surmised, was probably on top of the peak, ready to take astronomical observations, but seething at his laggard assistant, absent and carrying their scientific instruments. But unbeknownst to Preuss, Frémont was nowhere near the top. Nor, for that matter, was anyone else. Below where Preuss had fallen, two other men—Clément Lambert and Descoteaux—having succumbed to altitude sickness, were lying on the rocks. Frémont, too, was ill once again. Perched—along with Maxwell and climbing partner B. W. Ayers—on a makeshift resting spot on the mountain, he was suffering a recurrence of the previous night's headache and vomiting. "Finding myself unable to proceed," he recalled, "I sent the barometer over to Mr. Preuss, who was in a gap two or three hundred yards distant, desiring him to reach the peak, if possible."

Preuss, meanwhile, still assuming that Frémont was waiting for him on the peak, had regained another five hundred feet or so by the time Auguste "Johnny" Janisse, later that day, reached him with the barometer. Right away Preuss took an observation with the barometer—but, thoroughly fatigued, he could climb no further.

Kit Carson, meanwhile, climbing alone for much of the day, had been thinking for hours that he was about to reach the top of Snow Peak. Finally, feeling triumphant, he had reached a snowy summit on the main ridge—only to look upward to find Snow Peak still another eight hundred to a thousand feet higher!

As Carson wrestled with Snow Peak's Sisyphean frustrations, Frémont, still immobilized by illness, was sending Basil Lajeunesse and four other men back to the Camp of the Mules. "We were now better acquainted with the topography of the country," he recalled, "and I directed him to bring back with him, if it were in any ways possible, four or five mules with provisions and blankets."

An hour later, Frémont, Maxwell, and Ayers—hungry and cold—abandoned their rocky perch and returned to the previous night's camp at Island Lake. There, Frémont's illness persisted through the afternoon, but lifted toward sundown when Basil Lajeunesse—having completed his errand to Camp of the Mules—arrived with four other men, all mounted. To Frémont's delight, the men carried fresh provisions. As Frémont recalled Lajeunesse's lonely errand, "The men who had gone with him had been too much fatigued to return, and were relieved by those in charge of the horses; but in his powers of endurance Basil resembled more a mountain goat than a man." Lajeunesse's party, as Frémont had requested, had brought blankets and other provisions; and, soon enough, the men were enjoying coffee and dried meat. "We rolled ourselves up in our blankets, and, with our feet turned to a blazing fire, slept soundly until morning."[8]

In his journal, Preuss claimed that he fell to sleep that night with the impression that Frémont had had enough, that there would be no more climbing. Instead they would simply use the barometric reading Preuss had taken earlier that day, work up an altitude figure from it, and add another five or six hundred feet. That way, Preuss figured, they could leave this frigid zone with the satisfaction that they had measured, if not conclusively climbed, the Rockies' highest peak. At daybreak the next morning, however, Preuss awoke to find a newly sanguine Frémont rested and ready to climb. "Well, Mr. Preuss," he said, "I hope we shall, after all, empty a glass on top of the mountain."

There would be other surprises for Preuss that morning. For starters, Kit Carson, with whom Frémont had quarreled the day before, was gone. Acting on orders given him by Frémont the previous evening, Carson had set out before daybreak to return to Boulder Lake, taking with him all but six of the camp's men. For the final climb, Frémont had selected five men—Preuss, Lambert, Lajeunesse, Janisse, and Descoteaux.

With the men rested and fed and the mules refreshed from grazing in the meadow bordering Island Lake, Frémont and his party started off, up a long defile they had noticed the day before. Lajeunesse—having replaced Carson—led the way on foot. The others, as they ascended a small stream that flowed through the defile, rode mules. As the men and mules made their way over dangerous icy terrain, Preuss—rarely comfortable around animals—marveled at the mule's surefootedness. "Half a year ago I would not have believed that I could have dared to cross such ground on such a beast," he later confided to his journal.[9]

✻

The gorge into which they squeezed quickly narrowed—becoming almost sunless, hiding treacherously icy patches. But Frémont, soon enough, savored the satisfaction of gazing upon the dizzyingly high ridge from which rose the Wind River Range's highest peaks: "There at last it rose by our sides, a nearly perpendicular wall of granite, terminating 2,000 to 3,000 feet above our heads in a serrated line of broken, jagged cones."[10]

The men kept riding until they were directly below Snow Peak. Immediately before them, set in a chasm, the men also saw three small lakes—possibly today's Titcomb Lakes. Realizing that their final ascent to the peak would have to be on foot, they rode the mules into a meadow, about a hundred feet beyond and slightly above the lakes.

In the meadow—a green, grassy island amid the surrounding riot of granite—they turned the animals loose to graze. They also cached all equipment not absolutely necessary for the final climb. Now on foot, as Frémont recalled, the party moved slowly, methodically, husbanding their strength: "This time, like experienced travellers, we did not press ourselves, but climbed leisurely, sitting down so soon as we found breath beginning to fail."

On the way up, springs gushing from the rocks drenched the climbers. At about eighteen hundred feet above the lakes, they reached the snow line. From here on up, as conditions grew more perilous—more icy and vertical—they took no more breaks: "Hitherto," Frémont remembered, "I had worn a pair of thick moccasins, with soles of *parflêche*; but here I put on a light thick pair, which I had brought for the purpose, as now the use of our toes became necessary to a further advance."

As they neared the mountain's summit, Frémont—not about to let the moment slip away—worked his way in front of Descoteaux and Lambert who had been leading the climb. The party continued climbing until they reached an overhanging buttress that blocked their progress. The only way around it was a sheer precipice, a wall dropping hundreds of feet. Holding onto a narrow crack in the wall, Frémont, slowly, carefully, worked his way around the obstruction. Then, pulling himself up, he clambered onto the narrow peak above the wall—in his exhilaration, almost slipping over its other side.

The summit could hold only one climber at a time, so the men took turns standing atop it. Pistols were fired, toasts with brandy offered. Then the barometer was mounted and a reading taken. The peak's altitude, according to their readings, was 13,500 feet—a calibration not far off from the actual height of 13,517 of what is today called Fremont Peak. Unbeknownst to Frémont, however, he had erred in assuming the peak to be the highest in the Rockies; there are numerous other summits in the Rockies that rise higher than Fremont Peak—six in the Wind River Range alone. But was his ascent up what is now known as Fremont Peak? Or did he climb neighboring Woodrow Wilson or Gannett Peak? Historians and mountaineers can't agree. As in so many places along Frémont's trail, the historical record by now lies hopelessly entangled in myth and local lore.

After the barometer was put away, Frémont climbed back onto the summit, placed a ramrod in a crevice, and unfurled a special edition of Old Glory designed for the expedition. The flag had thirteen stripes and twenty-six stars and, across the field of stars, an eagle holding in its talons a clutch of arrows and a peace pipe.

❀

Snow Peak—what Frémont later renamed Fremont Peak—offered a commanding view: to the northwest the Great Tetons, to the northeast the Wind River valley, and to the southeast the mountains from which rose the North Platte River's headwaters. Years earlier, Thomas Hart Benton had suggested raising atop the Rockies' highest peak a sign reading "Terminus"—a sign marking what, on that day in that oration, the senator asserted to be the American empire's proper western boundary. Now, two decades later, Benton's son-in-law, John Frémont, had unfurled an American flag on what he believed to be that very citadel. And, as Frémont stood in the Rockies' bracing winds that afternoon, limits—either his own or his nation's—were far from his mind. Likewise, months later, as word of his gesture spread, few Americans interpreted it as setting limits. More perceived it as an enticement for the nation to spread still farther west—to gather an American empire whose republican territorial breadth would surpass any previously imagined by Montesquieu, Jefferson, or Benton.

❀

It took all that day and most of the rest for everyone to get back to the fort at Boulder Lake. And when Frémont bedded down that night, he drifted to sleep satisfied that he had more than met the objectives placed on him by Senator Benton, Colonel Abert, and his other Washington sponsors. The next day—August 17—the reunited party began the journey home. With winter around the corner, Frémont set a brisker pace. Six days later, they were again encamped at Independence Rock. This time, however, Frémont took time to leave his mark at the famed emigrants' way station. Carving out a cross in the rock, he covered it with a preparation of Indian rubber. And—determined to get longitudinal and latitudinal positions missed at key junctures be-

cause of bad weather on their outward-bound trip—Frémont continued to take astronomical observations. But they were unable to
measure altitudes—the barometer had been broken beyond repair
shortly after they left the Wind River Range.

On August 23, the morning of the party's planned departure from
Independence Rock, Frémont reminded everyone that their orders
called on them to survey the North Platte River watershed if possible.
That same day, he ordered the India rubber boat inflated, and he and
several others tried without success to sail it down the Sweetwater
River's too-shallow channel. The following day, the party was approaching that river's confluence with the North Platte when Frémont, noticing how the Platte had now becoming a rushing and
deeper river, once again ordered the rubber boat inflated. To accompany him downstream, Frémont selected "five of my best men"
—Lambert, Lajeunesse, Honoré Ayot, Leonard Benoit, and Descoteaux. Designating a series of downstream locales as possible points
for their eventual reunion, Frémont put the land party under the command of Baptiste Bernier: Missing the river party at one place, he told
Bernier, go to the next.

This time, the craft floated: "We paddled down the river rapidly,
for our little craft was light as a duck on the water." But as they neared
the Sweetwater's junction with the North Platte, the men heard an
ominous roar in the distance: Could it be the waterfalls about which
they had heard rumors? As the boat, entering a canyon, gathered
speed, it narrowly missed crashing into a rock wall. Several men
jumped overboard and, clutching the boat, tried to slow it down. As
the river deepened and they found themselves in water up to their
necks, they decided to beach the boat and reassess their course.

After beaching the craft, the crew climbed onto a rocky promontory to survey the downstream course. From their vantage, they could
see continuous rapids ahead, along with a succession of small falls, but
nothing spectacular: "We saw nowhere a fall answering to that which
had been described to us as having 20 or 25 feet." Thus reassured, the
crew reembarked. As the river's waters rushed by the boat, however, it
became clear that the crew had only minimal control over the craft.
Even so, the boat and its crew managed to drop through three successive cataracts without capsizing.

By eight o'clock that morning, tired, hungry, and drenched, the men, upon spotting another beach, had stopped for breakfast. Once again, Frémont climbed to high ground to see what lay ahead. As he looked downstream, the river's waters seemed smooth for a mile or two. But beyond that stretch loomed what appeared to be a high ridge and the beginnings of another canyon. The men reembarked at nine o'clock but, minutes later, stopped again—this time at the canyon's mouth that Frémont had spotted earlier. Once more, he climbed to high ground to take a second look at what lay ahead:

> So far as we could see, the jagged rocks pointed out the course of the cañon, on a winding line of seven or eight miles. It was simply a narrow, dark chasm in the rock; and here the perpendicular faces were much higher than in the previous pass, being at this end two to three hundred, and further down, as we afterwards ascertained, five hundred feet in vertical height.

By now—there being no way to lift the boat and their provisions out of the chasm—it was too late to think about a portage; the canyon stretched seven or eight miles to the east; its walls rose two to three hundred feet at their present location and still higher downstream. Fearing the worst, Frémont asked Preuss to take the chronometer and move downstream on foot. But even that turned out to be impossible: setting off before the others, Preuss walked downstream no more than five minutes before the canyon's rocky shoreline completely disappeared.

Having espied a particularly "ugly pass" downstream, Frémont, before shoving off, had taken the precaution of tying a fifty-foot length of rope to the boat's stern. After Preuss had been plucked from his rocky perch, Lajeunesse and two other men climbed out of the boat and made their way up to the pile of rocks on which Preuss had been standing. There, holding the rope, the three intended to steady the boat's passage through the next set of rapids.

As the boat eased back into the river's main current, however, the water's powerful force jerked the rope out of the grip of two of the men. Lajeunesse—still holding the strand—was, in turn, pulled off the twelve-foot-high pile of rocks, headlong into the river. The boat —with Lajeunesse clinging to the rope—shot down the river "like an arrow," Frémont recalled. As the boatmen watched helplessly,

Lajeunesse plunged through the current, "exerting all his strength to keep in mid-channel—his head only seen occasionally like a black spot in the white foam." Farther down—Lajeunesse estimated a half mile down—the boatmen managed to turn their craft into an eddy; and Lajeunesse and the two other rope men reboarded.

All six now resumed their voyage; only this time, river and boat seemed blissfully compatible. "We cleared rock after rock, and shot past fall after fall, our little boat seeming to play with the cataract," Frémont recalled. "We became flushed with success and familiar with the danger; and, yielding to the excitement of the occasion, broke forth together into a Canadian boat song." Their bravado, however, soon gave way to panic: "Singing, or rather shouting, we dashed along; and were, I believe, in the midst of a chorus, when the boat struck a concealed rock immediately at the foot of a fall, which whirled her over in an instant. Three of my men could not swim, and my first feeling was to assist them, and save some of our effects; but a sharp concussion or two convinced me that I had not yet saved myself."

All of the men eventually made it to shore—even the three who could not swim. The boat's cargo, however, lay strewn in the river: "For a hundred yards below, the current was covered with floating books and boxes, bales of blankets, and scattered articles of clothing; and so strong and boiling was the stream, that even our heavy instruments, which were all in cases, kept on the surface, and the sextant, circle [an instrument used to measure angular distances], and the long black box of the telescope were in view at once." As Frémont climbed out of the water onto the rocks, he noticed that he was even missing one of his moccasins.

Once ashore, the men began scrambling downstream to recover the items. Frémont and Preuss inched their way down one side of the river, while three others descended the other side. Lajeunesse, meanwhile, uprighted the capsized boat and, joined by Descoteaux, paddled downstream on his own salvage operation. They eventually recovered some bedding, the circle, various buffalo hides, a tent, Preuss's journal, and a blue coat that belonged to Frémont. Everything else was gone—including the camera, the daguerreotype plates, the compasses, the telescope, the sextant, and, most important, the journals and registers containing the barometric and astronomical

readings. Except for a double-barreled shotgun that belonged to Frémont, all of their guns and ammunition in the boat were lost. "We
were," Frémont recalled, "entirely at the mercy of any straggling party
of savages, and not a little in danger of starvation." In the end, even
the boat was lost: it suffered a puncture and had to be abandoned.
With Frémont and Preuss now separated from the other four men by
the river's rushing, whitewater currents, the two groups were compelled to rely on sign language to communicate above the water's
roar—eventually agreeing to continue downstream as two separate
parties.

Frémont and Preuss eventually managed to climb out of the
canyon and, cut off from the others, continued moving downstream,
along a high ridge overlooking the river. Rocks cut Frémont's bare
foot, and he frequently had to stop and pull cactus thorns out of it, but
the two were determined to reach Goat Island, a grassy island in the
North Platte that lay about two days upstream from Fort Laramie. At
Goat Island, both Frémont and Preuss believed, they would find the
rest of the party waiting for them.

✤

Later that day, as the Platte reemerged onto the prairie, their path became easier and the river—now wider, shallower, and slower—more
accessible. That afternoon, Frémont and Preuss met up with Benoit,
who told them that the rest of his party was headed toward Goat Island on a more direct route, away from the river.

Benoit had some other good news: before leaving the canyon, his
party had fished a book out of the river, and, as Benoit described the
volume, Frémont and Preuss realized exactly what it was—the journal
containing their astronomical observations.

Their spirits raised, Frémont, Preuss, and Benoit picked up their
pace. Several times that afternoon, they forded or swam across the
North Platte. Before sunset, ascending a low red ridge just above Goat
Island, they spotted fresh human footprints and a button dropped in
the sand: "A shout from the man who first reached the top of the
ridge, responded to from below, informed us that our friends were all
on the island." As the three men approached the encampment on

Goat Island, they were greeted by the scent of roasting buffalo. That evening, for the first time in weeks, they enjoyed a hot meal and a good night's rest.

On August 26—two days after reuniting at Goat Island—the exploring party reached their North Platte River "cache camp," where, digging up their carts and provisions, they found everything undisturbed. "I have just put on a clean shirt—what a luxury! We have lived like dogs and pigs," Preuss crowed to his diary. "I can also enjoy a good pipe of tobacco again." As they descended the North Platte, buffalo meat, to the party's delight, again became a camp staple. Still more creature comforts awaited them when, on August 31, they neared Fort Laramie.

✸

It had been forty-two days since the party had left the fort; and though exhausted and ragged, the men, as they prepared to leave their camp that morning, were determined to look presentable. "The men have finished their toilet," Preuss wrote. "Anyone who still has a clean or an untorn rag has hung it on himself." Those, like Preuss, who had been on the North Platte boating misadventure looked the worst; Preuss himself wore two pairs of trousers, "so that one can cover the holes of the other." As for Frémont, doing his best to look the part of the dashing young lieutenant, he once again donned his by now ragged dress-blue army uniform.

They had been expected at Fort Laramie for the past two days, and as they approached the fort, a series of cannon volleys saluted their arrival. Frémont's men returned the salute with volleys from their own firearms. Once inside the stockade, the men reunited with their two young friends—Frémont's relatives on his wife's side of the family, Henry Brant and Randolph Benton.

Both boys seemed well—Brant had endured some ribbing at the fort after an Indian woman he had traded a horse to get left him amid rumors that she had found him an unacceptable sexual partner. Randolph, meanwhile, had witnessed some violent clashes between warring groups of Indians and found them interesting. But the glamorous daily task of winding Frémont's chronometer failed to assuage the general ennui of life at the fort. And both young men, suffice it to say, were glad to be leaving.

❀

The survey party left Fort Laramie on September 3. Now averaging twenty-five miles a day, the men made short shrift of the rest of their return trip down the North Platte valley. As they descended the North Platte, by then "a mere line of water among the sandbars," it was hard to believe that this was the same river—sometimes only inches deep—in which they had almost drowned.

As the party, minus Kit Carson, who had departed for Taos at Chimney Rock, descended the North Platte, its waters grew increasingly deep. Frémont—still afflicted by his hankering to descend the river by boat—while encamped on the point formed by the Platte's division into its North and South Forks, ordered the men to begin building a "bull boat," a craft fashioned from the skins of bulls:

> Men were sent out on the evening of our arrival, the necessary number of bulls killed, and their skins brought to the camp. Four of the best of them were strongly sewed together with buffalo sinew, and stretched over a basket frame of willow. The seams were then covered with ashes and tallow, and the boat left exposed to the sun for the greater part of one day, which was sufficient to dry and contract the skin, and make the whole work solid and strong. It had a rounded bow, was eight feet long and five broad, and drew with four men about four inches of water.

Perhaps Frémont had forgotten about the hapless voyageurs who had stumbled into their camp the previous June, after having abandoned their barges along this part of the Platte River because of its shallow currents. For on the morning of August 15, when Frémont, Preuss, and two other men set off in the bull boat, they quickly learned for themselves that the Platte's waters remained inhospitable to watercraft. "We dragged her over the sands for three or four miles," Frémont recalled, "and then left her on a bar, and abandoned all further attempts to navigate this river."

On August 22, the party arrived at a Pawnee village just above the Platte's confluence with the Missouri River, where the men made welcome purchases of corn and other vegetables. From there, Frémont dispatched Lambert and two other men to Bellevue—a trading post on the Missouri, not far from the river's confluence with the Platte—with a request that the post's carpenter build a wooden boat in which the exploring party could descend the Missouri, back to St. Louis.

The morning of October 1 found the party encamped on the densely forested point of land formed by the fork of the Platte and Missouri Rivers. Awaking before dawn, Frémont barely made out the faint sound of cowbells drifting through the night air. The ringing, as it turned out, emanated from a farm belonging to Peter A. Sarpy, the proprietor of nearby Bellevue.

When the party rode into Sarpy's trading post later that morning, the men were delighted to see that work on their boat was well under way. Over the next two days, as they waited for the boat to be finished, Frémont, as Sarpy's guest, enjoyed "the security and comfort of his hospitable mansion." He also found time to auction off the expedition's horses and most of its nonscientific equipment. On October 4, they boarded the boat—for which Sarpy was eventually paid $166— and sailed down the Missouri. On October 10, they stopped to conduct astronomical observations at the mouth of the Kansas River—ten miles from Chouteau's trading post, where exactly four months earlier they had commenced their trip.

The party reached St. Louis on October 17. After almost six months of travels, Frémont, eager to get back to Jessie and Washington, found himself in no mood to linger in St. Louis. He sold the expedition's remaining provisions and equipment and, the next day, left via steamboat for the East.[11]

THE FIRST REPORT
AND OREGON FEVER

WHEN, ON OCTOBER 29, 1842, John returned to Washington, Jessie, now eighteen years old, had not heard from him since the previous June, when he had vanished into, in her words, the "silence and the unknown." During John's long absence, Senator Benton tried to keep Jessie busy. In at least one instance, that meant—drawing on her erudition in languages, literature, and history—asking for assistance with his own work. "My father," she later recalled, "knowing idleness was bad for me in my lonesome condition pretexted his need for some translations from Bernal Diaz' Conquest of Mexico, and this occupied my mornings."

Frémont, however, did arrive just in time for the birth of his and Jessie's first child. The baby girl was named Elizabeth Benton but was called Lily by the family. Typical of Victorian women who had domestic help, Jessie remained in bed for several weeks after the delivery. During that period, John joined his father-in-law in trying to keep Jessie's spirits up; in one instance, as she later recalled, the young lieutenant came into her room and presented her with a souvenir of his recent expedition: "Spreading over me a wind-whipt [*sic*] flag, he said, 'This flag was raised on the summit peak of the highest point of the Rocky Mountains. I brought it to you.' "[1]

The family's joy over the new daughter, however, could not allay their sadness over another event. Shortly after John's departure for the West, Mrs. Benton had suffered a stroke that left the once vivacious Washington hostess a mentally damaged woman who now spoke haltingly and slowly. Each day, Jessie watched in sadness as her father tried to console his wife, only to later retreat to his room in despair. Compounding Jessie's grief was her own conclusion that the stroke had been caused by her mother's habit of calling in an old family physician to bleed her whenever she felt the slightest discomfort. The old doctor eventually retired, and a new one, less given to bleeding patients, was brought in. But the damage, as she recalled, was already done: "Thirty-three times, my father told me, was my mother bled!"[2]

For Frémont, however, things were looking up. The accolades bestowed on him upon his return to Washington convinced him that he would soon be leading another expedition. Indeed, Senator Benton— understating the next venture's gestation time—later recalled that the explorer had "barely finished" the First Expedition before he "sought and obtained orders for a second one." Obscuring for posterity Frémont's earlier survey work, Benton and other contemporaries began their count with the South Pass expedition. Historians and biographers thus still call the South Pass trip the "First Expedition."[3]

Assuming that his next outing, the "Second Expedition," would be sooner than later, Frémont plunged into the work of pulling together the First Expedition report, maps, and statistical tables for which his boss, John Abert, was eagerly waiting. Frémont understood the value of such reports—understood their value so well that, like Lewis and Clark before him, he forbade exploring-party members on all his expeditions from keeping or publishing journals. While several journals by members of Frémont's exploring parties have found their way into print, all were published years after the journeys they recount.[4]

Frémont's government-published report on his Des Moines River expedition had been brief and straightforward—a stark recitation of places visited and things seen, with little anecdotal content—and it attracted little notice. But as Frémont worked on his First Expedition report, it seems clear that, from the start, he intended to produce a very different kind of document, one capable of reaching a broad audience. Frémont was, after all, a longtime admirer of the literate travelogues of Alexander von Humboldt. And so he readily accepted Senator Benton's suggestion that the expedition report take the form of a guidebook, and that, in addition to a general map, it also include a series of maps which, beyond depicting the country, would supply such practical information of interest to emigrants as where water, grass, and wood could be found, and where hostile Indians might pose problems.

Sadly, most of the specimens collected during the expedition had been lost in the boat accident on the Sweetwater River. Frémont forwarded the rocks and soil samples that did survive to James Dana, a Yale University professor who had recently accompanied explorer Charles Wilkes on a federally financed maritime exploring expedition to Antarctica, the South Seas, and North America's Pacific Coast. Frémont sent his surviving plant specimens to botanist John Torrey, then at the College of New Jersey—now Princeton University—who had agreed to catalog and classify them. In Frémont, Torrey saw an opportunity. "He expects," Torrey wrote his colleague Asa Gray, "next year, to continue the exploration to the Pacific & offers me what he collects. So here is a chance for you to get seeds &c. How would it do to send a collector with him." Not that Torrey had any desire to join the expedition; for that task, he had in mind their colleague Melines C. Leavenworth, a botanist and surgeon, recently retired from the U.S. Army. "Leavenworth," Torrey wrote, "wishes to go somewhere—& this place might suit *him*—but not *us*—in all respects."[5]

❋

Though John began his work on the report soon after his return to Washington, recurring headaches and nosebleeds stymied its progress. "The horseback life," Jessie recalled, "the sleep in the open air, had unfitted Mr. Frémont for the indoor work of writing." Frustrated, he asked Jessie to assist him. At the Bentons' C Street home, as Jessie later recalled, the couple soon settled into a routine: "Every morning at nine I took my seat at the writing table and left it at one. Mr. Frémont had his notes all ready and dictated as he moved about the room."[6] With Jessie taking down his words, John found it easier to recall scenes, people, and events. "I write more easily by dictation," he later recalled. "Writing myself I have too much time to think and dwell upon words as well as ideas."

As Jessie quietly listened to John's firsthand stories, drawing on her own secondhand knowledge of the West, she was able to ask the sort of questions that, prodding her husband's memory, stimulated greater details in his recollections of events, people, and places. As John re-called, her questions prompted a type of "discussion impossible ex-cept with a mind and purpose in harmony with one's own and on the same level." "And so," Jessie recalled, "swiftly, the report of the first expedition was written." The manuscript was sent out for typesetting, and the page proofs were returned for Jessie to correct. "This too I mastered," Jessie recalled, "all the queer little signs that must be ac-curate, and behold! Mr. Frémont's first book was finished!"[7]

By March 1, the report had been delivered to John J. Abert, head of the Corps of Topographical Engineers, who, the next day, for-warded it to Secretary of War John Canfield Spencer. In a cover letter, Abert explained that any lapse in the document's completion "was not owing to any want of industry on the part of Lieut. Frémont, but to the great amount of matter which had to be introduced in the report and the many calculations which had to be made, of the astronomical & barometrical observations; the necessary labor on these accounts has delayed the completion of the report until today."

That same day, Senator Lewis Linn rose in the Senate to praise the report, and, the following day, his legislative colleagues ordered the printing of one thousand copies of the document. Rushed into print as Senate Document 243, 27th Congress, 3rd Session—*A Report on an Exploration of the Country Lying between the Missouri River and the Rocky Mountains on the Line of the Kansas and Great Platte Rivers*—the 215-page document proved an instant success. Passed along from reader to reader and widely excerpted in newspapers around the country, the *Report* further nourished the growing public interest in the West al-ready stoked by the painter and writer George Catlin and such other writers as James Fenimore Cooper and Washington Irving.[8]

Frémont's colorful expedition narrative took up only 76 pages of the 215-page document. The remainder of the *Report* consisted of John Torrey's exhaustive illustrated catalog of the expedition's plant specimens, as well as Preuss's exhaustive charts recounting day-to-day longitudinal and latitudinal positions, altitude, and weather. The ac-companying map had been meticulously sketched from latitudinal and longitudinal determinations, then filled in with details taken from Preuss's daily sketches, compass bearings, and recorded distances. And as promised, James Dana, drawing on the soil and rock specimens that survived the raft accent, helped Frémont incorporate geological information into his narrative. The final published map was then printed from a lithographer's plate crafted by engravers at Baltimore's E. Weber & Co. Though reaching only to the Continental Divide, the map—with its finely inscribed lines, its elegant hachuring of the region's mountains, and its small, tidy lettering—nonetheless provided prospective emigrants, as well as armchair adventurers, dependable guidance down the Oregon Trail as far as South Pass.[9]

The *Report*'s narrative and accompanying map also helped to undermine stereotypes propagated by Zebulon Pike, Stephen Long, and others of the Upper Missouri and Platte valleys as a parched Great American Desert. With the publication of the First Expedition *Report* and map, areas once dismissed as wastelands by Washington policymakers and the Eastern public were revealed as far more amenable to human settlement and agriculture than previously imagined.

Debunking yet another misconception, the *Report* and map challenged the long-held belief in a common origin in the Rockies of the West's great rivers. This erroneous concept posited a symmetrical continental topography in which North America's four key rivers flowed, from a common origin, in the four cardinal directions. But instead of imagining a linear "continental divide" separating the river basins, early North American travelers—explorers as well as fur traders—conceived of the streams falling from a pyramidal height of land, somewhere in the northern Rockies. The concept's key American proponent was the Connecticut-born French and Indian War veteran and Western traveler Jonathan Carver, whose *Travels Through the Interior Parts of North America in the Years 1766, 1767, and 1768*, published in 1781, influenced generations of geographers and policymakers. According to Carver, the "four most capital rivers of the Continent of North America viz. the St. Lawrence, the Mississippie, the River Bourbon [the Nelson], and Oregan [*sic*], or the River of the West have their sources in the same neighborhood."

In that same region, Carver suggested, the source of the Missouri also lies. Find the Missouri's headwaters, he suggested; make a short hop over the apex of the topographic pyramid, and you will soon find yourself on the waters of the Columbia—Carver's "River of the West." Like his contemporaries, Carver underestimated the breadth of the

Rockies and North America's east-to-west expanse—miscalculations eventually corrected by Frémont's explorations.

Carver's version of the "Dividing Waters" shaped the thinking of generations of adventures and policymakers—among them Thomas Jefferson, who embraced a modified version of the theory of the pyramidal height of land. The centerpiece, after all, of President Jefferson's instructions to Lewis and Clark had been for them to find the headwaters of the Missouri and thus locate a "practicable" water route across the continent; as he was under the spell of Carver's theory, it never occurred to the President that—as he soon learned from Lewis and Clark—the Missouri's headwaters and the transcontinental route he sought might lie in two different places.[10]

By the early 1840s, when Frémont surveyed South Pass, Jonathan Carver's pyramidal height of land theory of 1781 had, among American geographers, come down to a belief in the common mountainous origins of at least five Western river systems—the Platte, the Colorado, the Missouri, the Columbia, and the Buenaventura. But when Frémont, in August 1842, climbed atop Fremont Peak—the *Report* still called it Snow Peak—he reported a slightly different view:

> On one side we overlooked innumerable lakes and streams, the spring of the Colorado of the Gulf of California; and on the other was the Wind river valley, where were the heads of the Yellowstone branch of the Missouri; far to the north, we just could discover the snowy heads of the *Trois Tetons*, where were the sources of the Missouri and Columbia rivers; and at the southern extremity of the ridge, the peaks were plainly visible, among which were some of the springs of the Nebraska or Platte river.[11]

Missing—correctly so—from Frémont's overview of the northern Rockies hydrology were three rivers whose headwaters had traditionally been assigned to the region: the Rio Grande and the Arkansas, which originate far to the south, and the Buenaventura, a myth-shrouded river reputed to flow west from the Rockies all the way to the Pacific.[12] Frémont's removal of those three rivers from the Rockies' "Dividing Waters" constitutes the most important scientific achievement of his First Expedition. In a time in which topographical features rooted in myth and hearsay still commonly appeared on maps, great cartography often had more to do with removing features from maps than with adding things to them. In that light, Frémont's greatest achievement as a mapmaker may lie in the things that do not appear on his maps. Frémont's 1843 map—eschewing anecdotes, legends, and other half-truths repeated from past maps—included only areas that he had personally seen and surveyed. Areas uncrossed by the expedition remained blank.

❋

In accord with the Corps of Topographical Engineers' scientific objectives, the *Report*'s narrative included descriptions of topography, geology, weather, and flora and fauna. That empirical sense of authority won readers—but so, too, did the *Report*'s style. The public had seen other expedition journals—including William Clark's and Patrick Gass's accounts of the Lewis and Clark expedition, Zebulon Pike's narratives of his own travels, and Edwin James's account of Stephen Long's expeditions. But those plodding works, generally lacking drama and literary polish, seldom drew widespread audiences. Literary qualities could be found in more popular works about the West—such as Washington Irving's *Adventures of Captain Bonneville* and *Astoria* and James Fenimore Cooper's Leatherstocking novels—but those were, at core, works of artistic imagination, with scant scientific value. By contrast, Frémont's *Report* possessed both factual integrity and, with Jessie's help, enough literary flourish to keep readers engaged.

Equally important, the *Report* seemed, by Victorian standards, sufficiently bare of obvious literary artifice to convince readers that they were beholding nothing less than a plein air document teeming with the dust and subhuman terrors of the Far West's most lawless roads. To a reviewer assaying the *Report* for the *U.S. Magazine and Democratic Review*, it seemed, "Many passages are powerfully written." But, concluded the critic, Frémont's opus nonetheless occupied a literary niche somehow *beyond* mere literature. "It is evidently the transcript of the notes made in the field. . . . The work betrays nothing in the style to derogate from the novelty and importance of the matter."

Nonetheless, "the whole can be read with pleasure, as well as benefit, by the man of taste and education."[13]

In truth, the work only purported to be an actual journal. Though its narrative was distilled from Frémont's notes, he wrote it in Washington, months after the end of the expedition. The narrative's journal format—with its tacit conceit that, at each turn, its author doesn't know what lies ahead—preserved an in medias res sense of drama. It also gave the Frémonts the freedom to structurally shape the narrative, to give the story the tautness of a good adventure novel. Indeed, to at least one critic—Ralph Waldo Emerson—that preoccupation with adventure gave the *Report* a preening quality. The "stout Fremont [*sic*]," the Concord philosopher complained, "is continually remarking on 'the group' or 'the picture' &c. 'which we make.' " There was, inveighed Emerson, "this eternal vanity of *how we must look!*"[14]

❋

Later detractors of John Frémont would claim that the authorship of his expedition writings belonged more to Jessie Frémont than to him. They argued that she was more ghostwriter than, to use the word the Frémonts used to describe her role, *amanuensis*—"one employed to take dictation or to copy a manuscript."[15] The accusation of false authorship, which persists to this day, arose from two factors: Jessie's acknowledged role in editing and shaping the writings after the trips were concluded and her own later success as a professional author.

No physical evidence, however, has come to light supporting such claims. The field notes from which the reports were distilled no longer exist, and the two surviving manuscripts we have—those from the Des Moines River expedition and the First Expedition—hardly resolve the matter. The former is in Jessie's hand, as are the first nineteen pages of the latter. But the rest of the 135-page draft of the narrative section of the First Expedition *Report* is in John's hand.[16] Perhaps more telling is the fact that although Jessie, in later years, often wrote and signed letters for her husband, the surviving letters in his own hand display a competently crisp prose style not dissimilar to that of the expedition narratives.

Jessie's own style, in her own letters and later published writings, bears—in most cases—little resemblance to that of the expedition writings. Certainly she served as an active editor. She also, one assumes, provided the reports' occasional Victorian rhetorical filigrees. More important, Jessie played a critical role in drawing out and shaping John's recollections. But in the end, the expedition writings are driven by a specificity of detail that would be tough sledding for a secondhand author to manage.

In at least one instance, however, it seems possible, even likely, that Jessie, John, or the two of them may have fabricated an incident—and one of the *Report*'s most celebrated incidents at that. After unfurling his American flag atop Snow Peak—later renamed Fremont Peak—John sits down to savor the moment, when his attention is arrested by "a solitary bee (*bromus, the humble bee*)," which came "winging his flight from the eastern valley, and lit on the knee of one of the men."

> It was a strange place, the icy rock and the highest peak of the Rocky mountains, for a lover of warm sunshine and flowers; and we pleased ourselves with the idea that he was the first of his species to cross the mountain barrier—a solitary pioneer to foretell the advance of civilization. I believe that a moment's thought would have made us let him continue his way unharmed; but we carried out the law of this country, where all animated nature seems at war; and, seizing him immediately, put him in at least a fit place—in the leaves of a large book, among the flowers we had collected on our way.[17]

The bee scene enchanted readers. "It touched my heart when he told me how a weary little brown bee tried to make its way . . . across a spur of snow," recalled the Western poet Joaquin Miller. And indeed, the incident might have transpired exactly the way Frémont described it. What raises questions, suggesting origins more literary than empirical, is that by 1842, the bee-as-advance-scout image already occupied an established berth in the imagery of American literature. In William Cullen Bryant's 1834 poem "The Prairies," for instance, he, like Frémont, accorded the bee—"a more adventurous colonist than man"—a role as advance scout of America's "westering" urge. Similarly, a year later, in Washington Irving's 1835 *Tour on the Prairies*, bees are once again pressed into service as "the heralds of civilization."

Frémont's expedition writings were hardly fraudulent—too much internal and external evidence supports their descriptions of places, people, and nature. While they do contain occasional incidents that strain credulity, most such passages involve political matters rather than descriptions of nature and day-to-day expedition life. But true or not, the bee story points up an important quality, as essential as anything else to John Frémont's appeal to his contemporaries: the degree to which John, or Jessie—or, more likely, both of them—possessed a pitch-perfect sense of their audience and their day's American mind. For in that season of growing official and public U.S. interest in the Trans-Missouri West, Frémont's *Report* struck a chord that resonated for decades.

A century later, another American explorer—surveying a place with mountains but no watersheds—thrilled the American public by unfurling Old Glory on the surface of yet another little-known realm. The American public of 1969 understood little of the science that had brought Neil Armstrong to the Sea of Tranquility. But it knew a triumph when it saw one—however symbolic—over its Cold War enemy, the Soviet Union. Likewise, Frémont's gesture atop Fremont Peak enthralled his contemporaries. Few of his admirers cared about, or understood, the South Pass expedition's scientific achievements. They did, however, understand—and revel in—bravura affirmations of American nationalism. And though it had been three decades since the American Revolution, Britain in 1842 remained very much a U.S. rival in North America—still occupying substantial territories, and allegedly lurking behind everything from hostile Indians to unexplained course changes by British merchant ships. So, to that era's American public, Frémont's gesture atop what he told them was the continent's highest peak swelled national pride. It was an act that constituted a bold affirmation of American empire and a showy repudiation of two centuries of British condescension and bullying.

Beyond that, Americans thrilled to learn that there rose in the West lofty snow-covered mountains that dwarfed the Appalachians, few of whose peaks exceeded five thousand feet. Here were mountains in every sense equal to Europe's storied peaks. Even the chauvinistic

German-born Preuss was convinced—ultimately finding in the Rockies a wildness, a sublimity, unfound among the summits of his native land. "It is apparent these mountains cannot be compared to our Alps. Yet they are hardly less remarkable in their way."[18]

Years after Frémont's famous climb, the poet Joaquin Miller—with a memory conflating two expedition reports into one—recalled reading the *Report* as a nineteen-year-old farmboy: "I fancied I could see Frémont's men hauling the cannon up the savage battlements of the Rocky Mountains, flags in the air, Frémont at the head, waving his sword . . . with unknown and unnamed empires at every hand. . . . Now I began to be inflamed with a love for action, adventure, glory and great deeds away out yonder under the path of the setting sun." Similarly, Henry Wadsworth Longfellow, hearing his wife read the *Report* aloud over several evenings, became so captivated that he considered composing an epic poem about the expedition. "Frémont has particularly touched my imagination," he confided to his journal. "What a wild life, and what a fresh kind of existence! But, ah, the discomforts!" Longfellow never wrote his Frémont epic, but in writing his great epic poem *Evangeline* he relied heavily on Frémont's writings to create prairie scenes. He even gave that poem's chief male protagonist a surname borrowed from one of Frémont's favorite expedition members—Lajeunesse.

Years later, yet another Frémont admirer, Walt Whitman, in "Passage to India"—his paean to the Benton-Frémont project of empire—found himself similarly borrowing from the *Report*'s Western landscape:

> I see in glimpses afar or towering immediately above me the great mountains, I see the Wind river and the Wahsatch mountains, . . .[19]

❁

Frémont's *Report* boosted a growing national interest in the West—particularly Oregon. "The Oregon fever is raging in almost every part of the union," the *Niles National Register* exclaimed that May. "It would be reasonable to suppose that there will be at least five thousand Americans west of the Rocky Mountains by next autumn."[20]

Though President Tyler made it clear in December 1842 that, until Britain and the United States reached a permanent territorial settlement regarding Oregon, the United States should grant no land titles there, to Benton and Linn it seemed a propitious moment to lobby for a more aggressive U.S. policy in Oregon. As early as March 1, when Linn rose in the Senate to praise Frémont's expedition, he made it clear that the ultimate value of the route lay in its being "on the way to the Oregon,"[21] More perhaps than his friend Benton, Linn displayed interest in the agricultural potential of the West's interior. But like Benton, his primary concern lay in establishing a continental link to the Pacific coast.

In early 1843, Linn introduced a bill calling for the construction of a line of at least five stockades and forts, "from some point on the Missouri and Arkansas river into the best pass for entering the valley of the Oregon; and, also, at or near the mouth of the Columbia River." The bill also called for the granting of 640 acres to every white male inhabitant willing to cultivate land in Oregon for five years.[22]

Rebuffing President Tyler, the Senate, in February 1843, passed Linn's Oregon bill, but only barely—by a 24–22 margin. Though the measure later failed in the House of Representatives, the Senate's action nonetheless emboldened the Oregon lobby. "The vote of the Senate," as Benton later recalled, "was sufficient encouragement to the enterprising people of the West."[23] And as Benton and Linn waged their public legislative war for Oregon, they were also quietly working to circumvent the White House's opposition to any provocative actions in the Northwest.

Indeed, of Frémont's Second Expedition, Benton later boasted that the Tyler administration was both "not entitled to the credit of its authorship" and "equally innocent of its conception."[24] Frémont's orders—issued by Abert on March 11, 1843—called for him to find another route, south of South Pass, across the Rockies. From there, he was to explore south of the Columbia River, including southern Oregon and the country between California and the Rockies. He was also to link up his survey of the continent with that of Commander Charles Wilkes, who a year earlier, from the Pacific, had penetrated Oregon and the Columbia River as far as Fort Walla Walla.

Frémont's task was to link his survey with Wilkes's survey, thus giving U.S. policymakers their broadest yet comprehension of the Pacific Coast, as well as the Far West's hinterlands. "This circuit," Abert wrote, concluding his description of the survey he wanted Frémont to conduct, "would embrace within its limits the heads of the Colorado, the Columbia, some of the heads of the Missouri proper, the Yellowstone and the Platte."[25]

❈

Once it became clear that John would be leading another expedition, it was decided that, as Mrs. Benton's health had improved, the Bentons—minus Senator Benton—would accompany him west as far as St. Louis. As Congress began its recess in early March, Senator Benton went ahead of his household to St. Louis, to deal with constituent political matters. While the rest of the family prepared for the trip, Frémont hastily began acquiring equipment and provisions for the next expedition.[26]

The most curious acquisition came after Frémont wrote Stephen Watts Kearny, commander of the Third Military Department at Jefferson Barracks, near St. Louis, describing his planned line of travel: "I shall be led into countries inhabited by hostile Indians, so that it is absolutely necessary to the performance of this service that my party . . . be furnished with every means of defense which may conduce to its safety." To arm what he expected to be a thirty-man exploring party, Frémont requested four pistols, thirty-three carbines, five kegs of gunpowder, a mountain howitzer, and five hundred pounds of artillery ammunition.[27] By any measure, a cannon and five hundred pounds of ammunition for it were odd selections for a scientific exploring expedition. But whatever reservations Kearny had, he put aside. Because Frémont was leaving the next day, Kearny told Captain William H. Bell, who ran the Army's St. Louis arsenal, that there was no time to check with Washington about the matter and to fill the order immediately. Bell filled the order. But suspicious of Frémont—why did he need a cannon?—he reported the incident to Lieutenant Colonel George Talcott of the Ordnance Office in Washington. Also, on April 22 and May 15, John Abert sent letters to Frémont, reminding him that there were limits on what he might spend, and that he assumed Frémont would stay within those limits.[28]

❋

Weeks earlier, when Frémont had returned to Washington from New York, he had found Jessie and the rest of the family packed and ready for the trip to St. Louis. The travel party included John, Jessie, and Lily Frémont, Mrs. Benton, Charles Preuss, and Jacob Dodson, a tall eighteen-year-old black man—"born free," according to Frémont, and employed as his personal valet. Dodson, captivated by stories from the First Expedition, had persuaded Frémont to let him accompany the next expedition.

Once in St. Louis, Frémont, assembling his expedition force, recruited several men from the First Expedition—including Alexis Ayot, Basil Lajeunesse, Louis Ménard, and Raphael Proue—and at least one veteran of Nicollet's exploring corps, the Prussian artillerist Louis Zindel. To assist in finding an alternate pass across the Rockies south of South Pass, Frémont hired Lucien Maxwell, a veteran of the First Expedition, who would guide them as far as the headwaters of the Arkansas River, where, they assumed, such a pass would be found—if it existed. To lead them through the Rockies and beyond, Frémont hired Thomas Fitzpatrick, a well-known mountain man, as the expedition's chief guide.

Frémont and the party left St. Louis and, on May 17, reached Westport Landing, where he intended to fatten his animals and tend to final preparations. Before leaving for Westport Landing, Frémont had put his wife, who was still in St. Louis, in charge of any correspondence that might arrive in his absence. Should any important letters arrive, she was to get word to him before his departure for the frontier. It was in that role that Jessie, in late May, opened a distressing letter, dated May 22, from John J. Abert to John: From what he had heard, Abert inveighed, Frémont had exceeded the limits that had been placed on expenditures for the expedition. Even worse,

I hear also that among other things, you have been calling upon the Ordnance Department for a Howitzer. Now Sir what authority had you to make any such requisition, and of what use can such a piece be in the execution of your duties. Where is your right to increase your party in the numbers and expense, which the management and preservation of such a piece require. If the condition of the Indians in the mountains is such as to require your party to be so warlike in its equipment it is clear that the only objects of your expedition[,] geographical information[,] cannot be obtained.

The object of the Department was a peaceable expedition, similar to the one of last year, an expedition to gather scientific knowledge. If there is reason to believe that the condition of the country will not admit of the safe management of such an expedition, and of course will not admit of the only objects for accomplishment of which the expedition was planned, you will immediately desist in its further prosecution and report to this office.[29]

To Jessie, John J. Abert's letter suggested a conspiracy bent on jeopardizing the success of her husband's expedition. More specifically, she suspected that James W. Abert, the son of the letter's author, was scheming to have Frémont fired so that he could take his place. "The report," she later wrote, "had given immediate fame to Mr [*sic*] Frémont—then why not the same to another officer?" She would, she decided, have to take matters into her own hands. "I saw at once that this would make delays, which would involve the overthrow of great plans, and I felt there was a hidden hand at work. Fortunately my father was absent from St. Louis, and I could act on my own instinct."[30] Jessie told no one about the letter and hid it away. Then, knowing that a Canadian voyageur, Baptiste Derosier, was about to leave for Westport with some last-minute provisions for the exploring party, she asked him to carry her own letter to her husband; telling John that *"he must not ask why,"* she instructed him to "start at once, ready or not ready. The animals could rest and fatten at Bent's Fort."[31]

PART III

THE SECOND EXPEDITION

SPRING 1843–WINTER 1845

We were in that older time when there was no telegraph to paralyze individuality. Else the grand plan with its gathered strength and fullness, ripening and expanding from Jefferson's time to now, almost its culminating hour, would have fallen before petty official routine.

—Jessie Benton Frémont

RETURN TO THE ROCKIES AND
EXPLORATION OF GREAT SALT LAKE

PON RECEIVING JESSIE'S LETTER, John ordered the men
to pack for an immediate departure—such was his confidence in her judgment. They reached the settlement of Elm
Grove on May 31. Situated on a well-traveled emigrant and trade corridor, Elm Grove lay a few miles east of where the Santa Fe and Oregon Trails diverged. The party that night shared its campground with
an assembly of about thirty men plus numerous women and children—all members of a California-bound emigrant party, under the
leadership of entrepreneur Joseph B. Chiles. It was, in fact, the first
U.S. emigrant party to travel by wagon to California; as Frémont recalled the scene, "The wagons were variously freighted with goods,
furniture, and farming utensils." Some even contained equipment for
a mill that Chiles hope to erect along the Sacramento River.

Whether the young lieutenant realized it or not, an irony thick as
the campfire smoke hung over that spring evening of 1843. When Frémont's exploration party—ostensibly the advance guard of American
empire—reached Elm Grove, the explorers, traveling behind Chiles's
emigrant party, had to settle for a second-choice campsite. In 1842,
when John Frémont had set out to survey the Oregon Trail's eastern
half, about 125 emigrants traveled down that corridor. When Frémont's party reached Elm Grove in May of 1843, a vast groundswell of
U.S. interest in the West—a trend nourished by Frémont's own *Report*
and map—was drawing more and more emigrants into the region. By
the end of 1843, the annual number of Oregon emigrants would jump
to 875, and by the end of the following year to 1,475. And for the du-

ration of his exploring career, Frémont would, in a sense, be locked into a race—trying to keep up with the very forces that he himself had helped put in motion, forces which over the next few years seemed, at every bend, about to overtake him.[1]

❦

At Elm Grove, Frémont's party picked up one more member—William Gilpin. A soldier, an entrepreneur, and Missouri journalist, Gilpin was also a close friend of Senator Benton, and, in those days, an enthusiastic proponent of American settlement in Oregon. Pining for a firsthand look at the American settlements beginning to spread down Oregon's Willamette River valley, Gilpin had persuaded Frémont to let him accompany the exploring party to Oregon.

Both parties—Frémont's and Chiles's emigrant wagon train—left the next morning and over the next two days followed the same Oregon Trail route—busier now—of Frémont's previous year's expedition. "Trains of wagons were almost constantly in sight; giving to the road a populous and animated appearance," he recalled. On June 3, where the Emigrant Road, snaking off to the north, forded the Kansas River, Frémont's men bid farewell to the Chiles party and the other emigrants.

Determined to fulfill his orders to find a new pass over the Rockies—one south of South Pass—Frémont struck out on a course up the Kansas River. But as the party moved out over the plains of today's south central Kansas, incident upon incident reminded him that his cadre included more than a few greenhorns. On June 5, for instance, Frederick Dwight—a travel-hungry former Harvard College law student who had thrown in with the expedition in hopes of reaching the Pacific and catching a ship to the Sandwich Islands and China—let his horse get away from him. The next morning, Lucien Maxwell—alarmed at the specter of losing not only a horse, but the saddle, bridle, and pistols it was carrying—hung back to look for the lost mount.

That afternoon, while crossing a stream nine miles from that morning's camp, the explorers were surprised by the sudden appearance of Maxwell riding toward them at full gallop, with a war band of Osage Indians in pursuit. The Indians, who had shaved heads and wore red

blankets, were apparently unaware of the larger party traveling with
Maxwell. Nevertheless, they managed to throw the exploring party
into confusion and, amid the chaos, drive off several of Frémont's
horses. The Indians eventually withdrew, and the horses were recovered. But the experience gave Frémont pause; it was, he later recalled,
"a first fruit of having gentlemen in company—very estimable, to be
sure, but who are not trained to the care and vigilance and self-
dependence which such an expedition required, and who are not subject to the orders which enforce attention and exertion." As for the
object of Frémont's lament, Frederick Dwight, by that August even
he had decided that he had had enough. When Dwight elected to
leave the party, his departure apparently inspired no regrets from its
other members. As Theodore Talbot confided to his journal, "His is no
great loss for he had not messed [eaten] with us since we left Fort
Laramie."[2]

By June 8, the party had reached the point where the Republican
River and the Smoky Hill Fork converged to form the Kansas River.
Because neither tributary streams seemed fordable, the party had to
construct a raft, a task that, along with a bout of stormy weather, delayed them for three days. Afterward they continued up the Republican, but conditions in the valley, damp from the heavy spring rains,
hindered their progress. They were now averaging only five or six
miles of travel per day; and, as they slogged along the river's banks,
carts got stuck and makeshift bridges had to be built over swollen tributary streams. On June 14—by now 1,520 feet above sea level and 265
miles from the mouth of the Kansas River—they found themselves
encamped at a tribal gathering place along the Republican that the Indians called Big Timber.

To quicken their pace, Frémont, while at Big Timber, divided the
party into two groups. The smaller of the two—comprising fifteen
men—which he would lead, was to move ahead of the other group.
The other group—comprising 26 men and transporting most of the
party's provisions—was to follow, but at a slower pace. As the men unpacked, divided, then repacked their provisions, artillerist Louis Zindel took advantage of the layover to get in some target practice with
the mountain howitzer—at one point, impressively hitting a four-foot
post from a distance of a quarter mile.

On June 16, both parties moved out from Big Timber. As Frémont's contingent worked its way still farther up the Republican River valley, he did his best to sort out and make notes on the profusion of wild flowers and grasses that the group passed—from bunch grass to buffalo grass, from dwarf lupine to various wild roses. Now in largely treeless prairie country, the men took particular delight in the shade offered by riparian groves of oak, ash, elm, and cottonwoods that traced the Republican and its myriad feeder streams.

By June 21, the party was in higher and more westerly country, and game—first antelope, then buffalo—became more plentiful. Two days later, camped beside a Republican tributary, they found the area so dense with prairie dogs that Frémont named the stream Prairie Dog River. For him the stream offered a welcome antidote to the stillness of the otherwise arid surrounding country: "It was musical with the notes of many birds, which, from the vast expanse of silent prairie around, seemed all to have collected here."[3]

❀

However sylvan the immediate country, the party, somewhere east of Prairie Dog River, had already crossed the hundredth meridian—the traditional longitudinal marker for the commencement—or end—of the arid West. Accordingly, as they continued their ascent of the Republican River valley, they increasingly found themselves in a much drier realm—a landscape of undulating, largely treeless sand hills. Bending to a northwesterly course, the party by June 30 found itself encamped in the South Platte valley. On July 1 the men caught their first glimpse of Long's Peak; and at noon three days later, they reached St. Vrain's Fort just in time for a bountiful Fourth of July feast.

The repast was sumptuous; and Frémont, once again, reveled in St. Vrain's generous hospitality. But otherwise he found the fort in an "impoverished" condition. Their hosts offered the exploring party some flour and a few pounds of powder and lead, but they were a far cry from what Frémont had hoped to obtain. What they needed was mules: "We could not proceed without animals, and our own were not capable of prosecuting the journey beyond the mountains without relief." At St. Vrain's, Frémont did hear that a herd of mules, driven from California, had recently arrived at Taos. Lucien Maxwell had already planned to leave the exploring party at St. Vrain's to travel to Taos to visit some family members living there. So Frémont commissioned him, while in Taos, to purchase ten or twelve mules, pack them with some provisions, and meet the exploring party at the mouth of the Fontaine-qui-bouit—today's Fountain Creek, a tributary of the Arkansas River.

At St. Vrain's, Frémont also made some changes in the exploring party's composition. Oscar Sarpy, a member of the party, had decided, and Frémont had agreed, that he was, by temperament and experience, ill-prepared for the explorer's life. Accordingly, Frémont officially discharged Sarpy, providing him with arms and a mount to get him back in one piece to Fort Laramie, whence he could find transportation back to the East with a returning party.

At daybreak on July 6, Maxwell left St. Vrain's for Taos, and Frémont and his party resumed their journey up the South Platte. To their relief, they found the river valley well-timbered. And ten miles from St. Vrain's, the party reached Fort Lancaster, also known as Fort Lupton, after its proprietor Lancaster P. Lupton. Though situated in isolated prairie country, Lupton's trading post, to Frémont, offered an agreeable domestic ambience: "His post was beginning to assume the appearance of a comfortable farm: stock, hogs, and cattle, were ranging about on the prairie; there were different kinds of poultry; and there was the wreck of a promising garden, in which a considerable variety of vegetables had been in a flourishing condition, but it had been almost entirely ruined by the recent high waters."[4]

After riding a few miles up the river the next day, the men encountered several Arapaho tribesmen from a nearby village, composed of about 160 buffalo-skin lodges. "It appeared," Frémont recalled, "extremely populous, with a great number of children; a circumstance which indicated a regular supply of the means of subsistence." The village's elders welcomed the party, "throwing their arms around our necks and embracing us." Frémont, for his part, felt embarrassed that he had only meager gifts to offer their hosts. But, he assured them, the larger party, following behind, would have more gifts.

After visiting with the Arapahos, the exploring party continued west, camping that night a little above Cherry Creek's junction with the South Platte, a site now occupied by today's Denver, Colorado. Continuing up the South Platte the next day, they found themselves in increasingly broken country; immediately before them lay the Front Range of the Rockies—"like a dark corniced line, in clear contrast with the great snowy chain which, immediately beyond, rose glittering five thousand feet above them."

On July 9, with provisions running low and hoping to find buffalo, the party moved along the divide separating the South Platte and the Arkansas River. Frémont found the topography delightful—a country of dazzling wind-sculpted hills, colorful flowers, and verdant grasses. Not until late that afternoon, however, did they find or kill a single bull buffalo. Heavy snow fell that night, but as the sky cleared, the men awoke to see Pike's Peak glistening in the morning's light.

Later that day, after establishing camp along Bijou Creek, a tributary of South Platte River, Frémont found time to indulge a longstanding curiosity. Noticing a prairie dog village, he and several men began digging into its holes. With all the obsessive energy that he and Joseph Nicollet had once brought to establishing that various river drainages connected, Frémont labored to prove that a connection linked all the prairie dogs' myriad burrows and tunnels: "After descending, with a slight inclination, until it had gone the depth of two feet, the hole suddenly turned at a sharp angle in another direction for one more foot in depth, when it again turned, taking an ascending direction to the nearest hole. I have no doubt that all their little habitations communicate with each other."[5]

❈

In hopes of finding buffalo, Frémont, over the past few days, had made a slightly eastward detour. But that gambit had yielded no herds. And so, on July 12, the party again changed course and headed toward the wagon road connecting St. Vrain's and Bent's Forts. They followed Fountain Creek to its junction with the Arkansas River, where, on July 14th, they pitched camp just below the settlement of Pueblo—site of today's Pueblo, Colorado, but then a cluster of log and adobe buildings, established a year earlier by mountain man Jim Beckwourth.

Pueblo's sparse population consisted largely of American mountain men and traders and their Mexican wives. Because the fur trade had largely collapsed, the settlement's families survived through farming and what survived of the Santa Fe trade. That trade, as Frémont learned at Pueblo, had been recently disrupted by an uprising among local Indians against whites in the area. Still more distressing, while at Pueblo, the party also learned that Lucien Maxwell, whom Frémont had dispatched to purchase mules, had left Pueblo for Taos on July 9, before word had reached them of the Indian uprising. Maxwell, Frémont was told, had probably been captured by the Indians; and it was also safe to assume that, even if Maxwell had eluded capture, he risked trouble with any Mexican soldiers he might have encountered—as Mexican hostilities toward Americans had been stirred anew by ongoing military actions by the Republic of Texas against the Mexican province of New Mexico.

Because the settlers at Pueblo were themselves low on provisions, they declined to sell Frémont the items he needed. They did, however, offer, as he recalled, all the "rude hospitality their situation admitted"—including allowing the exploring party to feast on fresh milk drawn from the settlement's cattle herds.[6]

At Pueblo, Frémont also had a welcome reunion with his old friend Kit Carson. At the end of the first Expedition, Carson had offered his services to Frémont for whatever next journey he might lead. But months later, Frémont prepared for his new expedition with no way of locating Carson—he had reluctantly assumed that he would have to make the trip without his friend. As it turned out, Carson had been at Bent's Fort—due east of Pueblo, down the Arkansas River—when he heard that Frémont was at Pueblo. He immediately rode the seventy-five-mile distance to Pueblo. Delighted to see Carson again, Frémont promptly rehired him as a scout and hunter at his old salary of one hundred dollars per month. Frémont also hired Charles Town, a native of St. Louis who had "many of the qualities of a good voyageur."

The exploring party remained at Pueblo until the morning of July 16—the deadline Frémont had given Maxwell for meeting them. Before leaving, Frémont dispatched Carson back to Bent's Fort, where he hoped there might be a herd of purchasable mules. Carson was to bring whatever animals he obtained to St. Vrain's Fort, where the exploring party would be waiting for him. Before leaving Pueblo, Frémont also took time to write and leave behind a note for Lucien

Maxwell, instructing him also to come to St. Vrain's Fort. Frémont would, he wrote, wait for Maxwell at St. Vrain's until July 26.[7]

✸

From Pueblo, the exploring party headed up Fountain Creek— Fontaine-qui-bouit River—toward the stream's namesake, Boiling Springs. At the foot of Pike's Peak, Boiling Springs, in today's town of Manitou Springs, Colorado, then ranked as one of the West's most celebrated natural attractions. "The water," Frémont recalled, "has a very agreeable taste." Even the inveterate complainer Preuss agreed—finding its taste "much to resemble that of the famous Seltzer springs in the grand duchy of Nassan." From Boiling Springs, the expedition rode north, arriving, on July 23, once again at St. Vrain's Fort. There, Frémont's contingent found not only Carson with ten mules that he had purchased at Bent's Fort but also Fitzpatrick and the expedition's main party. As it turned out, Fitzpatrick's party had been at the fort for a week—using the time to rest and refit for the expedition's next, more westerly leg. Giving cause for still more elation, the experienced Fitzpatrick had managed to get both men and beasts to St. Vrain's in reasonably good health. Moreover, his jealous watch over the provisions had preserved an abundance of flour, rice, and coffee.

At St. Vrain's the reunited party enjoyed a feast. And Frémont, while at the fort, purchased, for thirty dollars, a new lodge and poles. He also made still more changes in the party's makeup. The two Delaware hunters who had been traveling with the party reminded Frémont that, upon reaching St. Vrain's, they had gone as far as they had promised to go with the expedition. Regretfully, the lieutenant said goodbye to the two men. At Pueblo, Frémont had hired Charles Town as a new hunter for the party. So now, to fully make up the loss of the two Delaware hunters, he also engaged Alexis Godey a seasoned mountain man who happened to be at St. Vrain's Fort and wanted to join the expedition. Brave and ruggedly handsome, Godey, then twenty-six years old, was of French-Canadian descent and, in time, would become one of Frémont's favorite men.

While the party was at St. Vrain's, one other man joined the expedition—Thomas Fallon, an intense, quick-tempered voyageur who, as if to prove that attribute, had killed a fellow mountain man during the fort's Fourth of July celebration. Curiously, at St. Vrain's Fort the party was also joined by the Shoshone widow of the man Fallon had stabbed to death, as well as her two children. After agreeing that she and the children could travel with the expedition as far as her tribal homeland, Frémont arranged for her baggage to be transported on some pack mules and provided her with a small tent that he had been using.[8]

✷

At St. Vrain's Frémont had heard many suggestions as to where he might find the suitable pass for wagons somewhere south of South Pass that Abert's instructions had ordered him to find. But, after two full months of travel, he was beginning to wonder whether any such gap existed. After conversing with Fitzpatrick and Carson, Frémont, drawing on their best hunches as to where such a pass might be found, decided that he would lead a small party up the Cache la Poudre River, to its headwaters near Long's Peak and, from there, try to locate a pass over the Rockies. Once over the mountains, they would then find their way to Fort Hall, a Hudson's Bay Company post along the Snake River, in today's southern Idaho. Led by the seasoned trapper Thomas "Broken Hand" Fitzpatrick—the sobriquet derived from a rifle accident that had shattered his left wrist—the other, larger party, traveling with the carts and supplies, would take the more familiar South Pass route over the mountains, then reunite with Frémont's contingent at Fort Hall.

For his own party, Frémont gathered fourteen men, including Carson, Preuss, and Lajeunesse. Setting out on July 26, the party managed to cross the swollen South Platte River and, over the next days, began working its way up the wearyingly steep Cache la Poudre River canyon:

> Towering mountains rose about; their sides sometimes dark with forests of pine, and sometimes with lofty precipices, washed by the river; while below, as if they indemnified themselves in luxuriance for the scanty space, the green river bottom was covered with a wilderness of flowers, their tall spikes sometimes rising above our heads as we rode above them.

By July 29—near today's city of Fort Collins, Colorado—the party had reached snowy elevations in excess of fifty-five hundred feet. But the higher the men got, the deeper the river's chasm became and the more difficult it became to find anything resembling flat ground on which to walk: "We were compelled by the nature of the ground to cross the river eight or nine times at difficult, deep and rocky fords, the stream running with great force, swollen by the rains—a true mountain torrent, only forty or fifty feet wide."

Finally, on July 30, giving up on reaching the Cache la Poudre's headwaters, the party began pushing northwest. In bending to the north—toward the North Platte valley and South Pass—Frémont had effectively abandoned all hopes of finding the south–of–South Pass wagon crossing that he had been ordered to find.[9]

❀

By noon on August 2, they were, once again, in high prairie country, halted along a tributary of the Laramie River, where Frémont watched curiously as the Shoshone Indian woman traveling with them dug up yampah plants, a culinary mainstay of Indians in the region. "To us, it was an interesting plant," Frémont recalled, "a little link between the savage and civilized life. Here, among the Indians, its root is a common article of food, which they take pleasure in offering to strangers; while with us, in a considerable portion of America and Europe, the seeds are used to flavor soup."

After crossing the northern fork of the Laramie, and the Medicine Bow Rivers, the party, on August 3, found itself, once again, in country teeming with buffalo. Assuming that the beasts would become scarce in the coming days and weeks, Frémont called a halt to the explorers' march; and over the next two days, hunters were dispatched, scaffolds built, and fires made, and buffalo meat was cut into thin slices and dried over the fires.

❀

On August 9—striking, to their relief, the Sweetwater River—the men soon found themselves back on the rut-worn traces of the Emigrant

Road. After two grueling days in dry, rough, ravine- and sagebrush-choked country, the party was glad to be on relatively benign terrain. Frémont also recalled it was "a happy exchange to our poor animals for the sharp rocks and tough shrubs among which they had been toiling so long." Moving west now, up the Sweetwater, the party, on August 13, crossed the Continental Divide—"very near the Table Mountain at the southern extremity of the South Pass, which is near twenty miles in width and already traversed by several different roads." For Frémont, the return to South Pass marked a bittersweet moment: the men were no longer hungry, no longer wandering about half-lost on terra incognita; he was now halfway across the continent, and all of Oregon—and who knew where else—lay before him. But in passing over the Continental Divide at South Pass, he was retracing old ground—he had failed to find a new, more southerly pass.

✸

From South Pass, the party marched down a gently sloping hollow that took the group to the Little Sandy, then the Big Sandy Rivers, then along the Green River. After too many days on an arid, sandy landscape of rocks and sagebrush, the men were glad to be beside the Green River—delighted to discover that the "broad river, with its timbered shores and green-wooded islands" more than lived up to its name.

By Frémont's reckoning, they had now left the United States and crossed onto foreign—Mexican—soil. Because they constituted an officially sanctioned U.S. government exploring expedition, that passage was rife with diplomatic and political significance. But in his subsequent *Report* on the expedition, it registers only a passing reference ("and on the evening of the 15th we encamped in the Mexican Territory, on the left bank of the Green river . . ."). Likewise, Preuss's diary —often reflecting the camp's topics of conversation—makes no reference to the crossing. Frémont's indifference to the matter may be explained in part by the fact that Mexico's government had no real presence that far north. Beyond that, true to the habits he had cultivated under Joseph Nicollet, Frémont remained far more preoccupied with physiographic boundaries—watersheds, mountain ranges, and the like—than with borders defined by treaties.

❀

On August 18, still in Green River country, the party bid good-bye to their Shoshone traveling companion, who departed the expedition with her two children, bound for nearby Fort Bridger, to the south-west, where she hoped to find some of her people. The following day, Frémont dispatched Kit Carson northwest, to Fort Hall, with orders to purchase and bring back provisions for the party.

Moving west, on August 21 the party entered the lush Bear River valley. Compared to the wilderness they had just crossed, the country through which the party was now passing seemed relatively easy. The men were, after all, back on the Emigrant Road. That evening, they came upon and camped with a family of pioneers, lagging behind a larger party, encamped along a Bear River tributary. "It was strange," Frémont recalled, "to see one small family travelling alone through such a country, so remote from civilization. Some nine years since, such security might have been a fatal one; but since their disastrous defeats in the country a little north, the Blackfeet have ceased to visit these waters." The next day, still on the Emigrant Road, Frémont's party came upon an encampment of the main emigrant party:

> The edge of the wood, several miles along the river, was dotted with the white covers of emigrant wagons, collected in groups at different camps, where the smokes were rising lazily from the fires, around which the women were occupied in preparing the evening meal, and the children playing in the grass; and herds of cattle, grazing about in the bottom, had an air of quiet security, and civilized comfort, that constituted a rare sight for the traveller in such a remote wilderness.[10]

❀

Three days later, on August 25, now on the Emigrant Road's Bear River corridor, the party reached Beer Springs, yet another of the geo-

logical wonders by which emigrants marked their westward passage.
The springs took their name from their effervescent, sulphurous waters, which reminded earlier travelers, starved for civilization's comforts, of a sorely missed beverage. But it was the general landscape of
Bear Valley—tortured by ancient volcanic actions, and teeming with
gurgling geothermal activity—that truly enticed Frémont; and, to give
himself a chance to explore the area, he camped with the party there a
full day. He and Preuss used the time to examine the local lava formations and tufa—sedimentary rock distilled from waters rich in lime,
calcium, and carbonates—encrusting the area's geothermal basin. Local geysers also enhanced Frémont. Not far from Beer Springs, for instance, they stumbled upon a geyser that, at regular intervals, ejected
a three-foot-high water plume. Accompanying each eruption was a
rumbling noise that, the men agreed, sounded much like a steamboat
engine: hence the name they gave the geyser, Steamboat Spring.
Sadly today, however, both Beer Springs and Steamboat Spring lie
drowned under the reservoir at the town of Soda Springs, Idaho.

During his travels with Nicollet, Frémont had spent time with
Etienne Provôt, often credited with being the first white man to visit
the Great Salt Lake, and doubtless recalled stories the old trapper had
told him about the place. So now, as the exploring party ventured
down the Bear River valley, the conversations increasingly turned toward the physical mysteries of this country. "We were now entering a
region which for us possessed a strange and extraordinary interest,"
Frémont recalled. "In our occasional conversations with the few old
hunters who had visited the region, it had been a subject of frequent
speculation; and the wonders which they related were not the less
agreeable because they were highly exaggerated and impossible."
This was a region, after all, whose rivers drained not in any ocean, but
into a vast and, except among Indians, little known inland sea—the
Great Salt Lake. Except for Provôt, only a handful of trappers had visited the lake—and none had conducted scientific studies of it:

Its islands had never been visited; and none were to be found
who had entirely made the circuit of its shores; and no instrumental observations or geographical survey, of any description,
had ever been made anywhere in the neighboring region. It was

generally supposed that it had no visible outlet; but among the trappers, including those in my own camp, were many who believed that somewhere on its surface was a terrible whirlpool, through which its waters found their way to the ocean by some subterranean communication.

Great Salt Lake—lying physically and metaphorically far off Thomas Hart Benton's Road to India—played no role in any of any of the senator's Oregon- and trade-related objectives. Nor was there anything in Frémont's orders from Colonel Abert that could be construed as a license to visit Great Salt Lake. But Frémont had heard one too many stories about this mysterious salt-water-filled depression in the desert. And so, on August 26, at the head of Bear River valley, he decided to backtrack down the valley toward Great Salt Lake.[11]

❀

Frémont had hoped that Carson, by now, would have returned from Fort Hall, with the provisions needed by the party. But rather than waiting any longer for Carson's return or simply heading toward Fort Hall himself, Frémont sent expedition member Henry Lee on to the post, with instructions for Carson to overtake the party on the Bear River, along their march toward Great Salt Lake.

Frémont's march toward the lake was tough. The party fought its way over one steep grade, only to be confronted with another. The men soon found themselves hacking their way through dense brush. Though flocks of geese often filled the sky, the boat party managed to kill only a few birds; and efforts at catching fish proved no more successful. Desperate for game, one evening the explorers found themselves supping on skunk.

On September 1, when the men set up camp at the junction of the Malad and Bear Rivers, they had yet even to glimpse the lake. Though they could see several mountains which they thought might be islands rising from the lake, the explorers could never be sure. Frustrated by their slow overland pace, Frémont, the next day, decided to try his luck with the rubber boat. With hopes of reaching the lake that day and, by nightfall, rejoining the party with good news, he and Lajeunesse set off down the Bear River. Floating downstream, the men that day spotted several Indian families, encamped and fishing with nets fashioned from rushes and canes, along the river's shore. But the explorers found no lake that day: "Our boat moved so heavily, that we made very little progress; and, finding that it would be impossible to overtake the camp, as soon as we were sufficiently far below the Indians, we put to the shore near a high prairie bank, hauled up the boat, and *cached* our effects in the willow."

Upon climbing onto the riverbank, however, the two realized that their efforts had taken them only a few miles. Leaving the boat behind, they found the expedition party's trail and, after walking about fifteen miles, caught up with the others, already encamped for the night. Lajeunesse and several others retrieved the boat the next morning, and the party resumed its southward march. As they were breaking camp the next morning, September 4, the men greeted the welcome sight of Kit Carson, hauling enough flour and other provisions to last them for three days. But the news Carson brought was less encouraging: supplies at Fort Hall were scarce, he said, and, when he left the Hudson's Bay Company post, Fitzpatrick and the main party had yet to arrive there.[12]

On September 6, still marching south, the expedition climbed the hill that rises from the peninsular ridge dividing the Bear and Weber Rivers—a grassy butte, today known as Little Mountain, located southwest of today's Ogden, Utah.[13] At the hill's summit, Frémont beheld the object of their long search:

> the waters of the Inland Sea, stretching in still and solitary grandeur far beyond the limit of our vision. It was one of the great points of the exploration; and as we looked eagerly over the lake in the first emotions of excited pleasure, I am doubtful if the followers of Balboa felt more enthusiasm when, from the heights of the Andes, they saw the great Western ocean.

From the hill, Frémont noticed that the lake's shores visible to him were largely treeless. With that in mind, he resolved that the party, while following the river toward the lake, had to find a campsite for that evening as close to the lake as it could get before the trees disappeared. The men camped that night on the Weber River; and, the next morning, their latest round of provisions now exhausted, Frémont sent seven men, under the leadership of Basil Lajeunesse, back to Fort Hall to buy still more supplies. Among those who remained behind, Frémont, Carson, Preuss, Lajeunesse, and Bernier would explore the lake by boat; and the three other men would stay behind to tend the Weber River camp.

The next day, September 8, the party shoved off toward the lake in the rubber boat. Frémont and the four mariners—dawdling along the way to shoot at waterfowl and delayed by sandbars in the ever-widening, increasingly shallow Weber River delta—spent all of that day and most of the next covering the remaining few miles to the lake. In time, the river grew so shallow that the men removed their clothes, and began dragging the boat:

> After proceeding in this way about a mile, we came to a small black ridge on the bottom, beyond which the water became suddenly salt, beginning gradually to deepen, and the bottom was sandy and firm. It was a remarkable division, separating the fresh water of the rivers from the briny water of the lake, which was entirely *saturated* with common salt. Pushing our little vessel across the narrow boundary, we sprang on board, and at length were afloat on the waters of the unknown sea.[14]

Arbitrarily picking a destination, the men began rowing toward an island with a crater-shaped mountain rising from its middle: "Although the day was very calm, there was a considerable swell on the lake; and there were white patches of foam on the surface, which were slowly moving to the southward, indicating the set of a current in that direction, and recalling the recollection of the whirlpool stories"— though it seems difficult to believe that Frémont seriously believed such stories. The rough waters, in time, proved to be no more than that—no vortex, no subterranean passage to the Pacific, just rough waters, ruffled by a strong south wind. Another, more tangible, threat, however, soon captured the men's attention. About halfway to the island, the boat began losing air, and only the constant pumping of bellows kept the rickety craft afloat.

By noon, they had reached the island: "It was a handsome broad beach where we landed, behind which the hill, into which the island was gathered, rose somewhat abruptly." But though the island, on which they later built several campfires, had a peculiar naked beauty, it also seemed, to Frémont, curiously devoid of wildlife: "We did not meet with any kind of animal; a magpie, and another larger bird, probably attracted by the smoke of our fire, paid us a visit from the shore, and were the only living things seen during our stay." Crestfallen —perhaps recalling the lush South Carolina barrier islands of his boyhood explorations—Frémont named the place Disappointment Island. Ironically, however, seven years later, when explorer Howard Stansbury came through the area, surveying a route for the transcontinental railroad, he gave the island the name it retains to this day—Frémont Island.

Soon after reaching Frémont's Disappointment Island, the men climbed to the top of the hill that dominates the tiny landmass—a bare, rocky peak, eight hundred feet in height. There, Frémont spent much of the rest of the day conducting scientific observations and taking in the view. Gazing down on the lake, he was sufficiently familiar with previous maps of the area to notice that most of the landforms depicted on paper as islands in the lake were, as he could clearly see, not islands at all, but peninsular mountains, jutting narrowly into the water. It was a misconception that he would later correct in his official *Report*.

From his mountain perch, Frémont also noticed the lengthening snow cover now finding its way down the slopes of the surrounding mountains. He was eager to explore the lake more fully, but the lengthening white sheets offered a chilling reminder of the advancing season. And, given their experience with the air leaks the previous day, he thought it risky to take any more chances than necessary with the rubber boat. Reluctantly, he concluded, discretion dictated that they not linger on or around the Great Salt Lake. They needed to get to Fort Hall as soon as possible and, from there, complete their transit down the Snake and Columbia Rivers to the Pacific.

By sundown, the men had returned to the island's beach. Frémont and Preuss took observations once again; and, that night, within the

glow of several campfires, the party slept in three-sided lodges fashioned from driftwood gathered along the beach:

> The evening was extremely bright and pleasant; but the wind
> rose during the night, and the waves began to break heavily
> on the shore, making our island tremble. I had not expected in
> our island journey to hear the roar of an ocean surf; and the
> strangeness of our situation, and the excitement we felt in
> the associated interests of the place, made this one of the most
> interesting nights I remember during our long expedition.

The next morning, upon striking out again in the rubber boat, the
men braved even choppier waters than those of the previous day: "It
roughened as we got away from the island, and it required all the efforts of the men to make any head against the wind and sea; the gale
rising with the sun, and there was danger of being blown into one of
the open reaches beyond the island." Once ashore, Frémont dispatched Preuss and Lajeunesse back to the main camp, to bring the
horses needed to retrieve their boat and lakeside baggage. But because of continuing storms and Frémont's determination to conduct
some final observations, the party lingered by the lake another day.
While there, he used the extra time to boil down five gallons of water
he had collected into "fourteen pints of very fine-grained and very
white salt." The water was for drinking, the salt for their provisions,
but he also wanted to analyze the water's salt content.[15]

Over the next few days, as the party marched toward Fort Hall, the
men were almost always hungry. On the fourteenth, Frémont allowed
them to kill a fat young horse purchased from a group of Snake Indians. At least two in the party—squeamish at the thought of eating
horsemeat—elected to forgo the feast. "Mr. Preuss and myself," Frémont recalled, "could not yet overcome some remains of civilized
prejudices, and preferred to starve a little longer; feeling as much saddened as if a crime had been committed." Later that day, meeting a
solitary Indian on horseback, the men traded some gunpowder and
musket balls for a recently killed antelope.

On the morning of September 18—upon spotting in the distance
the Three Buttes, a well-known emigrant landmark—Frémont knew

they were close to Fort Hall. Still later that afternoon, their hearts rose as they glimpsed in the distance that post's "glistening white walls." Fort Hall had been established in 1834 by Nathaniel Wyeth, an ambitious Yankee trader, who two years later, with funds running low, had been forced to sell the post to the Hudson's Bay Company. Old Glory, which had flown over the post, came down. In its place rose the Union Jack.

Even more gratifying to Frémont's men, Fitzpatrick's entire party were camped outside the trading post. At Fort Hall the next morning, Frémont persuaded the post's proprietor, Richard Grant, to sell them what turned out to be several "indifferent horses, and five oxen in very fine order." Though it snowed that night, the men feasted on one of the oxen.

Fitzpatrick's main party of the expedition, as it turned out, had reached Fort Hall five days before Frémont's party. Fitzpatrick's men had suffered no major mishaps since Frémont had last seen them, but, they had, over the past seven weeks, faced spartan conditions. "They too," Frémont recalled, "had had their share of fatigue and scanty provisions, as there had been very little game left on the trail of the populous emigration." The good news was that, once again, the ever frugal Fitzpatrick had been able to conserve the expedition's staple supplies: "Mr. Fitzpatrick had rigidly husbanded our stock of flour and light provisions, in view of the approaching winter and the long journey before us."[16]

Pinned down by an early winter storm, the men remained for another four days at Fort Hall. They used the time to make repairs and acquire what provisions they could from the post's scant inventories. Astronomical observations were taken; and Frémont also found time to take soil samples and to size up the area's possible value to the United States: not only would this area be a suitable site for a post to assist and protect Oregon-bound American immigrants, he concluded, but it would also be ideal for agriculture and settlement.

At sunrise, on September 21, the Snake, as well as Blackfoot and Portneuf Rivers remained frozen, with no sign of any break in the weather. Frémont knew that conditions from here on could only get worse. Moreover, grievances among the men were growing louder, and he knew he needed to do something to restore the party's flagging morale. So, on the morning of September 22, Frémont told them that he had no intention of allowing the harsh weather to slow their progress; if any men wanted to leave, he said, now was the time to go.

Unlike at Fort Laramie a year earlier during the First Expedition, when Frémont made a similar offer to tamp down dissent and, to his relief, only one man had stepped forward, this time eleven men elected to leave—including Basil Lajeunesse, "one of the best men in my party, who was obliged, by the conditions of his family, to be at home in the coming winter."[17] Later that same morning, Basil Lajeunesse and the ten others who had elected to leave—carrying guns and twelve days' provisions to get them to buffalo country—departed for St. Louis. In one of their saddlebags, they carried a bundle of letters from Frémont, Talbot, and others for friends and loved ones back East. After seeing off Lajeunesse and his east-bound detachment, Frémont and the remaining men in the party set out on their own northwesterly Oregon-bound course.[18]

OREGON

ROM FORT HALL, the Emigrant Road made a dramatic northwestern bend, drawing travelers on to the tortured landscape
of the Columbia River plateau, a sprawling tableland stretching south to north from today's southern Idaho to central British Columbia. Covering the plateau are thick accretions of basalt—in some
cases, two miles deep—laid down by successive lava flows since time
immemorial. Rivers originating high in the snow-packed mountains
that bound the plateau—the Rockies to the north, south, and east, and
the volcanic Cascade Range to the west—later penetrated the lava
sheets. The waters of capillary-like creeks in the highlands eventually
joined into one mighty, twelve-hundred-mile west-flowing river—the
Columbia.

Of all the river systems flowing into the Columbia, the Snake's watershed covers the most ground, draining 40 percent of the Columbia
plateau; and it was the harsh conditions that prevailed across that
basin—much of which consisted of a parched forbidding plain—that
weighed on Frémont's mind that frigid September of 1843 as he
packed to leave Fort Hall. Thomas "Broken Hand" Fitzpatrick, who
had been here before, told Frémont what lay ahead: for the next four
hundred miles, the road ran through the broken volcanic country of
the southern half of the Snake River valley, a canyon dense with sagebrush and dark volcanic rocks. Inside, the gorge offered no grass for
the animals; and its rocky terrain rendered travel difficult for both man
and beast. And though the road ran along a river, getting down to its
waters proved difficult if not impossible. Preuss later complained of

"steep, volcanic, rocky shores along which one can travel for days without being able to find a place to get down to the stream."[1]

Where the Snake now forms the boundary between Idaho and Oregon, the river dips into Hell's Canyon—reaching depths of eight thousand feet. Just before that drop, however, the Emigrant Road bent to the northwest, thus avoiding Hell's Canyon on the river's final approach to the Columbia.

On September 22, 1843, Frémont's party left Fort Hall. Two days later, while passing along a particularly rough stretch of country, the men stumbled upon some wagon ruts veering away from the river. The Oregon Trail, after all, never existed as a discrete single road. Historians have called it a "trail corridor." Wagons often traveled in columns a half mile apart and carved out numerous shortcuts. Like a well-worn rope, the main trail frayed at either end into myriad smaller strands; still other trails veered off from its middle passages. Even along the trail's main corridor, it wandered from year to year, under changing weather conditions.

Frémont's party followed the ruts for several miles until, to the men's surprise, the tracks suddenly veered away toward a mountain pass to the south. The tracks, the men suddenly realized, belonged to the Chiles emigrant party with whom they had, months earlier, shared their camp at Elm Grove. The mountain man Joseph Walker, then serving as a scout for the emigrant party, and Chiles had decided to split their party.

A small group consisting of the Chiles party's strongest men was to ride toward Fort Boise, where they hoped to finagle some supplies from its proprietor. The rest of the party, led by Walker, would dip south, and, picking up the Humboldt River in today's Nevada, follow it west to its terminus at Humboldt Sink, a desert depression where the river's waters evaporate just below the Sierra's eastern slope. There the group would await the relief party from Fort Boise; the reunited party would then move south, and cross over through its scout's namesake route—Walker Pass. Six years later, after the discovery of gold in California, the Humboldt River part of Walker's route would become a major leg of the "California Trail," the main overland route to California. Fort Hall thus became the West's great fork in the road—the point where travelers had to decide, if they had not already, whether they wanted to go southwest to California or northwest to Oregon. Before that happened, however, Frémont would have his own extensive and complex dealings with Walker.[2]

✱

By that late September of 1843, as Frémont's party marched down the Snake River Valley, it had become difficult to find places suitable for either its afternoon halt or its evening camp. "The road had frequently been very bad; the many short, steep ascents, exhausting the strength of our worn-out animals, requiring always at such places the assistance of the men to get up each cart, one by one; and our progress with twelve or fourteen wheeled carriages, though light and made for the purpose, in such a rocky country, was extremely slow," Frémont complained. To hasten the pace, Frémont, on September 27, once again divided the party in two. While Frémont and his smaller group would scout the road ahead, Fitzpatrick, as before, would follow with the larger party and the wagons.

This stretch of the Snake—from Fort Hall to Hell's Canyon—then abounded in waterfalls, which the party reveled in gazing upon, particularly the so-called Thousand Springs. "Immediately opposite to us," Frémont recalled, "a subterranean river bursts out directly from the face of the escarpment, and falls in white foam to the river below." There in those days—and still today, though with a greatly reduced flow—the waters of eastern Idaho's Lost River, after disappearing into a desert sink north of today's Pocatello, Idaho, reemerged, spewing like a thousand springs from the Snake's steep and porous volcanic banks.

Frémont's party camped the night of October 1 near several lodges of Snake Indians about a mile below a series of cataracts that Frémont later named Fishing Falls. The huts, fashioned from willow branches thatched over with straw, had a semicircular shape, open to the south. The falls, Frémont learned, were a popular place for spearing salmon. In the spring, the tribesmen needed only to throw their spears at random into the river to catch a meal. Frémont found the tribesmen themselves to be, "unusually gay savages, fond of loud laughter; and, in their apparent good nature and merry character, [they] struck me as being entirely different from the Indians we had been accustomed to see." That night, when several of the Indians showed up in the expedition party's camp, Frémont gave them some trade goods in exchange for dried salmon: "At this season they are not very fat, but we were easily pleased."[3]

Over the next several days, after a harrowing crossing of the powerful Snake River, the party followed a strand of the Emigrant Road which ran parallel to but above the Salmon River Range's eastern edge. On October 7, the party descended a spur of the Salmon River Range and struck the Rivière Boisée, or "wooded river"—today's Boise River—where the explorers later set up camp in a stand of cottonwoods along its banks. After weeks in the Snake valley, the men delighted to be beside an approachable stream swathed in inviting woodlands: "Such a stream had become quite a novelty in this country, and we were delighted this afternoon to make a pleasant camp under fine old trees again."

The party that afternoon and over the next two days marched fifty miles down the Boise River valley—arriving on October 10 at Fort Boise, a once busy Hudson's Bay Company post. By 1843, however, when Frémont arrived at the forlorn post, the fur company's activities in the Snake River valley were waning; and its factor François Payette's management of it involved no ambitious visions: to meet his own needs, he had a small dairy and vegetable garden, but most of his income came from the sale of salmon. Payette was hospitable but had few items to sell—mostly dairy products; Frémont was glad to purchase some butter. But he left with an unfavorable impression of the Indians who gathered around the post:

> During the day we remained here, there were considerable numbers of miserable half-naked Indians around the fort, who had arrived from the neighboring mountains. During the summer, the only subsistence of these people is derived from the salmon, of which they are not provident enough to lay up a sufficient store for the winter, during which many of them die from absolute starvation.

Before leaving Fort Boise, Frémont left behind for Fitzpatrick and the larger party a bullock, a castrated bull, purchased at the fort, as well as the rubber boat. After leaving the post, the exploring party crossed the Boise River, then the ridge dividing the Burnt and Powder River valleys. While descending into the Powder River valley, Frémont kept an eye out for a landmark described to him days earlier by Fort Boise's factor Payette. *L'arbre seul*—the lone tree—had stood for years as a beacon to mountain men, emigrants, and other travelers through the area. But to Frémont's disappointment, when he reached the valley, the tree turned out to be just another reminder of the fact that, though an explorer, he was passing down an increasingly crowded overland corridor: "On arriving at the river, we found a fine tall pine stretched on the ground, which had been felled by some inconsiderate emigrant axe."[4]

✸

When does a hunch ripens into a full-blown theory? In the Second Expedition *Report*'s entry for October 13, Frémont offered his first exposition of what would become one of his greatest contributions to our understanding of North American geography. While passing over an eighteen-hundred-foot ridge between the Snake and Columbia River basins, he paused to take in the view. Before him lay a dog's breakfast of mountain ranges stretching toward the horizon.

By now, Frémont possessed a jeweler's eye for sorting out the complexities of landscape. And as he pondered the tangled tableau of mountains before him, he deduced that the ranges to the south and west seemed somehow connected to what, in the distance, he assumed to be the "California" range—the Sierra Nevada.

Reflecting upon all that he had already seen of, and read and heard about, the West, an image—a grand concept—began to materialize in Frémont's mind: from the Wasatch Range that towers above the Great Salt Lake's eastern shore, which he had visited four weeks earlier, to the Sierra's eastern slope, it seemed to him, there stretched a vast landlocked zone—bounded by mountains on all sides, and whose trapped rivers were unable to drain into any ocean. Contemplating that image, Frémont, in his October 13 *Report* entry, invoked for the first time his own coinage for that vast realm, the term by which it is to this day still known—the Great Basin—"a term which I apply to the intermediate region between the Rocky mountains and the next range, containing many lakes, with their own system of rivers and creeks, (of which the Great Salt is the principal,) and which have no connexion with the ocean, or the great rivers which flow into it."[5]

At this point, though, Frémont's hunch had to remain just that— only an idea that he tried on for size—nothing more. For in order to establish that such a landlocked basin existed, he had to first establish that no river, breaking through the Sierra, drained the region's waters into the Pacific.

❉

Over the past few weeks, as the party passed through the Snake River valley, the men had grown accustomed to cold nights and warm days. But now, as they moved still farther north and into autumn, the birches and other deciduous trees had lost their leaves. The nights were getting colder; and on the morning of October 16, while camped in the Powder River valley, Frémont woke to find that a quarter-inch sheet of ice had formed in his lodge. The temperature stood at 16 degrees.

By the next day, the party had reached eastern Oregon's steep but well-timbered and -watered Blue Mountains; and later that day, they dropped into that range's Grand Ronde—a circular valley, about twenty miles in diameter and lush with timber, water, and good grass for pasturage. "It is a place," he wrote "—one of the few we have seen in our journey so far—where a farmer would delight to establish himself, if he were content to live in the seclusion which it imposes." The next morning, with Frémont now determined to find a "a more direct and better" route out of the Grand Ronde and across the Blue Mountains, the exploring party, abandoning the Emigrant Road, continued north up the valley along an Indian trail.[6]

The next day, October 19, they followed a trace along a rocky stream that returned them into the Blue Mountains. Their path proved difficult, often blocked by large fallen trees as well as small living trees, which they had to cut down. Large evergreens abounded; and Frémont, dazzled by their size, walked about, tape measure in hand, periodically stopping to measure them—one white spruce measured twelve feet in circumference.

On October 22, by now nearing the Blue Mountains' western slope, the party emerged onto a bald with a commanding view of country to the west, and Frémont could see what he knew to be the Walla Walla River. The following morning, while descending one of the Blue Mountain's spur ridges, the men snagged their first glimpse of Mt. Hood, one of the principal peaks of the high snow-covered Cascade Range to the west. By the day's end—now only a few miles from the Walla Walla's confluence with the Columbia—they had reached Marcus Whitman's famous mission.

A physician from Upstate New York, Whitman had first come to Oregon, in 1834, along with a cadre of New England missionaries. These Protestant evangelicals, soon followed by others, constituted the first wave of American emigration to Oregon. They had ventured west in response to a request for the "white man's Book of Heaven" issued by a delegation of Nez Perce Indians visiting the East and established a Presbyterian post on the Willamette River, about ten miles north of today's Oregon state capital, Salem.

Two years later, in 1836, Whitman and his wife founded their own mission—at the site of today's Walla Walla, Washington—to minister to the local Cayuse Indians. Over the next decade, the Whitmans' mission proved to be a popular way station for Oregon-bound emigrants. Many Cayuse, however, perceived the ministry as disdainful of their culture; and, in 1847, local tribesmen would massacre the missionaries.

Upon reaching the Whitmans' mission, Frémont and the survey party learned to their disappointment that the famous post consisted of a lone adobe house. Preuss was particularly crestfallen: "I was so disappointed after all that to-do about the Walla Walla settlement. I actually believed we would find a sort of paradise. But it is not much better than all the miserable country which we have crossed. There is so little timber along the river that the Indians have to drag up firewood with pack horses."

They also learned that Marcus Whitman was away on business, and that the post had no supplies of corn or wheat to spare. Frémont did, however, acquire a bountiful supply of potatoes—an acquisition that even lifted the spirits of the normally doleful Preuss. "Last night we ate them twice," he confided to his journal while at the mission.

"Kit put another potful on the fire before we went to sleep." But though Frémont found the mission itself a disappointment, the sight of new Oregon emigrants passing through the settlement enthralled him. In particular, he was delighted to meet "a fine-looking large family of emigrants, men, women and children in robust health."

The next morning, October 25, after venturing four miles down the Walla Walla River to the Hudson's Bay Company's Fort Walla Walla, the party won its first look at the Columbia. To Frémont, the waterway, about twelve hundred yards wide at that spot, seemed "a fine navigable river." Even so, "the appearance of the post and country was without interest," he recalled, "except that we here saw, for the first time, the great river on which the course of events for the last half century has been directing attention and conferring historical fame." Preuss, characteristically, felt even more let down. "A drearier region is hardly imaginable," he wrote. "The fort is built close to the stream on bare sand, resting, to be sure, on rocks. No tree, no grass, nothing green in sight." As for the Nez Perce Indians gathered nearby, "They are the slaves of the Hudson's Bay Company, which uses them for all kinds of labor. For small trifles their daughters are bought as servants or concubines. Horses are their only wealth; a multitude rove about like wild [sic]. Good Indian horses are sold by the Company for $10.00."

While at Fort Walla Walla, Frémont also watched with curiosity as a tall Missourian named Jesse Applegate, the leader of an emigrant party passing through the post, supervised the construction of a group of Mackinaw boats, flat-bottom vessels built for the purpose of descending the Columbia Fearing the river's long-stretches of treacherous rapids, most emigrants chose to travel beside the Columbia rather than on its waters. But Applegate and his party were eager to get to the Willamette valley. So now, having recently abandoned their wagons and sold the cattle they had been driving, they planned to conquer the Columbia by boat.[7]

That night, Fort Walla Walla's factor, Archibald McKinlay, invited Frémont and the leaders of several emigrant parties to dinner. In Frémont's subsequent expedition *Report*, he gave no indication of what was discussed that evening. But certainly he questioned his host about all the overland and river traffic that McKinlay had watched pass by

his sandy domain. Fort Walla Walla, after all, lay at the western terminus of the Emigrant Road's long path over the Rockies.

Beyond that, since 1818—the year the Hudson's Bay Company
had established the post—the company's explorers and trappers, operating from Fort Hall, had been relentlessly probing the Snake River
and the western Rockies on increasingly broad and deep forays into
the watersheds of both the Snake and the Green Rivers, north as far as
Blackfoot Lake, south as far as eastern Utah's Bear Lake. A company
directive, issued in 1824, had commanded brigade leaders to trap
out the area's beaver population, thus reducing the region to a "fur
desert." By eliminating beavers from the Snake, Hudson's Bay Company officials hoped to discourage American trappers operating in the
southern Rockies from fanning north, up the Snake River and north of
the Columbia River.[8]

During their explorations, the trapper Peter Ogden and other Hudson's Bay Company explorers had determined that much of the Snake
River was navigable—thus tightening still more the bonds linking the
Snake basin to England's far-flung trade empire. Since 1813, when the
English seized Astoria—soon renaming it Fort George—at the Columbia's mouth, fur-laden English boats had ascended the broad river,
stopping along the way at the company's Fort Vancouver, across from
the mouth of the Willamette. After 1818, they also stopped at Fort
Walla Walla to pick up pelts harvested deep in the Rockies. From Fort
Walla Walla, the Hudson's Bay Company voyageurs resumed the firm's
traditional route back to the East in today's British Columbia. From
there, company agents crossed the Canadian Rockies and sailed east,
down the Saskatchewan River to the company's Cumberland House,
on Lake Winnipeg's northern shore. From there, the furs were taken
to Montreal, then shipped to Europe.

Fort Walla Walla thus constituted a vital knot both in the wide web
of British enterprise and in Senator Benton's vision of American empire. This spot also linked Frémont's already-surveyed overland route
from Missouri through South Pass to the Columbia River, which Benton hoped that American commercial traffic would soon dominate—
thus completing his long-contemplated Road to India. As Frémont
well understood, if Benton's theory of successive world empires
proved correct, it would be here that Britain's imperial pride must give

way to a new American empire—one reaching east to St. Louis, New York, Boston, and Europe, and west to the storied gold- and silver-rich ports of Asia:

> The union of two large streams, coming one from the southeast, and the other from the northeast, and meeting in what may be treated as the geographical centre of the Oregon valley, thence doubling the volume of water to the ocean, while opening two great lines of communication with the interior continent, constitutes a feature in the map of the country which cannot be overlooked; and it was probably in reference to this junction of waters, and these lines of communication, that this post was established. They are important lines, and, from the structure of the country, must forever remain so—one of them leading to the South Pass, and to the valley of the Mississippi; the other to the pass at the head of the Athabascan river, and to the countries drained by the waters of the Hudson Bay.

But although the Columbia and Snake confluence lay only nine miles from Fort Walla Walla Frémont, in the end, decided to pass on the trip—being, as he put it, "pressed for time."[9]

❀

On the morning of Saturday, October 28—reinforced with eight fresh horses, along with potatoes, dried salmon, and beef obtained at Fort Walla Walla—the party began its march down the Columbia River. Guided by a hired Indian boy, the men marched along the river's south bank, over sand and rough volcanic rocks. Their transit was slow and difficult—conditions underscored for them, one afternoon, when they spotted Jesse Applegate and his flotilla of Mackinaws constructed at Fort Walla Walla, gliding by on a smooth stretch of the river.

Over the next three days—as the river, passing out of the Columbian plateau, began cutting through the Cascades—the river's banks became higher and steeper. By November 2, the Columbia had sunk into a gorge that offered no bank at all on which the men could walk. Leading the party above and away from the river, Frémont took the men to what turned out to be more pleasing terrain—grassy hills and valleys—and that afternoon they forded the Columbia's John Day River tributary. The next day, the party's ever-westward march took them to yet another Columbia tributary, the Deschutes, which Frémont called the Fall River. Without being able to see the falls, the men listened in awe as the Deschutes's waters tumbled over an unseen precipice into the Columbia, far below them. Fording this Deschutes, it was obvious, posed dangers. Beyond that, Indians were congregated alongside the river's cataracts, apparently a favorite fishing spot.

Days earlier, while encamped at Whitman's mission, Frémont had heard reports of the "unsettled character" of the Indians along this stretch of the Columbia. Just recently, according to one story, a band of fourteen emigrants had been robbed of numerous possessions, including their horses. Since leaving Fort Walla Walla, Frémont's party had encountered numerous Indians. They had traded with some of them, but others had been hostile. Some even tried to steal their horses. So, as the party approached the Deschutes fording spot, Frémont steeled himself for the worst. But to the party's relief, none of the Indians showed any interest in the explorers. And while the fording of the river proved difficult—the howitzer went underwater several times—all of the men, animals, and equipment reached the other side unscathed.

Walking above the river the next day, the explorers spotted below them the Columbia's famous rapids, The Dalles. Climbing down to the river for a closer look, Frémont learned that even when the river's water levels were low, as they were that day at The Dalles, the currents—rife with barely visible whirlpools and other fatal currents—posed grave risks for travelers. Indeed, Frémont learned that, during the Applegate party's recent passage through here, one of their boats had overturned, drowning three people—including two of Jesse Applegate's sons.

Below The Dalles, the Columbia fanned out into a wide valley, through which, after traveling three or four miles, the party reached a mission. A lonely outpost of Methodism, The Dalles Mission included two wooden farmhouses, a large schoolhouse, stables, a garden, cleared fields, and, between the houses and the river bank, the wooden huts of an Indian village.

To Frémont—missing Jessie, Lily, and their more commodious life in Washington—the mission conveyed "the cheerful and busy air of civilization, and had in our eyes an appearance of abundant and enviable comfort." Even the surrounding forests seemed welcoming: "The character of the forest growth here changed, and we found ourselves, with pleasure, again among oaks and other forest trees of the east, to which we had long been strangers; and the hospitable and kind reception with which we were welcomed among our country people at the mission aided the momentary illusion of home."

❋

The Dalles Mission, Frémont decided, would be for all practical purposes the expedition's western terminus. Most of the party would remain at The Dalles, while he and a few others would pay a quick visit to Fort Vancouver, the famous Hudson's Bay Company post on the lower Columbia. Frémont knew of no good road connecting The Dalles and Fort Vancouver; and, with winter approaching, he decided it would be imprudent to take all of the men to Fort Vancouver.

The fort sat ninety miles downstream from The Dalles, along the Columbia's densely forested, less traveled northern bank. Since 1825, the post had played a critical role in Columbia River affairs. The headquarters for British fur-trading activities in the Northwest, it was also the region's largest white settlement. And for American emigrants arriving in the region, it served as a way station, from which, replenished with supplies, they crossed the Columbia and fanned out south, down the Willamette River valley. Equally important for Frémont, Fort Vancouver had been famously visited by members of Charles Wilkes's recent expedition. What better way, then, for Frémont to dramatize his accomplishment of his expedition's primary objective—of linking up his survey with that of Wilkes?

As a measure of the importance that Frémont attached to the visit, prior to his arrival at Fort Vancouver, Frémont angered Preuss by requesting that he shave his beard. We have no way of knowing who won that skirmish, but, according to Preuss's diary, he vigorously resisted the idea. "Nothing doing!" he vowed. "That would be the last straw, to have the disagreeable feeling of a growing beard for two weeks just for the privilege of a few dinner invitations. No! No! I'd rather stay with the Indians in the tent, especially since we have good bread, butter, milk, and potatoes."[10]

❀

It was now early November, and Frémont, increasingly preoccupied with winter's onset, knew that a Hudson's Bay Company bateau carried mail on its regular runs from Fort Vancouver up the Columbia. So, from The Dalles, he dispatched a letter to Fitzpatrick in care of Fort Walla Walla. Frémont had not seen Fitzpatrick since the expedition party had split into two groups. But he assumed that Fitzpatrick—if he wasn't there already—would soon be reaching the Walla Walla post. He instructed Fitzpatrick to abandon the carts there and, as soon as the requisite number of saddles could be made, to descend to The Dalles.

After writing Fitzpatrick, and before leaving the Dalles with the party he had selected for the Fort Vancouver trip, Frémont put Kit Carson in charge of the men who would remain behind at the Dalles. In his absence, Frémont told Carson, he and the other men should spend their days making packsaddles and repairing equipage, in preparation for their coming travels.

Having put his orders in motion, Frémont and three Indians plus Preuss, Bernier, and Dodson glided away from The Dalles Mission in a canoe obtained from local Indians. Weary of tough overland marches, Frémont considered canoe travel nothing if not idyllic: "We were a motley group, but all happy: three unknown Indians; Jacob, a colored man; Mr. Preuss, a German; Bernier, creole French; and myself." Downstream, the river's channel opened into a wider valley only to, later that day, close in once again, as it penetrated the towering, snow-cloaked Cascade Range. That evening, the party stopped along the shore and, drawing on the supplies it had acquired at The Dalles Mission, savored a repast of salmon, coffee, potatoes, bread, and sugar.

So peaceful had been that day's travel, and so eager was Frémont to get downstream, that they shoved off again, right after dinner: "I deemed it necessary to economize time by voyaging in the night, as is customary here, to avoid the high winds, which rise with the morning, and decline with the day." Floating downstream over the next few days, Frémont reveled in the Columbia's stunning views: "The beauty of the scenery was heightened by the continuance of very delightful weather, resembling the Indian summer of the Atlantic." On their second day out, with Mts. Hood and St. Helens and other high peaks now clearly in view, they approached the Cascades, the treacherous set of rapids situated where the river breaks out of the surrounding mountain range that bears its name. Spotting a small Indian village along the river's left bank, the party pulled ashore. There—in accord with a custom among travelers passing through the area—Frémont asked his three Indian guides to hire some tribesmen to assist in the two-mile portage along the south bank's grassy bottom, to a spot below the rapids.

Later that afternoon, the party passed by a rocky point known to river pilots as Cape Horn, extending from the river's south bank. "It borders the river," Frémont wrote, "in a high wall of rock, which comes boldly down into deep water; and in violent gales down the river, and from the opposite shore, which is the prevailing direction of strong winds, the water is dashed against it with considerable violence." To Frémont, one of their Indian guides recalled an earlier upstream voyage, during which he was detained for two weeks at Cape Horn before eventually giving up and returning to Fort Vancouver.

Toward the day's end, the men caught the faint but unmistakable sound of a sawmill—a sound which they deduced was coming from Fort Vancouver. But hopes of reaching the Hudson's Bay Company post that night were soon dashed by the sight of storm clouds gathering overhead. They camped that night on the river's northern shore. About midnight, it began to rain.

The following morning, November 8, after paddling a mile downstream—confirming their earlier estimation of Fort Vancouver's proximity—the men spotted the English bark *Columbia* lying at anchor below a massive citadel of upended logs, seven hundred by three hundred feet in dimension. Twenty-two buildings sat behind the fencing, a self-sustaining settlement that, in addition to residences for Hudson's Bay Company officers and clerks, included an Indian trading post, two churches, a bakery, a granary, a blacksmith shop, a jail—and the sawmill they'd heard the night before.

Upon arriving, Frémont immediately sought out the fort's famously hospitable director, John McLoughlin. As director of Hudson's Bay Company activities in the Pacific Northwest, McLoughlin ranked as the most powerful British official in these parts. Naturally, then, he took a keen interest in the activities of Americans and other nationals in Oregon, diligently reporting all that he saw and heard to his superiors in Montreal and London. And because—the "joint occupation" treaty notwithstanding—the British regarded the Columbia River as a de facto U.S.–British boundary, with the British occupying the area north of the river, McLoughlin did his utmost to direct American settlers to areas south of the river.

Even so, the fur company executive also enjoyed a reputation for unstinting courtesy among all who visited his remote post, regardless of nationality. To Frémont, he offered a room in the post and an invitation *"to make myself at home while I staid* [*sic*]*."* More important, "I was immediately supplied by him with the necessary stores and provisions to refit and support my party in our contemplated winter journey to the States; and also with a Mackinaw boat and canoes, manned with Canadian and Iroquois voyageurs and [local] Indians, for their transportation to the Dalles of the Columbia." Frémont thanked McLoughlin for the offer, but assured him that the U.S. government would defray all bills charged by the party. The post's director did manage to give Frémont a letter of recommendation for credit that could be presented to any Hudson's Bay Company officer on the group's homeward route.

✸

After two days at Fort Vancouver, Frémont's resupplied party was ready to return to The Dalles. Though the fort lay only fifty miles from the Columbia's mouth on the Pacific Ocean, he decided that— his own curiosity notwithstanding—he could not justify the extra time the trip to the coast would take:

It would have been very gratifying to have gone down to the Pacific, and, solely in the interest and in the love of geography, to have seen the ocean on the western as well as the eastern side of the continent, so as to give a satisfactory completeness to the geographical picture which had been formed in our minds; but the rainy season had now regularly set in, and the air was filled with fogs [*sic*] and rain, which left no beauty in any scenery, and obstructed observations.

Beyond that, Frémont again noted, "the object of my instructions had been entirely fulfilled in having connected our reconnaissance with the surveys of Captain Wilkes."

✸

Frémont's bland claim that the exigencies of time and weather precluded a trip to the Columbia's mouth seems out of character, if not disingenuous. Given his fondness for symbolic acts why, after traveling thousands of miles, would he deny himself the pleasure of punctuating his transit of the North American section of Senator Benton's Road to India with a swim in—and a flag-unfurling ceremony beside—the Pacific Ocean?

The answer to that question lies in the simple fact that by the time he reached The Dalles, thirty-year-old Frémont—with his low threshold for boredom—was feeling jaded beyond his young years. The compensatory moments of glory and high purpose that had offset the trip's daily tedium and miseries now seemed increasingly few and far between. In the *Report*, as Frémont moves his force down the Emigrant Road, dutifully checking off the route's various landmarks—Beer Springs, the Red Buttes, the Lone Tree, the American Falls, The Dalles and the like—there emerges the sense of a man increasingly worried that he has become more tourist than explorer. And exploring reputations, as Frémont well knew, rarely arise from expeditions guided by the footsteps of others.

In the *Report*, for instance, Frémont recalls how—while standing along the Deschutes River and hearing but not seeing its waters plunging into the Columbia, far below—he had been tempted to climb down to the Columbia to snatch a look at the falls. But while it would have been "very interesting" to gaze up at the then famous (and now drowned) "Falls of the Columbia," he ultimately vetoed the side trip.

Time, he recalls, was pressing; beyond that, the falls "had been seen and described by many." No doubt, a similar feeling registered when, as the party worked its way down the lower Columbia, Frémont, during his trading with local Indians, noticed their apparent knowledge of the "real value of goods" and "the equivalents of trade."[11]

Beyond whatever ennui Frémont felt creeping over him, by November 1843 he had grown distracted from Senator Benton's ocean-going vision of American empire. Though the explorer had grown up beside an ocean and spent his adolescence exploring the secrets of Charleston Harbor, he was also the same young man who, seven years earlier, had declined a naval appointment in order to assist an overland survey of the Appalachians. So for Frémont, the Pacific Ocean held scant attraction. It was the West's interior, not its coast, that enchanted him. In the end, Frémont's interest in—and comprehension of—the West had grown broader than those of Benton.

More to the point, Frémont cultivated a growing fascination with the steady trickle of emigrants, who were, in his mind, inexorably eroding Thomas Hart Benton's comprehension of the interior American West as little more than a series of arid way stations on the way to the Pacific Ocean. How then could Benton's imagined empire ever compete with the more vivid American activities that were already occurring on the Columbia before Frémont's very eyes? Each month, after all, new settlers—with no thoughts of China's and India's riches—were arriving in the Willamette valley and setting up new farms and mills.

At Fort Vancouver, Frémont wrote, "I found many American emigrants at the fort; others had already crossed the river into their land of promise—the Walahmette [sic] valley. Others were daily arriving." Similarly, on November 14, as the survey party watched a portage of one of the Hudson's Bay Company express boats around The Dalles, Frémont's attentions fell not on the goods being carried downstream, but on the travel-worn emigrants waiting ashore for the resumption of their down-river passage: "The portage ground was occupied by emigrant families; their thin and insufficient clothing, bare-headed and barefooted children, attesting to the length of their journey."[11]

Long before Frémont reached The Dalles and Fort Vancouver, plans that strayed far from his official orders and Benton's Road to India weighed on his mind. According to Preuss, as early as October 16 Frémont talked about bending away from Oregon toward sunnier climes to the south: "The latest plan now is to turn south from Fort Vancouver through Mexican territory. There we shall have to find the route from Monterey to Santa Fé and follow it. We hope to find sufficient grass for the animals there."[12]

Much of the explanation for Frémont's straying, geographically and intellectually, from Benton's preoccupations lies no doubt in the long shadow that Joseph Nicollet cast over him. Senator Benton had been instrumental in gaining Frémont his exploring commissions, had helped to shape his political and historical worldview, and, no doubt, had helped to sharpen his cunning as a thwarter of bureaucratic directives. Even so, Nicollet, in the end, proved the more formidable influence. Nicollet had helped Frémont to become a keen observer of watersheds and other natural borders. But he also nourished his indifference to paper borders created by maps, wars, and treaties. For those and other reasons, Nicollet's legacy—broader and more open-ended than that of Senator Benton—would, over the next three years, take Frémont far beyond, in both geography and spirit, the vision of American empire contemplated by Benton, Linn, and Washington's other "Western men."

❋

November 11—the party's second day on the Columbia after departing Fort Vancouver—dawned cold and rainy, but high winds kept the flotilla moving at a good clip. By the day's end, the Indians had even mounted a sail on Frémont's canoe. But on their third day out, November 12, as the men approached wind-whipped Cape Horn, the river's white caps snarled so violently that the party's Iroquois pilot, with Frémont's assent, ordered all of the boats ashore for the rest of the day. By late afternoon the next day, as they approached the Lower Rapids, the currents roiled so turbulently that Frémont's party was forced to "cordelle" the boats—to haul them upstream with ropes that the men pulled while standing atop the rocks along the river's south bank. As night fell, they stopped at the northern end of a long island, where they watched as the three Indians, traveling in lighter canoes, paddled upstream into the distance. Remembering that the canoe the Indians paddled contained the lodge purchased at Fort St. Vrain's as well as most of the explorers' bedding and provisions, Frémont's men shouted and fired guns, but to no avail. The faster-traveling Indians could not hear them above the river's roar.

Without their provisions, Frémont's party spent a cold night in a ceaseless rain. "The old voyageurs," Frémont recalled, "did not appear to mind it much, but covered themselves up as well as they could, and lay down on the sand beach, where they remained quiet until morning. The rest of us spent a rather miserable night; and, to add to our discomfort, the incessant rain extinguished our fires; and we were glad when at last daylight appeared, and we again embarked." The next morning, November 14, they paddled across to the north bank, where, against the rushing rapids, they cordelled the boat for the remainder of their upstream passage—"there being no longer any use for the paddles." In a small inlet just above the rapids, they found the Indians: "Here we found the lodge pitched and about twenty Indians sitting around a blazing fire within, making a luxurious breakfast with salmon, bread, butter, sugar, coffee, and other provisions." As Peter Burnett—an Oregon emigrant from Missouri and future California governor then traveling upriver with the party—recalled, Frémont, enraged upon learning that he and the others had spent a night in the rain, while the tribesmen slept dry and comfortable in the lodge, promptly rushed them out of the teepee.[13]

As the explorers waited for their boats to be hauled up to the cove, Frémont was visited by Friedrich G. J. Lüders, a German botanist then conducting his own survey of the Columbia: "I was delighted to meet at such a place a man of kindred spirits; but we had only the pleasure of a brief conversation, as his canoe, under the guidance of two Indians, was about to run the rapids; and I could not enjoy the satisfaction of regaling him with a breakfast." Shortly after the botanist's departure, his canoe, piled high with baggage and scientific instruments and specimens, capsized in the rushing waters. As Frémont recalled, "By the carelessness of the Indians, the boat was drawn up into the midst of the rapids, and glanced down the river, bottom up, with the loss of every thing it contained." Out of sympathy for the hapless scientist, Frémont named the cove Lüders' Bay.

Rains continued over the next few days. Whether the men were portaging or cordelling, the weather made the banks slippery and their work difficult. But Frémont proved a relentless taskmaster. Occasionally, the Indians—fatigued after long hours of labor—would stop, build a fire atop one of the dry rocks projecting into the river, and sit or lie down for a rest. Upon catching up with them, Frémont did whatever was required to get them back to work. "When nothing else would avail," Burnett recalled, "he would put out their fires. Finding it necessary to work or shiver, they preferred to work."[14]

✱

By the afternoon of November 18, the canoe's passengers had reached their own awaiting party's camp near The Dalles. "Carson," Frémont recalled, "had removed the camp up the river a little nearer to the hills, where the animals had better grass. We found every thing in good order, and arrived just in time to partake of an excellent roast of California beef." Frémont also found waiting for him the journalist and Oregon promoter William Gilpin, who had joined the exploring party the previous April at Elm Grove. More recently, Gilpin had been traveling with Fitzpatrick; but, eager to get to Fort Vancouver, he, while at the fort, had traded his mule for a canoe, horsemeat, and other provisions and had headed out, in front of Fitzpatrick and the main party. Gilpin had gone west to get a firsthand look at the Oregon country he had so long championed; and in the intervening months, according to Frémont, he had seen nothing to dispel his optimism: "His object in visiting this country had been to obtain correct information of the Walahmette [sic] settlements; and he had reached this point in his journey, highly pleased with the country over which he had travelled, and with invigorated health."

On the following morning, after Gilpin discovered his canoe had been stolen during the night, he accepted a ride in the flotilla returning to Fort Vancouver. From there, Gilpin later made his way back to the American settlements on the Willamette. There, over the next few months, he would become a chief voice among the valley's American settlers, who were increasingly agitating for self-government and U.S. affiliation. In the spring of 1845, it would be Gilpin who delivered to Congress the Oregonian Americans' official petition for federal recognition. Then and later, he remained a vigorous promoter of the West and debunker of Stephen Long's Great American Desert theory. In 1861, Gilpin became Colorado's first territorial governor.

✸

On November 21, upon Fitzpatrick's and the main party's arrival at The Dalles, final preparations for the expedition's next leg began in earnest. At The Dalles, Frémont purchased from Indians and others around the mission a total of 104 mules and horses. To further assist the party, H. W. Perkins, the proprietor of The Dalles mission, hired two Indians as guides to escort the men to Upper Klamath Lake— "one of whom," Frémont recalled, "had been there, and bore the marks of several wounds he had received from some of the Indians in the neighborhood; and the other went along for company."

Over the next few days, Frémont, Preuss, and Perkins made several hikes into the surrounding mountains to gaze out across at, and orient themselves with, the Cascades' seven great peaks. Clouds, however, obscured the view, "and we obtained bearings only to three that were visible: Mount Regnier, St. Helens, and Mount Hood. . . . In order to determine their positions with as much accuracy as possible, the angular distances of the peaks were measured with the sextant, at different fixed points from which they could be seen." Before leaving, Frémont also agreed, at Perkins's request, to take along with them a nineteen-year-old Chinook Indian, known to them as "William," who wanted, as Frémont recalled, to " 'see the whites' and make some acquaintance with our institutions."[15]

TO THE BANKS
OF THE BUENAVENTURA

O N NOVEMBER 25, 1843, as snow flurries powdered their shoulders, it was time for the exploring party to leave The Dalles, the Columbia River, and the Oregon Trail. Up until now, most of the expedition's travels had been over a more-or-less established route. Now, realizing that rougher, less-traveled terrain lay ahead, Frémont knew that wheeled vehicles would prove impractical. So, at The Dalles, he had abandoned their instruments wagon and donated it to the mission. And so, as they bid adieu to their friends at the mission, the howitzer now constituted the exploring party's only carriage.

Pushing south, up into the Cascades, on a route parallel with the Deschutes River, Frémont savored the surrounding sublime country: "At every place where we come in the neighborhood of the river, is heard the roaring of falls." He also reveled in the snowy hardwood forests along the whitewater streams that threaded the uplands; and above the timberline, the pristine views of Mts. Hood, St. Helens, and Rainier. The journey, however, proved arduous.

On December 9, still moving south, they left the Columbia River's watershed and, the next day, reached a watery meadow surrounded by timbered mountains. Assuming he had reached Klamath Lake—what is now known as Upper Klamath Lake, in southern Oregon—Frémont savored the lake and the bountiful grass on which the expedition's animals grazed. But he was also puzzled: "The broad sheet of water which constitutes a lake was not to be seen." Though Frémont assumed he had reached Upper Klamath Lake, he had actually arrived at Klamath Marsh, about thirty miles north of that lake.[1]

The party set up camp on a low, pine-covered neck of land jutting into the marsh. Because the Klamath Indians who inhabited the area had a reputation for hostility toward whites, Frémont posted guards for the night and ordered the horses and mules to be hobbled in a nearby meadow, visible to the sentries. For good measure, when the party spotted plumes of smoke rising from the lake and from its opposite shore, Frémont ordered that the howitzer be fired:

> It was the first time our [Indian] guides had seen it discharged; and the bursting of the shell at a distance, which was something like the second fire of the gun, amazed and bewildered them with delight. It inspired them with triumphant feelings; but on the camps at a distance the effect was different, for the smokes in the lake and on the shore immediately disappeared.[2]

The next morning, following their Indian guides, the men headed around the marsh to where they had spotted smoke the day before. They had come within a half mile of a settlement of thatched huts when they saw two persons advancing toward them. As the party's guides galloped out ahead to meet the two tribesmen, Frémont and the rest of the party—forming into a long line, riding abreast—followed. Upon catching up with the guides, Frémont learned, to his surprise, that one of the two strangers was a woman: "They were the village chief and his wife, who, in excitement and alarm at the unusual event and appearance, had come out to meet their fate together. The chief was a very prepossessing Indian, with very handsome features, and a singularly soft and agreeable voice—so remarkable as to attract general notice." Invited by the chief to visit the nearby settlement, Frémont found a cluster of huts, each twenty feet in diameter, with rounded tops, on which were doors through which the tribesmen entered the structure's interior.

The language spoken by these Klamath Indians differed from any that the explorers had heard among the Shoshone and other Far Western tribes that they had encountered. So only through physical gestures could the men communicate with their hosts. But through gestures, they came to understand that these tribesmen were at war with another people—presumably, the Modocs—who lived to the southeast of Klamath Lake.

At the Klamath village, Frémont was impressed by how the tribes-men exploited their environment: "Great quantities of [fish] . . . that had been smoked and dried, were suspended on strings about their lodges. Piles of grass and rushes abounded, from which they fashioned their shelters, plus sleeping-mats, hats, baskets and shoes." But typi-cal of those of European descent in the American West, Frémont's admiration for the Indians' crafts came with a lofty condescen-sion: "Almost like plants, these people seem to have adapted them-selves to the soil, and to be growing on what the immediate locality afforded."[3]

During the visit, Frémont also took notice of the "singular-looking dogs, resembling wolves" sitting atop many of the Klamath's huts; and, before leaving, he purchased several sleeping mats—to use for sleeping and as tablecloths—as well as one of the young dogs, "which, after its birthplace, was named Tlamath." Frémont's spelling of the dog's name reflected what he—in the best Nicollet tradition—insisted was a more faithful rendering of the way in which local Indians pro-nounced the name generally spelled "Klamath."

The party spent an hour at the Klamath settlement, then returned to their marshside camp. Finding time to conduct celestial observa-tions, Frémont and Preuss recorded that their camp was at latitude 42°56′51″—still in Oregon, but just barely north of the Mexican province of Alta California. Increasingly distracted, but still trying to meet the observational directives of his orders, Frémont also dutifully recorded his impressions of the area's strategic, commercial, and mili-tary significance: "Situated near the head of three rivers, and on the line of inland communication with California, and near to Indians noted for treachery, it will naturally, in the progress of the settlement of Oregon, became a point for military occupation." Bending away from military matters, he also noted the region's agricultural fecundity: "It is a picturesque and beautiful spot; and, under the hand of cultiva-tion, might become a paradise. Game is found in the forest; timbered and snowy mountains skirt it, and fertility characterizes it."[4]

❀

Likely aware that, a decade earlier, Hudson's Bay Company trapper-explorer Peter Ogden had visited Upper Klamath Lake, Frémont later noted that it was only after the survey party left the area that "our voyage assumed a character of discovery and exploration." Even now, Frémont's precise plans for that season remain murky; indeed, they were subject to much vacillation. One thing that does seem clear, however, is that Frémont hoped to solve a riddle that had, for generations, dogged American explorers and geographers. It concerned the river—usually but not always called the San Buenaventura—that supposedly arose in the Rockies and, after running across the West's plains and deserts, sliced through the Sierra Nevada and drained into the Pacific.

The Buenaventura's conceptual headwaters lay in reports sent back by Silvestre Vélez de Escalante and other Spanish explorers in the late eighteenth century. From such reports and maps, the river later found its way onto American maps. Most significantly, Alexander von Humboldt—departing from his usual empirical rigor and drawing on Spanish sources—published, in 1804, a map of Spain's New World holdings, depicting the river. That same year, the German geographer personally delivered a copy of his map to President Thomas Jefferson. The map impressed the President, who dutifully discussed its contents—including the Buenaventura—with Lewis and Clark before sending them on their transcontinental expedition. In Oregon, the two explorers found their own Buenaventura in a stretch of river—actually, unbeknownst to them, part of the Willamette—that they called the Multnomah. The river allegedly rose from the Rockies and flowed to the Pacific, they heard from local Indians. Likewise, Humboldt's map also impressed Zebulon Pike, who, in 1810, used it as a foundation for his own published maps of Spanish North America. Through Humboldt, Jefferson, Pike, and other tributaries, then, the Buenaventura found its way into the mainstream of American geographical speculation.

In a sense, the Buenaventura represented a last fleeting chance for those explorers and other travelers who remained bound and determined to find a water route across North America. During the early nineteenth century, a succession of explorers, trappers, and traders—upon confronting a stretch of river they could not identify—rushed to the hopeful conclusion that they had stumbled upon the fabled river. As cartographers, in response, incorporated those reports into their work, the elusive river—never staying put in any established channel—wandered all over America's maps.

By 1843, however, many experts had come to question the river's existence. Six years earlier, Albert Gallatin's map of the West had erased it completely. Even so, reports of the river's existence persisted. Gallatin, after all, had never been in the Far West—and his erasure of the river was as steeped in conjecture as the assertions that it existed. Until someone made a systematic traverse of the Sierra—and proved or disproved the river's existence—the Buenaventura would remain alive and well as a geographical conundrum.[5]

In his Second Expedition *Report*, Frémont would recall how, in commencing his crossing of the arid country southeast of Upper Klamath Lake, he longed only "to pass safely across the intervening desert to the banks of the Buenaventura, where, in the softer climate of a more southern latitude, our horses might find grass to sustain them, and ourselves be sheltered from the rigors of winter and from the inhospitable desert." Among historians—some of whom find this Buenaventura paean disingenuous—it has been suggested that Frémont, well-versed in his day's geographical literature, could not have truly believed in the Rio Buenaventura's existence. It has even been suggested that his alleged search for the river in the pages of his *Report* was an attempt to infuse additional drama into his narrative.[6]

But that assertion discounts the degree to which the question of the Buenaventura's existence remained in that day a subject of active debate. The assertion that Frémont, deferring to expert opinion, never believed in the river's existence discounts the substantial voices that, as late as 1844, still held for its existence—among them, Frémont's idol Alexander Von Humboldt and, of more immediate relevance that fall, the Hudson's Bay Company's John McLoughlin.

McLoughlin, then in his sixties, knew volumes about the West's geography. And, according to an account penned years later by Senator Benton, the Hudson's Bay Company officer strongly encouraged Frémont to find the elusive river. He even indulged in a bit of ad hoc cartography to help the explorer locate it:

Governor McLaughlin [*sic*] believed in the existence of this river, and made out a conjectural manuscript map to show its place and course. Frémont believed in it, and his plan was to reach it before the dead of winter, and then hibernate upon it.

As a great river, he knew that it must have some rich bottoms; covered with wood and grass, where the wild animals would collect and shelter, when the snows and freezing winds drove them from the plains: and with these animals to live on, and grass for the horses, and wood for fires, he expected to avoid suffering, if not to enjoy comfort, during his solitary sojourn in that remote and profound wilderness.[7]

If Frémont were to find the Buenaventura—a new transcontinental conduit, surpassing even South Pass—great glory would be his. But, then again, if—after making a thorough reconnaissance of the Sierra— he failed to find the river and thus became the cartographer who definitively erased this faded shred of myth from the maps, there would be glory in that as well. Also, by showing that no river drained the landlocked deserts of the West, he would be able to replace it with his own original contribution to North American geography—the Great Basin.

❋

On December 11, once Frémont and his men bid good-bye to the Columbia River Indians who had taken them this far, he tried in vain to persuade the nearby band of Klamath Indians to furnish them some guides, if only for a few days. Their chief, however—citing a shortage of horses, the snow that they would soon be in, and sickness in his own family—declined the request. The Indians did, however, tell the explorers that two days of eastward travel would take them to a large lake.

On the morning of December 12, Frémont's party departed Klamath Marsh. For the next two days, moving on an easterly course into higher country, they braved punishing winds and crossed over frozen ponds and snow up to a foot deep. Pack animals fell frequently and required assistance from the men to get back up with their loads. On December 13, while passing through an open pine forest in the highlands, the men suddenly heard the sound of horses galloping toward them. The horses, it turned out, belonged to a party of Indians led by the Klamath chief to whom they had, days earlier, said good-bye. "He seemed," Frémont recalled, "to have found his conduct inhospitable in letting the strangers depart without a guide through the snow, and had come, with a few others, to point us a day or two on the way."

The route, however, soon lifted the party into higher, snowier terrain for which the Indians were ill-clad; and, on the evening of December 14, the chief indicated to Frémont that they could go no farther—they must return to their village. The next day, the party crossed a river that Frémont mistakenly assumed to be the headwaters of the Sacramento River. Because, however, they were still in the Upper Klamath Lake watershed, it was more likely the Beaver Creek branch of the Sycan River, in southeastern Oregon. They spent the rest of the day crossing icy swampland that by late afternoon had given way to a dense, snow-covered pine forest: "We were slowly but gradually ascending a mountain; and, after a hard journey of seven hours, we came to some naked places among the timber, where a few tufts of grass showed above the snow, on the side of a hollow; and here we encamped. Our cow, which every day got poorer, was killed here, but the meat was rather tough."[8]

By December 16, as the party continued its ascent, the snow lay three feet deep, hard with a crustiness that cut the hoofs of their mules and horses. Toward noon, however, the explorers confronted a sight that gladdened their hearts: just ahead, the dark forest seemed to terminate in a wall of sky. Upon reaching the mountain's summit, the men gazed upon a welcome scene: "At our feet—more than a thousand feet below—we looked into a green prairie country, in which a beautiful lake, some twenty miles in length, was spread along the foot of the mountains, its shores bordered with green grass. Just then the sun broke out among the clouds, and illuminated the country below, while around us the storm raged fiercely. Not a particle of ice was to be seen on the lake, or snow on its borders, and all was like summer or spring."

Then and there, Frémont recalled, they named the snow-whipped ridge on which they stood Winter Ridge and the lake glistening below them Summer Lake: "We were now immediately on the verge of the forest land, in which we had been traveling so many days; and, looking forward to the east, scarce a tree was to be seen." Looking east and south, Frémont, once again, returned to his speculation about the Great

Basin: "Broadly marked by the boundary of the mountain wall, and immediately below us, were the first waters of the Great Interior Basin which has the Wahsatch [*sic*] and Bear river mountains for its eastern, and the Sierra Nevada for its western rim; and the edge of which we had entered upwards of three months before, at the Great Salt Lake."

Darkness had fallen across the lake by the time all the men had descended to its shore. The next morning, December 17, Frémont and Preuss determined that their camp along the lake's western shore sat at latitude 42°57′22″—still north of the forty-second parallel that marks the Oregon-California border.

On December 20—by now on a southeasterly course but still in today's southeastern Oregon—the men, upon reaching the summit of a volcanic ridge, gazed down upon yet another "handsome sheet of water"—this one some twenty miles in length. Seizing the opportunity to pay homage to the nominal sponsor of his expeditions, Frémont named it Lake Abert. As they descended the ridge, however, closer inspection revealed a less inviting scene: "The white efflorescences which lined the shore like a bank of snow, and the disagreeable ordor [*sic*] which filled the air as soon as we came near, informed us too plainly the water belonged to one of those fetid lakes which are common in this region." Though they eventually found a spot from which they could scramble down to the lake, they found the lake water undrinkable. That night, however, after digging holes along the lake's shore, the men eventually drew a filtered substance that some of them, including Frémont, managed to down.

The next morning, resuming their northern march along the lake, they soon found a grassy grove where the animals could feed. When they also discovered, in the same vicinity, several freshwater springs, Frémont ordered the party to camp and remain there for the day, to allow the animals to recoup. He, meanwhile, used the afternoon to better survey the surrounding area: "I rode ahead several miles to ascertain if there was any appearance of a watercourse entering the lake; but found none, the hills preserving their dry character, and the shore of the lake sprinkled with the same white powdery substance, and covered with the same shrubs. There were flocks of ducks on the lake, and frequent tracks of Indians along the shore, where the grass had been recently burned by their fires."

Three days later—now on a southerly course—the party, from yet another ridge, spotted what turned out to be a more beneficent lake—in all likelihood, one of the Warner Lakes, in today's northern Nevada—a locale that offered "tolerably pure water" and good grazing grass. The next day, Christmas morning, the party, on Frémont's orders, was roused by shots from small arms and the howitzer. Breakfast included the usual libational consolations by which Frémont marked important holidays: "Always, on days of religious or national commemoration, our voyageurs expect some unusual allowance; and, having nothing else, I gave them each a little brandy, (which was carefully guarded, as one of the most useful articles a traveller can carry,) with some coffee and sugar, which here, where every eatable was a luxury, was sufficient to make them a feast."[9]

On December 28—still moving south and now ten miles east of today's California line, but still on Mexican soil—the party experienced its closest encounter thus far with the area's Indians: "Riding quietly along over the snow, we came suddenly upon smokes rising among these bushes; and, galloping up, we found two huts, open at the top, and loosely built of sage, which appeared to have been deserted at the instant; and, looking hastily around, we saw several Indians on the crest of the ridge near by, and several others scrambling up the side. We had come upon them so suddenly, that they had been well-nigh surprised in their lodges."

At the abandoned site, the party found a smoldering sagebrush fire, baskets and rabbit skins, and piles of grass where the Indians had apparently been lying. As the party inspected the site, it suddenly heard, apparently from Indians gathered on a hill above them, the cry of a word that Carson understood to be the Shoshone word for "whites." The Indians, it turned out, had been watching the whites; and Carson and Godey rode off in pursuit.

Most of the Indians managed to escape Carson and Godey—all except a woman and two children. When Carson caught up with the three, hiding in sagebrush, the woman began screaming, shutting her eyes in fear:

By dint of presents, and friendly demonstrations, she was brought to calmness; and we found that they belonged to the Snake nation, speaking the language of that people. Eight or ten appeared to live together, under the same little shelter; and they seemed to have no other subsistence than the roots or seeds they might have stored up, and the hares which live in the sage, and which they are enabled to track through the snow, and are very skilful [*sic*] in killing. Herding together among bushes, and crouching almost naked over a little sage fire, using their instinct only to procure food, these may be considered, among human beings, the nearest approach to the mere animal creation. We have reason to believe that these had never before seen the face of a white man.[10]

❋

Since descending into the Great Basin, Frémont, beyond watching for the Buenaventura, had been keeping an eye out for yet another elusive figure of this region's mythical geography, a lush, reed-lined respite from the surrounding aridity called Mary's Lake. Somewhere to the southeast of Mary's Lake, Frémont believed, he would find the Buenaventura; and, from there, the party would triumphantly head east.[11] But by December 30, having found neither Mary's Lake nor the Buenaventura, he began to worry. As the party worked its way south, all but a few of the lake and stream beds that the men stumbled upon turned out to be dry. Making matters worse, the animals were suffering from lack of grass, and from the rocky terrain. By December 31, the party had reached the edge of Black Rock Desert—in today's northwestern Nevada—where, that afternoon, after descending several hundred feet into a long broad basin, they found the frozen stream by which they spent New Year's Eve: "Here we concluded the year 1843, and our new year's eve was rather a gloomy one. The result of our journey began to be very uncertain."

By January 3, by now traveling almost due south along a foggy ridge in northern Nevada's Granite Mountains, Frémont was even more worried: "We had reached and run over the position where, according to the best maps in my possession, we should have found Mary's lake, or river. We were evidently on the verge of the desert which had been reported to us; and the appearance of the country was so forbidding, that I was afraid to enter it, and determined to bear away to the southward, keeping close along the mountains, in the full expectation of reaching the Buenaventura river." Before leaving camp that morning, Frémont, concerned about the worsening condition of the horses and mules, ordered every man to proceed on foot; "and in this manner lightened by distribution the loads of the animals."[12]

On January 7, Frémont headed toward what they assumed were hot springs vapors rising from a nearby valley. "This is the most extraordinary locality of hot springs we had met during the journey," he recalled upon reaching the waters, near today's Gerlach, Nevada. "The basin of the largest one has a circumference of several hundred feet; but there is at one extremity a circular space of about fifteen feet in diameter, entirely occupied by the boiling water. It boils up at irregular intervals and with much noise." Once collected and allowed to cool, the water turned out to be slightly salty, but not so much that they couldn't cook with it. If they added snow, it was even fit to drink. But Frémont's worries continued to grow. Since leaving The Dalles, he had lost fifteen animals: two had been stolen, and malnourishment had killed the others. To better husband the expedition's resources and energies, "I therefore determined, until we should reach a country of water and vegetation, to feel our way ahead, by having the line of route explored some fifteen or twenty miles in advance, and only to leave a present encampment when the succeeding one was known."

The next morning, Frémont, Carson, and Godey, leaving the others behind in camp, rode out to scout the surrounding country. To their delight, they discovered, in a neighboring valley, a lush, spring-nourished ravine full of cottonwoods. Not having seen the species in a while, Frémont took their reappearance as a botanical harbinger of a greener country: "To us, they were eloquent of green prairies and buffalo."

As the rest of the company relocated to the cottonwoods camp, Frémont and Carson set out on another scouting expedition. The next day, they found yet another verdant spot—this one on the basin's edge, in the hollow of an adjoining mountain. Leaving behind a signal for the rest of the party to encamp there, the two, eager to see what lay ahead, began ascending the hollow toward the mountain's peak.

Once atop the peak, Frémont and Carson could not believe their eyes: "Beyond, a defile between the mountains descended rapidly about two thousand feet; and, filling up all the lower space, was a sheet of green water, some twenty miles broad. It broke upon our eyes like the ocean." Hungry to see more, the two men scrambled up a still higher neighboring summit: "The waves were curling in the breeze, and their dark-green color showed it be a body of deep water. For a long time we sat enjoying the view, for we had become fatigued with mountains, and the free expanse of moving waves was very grateful. It was like a gem in the mountains, which, from our position, seemed to enclose it entirely." Frémont initially believed he had stumbled upon Mary's Lake. But as he and Carson took in the scene, he realized that the mountains that surrounded the lake in no way comported with the "low rushy shores and open country" that he had been told fringed Mary's Lake.

The next morning, January 11, the two explorers completed their trek down to the emerald-green lake, and Frémont dutifully recorded notes on all that he could take in. "The water is so slightly salt[y]," he recalled, "that, at first, we thought it fresh, and would be pleasant to drink when no other could be had. The shore was rocky—a handsome beach, which reminded us of the sea. On some large *granite* boulders that were scattered about the shore, I remarked a coating of a calcareous substance, in some places a few inches and in others a foot in thickness."[13]

After the rest of the party reached the lake, the men began working their way south, along the lake's eastern shore, on an Indian trail that, as the beach receded, soon swept upward along three-thousand-foot-high precipices overlooking the lake. Boulders often obstructed their passage; and to make matters still worse, "during a greater part of the morning the lake was nearly hid by a snow storm, and the waves broke on the narrow beach in a long line of foaming surf, five or six feet high." Two days and twenty-one miles later, the party found itself beside the lake across from a striking pyramid-shaped island: "It rose, according to our estimate, 600 feet above the water; and, from the point we viewed it, presented a pretty exact outline of the great pyramid of Cheops." At their campsite that night beside the body of water—in today's Washoe County, Nevada—that Frémont soon named Pyramid Lake, they killed the last of the cattle they had driven from The Dalles.

The next day, the men spotted several "poor-looking Indians" lurking nearby, and coaxed one of them into their camp. The tribes-men, naked except for a tunic of rabbit skins, spoke what to Carson sounded like a dialect of the Snake language. And though the explor-ers found the dialect largely indecipherable, they understood the tribesmen to tell them that, though he lived in some nearby rocks along the lake, a river could be found at the body of water's southern end. The men were unsure as to whether the Indian was saying that the river ran into, or out of, the lake. But even from their campsite, Frémont could see a dense grove of cottonwoods at the lake's south-ern end, suggesting a sizable stream.

As they reached the cottonwoods and what turned out to be the in-let of a river, a group of Indians appeared on the trail, greeting the ex-plorers. In sign language, the chief invited the exploring party to visit their village, situated along the river. Frémont's party set up camp in a grassy bottom along the river, then took up the invitation to visit the village, a collection of straw huts a few hundred yards just up the stream. When one of the Indians brought in a large fish to trade, one of the men noticed that it was what Frémont called a "salmon trout"— actually, a cutthroat trout, a species that tolerates alkaline waters: "The Indians were amused with our delight, and immediately brought in numbers; so that the camp was soon stocked. Their flavor was excellent—superior, in fact, to that of any fish I have ever known. They were of extraordinary size—about as large as the Columbia river salmon—generally from two to four feet in length."[14]

However, as the Indians soon became regular visitors at his camp, Frémont—discomfited by the arms that they carried—stipulated that, to enter the camp, they must come unarmed. He wondered whether these Indians had ever seen white people before. But from the brass buttons that one of the tribesmen wore and from other manufactured items he noticed, he assumed that, at the least, they had relations with other Indians who had dealt with whites. When, however, Frémont tried to obtain geographical information from the tribesmen, language difficulties interfered. In the dirt, the Indians drew a map of their river, showing it originating in another lake in the mountains, about three or four days distant, in a direction slightly west of south. Beyond that lake, they drew another mountain, and beyond it, two more rivers, on which whites lived. But whether the Indians were referring to the Mexican and American settlements along the Sacramento River, or to some American party that had crossed the Sierra, Frémont could not be certain.

On January 16, heeding the Indians' directions, the explorers began an upstream march, south alongside the river beside which the tribesmen lived. The next day, now approaching the defile where what Frémont called the Salmon Trout River—today's Truckee River—fell from the Sierra, the explorers abandoned the stream as they continued their southward course: "With every stream I now expected to see the great Buenaventura; and Carson hurried eagerly to search, on every one we reached, for beaver cuttings, which he always maintained we should find only on waters that ran to the Pacific."

After abandoning the Truckee, another twenty miles south brought them to another river—a stream that Frémont later named the Carson River. The party followed the Carson west toward the mountains. Once again, however, finding no trace of beaver, they concluded that it was not the Buenaventura.

❋

Until now, Frémont had apparently planned to make a wide sweep south, along the Sierra's eastern slope, before returning home across the Great Basin. But as the party dipped south, he apparently had a change of heart. Later that afternoon, January 18, after the party had set up camp along the Carson River, Frémont and Carson rode out to see what they could discover about the origin of the smoke signals they had noticed during the day. Fatefully, in his subsequent *Report*, Frémont claimed that, upon returning later that day, he inspected the condition of the party's animals:

> I found their feet so much cut up by the rocks, and so many of them lame, that it was evidently impossible that they could cross the Rocky mountains. Every piece of iron that could be used for the purpose had been converted into nails, and we could make no further use of the shoes we had remaining. I therefore determined to abandon my eastern course, and to

cross the Sierra Nevada into the valley of the Sacramento, wherever a practical pass could be found.

Once in the valley, the party would proceed immediately to a fort and trading post, at the confluence of the American and Sacramento Rivers. There, the men would rest and acquire supplies for the trip back to Missouri.[15]

WINTER SIERRA 12

I N JANUARY 1844, when John Frémont, barely thirty-one years
old, gathered his men together at their camp on the Carson River
to announce his decision to cross the Sierra Nevada, there had
been no recorded winter crossing of the range. Even so, he later
claimed, "My decision was heard with joy by the people, and diffused
new life throughout the camp." Nonetheless, Frémont's stated reasons for reaching that decision have led historians, over the years, to
speculate that it originated from other, perhaps clandestine, considerations than those recounted in his official *Report*.

Such suspicions arise as much from the Sierra's rugged conditions—in winter, snows reach depths exceeding twenty feet—as from
Frémont's subsequent actions. The Sierra Nevada, the high glaciated
mountains that rise between California's Central Valley and the
mountain-and-desert country that Frémont called the Great Basin are
a "fault-block" range—a range created by a buckling of tectonic plates
along the earth's fault lines. Driven by heat deep in the earth, one
plate, or "fault-block," dives under another, which rises, tearing the
earth's crust and creating a new range of mountains. The Sierra range
runs north to south from Tehachapi Pass, just above Los Angeles, to
the Feather River valley, just south of Mt. Lassen. The range's loftiest
elevations, such as Mt. Whitney—at 14,495 feet, the Sierra's highest
peak—lie along its southern half. But even in the range's northern ex-
tremities, its peaks routinely exceed 11,000 feet.

While the Indians of western California made routine forays into
the foothills of the Sierra's less steep western slope, they rarely

climbed into its higher altitudes. And while European settlement in California had begun in the eighteenth century, most whites stayed close to the coast, viewing the Sierra as an impenetrable barrier. Likewise, the Shoshone, Paiutes, and other Indian peoples below the range's steeper, eastern slope, rarely ventured into the mountains.

The first known crossing of the range by a non-Indian—by explorer and trapper Jedediah Smith—occurred in 1827, sixteen years before Frémont first gazed upon the range. In 1834, the trapper Joseph Walker crossed the range somewhere on the divide between the Tuolumne and Merced Rivers; the following year, he made the first west-to-east crossing, through the relatively low Walker Pass (5,250 feet), near the range's southern terminus. And, in the fall of 1843, a branch of the emigrant party led by Joseph Chiles would, with Joseph Walker as its guide, become the first group to cross the mountains with wagons.

❋

Efforts to explain Frémont's reasons for crossing the winter Sierra have led to speculation that he was operating on secret orders. Biographer Allan Nevins has surmised, "It is barely possible that the expansionist senators, and Benton and Linn in particular, had reached an understanding with Frémont that he was to enter California and spy out the land." But, in the absence of concrete evidence supporting that conclusion—and none has surfaced—Frémont's own explanation, that he was low on supplies and feared dire consequences if the party remained in the Truckee River area, remains the most plausible reason for his decision. Years later, after all, Kit Carson corroborated Frémont's explanation: "We were nearly out of provisions and cross the mountain we must, let the consequences be what they may," he recalled to his biographer.[1]

The suggestion has also been made that Frémont would have been wiser to have wintered in the Truckee River valley, with its bountiful supply of trout, antelopes, pine nuts, and abundant grass for the party's animals. There, so the suggestion goes, the only real danger the party faced was the possibility that Indians in the area might steal their mules and horses one by one—thus stranding the party. But that suggestion discounts Frémont's quite reasonable fears of Indian attacks. Upon reaching Pyramid Lake, the party, for days, saw ominous smoke signals in every direction. And whether his fears were justified or not, Frémont perceived the Indians of the Sierra's eastern slope as a genuine threat to his party's safety. "Strict vigilance," he recalled, "was maintained among the people, and one-third at a time were kept on guard during the night. There is no reason to doubt that these dispositions, uniformly preserved, conducted our party through Indians famed for treachery."[2]

One other factor, unmentioned in any of Frémont's writings, warrants mention—his by then well-advanced sense of his own importance and talents. Though not yet an internationally renowned figure, by the winter of 1844 Frémont enjoyed a high degree of celebrity and public admiration. Emblematic of that adulation, even before his return from the Second Expedition, newspapers back East—albeit probably unbeknownst to Frémont—were reporting that, in distant Oregon, he was accomplishing imperial objectives that had eluded generations of American policymakers: "Fort Hall, on the Oregon, has been delivered up to Lieut. Frémont, and it is believed that Fort Vancouver soon will be," reported the New York *Spectator*, on December 13, 1843, in one such dispatch.[3] Given that level of public confidence, which no doubt swelled Frémont's own sense of his abilities, it is not difficult to imagine how he might readily assume that the winter Sierra would prove no obstacle to him.

❁

From their camp on the Carson River, the party, on January 19, set out to cross the Sierra. But instead of following the West Fork of the Walker River, they took a route up the river's East Fork to the area of today's Bridgeport, California. Perhaps making one last effort to find the Buenaventura, the party had drifted south of where Frémont wanted to be in order to cross the mountains. On January 25, they reached the site of today's Bridgeport, California. From there, Frémont and Carson—leaving the others behind for a day of rest— set off on a westerly scouting expedition, which, two days later, took them through a gap called Devils Gate, which Frémont thought, incorrectly, passed over the crest of the Sierras.

The following day, after he and Carson had rejoined the main party, Frémont led the entire expeditionary force through Devils Gate. But instead of descending into the canyon, the party ascended a ridge rising from the Walker River's west fork. On January 29, by now at altitudes exceeding seven thousand feet, as the party struggled to ascend the ridge, Frémont was forced to abandon the mountain howitzer that they had by then hauled over three thousand miles—an act that inspired one of the longest-running scavenger hunts in American history, as Sierra mountaineers, to this day, still search for the lost cannon.

That night, Frémont sought to draw out knowledge of the area from some local Indians. One of the Indians, an elderly man, said that, in the season before the snow fell, a crossing of the range took "six sleeps"—eight days of travel. Then, repeating gestures the explorers had seen before, the old Indian indicated that the snows were deeper than Frémont was tall—it would be impossible to cross at this time of year. Better, he suggested, that Frémont follow a nearby river to a snowless lake. There—in all likelihood, Pyramid Lake—people lived and there were many large fish to catch. Stressing what they saw as the folly of Frémont's intentions, the Indians kept repeating the word *Tah-ve*, which the lieutenant soon came to understand meant snow.

But Frémont would have none of it; assuring the Indians that his horses were strong, he indicated that he would, if necessary, break a passage through the snow. Then, unraveling a bale of scarlet cloth and trinkets, he showed the Indian what he would give for a guide. The elder conferred with the other tribesmen, left the lodge for a few minutes, then returned with a young man who, to Frémont, had a "very intelligent appearance." This young man, said the elderly Indian, had been to the place of the whites across the mountains, the place where Frémont wanted to go. He might, said the old man, be willing to guide Frémont's party there. "With a large present of goods," Frémont later recalled, "we prevailed upon this young man to be our guide, and he acquired among us the name of Melo—a word signifying friend, which they used very frequently." The next morning, sharing his latest plans with the entire party, Frémont told the men that their destination, Sutter's Fort, lay only seventy miles due west and reminded them of Carson's vivid descriptions of the Sacramento River valley and its benign climate and abundant game: "I assured them that, from the heights of the mountain before us, we should doubtless see the valley of the Sacramento river, and with one effort place ourselves again in the midst of plenty."

Snow, however, intermittent during the previous evening, was by that morning falling steadily. As it became obvious that they would be unable to travel that day, Frémont ordered the men to begin repairing leggings, moccasins, and other clothing for what lay ahead. Their food provisions by now were perilously low; and it had been awhile since the men had enjoyed a good meal. So, that night, Frémont acceded to the men's request to kill one of the three dogs in their camp: "Spread out on the snow, the meat looked very good; and it made a strengthening meal for the greater part of the camp. Indians brought in two or three rabbits during the day, which were purchased from them."[4]

The next day the party set off, but as the men reached altitudes exceeding five thousand feet, the snows eventually grew so deep that it became necessary to break a road through the white drifts: "For this service, a party of ten was formed, mounted on the strongest horses; each man in succession opening the road on foot, or on horseback, until himself and his horse became fatigued when he stepped aside; and the remaining number passing ahead, he took his station in the rear."

On February 4, Frémont and two or three other men, each with a horse to break a road, set out on a scouting expedition up a steep, snow-covered Indian path to Charity Valley. That afternoon, pointing to the west, the Indian guide Melo, to Frémont's relief, indicated the pass that would lead them into the Sacramento River valley: "The summit line presented a range of naked peaks, apparently destitute of snow and vegetation; but below, the face of the whole country was covered with timber of extraordinary size." The break in the mountains that Melo pointed out—later named Carson Pass—would, five years later, become the main passage over the Sierra's crest for thousands of emigrants streaming into California in search of gold, a new life, or both. From Frémont's elevated vantage that afternoon—what are today known as Charity and Faith valleys—the gap in the ridge lay only 4.5 miles ahead, so tantalizingly close that, then and there, he decided to try to "force" a road to it that same day.

After, however, covering that day only two or three hundred treacherous yards—and witnessing the horses give out, refusing to go any farther, and Melo cautioning that still deeper snows lay ahead—Frémont decided to head back and warn the main party before it proceeded any farther. But after backtracking only a short distance, Frémont encountered Fitzpatrick—himself headed toward the advance party and bearing still more discouraging news. "The camp had been occupied all the day in endeavoring to ascend the hill, but only the best horses had succeeded," Fitzpatrick told Frémont. Learning that the entire distance between where the two men stood and the previous night's camp lay strewn with camp supplies and horses—all floundering in the snow—Frémont instructed Fitzpatrick to move the entire party back to the previous night's camp at Grover Hot Springs.

Camped that night in Charity Valley's lower end, under an open grove of pines, the men built a fire and spread their blankets over the boughs in the snow. Two Indians visited them during the night. Upon learning of Frémont's plans, the older of the two tribesmen began, in Frémont's words, to "harangue" the white men: "We had now begun to understand some words, and, with the aid of signs, easily comprehended the old man's ideas. 'Rock upon rock—rock upon rock—snow upon snow—snow upon snow,' said he; 'even if you get over the snow, you will not be able to get down from the mountains.' "5

According to Frémont, by the end of the old man's jeremiad, William—the young Chinook Indian who had joined them at The Dalles—had his head buried in his blanket and could be heard loudly weeping: "Seated around the tree, we presented a group of very serious faces." Riling Frémont, Melo—determined to return to his own people—deserted the next morning: "His bad faith and treachery were in perfect keeping with the estimate of Indian character, which a long intercourse with this people had gradually forced upon my mind."

Over the next five days, part of the exploring party busied themselves collecting the camp equipment scattered between Charity Valley and Grover Hot Springs. The other half, encamped at Grover Hot Springs, began making the snowshoes and sledges needed to get their equipment over the crest of the Sierra.

❋

On February 6, Frémont, joined by Fitzpatrick and several others, set out on snowshoes to scout out a route for their final ascent of the range. Marching single file to break a path in the snow, the men found their way to a high peak—now called Elephants Back. As a boy, Kit Carson had accompanied the trapper Ewing Young on a hunting expedition to California in 1829–30. Now, as he stood with Frémont atop Elephants Back, a tide of memories rushed forward: gazing west, beyond the Sierra's eastern slope and the Central Valley, Carson spotted Mt. Diablo and the Coast Range. " 'There,' said he, 'is the little mountain—it is 15 years ago since I saw it; but I am just as sure as if I had seen it yesterday.' " Even closer—Frémont estimated the Sacramento valley some thirty miles distant—the men could see a dark line, which they assumed to be the Sacramento River, streaking across the valley floor.

The next morning, eager to find a campsite below Carson Pass, Frémont set out again, with a scouting party that now included Preuss, Carson, Dodson, and Theodore Talbot. The men found their way to a spot about two miles southeast of Carson Pass, near today's Red Lake reservoir. There, on February 10, Frémont established what he came to call his Long Camp, in sight of the pass, on a dome-shaped hill covered with snow, but close to exposed patches of grass, where the party's animals could graze.

❄

By February 10, the road-building process had the party strung out along an icy route stretching some twenty miles—from today's Markleeville to Grover Hot Springs to Frémont's Long Camp, near Carson Pass. As an eastbound group worked to break a road from the Long Camp back to Charity Valley; another detail, under Fitzpatrick, oversaw the work up from Grover Hot Springs to Charity Valley.

The work went anything but smoothly—on February 11, as Fitzpatrick's party tried to lead the animals up a canyon wall just west of Grover Hot Springs, he watched in horror as the animals sank into deep, entrapping snow—some all the way up to their ears. The next morning, even as Frémont learned of Fitzpatrick's plight, a work crew under his leadership, laboring to reinforce the road down the mountain, was working its way down to the accident site. "We made mauls," Frémont recalled, "and worked hard at our end of the road all the day. The wind was high, but the sun bright, and the snow falling." After stamping down the snow with their mauls, they covered the path with thick pine boughs to increase traction. Frémont, meanwhile, ordered five men to go back to Fitzpatrick's camp in Grover Hot Springs and slaughter several of the horses. The horsemeat was to be brought up on improvised sledges to the increasingly undernourished men. The remaining horses at Grover Hot Springs would be taken back to Markleeville, with its abundant grass, and kept there until the road was complete.

By February 13, the work seemed nearly finished. Looking east, about three miles distant, Frémont, while supervising his eastbound work party, spotted Fitzpatrick's westbound party, working their way down an opposite hill. Still later that same day, Fitzpatrick, confirming hopes that the two parties were about to meet up, visited Frémont to report that all was going well. Further buoying Frémont's spirits, he and his men had encountered a group of snowshoe-clad Indians, carrying fishing equipment and headed west: "This was an indication that the salmon were coming up the streams; and we could hardly restrain our impatience as we thought of them, and worked with increased vigor." Apparently, they were now on the Indian path that Melo had told them about.

Later that day, February 13, when the expected sledge of meat failed to arrive at the Long Camp, Frémont ordered the slaughter of Tlamath, the dog he had purchased from the Klamath Indians. Alexander Godey, as Preuss recalled, killed and prepared the dog: "It was prepared Indian fashion: the hair singed off, and it was scalded (horrible stench in our kitchen); the skin was washed, first with water and soap, then with snow." Shortly after the dog had been killed, however, the sledge did arrive. As measure of their growing desperation, the men supped that night on pea soup, mule, and dog.[6]

When the road was in place, the rest of the party, over the next few days, streamed into the Long Camp. Frémont, meanwhile, explored the surrounding country. On February 14, he and Preuss climbed one of the nearby mountains—Red Lake Peak—overlooking the camp. Though mists obscured much of the view, with their telescope they managed to spot, in the distance, a vast body of water, called Mountain Lake by Frémont—known since the late 1860s as Lake Tahoe. On February 16, Frémont set out on another two-day reconnaissance—this one with Jacob Dodson, down the Sierra's western slope, along a series of spur ridges. Along the way, Frémont dutifully noted any open, grassy areas where the main party might graze their animals on the final descent.

Toward dusk, upon reaching a mountain stream, they set up camp for the night. Lacking snowshoes and seeking to avoid snow, Frémont and Dodson spent much of the next day walking on the creek's frozen surface—until its ice cracked, tossing them into the frigid stream. They built a fire, dried their clothes; and, afterward, the two walked a few more miles downstream—far enough to convince Frémont that he had reached a tributary of the river for which he had been searching. Frémont had struck the headwaters of the American River—and it was at that stream's confluence with the much larger Sacramento River, which drains the Central Valley's northern half, that the Swiss-born entrepreneur Johann Sutter had built his famous redoubt.[7]

Reversing course, Frémont and Dodson made a "hard push" back—returning to the Long Camp that night, February 17: "Here we had the pleasure to find all the remaining animals, 57 in number, safely arrived at the grassy hill near the camp." Two days later, all of the men, equipment, and animals had reached the top of Carson Pass.

On February 21, they began their descent—gingerly working their way through the snow accumulations atop the narrow spur ridge that guided their downward course. The party covered six miles that day, then set up camp late that afternoon, in a grove of pines. Frémont and Carson, meanwhile, used the remaining light to climb a neighboring mountain and scout out the next day's route. Though they clearly still faced some hard traveling, the two were pleased to see that, compared to their course up the range's eastern side, this route down the western slope descended rapidly. And, to Frémont' delight, before sunset, they had the added satisfaction of spotting, in the distance, a shining line of water that led directly into a much broader sheet:

> We knew that these could be no other than the Sacramento and the bay of San Francisco; but, after our long wandering in rugged mountains, where so frequently we had met with disappointments, and where the crossing of every ridge displayed some unknown lake or river, we were yet almost afraid to be-

lieve that we were at last to escape into the genial country of
which we had heard so many glowing descriptions, and dreaded
again to find some vast interior lake, whose bitter waters would
bring us disappointment. On the southern shore of what appeared to be the bay could be traced the gleaming line where
entered another large stream; and again the Buenaventura rose
up in our minds.

The other large stream—the "gleaming line" striking out from San
Francisco Bay, south down the valley—was in fact the San Joaquin
River, not the Buenaventura. As Frémont later recalled, Carson, during his passage through California fifteen years earlier, had reached
the Sacramento River valley from the south, via the San Joaquin—
"but the country then was so entirely covered with water from snow
and rain, that he had been able to form no correct impression of watercourses." Even more tantalizingly, as night fell, the men spotted several flickering fires—flames so vivid that they initially presumed them
to be on the next ridge. But as they moved north and, when looking
west, saw the same fires each night, they concluded they must be tu-
larés burning—reeds set aflame by the Miwok Indians, along the
fringes of the Sacramento delta.
On February 23, the party faced what Frémont called the most difficult day of their travels:

We were forced off the ridges by the quantity of snow among
the timber, and obliged to take to the mountain sides, where,
occasionally, rocks and a southern exposure afforded us a
chance to scramble along. But these were steep, and slippery
with snow and ice; and the tough evergreens of the mountain
impeded our way, tore our skins, and exhausted our patience.
Some of us had the misfortune to wear moccasins with *parflêche*
soles, so slippery that we could not keep our feet, and generally
crawled across the snow beds.

Later that day, while he and Carson moved ahead of the main party
to, as Frémont put it, "reconnoitre [*sic*] the road," the two men were
crossing a rock-strewn river when Frémont, slipping on one of the

stones, fell into the icy stream. After some frightening moments in the swift currents, he pulled himself out—but not before Carson had already jumped in to save him. The two built a fire, dried themselves off, and returned to the main party that day. Still later that afternoon, Frémont and the entire party used horses to break a path to the stream into which he had fallen—the South Fork of the American River, near today's Strawberry, California.[8]

The next morning, February 24, the party set off down the American River's South Fork. Though Frémont knew that the worst parts of the Sierra crossing lay behind them, the condition of the men and animals could not have been worse. For food that night, the men killed another of their horses. The next morning—leaving Fitzpatrick in charge of the main party with orders to move at a slower pace—Frémont, leading a detail that included Preuss, Carson, Talbot, Derosier, Town, and Dodson, set out for Sutter's Fort, to bring back fresh animals, food, and other supplies to the others.

Frémont's advance party delighted as the snows of the past two months gave way to flowering meadows and green groves of pines and oaks. By March 6, they had reached the valley floor. There, they soon stumbled upon an Indian village, where they encountered a vaquero—a Spanish-speaking Indian cowboy—who told them that the river they were following was called the "Rio de los Americanos"—the American River—and that about ten miles below, it joined the Sacramento River. Even closer to where they now stood, said the tribesman, they would find Captain Sutter's fort. Later, upon reaching the post, they found Sutter himself, walking outside its walls. The exploring party, for their part, as Carson recalled, presented an image anything but impressive: "When we arrived at the fort we were naked and in as poor condition as men possibly could be."

❋

The forty-one-year-old Johann August Sutter enjoyed company but was suspicious of strangers. Even so, as he recalled, "I received him politely and his company likewise, as if an old acquaintance." Frémont, for his part, offered an equally rosy account of the evening: "He gave us a frank and cordial reception—conducted us immediate to his residence—and under his hospitable roof we had a night of rest, enjoyment, and refreshment, which none but ourselves could appreciate."

But, eager to get back to Fitzpatrick and the main party, the advance party, after purchasing from Sutter about sixty mules and twenty-five horses, left the post the next morning. Two days later, they found the main party just below the forks of the American River. Aside from acorns and a deer they had killed, Frémont recalled, the men had barely eaten for days:

> They were all on foot—each man, weak and emaciated, leading a horse or mule as weak and emaciated as themselves [*sic*]. They had experienced great difficulty in descending the mountains, made slippery by rains and melting snows, and many horses fell over precipices, and were killed; and with some were lost the *packs* they carried.

One of the lost mules had carried a pack containing all of the plant specimens collected since the party had left Fort Hall. All in all, of the sixty-seven horses and mules with the expedition when they began their Sierra crossing, only thirty-three remained when they reached the Sacramento Valley—and none was in a condition to ride. From the supplies that Frémont brought back from Sutter's Fort, the party prepared a hearty feast that evening. The next day, the entire party made camp at the junction of the American and Sacramento Rivers, just beyond Sutter's post. And that afternoon, as Frémont negotiated the purchase of more supplies and animals from Sutter, the rest of the exploring party began gathering the wood needed to make new packsaddles for the long trip back to Missouri.

During their stay near the post, Frémont also reunited with emigrant party leader Joseph Chiles. The previous spring at Elm Grove, Frémont's party had shared a camp with Chiles's California-bound pioneers—the first emigrant group to reach California overland with wagons. And the explorers, reaching Fort Hall soon after Chiles's entourage had passed through there, had barely missed seeing them again in Oregon. At Sutter's Fort, Chiles, now with a grant of land from California's Mexican government, was in the process of selecting a site for the ranch he planned to build. Though the two men, then, had no way of knowing it, political events would bring them together again soon enough—albeit under altogether different and more complex circumstances.

At Sutter's Fort that winter of 1844, most of Frémont's dealings with the post's namesake went smoothly. One incident, however, was destined to shadow the two men's future relationship. While there, Frémont accused three of his own men of stealing sugar. Upon learning of the allegations, Sutter—as an alcalde of the Mexican government, a civilian official with broad responsibilities—decided to himself try the accused men, eventually acquitting all three. Frémont resented the verdict, as well as what he viewed as Sutter's judicial intrusiveness. Moreover, while Frémont wanted to banish the three men from his midst, Sutter compounded the affront by hiring all or one— sources differ—of the three men.[9]

The exploring party left Sutter's Fort two weeks later, on March 24. Had Frémont been aware of another incident—one that transpired after he had left the fort—he might have been more forgiving of Sutter's adjudication of the alleged sugar thieves. Sutter, by then divided his loyalties between Mexico and the United States. Accordingly, after Frémont's arrival, he notified Thomas Larkin, the U.S. consul in Alta California's provincial capital of Monterey, of the exploring party's presence.[10]

As a Mexican official, however, he felt obliged to report the explorer's presence to the Mexican government. But before Sutter could comply with that requirement, he learned that the province's governor, General Manuel Micheltorena, upon hearing reports of Frémont's arrival, had already dispatched a detail of soldiers to the fort to question the visitors. Upon learning of the soldiers' imminent arrival, but apparently not sharing his news with Frémont, Sutter "hurried Frémont off before they came." As Sutter recalled years later, only after Frémont's departure did he officially notify Mexican officials of Frémont's presence.[11] It would not be the last time that Sutter saw Frémont, and not the last time that Frémont would bring Sutter into precisely the sort of conflict that he preferred to avoid.

CALIFORNIA IDYLL, AND BACK

B Y LATE MARCH OF 1844, spring lay robustly abloom down the length of California's Central Valley, which John Frémont called the California Valley—a riot of orange California poppies, deep blue lupines, bird's-eye gilia, and countless other wild flowers. It was on March 24 that his party, now numbering twenty-one men, finally departed Sutter's Fort and marched south, up the San Joaquin River. With the green Coast Range on their right and the much higher, snow-capped Sierra Nevada to their left, the men relished the scene: "Our road was now one continued enjoyment; and it was pleasant, riding among this assemblage of green pastures with varied flowers and scattered groves, and out of the warm green spring, to look at the rocky and snowy peaks where lately we had suffered so much."

Before turning east, Frémont intended to make a five-hundred-mile southeasterly jaunt, parallel with the San Joaquin River, to the southern end of the the Central Valley. There, where the Sierra Nevada lies relatively low, he would cross the range, then drop into the vast, largely unsurveyed country—his suspected Great Basin—that stretched east from the Sierra's eastern slope to the Great Salt Lake and the Wasatch Mountains that border the lake's eastern shore. The passage down the valley would also, he hoped, allow him to settle, once and for all, the debate over whether or not the Buenaventura was a real or a mythical river.

On April 8, the southbound party reached southern California's King's River. There, while the men were searching for a fording spot, some Indians appeared on the river's opposite bank. Initially, the tribesmen feared the whites, suspecting them to be Mexican soldiers. Having lived in Mexican missions, several of the Indians spoke Spanish; and, once assured that Frémont's men were not Mexican soldiers, the tribesmen showed the exploring party a good crossing point several miles upstream. Once across, the party was greeted by still other Indians, from a nearby village; Frémont recalled the tribesmen as "dark-skinned, but handsome and intelligent." He gave them some gifts and invited them to visit his camp. When the Indians showed up at the campsite, they bore various trade goods—including otter skins, bread made from acorns, and several kinds of fish.

By April 13, the explorers had reached the southern end of California's Central Valley. As the men worked their way up Oak Creek into the Tehachapi Mountains, oaks and pines reappeared. That night they were visited by a Spanish-speaking Indian, on leave from one of the coastal Jesuit missions which lay two or three days to the south. The Indian had obtained permission from the mission priests to visit relations in the Sierra and had been above and ahead of Frémont's party when he spotted the white men and decided to backtrack down the trail for a visit. To Frémont, "It was an unexpected apparition, and a strange and pleasant sight in this desolate gorge of a mountain—an Indian face, jingling spurs, and horse equipped after the Spanish manner."

Learning that Frémont planned, after descending the Sierra's eastern slope, to travel directly across the desert and mountain country toward the Great Salt Lake, the Indian offered some advice: the country east of the Sierra was harshly arid and forebidding; it had defied all attempts by Indians to cross it. Instead, the Indian advised, once across the Sierra, go south down an old Indian trail, to its junction with the Spanish Trail, which connected the pueblo of Los Angeles with Santa Fe. As it happened, the Indian added, he was en route to the San Fernando mission and, for the next two days, would be traveling the same route he had just commended to Frémont; he would be glad to take the survey party as far as the Indian trail's junction with the Spanish Trail.

The next day, April 14, their new guide leading the way, the party, as Frémont recalled, resumed their march up Oak Creek Pass:

Our cavalcade made a strange and grotesque appearance . . . guided by a civilized Indian, attended by two wild ones from the Sierra; a Chinook from the Columbia; and our own mixture of American, French, German—all armed; four or five languages heard at once; above a hundred horses and mules, half wild; American, Spanish, and Indian dresses and equipments intermingled—such was our composition. Our march was a sort of procession. Scouts ahead, and on the flanks; a front and rear division; the pack animals, baggage, and horned cattle, in the centre; and the whole stretching a quarter of a mile along our dreary path. In this form we journeyed; looking more like we belonged to Asia than to the United States of America.[1]

Later that day, the party reached the summit of Oak Creek Pass (4,834 feet), a critical juncture,[2] and one that conjured a bittersweet moment. Though Frémont and his men were glad to be homeward bound, they had, over the past few weeks, found themselves enchanted by the Central Valley's lush landscape and beguiling climate. But now, as they gazed southeast from the crest of the Tehachapi Mountains, the desolate Mojave Desert lay before them; and farther south, running east to west, the rocky San Bernardino and San Gabriel Mountains rose from the desert floor. The plant life they saw later that day, during their descent down the ridge, Frémont recalled, only heightened their concerns:

Crossing a low sierra, and descending a hollow where a spring gushed out, we were struck by the sudden appearance of *yucca* trees, which gave a strange and southern character to the country, and suited well with the dry and desert region we were approaching. Associated with the idea of barren sands, their stiff and ungraceful form makes them to the traveller the most repulsive tree in the vegetable kingdom.

The party's passage through Oak Creek Pass demarcated the end of its search for the San Buenaventura River. Having made a complete north-to-south transit of the region, from the Columbia River to the terminus of the Sierra, Frémont could now consign the Buenaventura

A young—and in this rare portrait, beardless—John Frémont. For the background, American portraitist George P. A. Healy copied an illustration of Wyoming's Wind River Range by Frémont expedition artist Charles Preuss. (Union League Club of Chicago)

A young Jessie Benton Frémont in a portrait by T. Buchanan Read. She shared with her husband keen intelligence, grand ambitions, and a taste for rebellion. (Author's collection)

Senator Thomas Hart Benton in a lithograph by Lehman and Duval based on a drawing by Charles Fenderich. As Frémont's father-in-law, mentor, and political sponsor, the Missouri senator helped to shape the explorer's career. (Henry E. Huntington Library and Art Gallery)

Class roll. As a College of Charleston student, Fremon— as he then spelled his surname—excelled in mathematics and classics but frequently missed classes. He was expelled three months before he was to graduate. Five years later, however, in 1836, the college granted him the degree. Note here the professor's reversal of the future explorer's first and middle names but his prescient spelling of his surname. (College of Charleston)

Joel Poinsett was one of Frémont's earliest mentors. He nurtured Frémont's opposition to slavery and beliefs in Unionism and Western expansion, and, as Secretary of War, secured his first exploring commissions. (Bancroft Library)

The French-born explorer Joseph Nicollet (1798–1843) is depicted in this rare image of unknown origin. During the late 1830s, Frémont assisted Nicollet's map-making surveys of the Upper Mississippi Valley. Through Nicollet's tutelage, the young Frémont polished his skills in geodesy and other exploration sciences. (Minnesota Historical Society)

I stood on a narrow crest, about three feet in width, with an inclination of about 20°, north 51° E. As soon as I had gratified the first feelings of curiosity, I descended and each man for I would only allow ~~one~~ or ascended in his turn, one at a time, to mount the unstable and precarious slab, which it seemed a breath would hurl into the abyss below. We mounted the barometer in the snow of the summit, and fixing a ram rod in a crevice, unfurled the national flag, to wave in the breeze where never flag waved before. During our morning's ascent we had met no sign of animal life, except the small sparrow like bird

A page in Frémont's handwriting from the only remaining draft of his engaging First Expedition *Report* published by the U.S. Senate in 1843. Here, he describes his ascent of what he later named Frémont Peak. (National Archives)

(*above*) Frémont ascending what he incorrectly assumed was the Rockies' highest peak. This heroic portrait appeared in a campaign biography by John Bigelow, designed to bolster Frémont's 1856 presidential bid. (Author's collection)

(*right*) A commemorative stamp issued during William McKinley's presidency in 1898 depicting Frémont triumphantly atop Wyoming's Frémont Peak.

An illustration from John Bigelow's 1856 Frémont biography depicting Frémont trying out an experimental rubber raft along the Sweetwater River's confluence with the Platte. (Author's collection)

Frémont's "Long Camp" in the Sierra Nevada Range, as depicted by Charles Preuss. During the Second Expedition, Frémont and his party were reduced to eating their pack mules and even their mascot dog. (Author's collection)

Artist and topographer Charles Preuss. The irascible German-born artist's maps and illustrations provided a compelling visual complement to Frémont's travel narratives. (Bancroft Library)

to the annals of mythical geography: "No river from the interior does, or can, cross the Sierra Nevada—itself more lofty than the Rocky mountains." With that settled, Frémont, over the next few weeks, would turn his attention toward demarcating his own contribution to the cartography of the West—the Great Basin.

❁

April 17 found Frémont and his weary band of of travelers standing along the banks of a small salt lake set in a lonesome desert valley. It was here, said their guide, that he must pick up the trail to his mission to the south. Before leaving, however, eager to make sure that the white men understood the route he had described, the Indian pointed to a barely visible trail, stretching east across the desert. Then, pointing to a black butte along the same route, he told them that they would find water there and a good campsite for the night. Frémont thanked their friend and, for good measure, before they parted, gave him some knives and scarlet cloth.

Following the Indian's directions, the party commenced their crossing of the Mojave Desert. On April 19, a few miles north of Cajon Pass, near today's Victorville, California, the party struck the trail. Though the landscape was barren, the men were glad to be on the trail. Since last November when they had left the Columbia River valley, the party, as Frémont viewed its situation, had been forced ever southward by mountains and deserts. Now, as the expedition began its passage down the Spanish Trail, Frémont savored the knowledge that they would soon be northbound, and eventually eastbound.[3]

Thirteen miles down the Spanish Trail, the party struck the Mojave River. Cottonwoods, willows, and hearty grass thrived along the river, and the party's animals were looking shriveled, so Frémont ordered that camp be set up there for the night. Though they slept beside a river that night, concerns about the availability of water increasingly weighed on Frémont: between their present position and the Colorado River, he knew that the country offered only isolated pockets of grass and water. Moreover, the recently departed Indian scout had warned that they would face numerous *jornadas* (day's journeys) in which they would go for forty to sixty miles without water. On those *jornadas*, he had said, bones of dead animals constituted the main road markers.

❋

The Spanish Trail—now called the Old Spanish Trail—remains one of the least known of the many trader and emigrant paths that once snaked across the West. From Los Angeles, the main trail climbed through Cajon Pass (4,301 feet, twenty miles north of today's San Bernardino, California), wandered into the Mojave Desert and northeast into the Great Basin, then continued northeast—thus bypassing the Grand Canyon—across the Sevier, Green, and Colorado Rivers of today's Utah, before crossing the Continental Divide in today's northern New Mexico and dropping southeast, down the Rio Chama Valley, to Santa Fe. Though sections of the route dated back to at least the mid-eighteenth century, it never became the object of systematic surveys and mapmaking efforts such as those conducted by Frémont. When he traveled the Spanish Trail, Frémont complained that it often seemed more a rumor than a known passage—a barely marked series of traces connecting an even more dispersed and obscure collection of springs and meadows.

Though, while in California, Frémont had heard many travelers' tales about the trail, most of the information proved unreliable: "The rivers that we found on it were never mentioned, and others, particularly described in name and locality, were subsequently seen in another part of the country." Beyond that, though Frémont had heard the path described as a "tolerable good sandy road, with so little rock as scarcely to require the animals to be shod," once on the trail he "found it the roughest and rockiest road we had ever seen in the country, and which nearly destroyed our band of fine mules and horses."

But luckily for Frémont his timing was good: it was early April, and the annual processions of trade caravans had yet to pass by, which meant that the campsites the explorers did locate still offered abundant water and grass: "A drove of several thousand horses and mules would entirely have swept away the scant grass at the watering places; and we should have been obliged to leave the road to obtain sustenance for our animals."

On April 22, the party was still following the Mojave River; but, though the men were following the stream's downstream course, rather than growing in size, it shrank as the surrounding sands absorbed its waters—typical of Great Basin streams. They camped that night along the river, about sixteen miles southwest of today's Barstow, California.[4] The next morning, as the party continued its passage down the Mojave—which explorer Jedediah Smith called "the inconstant river"—the river's waters entirely disappeared, only to reappear in small pockets another sixteen miles down the otherwise dry riverbed. That afternoon, finding another campground shaded by willows and cottonwoods, they stopped for the night.[5]

April 24 found the party still following the mostly dry Mojave River but camped that afternoon beside a welcome collection of water holes when some visitors came into its midst: two Mexicans, a man and an eleven-year-old boy. Frémont welcomed them into the camp; and later, joining the others by the campfire, the man, Andreas Fuentes, unraveled a horrific tale: he had belonged, he said, to a party of six, traveling with about thirty horses, from Los Angeles. The six belonged to and were traveling ahead of a much larger caravan from Los Angeles; they had gone only as far into the desert as they felt they could safely venture with such a small party, when they decided to stop at the Archilette—today's Resting Springs, California, east of the town of Tecopa—then one of the Spanish Trail's better-known campsites. There, they had planned to await the arrival of the caravan's main party.

Several days later, still waiting for the main caravan party, Fuentes's vanguard party came under attack by a group of perhaps a hundred Indians. As it happened, Fuentes and the boy, Pablo Hernandez, were on horseback on the camp's outskirts when the ambush occurred. Things happened so suddenly that the two could do nothing for their four compatriots. Somehow, however, the two—knowing that it was, in all likelihood, their thirty horses that the Indians wanted—did manage to drive most of their herd to a watering hole, about sixty miles distant, called Agua de Tomaso, today's Bitter Spring, within the Fort Irwin Military Reservation. Without stopping to rest, they then rode west, hoping to meet up with the larger eastbound caravan. They had, in fact, been riding west when they spotted Frémont's campsite and decided to stop. Frémont listened sympathetically to their story, then told them that they could join his party: he would, he promised, feed them and do everything in his power to assist them.

The next day, April 25, abandoning the Mojave River, the party turned north and, within a few miles, regained the Spanish Trail. Desert plains interrupted by black, rocky ridges barren of timber now dominated the course of travel; and, as the party passed dry riverbeds, the men learned to look for holes freshly dug by coyotes, which were able to sniff out subterranean pockets of water. "They were," Frémont recalled, "nice little wells, narrow, and dug straight down, and we got pleasant water out of them."

To Frémont—determined, arid climes notwithstanding, to sustain his vision of the West's ecological variety—even the desert's stunted flora offered unexpected gifts. He was particularly taken with a shrub with bright purple flowers that he identified as a new variety of *Psoralea*—properly known as *Psorothamnus fremontii*: "Throughout this nakedness of sand and gravel, were many beautiful plants and flowering shrubs, which occurred in many new species, and with greater variety than we had been accustomed to see in the most luxuriant prairie countries; this was a peculiarity of this desert. Even where no grass would take root, the naked sand would bloom with some rich and rare flower, which found its appropriate home in the arid and barren spot."[6]

Later that day, after covering over twenty-five miles, the party reached Agua de Tomasa, the watering hole where Fuentes had left his herd of horses. After setting up camp and making a sweep of the area, they concluded that the Indians had driven off the horses. That afternoon, Carson and Godey volunteered to go with Fuentes in search of the thieves and the horses. Early that evening, his horse having given out, Fuentes returned to the camp. Carson and Godey, he reported, were still riding, still searching.

That night, Frémont and Preuss stayed up late to conduct astronomical observations and determined their Agua de Tomaso camp to be at longitude 116°23′28″ and latitude 35°13′08″. Except during December and January, when the expedition's chronometer stopped while they were passing through western Nevada, the two had performed this observational ritual, weather permitting, twice daily since leaving Missouri the previous May. The chronometer had been restarted at New Helvetia—and Frémont had been amazed at how "remarkably well" it had since worked.

As it happened, the chronometer failed again soon after the party left Agua de Tomaso. Though Frémont's sextant still worked, and he continued to take midday readings of the sun to get the expedition's latitude, he would take only five more longitudinal readings during the expedition's remaining days—and those without a chronometer, using only the celestial heavens and his well-worn ephemeris.

✺

With Carson and Godey away, the rest of the expeditionary force remained at Agua de Tomaso a second day. That afternoon—as a loud Indian-style war whoop rang across the camp—Carson and Godey suddenly galloped into view, driving a herd of horses, which Fuentes immediately recognized as belonging to his party. Dangling from the end of Godey's gun, to the expedition's horror, hung two bloody scalps.

Once dismounted, the two told a story as grotesque as their war trophies: Carson and Godey had followed the Indians' trail up a mountain defile. Worried that they might lose the trail in the dark, the two, without building a fire, had settled down and slept in the defile until daybreak. Resuming their search the following morning, they found the Indians' campsite, which consisted of four lodges, and began creeping toward it. But when they came within thirty or forty yards of the camp, a nervous fidgeting of the captured horses alerted the Indians to Carson's and Godey's presence. Undaunted by the apparent numbers they confronted, the two—rifles blazing—charged into the Indians' camp. As Frémont recalled their story:

> The Indians received them with a flight of arrows shot from their long bows, one of which passed through Godey's shirt collar, barely missing the neck; our men fired their rifles upon a steady aim, and rushed in. Two Indians were stretched on the ground, fatally pierced with bullets; the rest fled, except a lad that was captured. The scalps of the fallen were instantly

stripped off; but in the process, one of them, who had two balls through his body, sprang to his feet, the blood streaming from his skinned head, and uttering a hideous howl. . . . The frightful spectacle appalled the stout hearts of our men; but they did what humanity required, and quickly terminated the agonies of the gory savage.

Carson and Godey had quickly gathered the surviving stolen horses—those the tribesmen had not yet slaughtered for the feast they were preparing when the ambush occurred. As if the story required any more pathos, Carson and Godey also recounted how an elderly woman—possibly the mother of the scalped tribesman, attempting to escape by climbing a nearby ledge—had watched the violence in horror from a perch above the fight. To Frémont, Godey and Carson had taught a "useful lesson to these American Arabs"; moreover—in the best Leatherstocking tradition—it marked a triumph of civilization over barbarism:

The time, place, object, and numbers, considered, this expedition of Carson and Godey may be considered among the boldest and most disinterested which the annals of western adventure, so full of daring deeds, can present. Two men, in a savage desert, pursue day and night an unknown body of Indians into the defiles of an unknown mountain—attack them on sight, without counting numbers—and defeat them in an instant—and for what? To punish the robbers of the desert, and to avenge the wrongs [against] Mexicans whom they did not know. I repeat: it was Carson and Godey who did this—the former an American, born in the Bonnslick [sic] county of Missouri; the latter a Frenchman, born in St. Louis—and both trained to western enterprise from early life.

Preuss, however, in his diary, took a different view of the incident:

Are these whites not much worse than Indians? The more noble Indian takes from the killed enemy only a piece of the scalp as large as a dollar, somewhat like the tonsure of a priest.

These two heroes, who shot the Indians [while] creeping up on them from behind, brought along the entire scalp. The Indians are braver in a similar situation. Before they shoot, they raise a yelling war whoop. Kit and Alex sneaked, like cats, as close as possible, Kit shot an Indian in the back . . .[7]

✸

By now, the expedition's path had carried the men deep into the arid desert and mountain country of Frémont's landlocked Great Basin. To lessen their exposure to its punishing sun, he adopted a practice of commencing their march in the late afternoon and traveling through the night.

After passing, on April 28, through a blinding sand gale, the party, the next day, reached and set up camp at the Spanish Trail's famed Archilette meadow. There, it found the mutilated corpses of the two adult men whom Fuentes and Hernandez had left behind. No sign of the two women left at the site could be found—presumably, they had been carried off by the Indian attackers. The next morning, before the expedition departed, its members penned an account of the attack and fastened it to a pole at the site, so that Fuentes's larger caravan party might learn the fate of their missing compatriots.

Continuing their northeasterly march along the Spanish Trail, the party, on May 3, reached a well-known campground of spring-fed streams and fertile meadows called Las Vegas—the meadows. The site, of course, offered none of the opulent casinos and hotels that would later rise there—many along downtown Las Vegas's main drag, Frémont Street. Even so, Frémont found the spot suitably commodious: "Two narrow streams of clear water, four or five feet deep, gush suddenly, with a quick current, from two singularly large springs; these, and other waters of the basin, pass out in a gap to the eastward. The taste of the water is good, but rather too warm to be agreeable; the temperature being 71° in the one, and 73° in the other. They, however, afforded a delightful bathing place."

The party set out early the next morning, and it was just as well—because the horse skeletons littering the trail suggested they faced a long *jornada*. They pushed on all day, hoping with each passing mile to find water. To slake their thirst, they sometimes stopped and cut into the desert's barrel cacti, whose pulp yields a bitterly acidic juice. Finally, after a rough, uninterrupted sixteen-hour march, their hopes rose when their mules began running ahead of the party; and, as Frémont recalled, "in a mile or two we came to a bold running stream—so keen is the sense of that animal, in these desert regions, in scenting at a distance this necessary of life."

The party had reached a stream called Muddy River, in Moapa Valley, two miles west of Glendale, Nevada. The men set up camp there but, after sunrise the next morning, discovered that, in the previous evening's darkness and fatigue, they had selected an unstrategic campsite: the river adjoined them on one side; but on their other side—about fifty yards beyond their camp—a rocky bluff looked down on them, leaving them vulnerable to Indian attack. The explorers could not prevent the Paiute Indians from gathering on the overlooking bluff and making threatening gestures. Assuming these were the same Indians who had murdered the Mexicans, Frémont had men to keep weapons in hand. For good measure, he also had the horses be driven away from the riverbank, where they had been grazing, and back into the camp.[8]

Save for breechclouts, the Indians were naked; and each had his hair gathered into a knot behind his head. Reinforcing what to Frémont's men seemed a fearsome savagery, each tribesman carried a quiver with thirty or forty arrows, as well as two or three arrows in hand. The arrows were tipped, Frémont recalled, with obsidian arrowheads, nearly as hard as diamonds—able, he speculated, to pierce completely through a man's body, killing him instantly. During the day, the Indians stole several animals. Even so, after a chief and several tribesmen bullied their way into the camp, Frémont—seeking to avoid violence—offered them a fatigued horse as a peace gesture. During the chief's visit, he surveyed the camp, and counted aloud the number of men in Frémont's party—there were twenty one. As Frémont recalled the incident,

the elder then gestured to the tribesmen surrounding the camp: "So many," said he, showing the number "and we—we are a great many." "If you have your arms," said he, waving his bow, we have these." I had some difficulty in restraining the people, particularly Carson, who felt an insult of this kind as much as if it had been given by a more responsible being. "Don't you say that, old man," said he; "don't you say that—your life's in danger"—speaking in good English; and probably the old man was nearer to his end then than he will be before he meets it.

But the confrontation never took place, and, the next day, a twenty-mile march took the exploring party to a campsite along the Rio Virgen—the Virgin River—a deep, swift stream, which Frémont called the dreariest river he had ever seen. As their three remaining steers had almost given out by now, Frémont ordered them killed.

That night, Indians watched the party's feast from the shadowed thickets that fringed the campsite. And, over the next few days, as the party continued its northeasterly course up the Virgen, the men noticed tracks of Indians along the river's sandy bottom.

On May 9, the much fatigued party reached an inviting meadow along the river, near today's Beaver Dam, Arizona, where it stopped to camp. As the other men rested, a weary Frémont settled down to arrange plant specimens. It was an ideal spot to contemplate plants, for the expedition had now reached a rich ecological zone, where three biological communities—those of the Mojave Desert, the Great Basin, and the Colorado Plateau—overlap in a banquet of ecodiversity. Even so, fatigued from the day's long march, Frémont soon drifted off to sleep in the hot midday sun.

At sundown, however, Carson woke him with troubling news. Party member Jean Baptiste Tabeau, without Frémont's permission, had ridden back to their previous night's camp in search of a lame mule and had not returned. Both men feared the worst; and, as they spoke, the two noticed a plume of smoke rising from a nearby cottonwood grove—a sight that both Frémont and Carson read as a signal alerting other Indians that a first blow against the white interlopers had been struck.

Determined to find the missing Tabeau, Carson and a small detachment set out that evening. When they returned after nightfall, they reported that they had found the lost mule. Standing in some bushes with an arrow in it, the animal had apparently been left to die by the Indians, who would no doubt be back to butcher it for food. Frémont, Fitzpatrick, and Carson, the next morning, rode to a spot where Carson, at dusk the day before, had noticed a puddle of blood. The puddle connected to a trail of blood, which the party followed for about twenty feet. Tabeau, Carson concluded, had been hit by an arrow, then—judging by the trail of blood and a pair of ruts marking the ground—had been dragged to, and thrown into, the river. Except for a piece of "horse equipment" found at the scene, the three men found no other vestige of their missing friend. The next morning found no Indians in the campsite's vicinity—a development that, to Frémont, indicated that the tribesmen, fearing retribution for Tabeau's death, had shrunk back into the wilderness.

A couple of days later, while hiking along the Santa Clara River—beyond the Beaver Dam Mountains, in the future state of Utah—they enjoyed their first rainshower in twenty-seven days. Though the march was arduous, they savored the increasingly verdant landscape, with its abundance of cottonwoods and good green grass. On May 12, just above their previous night's campsite, their route took the Virgin River's northern fork, Magotsu Creek. Paralleling the stream into the mountains, the party soon found itself atop the dividing ridge separating the Rio Virgen, which drains south into the Colorado, and the Sevier, which flows north and belongs to the Great Basin. Frémont correctly deduced that they were now walking along the eastern rim of the Great Basin.

Crossing the ridge, they immediately reached Las Vegas de Santa Clara, a lush meadow, long regarded as the end, or the beginning, of the desert portion of the Spanish Trail. The site—also known as Mountain Meadows—would, in 1857, became infamous as the place where a group of Mormons and Indians massacred a westbound emigrant party of 120 men, women, and children. Prior to that, however, the meadows were best known as the spot where Spanish Trail caravans traditionally halted for several weeks to rest. Even so, Frémont's party—eager to get home and declining to tarry in the meadows—broke camp the next morning, then descended into a broad valley drained by a tributary of Sevier Lake. The following day, going north, they caught a distant glimpse of the crenellated Wasatch Range, which, at its northern end, rises over the eastern shore of the Great Salt Lake.

The expedition had come full circle—and now Frémont faced some decisions: if getting back to Missouri was his most pressing concern, the men were close to what for Frémont was terra cognita. Their current position, after all, lay only a few days south of the Oregon Trail—and it would be relatively easy to follow it back to Missouri. If, however, exploring more ground remained a priority, there was still plenty of country due east of them that Frémont had yet to see. As it turned out, he would get some expert help in making those decisions.

Shortly after the party left Mountain Meadows, it was joined by the famed Western trapper and explorer Joseph Walker. A boisterous bear of a man—he weighed over two hundred pounds and stood six feet four inches tall—Walker, then in his mid-forties, enjoyed an unrivaled reputation among the West's mountain men. Handsome—invariably described as ruggedly elegant in the loose-fitting, silk-embroidered buckskin coats and jackets that he affected—Walker boasted a personal panache commensurate with his achievements as an explorer.

He had entered the Santa Fe trade in 1820 and, during the early 1830s, led Captain Benjamin Bonneville's expedition's into the Great Basin and California—explorations celebrated in Washington Irving's book *Adventures of Captain Bonneville*. Walker was, in all likelihood, the first white man to visit California's Yosemite Valley; and, in 1834, he had made the first known west-to-east crossing of the Sierra Nevada by a white man—passing over the range at its southern end, at the gap still known as Walker Pass. More recently—the previous September— Walker had passed through Fort Hall, leading a contingent of the Chiles emigrant party; and during his stay, he had conversed with Theodore Talbot, who was, at the time, leading a contingent of Frémont's party.

For the past few days, Walker, traveling behind Frémont with a trade caravan from Los Angeles, had noticed traces of the expedition's passage along the trail. Hoping to throw in with Frémont, he had rushed ahead, alone, to catch up with the exploring party. Frémont was delighted to see Walker. And aware of Walker's reputation as one of the West's ablest scouts, Frémont immediately hired him on as a guide.[9]

On May 16, the party reached a seven-mile-long lake—today, largely dry but still known as Little Salt Lake. Since April 20, the party had traveled 440 miles along the barely marked Spanish Trail. But now, it was time to forsake that established route—which, from Little Salt Lake, struck out northeast across the Markagunt Plateau. Abandoning the trail, the party, with Walker leading the way, now headed northeast, along the foothills of the mountains' western slope—and, soon enough, desert soon gave way to what Frémont considered a more hopeful landscape: "We had now," he recalled, "entered a region of great pastoral promise, abounding with fine streams, the rich bunch grass, soil that would produce wheat, and indigenous flax growing as if it had been sown."

On May 20, still moving along Utah's high plateaus, the party met the famous Ute chief Walkara—or "Walker," as whites called him. Since the 1830s, Chief Walkara—a cunning leader whose skills as a warrior were matched only by his talents as an ironfisted negotiator—had carved out a reputation as one of the West's most powerful Indian leaders. He led daring horse raids in California that brought thousands of stolen horses back to Utah; and he routinely collected tributes from weaker Indian tribes.

On that particular day when Walkara met Frémont and Walker, the chief was traveling with a small party of tribesmen—heavily armed with both rifles and bows and arrows—en route to the Spanish Trail, to exact his annual tribute from the Los Angeles trade caravans. Though Walkara enjoyed a reputation for brazen ruthlessness, Frémont, larding his recollection with characteristic egotism, later recalled their encounter as entirely civil: "He knew of my expedition of 1842; and, as tokons [sic] of friendship, and proof that we had met, proposed an interchange of presents. We had no great store to choose out of; so he gave me a Mexican blanket, and I gave him a very fine one which I had obtained at Vancouver."

Shortly thereafter, a gun accident cost François Badeau his life. But otherwise, the expedition's remaining days proved relatively uneventful. On May 24, the party reached Utah Lake, which Frémont assumed, incorrectly, to be a southern limb of the Great Salt Lake.[10]

❈

By the time Frémont reached Utah Lake, he was absolutely convinced that this vast, largely unmapped country had no outlet to any ocean— and that, in its entirety, it constituted a vast, internally drained "Great Basin." As he would write of that realm in his subsequent *Report*:

> Its existence is vouched for by such of the American traders and hunters as have some knowledge of that region; the structure of the Sierra Nevada range of mountains requires it to be there; and my own observations confirm it. Mr. Joseph Walker, who is so well acquainted in those parts informed me that, from the Great Salt lake west, there was a succession of lakes and rivers which have no outlet to the sea, nor any connexion with the Columbia, or with the Colorado of the Gulf of California.[11]

To Frémont, the Great Basin's deserts and mountains had become more than a physiographic anomaly, more than just the only part of North America not drained by an ocean. In his mind, the region became one of the West's, and North America's, most defining aspects —"a rare and singular feature." For if the heights of the Rockies represented a launch into a sublime of natural grandeur, one rivaling anything in Europe, then the Great Basin and its Native cultures—the Washo, Paiute and other so-called Digger people, so denigrated by whites because of their pursuit of roots and other plant foods—represented another, less ennobling sublime.[12] In Frémont's mind, the Diggers—unworthy of the romantic awe with which whites occasionally viewed Plains Indians—occupied the rock-bottom base of the hierarchic pyramid by which he ranked North America's indigenous peoples.

> The contents of this Great Basin are yet to be examined. That it is peopled, we know; but miserably and sparsely. From all that I heard and saw, I should say that humanity here appeared in its lowest form, and in its most elementary state. Dispersed in single families; without fire arms; eating seeds and insects; digging roots, (and hence their name)—such is the condition of the greater part. Others are a degree higher, and live in communities upon some lake or river that supplies fish, and from which they repulse the miserable *Digger*.

To Frémont, this Great Basin unsettled all previous assumptions about the continent and its peoples—and called for nothing less than a reimagining of the very idea of America and its inhabitants:

> The whole idea of such a desert, and such a people, is a novelty in our country, and excites Asiatic, not American ideas. Interior basins, with their own systems of lakes and rivers, and often sterile, are common enough in Asia; people still in the elementary state of families, living in deserts, with no other occupation than the mere animal search for food, may still be seen in that ancient quarter of the globe; but in America such things are new and strange, unknown and unsuspected, and discredited when related. But I flatter myself that what is discovered, though not enough to satisfy curiosity, is sufficient to excite it, and that subsequent explorations will complete what has been commenced.[13]

✸

By July's end, Frémont and the rest of the party were back at Westport, on the Missouri River. There he arranged local pasturage for his travel-weary animals, to allow them to recoup for the next expedition he hoped to organize. Afterward, he got on a steamboat headed down the Missouri.[14]

THE PATHFINDER 14

W HEN JOHN FRÉMONT'S STEAMBOAT, on August 7, 1844, returned him to St. Louis, he found Jessie, now twenty years old, still waiting for him. For fifteen months she had been haunted by fears of never seeing her husband again. After John's departure in the spring of 1842, Jessie had remained behind in St. Louis, expecting that he would be back by New Year's. That September, bolstering those hopes, two Indians brought her a letter from John, written on the plains the previous June, telling her that, though the exploring party had been delayed by rains, all was fine.

Two months later, she got another report—this one from Henry Lee, one of the men whom Frémont had discharged at Fort Hall. As it turned out, while swimming across a river on his homeward-bound trip, Lee had lost the letters he was carrying. But he told Jessie—neglecting to mention the foul weather, Indian troubles, and dire hunger that had bedeviled the party—that all was generally well with the explorers, news that she promptly passed along to Theodore Talbot's mother, Adelaide: They had perfect success in all their undertakings.

But, of course, neither Lee nor Jessie had any way of knowing that Frémont had prolonged the expedition by dipping south into California. Thus unaware, by February Jessie, expecting John's return any day, had transformed her life into a constant vigil "From the moment I open my eyes in the morning until I am asleep again I look for him," she wrote Adelaide Talbot. "I hurry home from a visit and from church & the first question is, 'Has he come?' "

By the spring of 1844, however, Jessie's optimism was giving way to brooding despair, a melancholy reinforced by a relapse in her mother's health problems and Lily's bout with whooping cough. Moreover, Senator Benton, that March, was injured in an accident aboard the U.S. Navy warship *Princeton*. President Tyler, Benton, and other dignitaries had been gathered on the ship's deck for a ceremonial cruise down the Potomac when a large cannon, during a firing demonstration, exploded. The accident injured numerous people, indeed killed several—including the Navy Secretary Thomas Gilmer and Secretary of State Abel Upshur. Senator Benton, for his part, was bloodied and badly shaken and permanently lost hearing in one ear.

In August 1844, fifteen months after John had departed, Jessie was staying at the home of a cousin whose husband was dying of tuberculosis, when she was roused one morning by a message that John had been spotted around town. Though Jessie initially questioned the report's veracity, it was soon echoed by Gabriel, the Benton family's coachman: he was sure, he said, that, in the previous evening's moonlight, he had seen John—"in his uniform and thin as a shadow"—walking toward the Bentons' home.

Suspecting a ghost, Gabriel recalled, he went out for a closer look—and ended up talking to the returning explorer. Frémont told Gabriel that he was eager to see Jessie and the family but, given the later hour, didn't want to wake up the house. Then, said Gabriel, John wandered off toward town, to await the dawn. As Jessie later recalled:

> The only green spot with trees was the open ground in front of Barnum's hotel, and there he sat on a bench for the slow stars to grow pale. One of the hotel people seeing the uniform came out and hospitably offered a room, when he recognized Mr. Frémont.[1]

✸

Two weeks after John's return to St. Louis, the Frémonts left for Washington and settled back into the Benton-Frémont family's C Street residence. Beyond reveling in his reunion with Jessie and Lily, John also had a chance to catch up with his mother, whom he had not seen in years: "To spare my time and be with me in the family surroundings she came to Washington and remained until the cold weather obliged me to take her back to the South."

Sadly, however, while Frémont had been away, death had claimed three of the most important members of his Washington circle of friends and supporters—Ferdinand Hassler, Senator Lewis Linn, and Joseph Nicollet. It saddened Frémont particularly to learn that Nicollet, his beloved mentor, had died alone, in a Washington hotel room: "It would have been a fitter end for him to have died under the open sky, and be buried, rolled up in a blanket, by the side of some stream in the mountains, than to have had life close in the night and alone at a hotel."[2] Nicollet's life ended in relative obscurity, but today's upper Midwest—particularly the Dakotas, Wisconsin, and Minnesota—abounds in places bearing his name. Indeed, in opening sequence to the 1970s television series *The Mary Tyler Moore Show*, set in Minneapolis, when Mary exuberantly tosses her cap into the air, she is standing in that city's downtown Nicollet Mall.

In Washington, now bursting with new tales of adventures in the Rockies, Oregon, California, and the West's barely known deserts, Frémont found himself much in demand. In quick order, he was received by General Winfield Scott and Secretary of War William Wilkins, The War Secretary, after hearing so much about the explorer, found himself surprised by his guest's youth—but, as Frémont later recalled, he "qualified this by saying that in my case it was a good failing, as young men never saw the obstacles."[3]

❋

Soon after Frémont's return to Washington, he put Preuss to work on the maps. In a Washington house he and his wife had recently purchased, Preuss found plenty of space in which to work. For Frémont, finding suitable work space was not so easy. He was besieged with visitors and letters requesting favors. To obtain needed privacy for his work, he rented a small two-story house a block from the Bentons' C Street residence. There, as Joseph Hubbard—a young astronomer and mathematician hired to calculate the *Report*'s statistical tables and charts—worked on the house's first floor, the Frémonts, settling into work space on the second floor, resumed their former collaboration.

Each evening, John would peruse his notes, thinking about the incidents that he wished to cover the following day. The next morning, at nine o'clock, he and Jessie would arrive at their office, then work straight through until they stopped at one o'clock for lunch. Each day, at that hour, the family's maid arrived with lunch and the couple's daughter, Lily, in tow. Then, often joined by Senator Benton—the only other guest allowed into the house—the family would sit down for a midday meal, invariably cold chicken, biscuits, and fruit. After playing with Lily, John and Jessie would take a walk to the Potomac. "A slight rain, we did not mind—only a rain storm," Jessie remembered. After their walk, John would return to the task of poring over his notes, preparing for the next day's session. "Talking incidents over," as he later recalled, "made her familiar with the minuter details of the journey, outside of those which we recorded, and gave her a realizing sense of the uncertainties and precarious chances that attend such travel."[4]

On occasion, when John and his young assistant, Hubbard, needed to verify an astronomical observation, he would fall asleep, then rise at some ephemeris-appointed wee hour and meet Hubbard on a stone carriage step before a nearby church to visually confirm the location of some moon or planet. After setting up their telescope, the two would sit on the stone slab, their backs against its riser, and wait for the appointed celestial body to appear. Once—after several consecutive nights of watching the two on the stone-step—a deacon living across the street called Senator Benton with, he said, "disagreeable information." As Frémont later recalled:

> He [the deacon] said that several nights he had seen his son-in-law in a state of gross intoxication lying on the pavement in front of the church, and apparently unwilling to allow a more sober companion who was with him to take him to the house.

But Benton, far from being grateful as the deacon had anticipated, instead scolded the man, lecturing him that he had "converted an honorable fact into a damaging falsehood."[5]

The Second Expedition *Report* turned out to be three times longer than its First Expedition predecessor. In March 1845, Frémont formally presented it to the Secretary of War; and, two days later, the

U.S. Senate ordered the printing of five thousand copies of a volume combining the reports from the First and Second Expeditions. Shortly thereafter, Pennsylvania's U.S. senator, James Buchanan—about to become Secretary of State in James K. Polk's newly elected presidential administration—ushered a motion through the Senate calling for an additional five thousand copies. To print the book, the Senate contracted with two Washington newspapers—the *Congressional Globe* and the *Daily Intelligencer*. Aware of public anticipation of the narrative, both papers soon publishing reviews of the new *Report* as well as lengthy excerpts from it; and those were, in turn, quickly reprinted in other papers around the country.

The actual book appeared later that year, won rave reviews, quickly became a best-seller, and was soon followed by privately published editions. Frémont's fame soon stretched from Walden Pond—where Henry David Thoreau, passing his second idyllic year there, found in the explorer's prose fodder for daydreams of pristine prairie flowers—to Germany, where a translated edition of the *Report* fed a voracious public curiosity about the American West.[6] In time, admiring publicity became so great that Frémont acquired a sobriquet, borrowed from the title character of a James Fenimore Cooper novel, that stuck to him for the rest of his life—the Pathfinder.

"They say," Jessie later wrote to John, "that as *Robinson Crusoe* is the most natural and interesting fiction of travel, so Frémont's report is the most romantically truthful."[7] To the expansionist zealots at the *U.S. Magazine and Democratic Review*. Frémont's Second Expedition, in its breadth and observational triumphs, even surpassed Lewis and Clark's epic transcontinental journey of 1804–06. "Certainly as first explorers, they were entitled to great merit," the magazine concluded, "but they lack the science which Capt. Frémont carried into his expeditions." The Cincinnati *Chronicle*, offering similar praise, called the Second Expedition "one of the most daring and romantic among the achievements of modern travellers." As an epochal triumph, the paper singled out Frémont's winter crossing of the Sierra. "It was," the *Chronicle* suggested, "not merely an expedition to Oregon, but it was the crossing of the great North American Andes, in the midst of winter—and a feat far exceeding the passage of the Alps, by the ancient or modern warriors."[8]

Critics, years later, questioned Frémont's title of Pathfinder. It was, however, a term that—except during his 1856 presidential campaign — he neither sought nor used; and, as he readily admitted, during most of his travels, he journeyed down paths blazed by others. What was new in Frémont's reports was their scientific maps and measurements, and their literary voice, transcending the prosaic flatness of previous Western tour books. In their eloquence, their geographic breadth, their attention to the sublime, and their reimagining of the American landscape, his narratives offered a fresh voice in American literature— and an imaginative new continental template for thinking, and writing, about America. Indeed, Frémont's voice sang with the same sense of enchantment with American landscapes that would later resonate in the works of such other varied American chroniclers as Walt Whitman, John Wesley Powell, Robinson Jeffers, Hart Crane, Willa Cather, Mark Twain, Robert Pirsig, John Muir, Georgia O'Keefe, Woody Guthrie, Jack Kerouac, Wallace Stevens, and Bob Dylan.

❋

Like its predecessor, the new *Report* included drawings by Preuss, as well as close to three hundred pages of exhaustive tables, recounting distances covered each day and meteorological and astronomical observations. But, unlike the first *Report*, this one also included a catalog, authored by New York paleontologist James Hall, of rocks collected by the expedition, with numerous engravings of fossil specimens. The *Report*'s catalog of plant specimens, written by John Torrey and Frémont, also featured myriad engravings. In an introduction to the catalog, Torrey noted that "about 1,400 species were collected, many of them in regions not before explored by any botanist." But, he lamented, of those, "more than half" were lost or destroyed before the party's return; beyond that, the *Report*'s publication deadline allowed him insufficient time to review all of the specimens. The explorer's next expedition, Torrey wrote hopefully, would allow Frémont to replace many of the missing specimens; and, in a subtle dig at Frémont, Torrey expressed the hope that the next trip would include a professional botanist, whose collecting activities would give "particular attention" to "the forest trees and the vegetable productions that are useful in the arts, or that are employed for food or medicine."[9]

Not surprisingly, much of the attention surrounding the *Report* focused on the new map that accompanied it. The map's coverage area—stretching from Westport (today's Kansas City) to the Pacific Ocean—depicted the survey routes of the First and Second Expeditions, as well as all the regions and places surveyed in both explorations. And like the earlier map, this one—with lots of white space—depicted only areas that the exploring party had actually surveyed, with one conspicuous exception: Frémont had not surveyed the California coast, but—drawing on the British explorer George Vancouver's 1792–94 marine survey—he included a line tracing the province's shoreline and also showed the province's principal coastal settlements.

The map did have its shortcomings: Frémont mistakenly assumed that Great Salt Lake and, to its south the freshwater Utah Lake constituted a single body of water. The map also mislocated the Sacramento River's headwaters and, like the 1843 map, offered an overly generalized depiction of several mountain ranges; indeed, many of the West's ranges would not be satisfactorily surveyed and mapped until after the Civil War.[10]

Those errors, however, paled beside the documents' larger contributions to geographical knowledge. The new documents continued Frémont's revelation of the West's topographical and ecological variety, as well as his dismantling of Jonathan Carver's symmetrical geography and Stephen Long's Great American Desert. On the latter front, for instance, Frémont—touting the West's agricultural potential—while commenting on the sagebrush that grew throughout the arid Snake River valley, noted that "I have been informed that in Mexico wheat is grown upon ground which produces this shrub; which, if true, relieves the soil from the character of sterility imputed to it." Similarly, Frémont's account of the Great Salt Lake basin—including his description of the region's "fertile and timbered" mountains and valley—was so vivid that Brigham Young, after reading it, became convinced that he had found a Promised Land for his beleaguered Mormon coreligionists; and, in 1847–48, he led them to the lake's shores.[11]

One of the map's most conspicuous achievements lay in a long line of vertical print—arcing like a drawn-string pulled away from California's bow-shaped Sierra Nevada—along the document's far western

side. Its triumphant announcement—whose splendid sense of geographical mystery sounded straight out of a Jules Verne novel—read:

> THE GREAT BASIN: diameter 11° of latitude, 10° of longi-
> tude: elevation above the sea between 4- and 5000 feet: sur-
> rounded by lofty mountains: contents almost unknown but
> believed to be filled with rivers and lakes which have no com-
> munication with the sea, deserts and oases which have never
> been explored, and savage tribes, which no traveller has seen or
> described. See Frémont's Report, pages 275, 6.

Equally important, the map showed no break in the Sierra Nevada
range—no Buenaventura River.

✹

As propaganda for Benton's Path to India, the new *Report* echoed the
senator's preoccupation with the Columbia River as the key to establishing U.S. trade links with Asian ports: "Commercially, the value of
the Oregon country must be great, washed as it is by the north Pacific
ocean—fronting Asia—producing many of the elements of commerce—mild and healthy in its climate—and becoming, as it naturally
will, a thoroughfare for the East India and China trade." Conversely,
the *Report* concluded that California had no role to play on Benton's
Road to India. For by dispatching the Buenaventura into the realm of
myth, Frémont also reached the conclusion that California's two great
rivers, the Sacramento and the San Joaquin, had no links to any Rocky
Mountain watersheds. And in his mind, that absence negated California's value as a future entrepôt for transcontinental and international
American commerce:

> There is no opening from the bay of San Francisco into the in-
> terior of the continent. The two rivers which flow into it are
> comparatively short, and not perpendicular to the coast, but lat-
> eral to it, and having their heads towards Oregon and southern
> California. They open lines of communication north and south,
> and not eastwardly; and thus this want of interior communica-

tion from the San Francisco bay, now fully ascertained, gives great additional value to the Columbia, which stands alone as the only great river on the Pacific slope of our continent which leads from the ocean to the Rocky mountains, and opens a line of communication from the sea to the valley of the Mississippi.[12]

But though nominally touting Benton's Path to India, Frémont was already reshaping that vision. Benton, for instance, had long championed the idea that much of the success of the mouth of the Columbia River as an American port would be driven by the export of locally raised wheat. But Frémont, while conceding that parts of Oregon could support the cultivation of wheat, asserted that the country in general paled when compared to the "Atlantic States" as a source of staple crops. As a place, however, to herd livestock, Oregon would be ideal:

Its grazing capabilities are great; and even in the indigenous grass now there, an element of individual and national wealth may be found. In fact, the valuable grasses begin within one hundred and fifty miles of the Missouri frontier, and extend to the Pacific ocean.[13]

Frémont's major straying from Benton, however, lay in the *Report*'s breadth and emphasis. In explaining its author's peripatetic rambling—Frémont's straying from his original orders into California and other locales—the *Report* often dissembled, contradicted itself, or simply ignored obvious questions. But as a day-to-day account of an extraordinary circumambulation of the continent, it was a vivid document. Of particular interest to the public were Frémont's colorful depictions of the American emigrants, scattered across the Trans-Missouri West, who were, with each new day, building a new world, a new America. Indians, of course, had no place in that new world. Indian removal—as it had been for his mentors Poinsett, Nicollet, and Benton—continued to be the sine qua non of Frémont's comprehension of white settlement in the West. The *Report* tacitly assumed that Indians eventually must disappear from the West's landscape. In the meantime, they existed to be sometimes feared, sometimes traded with, and occasionally admired for their crafts and studied as living artifacts—but, in the end, managed by an ever-growing military presence in the West; and, finally, dispersed into extinction.

Frémont's works won even more currency among emigrants after the Senate, in 1846, issued a series of seven maps—drawn from Frémont's explorations and created by Preuss—depicting, in sections, the entire length of the Oregon Trail, from Westport to the Columbia River. Besides gathering cartographic features from the two previous maps, the seven maps included practical information about where grass, water, game, and campfire fuel might be found, as well as remarks on weather and how to avoid Indian attacks ("Between the Red Buttes and Green River, the war ground of the Indians, particular attention should be paid as to guards and watches!").

Finally, in the Second Expedition *Report* and new maps—both the 1845 map and Preuss's 1846 seven-section map of the Oregon Trail—Frémont exercised, far more aggressively than previously, the explorer's prerogative of naming things. In his First Expedition *Report*, Frémont tended to defer to Indian appellations: "The names given by the Indians are always remarkably appropriate." Even so, that expedition's *Report* and map featured only a handful of Indian names; and unlike his mentor Nicollet, Frémont made no effort to sit down with tribesmen to find out what those names might be, and why. In most cases, he simply appropriated existing place-names, including, quite often, names accorded by earlier explorers—perpetuating, for instance, Lewis and Clark's names for the streams that form the Kansas River: the Republican, Solomon's Fork, the Grand Saline, and Smoky Hill. When, during that expedition, he did coin new names, they tended to be blandly generic—Hot Spring Gate, Goat Island, Island Lake, Snow Peak.

The Second Expedition *Report* and maps, however, found Frémont taking pleasure in branding lots of locales with what he called the "Frémont irons." For instance, Snow Peak, which he had famously climbed during the First Expedition—and which went unlabeled on the map generated from that trip—now became, on the newer maps, the clearly labeled Frémont Peak. Other coinages from the Second Expedition which today persist on modern maps include Summer

Lake, Pyramid Lake, and Lake Abert. Even so, his most prolific place-naming binge would come with his next expedition.[14]

❋

Soon after Frémont's return from the West—as if to punctuate the Second Expedition's triumphs—President Tyler, at General Winfield Scott's suggestion, promoted the young explorer, giving him a double brevet as first lieutenant and captain. By now, Frémont had become an even more-sought-after public figure, and that season's social calendar included engagements with such Washington dignitaries as former president John Quincy Adams; Britain's new minister to Washington, Richard Pakenham; and Massachusetts's U.S. senator Daniel Webster.

At the top of Frémont's busy schedule of dinners and meetings, however, was his and Senator Benton's visit with President-elect James K. Polk. Though Benton had supported former president Martin Van Buren as the party nominee the previous summer, the two hoped to develop a good working relationship. During their meeting, Frémont found a moment to talk about his recent expedition and the need for better geographical knowledge of the West—making his point that, too often, what passed for scientific knowledge about the region lay mired in rumors and legends. To Polk, Frémont recalled how he had recently, at the Library of Congress, drawn out from the map stand a map of North America, which showed once again— shades of Jonathan Carver's symmetrical geography—the Great Lakes connected to the Pacific Ocean by three great rivers, one draining into the Columbia River, another into the Gulf of Mexico, and the third —the Buenaventura—running straight through the Sierra Nevada. But the President-elect seemed skeptical of the young officer's information—seemed to, in Frémont words, respect " 'that ancient chaos' of the western geography as it existed on the old maps." As the explorer later recalled, far from being impressed by Frémont's authority, the President-elect "found me 'young' and said something of the 'impulsiveness of young men,' and was not at all satisfied in his own mind that those rivers were not running there as laid down."[15]

❋

As Frémont, during the summer of 1844, was completing his Second Expedition, political events were pushing expansionist issues to the fore. By that fall, Tennessean Polk had been elected president on a platform calling for the U.S. acquisition of Texas and for U.S. "reoccupation" of Oregon. For Benton and his expansionist brethren, the phrase "reoccupation of Oregon" evoked their long-standing conviction that U.S. title to Oregon had been acquired with the Louisiana Purchase in 1803 and had been frittered away by the U.S.–British "joint occupation" treaty of 1818. Heating up expansionist fevers still more, in March 1845, Congress had passed a joint resolution admitting Texas as a state—a move that most assumed meant war with Mexico.

Congress passed the Texas joint resolution only three days before its author, President Tyler, left office—presidential terms, in those days, ended on March 4. But it would be Tyler's successor who would have to deal with the act's consequences. Mexico's government, after all, had never recognized the independence of the Republic of Texas—still considered it a part of Mexico—and so regarded Congress's action as a bellicose act. Polk thus had inherited a diplomatic situation rife with troubles.

Benton and the new President were not close. Benton opposed two of the key planks in the platform on which Polk had been elected—the annexation of Texas and the settlement of the U.S. dispute with Britain over Oregon's boundary. Still, as one of the Senate's most venerable members, and as chairman of the Senate Military Committee, he remained—regardless of the nature of his relationship with Polk—very much in the middle of events.[16]

Benton enjoyed access to dispatches from U.S. diplomats in Mexico, many of which were translated into English by Jessie in the family's parlor—an arrangement that gave Frémont access to many confidential messages. He knew, for instance, that much of the speculation about possible war with Mexico centered on possible British reactions to such a conflict. Speculation was rife that, in the event of war, Britain would come to Mexico's side and, in the event of victory, take California or—more likely—Oregon for its prize. To preempt such British action, many expansionists believed, the United States must assert itself in the Pacific Northwest.

As Benton and his friends that season assessed the new White House administration, they found an ally in the new Navy Secretary,

George Bancroft. Forty-four years old, Bancroft was an erudite, Harvard-trained historian-turned-politician. During the 1830s, he had been, in his native Massachusetts, an enthusiastic supporter of President Jackson. More recently, he had helped to secure Polk's victory over Van Buren at the previous summer's Democratic Party convention. Once Polk took office, Bancroft quickly emerged as one of the new administration's leading lights—an astute voice to which the President often turned for counsel. Bancroft's work as a historian gave him no particular affinity for the sort of theories of empire that animated Benton. But he did share with Polk, Benton, and Frémont a deep suspicion of Britain, and British intentions in North America.

It had been more than two decades since Britain and the United States had been at war; and, despite disagreements over Oregon and other matters, Britain had given no indication of seeking military confrontation with America. But even in the absence of bellicose statements from London, Englishmen operating in North America were fully capable of stirring Anglophobic anxieties. Theodore Talbot of Frémont's Second Expedition, for instance, recalled how, during his stay, in September 1843 at the Hudson's Bay Company's Fort Hall, the post's proprietor, Richard Grant, had talked "of the country as British, the Indians in it, as serfs of the Hudson Bay Compy [sic], and soforth [sic], in the same strain."[17]

But beyond his anti-British sentiments, Bancroft also saw American territorial expansion as a positive good for the republic, as an adhesive binding its citizens to its social contract. The West's sprawling landscapes offered an opportunity to relieve crowded conditions in America's Eastern cities, resulting from the daily arrival of European immigrants. And building farms and ranches in the West, Bancroft believed, would bond those immigrants to their newly adopted nation. Beyond that, settlers would convert the West into a region of productive agriculture. Reflecting those views, Bancroft consistently advised President Polk to take a tough bargaining stance in his dealings with John Bull.

❋

For Benton and Frémont, Bancroft's appointment proved fortuitous. In contrast to Joel Poinsett, Secretary of War in the most recent Democratic administration—that of Martin Van Buren, who had left office four years earlier—William Marcy, Polk's newly installed War Secretary, had little interest in foreign policy or projects of territorial expansion. Compounding the Western cabal's growing alienation from the War Department, Frémont's recent behavior—particularly the incident with the mountain howitzer—had disenchanted Corps of Topographical Engineer chief John J. Abert. Benton and Frémont thus felt consoled that they did, at least, have the Navy Secretary's support— and he, in turn, had the President's ear. While Benton and his friends welcomed Bancroft's support, their newfound alliance with the Navy put them on what would be, for Frémont, a collision course with the U.S. Army bureaucracy that had once supported his explorations.[18]

❀

Amid growing U.S. anxieties about war with Mexico and a possible renewal of British military activities in North America, Frémont had little trouble obtaining permission to organize another expedition. Curiously, however—though he would later claim to have had an understanding with Benton, the Navy Secretary, and others that he was to enter California—Frémont's official orders from Abert, issued in February 1845, were bland and limited—calling for him to enter Mexican territory, but only for the purpose of surveying the watersheds of various rivers draining the eastern Rockies. Abert's orders not only contained no directive to enter California. They included absolutely no directives of a military nature:

> He will strike the Arkansas as soon as practicable, survey that river, and if practicable survey the Red River without our boundary line, noting particularly the navigable properties of each, and will determine as near as practicable the points at which the boundary line of the U.S. the 100th degree of longitude west of Greenwich strikes the Arkansas, and the Red River. It is also important that the Head waters of the Arkansas should be accurately determined. Long journies [sic] to determine isolated geographical points are scarcely worth the time and the expense which they occasion; the efforts of Captain Frémont will therefore be more particularly directed to the ge-

ography of localities within reasonable distance of Bents Fort, and of the streams which run east from the Rocky Mountains, and he will so time his operations, that his party will come in during the present year.[19]

Over the next two years, Frémont would do his best to balance Abert's orders with the directives—both real and imagined—he carried from Benton, Bancroft, and other expansionists. That challenge, politically, would prove to be a thin line as difficult as any he had before negotiated.

PART IV

THE THIRD EXPEDITION

SUMMER 1845–WINTER 1846

I skirt sierras, my palms cover continents.
—Walt Whitman

GREAT SALT LAKE, GREAT BASIN, AND HUMBOLDT RIVER

PON RECEIVING his new orders from John J. Abert, Frémont, that winter and spring of 1845, plunged himself into a
feverish burst of preparations for his next expedition. The
now thirty-two-year-old explorer managed to persuade his government sponsors that this mission called for a larger and better-equipped
party than those he had led in the past: "For this expedition ampler
means had been provided, and in view of uncertain conditions the
force suitably increased."

Theodore Talbot, who had proven himself a durable leader on the
Second Expedition, signed on to play a key role in the new expedition.
And while Frémont tied up affairs in the East, Talbot went ahead to St.
Louis to gather volunteers and provisions. Bolstered by Frémont's reputation, Talbot had no trouble finding recruits. Indeed, when Frémont
reached St. Louis on May 30, excitement ran so high that he felt
obliged to go into hiding. To fill out the exploring party's remaining
slots, he placed an ad in a St. Louis newspaper, inviting prospective recruits to a meeting inside the local Planters' Warehouse. On the appointed day of the meeting, however, the crowd grew so large and
boisterous that Frémont was forced to move the assembly outside.

By June 4, as the party prepared to leave St. Louis, fifty-five volunteers had signed up. Each was furnished, at government expense, a
Hawken rifle, two pistols, a knife, a saddle, a bridle, and two blankets.
Each man was also given a horse or mule for riding and was put in
charge of two pack animals.[1] At Westport, Frémont recovered his livestock, now healthy and rested after the grueling Second Expedition.
There, he got down to shaping this ragtag collection of men, many of

whom had never seen plains or deserts, into a workable exploring party.

The exploring party included familiar faces from earlier ventures—such as Talbot, Alexander Godey, Auguste Archambeault, Basil Lajeunesse, Lucien Maxwell, Joseph Walker, and Frémont's valet, Jacob Dodson. The party also included Lieutenant James Abert, son of John J. Abert; James McDowell, a cousin of Jessie's; and William, the Chinook Frémont had befriended in the Columbia River Valley. William, having spent the winter in Philadelphia with a Quaker family, now wanted to return to his own people.

The expedition also included nine Delaware Indians recruited in St. Louis. The plight of the Delaware underscored the debilitating trends put in motion by the arrival of Europeans in North America and accelerated by the growing U.S. interest in the American West. A large Algonquian tribe, the Delawares, during the mid-seventeenth century, had lived along the northeastern seaboard. Over successive decades, intertribal rivalries and various European peoples had pushed them increasingly westward. By 1835, most of those who survived found themselves living on a reservation in Kansas. Much of their traditional tribal life having collapsed by the 1840s, many hired themselves out to whites as trappers and hunters.

Conspicuously absent from this outing was Charles Preuss, whose wife had insisted that he decline Frémont's entreaty to accompany the new exploring party. In Preuss's place, acting as the party's topographer, was Edward Kern, a twenty-two-year-old artist from Philadelphia. Kern—idolizing Frémont, like many young men of his generation—considered him, as a young artist on a later expedition put it, "the beau ideal of all that was chivalrous and noble." Hoping to join his idol in the field, Kern had sent Frémont several illustrations and had impressed the explorer as "an accomplished artist . . . His skill in sketching from nature and in accurately drawing and coloring birds and plants made him a valuable accession to the expedition."[2]

❋

Their departure delayed by hard rains, the party, on June 26, finally left Westport on its westward journey. When the men, on August 2, reached Bent's Fort, on the Arkansas River, they found the post abustle with activity: a twenty-seven-wagon caravan of Santa Fe traders was camped outside, and another was expected any day. Also camped outside the fort was a village of Cheyenne Indians, at the post for a peace council with Delaware Indians.

More ominously—underscoring the increasingly charged circumstances under which Frémont was returning to the West—just three days before the exploring party's arrival, the post had hosted Colonel Stephen Watts Kearny and five companies of the U.S. Army's First Dragoons. From Fort Leavenworth, Kearny had taken his dragoons on a wide circle, to South Pass, then dropped south along the Rockies' eastern slope to St. Vrain's and Bent's Forts, before returning to St. Louis. With its show of force, the detail hoped to pacify plains Indians, but, anticipating war with Mexico, it also sought to test the ability of cavalry operating far from supply depots to engage in lengthy operations.[3] How much thought Frémont, upon hearing of Kearny's visit to Bent's Fort, gave to the colonel remains a mystery. But Kearny would soon play a major role in the explorer's life.

❋

At Bent's Fort, Frémont dispatched a separate party, under Lieutenant James (the son of John) Abert and William G. Peck, that was to survey, with Thomas "Broken Hand" Fitzpatrick as its guide, the Canadian River from its source to its junction with the Arkansas, as well as to investigate the Purgatoire River and the source of the Washita River.

From Bent's Fort, Frémont also dispatched a rider to the Cimarron, an Arkansas River tributary, where Kit Carson and another veteran trapper, Richard Owens, had recently established a ranch. At the end of the Second Expedition, Carson had promised Frémont that, if needed, he would be available for a third expedition; and he was as good as his word: he and his friend Owens, upon getting Frémont's message, sold the ranch and headed for Bent's Fort. "This was," Frémont later recalled, "like Carson, prompt, self-sacrificing, and true." Indeed, in Frémont's mind, Carson, Owens, and Alex Godey—all present for the Third Expedition—constituted an exemplary trio:

The three, under Napoleon, might have become Marshals, chosen as he chose men. Carson, of great courage; quick and complete perception, taking in at a glance the advantages as well as the chances for defeat; Godey, insensible to danger, of perfect coolness and stubborn resolution; Owens, equal in courage to the others, and in coolness equal to Godey, had the *coup-d'oeil* of a chess-player, covering the whole field with a glance that sees the best move.

Of course, one has little trouble ascertaining whom Frémont imagined as Napoleon.

❋

Frémont's Third Expedition, now comprising sixty men, departed Bent's Fort on August 16. Four days later, the party made a quick stop in Pueblo and, that night, camped on the Arkansas, at the mouth of Fountain Creek. There, Frémont took observations and established one of the four positions on which depended "the longitudes of the region embraced in the expeditions." August 20 brought them to a settlement called Hardscrabble, where trapper Bill Williams joined the expedition, and where Frémont staged a shooting match among the men, to award several specially made Hawken rifles he had acquired in St. Louis.[4]

September 5 found the party camped beside the Piney River, a tributary of the Grand River, just west of today's Denver, Colorado. "We caught here," Frémont recalled, "a singular fish, which was called buffalo-fish from a hump on the back, rising straight up immediately behind the head." In his later description of the area where he had hooked the fish, Frémont took pleasure in ridiculing an earlier description of the locale as a barren wasteland:

These wood-clothed ranges, with their abundant game and healthful air, we have seen described as "impenetrable deserts whose rugged inaccessibility barred all passage, amid whose parched sterility unfortunate travellers were exposed to death from thirst and hunger."[5]

Moving west, the party forded the Colorado River to the upper White, along which Joseph Walker, fresh from transporting a load of Rocky Mountain fur pelts to Fort Laramie, rejoined Frémont. On October 10, they reached Utah Lake. And after spending three days exploring Utah Lake, the party moved north to the Great Salt Lake.[6]

The lake's waters stood low that season, and Indians along its southern shore informed Frémont that a large nearby island could be reached on horseback. So, on October 18, Frémont, Carson, and a handful of other men left their camp on the lake's southeastern shore and rode out through its briny waters. Exploring the island, Frémont found his way to its highest point and took its latitude—40°58´48´´. During the day, the men found grass, fresh water, and numerous antelope, several of which they killed for food. Today, the island retains the name Frémont gave it—Antelope Island.

Upon leaving, the party encountered an old Indian who had been watching them that day. Gesturing toward the island, the old man informed Frémont that all of the antelope on the island belonged to him and that the white men must reimburse him for the game they had taken. "He was very serious with us," Frémont recalled, "and gravely reproached me for the wrong which we had done him. Pleased with his readiness, I had a bale unpacked and gave him a present—some red cloth, a knife, and tobacco, with which he declared himself abundantly satisfied for this trespass on his game reserve."[7]

Frémont used the two weeks at Great Salt Lake to make a thorough investigation of the area, studying its lacustrine ecology—all the while, mindful of ways in which his own studies might supersede those of past explorers. Stumbling, for instance, across an exposed salt deposit along the headwaters of a mountainous stream above the lake's eastern shore, he noted:

> It was found by us in the place marked by Humboldt on his map of New Spain as derived from the journal of the missionary Father Escalante, who towards the close of the last century attempted to penetrate the unknown country from Santa Fé of New Mexico to Monterey of California. But he does not seem to have got further in his adventurous journey—and this at that time was far—than the south end of the Timpanogos.

Late that October, shortly before the party left the Great Salt Lake, veteran trapper Bill Williams left the expedition, leaving Kit Carson and Joseph Walker as its most experienced scouts.[8]

❋

By now, time and winter's onset increasingly weighed on Frémont. And, haunted by the travails of his winter 1843–44 crossing of the Sierra Nevada, he was eager to cross that range before snows blanketed it. But what was the quickest route to California? From all of the mountain vantages around the Great Salt Lake, the view to the west presented endless mountains. After contemplating the matter for several days, Frémont selected a route over a flat, sagebrush-filled plain. The expanse—the Great Salt Lake Desert—loomed before them, dry and forebidding. Local Indians told Frémont that no one had ever crossed it; and among the exploring party, only Walker had any familiarity with it—and that only as a lost man in 1833.

One afternoon, while gazing down his intended line of travel, Frémont had spotted a solitary towering peak that appeared to be some fifty to sixty miles distant. Almost like an obelisk in its starkness, the peak seemed like a reasonable destination for the first leg of their foray across the Great Basin. After inducing a local Indian to go along as a guide, Frémont ordered Carson, Archambeault, and Maxwell to set out at night for the mountain. If they found water there, they were to build a signal fire; Frémont and the rest of the party would leave the next day and, after making a single camp in the desert, reach the mountain the following day.

Carson's party set out that night, and Frémont and his men followed the next afternoon. Frémont's men, encamped on the desert on their first night away from the Great Salt Lake, built a fire to alert Carson's party to their location. Near daybreak, they were awakened by the jangling of Archambeault's spurs as he rode into camp with news that Frémont's hunch had proven correct—the mountain did offer abundant water, grass, and wood. The party quickly broke camp and soon joined Carson and company at the foot of the mountain that Frémont named Pilot Peak—even today a conspicuous landmark along U.S. Interstate 80.

On November 1, the party resumed its journey. Though deep in the Great Basin, the men's travel was eased by the basin-and-range system that dominates the region. Here, tectonic pressures had stretched the landscape to the point of cracking. As those cracked pieces slowly sank, a corduroy-like succession of fault-block mountains, plains, and valleys was created across the Great Basin—for the explorers, a fortuitous result. Rather than having to struggle over the mountain ranges stretching across the region, the men simply bypassed them through connecting valleys.

Though now moving at a good pace, Frémont worked to balance his desire to observe the country against his worries about being overtaken by winter. Thus, while encamped at a place that he named Whitton Springs after one of his men, but that is now called Mound Springs, Frémont once again divided the expedition into two parties.

The larger party—led by Talbot, guided by Joseph Walker, and with Edward Kern acting as topographer—would move west through the Great Basin along the Mary's River—later renamed the Humboldt by Frémont—toward the Sierra. This route along the Humboldt River—later called by Mark Twain "the great highway of the West"— had already been explored during the 1820s by the Hudson's Bay Company's Peter Ogden. Whether or not Frémont knew of Ogden's exploration remains a mystery. But if he was aware of it, then Frémont's renaming of the river after his idol, the German geographer Alexander von Humboldt, constitutes one of his most arrogant acts. For Ogden had already named the river after his wife—named it the Mary's River.

✸

The plan was that, while the larger party followed the Humboldt River, Frémont's smaller party would dip southwest, bending away from the California Trail toward a large salt lake near today's Hawthorne, Nevada. This body of water, which Frémont later named Walker Lake, would be their point of rendezvous. Frémont's short-cut later became infamous after scout Lansford W. Hastings began publicizing it as the Hastings Cut-Off and leading emigrant parties along it—including the ill-fated Donner party of 1846. That summer, a series of time-consuming misadventures along the route caused the Donner party to become tragically trapped in the winter Sierra, where they eventually succumbed to starvation and cannibalism. The Donner experience discredited the route for several years, but the California gold rush of 1849 soon brought it back into use.⁹

✤

Frémont's smaller party consisted of ten men—including several of the Delaware hunters. As the party marched south, the hunters tended to scatter out, away from the main brigade, scouring the country for game, then firing a signal shot anytime they encountered anything of interest. One afternoon, the party startled a solitary Shoshone Indian as he prepared a stew of squirrels in a small earthen pot. Fearful for his life, the surprised Indian offered Frémont a sampling of his campfire fare, an invitation the captain declined. Before the expedition moved on, however, Frémont—upon learning that several Delawares had confiscated the Shoshone's bow and arrow—ordered the weapons returned.

Several days later, at another campsite—named Sagundai after the Delaware who had found the spot—Frémont's men had just finished a lavish feast of elk and were drifting off to sleep when Carson noticed an elderly, emaciated Indian woman, nearly naked, standing over their fire. Stumbling toward the fire, she had mistakenly thought the gathering an encampment of her own people and had already commenced speaking in her own tongue when she realized her error.

She moved to run away, but the men obstructed her. Later, as her fear gave way to cold and hunger, she indicated that she had been abandoned by her tribe and left to die because she was old and no longer able to gather food. The men in the exploring party gave her a substantial portion of their elk, intending for her to roast it over their fire. Instead, clutching the meat, she darted away, disappearing into the surrounding darkness. "Starvation," Frémont recalled, "had driven her to us, but her natural fear drove her away as quickly, so soon as she had secured something to eat." Before leaving the next morning, the men left behind, for her, their still burning fire and a small supply of pine nuts gathered in the mountains.

✤

That fall of 1845, as the exploring party pushed across the desert, the task of looking for passes that might offer water and grass slowed its progress. November 8 found the explorers at a creek just south of to-day's Elko, Nevada, that Frémont named Crane's Branch, after the Delaware Indian who had found the site. As Frémont later recalled, the names of his desert camps in this country record "the rivalry of the men in finding good camps. It was the recurring interest of each day to prove their judgment of country as well as their skill as hunters." But many of the names Frémont sought to leave upon that arid terrain fell victim to the same vagaries of memory and hubris that removed Mary Ogden's name from the Humboldt River. More than a century after Frémont camped along it, his Crane's Branch is now lost to us. A re-cent guess is that Frémont, that evening, camped on Twin Creek or nearby Huntington Creek.[10]

The party crossed the Ruby Mountains via Ruby Pass and dropped into Diamond Valley, where, on November 11, it camped at Connor Spring, named after another of the Delawares. Still drifting southwest, the party dropped below today's Eureka, Nevada, then crossed the Monitor and Toquima ranges. They then crossed Big Smoky Valley and followed the eastern slope of the Toiyabe Mountains, making a path around the range's southern terminus.

They were now approaching Walker Lake and, by November 24, were camped along its eastern shore, where, four days later, Edward Kern's larger main party joined them. That night, after dinner, Frémont sat down with Kern, Carson, Godey, and his other best men and proposed yet another division of the party: the next morning, Frémont's small party, with Kit Carson guiding it, would move north to find a suitable pass over the Sierra and, beating the snow if all went as planned, find their way to Sutter's Fort.

The larger party, under Talbot, with Walker guiding the way, would move south, along the Sierra's eastern slope; then, via the pass that Walker had discovered ten years earlier, the party would push over the range into the California Valley. They would meet deep in the southern stretch of the San Joaquin valley, on what Frémont called the "Lake Fork of the Tularé Lake"—on today's King River at its junction with Tulare Lake, then the West's largest freshwater lake. In periods of high water, Tulare Lake once sprawled over more than seven hundred square miles, but today—thanks to modern water di-version projects—farmland covers almost all of the old lake bed. From there, the entire party would ride up the Central Valley, to its northern terminus. Frémont would thus have surveyed the valley's entire length and mapped two more Sierra passes.

The two parties separated again, on November 29; and, Frémont's party began working its way up the Truckee River, apparently following ruts left by the Stevens-Townsend emigrant party of 1844–45. Once again, Frémont found himself on a well-worn path.[11]

THE OPENING CLEAR BEFORE ME

16

O N THE AFTERNOON of December 4, 1845, Captain John Frémont and the fifteen men remaining with him—those not in Theodore Talbot and Joseph Walker's southbound party— pitched camp along the upper Truckee River, their planned route of ascent into the Sierra. As the chilled shadow of the range's steep eastern slope darkened their camp, Frémont turned his gaze toward the distant, snowy pinnacles. At sundown, the temperature stood at 34 degrees; as the mercury dropped during the night, recollections of the previous winter's Sierra crossing mingled with a sense of relief. "Our effort had been to reach the pass before a heavy fall of snow, and we had succeeded," he later recalled. They planned to resume their march in the predawn hours. But, if treacherous weather threatened, Frémont was prepared to decamp immediately. "All night we watched the sky, ready to attempt the passage with the first indication of falling snow."[1]

But the weather held, and the ascent began, as scheduled, before first light. As before, the Sierra's rocky steep eastern slope proved arduous. Clear skies, however, raised their spirits: "On our way up, the fine weather which we had left at the foot of the mountain continued to favor us." By sunrise, they stood at the crest of what is now known as Donner Pass—"7,200 feet above the sea, the sky perfectly clear, and the temperature 22°."

Frémont, mindful of how quickly mountain storms can gather, had no intention of dallying in the high country: "There was no snow in the pass, but already it showed apparently deep on higher ridges and

mountain tops."[2] The descent of the more gradual western slope began on an emigrant road, along the Bear River. But when that route
became difficult, the party turned south, into a grassy mountain
meadow, where it camped for the night. Following a north-south ridge,
the march resumed the next morning, soon entering a forest of towering pines. For Frémont, "the tall red columns standing closely on the
clear ground," as they filtered the sun's light, simulated "the dim religious light of cathedral aisles." Further brightening his spirits was the
satisfaction that "we had made good our passage of the mountain and
entered now among the grand vegetation of the California Valley.
Even if the snow should now begin to fall, we could outstrip it into the
valley."

Descending now along a series of smaller, less rugged spur ridges,
the men dropped four thousand feet within a few hours: "The country
became low and rolling; pines began to disappear, and varieties of oak
. . . became the dominating forest growth." The villages of local Indians, who relied on acorns as a principal food source, were scattered
through the oak forests: "They select places near the streams where
there are large boulders of granite rock, that show everywhere holes
which they had used for mortars in which to pound the acorns." In one
Indian settlement, a scattering of several huts, Frémont found time to
stop and sample the local fare—"the sweetest and best acorns, somewhat resembling the taste of Italian chestnuts." By that evening, December 8, Frémont and his cohorts had descended to an elevation of
five hundred feet above sea level. Under clear skies, with the temperature at 48 degrees at sunset, they camped for the night, beside a
stream that Frémont named Hamilton's Creek.

With Sutter's Fort now within a few days' ride, the men enjoyed
the luxury of a less strenuous pace: "After the rough passage and
scanty food of the [Great] Basin these lovely spots with the delightful
spring weather, fresh grass and flowers, and running water, together
with the abundant game, tempted us to make early camps." A few
days later, the men were in sight of Sutter's Fort. As the rest of the
party waited behind at the camp, Frémont and Kit Carson rode to the
fort.[3]

❀

When Frémont, in December 1845, returned to the Mexican province of Alta California, political crosswinds were battering that vast, sparsely populated realm. Spain's nominal rule of California, begun in 1797, had ended in 1821, with the victorious Mexican Revolution. Madrid, however, during its long reign, had shown only sporadic interest in California—and then only as a distant military buffer on the northwestern frontier of New Spain, Madrid's New World empire. Spain's outposts in Alta California—four presidios, various scattered pueblos (civil municipalities), a string of missions along the coast— lived geographically and administratively apart from the rest of Spain's overseas empire.

The province's ambitious landowners and merchants experienced their predicament as a sort of twice-removed colonialism—a compounded sense of estrangement from both Spain and New Spain. That, in turn, nourished an ardor for the sort of free-trade and liberation movements that were reshaping other Spanish colonies. Even after revolution had given Mexico's republicans title to California, the sense of isolation and neglect continued to grow. For those living within the far northern frontier of Mexico, the promise of more autonomous government under the new republican government was never realized. Alta California, along with Baja California, New Mexico, and Texas, continued to languish as provinces, ruled directly by Mexico's congress with appointed governors controlling both civil and military affairs. The screws grew tighter still after 1836, when a new constitution—converting all states and provinces to departments— centralized Mexico City's rule throughout the nation, singling out California and New Mexico, because of their frontier conditions, as requiring particularly strong central-government oversight.[4]

Immigration to California during Mexico's rule was never plentiful. In a lame attempt to reverse that trend, the Mexican government, between 1825 and 1830, shipped 150 convicts to California. Many of the soldiers posted at the province's presidios were recruited from Mexican jails. Frequently unpaid, the conscripts were left to steal from the local citizenry, exacerbating ill feelings between rulers and ruled.

Commencing in 1825, as an outgrowth of the Mexican Revolution's anticlericalism, the ongoing secularization of California's twenty-one Franciscan missions and the withdrawal of public support for their upkeep reinforced the sense of malaise. The missions, after all, had been the main foundation of white settlement in the province. They had also helped to foster stable relations between Mexican citizens and Indians. But lacking public support, the missions soon fell into disarray. Whites and Indians who had been materially dependent on the settlements were compelled to look elsewhere for their livelihood. That quest became more difficult as successive California governors awarded, in the form of vast land grants, former mission properties to prominent supporters. For a select few, the land grants led to the rise of a lucrative economy of ranchos devoted to the raising of cattle for the tallow and hide markets. But for most Californios—Spanish-speaking Californians of European ancestry—the rise of the rancho economy only made life harder.

Political instability at both the federal and provincial levels also demoralized Californios. Mirroring ongoing turmoil in Mexico City, California, between 1822 and 1846, had twelve appointed governors. By December 1845, when Frémont returned to California, the province had recently witnessed the ousting of Manuel Micheltorena, California's last governor to be sent from Mexico. Micheltorena had angered many Californios by attempting to curry favor by dispensing land grants to John Sutter, John Marsh, and other wealthy Americans and Europeans living in California.

Micheltorena's ouster, however, only produced more discord. The provincial capital was moved from Monterey to Los Angeles. Governor Pío Pico, ruling from Los Angeles and nominally in charge of the province's legislation, became civil governor. José Castro—holding forth in Monterey and controlling the customhouse and treasury—became its *comandante*. As hostilities between Pico and Castro deepened—threatening to divide the province into two rival northern and southern fiefdoms—governmental ties to Mexico grew even frailer.

California, for all practical purposes, had become an independent nation-state on the brink of civil war. As the *Niles National Register*, that June, described the relationship between provincial officials and Mexico City, "They have no communication with Mexico, and are, in fact, independent of her." By 1845, the province's estimated population included fewer than 100,000 Indians, approximately 14,000 *gente de razón*—European Spaniards and people of mixed blood—and around

680 foreigners—for the most part, American-born immigrants.[5] Although many of the Americans had taken on Mexican citizenship and enjoyed cordial relations with local officials, there was growing discontent among California's English-speaking population.

That discontent would grow louder, that year, as another five hundred American emigrants on the Oregon Trail, upon reaching Fort Hall, elected to dip south down the California Trail and west over the Sierra, arriving in the province with hopes of establishing themselves as ranchers or in business.[6] By July 1845, their numbers had grown so large that Governor Pico feared an insurgency by Americans against California's fragile government. As the *Niles National Register* reported, "There will soon be more Yankees than Mexicans there, and they will, most likely, establish a government of their own, entirely independent of Mexico." To quash that possibility, Pico issued a formal ban on the further introduction into California of families "from the Missouri and the Columbia."[7]

A week later, he called for volunteers to erect defenses in all of the province's northern towns. To get a firsthand view of conditions, Pico, in November, conducted a military tour of northern California. Most of the settlers, he concluded, seemed industrious and free of seditious inclinations. Even so, he decided that, henceforth, the foreigners could remain in the province only on a provisional basis—a conclusion that increased ill feelings among the American settlers.

✳

From the outside, the growing anxieties nourished a perception that California was ripe for foreign conquest, with Britain, France and the United States, in particular, considered potential suitors. Ominously, on March 3, 1845—two weeks before Micheltorena was sent packing—outgoing U.S. President John Tyler signed the joint congressional resolution calling for U.S. annexation of the Republic of Texas, which Mexico still regarded as one of its northern provinces. By annexing Texas through joint congressional resolution, annexation advocates avoided having to get the two-thirds vote the Senate would need to ratify a treaty. Mexico, meanwhile, had vowed that any move by Texas toward U.S. annexation would bring war. Many in Washington, including Tyler's successor, James K. Polk, privately welcomed hostilities. Through war, or the threat of war, with Mexico, Polk reasoned, the United States could gain secure title over Texas and obtain—by conquest or purchase—Mexico's northern provinces of New Mexico and Alta California.

Polk desired California mainly for its access to the lucrative Pacific trade—a trade made more enticing after 1844, when, in the wake of the Opium War, five Chinese "treaty ports" opened to U.S. commerce. Beyond that, the President held the view, shared by many Democrats, that, if the United States failed to act, California would fall into British hands.

✸

On California and the perceived British claim to it, Senator Benton and Polk saw eye to eye. By now, Benton was prepared to welcome California into his vision of American empire, and he believed that the growing number of American emigrants made U.S. acquisition of the province inevitable. Fearing possible British action, Benton, in an October 1845 White House meeting, urged the President to enforce the Monroe Doctrine's strictures against the establishment of any new European colonies in the Western Hemisphere—particularly in California.

During their meeting, as Polk recalled in his diary, he and Benton also found time to discuss the senator's son-in-law's next exploring expedition:

> Some conversation occurred concerning Capt. Frémont's expedition, and his intention to visit California before his return. Col B. expressed the opinion that Americans would settle on the Sacramento River and ultimately hold the country. The conversation on the subject of Foreign Colonization closed by a general remark that no new Foreign Colony could be permitted on any part of the North American Continent, on which there seemed to be an agreement.[8]

The precise content of Polk and Benton's "conversation . . . concerning Capt. Frémont's expedition" remains a mystery. Neither left behind any more forthcoming recollection of what was said. Suffice it to say that the meeting and Frémont's subsequent actions in California probably yielded as many conspiracy theories as any other conversation in U.S. history.

❁

After Congress's joint resolution calling for the annexation of Texas failed to ignite war, Polk resorted to military provocation. In May 1845, two months before Texas officially accepted the U.S. annexation offer, the President was already trying to advance national interests by making Texas's long-standing border dispute with Mexico official U.S. business. He put U.S. warships off Texas's coast and ordered U.S. troops to occupy disputed lands below the Nueces River.

White House concerns about California also grew. On October 11, Polk received a report that Mexican troops, at England's suggestion, were being sent to California. Similar dispatches during that same period from other correspondents also alarmed the President. "Every thing coming from California, excites great interest here in the English circles," warned Dr. William S. Parrott, a secret agent in Mexico. "The British Legation is all alive on such occasions." There were reports that England was gathering a squadron in the Pacific to seize California in the event of U.S. war with Mexico; and that England was supporting a plan to settle Irish immigrants in California and establish the province as a British "protectorate."[9]

A letter the previous June from Navy Secretary George Bancroft to John Drake Sloat, commander of the Navy's Pacific Squadron, warning of possible war with Mexico, had asserted that, if the squadron commander should "ascertain with certainty, that Mexico has declared war against the United States," he should seize San Francisco and as many other California ports as his ships could reach. Sloat's new orders, sent in October, stated that he need not await a formal declaration of war. Another letter went to Consul Thomas Larkin, in Monterey, naming him a confidential agent and asking that he report on any evidence of foreign intrigue in California.[10]

❁

Having set military preparations in motion, the President then turned to diplomacy. In November 1845, as Frémont and his men were crossing the Great Basin, Polk dispatched diplomat John Slidell to Mexico City. Publicly, Slidell's mission called for him to negotiate the Texas boundary, and to arrange for the collection of outstanding claims of some three million dollars owed to American citizens whose properties had been destroyed or confiscated during the Mexican Revolution. Secretly, however, Slidell carried other instructions: to use the outstanding U.S. claims as leverage to entice cash-strapped Mexico to sell both New Mexico and California.

President Polk, when addressing U.S.–Mexican tensions and dispatching orders, tried to take into account the vast expanses of time and distance that lay between Washington, Mexico City, and other far-flung destinations. An order from Washington, after all, took weeks, often months, to reach its intended recipient in the field. In framing directives, Polk thus had to consider how such lapses in time before an order's arrival would alter the circumstances for which it was conceived. Toward that end, he sought to cast orders in a manner that gave field officers sufficient flexibility to accommodate changed conditions.

✸

That caveat concerning orders applied even more to Frémont, about whose precise whereabouts the President could only speculate. Frémont, in turn, was equally in the dark about the latest turns in U.S.–Mexico tensions. He had left St. Louis before Slidell was dispatched to Mexico. And as the explorer, in December 1845, reentered California, he, in all likelihood, had only vague notions about the current state of affairs between the United States and Mexico. Whatever he knew, it certainly gave him no pause about reentering Mexican territory.

Across the vast West, orally transmitted information enjoyed a life of its own; among the region's non-Indian residents and sojourners, ill-founded rumors frequently filled the gap left by the absence of promptly and regularly transmitted written communications. As California's first English-language newspaper, the *California Star*, would observe a few years later:

No where, we are confident, did ever rumor originate and circulate more freely, yet so singularly as in . . . California. To-day, a rumor arrives and remains undisputed; to-morrow, it is added to, or succeeded by another equally absurd, though perhaps altogether different in nature from the first, but to trace either to their origin would puzzle the shrewdest member of the bar, and defy the most scientific cross-questioner that ever wearied and annoyed a witness.[11]

Operating in the remote, sparsely settled West, government officials, soldiers, and others faced lapses counted not in weeks, but in months. And, as Frémont would soon learn, those lapses often became as important as a message's actual substance.

❀

Johann August Sutter had shown Frémont generous hospitality during the last visit to the fort. Even so, a brittle ambivalence riddled the explorer's feelings toward the Swiss entrepreneur. Frémont remained mindful that his host held appointed office in—and was, in complicated ways, reliant upon—the government of Mexico. On a more personal level, Frémont also recalled when Sutter had tried and acquitted the men in the Second Expedition exploring party accused by Frémont of stealing sugar; and afterward had hired several of them.

This time, when Frémont visited the fort, Sutter was away on business. John Bidwell, who had come to California in 1841 with the first overland party of Americans to reach the province, was left in charge. To Bidwell, then, Frémont—eager to replenish his supplies and to move on—listed his needs, an enumeration that included sixteen mules, flour, and saddles. He also requested the use of the fort's blacksmith shop to shoe his mules. Bidwell later recalled telling Frémont that he could fill only part of the order—"that we had no mules, but could let him have horses, and could make the pack-saddles; that he might have the use of a blacksmith's shop, but we were entirely out of coal."

According to Bidwell, Frémont reacted badly to that explanation—perceiving political motives behind the fort's inability to fill all of his requests: "He became reticent, and, saying something in a low tone to Kit Carson, rose and left without saying good-day, and returned to his camp." When Bidwell, later that day, hoping to assuage wounded feelings, rode out to Frémont's camp, he found the captain beyond consolation; as Bidwell later recalled, "he stated, in a very formal manner, that he was the officer of one government and Sutter the officer of another."[12]

Bidwell eventually did provide fourteen mules, some cattle, food for the exploring party, and the services of a blacksmith. For his own mount, Frémont selected a horse "reclaimed" from a wild herd. Thus resupplied, the party left Sutter's Fort on December 14.

When Sutter returned three days later, he promptly notified Mexican officials of Frémont's presence in California. To General Mariano Vallejo, he reported that Frémont had plans to spend the winter in California's benign climate before returning to Oregon. Always eager to keep all lines of alliance open, Sutter wrote another letter announcing Frémont's return to California, this one to U.S. Consul Thomas Larkin.[13]

❋

From Sutter's Fort, Frémont's party rode south for its rendezvous with Talbot, Walker, and the expedition's main party. Frémont knew the route from his earlier passage through the San Joaquin valley; most of the way, it hugged the Sierra foothills that rise along the valley's eastern edge. The rainy season, which commences in November, had not yet begun, so the men had little trouble fording the various bodies of water that lace the country: "We crossed wooded sloughs, with ponds of deep water, which near the foothills are running streams with large bottoms of fertile land; the greater part of our way being through evergreen, and other oaks."[14]

By December 19, the explorers had reached the headwaters of the Mariposa River. Along its banks, the men noticed a deeply worn trail of fresh horse tracks: "These and indications from horse-bones dragged about by wild animals, wolves or bears, warned us that we were approaching villages of Horse-thief Indians." The thieves, Frémont assumed, were coastal Indians once attached to Franciscan settlements, who, since the demise of the mission systems, had taken to stealing horses from coastal Mexican ranchos, and driving them into the mountains, partly to use as saddle horses, but principally to eat.

Fearing an Indian attack, Frémont dispatched Owens, Maxwell, and two of the Delaware Indians to ride ahead as scouts. But as signs of an Indian presence grow, Frémont decided to make an early halt for the day, beside a small stream, in an oak grove littered with horse bones, apparently the site of a recent Indian encampment: "We had barely thrown off our saddles and not yet turned the horses loose, when the intermittent report of rifles, in the way one does not mistake, and the barking of many dogs and sounds of shouting faintly reaching us, made us quickly saddle up again and ride to the sounds at speed. . . . In a short half mile we found ourselves suddenly in front of a large Indian village not two-hundred yards away. More than a hundred Indians were advancing on each side of a small hill, on the top of which were our men where a clump of oaks and rocks amidst bushes made a good defense." Owens, Maxwell, and the two Delaware Indians, before scampering up the hill, had dismounted and left their horses at its bottom; the Indians, meanwhile, who had the four men surrounded, were preparing to steal the explorers' horses when Frémont and his men rode into view: "Our shout as we charged up the hill was answered by the yell of the Delawares as they dashed down the hill to recover their [the explorers'] animals, and the report of Owens' and Maxwell's rifles."

As Frémont and his men rescued the scouts and their horses, Owens shot and killed one of the Indians. Several angry tribesmen then followed the party back to camp and, in Spanish, verbally harangued them for several hours—threatening another attack, with greater numbers, the next morning. Although Frémont divided the party into two watches who stood guard through the night, "Before midnight the Indians had generally withdrawn, only now and then [making] a shout to show us that they were on hand and attending to us."

The next morning came and went with no attack. Even so, Frémont concluded it prudent to alter the party's course from the forested foothills into the valley's open plains.

The men broke camp and rode "but a little distance" before they faced yet another confrontation. Close to where the San Joaquin River rolls out of the Sierra into the valley, the men spotted an Indian rushing toward them on horseback. Maxwell, riding ahead of the main party, assumed the Indian to be the advance rider of a larger, hostile party. At a full gallop, he began riding toward the lone Indian; and Frémont, Godey, and two of the Delawares quickly followed. "It was open ground over rolling hills," Frémont recalled, "and we were all in sight of each other, but before we could reach them a duel was taking place between Maxwell and the Indian—both on foot, Maxwell with pistols, the Indian with arrows. They were only ten or twelve paces apart." Frémont reached the combatants just as a single shot from one of Maxwell's pistols killed the Indian. "I would have taken him prisoner and saved his life," Frémont later claimed.[15]

❈

Taking the dead Indian's horse, the party continued its southeasterly course, "keeping a few men towards the mountain to give early notice of the approach of any Indians." On December 22, they reached the wide, timbered alluvial plain of the Tularé Lake River—today's King's River—their appointed point of rendezvous with the Talbot-Walker party. There, the men camped to wait for the missing party to arrive; besides, Frémont wrote, "the men, as well as the cattle and horses, needed rest."

Walker's party failed to show, and, on December 24, Frémont's men broke camp and rode west, following the King's River toward its Sierra headwaters. As they climbed higher into the mountains, reaching elevations of more than ten thousand feet, they became caught in an alpine blizzard. The men managed to keep their horses, but were forced to abandon the entire herd of cattle they had acquired from Sutter.

Moreover, the plight of the Walker-Talbot party, for which they were searching, weighed heavily on them. Frémont and the men marked New Year's Eve 1845 in their Sierra snowstorm: "The mountain winter had now set in, and we had some misgivings as we rode through the forest, silent now without a sound except where we came within hearing of water roaring among rocks or muffled under snow." When the storm passed, the men made their way back to Sutter's Fort.

❋

Reaching Sutter's Fort on January 15, Frémont consoled himself with the assumption that no harm had come to the missing Talbot-Walker party: "They were too strong to have met with any serious accident and my conclusion was that they had traveled slowly in order to give me time to make my round and procure supplies."

A Frémont letter to Jessie, that same month, painted a sunny portrait: "All our people are well," he assured her, "and we have had no sickness of any kind among us." Reflecting on past difficulties, he offered stoic rectitude: "Many months of hardships, close trials, and anxieties have tried me severely, and my hair is turning gray before its time. But all this passes, *et le bon temps viendra*."

The letter also depicted with enthusiasm the achievements of the current survey. As policymakers in Washington and American settlers in California contemplated possible U.S. acquisition of California, Frémont was already thinking about ways to physically link his most recent survey work with the new American clamor for California.

Anticipating, in his letter to Jessie, another federally published expedition report, John boasted of having now blazed a new, transcontinental route—one destined to supplant the Oregon Trail he had already popularized: "By the route I have explored I can ride in thirty-five days from the *Fontaine qui Bouit River* [Fountain Creek, along the Rockies' eastern slope] to Captain Sutter's; and, for wagons, the road is decidedly far better." From Sutter's Fort, Frémont added, he planned to survey a route up the Sacramento watershed to Upper Klamath Lake and the Willamette valley—"in this way making the road into Oregon far shorter, and a *good* road in place of the present very bad one down the Columbia. When I shall have made this short exploration, I shall have explored from the beginning to end *this road to Oregon*."[16]

❋

Although Frémont's letter to Jessie teemed with the exigencies of exploration, his actions revealed other concerns. Toward the letter's end, he wrote, vaguely, "I am now going on business to see some gentlemen on the coast, and will then join my people, and complete our survey in this part of the world as rapidly as possible." If exploration truly remained Frémont's obsession in January 1846, common sense suggests he would have remained at Sutter's Fort to await the Talbot-Walker party's return, and to collect provisions for the trip he had outlined.

Each passing day, however, brought new evidence that Frémont had grown distracted by his exploring duties. After only four days at Sutter's Fort, he and eight of his men sailed on a launch owned by Sutter for Yerba Buena, today's San Francisco. From there, they would travel by horse the remaining ninety miles to what he had decided, by then, was their primary destination—the coastal town of Monterey.

❋

Up to now, Frémont's party had kept a safe distance from Mexican officials. Now, anticipating interactions with the Mexicans, Frémont had obtained from Sutter a passport authorizing passage to Monterey.

By Frémont's account the men stayed "a few days" at Yerba Buena. During the visit, Frémont stayed at the home of William Leidesdorff, an American businessman, who served as U.S. vice-consul at the port. Like many American traders who had adopted Mexican citizenship, Leidesdorff enjoyed an enviable life—one that, for the homesick explorer, stirred forlorn comparisons. "His house," Frémont later wrote, "was one of the best among the few in Yerba Buena—a low bungalow sort of adobe house with a long piazza facing the bay for the sunny mornings, and a cheerful fire within the fog and chill of the afternoons." With William Hinckley, the port's captain—and another U.S.-born businessman who had adopted Mexican citizenship—Frémont found time to take an overnight trip, sailing to the south end of San Francisco Bay, to visit a quicksilver mine.

❋

Impressed, no doubt, by the growing presence of Americans in California, as well as by the natural bounty of the province's landscape, Frémont, by now, had apparently reconsidered his earlier dismissal of any role for California in the American empire. Pursuant to that new-found faith, Frémont, before leaving Yerba Buena, coined a sobriquet for the dramatic break in the Coast Range where the San Francisco Bay meets the Pacific Ocean. In a passing nod to Senator Benton's vi-sion of American maritime and mercantilist glory, Frémont pondered the passage's future importance as a trade link between far-flung na-tions. Then—"on the same principle that the harbor of *Byzantium* (Constantinople afterwards) was called *Chrysopylae* (golden horn)"— he bestowed upon the break a suitably imperial name—the Golden Gate.

Frémont's coinage Golden Gate anticipated the gold that he and Benton expected to be flowing *into* California from other climes. Little did they know that the gold would soon flow *out of* California. By then, of course, Frémont knew enough about California to give it the moniker it retains to this day—the Golden State.

❀

Late on the evening of January 24, Frémont's party left Yerba Buena. Accompanied by Leidesdorff, they rode onto the plain beyond the town's venerable Mission Dolores, and "in the darkness and the fog we lost our way." Their confusion ended later that night, when the barking of dogs punctuated their arrival at their immediate destina-tion, the ranch of Don Francisco Sánchez, in today's San Mateo County. The next night found them at the ranch of Don Antonio Suñol, in today's San Jose. As Frémont wistfully recalled years later, ranchers routinely extended "a cordial hospitality which in those days assured a good bed and a savory supper to every traveler."

Between Yerba Buena and Monterey, Leidesdorff nourished Fré-mont's enchantment with California's nature. "His descriptions of this part of the country were especially interesting to me," Frémont re-called. "He was a lover of nature and his garden at San Francisco was, at that time, considered a triumph." Indeed, Frémont remembered that, as he traveled about California, he found himself perpetually imagining a new home for Jessie and Lily, and his ailing mother: "I had before my mind the home I wished to make in this country, and first one place and then another charmed me."[17]

On January 27, the party reached Monterey. Set on a splendid bay,

Monterey, with its crumbling San Carlos Mission and its whitewashed adobe houses scattered about its gentle seaside hills, had been named California's capital in 1777. When Frémont arrived, its inhabitants were still smarting over Governor Pico's recent transfer of the provincial capital to Los Angeles: Monterey remained Alta California's strategic and business center. The province's treasury, customhouse, and key presidio were still there; and it remained the base of Pico's rival—and *comandante* of the province—General José Castro.

In Monterey Frémont stayed for several days at the home of Thomas Larkin, California's sole U.S. consul. Larkin's home, a two-story New England saltbox that incorporated features of the California rancho style, aptly summed up the consul's own life story: a forty-four-year-old native of Massachusetts, Larkin had been in California since 1832. A mild-mannered but shrewd businessman who had amassed a fortune as a general merchant and as a trader in hides and tallow, Larkin, unlike many other Americans in California, had declined to adopt Mexican citizenship. An outspoken advocate for free trade, he had been appointed the U.S. consul at Monterey.

❈

On January 28, the day after Frémont arrived in Monterey, Larkin, on behalf of the U.S. government, advanced his houseguest eighteen hundred dollars to cover purchases of supplies.[18] The party's presence in and around Monterey was, of course, bound to draw official attention; and on January 29, the district's prefect, Manuel de Jesús Castro, wrote to Larkin, asking why a U.S. "Officer (lodging in your house) came to this District with Troops of the United States." In his response that same day, Larkin assured the prefect that the visitors were "hired men (not of the United States Army)" who had come "for the purpose of resting themselves and [their] animals." Frémont, he wrote, had "come himself to Monterey to obtain clothing, and funds to purchase animals and provisions, and when his men are recruited [rested], intends to continue his journey to the Oregon Territory."[19]

Accompanied by Larkin, Frémont made a round of personal calls on Mexican officials—including the province's commanding general Don José Castro. To each, Frémont repeated the same explanation for his visit—"that I was engaged in surveying the nearest route from the United States to the Pacific Ocean"; they had come, he said, "in the interests of science and commerce," and were "citizens and not soldiers." As for his presence in Monterey, one single objective motivated his visit: "I had come to Monterey with the object of obtaining leave to bring my party into the settlements in order to refit and obtain the supplies that had now become necessary. All the camp equipment, the clothes of the men and their saddles and horse gear, were either used up or badly in want of repair."[20]

The Mexican officials acceded to his request: "The permission obtained I immediately set about arranging for supplies of various kinds and for sending fresh horses to meet our people." Gathering his men, Frémont led them about sixty miles north, where they established camp near the pueblo of San José.[21]

At some point after setting up camp near San Jose, Frémont's men crossed paths with William O. Fallon, a mountain man and fur-trade veteran then on one of his regular perambulations through California. Not long afterward, Fallon, while passing through the Central Valley, encountered William Walker and "Fabbol"—his full name is lost to us—both of the Talbot-Walker party. By then, having abandoned hope of finding Frémont on the King's River, the party was returning north to Sutter's Fort. But from Fallon, as Talbot-Walker party member Edward Kern later recalled, "we learned that the captain was at the pueblo of San José with the rest of his camp." Talbot immediately dispatched Walker to Frémont's camp, and the rest of the party soon followed. Frémont, in turn, sent out fresh horses to the band, and a few days after the encounter with Fallon, the entire party was reunited at San Jose.[22]

❋

While Frémont had correctly assumed that no harm had come to the missing party, he had overestimated Walker's familiarity with California. As it turned out, after the Frémont and Talbot-Walker parties had, on November 29, bid adieu to one another alongside the shores of Walker Lake, Talbot's division had lingered by the lake another week, resting their livestock. Afterward, as planned, they had ridden along the Sierra's eastern eastern slope, then westward into the Sierra, toward California. On January 19, after encountering two-and-a-half feet of snow along the way, they reached what is now known as Walker Pass, where they gained their first glimpse of California's Central Valley. "It lay beneath us," Kern recorded in his journal, "bright in the sunshine, gay and green, while about us everything was clothed in the chilly garb of winter."

Their good cheer, however, soon gave way to frustration. As supplies and patience dwindled, they spent weeks searching for Frémont along what they believed was the King's River. In fact, they were several hundred miles south of where on the King's River they were supposed to meet the Frémont party. As hopes of finding Frémont faded, the party had just broken camp and was en route to Sutter's Fort when they encountered mountain man Fallon, who told them that Frémont was at San Jose.

❋

By the time the Talbot-Walker detail caught up with Frémont's party, Frémont had already moved his men six miles south of San Jose, where they had set up camp at Rancho La Laguna Seca. The then-empty ranch belonged to William Fisher, a Boston sea captain. After six weeks of separation, the reunion lifted the men's spirits. But the party's swelled numbers—it now boasted sixty well-armed men—discomfited Californio officials. Three days after the Talbot-Walker party reached the party's new encampment, Governor Pico wrote to Prefect Manuel de Jesús Castro, asking him to keep a close watch on the Americans and to determine if they had any intentions beyond exploring Oregon.[23] On February 20, José Dolores Pacheco, San Jose's alcalde, wrote Frémont, charging that the Americans had stolen livestock from a local resident. When the alleged owner of the animals visited the camp to demand the livestock's return, Frémont compounded difficulties by treating the man rudely and ordering him to leave.[24]

In a letter to Pacheco the next day, Frémont, denying the charge of theft, defended the treatment accorded the camp visitor and, for good measure, asserted that the complainant "should have been well satisfied to escape without a severe horsewhipping." He also put the alcalde on notice that "any further communications on this subject will not . . . receive attention. You will readily understand that my duties will not permit me to appear before the magistrates of your towns on the complaint of every straggling vagabond who may chance to visit my camp."[25]

In a more ominous rebuke of Mexican authority, Frémont, upon leaving San Jose in late February, headed south—implicitly violating the terms under which he had been allowed to linger in California. He had, after all, assured officials in Monterey that he would stay in California only long enough to resupply his men for more travels, "in the interests of science and commerce." But by February 22, contradicting all of Frémont's assurances to Mexican authorities, his party was headed not toward Oregon or the Sierra, but, once again, southwest toward Santa Cruz and Monterey.[26]

❋

On the move again, Frémont delighted in California's sun-dappled forests, now breathing new life into an early spring. Beyond that, the explorer, who had passed on an opportunity to see the Pacific during the Second Expedition, was now eager to feel the ocean's "invigorating salt breeze which brings with it renewed strength." Recovering his childhood ardor for things marine, he recalled, "For me, the shore of 'the sounding sea' was a pleasure of which I never wearied."

On February 25, as he and his men descended from the Coast Range to Monterey Bay's northwestern end, Frémont got his salt breeze—along with a sudden turn in the weather, toward cold and rain. After waiting out the rains for a week at their seaside camp, the men, on March 1, resumed their southerly course. Two days later, near Monterey Bay's southern end, they set up camp at a ranch owned by Englishman William E. P. Hartnell.

With Mexico and the United States drifting toward war, sixty armed Americans encamped twenty miles from the provincial capital of Monterey were bound to spark a sharp reaction. On March 5, a Lieutenant Chávez—"somewhat rude and abrupt," Frémont charged—arrived at their camp with letters from General Castro and Monterey's prefect, Manuel de Jesús Castro, ordering the Americans to leave California immediately.

Frémont declined to answer either letter directly. His only response came, indirectly, in a letter the next day from Larkin to the two Mexican officials. Ignoring questions about Frémont's intentions in California, Larkin's letter focused instead on reports that three of the Americans, on a visit to Manuel Castro's ranch, had treated his daughter rudely; the U.S. consul asked that the Americans "not be unjustly or unnecessarily harassed from causes that may arise from false reports, or false appearance."

Frémont, meanwhile, preparing for a confrontation with General José Castro, on the same day he had received the letters ordering him to leave California, had moved his party about eight miles north to a defensible position, atop Gavilán Peak, in the Coast Range, northeast of Monterey.

On March 8, General Castro, seeking volunteers for a military attack on Frémont's camp, issued a proclamation:

In the name of our native country I invite you to place yourselves under my immediate orders at headquarters, where we will prepare to lance the ulcer which (should it not be done) would destroy our liberties & independence for which you ought always to sacrifice yourselves.[27]

Though Frémont had no way then of knowing it, that same day General Zachary Taylor's troops had crossed the Nueces River into territory contested by the United States and Mexico, thus rendering war between the two nations inevitable.

✸

Frémont's camp atop Gavilán Peak afforded the men water and timber, grass for the livestock, and a commanding view of the coastal plain.[28] Beyond that, the peak's eastern slope offered a route of retreat into the San Joaquin Valley, should it be needed. "Arriving at the summit, I proceeded immediately to build a rough but strong fort of solid logs, for which we found good trees abundant on the ridge," Frémont recalled. "While this was being built a tall sapling was prepared, and on it, when all was ready, the American flag was raised amidst the cheers of the men"—an event later celebrated as foreshadowing the U.S. conquest of California.

Larkin, meanwhile, through messages sent via a courier, kept the Americans abreast of Mexican troop movements. A March 8 dispatch to Frémont reported that General José Castro, the previous evening, had gathered about sixty men on the plains below Frémont's mountain camp. "At this moment," Larkin added, "some forty men are preparing to leave Monterey to join the party. I should think tomorrow he might have two hundred men or perhaps more."[29]

Frémont answered Larkin's message with resolute bravado, writing to him that, with field glasses, they were observing the Mexican forces mustering below them at nearby Mission San Juan Bautista, but that his men were prepared for the worst: "We have in no wise done wrong to the people or the authorities of the country, and if we are hemmed in and assaulted, we will die every man of us, under the Flag of our country."

For all their bravado, however, Frémont's pronouncements betrayed thinking as muddled as that which had brought him to the mountain in the first place.

❋

As the Gavilán Peak crisis deepened, Thomas Larkin tried to defuse the standoff through quiet diplomacy. In a letter to Frémont, he offered to ask the Mexican officials if they would abandon threats of military action if, in exchange, the Americans would move to another camp in California, more distant from Monterey. To Monterey's alcalde, Manuel Díaz, Larkin, in a March 10 letter, asserted, "I have reason to believe that Captain Frémont only waits a few days to rest his horses (having purchased his provisions) and intends to remove immediately from California. Yet it may be impossible for him to do so while surrounded by people with hostile intentions toward him."[30]

Even as Larkin discreetly sought to end the stalemate, Frémont himself—vainglorious rhetoric aside—was also looking for a face-saving way to extricate himself from the standoff. Then, on March 9, the camp's flagpole fell to the ground: "Thinking I had remained as long as the occasion required, I took advantage of the accident to say to the men that this was an indication for us to move camp, and accordingly I gave the order to prepare to move." That night, their campfires still burning, he and all his men but Walker quietly left Gavilán Peak. Disgusted with what he regarded as Frémont's cowardice in abandoning the mountain, Walker, a man with a long-standing taste for violent scrapes, had quit and gone south.[31]

❊

Back in Washington, President Polk had no knowledge of the Gavilán Peak standoff; and, even if he had, the episode would have had little if any influence on the administration's actions as it pursued diplomacy with Mexico but prepared for war. The same day that Frémont abandoned Gavilán Peak, Thomas Larkin forwarded to John Parrott, the U.S. consul in Mazatlán, an open letter to "the commander of any American Ship of War," asking that a sloop of war immediately be sent to Monterey. That same day in a letter to Secretary of State James Buchanan, Larkin noted that those in Frémont's party were "all men of confidence and remarkably well-armed," but that he feared their bluster. None seemed to "have any fear respecting the result from the present state of affairs. Yet the result for or against him may prove a disadvantage to the American residents in California." Beyond that, "Although the life of captain Frémont may require it, I hardly know how to act."

Larkin's March 8 letter to Frémont had expressed the same unsettled comprehension of affairs: "In all probability they [the Mexican Army] will attack you. The result either way may cause trouble hereafter to Resident Americans. I myself have no fear on the subject, yet believe the present state of affairs may cause an interruption of business."

But despite Larkin's own high-level Washington contacts, he also assumed that he was quite likely ignorant of the true nature of Frémont's mission—and was thus impotent to advise him: "It is not for me to point out to you your line of conduct. You have your Government Instructions. . . ." If secret orders did indeed compel Frémont to remain in California, Larkin urged him to beware of potential traitors: "I therefore only wish you to suppose yourself in a situation where you must take every measure to prevent a supprise [sic], from those you may consider partially friends."[32]

TO PROMOTE THIS OBJECT
OF THE PRESIDENT

AFTER ABANDONING THEIR CAMP on Gavilán Peak, on March 11, 1846, the party reached the Sacramento valley ten days later. It was this valley, the northern half of the Central Valley, that the thirty-three-year-old Frémont longed to explore. On March 22, looking for a spot to rest their horses, the party camped at a "favorite spot" along the American River, not far from Sutter's Fort, opposite a ranch owned by American merchant Eliab Grimes. Upon reaching Sutter's Fort the next day, Frémont, aware that the party needed a fresh set of supplies, dispatched Talbot to Yerba Buena in a launch owned by Sutter that made regular runs west, from a dock on the American River, just beyond the walls of Sutter's New Helvetia redoubt.[1]

Two days later, on March 24, their horses rested, the men struck out on a northerly course toward the Feather River: "The route lay over an undulating country—more so as our course brought us nearer the mountains—wooded with oaks and shrubbery in blossom, with small prairies intervening." The bright orange California poppies were "unusually magnificent," Frémont remembered. "The blue fields of the nemophyla and this golden poppy represent fairly the skies and gold of California."

On March 26, the party struck the Feather River, then followed it upstream to its junction with the tributary Yuba River. Of the Yuba, Frémont wrote, "The river has high banks—twenty or thirty feet— and was here one hundred and fifty yards wide, a deep navigable stream. The Indians aided us across the river with canoes and small rafts." That night, the party camped at a ranch owned by Theodor Cordua, a successful German-born wheat farmer. There, Frémont found still more evidence of California's agricultural potential; Cordua, he recalled, "informed me that his average harvest of wheat was twenty-five bushels to the acre, which he supposed would be about the produce of the wheat lands in the Sacramento valley. The labor on this and other farms in the valley is performed by Indians."

On March 30—by then, approaching the Central Valley's northern end—the party reached Peter Lassen's ranch on Deer Creek, east of today's Corning, California. There, in the wheat fields, vineyards, and experimental cotton fields cultivated by the Danish-born Lassen, Frémont again found reinforcement for his growing belief in California's agricultural potential. Even so, he reflected, "The seasons are not yet sufficiently understood, and too little has been done in agriculture, to afford certain knowledge of the capacities of the country."

The party stayed at Lassen's ranch for six days, resting, and feasting on the abundant salmon they caught in local streams. "The salmon," Frémont recalled, "crowd in immense numbers up the Umpqua, Tlamath [Klamath], and Trinity Rivers, and into every little river and creek on the coast north of the Bay of San Francisco; and up the San Joaquin River, into the Stanislaus, beyond which the Indians say they do not go."[2]

✸

News of Frémont's standoff at Gavilán Peak with Castro's army had rippled quickly across California, inspiring hopes among American settlers that he might be willing to lead an insurgency against the provincial government. As word spread, more and more American settlers began finding their way to Frémont's camp. In early April, reports reached him and the American settlers gathered around his camp that Indians in the Sacramento valley had attacked several Americans and were planning other assaults. Upon hearing the news, many of the settlers began asking Frémont to lead a preemptive strike against the Indians. Frémont would later claim that he had accepted the invitation. But expedition member Thomas Martin—possibly a more credible source on the episode—recalled a more aloof Frémont. As the settlers' fears grew, Martin recalled, they "asked Frémont to protect them." In the end, however, Martin recalled, "he refused as he had no right to fight the inds. [*sic*] but he told us that those who wished [to] take part in an expedition against those Indians he would discharge, and take us again afterwards."

From Lassen's ranch, the raiding party, comprising about fifty men, set off—riding north, up the Sacramento River, where plentiful fish and acorn-bearing oaks, that season, made the river's shore a popular site for Indian settlements. The men attacked the first village they came to—a settlement near today's Redding, California, at the confluence of the Sacramento River and Cottonwood Creek—shooting several Indians to death. Other villagers, both wounded and unwounded, scurried away into nearby riparian groves of oaks and willow, or into the river—swimming across to the other side or disappearing into the tularé reeds to hide.[3]

Of the raid, Kit Carson later recalled, "[We had] accomplished our purpose and given the Indians such a chastisement that it would be long before they would again think of attacking the settlements." Thomas Martin, likely exaggerating, later claimed that in one three-hour engagement, they had killed over 175 Indians. As to how the men felt afterward, neither Frémont's nor Carson's recollections provide many specifics. "I do not know how many we killed," Carson recalled. "It was a perfect butchery." Frémont, possibly overstating his role in the action, offered a similar assessment. "This was a rude but necessary measure to prevent injury to the whites," he later recalled. "And it had the effect which I intended."[4]

❀

In the wake of the raid on the Indian settlement, Frémont's party once again headed north, crossing the Sacramento the next day in canoes loaned to them by a local farmer. As they crossed the wide river, Frémont once again reveled in thoughts of California's nature harnessed to commerce. A year earlier, he had deemed the San Joaquin unfit for commercial navigation and had dismissed both it and the Sacramento—each lacking in linkages to the watersheds of the Rockies—as irrelevant to America's commercial future.

By the spring of 1845, however, Frémont was willing to ponder a role for the Sacramento in America's commercial future—as a Far Western branch of American empire. "The Sacramento was here," he recalled, "about one hundred and forty yards wide, and with the actual stage of water, which I was informed continued several months, navigable for a steamboat." He had, after all, seen wheat, grapes, and other crops rising from the Central Valley's rich alluvial soil. Might not, then, a rich internal California commerce—one nourished by the province's major rivers—also arise around those crops?

✳

More sublime thoughts crowded Frémont's mind the next day, April 7, as majestic Mt. Shasta—reaching 14,162 feet above sea level—rose into view. As the men marveled at Shasta and other mountains of the volcanic Cascade Range to their east and the Klamath Range to their west, Frémont's eye fell on yet another noble peak in the Cascades. The peak seemed worthy of recognition, so he named it Mt. Linn, in homage to Missouri's U.S. Senator Lewis Linn, who had died three years earlier. By thus christening the mountain, Frémont later wrote, he hoped it would stand "as an enduring monument to recall the prolonged services rendered by him in securing to the country our Oregon coast."

The next day, as the party moved into the Sacramento valley's far northern end, hard rains delayed its progress, he recalled: "We were now near the head of the lower valley, and the face of the country and the weather began sensibly to show the influence of the rugged mountains which surround and terminate it." The men were moving away from the bright fields of poppies and gentle foothills to the south into a wetter, higher, and colder domain of high snowbound mountains—a realm better known to trappers than to cultivators of the soil.

Once the rain that had delayed the party stopped, the men resumed their journey, now on an eastward course toward the Sierra. Soon they were well over a thousand feet above sea level, and foul weather returned. Hailstones "the size of wild cherries" pummeled the party, scattering their livestock. Snow followed, and "the evening closed in with rain, and thunder rolling around the hills."

At sunrise on April 10, the temperature stood at 33 degrees: "The surrounding mountains showed a continuous line of snow, and the high peaks looked wintry." Faced with those conditions, Frémont decided to return to Lassen's ranch. And as he soon learned, as still more men arrived at his camp, the news of his standoff with Castro's army was continuing to inspire talk among the American settlers of an insurgency against California's Mexican government.[5]

❀

Feeling put upon by Mexican officials, the settlers welcomed any reports of defiance—even if merely symbolic—against their host country's authorities. And nowhere were such reports more welcome than among the American settlers of the Napa and Sonoma valleys, to the north of Yerba Buena. Typical of such settlers, only twelve days after Frémont had established his makeshift fort on Gavilán Peak, the American trapper and explorer James Clyman, then living in the Napa valley, upon hearing of the incident, wrote in his diary of the "alarm . . . created by Mr. Freemont having raised an american flag at his camp." Four days later, Clyman wrote Frémont, offering his services as a soldier.[6]

By late April, a group of Americans—ready for military action—were considering an attack on the town of Sonoma, the Mexican government's most northerly California outpost. The site of a small army garrison and mission, Sonoma had originally been established as a buffer against Fort Ross—Russia's most southerly North American outpost—which had been abandoned seven years earlier. With the dismantlement of Fort Ross in 1841—Johann Sutter had purchased its contents and hauled them back to Sutter's Fort—Sonoma had, in the eyes of most Mexican officials, lost its raison d'être.

Sonoma's garrison, however, remained open, under the command of General Mariano Vallejo, a prominent rancher who enjoyed close ties to many American settlers. Although Vallejo was rumored to favor U.S. annexation of California, such talk did nothing to diminish, among the settlers, their perception of Sonoma's strategic value. By taking Sonoma, they believed, they could, "gain control of all the country north of the Bay." They also believed that "any action on our part leading to the overthrow of Mexican rule over California would be sanctioned by the Government at Washington."[7]

Two American settlers served as the movement's early catalysts—

Granville Swift and a "Mr. Kelsey," one of two Kelsey brothers involved in later actions against the Mexican government. The two decided to send a delegation to the Sacramento Valley, to try to enlist Captain John Frémont of Gavilán Peak fame to head their revolt. By linking up with the illustrious Pathfinder, the settlers hoped their insurgency would become a beneficiary of what many perceived to be a grand but still officially secret U.S. military campaign. As William Hargrave, one of the settlers sent to the Sacramento valley, recalled, "Frémont, being a U.S. officer of rank, must certainly be acting under instructions from Washington and in cooperating with him we must be perfectly safe and sure of ultimate further support."

In late April, Hargrave and three other settlers set off for the Sacramento valley, stopping en route at a ranch along the Napa River owned by George Yount, an American-born settler who had taken on Mexican citizenship. At Yount's ranch, they were joined by five or six men from the lower Sacramento valley, also hoping to find Frémont, and "bent upon the same errand." Upon reaching Sutter's Fort, the expanded party learned that Frémont and his men were encamped to the north, along the Feather River.[8]

When William Hargrave and his fellow Napa and Sonoma valley settlers caught up with Frémont, they assumed they had finally found a leader for their planned attack on Sonoma. But they were quickly disillusioned. Frémont told them that he had no inclination to lead or even countenance such a venture. Beyond that, as Hargrave recalled, "He peremptorily refused to take any responsibility for sudden action on our part and endeavored to delay or frustrate our efforts." Afterward, Hargrave and his friends returned to the Napa and Sonoma valleys, vowing to continue the "agitation"—"most of us somewhat disgusted with the result of our interview."[9]

❖

During his party's two week stay at Lassen's ranch, Frémont set up his surveying equipment and, on two nights, conducted lunar observations. During the respite, Talbot returned from Yerba Buena with the supplies requested by Frémont; and Thomas Martin, Alexander Godey, and four Delawares were sent out to trade for horses—horses presumed by Sutter, when he learned of the purchases, to have been stolen. Irate, Sutter, who had been waging a campaign to halt such thefts, dashed off an irate protest to Frémont. "I wrote him," Sutter later recalled, "demanding that he should leave the stolen horses and not drive away property belonging to others. He made no reply to my letter."

Sutter's myriad duties as an alcalde of the Mexican government required him to condemn purchases of stolen horses. But Frémont took a more cynical view of Sutter's actions. The explorer had never trusted the emperor of the Sacramento valley, and although Frémont never answered Sutter's letter about the allegedly stolen horses, the missive, according to Sutter, left an unbridgeable chasm between the two men: "This act Frémont never forgave me."[10]

Sutter's suspicions, in fact, had grown far beyond concerns about trafficking in stolen horses; and in an April 1 letter, he warned General Castro of Frémont's increasingly erratic movements; after stopping at Sutter's Fort on March 23, Sutter wrote Castro, Frémont had spent the next four weeks on a strangely peripatetic tour of the Sacramento River valley: "Every few days he would move his camp farther and farther up the valley," Sutter recalled in a later memoir. "Flitting about the country with an armed body of men[,] he was regarded with suspicion by everybody."[11]

❋

On April 24, Frémont's party left Lassen's ranch "to penetrate the country, along the Cascade ranges north into Oregon, and connect there with the line of my journey of '43." Though Frémont was unaware of it, that same day the long-expected military confrontation between the United States and Mexico had finally taken place. Forces between the two countries had clashed along the Rio Grande.

Retracing its earlier route up the Sacramento River, in two days Frémont's party reached the valley's northern head. On the morning of April 26, bending to a northeasterly course out of the valley, the party left the Sacramento River at Battle Creek, south of today's Redding, and southeast of Mt. Shasta. Over the next week, the party crossed the Cascades onto far northeastern California's small share of the Columbia River's high, volcanic plateau country. There, from the Pit River, the party moved straight into Oregon.

On May 6, at the junction of Klamath River and Upper Klamath Lake, the explorers came upon the first Indians they had encountered since leaving California. "It was a bright spring morning, and the lake and its surrounding scenery looked charming," Frémont wrote. "It was inviting, and I would have been glad to range over it in one of the Indian canoes. The silent shores and unknown mountains had the attraction which mystery gives always. It was all wild and unexplored, and the uninvaded silence roused curiosity and invited research."

Mindful of the massacre that had befallen Jedediah Smith's party along southern Oregon's Umpqua River in 1828, which left fifteen of eighteen men dead, Frémont's men approached the tribesmen cautiously.[12] But though the explorers' arrival startled the Indians, the tribesmen received the interlopers warmly. While Kern stole a moment to make a quick sketch of the scene, the party traded with the Indians to obtain dried fish and salmon; and, later that day, the Indians assisted the party's ferrying of the Klamath River. That day and the next, the party rode west, then north along the lake's shore, hugging the high Cascades' eastern slope. As they ascended into higher country, they climbed across mountain spurs, trudged through riparian marshes, and penetrated the dense evergreen forest that limned the lake's coves and inlets. As fallen timber and snow often obstructed their passage, a rigorous day of travel typically took the men only a few miles. Except for an occasional glimpse of a solitary Indian canoeing on the lake, the country seemed empty—to Frémont, ripe for exploration:

> Except for the few trappers who had searched the streams leading to the ocean, for beaver, I felt sure that these mountains were absolutely unknown. No one had penetrated their recesses to know what they contained, and no one had climbed to their summits; and there remained the great attraction of mystery in going into unknown places—the unknown lands of which I had dreamed when I began this life of frontier travel.[13]

Upon his return to the Klamath country, Frémont's thoughts initially focused on merely connecting his present explorations with his earlier survey of southern Oregon's interior. Now—perhaps suddenly mindful, once again, of the maritime visions of Senator Benton's Road to India—Frémont suddenly began thinking about finding his way through the Cascades, of crossing over them to the Pacific: "And possibly, I thought, when I should descend their western flanks some safe harbor might yet be found by careful search along that coast, where harbors were so few; and perhaps good passages from the interior through these mountains to the sea." While they waited for the amount of snow to decrease, Frémont mused, they might survey the country along the base of the mountains and link up their current explorations with his earlier Klamath country survey: "And if we could not find game enough to live upon, we could employ the Indians to get supplies of salmon and other fish."

✹

On the evening of May 8, Frémont was standing alone by his campfire, savoring its warmth against the lakeside mountain chill: "Suddenly my ear caught the faint sound of horses' feet, and while I was watching and listening as the sounds, so strange hereabout, came nearer, there emerged from the darkness—into the circle of the firelight—two horsemen, riding slowly as though horse and man were fatigued by long travelling."

As the two rode into the campfire's glow, Frémont recognized both men. One was his former exploring partner Samuel Neal, one of the Second Expedition explorers who had left the party at Sutter's Fort in the winter of 1844. Neal since then had become a prosperous rancher. The other man was Neal's associate, Levi Sigler. "After their horses had been turned into the band and they were seated by my fire, refreshing themselves with good coffee while more solid food was being prepared, Neal told me his story."

The two were exhausted, having ridden almost one hundred miles in the past two days. They had been sent by—and were riding ahead of—Lieutenant Archibald Gillespie of the U.S. Marines, who had traveled all the way from Washington with messages for Frémont. At Gillespie's request, out of shared concerns about dangers posed by hostile Indians, the men, two days earlier, had left Gillespie and three other slower riders behind—somewhere south of Upper Klamath

Lake. En route to the lake, following Frémont's trail, Neal and Sigler, upon realizing that a party of Indians was on their trail, had eluded their pursuers by crossing to the Klamath River's west bank. They had, Frémont recalled, "escaped only by the speed and strength of their horses, which Neal had brought from his own rancho."

Seated in the campfire's glow that night, Neal surmised that it was very likely too late to save Gillespie. Frémont, however, was adamant that they try to reach him; the trail along the lake, at the foot of the mountains, would be impossible to negotiate in the darkness, but Frémont made plans to leave at dawn—selecting ten of his best men for the relief party, including Kit Carson, Joseph Stepp, Dick Owens, Alex Godey, Basil Lajeunesse, and four of the Delaware Indians: "When the excitement of the evening was over I lay down, speculating far into the night on what could be the urgency of the message which had brought an officer of the Government to search so far after me into these mountains."

Frémont and the relief party left at dawn. They saw no Indians, but snow and fallen timber again slowed their progress. That afternoon, May 9, after riding forty-five miles, they stopped in a glade, an open meadow, along the lake's southern shore: "I knew that this was the first water to which my trail would bring the messenger, and that I was sure to meet him here if no harm befell him on the way." After a wait of several hours, Gillespie and the three other riders finally appeared.

❋

Archibald Gillespie's long road to his lakeside encounter with John Frémont had begun eight months earlier. In October 1845, the thirty-three-year-old officer had been named a confidential agent for U.S. Navy Secretary George Bancroft and ordered to carry several letters to U.S. officials in California. That same month, shortly before leaving, Gillespie had had a private meeting with President Polk, following which the President cryptically confided to his diary:

> I held a confidential conversation with Lieut. Gillespie of the
> Marine Corps, about 8:00 O'Clock P.M., on the subject of a se-

cret mission on which he was about to go to California. His secret instructions & the letter to Mr. Larkin, U.S. Consul at
Monterey, in the Department of State, will explain the object
of his mission.[14]

Traveling with his black servant, Benjamin Harrison, Gillespie, on
October 30, sailed from New York harbor aboard the U.S. Navy brig
Petersburgh, bound for Vera Cruz. The Marine officer carried several
documents—including a general letter of introduction from Secretary
of State Buchanan, personal and official letters for Frémont, and a letter for Commodore Sloat of the Pacific Squadron. He also carried, from
Secretary of State Buchanan, a letter for Thomas Larkin, naming him
a confidential agent of the U.S. government. In case Gillespie was
searched by Mexican officials, he also carried a letter of introduction
attesting (falsely) that he was working for William Appleton & Co., a
Boston trading house.

❋

With Gillespie posing as an ailing trader, he and his servant Harrison
reached Vera Cruz on December 10. There, while waiting for a stagecoach to Mexico City, Gillespie had the chance to observe local conditions and to take a measure of Mexican attitudes toward its neighbor
to the north: though he found the local population eager for war with
the United States, the troops he saw seemed utterly unprepared for
that eventuality—undisciplined, ragged, divided in loyalties. Some
remained loyal to the deposed former Mexican President Antonio
López de Santa Anna. Even more were devoted to General Mariano
Paredes y Arrilaga, a monarchist who, it was widely assumed, was
about to launch—or had already launched—a revolution to topple
Mexico's incumbent President José Joaquin Herrera.[15] Gillespie and
Harrison left Vera Cruz later that month. Gillespie had envisioned a
brief stopover in Mexico City, but political turmoil—the expected revolution that installed Mariano Paredes as Mexico's new President—
delayed them for four weeks. Once again, Gillespie seized the
opportunity to observe and report to Bancroft on local conditions.
Writing on January 16 to the Navy Secretary, Gillespie again noted

the poor state of the Mexican army—"the most miserable Troops I have ever seen." He also noted that the new government was too preoccupied with its own survival and ongoing U.S.–Mexican disputes over Texas to expend much attention on California. Gillespie recalled that, during his second term as California's governor (1845–46), Pío Pico had refused to recognize President Herrera's authority.

Herrera, in turn, had sent funds to General Paredes to pay the costs of outfitting an expeditionary force to impose Mexico City's will upon the errant province. Parades, Gillespie recalled, instead used the funds to pay troops that, as part of his revolution, marched on Mexico City.

Although Gillespie expected the Paredes government to show little interest in California, he also doubted that diplomacy would result in a sale of the province to the United States. After all, "one of the strongest reasons given for the overthrow of the Herrera Government was, its having thought of entering into a Treaty with U. States for the sale of Texas." Beyond that, the government's new Minister of War, Juan Almonte, was eager to make a military advance upon Texas. Thus, when Gillespie departed Mexico City, on January 21, the young officer left convinced that there was little chance that President Parades would agree to meet with President Polk's emissary, John Slidell. Although Slidell had been in Mexico since November 30, he had yet to gain an audience with any high government officials. If the United States was to acquire California, Gillespie concluded, it would have to be through war—or through diplomacy conducted after a war.[16]

In Mexico's Pacific port of Mazatlán, Gillespie delivered Buchanan's letter to Commodore Sloat ordering him, upon hearing of "actual hostilities" between the United States and Mexico, to immediately seize San Francisco and as many other California ports as possible.

❋

After Sloat had received Buchanan's letter, the *Cyane*, a U.S. Navy brig, on Sloat's orders, on February 22, picked up Gillespie and Harrison and took them via Honolulu to Monterey, where they arrived on April 17. At Monterey, after meeting with Gillespie aboard the *Cyane*,

Thomas Larkin invited the young officer to stay at his home. There, Gillespie recited his letter from Buchanan, naming Larkin a confidential agent. To ensure that the contents of the letter to Larkin did not fall into the hands of Mexican officials, Gillespie had taken the precaution of memorizing, then destroying the letter. The role of confidential agent—with compensation of six dollars a day—cast Larkin into a pivotal role in the Polk administration's ongoing effort to acquire California. In his letter of appointment, Buchanan wrote, "You will not fail by every safe opportunity to keep the Department advised of the progress of events in California, and the disposition of the authorities and people toward the United States and other Governments."[17]

During his stay in the provincial capital, Gillespie talked extensively with Larkin and other foreigners. On April 18—only a day after he reached Monterey—the dutiful agent penned a long letter detailing the latest California news to Navy Secretary Bancroft. The *Cyane*, at Larkin's request, postponed for one day its return voyage to Mazatlán in order to give both Gillespie and Larkin the opportunity to send official reports to Washington.

In his letter to Bancroft, Gillespie described the fractious state of California politics. "Don José Castro," he reported, "is a man devoid of principal, and is now endeavoring to get up a revolution to depose the Governor of California, Don Pío Pico, who resides some four hundred miles south of this, at the Pueblo de los Angeles." As for Frémont's recent standoff with Castro's army at Gavilán Peak, Gillespie sent the encouraging news that, though the exploring party had ultimately capitulated, "Three hundred Riflemen offered their services to Cap't Frémont, who, had he pleased, might have taken the country."

Gillespie, in his letter to Bancroft, downplayed the influence of European governments in the province. Continued emigration by Americans, Gillespie predicted, would shape California's future: "The tide of Emmigration [*sic*] will continue to flow on rapidly, and will place beyond doubt or fear any European interference. It would be perfectly impossible for any European Power to take possession of the country, unless it were over run by an Armed force"—and Gillespie saw no evidence of that possibility.[18] Larkin, writing to Buchanan that same week, echoed Gillespie's conclusion. He counseled policymakers not to worry about rumors that General Castro planned to take two to three hundred soldiers to the Sacramento valley for the purpose of blocking the new arrivals: "Should he be, he only hastens the crisis." Both men hoped that California would be spared in any military confrontation between the United States and Mexico.

❁

Gillespie was, no doubt, impressed by what he had learned about Frémont. But he apparently still considered his meeting with Larkin the major stop on his long trip. Contemplating his mission to Frémont, the young marine officer anticipated neither a long trip nor, for that matter, momentous results. To Bancroft, he wrote, "Cap't Frémont has gone to the North, whither I shall proceed immediately, and will no doubt overtake him in four days, & will be able to return here in time for the next ship; which I expect will reach this [place] in the course of a few days or two weeks; and should I obtain from him any thing of importance, will send a Courier across the Southern country as you directed."

Supplied by Larkin with horses and a guide, Gillespie and Harrison left Monterey in late April, reaching Yerba Buena on April 24. Gillespie carried a letter of introduction to William A. Leidesdorff— Yerba Buena's vice-consul and Frémont's former host—who helped Gillespie and Harrison prepare for the rest of their trip in search of Frémont. Before Gillespie's departure, Leidesdorff shared with him the recently arrived news, in a letter from Larkin to Leidesdorff, that the United States and Mexico were closer to official war.

At Larkin's request, the U.S. sloop-of-war *Portsmouth* had put in at Monterey two days after Gillespie's departure; and its commander, John B. Montgomery, Larkin informed Leidesdorff, "is of the opinion that Commodore Sloat may, by the next mail which would be within six or eight days have a declaration on the part of the United States against Mexico, in which case we should see him in a few days to take the country." Leidesdorff, in his response to Larkin, called the report "glorious news for Capt. Frémont. I think I see him smile."

Gillespie left Yerba Buena on April 25, and reached Sutter's Fort three days later. To Gillespie, Sutter showed his usual hospitality, but he also reported the American's presence to Castro. Sutter told the general that although Gillespie (modifying his previous assumed identity) had claimed to be an ailing retired officer, he didn't believe the story. Sutter believed the mysterious traveler to be an active U.S. Army officer, carrying official orders for Frémont.[19] Learning, while at Sutter's Fort, that Frémont was two weeks ahead of them to the north, Gillespie and Harrison hurried on up the valley. On May 1, they reached Lassen's ranch.

The next morning, defying reports of belligerent Indians to the north, Gillespie, Harrison, and five others, who joined with them at Lassen's ranch, set out to catch up with Frémont. On May 6, as evidence grew of the presence of hostile Indians along the route, they decided that two of the more experienced riders in the entourage, Samuel Neal and Levi Sigler, would ride ahead to find Frémont. Gillespie and the other three men in the party would follow.

❋

At dawn on May 9, in a glade along Upper Klamath Lake's south shore, Gillespie's party caught up with Frémont. As Gillespie and the other three riders emerged from the gloaming, "we greeted him warmly," Frémont recalled. "All were glad to see him, whites and Indians. It was long since any news had reached us, and every one was pleased to see him as if he had come freighted with letters from home, for all. It was now eleven months since tidings had reached me."

For Frémont, Gillespie's arrival marked a turning point—away from exploration, toward operations fraught with more dangerous and complex military and political consequences.

The mission on which I had been originally sent to the West was a peaceful one, and Mr. Bancroft had sent Mr. Gillespie to give me warning of the new state of affairs and the designs of the President. . . . Through him I now became acquainted with the actual state of affairs and the purposes of the Government. The information through Gillespie had absolved me from my duty as an explorer, and I was left to my duty as an officer of the American Army with the future authoritative knowledge that the Government intended to take California. I was warned by my Government of the new danger against which I was bound to defend myself; and it had been made known to me now on the authority of the Secretary of the Navy that to obtain possession of California was the chief object of the President.

Precisely what Gillespie told Frémont that night and the contents of the letters he brought remain a mystery. Frémont later insisted that, collectively, what he read and heard by the lake that night gave him discretion from the Polk administration to commence military operations against California's Mexican garrison. The precise "designs of the President"—or at least those communicated to Frémont—however, remain unclear, and largely undocumented. Few of the letters have survived; and we have only Frémont's vague, largely unverified, and often contradictory account of what Gillespie told and showed him.

❀

Frémont's account of events, even if believed, offers scant reason to conclude that the Polk administration had sent concrete orders for him to begin military actions. Even Frémont's *Memoirs*, written three decades after the episode, balk at claiming that a single document ordered him to begin military operations. Those instructions, Frémont insisted, he inferred from the totality of the letters and verbal information conveyed by Gillespie. Beyond that, he insisted that his conversations with Gillespie, and his understanding of the letters Gillespie had brought, must be comprehended in the light of prior understandings with the letters' authors—Buchanan and Benton.

The few letters that do survive offer little to support Frémont's claims. Buchanan, for instance, sent Frémont a perfunctory letter of introduction to Gillespie—a letter Buchanan did not even expect Frémont to receive: "I do not deem it probable that he will fall in with you; but if he should, allow me to bespeak for him your friendly attention. He will be able to communicate to you information on the health of Mrs. Frémont and Col. Benton and his family." Buchanan's bland dispatch contains nothing of substance, but in Frémont's *Memoirs*, it becomes a clarion call to arms:

From the letter itself I learned nothing, but it was intelligently explained to me by the accompanying letter from Senator Benton and by communications from Lieutenant Gillespie.

The officer informed me that he had been directed by the Secretary of State to acquaint me with his instructions, which had for their principal objects to ascertain the disposition of the California people, to conciliate their feelings in favor of the United States; and to find out, with a view to counteracting, the designs of the British Government upon that country.

Frémont gave a similar interpretation to the letter—now lost—from Senator Benton. "While apparently of friendship and family details," the missive nonetheless, Frémont claimed,

contained passages and suggestions which, read by the light of many conversations and discussions with himself and others at Washington, clearly indicated to me that I was required by the Government to find out any foreign schemes in relation to California and, so far as might be in my power, to counteract them.

Historian Hubert Howe Bancroft—no relation to the Navy Secretary—probably got things right, in 1886, when he surmised that the orders contained in Buchanan's letter to Larkin were very likely identical to those conveyed to Frémont: Why, after all, would Polk give contradictory orders to his only two agents posted on California soil?

Beyond Frémont's labored attempts at self-justification, however, evidence does exist that he might have reasonably concluded that he enjoyed, at the least, conditional authority to begin military operations. Among the communications Gillespie brought was his memorized version of the letter he had discreetly destroyed three weeks earlier, from Buchanan to Larkin, naming the consul a secret agent of the U.S. government. It was that letter, Frémont recalled, which included the directive to "find out, with a view to counteracting, the designs of the British government upon that country"—a mandate whose burden Frémont naturally assumed he was also expected to carry.

Gillespie, "who had been purposely made acquainted with their [the messages'] import," in all likelihood, also told Frémont about a message from Navy Secretary Bancroft that Gillespie had delivered to Commodore Sloat. That dispatch called on Sloat, in the event of "actual hostilities" by Mexican—by Californio—forces, to at once begin military operations.

✸

Gillespie, no doubt, also updated Frémont on deteriorating U.S.–Mexico relations and the likelihood of war, and informed him of the collapse of Polk's hopes of purchasing California. And while Gillespie himself dismissed the possibility of British conquest of California, Secretary of State Buchanan's letter to Larkin stressed the administration's fears of such Anglo intrigues.

Learning that the Polk administration considered British intrigue in California a casus belli, Frémont—who, by then, had adopted his father-in-law's Anglophobia—had no trouble, over the coming days and weeks, identifying what he considered evidence of John Bull's mischief on the Pacific coast. Thus, while it appears doubtful that President Polk's administration gave Frémont direct orders to begin military operations, it does seem likely that the administration did convey—directly or indirectly—conditional instructions under which Frémont might reasonably have concluded that such aggressive actions would be sanctioned. Or, as he put it, the directives gave him the opportunity, "where uncertainties arose, to give my own country the benefit of any doubts by taking decided action."[20]

✸

Over the years, Frémont as a soldier earned a reputation for occasional indifference to official orders. Given his sensitivity to that reputation, his *Memoirs*, published in 1887, are best read as an apologia written forty years after his fateful Upper Klamath Lake meeting with Gillespie—and a rhetorically duplicitous apologia at that, one in which we find Frémont at once claiming credit for and disowning responsibility for certain controversial acts. During his meeting with Gillespie, for instance, Frémont asserted that, in May 1846, he was acting as a man who knew his nation was *at* war; a few pages later, however, he made reference to the *likelihood of* war. In fact, war had already begun, at Matamoros, Mexico, two weeks before Gillespie reached Frémont— but neither of the two men had knowledge of that fact.

Historians, with good reason, have speculated that Frémont, prior to meeting Gillespie, was marking time in California and Oregon— awaiting official orders from Washington to begin hostilities, or else news of official war with Mexico. Whether or not that is true, clearly Frémont's appetite for war in California existed long before he met Gillespie. The origins of Frémont's decision to commence military actions in California, then, in all likelihood lay not in any single order, but rather in the set of general plans, ambitions, and visions that he had carried across the continent. Frémont viewed himself not as an agent for a presidential administration but for a far grander project— the quest for American empire. And by 1846—drawing on his own experiences and reflections—he had arrived at a view, vastly different from that of Senator Benton, as to how that quest should proceed.

Frémont and his father-in-law still had much in common: both manifested a disdain for what each viewed as the pettiness of government officials and their directives—and both viewed the American state as less a temporal set of elected officials and laws than an abstract conception of a people on the move—a people literally and metaphorically on the move—in and *through* history. Put another way, President Polk, James Buchanan and other administration officials saw the migration of Americans to the Pacific slope as advancing *the interests of* the American nation. Frémont, by contrast, saw those people and that movement *as* the American nation.

Frémont's personal loyalties were to Senator Benton; and through Benton—who had opposed Polk's nomination as the Democratic standard-bearer—Frémont considered himself linked to a grand historical procession far more important than any single administration. That course of empire stretched back to Jefferson, and to Lewis and Clark—and, beyond them, to England, Rome, Phoenicia, and the dawn of civilization. Cast by Frémont in what he considered their proper historical light, Gillespie's messages to the young captain merely confirmed the obvious—that U.S. acquisition of California was inevitable; and it culminated a process set in motion by grand forces of history long before Polk came to office. As Frémont put it,

Looking back over the contingencies which had been foreseen in the discussions at Washington, I saw that the important one which carried with it the hopes of Senator Benton and the wishes of the Government was in the act of occurring, and it was with thorough satisfaction I now found myself required to do what I could to promote this object of the President.

Gillespie, no doubt, also updated Frémont on developments in Oregon and the continued migration of Americans to the Pacific Northwest—news that further swelled Frémont's sense of historical self-importance. His explorations, after all, had already guided liberty into Oregon; and now California was summoning him to the same task.

That night by Klamath Lake, after everyone else in the party had fallen asleep, Frémont lay awake by his campfire, pondering the coming days. "I saw the way opening clear before me," he recalled. "War with Mexico was inevitable; and a grand opportunity now presented itself to realize in their fullest extent the far-sighted views of Senator Benton, and make the Pacific Ocean the western boundary of the United States. I resolved to move forward on the opportunity and return forthwith to the Sacramento valley in order to bring to bear all the influence I could command."[21]

NEUTRAL CONQUEST

18

B Y MIDNIGHT ON MAY 9–10, 1846, encamped beside Upper Klamath Lake, John Frémont lay snug in his blanket, contemplating the letters he had received that night and his ensuing conversations with Archibald Gillespie. Several campfires still burned. Close to each fire, though beyond range of the firelight, each member of the party had found a cedar with low branches under which to sleep. As Frémont later put it, "One always likes to have his head sheltered, and a rifle with a ramrod or a branch or bush with a blanket thrown over it answers very well where there is nothing better." But as Frémont indulged in his solitary reverie, he thought that he heard a noise of movement among the party's hobbled mules, down by the lake. Departing from his usual routine, he had posted no sentries that night—"Lieutenant Gillespie had told me that there were no Indians on his trail, and I knew there were none on mine." Deciding to investigate, but preferring not to awake the others, he drew his revolver and quietly walked to the lakeshore—"but nothing seemed stirring, and my presence quieting the animals I returned to the fire and my letters."

A while later, Frémont had barely fallen asleep when he was awakened by Kit Carson, calling to Basil Lajeunesse about more noises. Carson heard no answer. But, seconds later, he and Owens, who had been sleeping under the same tree, roused the entire camp. "Indians!" they shouted in unison. Scrambling to their feet, rifles in hand, the other men soon learned, to their horror, that the noise that had roused Carson and Owens had been the sound of an ax being driven into Basil Lajeunesse's head. Close to Lajeunesse's corpse lay the lifeless body of Denny, a Métis member of the party, killed by Indian arrows.

A band of Klamath Indians charged into the campfire's light. In the first moments of combat, Crane, one of the Delaware Indians, fell with five arrows in his body. Moments later, the crack of the exploring party's rifles rang through the camp. After a bullet struck and killed the attacking Indians' leader, his followers retreated back into the surrounding darkness and continued to fire arrows into the camp: "We threw a blanket over Crane and hung blankets to the cedar boughs and bushes near by, behind my camp-fire, for a defence against the arrows." The arrows stopped. But the men remained awake through the night, rifles in hand, behind their blanket defenses.

The next morning, inspecting tracks leading to the camp, the exploring party concluded that some fifteen to twenty Klamaths had taken part in the attack; all but one had escaped. Among the exploring party, three men—Crane, Denny, and Lajeunesse—had died, the last man, one of Frémont's favorite expedition members. As they inspected the dead Indian in their camp, Carson noticed that the corpse carried an English-made hatchet. Impulsively, he seized the tool and "knocked his head to pieces." Finishing the job, James Sagundai, one of the Delawares, then scalped the skull. No burial was made of the fallen Indian. "He was," Frémont recalled, "left where he fell."

"This event cast an angry gloom over the little camp," and—piquing shared Anglophobia—the men noticed that the dead Indian carried arrows with "lancet-like" metal tips that they assumed had come from the nearby Hudson's Bay Company post, on the Umpqua River. Their ire grew still stronger after they concluded that the attackers belonged to a band of Indians to whom they had, days earlier, given meat, tobacco, and knives. "For the moment," Frémont recalled, "I threw all other considerations aside and determined to square accounts with these people before I left them."[1]

❋

In avenging the attack, Frémont proved true to his word. After breakfast, draping their dead comrades across the party's mules, they broke camp and rode back to the main party. En route, they buried the corpses in a shallow grave in a grove of laurels by the lake.

The party spent the next several days making a violent, clockwise circuit of the lake, killing Klamath Indians along the way. On several occasions, they picked off individual tribesmen or small groups of them, with their rifles. In one particularly bloody scene, they made a surprise nighttime assault on an Indian village: "Their arrows were good at close quarters, but the range of the rifle was better. The firing was too severe for them to stand it in open ground and they were driven back into the pine woods with a loss of fourteen killed."

To Frémont, more than personal honor required revenge. He wanted to create a cautionary tale—a study in the violent consequences that befall those who ambush an exploring party. "It will be," he predicted, "a story for them to hand down while there are any Tlamaths on their lake."

✸

After leaving Oregon, the party stopped for two days at Lassen's rancho. While there, Frémont learned about a series of decrees, issued on April 11, in which Castro and other Mexican officials—reacting to the Gavilán Peak episode and what they now viewed as "imminent risk of an invasion founded on the extravagant design of an American Captain"—urged preparations for war. At Lassen's, Frémont, on May 24, took time to write to his father-in-law, Benton, telling the senator about his latest explorations and the Indian attack at Upper Klamath Lake. Curiously, in closing the letter, he wrote, "I shall now proceed directly homewards, by the Colorado, but cannot arrive at the frontier until late in September."

One can only assume that Frémont's declaration of his intention to return to the East immediately was a ruse intended to throw off any Mexican authorities who might intercept the letter. For, the following day, he penned a document auguring very different intentions. It was a letter ordering Gillespie to go to see John B. Montgomery, captain of the U.S.S. *Portsmouth*, then anchored at Yerba Buena. In the letter, Frémont—still calling his entourage "the Exploring Party"—described his men as "almost entirely destitute" and asserted that "the unfriendly disposition of this Government in the present doubtful position of affairs, has made it very difficult for me to obtain provisions." The letter requested soap, tobacco, sugar, flour, and other camp-life necessities of any exploring party. But it also asked for three hundred pounds of musket-ball lead, a keg of gunpowder, and eight thousand percussion caps.[2]

❊

After leaving Lassen's rancho on about May 26, the exploring party rode on to Samuel Neal's Rancho. Neal was away when they arrived, but area settlers and their families soon gathered at Frémont's camp— and reported that the Indians usually employed at ranches in the area had, over the past few weeks, departed for the mountains. To the settlers, the Indians' mysterious abandonment of their agricultural labors augured an attack. Dramatizing their point, the settlers told Frémont about an Indian boy reportedly killed after refusing to take to the mountains.

Shortly after Frémont's arrival at Neal's rancho, a courier arrived from Sutter with a message that seemed to confirm the settlers' worse fears: according to Sutter, two Mexican officials had been sent by General Castro to stir up antisettler sentiments among the Indians. When Samuel Neal and his friend Samuel Hensley, another American settler, returned to the ranch, they provided still more rumors of Mexican government intrigue among the Indians. Hensley told of witnessing, while at Sutter's Fort days earlier, an interrogation of a Maidu chief from the Cosumnes River area, south of the fort.

The interrogation concerned a conversation that allegedly had taken place when General Castro had recently passed through the area. According to Hensley, the Indian said that his fellow tribesmen had been promised great rewards by General Castro in exchange for burning the wheat crops of the American settlers. Hensley, after sharing his tale, offered Frémont a stark conclusion: "that the American residents would have to leave the country or fight for the homes which they had made."[3]

In addition to the threat of Indians, the location of Castro's actual troops still weighed on Frémont's mind. As Frémont contemplated the threat of an Indian attack, he pondered whether, planning an ambush, Castro's troops were possibly by then in California's north, marching up the valley, bent on attacking Frémont and his men. To investigate any possible Mexican troop movements in the valley, Frémont dispatched Samuel Hensley to visit John Marsh, the American-born rancher who owned the vast Rancho Los Meganos, below Mt. Diablo. Marsh's rancho, south of Suisun Bay on the Central Valley's eastern fringe, put him in an ideal position to observe traffic within the Central Valley as well as movements between the valley and San Francisco Bay.[4]

✸

As Frémont's party resumed its southerly course through the widening Central Valley, they delighted in the increasingly warmer weather, and in watching the shrinking snow cover in the Sierra heights to their east. Neal and Hensley, who had left Neal's rancho with Frémont's party, meanwhile rode apart from the main party, crisscrossing the valley, urging settlers to join the advancing Americans. "My camp," Frémont recalled, "wherever it might be, was appointed the place of meeting."[5]

✸

Widening reports, meanwhile, of the gathering American insurgency only increased tensions between California's rival rulers, Pío Pico and José Castro. In late March, in the wake of his army's standoff with Frémont at Gavilán Peak, General Castro had called together, at Monterey, a junta of military strategists, to evaluate California's military situation, and to end the Castro-Pico tensions by clarifying the province's political leadership. Immediately upon convening, the junta recognized Paredes as Mexico's new president. And, that April, when decrees were issued urging preparations for war—a responsibility that fell more naturally to General Castro than civil leader Pico—many perceived them as intended to weaken the powers of Pico's government in Los Angeles. Moreover, the junta placed Castro at the head of efforts to resist the American insurgents—calling on him to mobilize soldiers for that effort and to fortify all of the northern settlements vulnerable to attack. Pico was called to come to Monterey and assist the defensive efforts. But if Pico failed to come, Castro was himself to go to Santa Clara and there take full command of all mobilization efforts until the arrival of reinforcements from Mexico proper. Pico, however, believed that Castro was using American aggressiveness as a pretext to raise an army to vanquish Pico's rival regime in Los Angeles. He rejected the junta's entreaty, then appealed to Mariano Vallejo, the long-term *comandante* at Sonoma, for support. But Vallejo would have none of it—informing Pico that the American threat was real, and that he planned to support Castro.

Pico, however, remained defiant. He decided to raise his own army in Los Angeles, then take it north—ostensibly to aid Castro's resistance, but in fact to seize Castro and remove him from office. Pico also called on representatives from both the north and the south to gather at Santa Barbara on June 15 and formulate a comprehensive plan for resisting the Americans, thus restoring political order in the province. Although the Santa Barbara council never sat, Pico's call for the meeting inspired, over the next few months, numerous rumors of European intrigue. Many American settlers even came to view the meeting as a venue for transferring title to California to Great Britain. General Castro, meanwhile, increasing settlers' fears, spent much of May scouring northern California in search of volunteers for the army he was raising at Santa Clara.

❋

Continuing south down the Sacramento Valley, on May 30 Frémont's party established a camp west of the Feather River, at Sutter Buttes, where they camped for the next ten days. A volcanic mountain range, no more than a half mile in length and twenty-seven hundred feet above sea level, the dark, craggy Sutter Buttes, then as now, rise ominously—visible from Interstate 5, just north of Sacramento—from the surrounding flatness of the Sacramento valley.

After initially setting up camp along the Buttes' southeastern edge, the party moved, a few days later, to another spot, on the range's northeastern margin. There, Frémont found time to take what would be the trip's final astronomical measurements. Of his final, June 7, register entry of astronomical observations, he later wrote, "Here terminated the geographical work of the expedition."[6]

❋

By now, new rumors were reaching Frémont at Sutter Buttes about an imminent attack by General Castro. One report had the general planning an advance upon the settlers with up to three hundred soldiers; another had Castro scheming to build a fort in the Sierra's Donner Pass to prevent the arrival of new non-Mexican settlers. The most persistent reports, however, involved Indians—the valley's wheat crop was now dry, and according to the latest rumors, Indians, whipped up by Castro, were about to descend from the Sierra foothills to torch the crops.

These newest rumors nourished fresh hopes that Frémont might finally join in supporting aggressive measures against the Mexican army. Soon afterward, William Knight, owner of a nearby ranch, reached Sutter Buttes with still more startling news: two Mexican officers, he reported, had just passed by his ranch on the Sacramento north of Sutter's Fort. Fording from the ranch to the river's western bank, the officers were driving a herd of about two hundred horses. The horses, it was said, had been acquired from General Vallejo in Sonoma and were being driven to General Castro's current headquarters in Santa Clara. Castro, Knight said, planned to use the horses in an assault on the settlers.

Suddenly ablaze with talk of stealing the horses, the settlers called on Frémont to lead a raid on the Californios. When he refused, Ezekiel Merritt, a tall, blunt-speaking settler, volunteered to lead the raid. Frémont later called Merritt "my Field-Lieutenant among the settlers"—a man who took "delight in incurring risks, but tractable and not given to asking questions when there was something to do." Another acquaintance, however, offering a harsher view, called Merritt "a brawny, stern man of forty years of age; he is hard-featured[,] has blood-shot eyes and a peculiar stuttering speech. His whole appearance and manner was that of a man moved by some revengeful intoxicating passion."[7]

Merritt recruited a small raiding party comprising about ten men—and quickly set out to to steal the Californios' animals.[8] Riding south, he made a quick stop at Sutter's Fort. Fortunately for the Americans, the two Mexican army officers had stayed at the fort on the evening of June 8—and, while there, during conversations with Sutter, had been boastful, as well as indiscreet. Sutter gladly shared with Merritt the details of the Mexicans' planned route.

The Americans—just before dawn on June 10—wildly yelling, burst into the Californios' camp on the Cosumnes River's south bank and quickly confiscated their weapons and the herd of horses. In the ambush's wake, Lieutenant Arce—one of the two Mexican officers—claimed that, without the element of surprise—if, in other words, there had been an actual battle—the Americans would have been the losers. Taking up Arce's challenge, the boastful Merritt—so he later claimed—offered to return both horses and weapons, leave, then restage the attack. Arce and his his fellow officer, Blas Alviso, declined the offer. Merritt returned their weapons and released them with their personal mounts to return to Santa Clara. Before parting, Merritt boastfully told the two officers to tell General Castro that by the time they got back to Santa Clara, the Americans would control Sonoma, and that Mariano Vallejo would be their prisoner.[9]

❋

Not surprisingly, word of Merritt's brazen deed quickly circulated through the province—discomfiting not only General Castro and other Mexican officials, but also Americans and other foreigners who still hoped for a peaceful U.S. annexation of California.

For wealthy California landowners—such as the Americans John Marsh and Abel Stearns, the Swiss-born Sutter, and even Mexican officials such as Mariano Vallejo—hopes for U.S. acquisition of the province arose, as much as anything, from fears of societal breakdown and a desire for social, political, and economic stability. "For a country not containing fifteen thousand people," merchant Larkin complained to his friend Stearns, "it's the most excitable & combustible one in the world."[10] Hoping for a smooth transition to U.S. dominion, these men tended to disdain any actions that seemed to augur violent social upheaval and, equally important, disrupt day-to-day commerce—particularly when such actions were instigated by society's unlanded elements. Typifying the class-based distaste for the insurgents' actions, Larkin, on June 14, wrote General Castro, offering to help, "if any feasible method can be pointed out to him," in the recovery of the stolen horses.[11]

❁

Historical sources on Frémont's activities in the wake of Merritt's departure with the raiding party are fragmentary, often contradictory. Frémont and his defenders later claimed that, during this period—mindful of limits imposed by his position as a U.S. Army officer—he quietly manipulated events, allowing others to claim credit for certain controversial actions that he actually instigated. By contrast, critics portrayed Frémont, during this period, as a man increasingly left behind by events, a man struggling—often in vain—to find his place in an ever-thickening web of intrigue and conflict. Whatever else happened during that spring of 1846, Frémont's leadership had clearly faltered. The sure-handed sense of mission he had brought to his scientific surveys had grown tentative and shaky—and his authority over the men he ostensibly commanded seemed increasingly hollow.

❁

By June 8, increasingly nervous about the quickening pace of events and determined to occupy "a more central position," Frémont decided to leave Sutter Buttes and relocate the party to its old American River campsite near Sutter's Fort.

Before and after Frémont's party left Sutter Buttes, it was joined by still more settlers—many drawn there by a letter that Frémont or some anonymous instigator, via an Indian messenger, had circulated in the Sacramento valley: "Notice is hereby given, that a large body of armed Spaniards on horseback, amounting to 250 men, have been seen on their way to the Sacramento Valley, destroying the crops, burning the houses, and driving off the cattle." Although the sheet bore no signature, it stated that "Capt Freemont invites every freeman in the valley to come to his camp at the [Sutter] Buttes." William Ide, one of the settlers who received the letter and took up the invitation, would later suggest that the absence of Frémont's signature was deliberate; to have signed it would have been "legal evidence of unwarrantable interference in the difficulties brewing in the country"— an action which, Ide claimed, Frémont subsequently *"uniformly and unequivocally declared he should refrain from."* [12]

✳

Among the settlers in Frémont's camp, the departure of Merritt's raiding party and growing fears of an attack by General Castro increased calls for military action. As they awaited Merritt's return, Frémont listened patiently as various settlers made their case for a preemptive strike.

William Ide's martial hopes, for example, had been bolstered by the initial reports, months earlier, of Frémont's arrival in California. But when Ide and other settlers finally met their putative liberator, they were ill-prepared for Frémont's less than forthright approach. According to Ide, Frémont's plans called for little more than encouraging provocative actions, by American irregulars, against Castro's army. Far from calling for a mass insurgency that he himself would lead, Frémont merely suggested that the Americans select "a dozen men who have nothing to lose, but everything to gain," and dispatch them—on their own—to steal Castro's horses. The party should also take several prisoners, "and thus provoke Castro to strike the first blow in a war" that, once word of the conflict reached Washington, the United States would promptly join.

Ide, with disdain, aptly called Frémont's proposal a strategy of "neutral conquest." And, as the settlers listened to the proposal, they, too, were unimpressed. When several dismissed it as too timid, Frémont angrily ended the meeting. A few minutes later, in another tent, the settlers continued their conversation—but this time without Frémont.

Now they talked about a revolt without Frémont's—or for that matter, Washington's—assistance. This fight, they finally decided, belonged to them and to no one else: "The United States may have cause of war against Mexico; but that is nothing to us. We have cause of war and blood—such as it is impossible for the United States to have received." By Ide's account, that steely resolve—to move ahead without Frémont—quickly spilled out of the tent and, circulating through the camp, won instant acclaim among the settlers. " 'Hurrah for Independence!' cried the whole camp." As war fever rose, several members of Frémont's original party—even Kit Carson—asked to be discharged so that they might join the planned campaign. As Ide recalled, "This was peremptorily refused. Frémont, in my hearing, expressly declared that he was *not at liberty to afford us the least aid or assistance; nor would he suffer any of his men to do so; that he would not consent to discharge any of them, as he had hired them expressly for, and needed their assistance on his journey over land to the States.*"

According to Ide, Frémont added that he had not asked for the settlers' assistance. If circumstances required it, his own men could defeat Castro's army—but they would not attack unless first attacked. In the meantime, Frémont's party would await the new supplies which Gillespie had been dispatched to Yerba Buena to obtain. Frémont expected the provisions would arrive within two weeks; afterward, he expected to, *"without further reference to what might take place here, be on his march for the States."*[13]

❀

On the morning of June 11 Merritt, driving the stolen herd, had returned to camp and turned over the horses to Frémont for safekeeping. Now, flushed with that victory, the settlers were abuzz with excitement about their next mission—another military errand on which Frémont was refusing to act. Their next objective was the capture of Sonoma: if the settlers could control Sonoma and the rest of the country north of San Francisco Bay, General Castro's planned operation against them would, in all likelihood, fail. And the Americans would have a secure base to which they could rally more of California's foreigners.[14]

❀

Fearful that he was about to be left behind by the men of his original party, Frémont called its members together and implored them to stay. According to survey-party member Thomas S. Martin, Frémont told the men that we had shared in common the dangers and hardships of our journey to that point and he hoped that no difficulty would occur to cause our separation, that he would make every concession in his power to prevent such an event, and he hoped that we would each one by doing his duty etc. contribute to that end; that we were about to enter upon a campaign in this country and that it was indispensable that there should be harmony between us and a determination to hold together come what would.

But, according to Martin, when Frémont sensed that his appeal to comradely loyalty was failing to move the men, he tried another tack—"that it being impossible for him under his present orders to assume the offensive with his command he proposed disbanding us, when we could recognize and choose a leader." At that point, Martin recalled, the party's members, seeking a little distance from their just-resigned leader, left their American River campsite and marched downstream a short distance until just opposite Sutter's Fort. "Here we were disbanded. We put the election of a leader to the vote and Fremont was unanimously chosen. He then told us that we could elect an officer and go and take Sonoma." Under his new commission—essentially that of a filibuster army beyond the purview of the U.S. Army—Frémont now allowed the men to move against Sonoma and try to thwart General Castro.

With Frémont having formally removed himself from a leadership position, the men were now compelled to select a new command structure. Putting the matter to a vote, they elected Merritt and Ide, along with fellow settlers Henry L. Ford and Granville Swift, as their leaders—with Swift as senior officer. Building from that nucleus, they quickly recruited several more volunteers—bringing their total ranks to twenty-one men.

Swift and the assault party left later that same day. Frémont, while expressing approval of the mission, once again stayed behind. To a large degree, events and men had moved beyond Frémont's control. Even so—testament to the loyalty he inspired among those who had followed him over the West's prairies, mountains, and deserts—none of the original members of the third exploring party peeled away to follow Merritt.[15]

BEAR FLAG

O VER THE PREVIOUS THREE MONTHS of 1846, thirty-three-year-old John Frémont had struggled mightily, at times desperately, to avoid being left behind by events in the Sacramento valley and the rolling country north of San Francisco Bay. To preserve his leadership, he had even been willing to affiliate himself with an insurgency bent on establishing an independent republic in California—a cause that enjoyed no sanction from Senator Benton and his friends, or from the United States government under whose flag Frémont had come to this distant Mexican province.

But what was Frémont's actual involvement in that insurgency? Twice in public testimony in Washington, shortly after concluding his military service in California, and still later in his *Memoirs*, he would claim to have played a major role in the Sonoma assault. As he put it before one Washington panel,

> In concert, and in co-operation with the American settlers, and in the brief space of about thirty days, all was accomplished north of the Bay of San Francisco, and independence declared on the 5th day of July. This was done at *Sonoma*, where the American settlers had assembled.

And in his *Memoirs*, Frémont—dispensing with the passive voice—baldly asserted, "Acting upon . . . necessity, I sent Merritt into Sonoma instructed to surprise the garrison at that place."[1]

But in making such claims, Frémont was apparently motivated

more by personal motives than by any fealty to the truth—for, in the end, the case for his leadership in what became known as the Bear Flag Revolt appears weak. Why would Frémont have misrepresented his role? By the conclusion of the California campaign, he had become known as the "Conqueror of California," so it hardly seemed appropriate for the province's Caesar to have commenced his actions as a nervous prevaricator. Beyond that, after the campaign, challenges arose concerning the legal and political legitimacy of Frémont's actions in California. To defend himself against such charges, it behooved him to place his military actions under the protective coloring of U.S. military authority at the earliest plausible date.

Whatever indirect role, if any, Frémont played in the decisions to undertake the capture of Arce's horses and the seizure of Sonoma remains unclear. His later statements regarding the two actions were either vague, contradictory, or both—and we have none from Merritt. Recall that Frémont, in his *Memoirs*, called Merritt "my Field Lieutenant among the settlers"—implying that he, Frémont, acted as chief commander among the American insurgents. According to Ide, Merritt, after stealing General Castro's horses, asserted that he had taken that action on Frémont's "advice."

But giving "advice" is hardly tantamount to commanding an operation—and even the idea that Frémont counseled the Americans to seize Sonoma seems questionable. It also is doubtful that Merritt played the subordinate role implied by Frémont. Weeks after the attack on the Mexican garrison, Merritt was described as "the cheif [*sic*] actor in the late Sonoma affair."[2] And according to Ide, as Merritt and his attack party left for Sonoma, their "conduct was highly applauded by Capt. Frémont." But Frémont, Ide added, nonetheless declined to "offer us the least protection or assistance."[3]

It also seems doubtful that Frémont secretly planned each of the two operations and then allowed others to execute them. Writing to his brother shortly after Merritt's party seized Sonoma, Edward Kern noted that the exploring party took no part in the action: "They had it all to themselves[,] our camp laying by as mere spectators." Frémont himself, in his *Memoirs*, tacitly endorsed that portrait of inaction, when he recalled his posture *after* the raid on Sonoma: "Affairs had now assumed a critical aspect and I presently saw that the time had come when it was unsafe to leave events to mature under unfriendly, or mistaken, direction. I decided that it was for me rather to govern events than to be governed by them."[4]

❋

More than anything Frémont did, it was simply the presence of a famous U.S. Army officer that emboldened the American settlers to act on plans contemplated long before his arrival. The settlers of the Napa and Sonoma valleys had struck on the idea of taking Sonoma even before Frémont's admirers began flocking to his camp in the Sacramento valley. Indeed, the settlers' gathering militancy not only antedated Frémont's arrival in California but continued in spite of his rebuff of their appeals seeking help for an attack.

Raising doubts about any presidential authorship of the attack on Sonoma is a letter dated September 1, 1846—two months after the Bear Flag was raised over Sonoma—overlooked by past Frémont biographers, from President Polk to Senator Benton. In it, Polk informed Benton that the State Department had just learned that Monterey had fallen to U.S. forces, after which he added:

> Information has also been received that a party or detachment from *Col. Frémont's* forces took possession of a frontier post called *Sonoma* to the North of San Francisco, that *Genl Castro*, the Commandant General attempted to dislodge them, but that after a slight skirmish and the arrival of *Col. Frémont* in person he *Castro* retreated.—The dates from Monterey are to the 6th of July and from the vicinity of that place to the 9th of the same month.—Supposing that you would be gratified to hear this intelligence, and particularly to learn Col. Frémont's whereabouts, previous to your departure from the West, I write you this note.—By calling at the State Department you can learn particulars.

The almost desultory tone of Polk's conveyance of the news about the assault hardly sounds like one conspirator congratulating his coconspirator on the realization of a long-planned intrigue.[5]

✺

Even as Frémont vacillated in the Sacramento valley, the movement by American settlers to seize Sonoma—and California—had already taken on a life of its own. As William Hargrave, one of the Napa valley settlers sent to entice Frémont into their conspiracy, recalled, "On our return to Napa Valley we found that the revolutionary movement had gained more ground and steps were taken at once to organize a force sufficient for our first enterprise—the capture of Sonoma."[6]

Contemporary critics and, later, historians have accused Frémont, during this period, of rank opportunism. Upon closer scrutiny, however, the record suggests more confusion than cunning. Frémont's equivocation suggests he had no firm grasp of events, and no thought-out set of plans. At best, he was improvising. At worst, he was floundering in a maelstrom of events beyond his control.

So why did Frémont's leadership falter? Until Frémont's standoff with General Castro, his toughest decisions had been made in desolate wildernesses, far from Washington or any other seat of government. Frémont's own life and those of his men might turn on decisions made in such remote climes. But beyond whatever immediate consequences his choices might have on himself and those under him, such decisions had few or no long-range consequences.

Consider, too, the size and type of army that, in the summer of 1846, suddenly clamored for Frémont's leadership. Preoccupied with watersheds, mountains passes, and other topographical priorities, Frémont the explorer had violated national borders with little or no reflection, and had often found himself in dangerous situations—ably confronting hostile Indians, hunger, foul weather, flooded rivers, and other perils. But in California he was suddenly confronting a set of circumstances for which nothing had prepared him—a complex configuration of choices, with stakes far higher, both for himself and for his nation, than any he had ever before faced.

Like a man sizing up a billiard shot with an infinity of possible ricochets, Frémont pondered his options. Beyond trying to accommodate the quicksilver republicanism of the agitated settlers who sought his leadership, he had to think about how his actions might be received by his own superiors in Washington. He also had to consider what reactions his decisions might provoke among the governments of Mexico proper, California, and England.

At Klamath Lake, after reading Gillespie's dispatches, Frémont had decided that he finally had the "license" to act on his and Benton's long-seasoned objective of bringing California into the United States. But that resolve had given the young captain no insight into how and when to advance that objective. And the communications were sufficiently vague to leave Frémont at tactical loose ends—groping for a strategy to translate his objectives into concrete actions.

❋

Riding from Sutter Buttes on the night of June 12–13, Ezekiel Merritt's ragtag army dodged the main road to Sonoma that wraps around San Pablo Bay's north shore. Taking a more northerly and circuitous route to preserve the element of surprise, and gathering more recruits along the way, the army, when it arrived in Sonoma at dawn on June 14, numbered thirty-two men.

The motley band arrived on Sonoma's town square and surrounded Mariano Vallejo's walled Casa Grande compound. To the general's sister, Rosalía Leese Vallejo, the men appeared to be "rough looking desperadoes." Bitterly recalling the scene three decades later, she recounted, "The majority of this marauding band wore buck-skins pants, some blue pants that reached only to the knee, several had no shirts, shoes were only to be seen on the feet of fifteen or twenty among the whole lot."

Three men then knocked on the entrance to Casa Grande—Merritt and Knight, joined by Robert Semple, a leader of the revolt and, later that year, cofounder of *The Californian*, California's first newspaper. When no one immediately answered, they began banging with hammers to defeat the lock that guarded the general's impressive two-story house. Situated on the square's north side, the walled adobe compound, 110 feet in length, featured a formidable *torreón*, a four-story tower which rose from its west wall. To the house's east sat the one-story adobe barracks that garrisoned the Mexican soldiers once, but no longer, posted at Sonoma. And next door to it lay the now crumbling Sonoma mission.

Vallejo was initially delayed as he put on his uniform. Rejecting his wife's pleas that he try to sneak out a back door and flee, when the general finally opened the door, he invited the insurgents inside. Until the general's American brother-in-law, Jacob Leese, arrived to translate, however, their talks made little progress.

Asked by Leese why Vallejo was being arrested, Robert Semple answered that they sought to make California an independent state— and that Vallejo commanded much influence, held substantial property, and owned a large arsenal of weapons, which they needed. To that, Vallejo countered that he was sympathetic to their objectives. He had, he said, always been a protector of the rights of foreigners. Beyond that, he added, their efforts would soon prove pointless; it was his understanding, he said, that California officials were planning to ask the United States to assume control over the province.

The three insurgents assured Vallejo that no harm would come to him or to anyone else in Sonoma. They also pledged to take no property—beyond that absolutely needed. To Vallejo's and Leese's suspicions that the settlers were acting under orders from either Frémont or the U.S. Army, the three Americans assured the two men that their ragtag army was acting on its own.

As the talks inside continued, the other insurgents, waiting outside, grew anxious. Eventually, John Grigsby, a settler rapidly emerging as one of the revolt's principal leaders, was appointed to go inside; and when he, too, failed to return, Ide was sent in. Later reports suggested that Vallejo's generosity with brandy prolonged that morning's meeting. When the articles of capitulation were finally presented, most of the Americans waiting outside scorned them—objecting to the negotiated provisions that allowed Leese, General Vallejo, his brother Salvador Vallejo, and another officer, Lieutenant Colonel Victor Prudon, to be paroled on their honor as gentlemen. Most of the insurgents preferred that the men be taken as prisoners to Frémont's camp—a demand to which all present, even the prisoners, eventually acceded.

That afternoon, there was much drinking, the local alcalde was locked up, and the invaders seized all the horses, weapons, and ammunition that they could locate. Semple, Ide, and other leaders, however, did successfully discourage any hunger among the men for wholesale plunder. As expedition artist, Richard Kern, in all likelihood reflecting Frémont's own misgivings about the purported revolutionaries, soon observed in a letter to his brother, "Had the revolutionaries been left to themselves[,] a few weeks would have settled the business by their defeating themselves." To Kern, most of the insurgents seemed "moved by nothing but the chance of plunder without the slightest principle of honor."

That same day, William L. Todd—a twenty-six year old American settler, and a cousin of Mrs. Abraham Lincoln—designed a flag. Taking a piece of light brown cloth, with either red paint or berry juice— accounts disagree—he drew a broad stripe across its bottom and a star and a grizzly bear across its top. Across the middle of the cloth, in black letters, he painted the words "California Republic." To the hurrahs of the settlers, the banner—of what was quickly christened the Bear Flag Republic—was raised on the staff in Sonoma's town plaza, where, up until that morning, the flag of Mexico had flown. A stylized version of the flag was later adopted as, and remains, the official flag of the state of California.[7]

✤

As the settlers that day had advanced toward Sonoma, Frémont's party, once again, had also been on the move—this time, toward Sutter's embarcadero, at the confluence of the American and Sacramento Rivers. Because he had spent years leading wilderness expeditions, Frémont's attentions rarely strayed far from the material needs—from clothing to food, from tobacco to whiskey—that sustain any mobile party. Thus, even as he wrestled with his ambivalence about the settlers' war on the Californios, he was eagerly awaiting the supplies he had requested from Captain John B. Montgomery of the U.S.S. *Portsmouth*, still anchored at Yerba Buena.

Reaching Sutter's embarcadero on June 15, Frémont and his men found Gillespie, his servant, Benjamin Harrison, and several of the *Portsmouth*'s crew waiting for them. The supplies they had brought were still aboard the launch sent out by Montgomery. The vessel had arrived around midnight on June 13–14, a full day before Frémont's men reached the embarcadero—though apparently none too soon:

"He and his party are very much sunburnt, and are the most ununi-
form and grotesque set of men I have ever seen," recalled Marius Duvall, the *Portsmouth*'s surgeon. "Their buckskin dresses, with fringes at
the seams, are something peculiar." After the men set up camp in a
nearby grove of oaks, the long-awaited supplies were brought off the
launch: "The flour barrels, tobacco boxes, tea and coffee cases were
opened with all dispatch, and their contents served out to watery
mouths."[8]

Although the stores sent by Montgomery included a large cache of
weapons and ammunition, Frémont, even at this late date, still insisted, for the record, that he had no role to play in any insurgency
against the Californios. In a June 16 letter thanking Montgomery for
the supplies, he portrayed himself as an innocent—a man of science,
unfairly linked to the belligerency of others. Even while professing
admiration of those who "have made some movements with the view
of establishing a settled & stable Government, which may give security to their persons & property," Frémont stuck to his claim of strict
neutrality. "The people and authorities of the country persist in connecting me with every movement of the foreigners, & I am in hourly
expectation of Genl. Castro." He planned, he assured Montgomery, to
spend the next few weeks resting his animals and preparing for a departure in early July for the East; he planned, he wrote, to be back in
Missouri by September.

The confusion reflected in such pronouncements was equally evident in Frémont's actions. For instance, he professed sympathy for the
seizure of Sonoma. But, according to Duvall, when the prisoners taken
there arrived at Frémont's embarcadero encampment, he treated them
as anything but prisoners: "Capt. Fremont received them as they dismounted, shook them by the hand and invited them into his 'lodge'
[teepee]." The next day, while visiting Sutter's Fort, Duvall found the
Americans' chief prisoner more perplexed than frightened by recent
events. "General Vallejo remarked that he considered himself his (F's)
prisoner, that he regretted he had no sword to deliver to him—but
having been so taken by surprise and hurried off, that he had not had
time to procure it. Capt. F. endeavoured to dissuade him from the
idea, that he was his prisoner, but unsuccessfully." Afterward, Frémont ordered a group of Delaware Indians to escort his guests to Sutter's Fort, where they were to be held until further notice.[9]

Montgomery likewise could be forgiven if he found mixed signals in Frémont's professed intentions: in an earlier letter sent via Gillespie, for instance, Frémont had speculated to Montgomery about the possibility of taking his exploring party to Santa Barbara and had asked if the *Portsmouth* might anchor there to wait for them. In a June 10 letter accompanying the supplies he sent to Frémont, Montgomery had answered that he would be willing to sail to Santa Barbara or any other Pacific port. Answering Montgomery's offer, Frémont now asked him to keep the *Portsmouth* anchored at Yerba Buena, "where your presence will operate strongly to check proceedings against us." Although Frémont stated he planned to leave, within weeks, for Missouri, "if, therefore, any hostile movements are made in this direction, I will most assuredly meet or anticipate them; and with such intention I am regulating my conduct to the people here."[10]

For weeks, unsure of his proper course of action, Frémont had tried to stay above the fray. Now, by accepting the Sonoma prisoners, he had moved irrevocably beyond the strained professions of evenhandedness that had characterized his initial response to California's growing American insurgency. Johann Sutter, relating a recent conversation with Frémont to surgeon Marius Duvall, declared that Frémont was now "throwing aside the vacillating policy which has thus far characterized his conduct . . . [and] had openly declared for the side of the foreigners."[11]

✺

In dispatching his prisoners to Sutter's Fort, Frémont reached for a mantle of authority over the settlers that, days earlier, had seemed to be slipping away from him. But how would Sutter—essentially being forced to act as the prisoners' jailer—react to being thus implicated in the revolt?

The relationship between Frémont and Sutter, never easy, suffered fresh strains, when Frémont arrived with the Sonoma prisoners on June 19. Sutter—even as a Mexican official—had long favored U.S. acquisition of California and seemed delighted with the insurgency at Sonoma. Even so, Frémont insulted him by treating him as anything but an ally. Shortly after Frémont's arrival at the fort, Sutter emerged in tears from a private meeting with his American visitor. The explorer had informed Sutter that "he was a Mexican, and that if he did not like what he (Frémont) was doing he would set him across the San Joaquin River and he could go and join the Mexicans." Before leaving, Frémont made it clear that if any prisoners escaped, Sutter would be held responsible; for good measure, he put a member of his own party, Edward Kern, in charge of the fort.

❋

At least partially, Frémont's newfound zeal for the insurgency arose from his awareness of the size of the enemy forces stirred by the attack on Sonoma: "Against the Mexican Government, with which I knew we were contending, the individual action of the settlers could have only a temporary success, to result in inevitable disaster so soon as the government troops were brought to bear upon them." Frémont's assumption that U.S. forces would soon join the fight also nourished his growing boldness. "I represented the Army and the Flag of the United States," he later grandiloquently claimed. "And the Navy was apparently co-operating with me. This gave to my movements the national character which must of necessity be respected by Mexico, and by any foreign power to which she might ally herself." Still, self-doubts dogged Frémont: lest the U.S. government later have any reason to disavow his actions, he took the precaution of drawing up a letter of resignation from the U.S. Army, to be sent via Senator Benton to the War Department, "in the event of such a contingency."[12]

❋

Over the coming days and weeks, however, new developments weaned Frémont away from such doubts. On the positive side, the success of the assault on Sonoma encouraged martial ambitions; as word of the attack and a republican-styled "Bear Flag" declaration of independence hastily written by Ide circulated through northern California, more settlers were flocking to Sonoma. On the negative side—but no less useful in recruiting volunteers—word also arrived at the camp of a new proclamation by General Castro, ordering all foreigners "to leave the country at any date fixed by the government or they would otherwise be driven out by force." There were also fresh rumors of intrigues by Californio officials among the Indians, encouraging them to attack the Americans.

On June 20, word reached Frémont that General Castro was organizing a force, composed of soldiers and Indians, to attack Frémont's camp. Frémont got still more incentive to abandon his American River camp when John Neal, a courier dispatched from Sonoma by Henry L. Ford, reported that the Bear Flaggers had begun to doubt William Ide's leadership; still more worrisome, a large force of Californios under Joaquín de la Torré was gathering at San Rafael, with plans to attack Sonoma. The de la Torré party, consisting of about seventy men, had been dispatched by General Castro from his temporary base at Santa Clara, about two days' ride from Sonoma. After hearing of the assault on Sonoma, Castro had pulled together about four hundred recruits at Santa Clara.[13]

Answering "urgent appeals made by the settlers for assistance," Frémont and some ninety men, on June 23, set off for Sonoma. His force consisted of his original party; Sutter's chief clerk, Major Pierson B. Reading; six of Sutter's trappers; and Samuel Hensley and his settler followers. James W. Marshall, who would later gain fame by discovering gold in California, recalled the departing party: "There were Americans, French, English, Swiss, Poles, Russians, Chilians [sic], Germans, Greeks, Austrians, Pawnees, native Indians etc. . . . Well if they [Castro's army] whip this crowd they can beat all the world, for Castro will whip all nations, languages and tongues!"[14]

Upon reaching Sonoma two days later, Frémont learned that, days earlier, two Americans traveling from the coastal town of Bodega to the west, en route to Sonoma, had been captured by a group of Californios, who "had tied them to trees and butchered them with knives." Frémont also heard that that Captain de la Torré's army, mustering at nearby Mission San Rafael for the attack on Sonoma, was awaiting reinforcements under General Castro. By noon the next day, June 26, Frémont—with an army 130 men—was en route to San Rafael. They reached the mission at 3:00 that afternoon but found its buildings deserted. Upon learning that Castro's army was now at Point San Pablo, on San Pablo Bay's eastern shore, waiting to cross the Bay,

Frémont and his men headed toward the coast. Two days later, on Sunday, June 28—after the party spotted a boat crossing the bay, sailing west toward San Quentin, along its western shoreline—Kit Carson and several others rode off to intercept the vessel. At San Quentin, the boat stopped long enough before returning to San Pablo for three Californios to step ashore. The three men were Francisco and Ramón de Haro, twins in their twenties; and an older man, their uncle José de los Reyes Berreyesa, whose son, the alcalde of Sonoma, was at that moment a prisoner of the Bears.

As they—all unarmed—came within fifty yards of the waiting Americans, the Americans opened fire, killing all three men. Conflicting accounts cloud efforts to understand why the shots were fired—and by whom; according to one oft-quoted account, as Carson's party left Sonoma, Frémont had warned them that he had "no room for prisoners"—an admonition that Carson, it has been suggested, took as license to kill all three of the approaching Californios. But accounts fail even to consistently place Carson at the scene of the killings. Yet another account claimed that the three men were killed after they resisted capture. Frémont himself attributed the deaths to an inadvertent shooting by his Delawares out on a round of scouting.[15]

❀

That same afternoon, a scouting party led by Frémont intercepted an Indian carrying a letter indicating that de la Torré was planning an attack on Sonoma for the next day. Alarmed, Frémont's men backtracked the approximately thirty miles to Sonoma that night.

But, as it turned out, the party sent by Castro had returned to its base in Santa Clara. The intercepted letter had been a ruse, designed to tie up Frémont on a fool's errand back to Sonoma, thus buying de la Torré's army time to escape. While Frémont and his men headed to protect Sonoma, de la Torré's army rode to Sausalito. From there, in a borrowed schooner, they crossed San Francisco Bay to Yerba Buena.

Upon learning of the trick, Frémont rushed to Sausalito—only to learn that his quarry had already slipped across the bay. The next morning—July 1—he and the twelve men traveling with him persuaded Captain William D. Phelps of the American bark *Moscow* to ferry them across to Yerba Buena. Once ashore, they found no soldiers in the settlement's crumbling presidio. Determined to leave *some* kind of mark, they contented themselves with spiking the ten long-abandoned Spanish brass cannons at the old castillo at the mouth of the bay—the break in the Coast Range that Frémont had, months earlier, named the Golden Gate. The next day, ten men of the Bear Flag insurgency joined Frémont's party at Yerba Buena. Increasingly brazen, the occupation force arrested Robert Ridley, a Mexican-born naturalized Englishman, and captain of the port.

Up to now, Frémont's involvement in actual military actions had been minimal. Now, he suddenly commanded a movement that claimed control over all of California north of San Francisco Bay, and eastward from the ocean to Sutter's Fort.[16]

✺

Frémont's forces returned to Sonoma on July 4—just in time for a buoyant celebration of Independence Day, complete with cannon volleys, a fandango, and a reading of the Declaration of Independence. The next day, Frémont called a public meeting at Vallejo's house: "It had now become necessary to concentrate the elements of this movement, in order to give it the utmost efficiency of which it was capable." Ide and his followers sat in one room, Frémont and his in another. Sprinkled through each group were a handful of U.S. Navy men. Frémont addressed the assembly but, according to Ide, fell short of calling for California's independence from Mexico. Instead, Ide reported, Frémont wanted merely to capture General Castro—as vengeance on the Californio general for the Gavilán Peak episode.

Whatever differences divided those at the meeting—accounts differ—they settled on Frémont as their leader. To hammer out an official statement of purpose, a committee was appointed consisting of one Bear (Ide) and two of Frémont's men (John Bidwell and Pierson B. Reading). Frémont, eager to exorcise memories of past vacillations, persuaded the assembly to date the beginning of California's independence not from June 15—when Sonoma was actually taken—but from July 5, the day of their meeting, when Frémont assumed formal command over the insurgency. That way, Frémont's leadership would, as he later noted, "begin at the beginning."

As the fledgling republic's ragged army assumed a formal structure,

Frémont—borrowing the Spanish word for *bear*—became "Oso 1" and Gillespie "Oso 2." The army of 224 was split into four companies: Richard Owens led a company composed mainly of Frémont's men. The other three companies—comprising mainly settlers—were led by Henry L. Ford, John Grigsby, and Granville P. Swift.

The next day, the prolific Ide wrote out the conditions by which the new republic might be annexed by the United States. California, Ide's decree stated, must enjoy all privileges enjoyed by other states. It must also retain its public lands, and the United States would have to agree to defray all costs of the war against Mexico. After the meeting, on Frémont's orders, the new army's four companies began rounding up all available horses and cattle. Scouring the area, they gathered seven hundred mounts—most of them from Vallejo's rancho, just outside Sonoma. Five hundred head of cattle were taken from a nearby government outpost.

Leaving behind Grigsby and a company of fifty men, Frémont and the rest of the army, on July 6, left Sonoma—dragging several small brass cannons—bound for their old camp on the American River. There, on the evening of July 10, a courier arrived with news that "electrified" Frémont and his men: three days earlier, Commodore Sloat had raised the Stars and Stripes over Monterey's main plaza, thus asserting U.S. possession of California. Captain Montgomery, on Sloat's orders, had raised the U.S. flag in Yerba Buena and had sent a flag to Sonoma to be raised over that settlement as well. Upon receiving the message, Frémont, following suit, quickly raised the U.S. flag over Sutter's Fort.

❋

What were Frémont's plans at that point? He later claimed that he had intended to march on General Castro's army. Whatever his plans, they were soon overtaken by other exigencies. The next day, another courier arrived with new orders directly from Commodore Sloat: Frémont was to leave immediately for Monterey. While Sloat now held Monterey, as he waited to negotiate a formal peace accord with Mexican authorities, he felt undermanned to keep civil peace in the area. To Frémont, the naval commander wrote, "Although I am in expectation of seeing General Castro, to enter into satisfactory terms with him, there may be a necessity of one hundred men, well mounted, who are accustomed to riding, to form a force to prevent any further robbing of the farmers' houses, &c. by the Indians."[17]

Frémont was being drawn deeper and deeper into matters that had little relevance to exploration and everything to do with the advance of the American empire.

A PAWN FOR EMPIRE 20

Y THE SUMMER OF 1846, John Drake Sloat, commodore of the U.S. Navy's Pacific Squadron fleet, then anchored at Mazatlán, had no stomach for war. A once-vigorous officer, he was now sixty-eight years old, in failing health, and waiting for word on a request for retirement already sent to Washington. In pondering the seizure of California's ports, Sloat was haunted by an embarrassing incident that, in October 1842, had befallen his Pacific Squadron predecessor, Thomas ap Catesby Jones: after getting false reports that California was about to be seized by English or French interlopers, Jones had seized Monterey and raised the U.S. flag over the port—only to have his actions rebuked by Washington.

As a result, Commodore Sloat, even after learning, on May 17, of the outbreak of U.S.–Mexican hostilities along the Rio Grande, had hesitated to act. Although he had orders, upon hearing of "actual hostilities," to move immediately to occupy Yerba Buena—by then increasingly known as San Francisco—and as many other California ports as he could reach, he waited for more reports. Not until June 7, when Sloat learned of the U.S. blockade of Vera Cruz, did he and his flotilla sail for Monterey.

The Pacific Squadron consisted of three frigates, the *Savannah*, the *Congress*, and the *Constitution*; two transport ships, the *Relief* and the *Erie*; and three sloops, each with forty-four guns, the *Warren*, the *Cyane*, and the *Portsmouth*. The squadron reached Monterey on July 2. Once again, however, Sloat hesitated to commence military operations. He made courtesy calls ashore, received the latest news on the activities of John Frémont and the Bear Flaggers, and allowed the ship's crew to go ashore for recreational purposes. Finally, on July 7, demanding the town's surrender, Sloat issued a proclamation declaring Alta California conquered: "Henceforward California will be a portion of the United States, and its peaceful inhabitants will enjoy the same rights and privileges as the Citizens of any other portion of that Nation, with all the rights & privileges they now enjoy, together with the privilege of choosing their own Magistrates & other Officers . . . and the same protection will be extended to them as to any other State of the Union."[1]

Though Don Mariano Silva, Monterey's local *comandante*, explained that he possessed no authority to surrender the town, the town's capture took place without a shot because no effective Californio troops were there. As a measure of how far California had drifted from Mexico City's consciousness, before the U.S. flag could be raised a Mexican flag had to be found; it had been months since one had flown over northern California's principal town. Once located, the Mexican flag was raised, then immediately lowered; and the U.S. flag, accompanied by a twenty-one gun salute, was promptly run up the same pole.

Captain Montgomery, upon receiving orders from Sloat, promptly affected a similarly smokeless capture of San Francisco. That same day, a contingent of soldiers dispatched by Montgomery reached Sonoma, where there was a public reading of Sloat's proclamation; the Bear Flag was lowered, and the U.S. flag raised.

✤

After declining to challenge the Bear Flaggers north of San Francisco, General Castro's army of 160 men returned to their temporary base of operations in Santa Clara. As the general pondered his next move against the Americans, he reflected on his long-standing rivalry with Governor Pico; with the Yankees now controlling much of northern California, Castro reasoned, perhaps it was time to make peace with his rival to the south. Pico, meanwhile, unaware of the magnitude of U.S. military operations in California, was at that very moment headed north, seeking a military confrontation with Castro.[2]

✽

On July 11, from Los Ojitos, northwest of Paso Robles, Castro dispatched a message to Pico imploring him to join in a shared effort "to save the country and the dignity of the national government." In his dispatch, Castro also included copies of an exchange between himself and Sloat, in which Castro had refused a demand of surrender from the American officer. "There is still time," Castro stressed in his entreaty to Pico; "the invaders have only occupied Monterey and San Francisco."

Castro's letter reached Pico—by then encamped at San Luis Obispo—that same day. Accepting the governor's offer of reconciliation, he immediately turned south. Countermanding earlier orders to seek a confrontation with Castro, Pico now ordered his officers in the field to direct all of the province's forces toward Los Angeles's defense.[3]

✽

After receiving Sloat's summons to come to Monterey, Frémont, on July 12, leaving his camp near Sutter's Fort, headed south, down the Sacramento River valley. Upon reaching the Mokelumne River, the party split into two groups. Gillespie and a small party continued down the valley and over the Coast Range, to Monterey. Frémont's contingent bent toward the west along a more direct route to Monterey—over the Coast Range and down the coast. Gillespie's contingent arrived at Monterey on July 16. Two days later, Frémont reached Mission San Juan Bautista, which, months earlier—from Gavilán Peak, during his standoff with Castro's army—he had gazed down upon, watching Californio troops assembling against him. But this time, Frémont's army found no enemy troops at the old mission; they did, however, find evidence that General Castro's army had passed through within the week. Moreover, in the adjacent village of San Juan, the Californios had left behind a cache of weapons—nine cannons, nineteen kegs of gunpowder, and 150 muskets that quickly fell into the Americans' hands. Recognizing a military need to hold San Juan Bautista—but at the same time, expecting no more enemy threats from the north—Frémont ordered only a small contingent of men to stay behind to hold the mission.

While at San Juan Bautista, Frémont's army was joined by thirty-five men—including Archibald Gillespie—dispatched by Sloat to keep communications open between Monterey and Yerba Buena. Gillespie reported to Frémont that Sloat, after taking Monterey, seemed disinclined to take further military actions in California. He did, however, plan in the coming days to relinquish his authority to Robert F. Stockton, a newly arrived commander eager to take such actions.

By all accounts, when Frémont's California Battalion reached Monterey, they created quite a stir. According to Frémont, "the rough and travel-worn" appearance of his men stood in stark contrast to that of Sloat's sailors, with their crisp white uniforms. To a British naval officer who witnessed the California Battalion's arrival in Monterey, its men appeared to be

> true trappers, the class that produced the heroes of Fenimore Cooper's best works. The men had passed years in the wilds, living upon their own resources; they were a curious set. A vast cloud of dust appeared first, and thence in long-file emerged this wildest wild part. Frémont rode ahead, a spare, active-looking man. . . . He was dressed in a blouse and leggings, and wore a felt hat. After him came five Delaware Indians, who were his body-guard, and have been with him through all his wanderings; they had charge of two baggage-horses. The rest, many of them blacker than the Indians, rode two and two, the rifle held by one hand across the pommel of the saddle. . . . The dress of these men was principally a long loose coat of deerskin, tied with thongs in front; trousers of the same, of their own manufacture.

"It was a day of excitement," Frémont recalled. "I was glad again to meet the ocean breeze and surf. Many of my men had never seen the ocean, or the English flag." Frémont, upon arriving—still believing that Britain had active interests in seizing California—was delighted to see, in the harbor, four U.S. men-of-war outnumbering a lone British ship, the eighty-gun *Collingwood*, flagship of Britain's Pacific Squadron.[4]

✸

English dreams of conquering California stretched back to 1579, when explorer-privateer Sir Francis Drake, upon making landfall somewhere north of San Francisco, christened California "Nova Albion," claiming it for Queen Elizabeth. And during the nineteenth century, John Bull continued to manifest interest in the province.

Ironically, however, by the mid-1840s, when political instability in California had made British acquisition of the province a plausible possibility, Foreign Minister Lord Aberdeen resolutely opposed any such action. During that period, he rejected several appeals from putative Californio insurgents; indeed, a rebuff came as late as August 1846—after the Mexican government, concerned about the financial costs of waging war with the United States, had offered to sell California to Britain in exchange for a war loan. In rejecting the deal, Aberdeen asserted that the offer came too late; given the instabilities that already plagued California, he wrote, the Mexican government was in no position to guarantee the province's transfer to a third party. Even the plans of an Irish priest named Eugene McNamara to establish an Irish colony in southern California—a proposition that fueled the Anglophobia of Frémont and other Americans in the province—failed to generate enthusiasm among British officials.[5]

Surviving correspondence suggests that the British fleet's main charge in the Pacific, during the period of U.S.–Mexican hostilities, was to prevent French encroachments on English interests in the Pacific Islands. In California itself, British naval attention tended to focus on gathering intelligence and protecting British nationals. Nonetheless, by the summer of 1846, Frémont, Sloat, and others were convinced that the British fleet was only biding its time, waiting for the right moment and opportunity to seize California.

✸

Admiral Sir George Seymour, having learned in mid-June, of recent U.S military movements in California, had thought it prudent to stop in at Monterey for a firsthand investigation. His ship, the *Collingwood*, arrived at Monterey on July 16. The visit proved routine: Seymour found the U.S. flag flying over the harbor, exchanged standard courtesies with the U.S. Pacific Squadron, then left for the Sandwich Islands.

Among the *Collingwood*'s passengers was none other than Father Eugene McNamara, carrying a letter signed by Governor Pío Pico granting him permission to locate three thousand Irish Catholic families that he hoped to bring over on a later trip, within a sprawling land grant in the San Joaquin valley. Because the letter was dated on July 4, 1846, however—only three days before the U.S. flag had been raised at Monterey, American officials suspected the document had been backdated and refused to recognize the land grant. And thus, in a fit of bickering over a document ostensibly validating McNamara's plan— what U.S. Army Corps of Topographical Engineers explorer William Emory later called "a perfect humbug"—so went the remaining vestiges of England's California dreaming.[6]

✸

In Frémont's mind, the arrival of American soldiers at Monterey had barely thwarted a British seizure of California. As he later recalled the mood of his troops upon reaching Monterey, "The men looked upon the *Collingwood* with the feeling of the racer who has just passed the winning post." When Frémont and Gillespie went aboard the *Savannah* for a private talk with Sloat, the *Collingwood*'s presence provided a unifying conversational topic: Sloat, as it turned out, shared Frémont's suspicions about British intrigue in California. But when the conversation turned toward less murky matters, it quickly ran aground.

For months, Frémont, like some perpetually bluffing, high-stakes poker player, had fostered the notion—or, at the least, allowed others to believe—that his actions in California had issued from some closely guarded, secret orders given to him by President Polk. Convinced that Frémont enjoyed such high-level confidences, Thomas Larkin and Ezekiel Merritt, among others, had declined to inquire as to the origin and nature of those orders. Sloat, however, was, at the age of sixty-eight, too world-weary to indulge such conceits and was hardly intimidated by the young explorer's airs.

Gillespie, en route to California, had met with Sloat in Mazatlán— and had given Sloat the same orders from Polk that Frémont soon received. Sloat now wanted a precise account of any additional orders Frémont carried: "I do not know by what authority you are acting, Mr. Gillespie has told me nothing," the old officer exclaimed to Frémont. "He came to Mazatlan, and I sent him to Monterey, but I know nothing. I want to know by what authority you are acting."

Frémont told Sloat "that I had acted solely on my own responsibility, and without any expressed authority from the Government to justify hostilities." At that, Frémont recalled, the veteran officer became irate—"and gave me distinctly to understand, that in raising the flag at Monterey he had acted upon the faith of our operations in the north."

All along, Sloat, a man who believed in an ironclad chain of military command, had assumed that Frémont had carried some secret orders from the highest levels of the federal government. And, believing that, the commodore, for the past few months, had been taking Frémont's lead. Now, an outraged Sloat was discovering that Frémont enjoyed no such high-level authority. The meeting between the two men ended abruptly, and there would not be another. Even so, Frémont remained convinced that the "die was cast" for continuing U.S. military operations in California:

> I knew that the men who understood the future of our country, and who at this time ruled its destinies and were the government, regarded the California coast as the boundary fixed by nature to round off our national domain. From Mexico it was naturally separated, and events were pointing to its sure and near political separation from that power.

Longing for any sort of sign that he had made the right decision, Frémont, while taking a walk on a pine-covered coastal promontory later that day, even drew solace from the name of one of the U.S. ships swinging at anchor in the bay—"thinking it a good augury that as Savannah was my birthplace, the birth of this new child of our country should have been presided over by this *Savannah* of the seas."

Gazing across the harbor at the five warships at anchor, he reflected, "There lay the pieces on the great chess-board before me with which the game for an empire had been played. At its close we had, to be sure, four pieces to one, but that one was a Queen. I was but a pawn, and like a pawn I had been pushed forward to the front of the opening of the game."[7]

❊

Up to now, Frémont had been a rogue soldier with a penchant for inferring from happenstance incidents the unfolding of a grand historical destiny in which, he believed, he was destined to play a pivotal role. In the months since he had returned to California, no incident or object—from a flagpole's collapse, to a British-made arrow, to the name of a ship—had been too insignificant, as Frémont searched for auguries to support his self-defined role as California's conqueror. With the arrival, however, of the American Navy along the province's coast, soon to be followed by the overland arrival of the U.S. Army, Frémont's days would soon be governed by more concrete forces. He would indeed become a pawn—a pawn caught not only between two warring nations, but also between a set of ambitiously scheming U.S. military commanders.

❊

According to Frémont, Sloat vowed that, until specific orders arrived from Washington, "he [Sloat] could do nothing." All Frémont could do was await Sloat's departure. Meanwhile, Stockton, Sloat's imminent successor, wrote to Sloat, advising him that it was important to capture General Castro or run him out of California. Might Sloat, Stockton asked, authorize him to order Frémont's army to sail south aboard the *Cyane* to catch up with the fleeing Californio army?

Sloat, still awaiting his official retirement orders from Washington, declined to formally relinquish his command. He was, however, willing to give Stockton command over Frémont's land forces, as well as the *Cyane*. Stockton had arrived at Monterey on July 15, aboard the U.S.S. *Congress*, with orders from Washington to gain intelligence on Mexican affairs in California and to do his best to cultivate good feelings toward the United States among the local populace. To his delight, Frémont soon learned that the new commander was as eager to take on the Californios as Sloat had been reluctant. Wealthy, vain, widely celebrated for his military prowess in the War of 1812, Stockton had visions of conquest that more than matched those of Frémont. Stockton seemed ready to revive the belligerent bravado of the Osos; to his father-in-law, Frémont wrote, "This officer approves entirely of the course pursued by myself and Mr. Gillespie."

With Stockton now his immediate commanding officer, Frémont and his forces, on July 23, were regularized into the U.S. Army as the "California Battalion." Frémont was accorded the rank of major; Gillespie became captain and adjutant. Frémont's troops—whose numbers Stockton hoped, in the near future, to increase, through reinforcements from the east, from 165 to 300—agreed to volunteer their services in exchange for ten dollars a month and rations, for as long as they were needed. Their orders called for them to embark for San Diego, aboard the *Cyane*, on the morning of July 26. Once there, they were to gather horses and remain encamped in the area. They were also to maintain daily communications with the *Cyane*—and to be prepared to march, at a moment's notice, on Los Angeles, where Castro was believed to be mustering new forces. In San Diego, Frémont would also be in a position to block any retreat by Castro over the mountains to the west, and south, along the Colorado River, back to Mexico.

Frémont would have preferred his original strategy—to ride, not sail, south with his army, gathering recruits and seizing towns along the way. But he was also convinced that Stockton's plan would win a quick victory. To Senator Benton, on the eve of his departure for San Diego, Frémont wrote that he expected to leave California by the end of August.[8]

✽

On July 26, Frémont and his California battalion—with the addition of some Marines now about 120 strong—sailed from Monterey aboard the U.S. sloop-of-war *Cyane*. Though the soldiers had eagerly anticipated "the novelty of a voyage," as they sailed down California's coast excitement soon gave way to boredom and, for some—including Carson—seasickness. At noon on July 29, after three days at sea, their spirits rose when they dropped anchor in San Diego's enclosed harbor.

The Americans captured the *Juanita*, a Mexican brig swinging at anchor in the harbor. Afterward the *Cyane*'s captain, Samuel F. Dupont, asked the town's officials to hoist the U.S. flag. When they declined, Dupont dispatched a squadron of U.S. Marines to perform the honors. Once ashore, Frémont's men encountered no hostilities: indeed, according to him, they were greeted by the port's captain, Santiago Argüello, and by Juan Bandini, one of the town's most prominent citizens.

Over the next week, the two Californios and other local residents guided Frémont's search of the surrounding countryside for horses needed for the planned assault on Los Angeles. For the Americans, the search through the verdant hills and valleys surrounding San Diego became a sort of idyll. As Frémont recalled, "The days were bright and hot, the sky pure and entirely cloudless, and the nights cool and beautifully serene. In this month fruits generally ripen—melons, pears, peaches, prickly-fig (*cactus-tuña*), and others of like kind."

Frémont enjoyed the countryside, but along with the original members of his exploring party, he found it difficult to adjust to their new role as subordinates in a larger organization: "Living an uncontrolled life, ranging prairies and mountains subject to no will but their own, it was a great sacrifice for these border chiefs to lay aside their habits of independence." Frémont had orders to remain near San Diego until he received further orders, but he found it hard to sit still, knowing that General Castro's army lay within a day's ride. At one point, Captain Dupont, reminding him of those orders, had to intervene to prevent Frémont from making a premature march on Los Angeles.[9]

❋

On July 29, the day that Frémont and the California Battalion arrived at San Diego aboard the *Cyane*, Commodore Sloat finally relinquished his command over the Pacific Squadron and departed California aboard the *Levant*. His replacement, Robert F. Stockton—now with both naval and land forces at his command—was eager to embark on a new strategy.

After seizing Monterey in July, Sloat had been content to see the U.S. flag raised over a handful of other coastal towns and simply await new orders from Washington. But Stockton had no intention of waiting for new orders: in a blistering proclamation issued on July 29, the same day he assumed command, he accused the Mexican government and army of unprovoked hostilities against the United States. He specifically accused General Castro of "hunting and pursuing . . . with wicked intent Captain Frémont of the U.S. army, who came here to refresh his men . . . after a perilous journey across the mountains, on a scientific survey."[10] That same day, Stockton made Montgomery commander of the district of San Francisco and New Helvetia and, at Larkin's suggestion, ordered Johann Sutter released from confinement.

With northern California secure, Stockton now turned toward the unfinished business of capturing the provincial capital of Los Angeles. On August 1, along with Thomas Larkin and 360 sailors and marines, he sailed from Monterey aboard the *Congress*, bound for San Pedro, just south of Los Angeles. En route, they anchored just long enough at Santa Barbara to seize the town, raise the U.S. flag, and leave behind a garrison of sixteen men.

The *Congress* reached San Pedro on the morning of August 6. Writing to Frémont that night, Stockton ordered him and his army to leave San Diego "as soon as you can" and to meet Stockton and his forces at Temple's Farm, an estate south of Los Angeles, close to where Castro's army was believed to be encamped. Stockton, upon landing at San Pedro, had learned that, a day earlier, 300 Californio troops—250 under General Castro, 50 under former governor Juan Alvarado—had evacuated Los Angeles and were headed toward Los Alamitos, a ranch owned by Abel Stearns (in today's Long Beach).

Seeking to avoid further bloodshed, Stockton hoped to persuade Castro and other Californios to repudiate Mexico's dominion over California—and to accept U.S. annexation of the province. If the Californios declined, Stockton and Frémont were prepared to wage war. Stockton's ultimatum was conveyed in letters from Thomas Larkin to Abel Stearns, the wealthy American-born Mexican citizen in Los Angeles. Larkin asked Stearns to talk with Governor Pico, General Castro, members of the provincial assembly, and other influential citizens. Stearns was to tell them that if they wanted to avert an attack on Los Angeles, they should dispatch, before the next day, a delegation composed of the province's highest officials, to San Pedro, to treat for peace.[11]

Stearns's reply to the ultimatum, in Larkin's words, "amounts to nothing." Through an emissary, on August 7, the Los Angeles merchant sent word that any communications about California's future must go directly to General Castro. Weeks earlier, when Sloat seized Monterey and sought an official exchange with Castro, the general had insisted that any such demands must be sent to the province's governor and assembly. Frustrated by what seemed to him deliberate prevarication, Larkin replied to Stearns that Stockton "can do [no] more and is determined to have no more correspondence on the subject. The U.S. & M are at war."[12]

However, the arrival of an emissary from General Castro's camp interrupted the rush to arms. The messenger asked if Stockton would be willing to receive two representatives of General Castro. Stockton, still willing to give diplomacy a chance, appointed Larkin and Lieutenant James F. Schenck to meet with the general's two agents.

The talks, however, foundered quickly. At their first meeting, Castro's delegates, Pablo de la Guerra and José María Flores, insisted that no formal negotiations could take place until all hostile actions ceased—a condition that Stockton quickly rejected. Stockton answered that, although he deplored war, "plain duty" required him to carry it on until California no longer belonged to Mexico.[13]

Castro reacted indignantly to Stockton's hard-line position but knew that California's days under the Mexican flag were numbered. Governor Pico—fulfilling the terms of his and Castro's long-discussed union of forces—had given Castro command of the provincial militia, but it was too little too late. Pico's unit consisted of a hundred untrained, unhappy, poorly equipped men—most of whom were waiting for the right moment to flee a force that they had been cajoled into joining.

To Pico, Castro, on August 9, wrote that California's conquest by the United States seemed inevitable:

After having made on my part every sacrifice that has been in my power, to prepare for the defense of the Department and to oppose the invasion that by land and sea has been made by the United States forces, today I find myself in the painful necessity of informing Your Excellency that it is impossible for me to do one or the other.[14]

Successful in finding horses for most of his men, Frémont, on August 8, received Stockton's directive ordering him to leave San Diego for Temple's Farm, the estate just south of Los Angeles. Later that day, Frémont and 120 of his men left for Los Angeles. En route, assuming that Castro knew that the two American armies planned to link up, Frémont feared an ambush by the Mexican general: "But with the exception of scattered horsemen occasionally seen, and disappearing as quickly, there was no demonstration of any kind." On August 13, encamped two miles south of Los Angeles, Frémont's army was joined by Stockton's forces. That afternoon, as they entered Los Angeles, the two armies encountered no enemy forces, no resistance—"our entry," Frémont recalled, "having more the effect of a parade of home guards than of an enemy taking possession of a conquered town."[15]

❋

While en route to Los Angeles, Frémont learned that Castro had already disbanded his army—right after penning his October 9 letter to Governor Pico, decrying the provincial capital's inevitable capture by U.S. forces. Pico, in turn, had, the next day, submitted a dispatch to the provincial assembly—telling them that he concurred with Castro's assessment that the pueblo was, by now, indefensible. At Pico's suggestion, the body permanently adjourned. As California's final vestiges of Mexican government collapsed, Castro and a small party fled Los Angeles, escaping through the San Gorgonio Pass, in the San Bernardino Mountains . . . and south to Mexico. Frémont dispatched a small party to track Castro down. Though the detail failed to overtake the general, it did recover ten artillery pieces hastily buried in the sand at one of Castro's campsites along the route of his retreat. Governor Pico, meanwhile, escaped to Baja California, from where he made repeated and fruitless appeals to the Mexican government to attempt a recapture of Alta California.

❋

On August 17, four days after Stockton and Frémont entered Los Angeles, Stockton issued his second proclamation in as many weeks. He declared California to be U.S. soil. He also announced that, in addition to his title as the new U.S. territory's commander in chief, henceforth, he was also its governor. Stockton pledged that all persons accepting the change in regimes would be protected, along with their property, by the new government. To underscore that pledge, the California Battalion would be kept intact to preserve the peace and punish law-breakers. Moreover, a curfew would be enforced from 10:00 p.m. to sunrise. Elections would be held to select civil officials. In places where that failed to happen, Stockton would appoint appropriate civil officials.[16]

Stockton hoped to have completed California's peaceful transition to U.S. rule by October. Toward that end, he planned to create what he called a system of "Organic Laws of the Territory"—to leave intact, as much as possible, the laws and institutions established by Spain and inherited by Mexican officials. To President Polk, he wrote, "I am of opinion that a mixed government of old and new forms will be at present most beneficial and wise."

Stockton's proclamation also contained a provision threatening deportation of any new arrivals to California unwilling "to pledge themselves to be, in all respects, obedient to the laws" of the territory. As Stockton explained to Polk, the provision was directed to the hundreds of Mormon emigrants—practitioners of polygamy, outlawed in the United States—soon expected in San Francisco. The Mormons, Stockton feared, were "likely to give me more trouble than our 'decided enemies.' . . . I have had my eye upon them."

Copies of Stockton's proclamation were sent to Montgomery and Gillespie, and its text was published in the *Californian*—California's first newspaper, which had published its premier issue on August 15, just three days after Stockton took Los Angeles.

✸

Beyond his frenetic haste to consolidate U.S. control over California, Robert Stockton, by mid-August of 1846, had other matters on his mind. From Mexican newspapers, he had just learned of President Polk's war proclamation, issued that May, against Mexico. Immediately, the commodore began envisioning a new role for himself in the widening conflict between the United States and Mexico.

California had accorded Stockton no small degree of stature. "My word is at present the law of the land," he had boasted to Polk. "My person is more than regal." But though sprawling and topographically spectacular, California was also far from the war's main theater—far from the battlefields of Mexico proper on which U.S. officers such as generals Winfield Scott and Zachary Taylor were capturing the nation's imagination—and securing their reputations.[17]

As for Frémont's future, Stockton's departure would certainly put the commander of the California Battalion in a far more independent, and powerful, role—thus giving him yet another chance at military glory.

❋

Deeming the U.S. conquest of California complete, Stockton, in an August 24 letter to Frémont, outlined his plans for the rest of the war: "Privateers will no doubt be fitted out to prey upon our commerce, and the immense value of that commerce in the Pacific Ocean, and the number of valuable men engaged in it, requires immediately all the protection that can be given to them, by the Ships under my command."

Stockton sought to get under sail "as soon as it can be safely done." Toward that end, he informed Frémont that he intended to name him governor of the territory, and Gillespie his second in command. To tighten the U.S. grip on the territory, Stockton also ordered Frémont to go to Monterey and San Francisco and find new recruits for the California Battalion. From the Monterey garrison, then under Captain Daingerfield Fauntleroy, and from the San Francisco garrison, still under Captain John B. Montgomery, Frémont was instructed to find recruits who would bring the California Battalion's ranks to three hundred men—fifty to garrison San Francisco, fifty for Monterey, twenty-five for Santa Barbara, fifty for Los Angeles, and twenty-five for San Diego. The remaining hundred men were to be kept together, so that the other garrisons could call upon them on short notice.[18]

To Frémont, it seemed, after so many vexing reversals, that everything—his own destiny entwined with that of America's expanding empire—was finally falling into place.

COMMANDANT OF THE TERRITORY

O N SEPTEMBER 2, 1846, Commodore Robert Stockton named John Frémont military commandant of the new U.S. territory of California. For good measure, Stockton also divided California into three military departments: Archibald Gillespie was put in charge of the southern department, which stretched from Los Angeles to Baja California. Lieutenant A. T. Maddox was to head the central department, which included Monterey, and Captain Montgomery, still anchored at San Francisco, was put in charge of the sprawling northern department, stretching eastward from San Francisco to Sutter's Fort.

Afterward, Stockton ordered Frémont to meet him in San Francisco on October 25. There, on the eve of Stockton's departure, he told the explorer that he planned to transfer the title of territorial governor from himself to Frémont. On September 3, Stockton sailed from San Pedro aboard the *Congress*, bound for Monterey and San Francisco.

❄

Prior to leaving Los Angeles, in letters to President Polk and Navy Secretary Bancroft, Stockton had outlined his plans for California's governance and his intention to chase Mexican privateers. To hasten delivery of the letters, Kit Carson was asked to make an overland journey to Washington. Neither letter, however, mentioned the most audacious aspect of Stockton's plans—plans that called for a much larger force than the enlarged three-hundred-member California Battalion that he had described to President Polk.

As Frémont later recalled, Stockton "had directed me, as soon as certain work about Los Angeles was completed, to go to the Sacramento valley." There, Frémont would increase his troop strength to the three hundred men originally requested by Stockton. Frémont was also to ascertain how many men might be recruited from the Sacramento valley for a bold land invasion that Stockton hoped to make—from Mazatlán or Acapulco, deep into Mexico. Emboldened by visions of himself as an American Admiral Nelson, Stockton sought nothing less than to "shake hands with General Taylor at the gates of Mexico." To mount the invasion, Stockton told Frémont, he needed an army of one thousand men. After his recruiting trip to the Sacramento Valley, Fremont and his enlarged army would meet Stockton in San Francisco. There, the commodore would take charge of his new recruits, make Frémont governor, and sail away toward new theaters of war.

On September 11, Frémont left Los Angeles for the Sacramento valley, leaving Gillespie behind to hold the pueblo. To assist with that task, Stockton, who had departed nine days earlier, had left behind at Los Angeles forty-eight men, along with twenty thousand dollars in scarce specie removed from the *Congress*. As before, the march north rekindled Frémont's ardor for California's nature: "It was just the weather for days on horseback when there is no special care to interfere with the enjoyment of fine weather and exercise."

In late September, when the battalion reached the Sacramento valley, Frémont joined other officers in scouring the area for recruits. They, however, soon learned that, among the valley's American settlers—many of whom were newly arrived and preoccupied with building homes—the idea of leaving for military action in Mexico held no appeal. While, Frémont recalled, "there was no difficulty in obtaining the aid of the immigrants to hold the country we had taken," few were willing to go any farther. Beyond that, "when appealed to by them for my own opinion, I did not have enough confidence in the enterprise to advise them to embark in it."[1]

Stockton's dream of orchestrating a land invasion of Mexico collapsed on October 1, when a courier from Archibald Gillespie informed him that, on September 22, the Californios of Los Angeles had rebelled against their American occupiers.[2] Gillespie, in Frémont's ab-

sence, had proven a harsh, inept military commander of the pueblo—
fueling popular resentments through arbitrary arrests and petty, lib-
erty-curtailing laws aimed at the Californios. Led by José María
Flores—violating an earlier parole after his capture during the U.S.
conquest of Los Angeles—and other former members of Castro's
army, the pueblo's citizenry had revolted, forcing Gillespie and his garrison to flee to San Pedro. There, after a delay of several days, they
had boarded the merchant ship *Vandalia* and sailed to the north end of
the harbor, where they anchored and awaited the arrival of reinforcements, requested in the message sent by courier to Stockton.

A cheer went up among Gillespie's men on October 6, when they
spotted the *Savannah*, now captained by William Mervine, sailing into
the harbor. Gillespie's men and three hundred from the *Savannah* attempted that day to fight their way back to Los Angeles. But all their
efforts were repulsed by the Californios. By dusk, the Americans had
fallen back to San Pedro. As most of the soldiers waited aboard the
Savannah, swinging at anchor at San Pedro, the *Vandalia* set sail for
San Francisco to alert Stockton to the worsening situation.

❀

Learning of the revolt in Los Angeles, Stockton sent word to Frémont, still in the Sacramento valley, to gather as many volunteers as
possible and come to San Francisco immediately. Though the valley's
Americans had shown little interest in joining Stockton's proposed
land invasion of Mexico, fighting Californios *in* California was a different matter. And Frémont had no trouble finding American settlers
ready to join the fight.[3] Launches from the *Portsmouth* and the *Congress*, dispatched by Stockton on October 10, returned from the Sacramento valley to San Francisco with Frémont and about 160 new
recruits. To fill out the rescue force, Stockton also drew men away
from Sonoma, San Jose, San Francisco, and Monterey.

On October 14, Stockton and Frémont set sail aboard separate
ships from San Francisco. Two days out, however, the two vessels lost
sight of each other in a heavy fog, and the *Sterling*, carrying Frémont
and his men, fell far behind the swifter *Congress*, carrying Stockton and
his forces. Stockton's grand strategy called for his own forces to land at

San Pedro and march upon Los Angeles. Frémont was to land at Santa Barbara, find horses for his men, then embark on what was normally a three-day overland ride to Los Angeles.

South of San Francisco, Stockton spotted the merchant ship *Barnstable*, whose crew passed along a dispatch from Lieutenant A. T. Maddox, in charge of American forces at Monterey, reporting that his garrison was under attack and required help. Answering the appeal, Stockton anchored the *Congress* at Monterey from October 15 to 19, leaving behind fifty men and several artillery pieces. At Santa Barbara, Stockton anchored long enough to determine that Frémont had not yet arrived. Had he lingered, the commodore might also have noticed that the small garrison, under Theodore Talbot—left earlier by Frémont to secure the port—had already departed the town amid rumors that a force of Californios from Los Angeles were headed its way. Stockton's *Congress* arrived at San Pedro on October 23 and joined Mervine's *Savannah*, still anchored in the harbor.

Two days later, Gillespie's irregulars, followed by Stockton's sailors, landed and retook San Pedro—only to be driven back the next day by four hundred Californio reinforcements, determined to hold Los Angeles. Frustrated by this latest setback and by Frémont's failure to appear in Los Angeles, Stockton transferred Gillespie's volunteers to the *Savannah* and, on October 30, sailed for San Diego where he would establish a fortified headquarters, plan his next move, and await word from Major Frémont.[4]

✦

On its second day out of San Francisco, a day after losing the *Congress* in a fog bank, the *Sterling*, carrying Frémont and his forces, had encountered the northbound *Vandalia*. From Archibald Gillespie—escaping his Los Angeles troubles on the merchant ship—Frémont learned of Mervine's initial retreat from Los Angeles. Acquiring even more problems, he also learned that the Californios, assuming that American reinforcements would require more mounts to recapture Los Angeles, had taken it upon themselves to drive most of the horses away from the coast. Concluding that, without more men and supplies, his own efforts would come to naught, Frémont ordered the *Sterling* to reverse course; and slowly the ship began working its way north, back up the coast to Monterey. There, Frémont reasoned, his forces could regroup for the planned assult on Los Angeles. The *Sterling* reached Monterey on October 27. From there, Frémont wrote to Stockton, promising to put down the local revolt by Californios, and gather horses and supplies, "so as to be in readiness to march to the southward immediately on the arrival of our reinforcements."[5]

❋

Buoyed by his newly recovered sense of independence, Frémont—from headquarters in Monterey threw himself headlong into the task of increasing the size of his army. His men began gathering what remaining horses they could find around Monterey—those not already driven by the Californios away from the coast. Owners of the requisitioned animals who were sympathetic to the cause got receipts, which could, in theory, be redeemed at a later date by the U.S. government. Individuals who resisted were treated rudely and got no receipts. Frémont, meanwhile, also sent letters asking for men and more mounts to Captain John B. Montgomery, aboard the *Portsmouth*, at San Francisco, and to Edward Kern at Sutter's Fort.

Sutter's Fort was already a beehive of recruiting activities. Weeks earlier, after hearing of the revolt at Monterey, Captain Montgomery, at San Francisco, had written Kern and asked him to send scouts out to look for recruits among newly arrived emigrants. Responding to Kern's appeals, Edwin Bryant, a journalist newly arrived from Kentucky, along with two other Americans, Andrew Grayson and Richard T. Jacob, recruited numerous newcomers. They also raised a company composed of forty Walla Walla tribesmen, as well as native California Indians. Jacob, the son of a prominent family in Kentucky, would, two years later, marry Jessie Frémont's sister Sarah.[6]

By mid-October, when Frémont, returning to Monterey, put out his own call for enlistees, recruiting had reached fever pitch. By November 16, he was writing Captain William Mervine, asking him to suspend any recruiting efforts not expressly directed by Frémont's own agents: "At present I am much harassed by numerous appointments of irresponsible men, who obey nobody, and are more often drunk than sober."[7]

Concerns about the quality of officers grew still deeper on November 16—the day before Frémont and the California Battalion left Monterey for nearby San Juan Bautista for a final muster of men and horses. That evening, two couriers arrived, bearing news that a regiment of twenty-two volunteers collected at Sutter's Fort by Captain Charles D. Burrass had engaged a party of Californios. The American forces had suffered unnecessary casualties because of the bravado of an insubordinate officer. Captain Bluford K. "Hell Roaring" Thompson—usurping Burrass's authority—had led the volunteers on a foolhardy assault. Burrass and three other Americans were killed and several more wounded. The engagement had offered a cautionary tale of the dangers posed by the battalion's shaky command structure. The Californios suffered the same number of casualties. "Their small loss," Frémont later wrote, "shows how heedlessly the action was fought on our side."[8]

The California Battalion prepared to depart for the south. Fearing the reactions of local Californios, American residents around Monterey began to worry about their own safety. To allay some of those fears, Captain Montgomery dispatched two couriers: James Griffith to Sonoma and Lansford Hastings, a California promoter recently returned to the province, to San Jose.[9]

By late November, the entire California Battalion, mustered at San Juan Bautista, came to 428 men, including Indians and servants. Some one thousand nine hundred horses and mules had been collected, as well as three hundred head of cattle.[10] Most of the battalion's members were either American settlers or newly arrived emigrants, though its ranks also included Germans, Englishmen, Canadians, Indians, and Californians. All in all, volunteer Edwin Bryant noted, the army displayed "little of the 'pomp and circumstance of glorious war.' ":

There are no plumes nodding over brazen helmets, nor coats of broadcloth spangled with lace and buttons. A broad-brimmed, low-crowned hat, a shirt of blue flannel, or buckskin, with pantaloons and moccasins of the same, all generally much the worse for wear, and smeared with mud and dust, make up the costume of the party, officers as well as men.[11]

✸

If Frémont, in mustering his new troops, displayed a fresh sense of initiative, he had good reason: upon reaching Monterey, he had learned of his recent promotion to the rank of lieutenant colonel. And not knowing Stockton's whereabouts, he was, once again, cut off from any superior command—and thus free to follow the whims of his perceived destiny. But he also recognized the limits of his actual powers. In a letter of November 27 to the *Savannah*'s Captain William Mervine, Frémont, in a moment of rank self-pity, noted the hollowness of his ostensible authority:

> I should feel it unnecessary to make these representations to you were the commission of Military Commandant of California received by me from Commodore Stockton, of any authority among his Officers: but under the actual circumstances I should feel myself humiliated by attaching it to my name.[12]

In that same letter, convinced that northern California lay securely under U.S. control, Frémont asked Mervine to suspend all military actions in that part of the territory: "Believing this to be the best as well as most humane course, and satisfied of the present peaceable disposition of the greater part of the inhabitants here, I have to request that you will sustain it by your influence and authority."[13] Two days later, Frémont and his enlarged California Battalion mounted up and rode away from San Juan Bautista.

✸

From the old mission at San Juan Bautista, the California Battalion moved up the San Benito River and over the mountains into the Salinas valley. Winter had already set in—and for days at a time, the ragged army slogged through cold, slashing rains. Nights found them in soggy bedding and tents. Because horses too weak for the trek were left behind, many in the battalion were forced to walk. Beeves— driven along with the column and slaughtered as they were needed— furnished the men's main diet. "Cold weather and the exposed marches," Frémont recalled, "gave wholesome appetites." But harsh conditions notwithstanding, "perfect order was maintained on the march and in the camp, and private property was respected absolutely. No man left the camp without a pass, and the column passed over the country without giving reasonable cause for complaint to any Californian."

On the morning of December 14, the battalion set up camp atop a mountain near the coastal town of San Luis Obispo. That afternoon, Frémont, accompanied by William Knight, went to a nearby point, where they could espy the town's namesake mission below them. When darkness fell, the battalion descended the ridge, surrounded the mission, and detained and questioned most of the Californio civilians inside. The mission's church was then opened, and most of the soldiers slept inside. Frémont allowed the soldiers to take some frijoles, vegetables, and crushed wheat that they found. Otherwise, he was determined to safeguard the mission and its property and, to that end, posted sentries around the buildings.

Drawing on information extracted from the mission detainees, the battalion soon rounded up some thirty Californio soldiers in the settlement. Among the soldiers captured was one Don José de Jesús Pico, a leader of the Los Angeles insurrection. Pico had been captured after the revolt and subsequently released on parole. The Americans held a hasty court-martial at which they convicted Pico of violating his parole and sentenced him to be shot. Just prior to the execution, however, Richard Owens appeared with Pico's teary wife and children, and Frémont, after hearing their appeals, decided to spare the prisoner. Upon learning of the commutation, Frémont recalled, Pico fell to his knees, crossed himself, and exclaimed, "I was to die—I had lost the life God gave me—you have given me another life. I devote the new life to you."

Before leaving San Luis Obispo, Frémont also had time to peruse a cache of letters found at the mission—including several from José María Flores, who had led the Los Angeles insurrection. One of the dispatches contained a reference—tantalizing but lacking in details— of a recent victory by the Californios over the Americans at a place called San Pasqual, north of San Diego. It had been two full months since Frémont had seen or communicated with Commodore Stockton, but apparently the war for control of southern California continued.

Upon leaving San Luis Obispo after three days, Frémont was concerned about possible ambushes by Californio troops. To lessen that risk, he decided to avoid the Mission Road, California's main coastal route; to keep to less well-known roads and trails, and even to use difficult cross-country routes—in some cases, routes over mountains. As battalion member and journalist Edward Kemble recalled:

> Every man, down to the Digger horse-thief Indians, knew that we were beating the air in our roundabout marches—that while we were wearing out our animals and exhausting the strength of our hardiest men by seeking out the roughest and most impracticable starvation routes southward, in the vain hope of stealing a march on the foe—his well-mounted spies knew all about our movements and where we encamped every night.

Christmas morning of 1846 found the battalion in a torrential downpour in the mountains overlooking Santa Barbara: "All traces of trails were washed away by the deluge of water, and pack animals slid over the rocks and fell down the precipices, blinded by the driving rain." By Frémont's own estimate, during their descent from the ridgeline, the battalion lost over a hundred horses. Beyond that, "baggage strewed along our tracks, as on the trail of a defeated army."[14]

When the troops finally entered Santa Barbara, they encountered, to their relief, no opposition—no trace of enemy soldiers, all of whom had apparently been withdrawn for the defense of Los Angeles. They spent the next several days resting, making repairs, and generally regrouping after a month of storm-vexed travels. One day during the respite, Don José de Jesús Pico came to Frémont with news that an elderly woman—a woman highly respected among the Californios, Pico assured him—was in the camp and wished to speak with Frémont. "I found that her object was to use her influence to put an end to the war," Frémont recalled. In what he later considered a precursor to the war's end, the mysterious woman asked him "to do so upon such just and friendly terms of compromise as would make the peace acceptable and enduring."

Yet another visitor had a more tangible offering. After the schooner *Julia* anchored, its captain, Lieutenant Edward A. Selden, presented the battalion with a four-pound cannon sent by Captain Mervine for McClane's artillery corps. Prior to the *Julia*'s departure, Frémont gave Selden a letter for Stockton, in which he said that he planned to leave Santa Barbara that day, January 3, then ride directly to Los Angeles. If he didn't find and fight the main party of Californios en route, he assured Stockton, he would certainly attack them at the pueblo.

As Frémont promised, the battalion departed Santa Barbara that day. And as he had told Captain Selden, on this final stretch of the march to Los Angeles, his route cleaved as close as possible to the sea. Indeed, just south of Santa Barbara, at Rincon Point, a fifteen-mile-long defile, breaking their line of march, would actually force the men onto the beach. There, Selden had warned, where the beach passage narrowed to about fifty yards, the battalion would be vulnerable to attack. Should any Californios, he said, install artillery blocking the beach, Frémont's men would be an easy target. To protect them during that passage, Selden told Frémont that the *Julia* would sail to, and anchor beneath, a steep cliff overlooking Rincon Point.

On their second night out from Santa Barbara, the battalion camped on the beach at Rincon Point, beneath the cliff, while, as Selden had promised, the *Julia* waited offshore. Though a party of Californios under Los Angeles insurrection leader José María Flores did begin work on a breastwork across the beach, a flanking movement above the beach by eighty of Frémont's men caused them to flee. January 9 found the battalion encamped somewhere between Rincon Point and Mission San Buenaventura when two couriers arrived with a letter for Frémont from Stockton.

The commodore, encamped north of San Diego at Mission San Luis Rey (near today's town of Oceanside), had heard that Frémont was at least as far south as Santa Barbara. Stockton wanted to let him know that he expected to be in Los Angeles by January 8 or 9, the day Frémont received the letter. Stockton warned that recent victories over U.S. forces commanded by Captain Mervine and Stephen Watts Kearny, Frémont's old nemesis (recently promoted to the rank of general) from the mountain howitzer episode, had emboldened the Californios: "You had better not fight the rebels until I get up to aid you, and you can join me on the road to [the] Pueblo [Los Angeles]. . . . In the art of horsemanship, of dodging, and running, it is in vain to compete with them."[15]

On January 11, riding east toward the San Fernando Mission, Frémont's battalion encountered two Californios carrying startling news: one day earlier, U.S. forces under Commodore Stockton and General Kearny had retaken Los Angeles. The decisive battles of the California campaign had already been won. Frémont's decision to avoid the Mission Road—his "backing & filling in those infernal Mountains," as Battalion member Louis McLane later griped—had led to their untimely arrival in the south and allowed the ultimate victory in the California campaign to fall into the hands of Frémont's rivals, Stockton and Kearny. The glory which—months earlier, atop Gavilán Peak—seemed within Frémont's reach had slipped away like an errant dream.

❈

In mid-May of 1846, General Kearny had been ordered to raise an army for the purpose of seizing the town of Santa Fe and protecting the American trade that gravitated toward the New Mexican capital. Two weeks later, President Polk had another idea: Why not order Kearny, after he seized Santa Fe, to continue to California? Now that war was officially declared, the President could openly express his determination to acquire California for the United States. And if Kearny's army could continue from New Mexico to the Pacific Coast, the general would be weeks ahead of any other land forces that might be dispatched from the East into the West.

To obtain reinforcements for his First Dragoons, Kearny was authorized to requisition troops from the governor of Missouri and, once in New Mexico and California, to recruit new troops among American settlers and from the ranks of Mormon emigrants then beginning to stream into the Far West. Additional weapons, ordnance, and supplies for the army would be shipped around Cape Horn to California. Kearny was also told to expect the arrival in California by sea of a volunteer regiment from New York. On August 18, facing no resistance, Kearny's sixteen-hundred-man Army of the West took Santa Fe. On September 24—having set up a U.S. government for New Mexico and divided his forces—Kearny, leading an army of about three hundred dragoons, set off from Santa Fe down the Rio Grande, bound for San Diego. On October 6, his Army of the West had just passed the town of Socorro, New Mexico, when it met a grizzled party of eight or nine men on horseback, yelling like Indians as they charged straight toward it. The leader of the party was Kit Carson—acting as Stockton's courier, taking a bundle of letters to Washington.

Kearny had expected that U.S. naval forces might, by then, have seized a handful of California's coastal settlements. But he also assumed that the province's conquest was not fully accomplished. Carson, however, had fresher news: California's conquest by the United States, he assured Kearny, was complete. The entire territory was secure, and Robert Stockton was its new governor, Frémont its new commandant. Because Carson had left California in the wake of Stockton's and Frémont's original conquest of Los Angeles in late August, he was unaware of the subsequent revolt by Californios in the pueblo weeks later. Upon hearing Carson's report, Kearny sent all but 121 of his men back to Santa Fe. Over his objections, Carson was ordered to reverse course and, acting as their scout, guide Kearny's army to California. As for the letters Carson was carrying to Washington, Kearny assigned the completion of that errand to veteran mountain man Thomas "Broken Hand" Fitzpatrick, who had been serving as Kearny's guide.

Kearny got still fresher news in late November, as his army, now riding west, approached the Colorado River. From intercepted letters and Californios fleeing the tumult along the coast, Kearny learned of the revolt in Los Angeles and was told that Stockton remained pinned down in San Diego, waiting for Frémont.

After crossing the mountains into California, Kearny, on December 2, encountered an English-born rancher and naturalized Mexican citizen who declared himself a neutral in the present conflict. Because the rancher was going to San Diego the next day, Kearny asked him to take a letter to Stockton. Kearny wrote that Santa Fe was in American hands, and he asked Stockton to send out a party to meet him as soon as possible.

Upon receiving Kearny's request the next day, Stockton immediately dispatched Gillespie and a party of thirty-seven riflemen. The following day, December 4, Gillespie's party found Kearny's troops and informed them that a band of Californio insurgents was gathered at the nearby settlement of San Pasqual, northeast of San Diego. On December 6, Kearny and Gillespie charged into San Pasqual. Though outnumbered, the Californios' lancers and tactics proved superior; and the Americans lost twenty-one men. The next day, demoralized and disoriented, Kearny's forces found their way to a ranch about ten miles down the road, toward San Diego—Rancho San Bernardo. There, they suddenly found themselves trapped between the mountains and armed Californios. That night, Carson and two others, slipping away from the ranch, managed to reach Stockton. The commodore dispatched a 180-man relief force, which, around midnight on December 10–11, reached Kearny. Suddenly outnumbered and outgunned, the Californios soon dispersed.

Less than two days later, on December 12, the Army of the West reached San Diego, where Stockton and Kearny immediately began organizing their joint force for the reconquest of Los Angeles. The joint force of six hundred men moved out of San Diego on December 29. While en route to Los Angeles, on January 4, they were approached by three Californio couriers with a cease-fire offer from the Mexican general José Mariá Flores. To avoid needless bloodshed, he proposed a cessation of hostilities long enough to give both sides time to investigate reports that the United States and Mexico had made peace. Stockton, however, rejected the offer. Any surrender, he vowed, must be unconditional, with the understanding that Flores must be turned over to American forces and executed.

On January 8 and 9, in fighting northeast of the pueblo, Kearny's and Stockton's forces defeated the Californios, forcing them to flee toward the modern-day city of Pasadena. The next day, the Americans reentered, and once again raised the U.S. flag over, Los Angeles.[16]

❋

In the aftermath of the American reentry into Los Angeles, many Californio troops left for their respective homes. Others gathered in small groups and repaired to nearby ranchos. On January 12, 1847—two days after U.S. forces reoccupied Los Angeles—John Frémont, still encamped with his troops at the San Fernando Mission, heard reports that Californio troops had gathered nearby, at the San Rafael and San Pasqual ranchos.

Aware that no treaty had ratified the apparent cessation of hostilities between U.S. and Californio troops, Frémont dispatched José de Jesús Pico, the Californio whose life Frémont had spared at the San

Luis Obispo court-martial, to Rancho San Rafael with a message to Don Andrés Pico—Jesús Pico's cousin, and now the Californios' senior *comandante*. Returning that evening, Jesús Pico reported that the Californios seemed amenable to talks. News of Frémont's peace overture also reached Manuel Castro and José Flores at the nearby San Pasqual rancho. Flores turned over his command to Andrés Pico and, along with Manuel Castro and several others, slipped away to Sonora.

The next morning, January 12, two emissaries dispatched by Andrés Pico rode into Frémont's camp. Peace commissioners for both sides were appointed, and Frémont declared a one-day truce while talks proceeded. The Californios were willing to abandon hostilities and accept U.S. governance, but they refused to accept Stockton's earlier demand of unconditional surrender.

Louis McLane, Pierson B. Reading, and R. Eugene Russell, Frémont's negotiators, were told by the Californios that, if they failed to come to terms with Frémont, the surviving remnants of their army were prepared to take to the surrounding hills and wage guerrilla warfare, which, as McLane recalled, would have been "a most serious war for us, without horses or regular troops. In such a mode of warfare the Volunteers would not be worth their keeping."[17]

As the talks progressed, Frémont's battalion moved south, to the Féliz family's farm, Campo de Cahuenga, on the plain north of Cahuenga Pass, near today's Universal City. There, on January 13, in an abandoned adobe ranch house, the peace commissioners, along with Frémont and Andrés Pico, agreed to seven "Articles of Capitulation." The Californios agreed to surrender their arms, disband, and return home. They were not required to swear an oath of allegiance to the United States until a formal comprehensive treaty had ended all U.S.–Mexican hostilities; but they agreed, in the meantime, to obey all U.S. laws. The Americans, in return, promised the Californios equal rights under U.S. law and protection of their lives and property. Frémont, Andrés Pico, and the various peace commissioners, the next morning, signed the Treaty of Cahuenga.[18]

Fourteen months earlier, Frémont had commenced U.S. hostilities in California without formal authorization. Now, with the stroke of a pen, he had ended the conflict in the same manner.

PART V

RECKONINGS

1847–54

You have a Sparta, embellish it!
—Daniel Webster

GOVERNOR FRÉMONT

HE NEXT MORNING, January 14, 1847, as John Frémont and his men broke camp, preparing for their short march south to Los Angeles, heavy rains pounded Campo de Cahuenga and the surrounding Santa Monica Mountains. En route to Los Angeles—slogging through the torrents and mud, down the Santa Monicas' southern slope—the ragged troops made an unseemly sight. Few had coats or hats; many lacked even shoes. "A more miserably clad, wretchedly provided, and unprepossessing military host, probably never entered a civilized city," volunteer Edwin Bryant recalled. "In all except our order, deportment, and arms, we might have been mistaken for a procession of tatterdemalions, or a tribe of Nomades from Tartary."

Upon arriving in Los Angeles, the company found it largely deserted by Californios, but, as expected, occupied by Stockton's and Kearny's forces. In Los Angeles, Frémont settled into temporary quarters, assigned to him by Stockton, at Government House. The rest of the California Battalion continued east, to Mission San Gabriel, where they were to be garrisoned for the time being.

❁

With California secure, Commodore Robert Stockton now looked forward to turning the office of governor over to Frémont, and leaving for Mexico proper. He had already, the previous September, made Frémont the commandant of all U.S. forces in California. With that honor, however, Stockton—as he surely must have known—had bequeathed to thirty-three-year-old Frémont a wholly unenviable predicament—a situation ripe for an inevitable confrontation with Stephen Watts Kearny, who outranked Frémont and, beyond that, considered himself commander of all U.S. troops in California. Though Kearny was a close friend of Senator Benton's, he and Frémont already had ill feelings toward one another that stretched back to the mountain howitzer incident at the outset of the explorer's Second Expedition.

For Kearny, a by-the-book career military man—indeed, author of a book of rules for U.S. dragoons—Frémont's request for the cannon had raised questions about his fealty to military regulations. And nothing in the intervening years had lessened his suspicions about the impulsive Frémont. Making matters worse for Frémont, Kearny—having been promoted the previous summer—now held the rank of brigadier general, thus rendering him an even more formidable foe.

Beyond such personal matters, however, the clash that was about to ensue arose from a conflicting set of orders, dispatched from Washington, which gave the Army commander Kearny and his naval counterpart, Stockton, two ambitious rivals, each the authority to organize California's civil government.

The Stockton-Kearny confrontation flared on January 16—two days after Frémont reached Los Angeles—when Kearny wrote the Navy commodore, challenging his authority to organize and to appoint officials to run California's civil government. In the same letter, Kearny noted that, just three days earlier, he had given Stockton a copy of orders, issued the previous June, by Secretary of War Marcy, delegating all such authority to Kearny. Against that background, Kearny wrote, he felt compelled to pose a question:

> I have to ask if you have any authority from the Presdt., from the Secty. of Navy, or from any other channel of the Presdt. to form such government & make such appts.? If you have such authority & will shew it to me, or furnish me with certified copies of it, I will cheerfully acquiesce in what you are doing.[1]

Answering the challenge, Stockton immediately dispatched his own missive, stating that California's government was a fait accompli—that its laws and the selection of its officials were already a matter of public record. Beyond that, Stockton wrote, he had no intention of surrendering one shred of authority to an officer on whose behalf, five weeks earlier, he had had to dispatch troops to save from certain oblivion at the enemy's hands. Stockton wrote that he intended to ignore Kearny's requests. He did, however, promise to relay the general's grievances to President Polk—along with a suggestion that Kearny be recalled from his command.[2]

On January 16, the same day that Kearny challenged Stockton, one of Kearny's officers dispatched a similarly blunt letter to Frémont. At Kearny's behest, Lieutenant William Emory wrote Frémont, ordering him to desist from making any further military appointments and, in the future, to submit all proposed actions to Kearny. For good measure, Emory enclosed a copy of the orders issued by War Secretary Marcy.[3]

After Emory received no immediate answer from Frémont, Kearny sent a much briefer letter the next day:

Dear Colonel:
I wish to see you on business. Yours,
S. W. Kearny
Brigadier General

That same day, January 17, when Frémont appeared at Kearny's quarters, he stood stiffly before the general's desk and said that, yes, he had received the orders in question. In fact, he had been up much of the night, writing a response to them. That letter was now, he said, with a clerk who was making an official copy of it. Moments later, Kit Carson arrived, carrying the letter. After inspecting the copy, Frémont signed it, then handed it to Kearney.

Kearny asked Frémont to have a seat while he read the document. In his letter, Frémont refused to obey Kearny's order; and he asserted that, as early as the previous July, Stockton had been holding California and commanding all U.S. forces in the province. That command, Frémont wrote, continued to be acknowledged in the day-to-day deference accorded Commodore Stockton by most U.S. officers in occupied California. On that point, Frémont noted, "I learned also in conversation with you, that on the march from San Diego recently to this place you entered upon & discharged duties implying an acknowledgment on your part of supremacy, to Commodore Stockton." Finally, Frémont asserted, though he felt "great deference" to Kearny's "professional & personal character," until higher authorities resolved the current dispute, "I shall have to report and receive orders as heretofore from the Commodore."[4]

❋

Kearny, then fifty-one years old, became livid at Frémont, who, only six days earlier, had turned thirty-four:

> I told Lieutenant Frémont, that I was a much older man than himself, that I was a much older soldier than himself, that I had great regard for his wife, and great friendship for his father-in-law, Colonel Benton, from whom I had received many acts of kindness, that these considerations induced me to volunteer advice to him, and the advice was, that he should take that letter back and destroy it, that I was willing to forget it.

Kearny warned Frémont that if he persisted in his behavior, he "would unquestionably ruin himself." But Frémont remained adamant: He would continue to view Stockton as his commanding officer. Beyond that, Frémont added, he expected, any day now, to be appointed by Stockton as California's new governor—and because he considered Stockton his commanding officer, he intended to accept and act on the powers implied by that appointment.

❋

Later that same day, Frémont learned that Stockton had indeed—in a proclamation penned the day before—named him California's new governor. From Los Angeles, Frémont—taking up the prerogatives of his new post—began issuing various gubernatorial proclamations, including, on January 22, a statement restoring civil authority in the territory. Three days later, anticipating a need for a larger U.S. force in California, he directed Army Captain John K. Wilson and Louis

McLane, who was now a major, to raise a second artillery company for "the California service."

Over the next two months, as California's putative governor, Frémont did his best to tend to the day-to-day responsibilities of his office—spending time at his headquarters, and also venturing out among the people to listen to their problems. "I lived in the midst of the people," he later recalled, "in their ancient capital, administering the government, as a governor lives in the capital of any of our States." Often seen wearing a sombrero, Frémont also tried to ease wounded feelings among Californios and reconcile them to the new U.S. government. Toward that end, he made prominent Californios advisers to his administration and appointed teams to investigate claimed losses of property of Californios.[5]

❖

But in naming Frémont governor, Stockton had conferred upon the explorer a title whose legitimacy was questionable and would prove problematic. During his own tenure as governor, Stockton could legitimately point out that he had been the key U.S. officer in securing U.S. dominion over California. Beyond that, Stockton's claim to dominance over Kearny was further bolstered by a ten-to-one troop ratio superiority over his rival. Frémont, by contrast, held no such advantages. He was a lieutenant colonel who was regarded as having won his rank through political and familial connections. As one soldier in Kearny's army—disparaging "Frémont's thirst for glory"—groused, "I only wish I could marry a Senator's daughter; I might then set at defiance the orders of my superiors and do as I pleased."[6]

Unlike Stockton, Frémont had played no significant role in the military actions around Los Angeles, and with the departure of Stockton's forces from California, the California Battalion now constituted the only troops under Frémont's command. Tilting the troop ratios even more against Frémont, Kearny's Army of the West, whose numbers in California then amounted to only about a hundred men, was about to be reinforced by the overland arrival of the U.S. Army's five-hundred-strong Mormon Battalion, and by another regiment from New York, under Colonel Jonathan Stevenson. And unfortunately for

Frémont, the men of both units would look on Kearny as the territory's governor.

Beyond those particulars, a certain logic dictated that the head of U.S. land forces in California, rather than his naval counterpart, run the occupied territory. Even if Stockton had not carried orders to establish a civil regime in California, because he had reached the province before Kearny's overland army it would have fallen to him to establish the first semblance of U.S. rule over California. But now, with Kearny on the scene—and about to be reinforced by still more land troops—it made little sense for a naval commander to continue to govern the new U.S. territory.

❀

An ongoing loss of allies further eroded Frémont's position. His very acceptance of the title of governor, after all, had marked the exit of his key ally in California, Robert Stockton. To make matters worse, Stockton's replacement, Commodore W. Branford Shubrick—who arrived only three days after Stockton named Frémont governor—quickly proved himself a staunch Kearny ally.

In distant Washington as well, tides were running against Frémont. The previous summer, his main administration ally, Navy Secretary George Bancroft, had left the cabinet to become U.S. minister to Great Britain. Replacing him was John Mason who, upon learning of the dispute in California, sent orders on November 6 expressing President Polk's desire that Kearny be accorded "the entire control" over all military matters on land, and all administrative functions in California.

❀

Almost a decade earlier, Senator Benton and the "Western men"— stymied by Congress in their efforts to promote Western exploration— had allied themselves with the U.S. Army's Corps of Topographical Engineers. Over the past three years, however, John Frémont's increasingly erratic behavior had alienated key U.S. Army officials— ranging from War Secretary William Marcy to Corps of Topographical

Engineers chief John J. Abert. In search of new supporters, Benton, Frémont, and their allies had turned toward the Army's interbranch military rival, the U.S. Navy. But now, with George Bancroft's departure and his replacement by John Mason, Benton and his friends suddenly had no firm supporters within the executive branch's bureaucracies. Even President Polk was by now reluctant to come to John Frémont's aid.

✺

It was in mid-February of 1847 that Kearny received Navy Secretary Mason's orders giving him full authority in California. Later that year, Frémont—accusing the general of trying to entrap him into an act of insubordination—would charge that Kearny had deliberately kept the contents of the Mason directive from him. To that accusation, Kearny would answer that, even if he had failed to share the letter's contents, he had violated no military regulations. "I am not," he would assert, "in the habit of communicating to my juniors the instructions I receive from my seniors, unless required to do so in those instructions."[7]

Whether or not Kearny had failed to properly notify Frémont of the orders, the general wasted no time in spreading the news of his newly reconfirmed stature. In early March, he and Shubrick issued a joint proclamation, trumpeting the President's orders; and, that same day, Kearny issued a second proclamation, declaring himself California's governor.

Emboldened by his enhanced position, Kearny, on March 1, ordered Frémont to gather all of the territory's public papers and archives in Los Angeles, and to bring them, "with as little delay as possible," to Monterey, newly restored by Kearny as California's capital.[8] In the same letter, Kearny passed along instructions from General Winfield Scott, stating that Frémont should not be detained in California any longer than it took to fulfill this last set of orders.

The dispatch also notified Frémont that his California Battalion would soon be superseded by a new Southern Military District—to be led by Lieutenant Colonel Philip St. George Cooke—a young West Point graduate, then commanding the Mormon Battalion. In the meantime, Frémont was instructed that all California Battalion members not already in regular U.S. Army service should be mustered into it, so that they could be paid and put under Cooke's command. Those unwilling should march to San Francisco to be discharged.[9]

Two weeks later, Cooke wrote Frémont, asking how many members of the California Battalion were under his new command. The same day that Frémont received the inquiry, his "secretary of state," William H. Russell, wrote the Mormon Battalion commander, telling him that not one member of the California Battalion had been mustered into Cooke's new command. Beyond that, Russell noted, "the Govr. considers it unsafe at this time, when rumor is rife with a threatened insurrection to discharge the Battn. and will decline doing so."[10]

Upon receiving Frémont's answer, Cooke immediately dispatched a courier to Monterey to notify Kearny of Frémont's continued recalcitrance.

❀

As Frémont and Kearny continued their shadowboxing through intermediaries, other problems weighed on the beleaguered Frémont. Many of the woes were financial: from Stockton, Frémont had inherited a chaos of unpaid bills, which, during Frémont's tenure in Los Angeles, had only grown in size. Whether or not Frémont's position as governor was legitimate, there were needs in Los Angeles that had to be met: the men of his California Battalion required food, shelter, clothing, and wages; he also needed funds to run a government that Kearny, even if he had funds to spare, had no intention of subsidizing.

To supply the California Battalion, Frémont, since January had taken on more than $10,000 in cash loans from wealthy Angelenos at interest rates of up to 3 percent per month. Most debts, as Frémont later estimated, arose from less orderly in-kind transactions—and, all combined, exceeded $600,000:

"From 3,000 to 4,000 horses, averaging thirty dollars each"—
$120,000
"3,000 head of cattle, averaging $10"—$30,000
"1,000 saddles, bridles, spurs, and horse equipments, averaging
$60"—$60,000
"400 rifles, at $30 each"—$12,000

"Drafts protested and obligations, including damages and interests"—$50,000

"Claims for provisions taken, and damages at *San Pedro* and *Los
Angeles*, examined and allowed by a commission before I left
California"—$29,584

"Provisions and supplies, to wit: flour, grain, coffee, sugar, vegetables, and other small items, to wit: sheep, wagons, gears,
damage to ranchos"—$100,000

"Services of the California battalion"—$100,000.[11]

Frémont—haunted by the previous year's uprising against Gillespie—feared another revolt by Los Angeles's Californio population.
While, by all accounts, he had conducted a conciliatory governance of
Los Angeles, edicts by Kearny, he later charged, had reneged on com-
mitments made in the Treaty of Cahuenga, thus stirring talk of revolt.
"Groups of armed men were constantly seen," he recalled. "The
whole population was in commotion, and every thing verged toward
violence and bloodshed."[12] As his problems festered, Frémont resolved to act. That February, to make his case in the East, he dispatched Kit Carson and fifteen riders to Washington. More fatefully, "I
determined to go to Monterey to lay the state of things before General
Kearny." Frémont later claimed that he merely sought to warn Kearny
of the possibility of another revolt in Los Angeles. But there are
equally strong reasons to believe that, fearing the consequences of his
refusal to obey Kearny's earlier order to disband the California Battalion, he sought an opportunity to repair damaged relations.

At dawn on March 22, along with Jacob Dodson and Don José de
Jesús Pico, Frémont set off for the territorial capital. Today their ride
is largely forgotten. Had Frémont's admirer Henry Wadsworth Longfellow chosen to spin a poem from their trip, perhaps the trio's long
ride would have achieved a more durable immortality. Even so, for
generations of Californians, Frémont's Los Angeles-to-Monterey circuit of spring 1847 remained a tale to tell: all in all, in time spent on
the road during their round trip the men would cover 840 miles in
eight days—including a day-and-a-half layover in Monterey. To maintain their pace, they had nine horses. As each man's mount tired, he
simply saddled up one of the loose animals.[13]

The three men reached Monterey on the afternoon of March 25;

and, that evening, Frémont went to General Kearny's headquarters in Thomas Larkin's home. There, joined by Larkin, he made a brief courtesy call on the general and arranged for a formal meeting the next day. From the start, that subsequent encounter went badly. Frémont opened by complaining of the presence in the room of Kearny's colleague, Colonel Richard Mason. To that, Kearny later recalled,

> I told him that Colonel Mason had been sent out by the War Department to relieve me in my command in California as soon as I thought proper to leave it, and that there was no conversation which I could hold with him, on public affairs, but that it was proper Colonel Mason should be present at.

But Frémont refused to drop the issue. Mason, he said, was there to allow Kearny to later take advantage of some "unguarded" remark their visitor from Los Angeles might make. As Kearny recalled the exchange, "His reply to me was offensive, and I told him that I could hardly believe that he would come in my quarters and intentionally insult me."[14]

By Kearny's account, only after he convinced Frémont that Mason was not leaving did the meeting turn to other matters. Kearny asked Frémont if he intended to obey Kearny's March 1 orders. At that, Frémont offered his resignation, but Kearny refused to accept it. When Kearny repeated his question and Frémont hesitated in answering, the general suggested that the young officer take some time before answering—up to an hour, if he needed it—for it was an important question. Taking up Kearny's offer, Frémont left, then returned an hour later. Yes, he said, he would obey Kearny's orders—he would disband the California Battalion.

✸

Frémont left Monterey that same day, reaching Los Angeles four days later—followed, within the week, by Mason, now carrying orders that essentially gave him all powers formerly claimed by Frémont. Looking for a way out of a bad situation, Frémont, on May 10, wrote Kearny, asking for permission to take sixty men and 120 horses, already rested for such a venture, and merge his forces with those of General Winfield Scott's, already in Mexico proper. By then, however, Kearny—now planning his own exit from California—had already concluded that he would take Frémont with him to the East and thus denied the request.

In the meantime, Frémont's and Mason's relationship continued to deteriorate. By April 14, things had gotten so bad that, when Frémont refused Mason's request for information about some recently requisitioned horses, Mason threatened, "None of your insolence, or I will put you in leg irons." Livid, Frémont challenged Mason to a duel— the terms eventually agreed to: double-barreled shotguns with buckshot at twenty paces. In the end, however, the duel never took place. Mason asked for a postponement until both men could meet at Monterey. And General Kearny, upon hearing of the challenge, ordered both men to "proceed no further" in the matter.[15]

❀

Finally fulfilling General Stephen Watts Kearny's orders to disband the California Battalion, John Frémont and the five hundred or so men remaining with him left Los Angeles that May of 1847, reaching Monterey on the twenty-seventh. Most of the battalion's men, however, chose to be discharged with no pay at all. Frémont, meanwhile, was ordered to take the men who wished to remain with him, and to follow General Kearny and his army back to the East. And so, on May 31, with only nineteen men of the original party he had brought to California, Frémont followed ingloriously behind Kearny's army, to Sutter's Fort to prepare for the overland trip.

While there, Frémont asked for permission to take a few men from his party and—paying their own personal expenses—move in advance of Kearny's army. Citing their long absences from their families, Frémont pointed out that, with his intimate familiarity with the intervening country, he and his men would be able to reach St. Louis some forty or fifty days ahead of Kearny's larger party. Kearny, however, denied the request. On June 17, Kearny's army left Sutter's Fort with, once again, Frémont and his men following behind. Below Donner Pass, where they crossed the Sierra's summit, they stopped, on

June 22, at Donner Lake, where they lingered long enough to bury corpses left behind by the lake's namesake emigrant party, the last of whose snow-trapped survivors had left the site only weeks earlier. By mid-July, Kearny's procession had reached Fort Hall, where it met the streams of emigrants by then pouring down the Oregon Trail.

Frémont later complained that, during the entire overland crossing, though never informed that he was under arrest, he and his men were nonetheless subject to protocols and indignities generally reserved for prisoners. Frémont had already complied with orders to turn over to one of Kearny's officers all of his scientific instruments and expedition specimens. And during the entire march east, he remained under the constant "surveillance" of Kearny's Mormon guard. It wasn't until they reached Fort Leavenworth, on the Missouri River, that—on August 22—Frémont's official status was finally revealed to him: as Kearny watched, a lieutenant read a statement to Frémont that, henceforth, he should consider himself under arrest; after settling final accounts with his men, he was to report to Washington to the U.S. Army's adjutant general.[16]

❋

Upon reaching Westport a few days later, Frémont found Jessie waiting for him on the town's wharf. Reunited after a separation of more than two years, the couple, as they continued their downriver trip to St. Louis, delighted in the cheers they received in the towns along their route. News of the dispute with Kearny had preceded the explorer's return, and public sentiment in Missouri ran solidly in Frémont's favor. Even so, once back in St. Louis, Frémont felt compelled, as a matter of military decorum, to decline an offer to stage a public dinner in his honor. On September 16, the couple reached Washington. The following day, after reporting to the Army's adjutant general's office, Frémont promptly left for Charleston, to attend to his ailing mother.

As it turned out, Frémont reached his mother's home in Aiken, South Carolina, a few hours after she died. After her funeral, he continued on to Charleston, where he stopped long enough to visit friends and to accept, from a local citizen's committee, a specially designed, ornately wrought sword, as a "memorial of their high appreciation of the gallantry and science he has displayed in his services in Oregon and California."[17]

❖

In Mexico, meanwhile, U.S. forces under General Winfield Scott were, that summer of 1847, pushing inexorably south toward Mexico City. On the morning of September 14, after fighting their way up the fortified hill of Chapultepec, American soldiers victoriously entered the national palace, over which they quickly raised Old Glory. In the wake of the U.S. victory, a debilitating stalemate settled over efforts by U.S. and Mexican diplomats to negotiate a formal conclusion to hostilities.

Back in Washington that same fall of 1847, Lieutenant Colonel John Frémont's own long stalemate of sorts with the U.S. Army was approaching its own high noon. At 12:00 o'clock on November 2, a thirteen-man panel of U.S. Army officers sat down at the old Washington arsenal to hear court-martial charges against him.

❖

At least as early as June 6, when Kit Carson—ordered the previous February to deliver military dispatches to the East—reached Washington, Jessie had learned of the Frémont-Kearny clash. She and the other Bentons immediately sprang into action, organizing a campaign on John's behalf. Indeed, the day after Carson arrived, Jessie, accompanied by Carson, went straight to the White House and President Polk. The President listened patiently as the two made their case, but, as Polk's diary makes clear, he felt no obligation to come to Frémont's aid:

> Mrs. Frémont seemed anxious to elicit from me some expression of approbation of her husband's conduct, but I evaded [making any]. In truth, I consider that Col. Frémont was greatly in the wrong when he refused to obey the orders issued by Gen'l Kearney [*sic*]. I think Gen'l Kearney was right also in his controversy with Com. Stockton. It was unnecessary, however, that I should say so to Col. Frémont's wife, and I evaded giving

her an answer. My desire is, that the error being corrected, the matter shall pass over quietly without the necessity of having an investigation by a Court Martial.[18]

Two months later, Senator Benton visited the President. The meeting took place on August 17, an hour before Polk's Tuesday cabinet meeting. During their exchange, Polk expressed his hope that the matter might be resolved without a court-martial. But Benton—not content to merely make his case and leave it at that—broadly hinted that perhaps a full public investigation by the U.S. Senate of the administration's entire course of conduct in California might be in order. Polk, by his own account, was unfazed by the threat: "I answered him with some spirit that so far as the administration was concerned I had nothing to fear from the most searching investigation, and indeed that [I] would court such an investigation that he proposed to institute."[19]

❋

During Frémont's trial, Captain John F. Lee, of the U.S. Army's Ordnance Department, served as the judge advocate, the prosecutor. Representing Frémont were Senator Benton and Benton's brother-in-law William Carey Jones. The defendant faced multiple counts on three charges: mutiny, refusing a lawful command from a superior officer, and conduct prejudicial to military discipline. Commencing on November 2, 1847, the trial—an object of continued public attention—finally ended on January 31, 1848, ten days after Frémont's thirty-fifth birthday.

In the defense, Frémont and his lawyers sought not only to impeach Kearny's veracity and motives, but also to show that the charges against Frémont had arisen from a dispute between two officers—Stockton and Kearny. More specifically, they attempted to show that because Stockton had reached California before Kearny and had begun establishing a civil government, Kearny's orders to set up a government were obsolete before he reached the territory. Beyond that, as Frémont insisted when, nudging lawyers Benton and Jones aside, he delivered his own closing argument, he had, throughout his time in California, always acted in good faith—to both the American people and the Californios who lived under his nominal governance:

My acts in California have all been with high motives, and a desire for the public service. My scientific labors did something to open California to the knowledge of my countrymen; its geography had been a sealed book. My military operations were conquests without bloodshed; my civil administration was for the public good. I offer California, during my administration, for comparison with the most tranquil portion of the United States; I offer it in contrast to the condition of New Mexico at the same time. I prevented civil war against Governor Stockton, by refusing to join General Kearny against him; I arrested civil war against myself, by consenting to be deposed—offering at the same time to resign my place of lieutenant colonel in the army.

I have been brought as a prisoner and a criminal from that country. I could return to [California], after this trial is over, without rank or guards, and without molestation from the people, except to be importuned for the money which the government owes them.

I am now ready to receive the sentence of this court.[20]

✸

Frémont, Benton, and Jones had waged a vigorous defense, but, in the end, the panel found the defendant guilty on all charges. Frémont was ordered dismissed from the Army.

President Polk, however, a month later, sent a letter, directing the famous explorer—"in consideration of distinguished services"—to resume his military career, "and report for duty with his regiment." The prideful Frémont, however, promptly declined the President's largesse—answering Polk that unless the conviction was lifted, he had no intention of remaining in the Army; it was, as Jessie recalled, "*justice*, not *clemency*," that the couple sought: "And as a month passed without further action by the President, Mr. Fremont notified him, he considered himself out of the army and would proceed to act accordingly."

With that, Polk accepted the resignation.[21]

MEASURING THE EMPIRE

OR THIRTY-FIVE-YEAR-OLD John Frémont, his court-martial constituted a profound personal setback. Even so, the expansionist forces that he had nudged along continued apace. On February 2, 1848, a month after the verdict against Frémont, President Polk signed the Treaty of Guadalupe Hidalgo, formally ending the Mexican War. Beyond recognizing the U.S. annexation of Texas, the treaty gave the United States title to New Mexico and California in exchange for eighteen million dollars. The Mexican cession, containing nearly 500,000 square miles of territory, along with the now clear U.S. title to Oregon south of the forty-ninth parallel, turned the rhetoric of Manifest Destiny into reality. The United States became an empire that spanned the continent. In the closing months of his administration, President Polk—acting to implement a territorial objective pursued by U.S. Presidents dating back to John Quincy Adams—quietly sought to purchase the island of Cuba. But when the New York *Herald*, in October 1848, disclosed the secret talks, embarrassed U.S. and Spanish officials abruptly ended their conversation. The mid-nineteenth-century's enlargement of the nation's hemispheric domain had reached its conclusion.

"You have a Sparta, embellish it!" With those words, the Whig Daniel Webster, during the 1840s, had challenged expansionist Democrats to look beyond their lust for new lands and to begin the work of consolidating their empire's new domain. And now the time had come to meet Webster's challenge. With the continental boundaries now in place, the time had come to consolidate—to learn about, to settle, and to integrate into the nation's life—the empire's new Western domain.[1]

❃

Court-martialed or not, Frémont, in the minds of many Americans as well as Europeans, deserved much of the credit for realizing this new empire. In the wake of his return from the Third Expedition, England's Royal Geographical Society awarded him its founder's medal for valorous service to geographical science; and Frémont's long-time idol, the geographer Baron von Humboldt, awarded him a similar gold medal from Prussia's government. According to Jessie Frémont, during that same season, John received at least two job offers from South Carolina—one for the presidency of the Louisville, Cincinnati, and Charleston Railroad, for which he had done survey work two decades earlier, and another for a professorial chair at the College of Charleston. If true, the latter offer culminated a particularly sweet vindication. This was, after all, the same institution that seventeen years earlier had expelled Frémont as a student. In 1836, five years after that expulsion, the college had, on the recommendation of its president, Jasper Adams, relented and granted the explorer a Bachelor of Arts degree. And now, according to Jessie, the college, in its efforts to lure Frémont as a professor, "added a thousand a year to the already good salary."[2]

For Frémont, however, lectern and deskbound jobs could not compete with his zeal to return to California. Before leaving the territory with Kearny's army, he had left three thousand dollars with Thomas Larkin to purchase a parcel of coastal property for him. But somehow, Larkin—through some misunderstanding, or simply underestimating the depth of Frémont's long-held dreams of owning an estate by the sea—had used the funds to purchase a wild seventy-square-mile tract in the Sierra foothills, over a hundred miles from the nearest coastline. Nonplussed, Frémont nonetheless began making plans to develop a working ranch in California—either on the property purchased by Larkin or, if a refund or swap could be arranged, on some other tract by the sea. Frémont contracted to have a house, corral, and barn built on his property. And by sea, he arranged to have shipped to the property various farm implements as well as the components for an entire sawmill.[3]

❃

Though his troubles with Kearny had cost Frémont many of his Washington patrons, many still considered him among the nation's greatest experts on the vast new territories that the United States had just acquired. As evidence of that durable popularity, in May 1848, after a year of public lobbying by Frémont, the U.S. Congress voted an allocation of $500,000 to pay off most of the debts incurred by him on behalf of the U.S. government during his occupation of Los Angeles. Equally important, the previous year, the Senate had commissioned him to write a brief narrative account of the Third Expedition. The document was to accompany a map of the Far West that Preuss had been commissioned to produce, using materials gathered from all three Frémont expeditions, as well as from other reputable scientific sources.

Not surprisingly, while writing the narrative, John grew distracted by preparations for his court-martial. Moreover, Jessie was pregnant again and in ill health; and, soon after work commenced on the report, she had to withdraw from her usual collaboration. On July 27, 1848, she gave birth to the couple's second child, Benton Frémont. They were glad to have a son, but the baby was sickly, racked by what a doctor told them were spasms that rushed blood to his tiny head. But Senator Benton, aware of the toll that recent events had taken on the child's mother, had another diagnosis: the child, he suggested, suffered from " 'the Court-Martial,' a family disease."[4]

John thus finished what he took to calling "the cursed Memoir" alone. The sixty-seven-page report—published in 1848 as a *Geographical Memoir upon Upper California in Illustration of His Map of Oregon and California*—lacked the flair and length of its predecessors; it also lacked any scenes even remotely comparable in drama to, say, the Snow Peak climb of the First Expedition *Report*. And unlike the two predecessor reports, the *Memoir* was not cast as a guidebook for prospective emigrants. Although the Senate issued twenty thousand copies of the *Memoir* and the accompanying map that Charles Preuss had been enlisted to draft, neither captured the attention, or sales numbers, of the earlier publications.[5]

Even so, the *Geographical Memoir*—often unjustly neglected by Frémont scholars—accomplished much. In addition to the usual tables of scientific data that attended Frémont's reports, it offered the

Charles Preuss's illustrations of the West appealed to the public taste for the sublime in nature. These two illustrations, the first of Wyoming's Wind River Range and the second of Frémont and his party encamped beside Nevada's Pyramid Lake, show Preuss's tendency to exaggerate the architectonic features of landforms. (Author's collection)

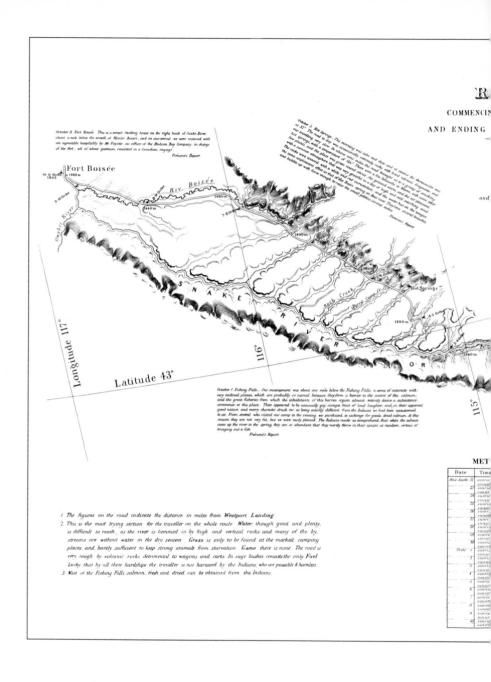

and

October 8. Fort Boisée This is a simple dwelling house on the right bank of Snake River, about a mile below the mouth of Rivière Boisée; and on our arrival we were received with an agreeable hospitality by Mr Payette, an officer of the Hudson Bay Company, in charge of the fort, all of whose garrison consisted in a Canadian engagé.
Frémont's Report

Fort Boisée

10 11 Octbr 1460 m
1843

9 40 Octbr

Riv. Boisée

1490 m

1440 m

7.8 Oct

1400 m

October 5. Hot Springs. The morning was calm and clear, and at sunrise the thermometer was at 32°. The road to day was occasionally extremely rocky, with hard volcanic fragments, and our travelling very slow... [Frémont's Report]

1360 m

Hot Springs

Rock Creek

Barrel Camp Cr.

4.5 Octbr

1360 m

3 Octbr

1340 m

S N A K E

R I V E R

O R

Longitude 117°

116°

115°

Latitude 43°

October 1. Fishing Falls.. Our encampment was about one mile below the Fishing Falls, a series of cataracts with very inclined places, which are probably so named, because they form a barrier to the ascent of the salmon: and the great fisheries from which the inhabitants of this barren region almost entirely derive a subsistance commence at this place. There appeared to be unusually gay savages, fond of loud laughter; and, in their apparent good nature, and merry character struck me as being entirely different from the Indians we had been accustomed to see. From several who visited our camp in the evening, we purchased, in exchange for goods, dried salmon. At this season they are not very fat, but we were really pleased. The Indians made us comprehend, that, when the salmon came up the river in the spring, they are so abundant that they merely throw in their spears at random, certain of bringing out a fish.
Frémont's Report

MET

1. The figures on the road indicate the distance, in miles from Westport Landing.
2. This is the most trying section for the traveller on the whole route. Water, though good, and plenty, is difficult to reach, as the river is hemmed in by high and vertical rocks and many of the by-streams are without water in the dry season. Grass is only to be found at the marked camping places, and barely sufficient to keep strong animals from starvation. Game there is none. The road is very rough by volcanic rocks, detrimental to wagons and carts. In sage bushes consists the only Fuel. Lucky that by all these hardships the traveller is not harassed by the Indians, who are peaceable & harmless.
3. West of the Fishing Falls salmon, fresh and dried, can be obtained from the Indians.

Date	Time
1843 Septbr 22	sunrise
	sunset
23	sunrise
	sunset
24	sunrise
	sunset
25	sunrise
	sunset
26	sunrise
	sunset
27	sunrise
	sunset
28	sunrise
	sunset
29	sunrise
	sunset
30	sunrise
	sunset
Octbr 1	sunrise
	sunset
2	sunrise
	sunset
3	sunrise
	sunset
4	sunrise
	sunset
5	sunrise
	sunset
6	sunrise
	sunset
7	sunrise
	sunset
8	sunrise
	sunset
9	sunrise
	sunset
10	sunrise
	sunset

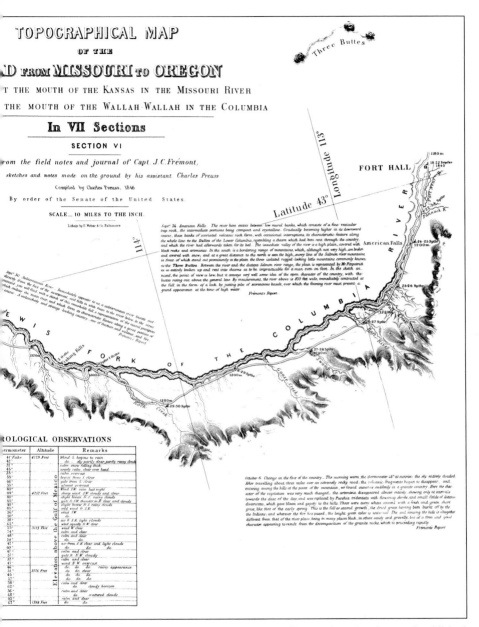

The sixth in a seven-map series generated by Frémont's explorations and published by the U.S. Senate in 1846. Beyond cartographic features, the maps included practical information for emigrants, such as where to find water and campfire fuel and how to avoid Indian attacks.

An illustration from Frémont's *Memoirs* published in 1887. It depicts an elderly Indian woman of the Great Basin who startled the Third Expedition at one of their campsites. (Author's collection)

Kit Carson's adventures with Frémont led to international fame for the former trapper. (Bancroft Library)

The short-lived Bear Flag Republic's namesake flag, of which California's state flag is a stylized version. The flag was designed and made by William L. Todd, a cousin of Mary Todd Lincoln. (Society of California Pioneers)

An engraving, probably based on a drawing by either Richard or Edward Kern, captures the desolate mood of the wintry San Juan mountains in 1848–49, during Frémont's disastrous Fourth Expedition. (Henry E. Huntington Library and Art Gallery)

The title page of sheet music for a song promoting Frémont's 1856 presidential campaign, which ceaselessly evoked reminders of Frémont's glory years as an explorer. (Bancroft Library)

Civil War daguerreotype of General Frémont in his dress blues. (State Historical Society of Missouri)

A daguerreotype of Frémont's friend, the American sculptress Vinnie Ream (1847–1914). Though Frémont was fifty-six years old and the artistic prodigy twenty-two when they met in Paris in 1869, the two soon shared a close friendship that—whatever its precise nature—never flared into scandal. But it and similar relationships with younger women nourished salacious gossip and speculation throughout the explorer's life. (Library of Congress)

Frémont, Jessie, and their daughter Lily posed in 1888 beside the General Frémont, an ancient tree named after him in what is now California's Henry Cowell Redwoods State Park. (Henry E. Huntington Library and Art Gallery)

general public a vividly comprehensive account of a place often better known through legends than in specific details. Shortly after the *Memoir*'s publication, historian James Rhoads, capturing the narrative's virtues, as well as the era's hyperbole, wrote in *Sartain's Union Magazine of Literature and Art* that Frémont's revealing of California ranked among the three most important events in U.S. history: "Columbus marked a pathway to a new-found world; Washington guided and sustained the patriots who consecrated that world to the advancement of human rights and human welfare; and Frémont lifted the veil which, since time first began, had hidden from view the real El Dorado."[6]

Beyond christening the Golden Gate, Frémont's new narrative corrected some earlier miscalculations concerning California's coast, as well as the Second Expedition *Report*'s erroneous depiction of the Great Salt Lake and Utah Lake as a single body of water. The *Memoir* also allowed Frémont to extend and refine his ongoing examination of the Great Basin—much of which, he again noted, seemed more Asiatic than American, greatly resembling the high country between the Caspian Sea and northern Persia. But, at the same time, he also urged prospective emigrants not to overlook the "fertile" lake- and river-watered meadows and pine forests to be found in the higher elevations of the Great Basin's mountains.

Turning his attention to the Great Basin's lower elevations, Frémont also noted, approvingly, that the Mormons, taking his earlier advice, had recently established a colony by the Great Salt Lake. He also anticipated the future value of the Humboldt River as the key overland emigrant corridor into California: "This river possesses qualities which, in the progress of events, may give it both value and fame. It lies on the line of travel to California and Oregon, and is the best route now known through the Great Basin, and the one travelled by emigrants."[7]

Perhaps most important, the *Geographical Memoir* served as a rousing finale to Frémont's meditation on American empire. In the Second Expedition *Report*, he had disparaged the long-range value of both the Sacramento and the San Joaquin Rivers. By 1847, however, Frémont correctly recognized that California—not Oregon—lay at the heart of America's Western dreams. In the *Memoir*'s closing passage, he proclaimed:

Geographically, the position of this California is one of the best in the world; lying on the coast of the Pacific, fronting Asia, on the line of an American road to Asia, and possessed of advantages to give full effect to its grand geographical position.[8]

That obligatory paean to maritime commerce, however, constituted a conspicuous exception in a document otherwise wholly preoccupied with the attributes of California's interior. In his Second Expedition *Report*, Frémont had enumerated California's natural attributes, evaluating each according to its worth in meeting the various commercial-, military-, and transportation-related exigencies of Benton's Road to India. Among other things, he had noted the defensive value of the Coast Range, as well as California's relative merits as a locus for international ports.

In the *Geographical Memoir*, by contrast, Frémont gave himself latitude to celebrate California's natural bounties without reference to such piecemeal criteria—or, for that matter, to any grand historical theories. He was now reading California's landscape on his, not Benton's, terms. Thus, while much of the *Memoir*'s narrative teems with the expected day-to-day journal "entries" detailing climate, flora, and geology, it also abounds in more general praise for a place that clearly enchanted him. On the subject of the territory's coast, for instance, his writing now swelled with a singular enthusiasm:

> The inhabitant of corresponding latitudes on the Atlantic side of this continent can with difficulty conceive of the soft air and southern productions [crops] under the same latitudes in the maritime region of Upper California. The singular beauty and purity of the sky in the south of this region is characterized by Humboldt as a rare phenomenon, and all travellers realize the truth of his description.[9]

Like the fellow in Wallace Stevens's poem "Anecdote of the Jar," who, after placing a jar on a hill, delights in watching the surrounding country rise to meet its glassy surface, Frémont now accorded California a centrality denied in his earlier writings.

In the Second Expedition *Report*, the economic potential of California's Central Valley—parsed by Benton's esoteric criteria—had been given short shrift. Stressing that it lacked a substantial river, Frémont had noted that the valley—largely landlocked and inconveniently situated between the Coast Range and the Sierra—could hardly compete with the Columbia River corridor. In the *Geographical Memoir*, by contrast, Frémont took a more sanguine view of the San Joaquin and Sacramento Rivers' navigability. Beyond that, the two rivers' respective valleys—combined, they formed the Central Valley—now constituted an organic masterpiece of topographical design:

> It is a single valley—a single geographical formation—near 500 miles long, lying at the western base of the Sierra Nevada, and between it and the coast range of mountains, and stretching across the head of the bay of San Francisco, with which a *delta* of twenty-five miles connects it. The two rivers, San Joaquin and Sacramento, rise at opposite ends of this long valley, receive numerous streams, many of them bold rivers, from the Sierra Nevada, become themselves navigable rivers, flow toward each other, meet half way, and enter the bay of San Francisco together, in the region of tide water, making a continuous water line from one end to the other.

Moreover, the Sierra's foothills that descend into the valley, offer many "pretty valleys"—many of which

> afford many advantageous spots for farms, making sometimes large bottoms of rich moist land. The rolling surface of the hills presents sunny exposures, sheltered from the winds, and having a highly favorable climate and suitable soil, are considered to be well adapted to the cultivation of the grape, and will probably become the principal vine growing region of California.[10]

To Frémont, grapes constituted only one parallel among many linking California to the Mediterranean—particularly Italy. Indeed, in the *Geographical Memoir*, Frémont invoked, for the first time, an analogy that—reinforced by countless acts over the next century—would become a critical part of California's identity. Long before early-twentieth-century California boosters self-consciously promoted Mediterranean themes in California's life, Frémont noted that, west of the Sierra, California is roughly the size of, and shares climatic similarities with, Italy. By his lights, only in California's superior hydrological design—a system of watersheds that promote unity over regionalism—did its geography markedly differ from that of Italy:

> Like Italy, it is a country of mountains and vallies: different from it in its internal structure, it is formed for *unity*; its large rivers begin concentric, and its large vallies appurtenant to the great central bay of San Francisco, within the area of whose waters the dominating power must be found.

Capping off the celebration of California, Preuss's map accompanying the *Geographical Memoir* bore, in the vicinity of Sutter's New Helvetia settlement, the label "El Dorado or Gold Region"—thus rendering it the first map with wide distribution to proclaim the territory's recent gold strike. Preuss had added the line upon learning of the strike, well after Frémont had already departed the East on another Western expedition. Even so, the timing resulted in false charges that Frémont knew about the strike before the general public, and that it thus served as the motivation behind his Fourth Expedition into the West.[11]

✸

Although the *Geographical Memoir* failed to garner the widespread public attention his earlier reports had won, Frémont had hardly dropped out of the news or escaped public controversy. The latest furor took place after Senator Benton and Frémont noticed, in the May 9, 1848, issue of the *National Intelligencer*, an article about the recent loss of a whaler off California's coast because, the paper said, of maps "now in general use."

Benton immediately sent a letter to the *Intelligencer*, noting that the error which placed California's central shoreline too far east had already been discovered and corrected by Frémont in Preuss's soon-to-be-published map of the Far West. Without mentioning him by name,

Benton was impugning the West Coast reconnaissance conducted during the conclusion of Charles Wilkes's naval expedition of 1838–42. Upon the *Intelligencer*'s publication of Benton's jibe, Wilkes answered with his own, charging that Frémont's alleged "correction" had been made by others as early as 1826.

Through his own letters to the paper, Frémont soon joined the fray—and, for the next month, he and Wilkes treated the *Intelligencer*'s readers to a blizzard of contentious letters on topics ranging from the accuracy of Wilkes's Oregon coast survey to Frémont's measurements of the Sacramento valley.[12] But even as he quibbled with Wilkes and completed his *Geographical Memoir*, Frémont was already contemplating yet another expedition.

❋

By the summer of 1848, there had been talk for several years around Washington of someday spanning the continent with a transcontinental railroad. Much of the speculation had been sparked by New York merchant Asa Whitney, who, in 1844, had launched an intensive campaign to build a line from Lake Michigan to the Pacific Coast. Although Senator Thomas Hart Benton and the ambitious entrepreneur would become bitter enemies, Whitney's career, in many ways, vindicated the very formula for success that Benton had prescribed for America. The son of a prosperous Connecticut farmer, Whitney had moved in about 1817 to New York, where he learned the dry goods business. As a buyer for American merchants, he traveled Europe for several years before returning to New York to start his own company. After the Panic of 1837 destroyed his business, he went to China, where, acting as an agent for U.S. firms, he became so rich that he won the freedom to spend much of the rest of his life promoting various railroad projects.

Like Benton, Whitney was convinced that the key to America's economic future lay in establishing some type of transcontinental thoroughfare that linked the Eastern United States to the Pacific and thence to the lucrative trade of Asia. But, in contrast to the hidebound Benton, who as late as 1848 still doubted that a railroad could ever cross the Rockies, Whitney had become a vigorous advocate of a transcontinental rail line. In January 1845, he asked the U.S. Congress for a land grant embracing a sixty-mile-wide swath along the corridor of his proposed line.

But with Oregon still under the Anglo–U.S. joint occupation arrangement and California still part of Mexico, the United States, during, the mid-1840s, held no title to any Pacific port that could serve as a Western terminus for such a line. As a consequence, Whitney's proposals received little serious attention. By 1848, however, all that had changed. The resolution of the Oregon question had given the United States claim to much of the Northwest; and the Guadalupe Hidalgo treaty had provided secure title to Texas, New Mexico, and California. Moreover, the entire nation was experiencing a boom. During the 1840s, the nation's population, swelled by European immigration, had grown from 17 million to 23 million. In Missouri, such trends were augmented by growing numbers of native-born U.S. citizens arriving from the East—almost doubling the state's population, from about 383,000 in 1840 to about 682,000 in 1850. St. Louis, which Benton had reached in 1815 and soon thereafter romanticized as the capital of a vast fur-trapping empire, had, by 1848, transformed itself into a busy metropolis whose far-flung commercial links trafficked in many products besides beaver pelts.

Energized by that economic expansion, the nation in general and the Western states more particularly had grown obsessed with competing plans for a transcontinental railroad. As *De Bow's Review* put it, "We want the road, finally, to complete for us that *commercial Empire* after which we have sighed—which has been indicated for us in every step of our progress, from the landing of the Pilgrim Fathers, and which appears to be *ours* by a manifest and inevitable destiny. *Shall we not then have it?*" [13]

In fact, several rail lines already stretched from the East Coast to the Mississippi River, so the most frenzied competition for being the jumping-off point for the new transcontinental line pitted various Midwestern cities against each other—each lobbying, publishing pamphlets, and sponsoring conventions to promote its town as the most logical eastern terminus for whatever line was built. Benton pitched for St. Louis, though he still questioned whether any steam engine could ever make it through the high, often snowbound Rockies. Any trains, he believed, would be forced to stop at the foot of the range and unload their goods onto sleighs for shipment over the mountains. Engineers, he was convinced, would have to be summoned to sort out such matters. In the meantime, he argued, whatever sort of "national road" was built, it should run from St. Louis to San Francisco, along a central line across the continent—west to east, intersecting the head of the Rio Grande, then crossing both the Rockies and the Sierra somewhere close to the thirty-eighth parallel. Indeed, over the next few years, Benton's advocacy of this thirty-eighth-parallel route—replacing his earlier obsession with South Pass—would become a fixation almost mystical in his devotion to it.

In order for his line to be built, however, Benton first had to make sure that Congress rejected Whitney's proposed line. That moment came in late July of 1848, after Connecticut's U.S. Senator John Milton Niles urged his colleagues to take up Whitney's proposal. Benton immediately urged that the measure be tabled. The government, he argued to his Senate colleagues, had no right to give away 100 million acres of land to any single man. Beyond that, "We must have surveys, examinations, and explorations made, and not go blindfolded, haphazard into such a scheme."[14] Months later, arguing for his proposed route at a St. Louis convention of railroad boosters, Benton would go out of his way to suggest the distance he himself had traveled since two decades earlier, when he had suggested raising a sign reading "Terminus" at the crest of the Rockies. Now, what he wanted to see, he said, was a statue of Columbus on a Rocky Mountain peak overlooking the road—"pointing with outstretched arm to the western horizon, and saying to the flying passengers, there is the East! there is India!"[15]

However, Benton's emphasis on the necessity of "surveys, examinations, and explorations" lacked the spirit of scientific detachment that it might have appeared to possess. For even as he offered that admonition, Benton was already seeking congressional funds to support an expedition to establish the practicality of his proposed thirty-eighth-parallel line. The senator, after all, understood that, before he could entice Congress to adopt the route, he had to establish that he had located a Rockies passage that would be practical in all seasons.

The discovery and mapping of such a pass lay at the heart of what Senator Benton and John Frémont hoped would be the explorer's next federally funded expedition. In the wake of the court-martial, Benton scuffled with the Polk administration on numerous issues and did not visit the White House for more than a year, alienating many congressional and administration allies. As a consequence, Benton and Frémont failed to muster sufficient congressional support to fund the expedition. While the Senate, that summer, eventually approved an allocation of thirty thousand dollars to fund the proposed expedition, the House of Representatives rejected the measure a week later. Undaunted, Benton, by summer's end, had arranged for a group of St. Louis businessmen—led by banker and merchant Robert Campbell, saddler Thornton Grimsley, and merchant O. D. Filley—to advance cash to fund the new expedition. Among trappers and explorers, Filley's name was particularly well-known, for it was cast on the Dutch ovens that he manufactured, long a popular item around Western campfires. Indeed, Filley eventually provided most of the expedition's camp equipment.[16]

❋

Frémont, meanwhile, had no intention of abandoning plans to develop his ranch in California, only to postpone it a bit. This new survey, after all, would take him back to California—albeit by a slightly circuitous route. Indeed, since learning of Larkin's purchase of land for him in the Sierra foothills, Frémont had corresponded with his friend in Monterey, and Larkin had agreed to refund Frémont's three thousand dollars and help find him, pursuant to his original wishes, some property along California's coast.

To prolong her time with John before he again vanished into the void, Jessie decided to take their infant son, Benton, their daughter, Lily, now six years old, and a family servant and accompany her husband all the way to Westport—the expedition's jumping-off point. By October 3, they had reached St. Louis and boarded the steamer *Martha* for the final leg of their shared journey. En route up the Missouri, however, tragedy befell the family when the infant Benton suddenly became ill and died. Devastated, as Jessie later recalled, she refused to give up the corpse: "Grief was new to me then and I could not bear to give him up." Only after the couple reached Westport did she finally relinquish Benton's tiny body to a cousin aboard the ship, who would arrange for its transfer to St. Louis for burial.[17]

At Westport, the couple once again said good-bye. Even without Benton's death, however, this parting differed from earlier ones, for the couple planned to reunite not in St. Louis or Washington, but in California. After saying good-bye, Jessie, Lily, and the servant boarded a downriver boat back to St. Louis and, from there, returned to Washington. If all went as planned, she would sail from New York in the spring, then take the overland route over the Panamanian Isthmus, and from there, sail to San Francisco. There, she would finally see for herself dazzling California, whose virtues John had for so long extolled to her.

✹

To take advantage of the warmer seasons, Frémont's earlier expeditions had all departed in the spring. This time, however, the point of their journey was to establish that they had located a passage over the Rockies that could be crossed at any time of the year—including the snowiest months of winter. And so, on October 21, only nine months after Frémont's court-martial—the exploring expedition left Westport, Kansas. Thirty-five men comprised the original party—including such veterans of past expeditions as Alexander Godey, Charles Preuss, Thomas Martin, Charles Taplin, and Raphael Proue. It also included Edward Kern of the Third Expedition, as well as his brothers Richard, also an artist, and Benjamin, a physician. Jackson Saunders, a free black man who worked as a servant for the Benton family, came along as Frémont's valet, and eighteen-year-old Frederick Creutzfeldt served as the expedition's botanist. To help keep costs down, several members of the expedition party agreed to serve without formal arrangements for pay, trusting Frémont to reimburse them later. According to Thomas Martin, the explorer, even after being rebuffed by Congress, still believed that the federal government might yet fund the expedition. "He promised us no wages," Martin recalled, "but said that when the work was finishing [the] Govt. would pay us."[18]

From Westport, the party moved quickly up to the Smoky Hill Fork tributary of the Kansas River. Riding up the Smoky Hill Fork valley, Frémont—mindful of the projected rail line's inevitable role in promoting settlement and agriculture within the continent's interior—was struck by the country's abundant forests, game and excellent grass and soil "of very superior quality." "This line," he wrote to Benton, "would afford continuous and good settlements certainly for four hundred miles, and is therefore worthy of consideration in any plan of approach to the mountains."[19]

On November 2, the party struck out on an overland course toward the Arkansas River. They were now on the plains and, that same day, spotted their first buffalo. Not that the pace Frémont set—on one day covering forty miles—left much time for sightseeing. "The life is damned hard," wrote Captain Andrew Cathcart, a former officer in Britain's elite Hussars regiment, who had signed on with Frémont in order to see the West. "We start at sunrise, having breakfasted by starlight and travel till near sun down, always camping in a strong position and keeping guard."[20]

Game was plentiful and the campsites were good, but the men found themselves discomfited by a group of Kiowa Indians who tagged along with the party for several days. On November 9, the exploring party even shared a campsite with the tribesmen—that night, offering the Indians various trade goods in exchange for buffalo meat. "They were," Richard Kern recalled, "a set of wild looking rascals, mostly clothed in Buffalo robes and carrying bows and arrows." To Richard's brother Edward, by contrast, the Indians seemed more cunning than primitive. "Picturesque, unsophisticated children of Nature, bah," he wrote, "they have plenty of mules and horses but want silver for them."[21]

Still more disturbing were the ubiquitous prairie fires, whipped by autumn's winds into a harrowing blaze, that the men passed by, forcing them to carefully thread their way over and around the rolling prairie's knolls and ravines. "These lines of *miles* of flames are a magnificent sight," Cathcart wrote, "but (especially at night) keeps you in perpetual anxiety." One evening, the flames edged so close that the men had to start a backdraft blaze to prevent the wind-driven fire from devouring their camp.[22]

On November 15—now traveling along the Arkansas's south bank—they camped at a spot across from Bent's Fort. Remaining at the campsite for two days, the men took time to write letters and purchase supplies—Frémont, to his relief, managed to find and buy a "good lodge." They also found time to rest and generally to prepare for the mountainous hardships that lay ahead. While camped there, the men enjoyed a fine view of Pike's Peak and the twin Spanish Peaks, which rise along the flank of south-central Colorado's Sangre de Cristo Range. But those vistas also augured difficulties for the days ahead. To Benton, Frémont wrote that both Indians and whites, with whom they talked while near Bent's Fort,

> say they have never known the snow so deep in the mountains so early, and that there is every prospect of a severe winter. But this does not deter us. I have my party well prepared, and . . . expect to overcome all obstacles.[23]

Three days later, after marching another seventy-five miles up the Arkansas River, the party reached the tiny hamlet of Pueblo, where, just across the river, they set up camp at Mormontown, a scattering of log cabins built by Mormon soldiers a year earlier. The soldiers—discharged, in May 1847, from service in General Kearny's army—had wintered at the site after being turned away from Pueblo by mountain men among whom Mormons were unwelcome.

At Pueblo, Frémont heard the same, by now familiar, description of conditions in the Rockies. As party member Micajah McGehee later recalled, "Most of the old trappers at the pueblo declared that it was impossible to cross the mountains at that time; that the cold upon the mountains was unprecedented, and the snow deeper than they had ever known it so early in the year." Faced with such predictions, Frémont, while visiting Pueblo, hired the renowned trapper Old Bill Williams—who had accompanied the Third Expedition as far as the Great Salt Lake—to serve as an expedition scout.[24]

❋

Williams, sixty-one when he joined Frémont's survey, never attained the immortality of such scouts as, say, Kit Carson and Joseph Walker. Nevertheless, in his day, Old Bill Williams enjoyed a reputation for possessing an unrivaled knowledge of the Rockies. He had grown up in Missouri and for several years had been an itinerant Protestant preacher before becoming, for twelve years, a trapper and trader among the Osage Indians. During the early 1820s, serving as an interpreter, he assisted the federal survey of the Santa Fe Trail. For the next two decades, he worked as an independent trapper and trader, scouring the Rockies as far north as the Yellowstone River, and venturing as far west as California. Typical of Rocky Mountain trappers, Williams had lived with, and married into, the Osage and Ute tribes.

He was tall and rangy, with red hair and a beard, and his legendary eccentricities stretched from his often incomprehensible speech to his wobbly gait to his trademark style of riding. "Scarce a horse or mule could unseat him," Micajah McGehee recalled:

> He rode leaning forward upon the pommel, with his rifle before him, his stirrups ridiculously short, and his breeches rubbed up to his knees, leaving his legs bare even in freezing cold weather. He wore a loose monkey-jacket or a buckskin hunting-shirt, and for his head-covering a blanket-cap, the two top corners drawn up into two wolfish, satyr-like ears, giving him somewhat the appearance of the representations we generally meet with of his Satanic Majesty.

Williams was also known for being willing and able to outdrink and outgamble any man among his trapper brethren. But such indulgences could not mask his very formidable skills as an expert marksman, rider, and trapper—talents surpassed only by Williams's self-knowledge of them. Emblematic of that pride, his pelts came tagged "William S. Williams, M. T."—for Master Trapper.[25]

❀

Frémont's party left Pueblo on November 22. As the men worked their way up the Arkansas into higher elevations, the prairie's fragrant sagebrush gave way to the sharper aromas of cedars and junipers. Even so, warm temperatures during the day graced their passage. The next day, after turning south and going about four miles along the

Arkansas's Hardscrabble Creek tributary, they reached the settlement of Hardscrabble, where its proprietor, Lancaster Lupton, once again welcomed Frémont.

The party remained at the post for two days—resting and purchasing supplies and fresh horses for their ascent into the Rockies. After having loaded all of their horses with corn, and the mules with the remaining supplies and equipment, they would walk into the Rockies. After the party had disappeared into the snow-capped mountains, Lupton, in a letter to his old friend Senator Benton, did his best to offer a sanguine view of the expedition's prospects. "The snow is unusually deep in the mountains," he wrote, "and many old mountainmen here have expressed a doubt whether he can get over with so large a cavalcade—about one hundred horses and mules and thirty-odd men; but I think he will do it."[26]

The party left Hardscrabble on November 25. The next day, still traveling on foot, the party entered the Wet Mountains, the first peaks of the outer Rockies. By November 27—now ascending the range inside a deep canyon thick with pines and aspens—they found themselves in three feet of snow. The next morning, November 28, they reached a ridge crest of the Wet Range, high above the spectacular Wet Mountain valley, bounded on its west by the high pinnacles of the Sangre de Cristo Mountains. Frémont planned to cross the Sangre de Cristos, then strike the drainage of the Rio Grande, then follow its tributaries into the San Juan Mountains, where they hoped to find their way over the Continental Divide somewhere close to the thirty-eighth parallel—most likely, through Cochetopa Pass.[27]

On December 3, the party reached the summit of the Sangre de Cristo Mountains' Mosca Pass—then called Robidoux Pass. Standing in the wind-hardened snow at the summit of the 9,175-foot-high pass, the men, gazing west, looked down on the San Luis Valley, walled in on its west by the San Juan Mountains' dome-shaped peaks, a legacy of their creation by volcanic action. Descending from Mosca Pass, the party's transit was made difficult by piles of snow-covered fallen trees scattered along its route, apparently the result of an earlier mountain tornado, or runoff from a thunderstorm.

Though often dramatically vivid, the fragments of diaries, letters, and other first-person reminiscences recounting the expedition offer puzzlingly vague and contradictory accounts of the survey party's pre-cise location on any given day. Even now, the expedition remains a subject of lively speculation among mountaineers and historians. On this much, however, sources agree: by mid-December, the men—in their determination to find a new, thirty-eighth-parallel route through the Rockies—found themselves struggling through deep snow as they worked their way across high ridges toward a summit they thought was the Continental Divide.

The evening of December 15 found the party camped a quarter mile below 12,944-foot-high Mesa Mountain. For the next two days, trudging through snowdrifts up to twenty-five feet deep, the men continued to press on—only to be pushed back by snow, high winds, and temperatures that, during the night, fell to thirty de-grees below zero. "Along these naked heights," Frémont recalled, "it storms all winter and the raging winds sweep across them with re-morseless fury." To make matters worse, on their first crossing at-tempt, they faced a violent *pouderie*—"dry snow driven thick through the air by violent wind, and in which objects are visible only at a short distance."[28]

By now, the expedition's supplies were dwindling—the corn for the mules was long gone—and the entire episode had acquired the character of an unyielding nightmare. "The snow became deeper daily," McGehee recalled, "and to advance was but adding dangers to difficulties. About one-third of the men were already frost-bitten more or less; some of the mules would freeze to death every night, and every day as many more would give out from exhaustion and be left on the trail, and it seemed like combating fate to attempt to proceed, but we were bent on our course and we continued to ad-vance."[29]

On December 17, after passing over Mesa Mountain, the party es-tablished a new camp—Camp Dismal—along that elevation's western slope, at the head of Wannamaker Creek, which Frémont, still think-ing he had crossed over the Continental Divide and that they were on the Rockies' western slope, thought belonged to the Colorado River's headwaters, but which actually belonged to the Rio Grande's drain-age. By now hungry, frost-bitten, and trapped in a violent snowstorm, Frémont knew he must find another route. "All movement was para-lyzed," he recalled. "To advance with the expedition was impossible:

to get back, impossible. Our fate stood revealed. We were overtaken by sudden and inevitable ruin."[30]

From Camp Dismal, Charles Preuss and several others had set off toward the west, hoping to locate a route out of the mountains. Those remaining in camp, meanwhile—building fires and digging holes in the snow—did their best to stay warm and conserve their supplies. But even as most of their remaining mules were dying of starvation and exposure, the men—not wanting to exert the extra labor of butchering the animals' frozen carcasses—began, in a wasteful act of indulgence, slaughtering their few remaining, and by now emaciated, living mules.

❋

By December 20—after Preuss's party had been unable to locate a western route out of Camp Dismal—the men counted fifty-nine mules still alive, fewer than half their original herd. On December 22, the party, by crossing over to Mesa Mountain's southern slope, began working its way off that elevation. By then, Frémont realized that they were already encamped along the headwaters of the Rio Grande. Thus, he reasoned, if he could dispatch a relief party down those headwaters to the Rio Grande, to the New Mexican settlements north of Taos, his expeditionary party, once resupplied, might yet return to the mountains and, via the Cochetopa route, make it through the Rockies.

Over the next three days, using mauls improvised from tree limbs, the men worked their way back and forth across the ridge, lugging their baggage and equipment to a campsite just above Rincon Creek, a Rio Grande tributary. Once all of the remaining equipment had reached the creek, the men, using "pots and dinner plates," scraped out a hole in the six-foot-deep snow, thus establishing what they called Camp Hope. And it was there—supping on a meal of rice doughnuts, biscuits, coffee, and mule-meat pie—that the men spent Christmas Day of 1848.

Years later, with the distance of hindsight, a journalist, after interviewing exploring party member Thomas E. Breckenridge, a veteran of the Third Expedition and the conquest of California, would compose a mock menu grimly lampooning the party's Christmas repast:

MENU

SOUP
Mule Tail.

FISH
Baked White Mule.
Boiled Gray Mule.

MEATS
Mule Steak, Fried Mule, Mule Chops, Broiled Mule,
Stewed Mule, Boiled Mule, Scrambled Mule, Shirred Mule,
French-fried Mule, Minced Mule.

DAMNED MULE
Mule on Toast (without the Toast).
Short Ribs of Mule with Apple Sauce
(without the Apple Sauce).

RELISHES
Black Mule, Brown Mule, Yellow Mule,
Bay Mule, Roan Mule, Tallow Candles.

BEVERAGES
Snow, Snow-Water, Water.[31]

❋

While at Camp Hope, Frémont named Henry King, a veteran of the
Third Expedition, to lead a small detail that was to move out ahead of
the main party, negotiate its way down the creek to the Rio Grande,
and follow the river to the nearest New Mexican settlement. There,
they were to acquire relief supplies, then return to rescue the others.
As most of the men remained behind, working to complete the task of
moving the party's baggage to Camp Hope, the relief party set out on
December 26. Two days later—having concluded there was no point
in lingering to await the return of the relief party—Frémont decided

that he and the other remaining men should set out on their own toward the Rio Grande. Toward that end, the men, after dividing themselves into three details, set out to find the Rio Grande, where, if things turned out as Frémont hoped, they would meet King's relief party somewhere downstream in the San Luis valley.

Though Camp Hope lay only about ten miles from the Rio Grande, the men, in their confusion, covered about forty miles over twenty days to reach the Rio Grande. Of the three groups, Frémont's party, which included Preuss and Godey, reached the baggage cache site first—on January 2. Over the next few days, as the members of the other, slower-moving two parties stumbled into their new camp, Frémont grew increasingly impatient for the return of King and the relief party.

Finally, on January 11, having concluded that the King party had been detained, or possibly killed by Indians, Frémont's party set off once again, ahead of the other two groups. Before leaving, he instructed the men left behind to finish packing the remaining baggage and to meet him farther down the Rio Grande, at its confluence with the Conejos River, which already had some New Mexican summer farming settlements. Toward that end, the men who would remain behind were divided into two details—one that included the Kern brothers and ended up remaining on the mountain, and one that spent much of its time transporting baggage down to the camp near La Garita Creek.

But, as McGehee later recalled, before leaving, Frémont also managed to sow ill feelings among the men by telling them that, "if we wished to see him we must be in a hurry as he was going on to California. By this time, being forced to abandon his projected route, he had determined to proceed to California by a southern route."[32]

✸

Five days after leaving the main party, Frémont's advance party, while marching along the Rio Grande, had the good fortune to encounter a friendly Ute Indian. In exchange for Frémont's rifle, his two remaining blankets, and "other promised rewards when we should get in," the Indian agreed to conduct the men to the closest New Mexican settlement and to bring along four horses to carry their remaining equipment.

On January 16, still farther down the river, Frémont's party stumbled upon Henry King's relief party—albeit without King. Frostbitten, starving, their sun-withered skin ravaged by sores, they were, Frémont recalled, "the most miserable object I had ever beheld . . . I did not recognize Creutzfeldt's features." The rescue party, as Frémont soon learned, had been, from its outset, star-crossed.[33]

✸

Less than two weeks after leaving Camp Hope, the men of King's relief party had eaten through their entire supply of food and then consumed candles, boots, belts and knife scabbards, as well as the provisions they had acquired en route—a crow, a mountain sheep, and a river otter. Apparently, much of the blame for their troubles lay with Bill Williams. From its start, the party had made slow time, but south of today's Monte Vista, Colorado, Williams had led the party away from the Rio Grande on what he stressed to them was a shortcut that would allow them to sidestep a time-consuming bend in the river. But Williams had another reason for taking the "shortcut." Only months earlier, he had been living with a band of Utes who lived along the river bend. And now—for good reason—he sought to avoid them; during the summer of 1848, he had, after a drinking binge in Taos, led a detachment of vengeful U.S. soldiers stationed in New Mexico to the settlement. Once there, the soldiers engaged in a massacre. For that, Williams feared, the Utes were out for his scalp.

Williams kept his scalp, but the route away from the river exposed the relief party to a desolate sagebrush prairie swept by blistering winds that left eyes blinded, fingers and feet frozen, and their leader, Henry King, dead of starvation, hypothermia, or both. Reports later surfaced that the other three men had eaten part of King's corpse—a report later given credence by Kit Carson, who allegedly observed that "in starving times no man who knew him ever walked in front of Bill Williams."[34]

✸

Gathering the three remaining survivors of the "relief party" onto their spare horses, Frémont's party continued its downstream course.[35] On January 20—the day before Frémont's thirty-sixth birthday—the expedition reached the New Mexican settlement—today's Questa, New Mexico—at the Rio Grande's confluence with its Red River fork. There the men soon dispersed, becoming guests at various homes scattered among two separate but closely tied communities in the area—Taos and Rio Colorado.

While Preuss and Theodore McNabb, soon joined by others, remained at the settlement. Frémont continued to Taos, to gather supplies for a party to rescue the men left behind in the mountains to transport the baggage down. They, too, had eventually escaped the mountains. But starving and delirious—their mules and provisions long gone and with no game in sight—they had been reduced to boiling and eating rawhide and ropes for sustenance.

For whatever the reason, however—perhaps simply fatigue and frostbite—instead of returning to the mountains, Frémont remained in Taos, recuperating at Kit Carson's house. "How rapid are the changes of life!" he wrote Jessie during his stay at Carson's:

A few days ago, and I was struggling through snow in the savage wilds of the upper Del Norte [the Rio Grande]. . . . Now I am seated by a comfortable fire, alone—pursuing my own thoughts—writing to you in the certainty of reaching you—a French volume of Balzac on the table—a colored print of the landing of Columbus before me—listening in safety to the raging storm without![36]

In the same letter, Frémont expressed undaunted confidence in Senator Benton's thirty-eighth-parallel route across the Rockies. *"The survey . . . has been uninterrupted up to this point,"* he wrote, *"and I shall carry it on consecutively."* To the extent that the expedition had encountered problems, Frémont laid the blame on Bill Williams—as did even Charles Preuss, normally given to blaming all problems on Frémont. Even as the party's plight grew increasingly desperate, Preuss, on December 15, wrote that Williams "kept insisting that we need only cross the mountain range in order to reach a snow-free tableland. We believed him, in spite of the fact that we saw here only snow on mountains and in valleys."

By all accounts, Williams and Frémont, at several junctures, had quarreled over which mountain routes to take. Afterward, Frémont believed that Williams had led them astray: "The error of our expedition was committed in engaging this man. He proved never to have known, or entirely to have forgotten, the whole country through which we were to pass."[37]

As Frémont recuperated at Carson's house, Godey, who had been staying at Rio Colorado, rounded up thirty horses and mules, enlisted several New Mexicans, and struck out up the Rio Grande to rescue the exploring party's remaining men. On February 9, he returned from the north, to the Red River settlement, with the expedition's remaining survivors: all in all, ten of the party's original thirty-two members who had entered the San Luis valley had died of starvation or hypothermia. From the Red River settlement, the party's remaining members pressed on, reaching Taos on January 11, where they rejoined a by-then-recuperated Frémont.

❀

Frémont had several friends in Taos—including Kit Carson, Dick Owens, and Lucien Maxwell—all of whom expressed eagerness to get him resupplied so that he could resume his journey to California. Of particular assistance was Major Benjamin L. "Old Ben" Beall, of the Army dragoons—in charge of all U.S. military forces in northern New Mexico—who, upon learning of Frémont's plight, promptly arranged to provide the survey party with fresh horses and provisions from the Army's commissary.

On January 13, only two days after the expeditionary party had regrouped and replenished their supplies, they set out for California. The party included all of the surviving members of the original expedition except for six men: Creutzfeldt was too weak to go on, and Cathcart decided he had seen enough of the West. As for Williams and the three Kern brothers, they were not invited to continue—a slight arising, in all likelihood, from previous tensions that had arisen and the rumors of cannibalism.

✸

From Taos, the party eventually found its way to Tucson, and thence to the confluence of the Gila and Colorado Rivers. There, Frémont caught up with a party of "several hundred" Sonorans—men, women, and children—all en route to California. Why California? Frémont asked.

Confirming a rumor that Frémont had heard in Santa Fe, the Sonorans told him that, weeks earlier, gold had been discovered in the foothills of California's Sierra Nevada. The Sonoran party included numerous experienced miners—all headed to the gold country to try their luck.[38] The strike, as it turned out, had been made by James Marshall, as he supervised the construction of a sawmill along the south fork of the American River, within Johann Sutter's vast New Helvetia domain. And, as Frémont marveled at the Sonorans' stories and pored over their maps, he noticed the proximity of the gold mines to Las Mariposas, his recently acquired property in the Sierra foothills. In his baggage, the explorer had all the documents needed to transact with Thomas Larkin the planned refund of the three thousand dollars he had paid for Las Mariposas. But now, as Frémont surveyed the Sonorans' maps, he began to have second thoughts.

On the spot, he offered to grubstake twenty-eight of the Sonoran men. If they would meet him at Las Mariposas and help mine the gold he suspected they would find there, they would evenly split any discovered riches. From the Colorado River, Frémont pushed north, finally disbanding the expeditionary party at, in all likelihood, Isaac Williams's sprawling Rancho Santa Ana del Chino, in today's Riverside County, California.

Before breaking up the party, Frémont did his best, given his meager resources, to stand its members in good stead. In Los Angeles, he made arrangements to provide each man with food and other supplies; he also gave each man a pony and a pack animal and invited each one, if he were game, to come and try his luck at placer gold mining at Las Mariposas. From Rancho Santa Ana del Chino, it is also likely that Godey set off with the twenty-eight Sonorans, to begin their work at Las Mariposas. Frémont, meanwhile, continued to San Francisco, where he expected to meet Jessie.[39]

✳

For Jessie, the wait through the fall and winter of 1848–49 seemed interminable. From Westport, in October of 1848, she returned to St. Louis. Still mourning the death of their infant, Benton, she blamed General Kearny and the court-martial for the baby's death.

President Polk, over Senator Benton's vehement opposition, had promoted Kearny to the rank of brevet major general. Within months after taking up his new command in Mexico, however, Kearny suffered a violent attack of dysentery and yellow fever and was transferred to St. Louis for medical care. From what became his deathbed there, the general—aware that Jessie Frémont was in town—summoned her, so that he might reconcile with her and John. But, for Jessie, the wounds of the court-martial remained too fresh for her to consider such a meeting. Declining Kearny's dying request, she told the general's doctor that "I could not forgive him. There was a little grave between us I could not cross." Kearny died on October 31.[40]

But though estranged in life, Frémont and Kearny, in posterity, maintain a close symbolic proximity. In Nebraska, as in several other states, towns, counties, or streets named after the two men lie close together. In San Francisco, Fremont and Kearny streets, though never intersecting, lie within a few blocks of one another—not far, for that matter, from Vallejo, Beale, Sutter, and Stockton streets.

✳

By the winter of 1849, Jessie was back in Washington, her thoughts focused on John and her own planned trip to California. Writing the previous November from Bent's Fort, John had optimistically predicted that by January he would be in California, where he would await her arrival by steamer. But she was discomfited by other reports reaching her that fall, that the snow in the Rockies that season lay deeper than usual. To get to California, she planned to take the new government-subsidized mail steamer from New York to Chagres, on Panama's Gulf of Mexico coast. From there, she would cross the isthmus by pole boat and mule caravan to Panama City on the Pacific coast, where she would board a California-bound steamer. Travelers described the overland trip as exceedingly unpleasant—with risks of contracting yellow fever, cholera, and malaria in tropical jungles and rivers.

Jessie, now twenty-four years old, had always been known for her independence. Even so, this would be her first trip on her own with little Lily, and as she occupied herself with preparations for the journey, she reflected on how she had, in some ways, lived a sheltered life:

> I had never lived out of my father's house, nor in any way assumed a separate life from the other children of the family—Mr. Frémont's long journeys had taken him from home more than five years out of the eight since we were married. I had never been obliged to think for or to take care of myself, and now I was to be launched literally on an unknown sea, travel toward an unknown country, everything absolutely new and strange about me, and undefined for the future.[41]

Compounding her anxieties were warnings from her father, other members of the family, and family friends—among them Secretary of State James Buchanan, who, during a visit to the family's C Street house dismissed the planned trip as "a cruel experiment."[42] Senator Benton, failing to dissuade Jessie from going, did insist that she and Lily not go alone. Just before their departure, her brother-in-law Richard Taylor Jacob was drafted to accompany her. To assist in her personal needs, a servant woman from New England was hired at the last minute. On March 15, sailing aboard the steamer *Crescent City*, the newly expanded entourage finally left New York. The ship, however, had barely left the port when the ship's captain had to take Jessie's freshly hired servant into custody after Jessie caught her stealing items from her baggage. Nine days after leaving New York, the *Crescent City* reached Chagres. There, the party boarded a pole boat owned by the steamship company to travel up the Chagres River.

By the standards of time and place, the Frémont party enjoyed a privileged transit across the isthmus. Their boat, after all, featured a palm-leaf canopy for shade, while most river travelers had to settle for dugout canoes. And rather than camping in the open jungle, Jessie's party stayed each night in a tent, at camps set up for workers on the cross-isthmus railroad then under construction. Even so, the mosquitoes proved merciless, the food terrible, and the heat relentless—so intense that Richard Jacob succumbed to sunstroke. Years later, Lily still blanched when she recalled the hospitality of a local alcalde along their route who treated them to the local delicacies of iguana and baked monkey—the latter dish, she recalled, "looking for all the world like a child burned to death!"[43]

By the time their boat reached its terminus at the inland village of Gorgona, it was clear that the ailing Jacob would have to turn back. After his departure, Jessie and Lily resumed their journey across the isthmus via a grueling twenty-mile muleback caravan trip through the mountains to Panama City. In April, upon reaching Panama City, Jessie's entourage initially settled into one of the town's makeshift canvas-walled hotels. But their stay there was brief, for upon learning that Jessie was in town, Señora Arcé y Zimena, an aristocratic Panamanian widow whose nephew Jessie had known when he was Panama's minister in Washington, insisted that she and Lily stay with her.

Arcé y Zimena installed her visitors on the cool second floor of her family's elegant tiled mansion. The accommodations proved comfortable. But as Jessie waited in Panama City for a California-bound ship, she fretted about her own situation, as well as John's. Vague but troubling reports about the railroad expedition had reached her. And though eager for definitive news, she feared what she might hear. In any case, she was unprepared when a letter from her husband caught up with her at the Arcé y Zimena mansion. Dated January 27, it had been written at Taos and began on a sanguine note: "I write to you from the house of our good friend Carson. This morning a cup of chocolate was brought to me, while yet in bed."[44]

❀

Soon enough, however, the letter plunged into a harrowing account of the expedition. While Jessie was glad to know that John remained alive, his descriptions of the expedition haunted her. Days later, on another morning, when an acquaintance brought her a newspaper report of the expedition, it all proved too much for her to bear. For, as she later recalled, when that same acquaintance returned that evening with yet another report, "he found me where he had left me in the morning—sitting upon the sofa with the unopened paper clasped in my hand, my eyes closed, and my forehead purple from congestion of the brain, and entirely unable to understand anything said to me." The doctors diagnosed her malady as "brain fever," but to Jessie, "it was a relief to become too ill to think."

Her lungs were infected, and she was coughing blood. Two doctors—one an American, the other a Panamanian—were summoned: while the American prescribed fresh air, blistering, and iced liquids, the Panamanian suggested a regimen of bleeding, hot drinks, and a closed room. "These two," she recalled, "with their contradictory ideas and their inability to understand each other fully, only added to the confusion of my mind and became part of my delirium." Fortunately, however, for the patient—no doubt recalling her own mother's experience with bleeding regimens—no leeches were available. And she managed to escape the episode with only a chest rubdown with croton oil, which produced the requisite blisters sought by the American doctor.

❦

The beginning of the end of Jessie's Panama City layover came on May 6, with horn blasts from two arriving steamers, the *Oregon* and the *Panama*, both fresh from California. Elated that she would soon be leaving for California, Jessie joined the crowd jamming the town's docks to watch passengers leave the two ships. Amid the crush, she heard a male voice call out her name. To her surprise, it was Major Edward Beale.

Although Jessie was glad to encounter any friend of her husband, Beale bore discouraging news: San Francisco, he told her, was engulfed in chaos. Housing and provisions were abysmal, vices rampant—it was, he said, no place for a lady. Moreover, John had injured his leg during the railroad survey and was expected to be returning east for treatment. She should turn back immediately, he advised her—go back to Washington and, there await her husband's return.

Ultimately, Jessie decided to ignore Beale's advice. She and John had agreed to meet in San Francisco, and she would stick to their plan. And so, on May 18, Jessie and Lily boarded the steamer *Panama* for the final leg of their passage to California. Though the ship was built to accommodate eighty passengers, with the crush of forty-niners, it was carrying four hundred travelers. To make matters worse, food was in short supply, and her and Lily's airless cabin revived Jessie's cough. To provide partial relief, a special tentlike room was set up on the deck for them.

Days later, when the *Panama* made a brief stop in San Diego, Jessie was so convinced that bad news of her husband's fate awaited her that she declined to go ashore with the ship's other passengers. Her fallen spirits, however, soon won a reprieve, when a gaggle of passengers—after going ashore and hearing reports of John's survival—rushed to her room with the good news. "The Colonel is safe," they shouted; "he was at Los Angeles this week and has gone on to meet you at San Francisco."[45]

On June 4—seventeen days after the *Panama* had sailed from Panama City—Jessie joined the steamer's other passengers in a rousing cheer as they spotted the narrow gap in the Coast Range that her husband had recently named the Golden Gate. But, as they sailed into San Francisco harbor and a dozen or so boats approached the steamer, her heart sank as she realized that John was not among the men boarding the *Panama* to greet its passengers. Instead, she was greeted by William Howard, a local merchant, who told her that John was not yet in San Francisco but was expected any day. Jessie and Lily were taken to quarters Howard had arranged for them at the commodious abode formerly owned by the late William Leidesdorff, now a private club for the city's more prosperous businessmen.[46]

When John reunited with Jessie and Lily ten days later, he could tell that his wife was not well. Concluding that she needed a warmer climate, he immediately began arranging to move the family south, to Monterey, which they reached by steamer, on June 20.[47]

In Monterey, oddly enough, the Frémonts rented a wing of a spacious adobe that had been the home of his old nemesis José Castro, then still in exile. There—with Señora José Castro, who with her children occupied the other half of the long, narrow building—the Frémonts settled into what, years later, Jessie would recall as a splendid domesticity: "This was my first house and my first housekeeping—without any of what we consider indispensable necessities of servant, or usual supplies, but most comfortable and most charming. We had the luxuries of life, if not its necessities."[48] Having defied her father, other family members, and friends in coming to California, Jessie now went about her affairs with a new self-confidence. Twenty-five years old when she reached California in June 1849, Jessie, by then, had been married for eight years and given birth to two children, one of whom had died in infancy. Even so, she had seldom strayed far from her parents' abiding attentions. Now, commencing a new life in California, she would begin to assert an independence and display a self-confidence commensurate with her long-standing intellectual and social precocity.

❋

John's hunch about Las Mariposas' geology, meanwhile, had proven correct. And, as the gold mined there by his Sonoran workers streamed back to Monterey and much of it was plowed into other investments, he became a wealthy man. From the family's home at Monterey, he soon found himself traveling much of the time between his various businesses. At Las Mariposas, his twenty-eight Sonorans during several months of placer mining washed out about a hundred pounds of gold per month—an amount worth about twenty-five thousand dollars, half of which went to Frémont. That autumn, however, the explorer had even better news when a rich vein more than five miles in length was discovered on his land. Even the lowest-grade ore from this strike, the Mariposa Lode, Frémont estimated, would fetch more than sixteen million dollars a year. To extract gold from a vein of that scale, however, required far more resources than he then possessed. To acquire the capital needed to mine the Mariposa Lode, Frémont began signing contracts with almost any parties who would agree to begin mining within six months or a year—with the lessor receiving the traditional one-sixth of all minerals extracted.

By August of 1850, Frémont had signed leases with at least seventeen parties. Beyond that—convinced by a business associate that English capital and capitalists were the key to fully exploiting his mineral resources—Frémont engaged David Hoffman, an American and a former law professor, then living in London, to represent his interests in Europe. Frémont's contractual partners, however, weren't the only ones mining Las Mariposas, for as news of the Mariposa Lode spread, growing numbers of squatter miners began descending on Frémont's properties.[49] Even as Frémont dealt with his mining operations at Las Mariposas, he also operated a sawmill at San Jose. And in San Francisco, he had purchased several properties and had other business interests.

The rigors of the court-marital and the deprivations of the railroad survey soon faded from Frémont's countenance. The journalist Bayard Taylor, meeting the explorer in California during that period, found him in good spirits and health, wearing a sombrero and "California jacket"—the waist-length coat favored by Californio men—"and showing no trace of the terrible hardships he had lately undergone." He had, Taylor recalled, seen in no other man such

> qualities of lightness, activity, strength, and physical endurance in so perfect an equilibrium. His face is rather thin and embrowned by exposure; his nose a bold aquiline and his eyes deep-set and keen as a hawk's. The rough camp-life of many years has lessened in no degree his native refinement of character and polish of manners. A stranger would never suppose him to be the Columbus of our central wildernesses, though when so informed, would believe it without surprise.[50]

When traveling along California's coast, John often took the family along—journeying in a special surrey that he had had shipped from the East around the Horn. With the stars their roof as they leisurely drifted along California's surf-pounded margins, for John the outings certainly must have brought back fond memories of similar trips years earlier, in the southern Appalachians, with his own parents. As Lily later recalled her and her parents' first years in California:

> We lived a nomadic life at first, driving back and forth between San Jose, Monterey, and San Francisco, very rarely sleeping even for one night under a roof. My mother had the cushions drawn together in the surrey so as to form a mattress, while I slept [on] in the boot. . . . My father and the other men slept in the open on their blankets, or in hammocks when trees were near enough for them to be hung.[51]

When, in late August, a letter arrived from President Zachary Taylor, naming Frémont to the commission established to survey the new U.S.–Mexico boundary, he accepted the offer—only to resign from the panel shortly thereafter. A Whig, a Mexican War hero, and a retired general, Taylor had, the previous year, defeated Senator Benton's friend and U.S. senator from Michigan, Democrat Lewis Cass, for the presidency. Savoring his new independence and wealth, Frémont, by resigning from the Boundary Commission, had made it clear to all that he had no interest in returning to the hardships of overland surveys. But why had he accepted the post in the first place?

Very likely, he had accepted the appointment as an implicit refutation of his court-martial conviction. In addition, Frémont—already involved in California's movement for statehood—was thinking about running for one of the seats that California would have in the U.S. Senate; and when he sought that office, the Boundary Commission post would be one more item to list among his qualifications for office.

That September, when a convention met in Monterey to draft a state constitution, John and Jessie hosted what one participant recalled as numerous "star-chamber meetings" in their adobe home. And John, as a delegate, joined the convention's majority in adopting a state constitution that banned slavery in California. Afterward, Frémont—building on the political momentum he had developed in the run up to the convention—began campaigning for the Senate.[52]

As a Senate candidate, Frémont—aligned with the Democratic Party's "Free Soil" wing, which opposed slavery's extension into the West—defended his actions in 1847 as California's territorial governor. He also made it clear that he still favored the central railroad route that he and Senator Benton had championed. That December, when the state legislature met in San Jose for its inaugural session, efforts to select the state's two U.S. senators bogged down in debates over slavery. In the end, striking a compromise, the lawmakers, to mollify proslavery forces, selected physician William Gwin, a former Mississippi congressmen, for one seat and, to accommodate Free Soilers, chose Frémont for the other seat. In a drawing of straws, however, Frémont got the shorter, staggered Senate term.

Months earlier, following September's constitutional convention in Monterey, the Frémonts had moved to San Francisco, where John had purchased an attractive Chinese house, imported from Asia in pieces and assembled like a puzzle with pegs rather than nails. But no sooner had the family settled into the new house, in the city's Happy Valley neighborhood—today's South of Market—than it was time, once again, to pick up and move back to Washington to begin Frémont's Senate career. When the Panama-bound steamer *Oregon*, on the rainy New Year's night of 1850, sailed from Monterey, it was carrying 280 passengers, including the Frémonts. The ship also carried more than one million dollars in California gold. We have no way of knowing if any of it belonged to the Frémonts. This, however, we do know: to make this trip John had no call to borrow money to pay his and his family's way, for he and Jessie were now rich.[53]

THE WAGES OF EMPIRE, AND THE FINAL EXPEDITION

B Y December of 1848, when President Polk publicly acknowledged the discovery of gold in the Sierras, thousands of fortune seekers were already streaming into California. Most came by land—many along the routes surveyed by Frémont. In Washington, meanwhile, questions about a transcontinental railroad by now turned not on whether such a line would be built, but on when and where. Determined not to be left behind in the quickening competition among Western cities to host the line's eastern terminus, Thomas Hart Benton, in February of 1849—undaunted by the disasters that had befallen Frémont in the San Juans—rose in the Senate, once again to champion his thirty-eighth-parallel, St. Louis–to–San Francisco route.

Blithely passing over the debacle of Frémont's survey, Benton described the expedition as an ongoing enterprise that had already accomplished the difficult task of probing various passes through the southern Rockies. The survey's only remaining work, he blandly added, was, "to complete the examination of the mountain passes, and of all the country between the Mississippi and Pacific." Lest anyone needed any reminding, Benton also noted that Frémont was surveying a route destined to become America's path to empire:

The bay of San Francisco, the finest in the world, is in the center of the western coast of North America: It is central, and without a rival. It will accommodate the commerce of that coast, both north and south, up to the frozen regions and down

to the torrid zone. It is central in that respect. The commerce of
the broad Pacific Ocean will center there. The commerce of
Asia will center there. Follow the same latitude across the country, and it strikes the center of the valley of the Mississippi. It
strikes the Mississippi near the confluence of all the great waters which concentrate in the valley of the Mississippi. It comes
to the center of the valley.

Benton also took time to rehearse his by-now-familiar theory about
the nature of historical empires, reminding his colleagues

that Asiatic commerce had been the pursuit of all western nations, from the time of the Phoenicians down to the present
day—a space of three thousand years; that during all this time
this commerce had been shifting its channel, and that wealth
and power followed it, and disappeared upon its loss; that one
more channel was to be found—a last one, and our America its
seat.

For his proposed road, Benton suggested, the federal government
should set aside a mile-wide right of way along its entire route. To allay any suspicions of inflexibility on his part, he stressed his willingness to entertain a variety of ideas about how his proposed road might
be built. "I propose to reserve ground for all sorts of roads—railway,
plane, macadamized," he said. He would even consider the idea, recently floated by an American inventor, of a "track [run] by magnetic
power." But whatever new technology the engineers eventually selected, Benton stressed, they should save room for the construction of
"a plain old English road, such as we have been accustomed to all our
lives—a road in which the farmer in his wagon or carriage, on horse or
on foot, may travel without fear, and without tax—with none to run
over him, or make him jump out of the way."[1]

In this—the promotion of Senator Benton's latest Western venture—his trademark zeal remained undiminished. But the tides of
politics and history were running away from the sixty-six-year-old senator. After thirty years, the aging Benton's pontifications on historical
empires had grown tinny, his political timing eccentric. His account of

the virtues of his proposed route, emphasizing the necessity of paralleling major rivers, belonged less to that day's expanding age of steam-driven railroads, more to the, by then, rapidly vanishing river-obsessed age of trappers, voyageurs, and fur magnates.

As Senator Benton touted his line through the San Juan Mountains, more practical leaders—chief among them, John J. Abert of the Corp of Topographical Engineers—were planning other railroad surveys, far south of the frigid San Juans into which Senator Benton had dispatched his son-in-law.

❀

As voices battling slavery's expansion into the West, Thomas Hart Benton and John C. Frémont would continue to play important roles in American politics. But by 1849, their day as key shapers of America's destiny had drawn to a close. Then again, perhaps Frémont already knew—knew it in his bones—that the curtain was falling on his glory days. A year earlier, writing to Benton from Bent's Fort—predicting that the Fourth Expedition would be his last—he complained that he had grown weary of the explorer's life. Weeks before that railway survey led him and his men into an icy labyrinth of frostbitten starvation, he had confided to his father-in-law:

I think that I shall never cross the continent again, except at Panama. I do not feel the pleasure that I used to have in those labors, as they remain inseparably connected with painful circumstances, due mostly to them. It needs strong incitements to undergo the hardships and self-denial of this kind of life, and as I find I have these no longer, I will drop into a quiet life.[2]

❀

Alas, the quiet life—though often tantalizingly close—continued to elude the Frémonts. Foretelling the sort of reversals that would stamp much of the rest of John's public life, his U.S. Senate career turned out to be pathetically brief—a mere twenty-one working days. The Frémonts reached Washington in the spring of 1850, but John had to wait until the following September, when California was formally granted statehood, to take his seat. As a freshman senator, he settled into legislative work on behalf of several issues relevant to the new state he represented—including gold-mining regulations, a transcontinental wagon road, and state land grants to support the construction of public universities. It was, however, his advocacy of Free Soil legislation—such as a bill to ban the slave trade in the District of Columbia—that made his name anathema among defenders of slavery in the U.S. Senate and far beyond Capitol Hill, and thus won Frémont a new batch of enemies.

✳

The nation's growing debates over the future of slavery in the West had come to a boil in 1849, as California sought to become a full-fledged member of the Union. That year's gold rush had already swelled the territory's population well beyond the requisite sixty thousand needed to qualify for statehood. So, once again, Congress faced the problem of finding a way to admit a new state and simultaneously preserve the balance between free and slave states. By 1848, there were thirty states in the Union: fifteen slave and fifteen free. But as California and New Mexico—neither with a tradition of black slavery—prepared to enter the Union, both seemed destined to upset that balance.

Hoping to prevent the crisis from festering, President Taylor tried to address it immediately. From his perspective, so long as slavery's status in the territories remained unclear, sectional tensions could only increase. To sidestep that predicament, he proposed granting immediate statehood to both California and New Mexico. The federal government could then sidestep the free-or-slave issue, which would be left to the citizens of each new state. And because Taylor believed slavery could never thrive in the Far West, he assumed that both California and New Mexico would be organized as free states. To initiate his plan, he dispatched federal agents to California and New Mexico and authorized them to help draft the necessary state constitutions.

Though Taylor never spoke publicly about his expectations that both of the new states would eventually exclude slavery, Southern politicians immediately suspected the President's plans. Fearing the creation of two new free states, Mississippi officials called upon slave-holding representatives from the South's states to gather in Nashville to formulate a regional strategy to oppose Taylor's plans. Some Southerners were even already advocating that the states of their region secede from the Union.

As the crisis deepened, Senator Henry Clay of Kentucky, author of the Missouri Compromise of 1820, offered yet another accommodation. In January 1850, he proposed that California be admitted to the Union as a free state; most of its American settlers, he reasoned, had come there without slaves and seemed to want slavery barred from the state anyway. The remaining lands won from Mexico should be divided into two new territories—New Mexico and Utah—and each allowed to settle the status of slavery by popular vote.

To mollify antislavery Northerners, Clay also proposed a ban on slave auctions in the nation's capital. Washington, D.C., to the embarrassment of opponents of slavery, had served as a principal slave market. As a sop to Southern planters, Clay proposed that slavery still be legal in the District of Columbia and that Congress pass a more stringent fugitive-slave law. All of these provisions became part of a single bill, the Omnibus Bill, which was, on January 29, submitted to Congress for debate. Now, it fell to the various representatives of the North and the South to come together and approve it.

❋

The Compromise of 1850's long, tortured path to eventual adoption by Congress revealed just how strained North-South relations had become. Neither side made concessions, and with President Taylor opposing the measure, it proved impossible to pass the eventual compromise as a single legislative package. Only after the President's unexpected death in July 1850, after eating tainted food, did the compromise, as separate measures—not a single Omnibus Bill—pass Congress. With Taylor's successor, President Millard Fillmore, a former Upstate New York congressman, supporting Clay's proposals, Congress, by September's end, had passed all of the separate items. But though Congress, in the end, embraced Clay's proposals, the debates surrounding the measures produce no spirit of compromise. Only about 20 percent of the congressmen voted for all of the parts of Clay's package. In the end—with zealots on both sides of the Mason-Dixon line voting along predictable lines—it was moderates from both North and South who made the difference.

Though no spirit of compromise had emerged, Congress had, for the moment, extinguished the latest outbreak of the sectional crisis. When representatives of the Southern states met at Nashville in the winter of 1850–51, those favoring secession found themselves isolated. Most Southern politicians, as well as the public at large, saw little reason to wreck the Union. At the same time, however, Southerners did not write off secession entirely. Many had come to believe that secession was legal—but simply questioned whether the time was right to act on that prerogative. Events during the next decade, however, would, in time, convince many white Southerners that secession was the only way for them to preserve slavery and what they called, from an increasingly defensive posture, the Southern way of life.

For those like Benton and Frémont aligned with the Free Soil movement, which opposed slavery's extension into the West, it was a perilous time. Benton's three-decade-long Senate career ended in February 1851, a month after Missouri's General Assembly declined to elect him for another term. As for Frémont, upon Congress's recess the previous fall he had rushed back to California via the isthmus, to thwart efforts by a growing proslavery faction to unseat him. But the political damage had already been done. When the legislature met that February, it went through 141 ballots—finally deadlocking on the question of who would occupy Frémont's old U.S. Senate seat. Until the following year, when the legislators would again take up the issue, California would have only one U.S. senator—the proslavery William Gwin.[3]

✤

By the winter of 1851, John Frémont had already concluded that he had no desire to wait another year to stand again for the Senate. Politics, he had decided was "too costly an amusement in this country just now."[4] Besides, he was now thirty-eight years old; Jessie, now twenty-six, was again pregnant; and business matters increasingly consumed his time and energies.

John was acquiring more and more properties. And, even as he worked to develop Las Mariposas, he still faced litigation challenging his title to the property. Moreover, while he had been away in Washington, a new wave of squatter prospectors had arrived at Las Mariposas. Complicating matters still more, he had recently signed a contract with the federal government to provide beef, from his Las Mariposas cattle, to local Indians who had been displaced from their lands.

On April 19, 1851, the couple celebrated the birth of their new son, John Charles II. But any illusions they entertained of settling into a cozy San Francisco domesticity literally went up in flames two weeks later, when a fire that destroyed much of the city barely missed the Frémonts' house. Eleven days later, another fire—like the first one, very likely set by arsonists—completely engulfed the family's house. Though John soon found another house in San Francisco for the family, Jessie had been badly shaken. John's business affairs, meanwhile, were going from bad to worse. At one point, he even considered selling Las Mariposas. By October of that year, he had decided that he and Jessie needed a respite from their troubles. Already planning to travel to Europe to raise more capital for Las Mariposas, he decided to take the entire family along on what evolved into an extended tour of Europe.

During their sojourn, Frémont won plaudits from Europe's elite society—including Queen Victoria, the Duke of Wellington, Hans Christian Andersen, Napoleon III, and Alexander von Humboldt. Even so, controversy still dogged him. On April 7, while the couple was out for an evening in London, four policemen seized and arrested Frémont. The charges arose from debts owed British creditors to whom he had, as California's governor, issued U.S. government vouchers. Though the British firms had supplied various provisions to the U.S. government in California, federal officials had never reimbursed them. A London friend of Frémont's posted his bail, and Washington officials eventually resolved the matter, but the experience soured the couple on England. In May, they relocated to Paris, renting a mansion on the Champs Elysées, between Place de l'Étoile and Rond Point. There, on February 1, 1853, Jessie gave birth to the couple's second daughter—Anne Beverley, named after John's mother.[5]

✳

By June of 1853, the Frémonts had returned to Washington, where they rented a house not far from Thomas Hart Benton's. Later that summer, when their new baby became ill with a digestive disease then sweeping Washington, Jessie took the children to the estate, in Silver Spring, Maryland, of Francis Preston Blair, patriarch of Washington's powerful Blair clan, long-standing friends and political allies of the Bentons.

The Blairs were distantly related to the Bentons; and Francis Preston Blair had been a political intimate of Senator Benton for more than three decades. Between 1831 and 1847, Blair had edited the Washington *Globe*, the Democrats' main newspaper in the nation's capital. But even without the *Globe*, Blair remained a formidable presence in Washington. Indeed, over the coming years, his influence with Presidents Buchanan, Lincoln, and Johnson would prove just as significant as it had with their predecessors, Andrew Jackson and Martin Van Buren.

That familial tradition of political activism would be sustained by the senior Blair's sons, Francis Preston Blair, Jr.—better known as Frank Blair—an able Princeton-trained lawyer; and Montgomery Blair. Further cinching the Frémont-Blair connection, Jessie considered Frank's and Montgomery's sister, Elizabeth Blair Lee, her closest friend, and the two, until political discords drove the families apart, maintained an intimate correspondence.[6]

✳

The Blairs' generous hospitality notwithstanding, little Anne Frémont died on July 11. John by then had become preoccupied with the idea of taking up his former vocation and was pondering another transcontinental expedition. Although Millard Fillmore had managed to secure the passage of the Compromise of 1850, growing divisions among the Whigs denied him his party's presidential nomination two years later. The fractured Whigs of 1852 eventually turned to General Winfield Scott. But, in the end, even Scott's status as a hero of the Mexican War could not elect him. That year, the Democrats nominated New

Hampshire's Franklin Pierce, who managed to keep his party's northern and southern members sufficiently united to win the presidency.

During the spring of 1853, shortly after the Frémonts had fled to Paris, John had learned that Congress had ordered President Pierce's Secretary of War, Jefferson Davis, to commission three survey expeditions, to explore northern, central, and southern transcontinental rail routes through the Rockies. Ever the loyal father-in-law, Thomas Hart Benton—who, in 1852, had won a seat in the House of Representatives—lobbied Davis to appoint Frémont to lead one of the surveys. Davis, however, a slaveholder who nursed fresh memories of Frémont's vocal opposition to slavery, refused the request.

Even so, federal interest in the Benton-Frémont central route persisted, and War Secretary Davis appointed a party, led by Captain John W. Gunnison, to explore it. Before Gunnison could depart, however, another survey party, led by Edward Beale, left Westport, in May 1853, to explore the same route. To publicize the expedition, Beale brought along his cousin, journalist Gwin Harris Heap. Subsidized with private funds raised by Benton and his friends, the Beale-Heap expedition successfully crossed the San Juan Mountains, eventually reaching California. A month after Beale took to the field, Gunnison's party left Fort Leavenworth, following the same route. But though that expedition also eventually reached California, tragedy befell the party. While it was encamped in the Sevier River valley, in today's Utah, a band of Paiute Indians attacked the party, killing Gunnison and all but a handful of the expedition's members. Among the dead were two veterans of Frémont's 1848–49 railroad survey—Richard Kern and Frederick Creutzfeldt. Charles Taplin, another veteran of Frémont's Fourth Expedition, managed to miss the massacre: a week or so earlier, when the party reached the Great Sand Dunes, his mind had become, he said, too crowded with memories of the Frémont fiasco for him to continue; and he had left the party.[7]

To Frémont, the fact that the two parties had crossed the San Juans in the summer hardly closed the chapter on the range's exploration. To fully establish the practicality of the thirty-eighth-parallel route, he believed, the San Juans must be crossed when snow covered them. Also, Gunnison had won his exploring commission from Davis, who opposed the thirty-eighth-parallel route. So how much confidence could Frémont and Benton have had in Gunnison's fidelity in accurately reporting his findings about the route?

Thus, even as the Beale and Gunnison parties were working their way across the continent, Frémont began organizing another expedition to attempt, once again, a winter crossing of the San Juans—with a few corrections, but otherwise along the same route that had led him to disaster in 1848–49.

✽

Frémont had attempted, during the First and Second Expeditions, to take up von Humboldt's challenge to photographically document an exploring survey, but both efforts had fallen victim to his lack of expertise with daguerreotype equipment. So, as he prepared for this next expedition, he not only purchased photographic equipment but also hired someone adept at using it—thirty-eight-year-old Solomon Nunes Carvalho. A painter, photographer, and devout Sephardic Jew, Carvalho had been born in Charleston. Fortunately for posterity, Carvalho—in defiance of Frémont's injunction against his men making such records—kept and, in 1857, published an account of his expedition in the San Juans, still among the least known of Frémont's journeys. Because we have no substantial account by Frémont of the outing, most of what we do know comes from Carvalho.

For the expedition's topographer, Frémont had hoped to again hire Charles Preuss. But when an ailing Preuss declined the job, Frémont turned to F. W. von Egloffstein, a twenty-nine-year-old Prussian immigrant. By August, Frémont was in St. Louis, hiring more men and purchasing more supplies. Though he worried that the party included too many greenhorns, those concerns were somewhat offset when Frémont's old friend Alexander Godey agreed to join the survey. By September, when the party assembled at Westport, Frémont's eagerness to move out had grown more urgent still, when word reached them that the Heap-Beale party—earlier dispatched by Benton to confirm the practicality of the thirty-eighth-parallel route—had already crossed Cochetopa Pass.

At Westport, Frémont rounded out the roster of twenty-two men, including ten Delaware Indians and two Mexicans, that comprised the final party. They left Westport on September 20, but two days later, while at the Shawnee Mission, Frémont suddenly became violently ill—struck with an inflammation in the upper part of his left leg, a searing pain that soon spread to his chest, throat, and head. Frémont and Max Strobel, the party's assistant topographer, headed back to Westport. Before leaving, Frémont put William Palmer, the brother of his San Francisco banker, Joseph Palmer, in charge of the party. His instructions to Palmer were to move ahead with a "Captain Wolf," one of the Delaware hunters, as their guide.[8]

Five days later, spotting a lone horseman riding toward them from the east, the survey party members hoped it was Frémont returning to join them. Instead, it was Strobel, with news of their leader's condition. Frémont had gone back to St. Louis for medical care, but—to Jessie Frémont's distress—expected to rejoin them soon. "I think he has done enough—but he does not," Jessie complained from St. Louis to Elizabeth Blair Lee. "If this ends well, I shall be glad for his sake it was done for he would have always regretted it—but nothing it can ever bring can reward either of us for its cost in suffering to him & anxieties to me."[9]

Through Strobel, Frémont instructed the men to go as far west as the Saline Fork of the Kansas River, and there—where both timber and buffalo were abundant—establish a camp. Once that was done, they were to send Solomon, a Delaware hunter, back to escort Frémont to the campsite. He expected to rejoin the men within two weeks.[10]

Obeying Frémont's instructions, Wolf and the party continued up the Kansas River valley. But when a fortnight passed with no sign of Frémont, they grew worried. Their concerns deepened still more when, on the afternoon of October 30, a dense prairie fire blackened the skies around them, destroying all traces of their passage. The next morning, however, despair gave way to relief when they spotted four mounted riders coming toward them at full gallop from the east's smoky horizon. It was Frémont; his doctor, a homeopath, Dr. A. Ebers; Solomon; and Albert Lea, a free black man hired as a cook for the expedition. To catch up with the main expedition party, the four men had beaten a path through fifty miles of ashes; and, as Carvalho later recalled, "no father who had been absent from his children, could have been received with more enthusiasm and more real joy."[11]

✽

Moving deeper into buffalo country, the party soon reached William Bent's new fort, at Big Timbers. Bent, four years earlier, had abandoned his original adobe fort thirty miles upstream after it became infested with a bad epidemic of cholera. The party spent a week at Bent's new fort, then continued up the Arkansas River. By November's end, the men had reached the Arkansas's confluence with the Huerfano River. There, Dr. Ebers and another party member turned back. The survey party then followed the Huerfano into the Rockies. Along the way, Frémont and Carvalho temporarily left the main party to examine Mosca Pass—though, in the end, the party used the more northerly Medano Pass to cross into San Luis valley.[12]

Like Beale's and Gunnison's parties, Frémont's men followed the Old Spanish Trail through the largely treeless San Luis valley. Leaving the valley, they found their way into the San Juans, where they picked up the path Gunnison had blazed. Because Gunnison, to clear a path for his wagons, had been forced to fell trees along his route, his expedition's path was easy to find. Following the route, Frémont's party ascended Saguache Creek and, on December 14, crossed the Continental Divide at North Cochetopa Pass, in the La Garita Mountains, a subrange of the San Juans marking its eastern edge. The widest of the many ranges comprising the Rockies, the San Juans stretch from the La Garitas west to the vicinity of Durango, Colorado.

On the lower ridges, the party had encountered snowbanks several feet deep, but at North Cochetopa Pass—at an elevation of 10,160 feet—frigid winds kept the snow to a dusting of inches. Once over the pass, they followed the Gunnison River on its westerly course, until deep Black Canyon blocked their way. By now—with shades of the disastrous 1848–49 railway survey haunting Frémont—the weather had turned irrevocably foul, their provisions were running low, and they soon began killing horses and mules for food. Moreover, they were increasingly doubtful about their location and how to find their way out of the mountains.[13]

Over the next few days, negotiating a labyrinth of defiles and streams, the men found their way toward the route that would take them to the Colorado River valley. In the Uncompahgre valley, the party bartered with a band of Utes for fresh venison. But when one of the tribesmen accused Frémont's men of eating his woman's horse, the exchange threatened to flare into violence. Bloodshed was averted when Frémont's men agreed to pay for the horse. But that payment only led to a demand for more goods—including a keg of gunpowder. Frémont refused the demand—simultaneously assuring his men that the Utes, because their families were present, would avoid a fight.[14]

The exploring party spent an anxious night, but no attack came. The next day, however, after the party had covered thirty miles and set up camp along the Colorado River—near today's Grand Junction, Colorado—the Ute warriors reappeared, but this time without their families. Demanding still more payments, they insisted that Frémont's party had paid the wrong persons for the horse. Throughout the exchange with the tribesmen, Frémont remained in his lodge—relaying his instructions via Carvalho, whom he told to refuse the Indians' demands. Frémont also instructed him to set up a target on a nearby tree and to give the visitors a demonstration of the firepower of the Navy Colt revolvers that the party members carried.[15]

Carvalho dutifully carried out the demonstration—even allowing one of the tribesmen to fire several shots. After the fifth or sixth shot, Carvalho discreetly replaced the weapon in its holster, then pulled out another, already loaded, revolver and resumed firing—leaving the impression that a single gun carried an infinite number of shots. Of the impression the demonstration left upon the Utes, he later recalled, it "scared them into the acknowledgement that they were all at our mercy, and we would kill them as fast as we liked, if we were so disposed."[16]

According to Carvalho, Frémont's self-confinement to his lodge during the encounter further projected an image of mystical powers. Whether or not that impression was deliberate, such reclusiveness had increasingly become part of Frémont's regimen. Perhaps feeling increasingly isolated, he would sit by himself in the lodge, calculating observations, writing letters, and contemplating the next day's movements. However strange such habits may seem in their retelling, to the men of the exploring party, Frémont in his lodge seemed a study in dignified self-possession:

Col. Frémont's lodge was sacred from all and everything that was immodest, light or trivial; each and all of us entertained the highest regard for him. The greatest etiquette and deference were always paid to him, although he never ostensibly required it. Yet his reserved and unexceptionable deportment, demanded from us the same respect with which we were always treated, and which we ever took pleasure in reciprocating.[17]

As the party, working its way west, approached the Green River country, Frémont' spirits must have risen, for he was now in line to reconnect with some of the same traces of the Old Spanish Trail that he had followed on his return from his Second Expedition. But somewhere just before the expedition reached the Green River, as conditions worsened and frostbite set in, shades of another, less pleasant, expedition—the Fourth Expedition—must have overtaken the men. Frémont gathered the party's members together and asked each man to make a sacred vow—that he would never, under any conditions, consume another party member's flesh.

By the time the men reached the Wasatch Range—even today formidable country in winter—they had eaten a porcupine, a beaver, and most of their horses. As Carvalho recalled their grim menu, the horses' "hide was roasted so as to burn the hair and make it crisp, the hoofs and shins were disposed of by regular rotation."[18]

In early February, upon reaching the crest of the Wasatch Range, Frémont got out his compass and determined they were within fifty miles of the Mormon village of Parowan. The calculation proved correct, for, on February 7, they struck a wagon trail that connected to the Mormon settlements below. That same day, the party experienced the expedition's first and only casualty—Oliver Fuller, who, consumed by frostbite and exposure, died in the saddle. The next day, the party straggled into Parowan.[19]

Over the next two weeks, Parowan's Mormon community extended to Frémont and his ragged party a generous hospitality, taking the men into their homes and nursing them back to robust health. There, Frémont also met Utah's territorial secretary Almon W. Babbitt, who, convinced of the explorer's credit-worthiness, arranged for a fresh herd of horses for the party. The Mormons, in Frémont's mind, had saved the lives of him and his men, and so won his everlasting gratitude. Indeed, years later, at a lecture in Los Angeles, he refused to introduce the anti-Mormon crusader and writer Kate Field.[20]

Frémont, once in the safety of an established community, conjured a bizarrely sanguine assessment of his recent misadventures. To territorial secretary Babbitt, about to travel to Washington, he entrusted several letters, including two to Benton, in which he noted that though the winter had been one "of extreme and unusual cold," he was nonetheless happy to report "our safe arrival," and "general good health" and the expedition's "reasonable success": "We went through the Cochatope [sic] Pass on the 14th December, with four inches—not feet, take notice, but inches—of snow on the level, among the pines." With that crossing, he concluded, Benton's thirty-eighth-parallel Road to India lay gloriously confirmed—indeed, as good as built: "I congratulate you on this verification of your judgment, and the good prospects it holds out of final success in carrying the road by this central line."[21]

Thanks to Carvalho's efforts, the 1853–54 outing would later be recalled as among the first photographically documented exploring expeditions. By all accounts, the images, printed from the daguerreotype plates in Mathew Brady's Washington studio, were magnificent; and Frémont planned to publish them in a separate volume on the expedition. But before that could happen, the plates were stored in a warehouse which, years later, burned to the ground. But fortunately, many of the images had already been made into engravings, which later appeared in Frémont's published memoirs. A century and a half later, Robert Shlaer, a photographer in New Mexico—using Carvalho's writings and the engravings based on his vanished daguerreotypes—scoured the San Juans, eventually located the vistas depicted in the original images, and reshot them—using daguerreotype equipment.

In what, had they known, would have been a bittersweet irony for Frémont and his exploring party, Shlaer's rediscovery of the sites Carvalho had shot was made possible because the region had been so little disturbed since the survey detail had passed through it. Though knowledge collected by other Frémont expeditions would later prove useful in developing the nation's transcontinental rail network, no rail line would ever be built along the thirty-eighth-parallel line that he and Benton championed.[22]

At Parowan, Carvalho and the topographer Eggloffstein left the party, to return to the East. Frémont, meanwhile, left the Mormon settlement on February 21, leading a newly constituted party of old and new members. Resuming their southward passage, following the Old Spanish Trail, soon known as the Mormon Road, they traveled eighteen miles to the new Mormon community of Cedar City, then crossed the largely unexplored Escalante Desert. Crossing today's Utah-Nevada border along the same line as today's Highway 2, they pushed past a barrage of snowstorms, until they reached the Sierra's western slope, just south of today's Bishop, California. Frémont had hoped to cross the range at Walker Pass, but finding it blocked by snow, the party drifted south until he found a more accessible gap. From there, the men found their way over the range's crest, into the Central Valley, where flowers were abloom and no trace of winter impeded their path.[23]

PART VI

FOR LIBERTY, UNION, AND COMMERCE

1854–64

All night above their rocky bed
They saw the stars march slow;
    The wild Sierra overhead,
    The desert's death below.

                . . .

Rise up, Frémont, and go before;
    The Hour must have its Man;
Put on the hunting-shirt once more,
    And lead in Freedom's van!
        —from "The Pass of the Sierra,"
        by John Greenleaf Whittier

FREE SOIL, FREE MEN, FRÉMONT

A S JOHN FRÉMONT had planned, his stay in California after
his 1853–54 railway survey expedition was brief. By early
May of 1854, he was back in Washington. On this trip, he
managed to bypass the rigors of the boat and muleback crossing of the
isthmus, for, only months earlier, the Panama Railway—foretelling a
more comfortable age in transcontinental transportation—had commenced operations. John returned to Washington in time to be there,
on May 17, when Jessie Frémont—two weeks before her thirtieth
birthday—gave birth to Francis Preston Frémont, named after Francis
Preston Blair, Sr. Though the birth of the baby, the Frémonts' fifth
and last child—soon known as Frank—delighted the couple, it came
amid what was otherwise a season of sorrows for the family.[1]

The previous August, Thomas Hart Benton, caught up in the increasingly divisive national debates over slavery, had been defeated in
his bid for reelection to the U.S. House of Representatives. The following month, after a long bout of illness after suffering sunstroke
during survey work in California, John's old trail companion Charles
Preuss committed suicide, hanging himself from a tree outside Washington. That same September, closer to home, Jessie Frémont's
mother and Thomas Hart Benton's wife—Elizabeth McDowell Benton—after feeling faint and asking to be helped to a couch in her husband's study, died in her sleep.

In California, meanwhile, in October of 1854, the local sheriff, in
an act culminating years of financial mismanagement and growing
debts, seized most of the parcels comprising the Frémonts' Las Mari-

posas estate, with orders to sell it to pay off a court judgment obtained by one of John's key creditors, the banking firm of Palmer, Cook & Co. Four months later, in February 1855, as Thomas Hart Benton was serving out his final days in the U.S. House of Representatives, his Washington home burned. The fire consumed Benton's entire library and nearly half of his only draft of the second volume of his memoirs of three decades in the U.S. Senate. The first volume of the work, *Thirty Years' View*, had been published the previous spring. Undaunted, Benton found new quarters and immediately set out to rewrite the destroyed portions of the second volume, which was eventually published in May 1856.

❋

For the nation, too, it was a season of turmoil. In May 1854, Congress had passed, and President Franklin Pierce had signed, the Kansas-Nebraska Act. The legislation opened the new territory of Kansas to slavery, violating the Compromise of 1820, which had banned slavery north of the thirty-sixth parallel. More broadly, the act destroyed seven decades of political handiwork by which Congress, to allay sectional tensions, had tried to balance the number of slave and free states brought into the Union.

Both north and south of the Mason-Dixon line, the Kansas-Nebraska Act brought simmering sectional hostilities to a boil. In Kansas, violent guerrilla warfare between slaveholders and antislavery activists provided the nation with a foretaste of the coming Civil War. For politicians such as Benton, representing constituencies split on the issue of slavery, the white-hot Kansas-Nebraska Act–fueled controversies constituted a particularly rocky shoal. Benton opposed the act—but in subsequent speeches he managed to alienate both sides in the controversy and was denied reelection to the House of Representatives.[2]

❋

During the fall of 1855, weary of Washington and its troubles, the Frémonts gave up their residence there and moved to New York City, where they rented a townhouse at 176 Second Avenue, between

Tenth and Eleventh streets. That spring and summer, John, traveling between Washington, New York, and Philadelphia, attended to various business matters. Determined to put Las Mariposas on a solid footing, he planned to return to California the following fall. Jessie, meanwhile, had been in poor health since the birth of Francis Preston the previous May. By July, she was taking opiates to relieve the pain of "neuralgia" coursing through the trunk of her body; and, that August, to escape the heat of summer in Manhattan, she took the children to Siasconset, on Massachusetts's Nantucket Island.[3]

❉

By that summer, it had become clear to the Democrats that their incumbent President, Franklin Pierce, was too damaged by the Kansas-Nebraska troubles to be reelected. Moreover, the Whig Party was nearing total collapse. Determined to find a new platform for their antislavery politics, various northern Whigs, joined by Free Soil Democrats and independents, had, for the past two years, been organizing the new Republican Party.

Further complicating affairs, many former Whigs and Democrats, sharing an opposition to the continued immigration of foreign nationals into the United States, had bonded into what they called the American Party. Virulently anti-Catholic and anti-Irish, the new party bore the aspects of a secret fraternity. When asked about its activities, members were instructed to answer, "I know nothing," hence the name by which the new party soon became known—the Know-Nothings. Although the new party planned to nominate its own candidate for President, few observers believed it had any chance of winning the nation's highest office. There was, however, a consensus that whichever party won the election, that party would have to appeal to anti-immigration voters who would otherwise support the Know-Nothings.

The Democrats, disenchanted with Pierce, were eager to find a fresh face with broad appeal. Toward that end, they had been sounding out Frémont about the possibility of his running as their party's 1856 presidential candidate. In October of 1855, such talk became more specific when the prospective candidate sat down with some key Democrats to discuss the matter. Due to his Free Soil sentiments,

Frémont ultimately declined the invitation. To his consternation, the entreaty carried a stipulation that, as their nominee, he would have to support the Kansas-Nebraska Act. Beyond that, he would be required to back the recently strengthened Fugitive Slave Law, which mandated the arrest and transport back to the South of runaway slaves who had managed to make it north of the Mason-Dixon line.[4]

The newly formed Republican Party was also seeking a fresh face for the 1856 election. Its partisans, too, had been feeling out Frémont about a possible candidacy on *their* ticket. With the Republicans, however, Frémont felt himself among politically kindred souls. This new party, after all, shared his opposition to the spread of slavery into the West.

It was Massachusetts congressman Nathaniel Banks—soon known as "the discoverer of Frémont as a Presidential Candidate"—who apparently first thought of approaching the explorer about the Republican nomination.[5] According to New York *Evening Post* editor and founding Republican John Bigelow, the approach to Frémont came after he, Banks, and several other Republicans had a conversation in which they agreed that their infant party had devised a sound platform of positions, but that they now needed to find an attractive individual "to incarnate our principles." But, then again, "men of national reputation were either committed to the other side or had been too active partisans for the Free-Soilers of opposing parties to unite upon." So what the Republicans needed, Banks and Bigelow agreed, was an appealing candidate who, while holding to Republican opinions, was not overly encumbered by past positions on controversial issues. The more Banks and Bigelow thought about that formula, the more they agreed that John C. Frémont might be just that man.

The subsequent meeting, between Banks, Bigelow, and Frémont, took place at Manhattan's Metropolitan Hotel. Bigelow, who had never met the explorer, recalled the encounter:

> He impressed me more favorably than I had expected. His manner was refined and dignified. Our conversation had no special political significance, though it was so directed that he could not fail to infer that our visit was something more than a formal call.

Encouraged, Banks and Bigelow scheduled another meeting with Frémont, this one attended by a wider circle of Republicans.[6]

Afterward, with Frémont's blessing, a group of Republicans led by Banks began promoting the explorer as the new party's only candidate with a real chance of winning the general election. Though Frémont had scant political experience, Republican strategists figured that meant he was less likely to alienate potential voters—or, as Horace Greeley put it, "A candidate must have a slim record in these times."[7] Moreover, the Republicans wanted a candidate who would appeal to younger voters. And on that score too, forty-three-year-old Frémont, with his romantic persona, seemed ideal. "I felt," Greeley recalled, "that Colonel Fremont's [sic] adventurous, dashing career had given him popularity, with our young men especially."[8]

By then, several other prominent Republicans had expressed interest in the party's presidential nomination—among them Ohio's Governor Salmon Chase, New York's U.S. Senator William Seward, and U.S. Supreme Court Justice John McLean. Chase failed to win support among any major political figures in the East, however; and his appeal to German immigrants, a major element in his campaign, was blunted outside Ohio by past connections with the Know-Nothings. Seward had the opposite problem: he had made too many statements attacking the Know-Nothings. As for McLean, having recently turned seventy, many considered him too old.

By late spring of 1856, Frémont's boosters included an impressive array of party officeholders, wire pullers, and journalists—among them New York *Tribune* editor Horace Greeley, Albany editor and New York power broker Thurlow Weed, and U.S. Senator Henry Wilson of Massachusetts. Though confident they had an attractive candidate, Frémont's supporters still worried that the American Party—the Know-Nothings—would siphon off votes from the Republican ticket in the general election. By that summer, the Know-Nothings had split into two factions—a proslavery wing, headed by their eventual presidential candidate, former president Millard Fillmore; and an antislavery wing, as yet unsettled on its presidential nominee.

It was the Know-Nothings' antislavery wing that most worried the Republicans. Like the Democrats and the Republicans, the antislavery Know-Nothings, earlier in the election season, had sounded out

Frémont about heading their presidential ticket. The Republicans worried that the antislavery Know-Nothings might beat the Republicans to nominating Frémont, a prospect that would drive immigrants and other anti-Know-Nothing voters away from the Republicans.[9]

As the antislavery Know-Nothings gathered that June in New York City, Frémont prepared a letter that, if the need arose, he would send to one of that party's key leaders, Ohio's Lieutenant Governor Thomas Ford, disclaiming interest in the party's nomination. The letter praised the Know-Nothings' opposition to the spread of slavery but rejected its antiforeign and anti-Catholic orientation. Pointedly, the missive also praised what Frémont considered a need for all opponents of slavery "to rise above all political animosities and prejudices of birth or religion."[10]

To counter the possibility that the nativists—the Know-Nothings —would siphon off otherwise pro-Republican votes in the general election, party strategists concocted a byzantine scheme: when the antislavery Know-Nothings assembled in New York, Republican stalwarts such as Henry Wilson, Preston King, and Isaac Sherman fanned out across the convention floor, talking up the candidacy of none other than their own party stalwart Nathaniel Banks. The Massachusetts congressman had been elected to his seat as a Know-Nothing, still harbored many anti-immigration views, and thus enjoyed wide popularity among the nativist party's rank-and-file. To further prop up Banks's candidacy, the Republican interlopers handed out substantial cash at the convention—as much as thirty thousand dollars, according to one later report.[11]

The ploy worked. The antislavery Know-Nothings made Banks their presidential candidate. For the vice-presidency, they selected former Pennsylvania governor William Johnston. In Philadelphia, the Republicans held their own convention. And on June 19, they made John Frémont their presidential nominee. For the vice-presidential slot on their ticket, the Republicans—passing over Abraham Lincoln, then a young former congressman—turned to Senator William L. Dayton of New Jersey.

The next day—executing the terms of the deal struck between Republican leaders and their antislavery Know-Nothing counterparts—Nathaniel Banks was allowed to withdraw from the Know-

Nothing ticket, and the nativist party made Frémont its official nominee. While Banks had planned all along to win, then decline the Know-Nothing nomination, his running mate William Johnston had made no such plans. Indeed, rumors circulated that, in the wake of Banks's withdrawal, Johnston would be made Frémont's running mate, on a Republican–Know-Nothing fusion ticket.

The matter of persuading Johnston to step aside and endorse his Republican counterpart, Dayton, for the vice-presidency posed a problem requiring great delicacy; and, over the next eight weeks, Republican operatives, often working on a state-by-state basis, sought to resolve the matter. The long process of nudging Johnston aside culminated in late August, after Senator Edwin D. Morgan of New York and other Republicans set up a meeting in New York between Johnston and Frémont. At the meeting, Frémont—in a deft bit of political surgery at odds with his reputation for political ineptitude—apparently implied to Johnston that, if he would withdraw from the race, and the Republicans won the White House, the Frémont administration, when it came time to dispense patronage, would look favorably on Johnston and his friends.

Of Frémont's conversation with Johnston, Morgan later wrote to an associate, "Though I know no promise was made to him, the Col said in case of his election he should give all his [Johnston's] friends who participated in it, fair play." With Johnston's subsequent withdrawal from the race on August 29, the antislavery Know-Nothings were officially lined up behind the entire Frémont-Dayton ticket.[12]

After Banks's withdrawal, a group of angry antislavery Know-Nothings, inflamed by pangs of betrayal, gathered and nominated as their presidential candidate Frémont's old California ally Robert Stockton. The retired naval officer's candidacy, however, failed to achieve any clear direction and, in the end, had little impact on that season's campaign.

❋

While the Republican platform called for the construction of a transcontinental railroad, John Frémont's official letter accepting the nomination—reflecting the candidate's growing distance from

Thomas Hart Benton, as well as the evolution of his own concerns—carried no references to international commerce or anything else remotely related to Benton's Road to India. Instead, expressing the Republican Party's priorities, the letter emphasized the need to prevent slavery from spreading into the West and vilified Southern slaveholders as betrayers of the nation's core principles:

> Nothing is clearer in the history of our institutions than the design of the nation, in asserting its own independence and freedom, to avoid giving countenance to the extension of slavery. The influence of the small but compact and powerful class of men interested in slavery, who command one section of the country, and wield a vast political control as a consequence in the other, is now directed to turn back this impulse of the Revolution, and reverse its principles.[13]

By the summer's end, the presidential contest had become a three-man race: the Democrats—meeting that June in Cincinnati, the first major political convention held west of the Appalachians—had nominated as their candidate former Secretary of State James Buchanan; and the proslavery Know-Nothings, joined by the remnants of the old Whig Party, had selected as their standard-bearer former president Millard Fillmore.

❀

To no one's surprise, Frémont's nomination prompted alarm among Southern slaveholders of a "Black Republican" conspiracy afoot in the land. Senator John Slidell of Louisiana predicted that if Frémont won the race, "the Union cannot and ought not be preserved." Even more belligerently, South Carolina Congressman Preston Brooks declared that, should Frémont win, Southerners should feel compelled not only to secede from the Union, but also to lay "the strong arm of Southern freemen upon the treasury and archives of the government."[14]

Even some Northerners joined the disunion chorus. Massachusetts Congressman Anson Burlingame, anticipating a Frémont victory, gleefully predicted that, upon his election, "then, if the slave Senate will not give way, we will grind it between the upper and nether mill-stones of our power." Similarly, Frémont supporter George W. Julian, decreed of the campaign, "It is not alone a fight between the North and the South; it is a fight between freedom and slavery; between God and the devil; between Heaven and hell."[15]

✸

Anticipating precisely such talk of disunion, Thomas Hart Benton, from the beginning, had urged Frémont to decline the Republican nomination. The Senator shared the Republicans' distaste for the Kansas-Nebraska Act. But as an old Jacksonian Unionist, he also re-garded the new party as a divisive sectional clique that risked driving the South to secession. Frémont's acceptance of the Republican nom-ination thus marked his final political break with his father-in-law.[16]

For Jessie Frémont, the growing chasm between her husband and her father posed an even more sensitive dilemma. "I write constantly to Father but have not had a line from him since I left there at Christ-mas," she lamented, that spring, to Elizabeth Blair Lee. "He always drops me that way when he is offended with Mr. Frémont."[17] Things became more strained after her father—putting aside a recent per-sonal feud with the Democrats' standard-bearer—endorsed James Bu-chanan at the Democratic convention and robustly campaigned for him that fall. Indeed, to give himself a more visible platform for his pro-Buchanan campaigning, Benton even accepted the nomination of the antislavery wing of Missouri's Democratic Party as its candidate for governor. The campaign had no chance of success, but the nomi-nation gave Benton a platform for a vigorous forty-day speaking tour of Missouri, stumping for Buchanan.

Closing that tour before a rally in St. Louis, Benton told assembled Buchanan supporters that he held the Republicans' presidential can-didate as dear as one of his own offspring: "There was nothing which a father could do for a son which I have not done to carry him through his undertakings, and to uphold him in the severe trials to which he has been subjected." But, Benton added, fearful of the dangers of dis-union posed by the Republican Party, he had also warned his son-in-law, a year earlier, not to expect his support as that party's presidential candidate: "I told him at once that I not only could not support him, but that I would oppose him."[18]

❋

Particularly painful to Jessie Frémont were the personal attacks directed against her husband—many of which came from, as Buchanan himself had once been, long-standing family friends. Over the summer of 1856, for instance, Senator William Bigler of Pennsylvania, challenging John's business ethics, called for a Senate investigation of his activities in California. Outraged, Jessie wrote to Elizabeth Blair Lee, "I am blazing with fever from the sudden anger I felt last night on reading Mr. Bigler's motion in the Senate. Mr. Frémont says if Father takes no notice of [the Bigler attack] & continues to work with them he will never speak to him nor any of his children."

But despite such rancor, Jessie remained resolute in her desire to preserve ties with her father—and to steer him and her husband away from confrontation. "I will let it make no outward difference," she wrote, in the same letter, of Bigler's charges and her husband's threat to break off ties with her father. "But I have just written a long letter to Cousin Sarah [Benton Brant] that she may tell it to Father—not what Mr. Frémont says—that I only tell you—you are my confessional—but telling him what I felt he ought to do."[19] In the end, Jessie preserved her relationships with both her husband and her father. Even more remarkably, thanks largely to her efforts, John and her father resumed at least polite relations once the campaign was over. But the two men's political break had also introduced a chill into their relationship that the coming years would not thaw.

❋

During the general campaign, rallying behind the slogan of "Free Soil, Free Men, Frémont," the Republicans did their utmost to exploit their candidate's heroic explorer persona. Allusions to the Pathfinder and his achievements abounded in handbills, editorials, songs, and speeches. The Quaker poet John Greenleaf Whittier wrote at least five poems promoting the candidate, including "The Pass of the

Sierra" and "A Song Inscribed to the Frémont Clubs." Besides poems, there were songbooks and lithograph portraits for sale. Journalist John Bigelow of the New York *Evening Post* and former Congressman Charles Upham each published lengthy biographies of the hero candidate. And, in yet another overture to posterity, towns were encouraged to change their names to Frémont. Though some of the monikers failed to stick, at least twelve U.S. towns—both east and west of the Mississippi—adopted the explorer's name.[20]

Keeping that era's custom among presidential candidates, neither Buchanan nor Frémont hit the campaign trail during the contest. Although both candidates conferred regularly with friends and supporters, Buchanan spent most of the campaign at his modest two-story home just outside Lancaster, Pennsylvania, while Frémont stayed close to home, at 56 West Ninth Street, the family's latest Manhattan address. A committee that included John Bigelow, Isaac Sherman, and Jessie Frémont tended to run the day-to-day Frémont-Dayton campaign, as well as handle its official pronouncements.

Jessie's acumen in electoral politics, though far from acute, was generally superior to that of her husband. Even in the campaign's public dimension, she played a role only slightly less prominent than that of the actual candidate. References to "Our Jessie" abounded in the campaign's slogans and songs. As one lyric captured the partnership, "We go for our country and Union, and for brave little Jessie forever."[21] As Jessie, from New York, playfully bemused by the new attention, wrote to Elizabeth Blair Lee during the campaign:

> Just here & just now I am quite the fashion—5th Avenue asks itself, "have we a Presidentess among us—" and as I wear fine lace and purple I am in their eyes capable of filling the place. So I go out nightly—sometimes to dinner & a party both the same night and three times a week to the opera where I hold a levee in my box.[22]

✸

Frémont made no major speeches during the general election race. His reticence, contrasting with Jessie's gregariousness, arose not from any lack of passion or conviction. John Frémont held long-standing

views on many public issues—particularly those concerning his twin
passions of preserving the Union and opposing slavery, views which
went back to his tutelage as an adolescent under the antislavery
Unionist Democrat Joel Poinsett. But while Frémont held firm convictions on those and other issues, he possessed limited knowledge of
many of the legislative particulars of national politics. And by keeping
his comments short during the campaign, he avoided the daily risk of
exposing that shortcoming.

There was a positive advantage, too, in limiting Frémont's campaign pronouncements. In a conventional sense, John Frémont was ill-
suited to electoral politics. No one would ever have accused him of
being a glad-hander. This was, after all, a man who, when confronted
with adversity, often retreated into a brooding silence—and, for this
outing, there would be no lodge into which he could disappear. But
that same aloofness also helped to preserve a long-burnished
charisma. Though Frémont could be thin-skinned and impulsive, in
one-on-one meetings, he projected an impressively dashing, commanding presence.

The same charismatic reticence that, years earlier in the months
before the Bear Flag revolt, had led Thomas Larkin and others to believe that explorer Frémont knew far more than he was telling conferred upon candidate Frémont an aura of quiet, knowing strength.
Republican strategists thus recognized that too much exposure would
diminish the Frémont mystique. Better to let the candidate continue
to seem the slightly aloof explorer. As an admiring acquaintance, during those years, recalled Frémont's presence:

> He is about forty-five years old, tall and slender, of modest de-
> meanor, and of quiet, undemonstrative manner. At first, he
> makes no strong impressions upon you, but in conversation, by
> degrees, you come to the conclusion that you are in the presence
> of no common man. There is a deep [intensity] of expression in
> his eye, which taken in connexion with his calm, measured
> words, forces upon you the conviction, that his extraordinary [ca-
> reer] is but a just reflection of his inherent character.

Even with Frémont physically absent from the campaign trail, his
managers had little trouble transferring that aura of "deep intensity"

to the countless mass rallies that they organized around the Northeast and Middle West. Fifty thousand supporters gathered at a Frémont rally in Indianapolis; twenty-five thousand at Massillon, Ohio; and thirty thousand at Kalamazoo. At Alton, Illinois, Abraham Lincoln, who proved a tireless speaker on Frémont's behalf, spoke to a state fair crowd estimated at thirty-five thousand people. Cannons fired, brass bands played, parades paraded; and in cities across America, banners, lithographs, transparencies, campaign biographies, and handbills, as well as mammoth torchlight processions, spread the Frémont gospel: "We Follow the Pathfinder," "No More Rule of Nigger-Drivers," "We Are Buck-Hunting," "Free Speech, Free Press, Free Soil, Free Men, Frémont and Victory."[23]

In addition to attracting former Whigs and Free Soil Democrats, the Frémont campaign galvanized constituencies heretofore uninspired by presidential campaigns—particularly abolitionists and women's rights advocates. Poet William Cullen Bryant, who actively campaigned for the Republican nominee, writing to his brother John, proclaimed, "A very large class of persons who never before took any interest in elections are zealous Fremonters now—among these are clergymen and Quakers and [past] indifferents of all sorts." Frederick Douglass predicted that a Frémont triumph "will prevent the establishment of Slavery in Kansas, overthrow Slave Rule in the Republic . . . and [put] the mark of national condemnation on slavery . . . and inaugurate a higher and purer standard of Politics and Government."[24]

Many of Frémont's supporters sensed something new in the air—a fresh departure from the past's politics. At forty-three, Frémont was, at that time, the youngest presidential candidate in U.S. history; and his opponent, James Buchanan, at sixty-five, among the oldest. The Democratic candidate—who had been a congressman, senator, diplomat, and Secretary of State—had been, after all, a public figure for three long decades. Some even called him "the Old Public Functionary."

❉

But despite the outpouring of public enthusiasm for the Pathfinder, the campaign, in the end, proved more of an ordeal than Frémont could ever have imagined. As John Bigelow, earlier that year, had begun preparing what became his dense, 480-page biography of Frémont, Jessie Frémont—because she knew the material better but very likely also out of familial sensitivity to a delicate topic—offered to write the volume's introductory chapter, summing up John's genealogy and early years. Her eventual chapter provided some new details about John's parents and their union, but it also falsely asserted that immediately after John Pryor's wife Anne Whiting Pryor had left him for Charles Fremon, John Pryor had been granted a divorce by a special act of the Virginia legislature; and that once her divorce from the cuckolded Pryor was granted, Anne and Charles Fremon had been legally married.[25]

As the campaign geared up, however, any hopes of having deflected the matter of the Republican candidate's "legitimacy" quickly faded. Of Frémont's parents, the Richmond *Dispatch*, typifying anti-Republican barbs, asserted, "We cannot say whether the parties were ever married." But, "certain it is that old Col. [*sic*] Pryor was never divorced from his wife." Given that, the paper said, "The question arises, could there have been a legitimate marriage without a divorce?" Answering its own question, the *Dispatch* concluded, "The life of the progenitor of the free-soil candidate for the Presidency, shows that he was at least a disciple of Free-love, if not of Free-soil."[26]

Other charges from the Buchanan camp accused Frémont of being a murderer (the shooting by Carson and others under Frémont's command, during the Bear Flag uprising, of the Californio twins Francisco and Ramón de Haro and their uncle José de los Reyes Berreyesa), of having been involved in cannibalism (a charge Frémont himself had leveled against Bill Williams and his relief detail during the 1848–49 railway survey), and of libertinism (alleged dalliances with, among others, the young woman in Greenville, South Carolina, with whom he supposedly had a tryst during his 1836 railway survey).

For good measure, the Democrats also accused Frémont of being a Roman Catholic. The candidate, of course, had been an Episcopalian since his confirmation as a youth into that church. The Catholicism charge arose partly from John and Jessie's wedding before a Catholic priest, partly from an incident depicted in the First Expedition *Report*, when Frémont scrawled a cross on Independence Rock.

Asserting that his religious convictions were a private matter, Frémont declined to publicly answer the charge of Catholicism. Campaign operatives, however, vigorously refuted the accusation; and the candidate himself, that September, hoping to defuse the issue, met with, and apparently impressed, a group of New York's most prominent Protestant ministers. As one of the clergymen, writing to Bigelow a week later, recalled:

> He did not speak with any bitterness or bigotry of any professed Christians, but for himself, he said, *I was born and educated in the Episcopal Church; and at the age of sixteen was confirmed as a member of that Church, and I have never had the shadow of a thought of changing it.*[27]

✸

Anticipating the 1860 presidential campaign that would be waged four years later, the 1856 race, in the end, evolved into two separate races—Frémont versus Buchanan in the North, and Fillmore versus Buchanan in the South. In only four slave states—all border states—did Frémont's name even appear on the ballot. In November's general election, the Frémont-Dayton ticket carried New York and most of the Northeastern states, but—failing to carry the swing state of Pennsylvania—lost the general election to Buchanan. Frémont's vote tally was 1,339,932—about a half million less than Buchanan's 1,832,955 total, and about a half million more than Fillmore's 871,731. In the end, too many former Whigs had gone for either Buchanan or Fillmore for Frémont to carry the race.

In their zeal to find a fresh-faced standard-bearer, the Republicans had settled on a man patently ill-qualified as a candidate and a prospective President. Although they had successfully exploited Frémont's aura as an explorer, in making him their nominee the Republicans had overlooked the fact that his gifts as a leader of small exploring parties and as a patient assayer of landscapes had few applications on the campaign trail.

In the end, even John Bigelow—who would soon, to Jessie's great regret, grow estranged from the Frémonts—came to doubt the candidate's abilities. In his journal, Bigelow later confided, "As a candidate for President in 1856, he did everything pretty much that he could do to bring his party into contempt though it was only partially discovered until after the election." Whatever alleged disclosure Bigelow was referring to remains unclear, but it seems apparent that, whether the story was true or not, he had come to believe that during the campaign John had "debauched" a servant girl in the Frémont household.

But beyond such lurid speculations, and beyond the Republicans' electoral defeat, the new party had made a promising start. As for the nation, by rejecting Frémont it had bought itself another four years of political union—for, with Buchanan the victor, there would be, at least for now, no secession of Southern states. Jessie Frémont later claimed that, had John won the 1856 presidential race, he would have been able to avert the crises of secession and Civil War. Drawing on his own and his wife's "large family connections through the Southern States, arrangements would have been entered into, preventing the resort to war." With a policy of "gradual abolishment" of slavery, with federal compensation for former slaveowners, President Frémont, she argued, would have been able to tamp down Southern discontents.[28]

Jessie's brave speculation aside, one can only wonder—perhaps shudder—about how Frémont would have handled the secession crisis that, four years later, would face the Republicans' first successful presidential candidate—Abraham Lincoln.

❋

In the months following his defeat, Frémont fell into a restless mood—contemplating a book about his two railroad surveys, even as he planned his next trip to California to tend to Las Mariposas business. Or, as Jessie described the latter objective in a letter weeks after the election, "Mr. Frémont . . . has already mounted his old hobby and is in full chase after his butterfly—this time with solid prospects of success."

For Jessie, however, the prospect of returning to life in the Sierra foothills held no allure. There, amid "the country life in California," she noted in a January 1857 letter to Elizabeth Blair Lee, even the routine tasks of domestic life—cleaning, laundry, and cooking—became a daily challenge. Contemplating the writing collaboration that John hoped to resume with her once they got back to Las Mariposas, she complained:

Mr. Frémont thinks of the climate & the sunrise over the fine mountain scenery, the spring flowers & horseback rides that send him with a vigorous appetite to breakfast & a clear healthy mind to write. I am to be ready to do that writing but I am to know & provide the component parts of that breakfast first.[29]

Beyond Jessie's general aversion to life at Las Mariposas, a growing distance had entered the couple's relationship; and she, feeling increasingly independent, no longer felt compelled to leave New York to follow John back to the Sierra foothills. "Mr. Frémont says I may live where I like & I like here," she reported in that same November letter.[30]

The following spring, in 1857, as John prepared for an extended trip to Las Mariposas, Jessie abruptly changed her mind about remaining behind in the East. In poor health, exhausted from the campaign, and dispirited by its toll upon familial relations, she decided that, while John was in California until the fall, she would take the children and leave on her own extended trip—to France. So, in mid-June, as John returned to California, Jessie, the children, and John's niece Nina left for France, where they settled into a comfortable country villa in Saint-Germain-en-Laye, just outside Paris.[31]

That fall, however, after hearing that Jessie's seventy-five-year-old father was ill—suffering severe paroxysms of pain with what had been diagnosed as "an obstinate constipation"—the entire family returned to the East Coast. By coincidence, John and Jessie both reached New York harbor on November 3. Over the next five months, dividing their time between New York and Thomas Hart Benton's house in Washington, the Frémonts did their best to console the ailing retired senator.[32]

As much as they doted on him, the couple hardly realized how ill he was. Had they known he was dying of cancer of the bowel, the Frémonts, including Nina, in all likelihood, would not have left, on March 20, 1858, to return by steamer to California. On April 10, the former senator drew his final breath. Jessie's absence from her father's side at his death would haunt her for the rest of her life.[33]

❋

Eager to remove himself from public life, John Frémont, with his family, had moved to Las Mariposas by April 24. There, John settled with renewed vigor into the task of developing his vast properties. In 1855, the U.S. Supreme Court, ending a protracted legal battle over the legality and boundaries of Las Mariposas, had ruled in Frémont's favor. By now his enterprises at the 44,386-acre spread included mining, lumber-milling, and ranching operations and several small settlements—including the tiny company town of Bear Valley, where John maintained his offices at the Oso Hotel, the settlement's only substantial building. The slightly larger town of Mariposa—beyond Frémont's land grant and seat to the recently created Mariposa County—lay about ten miles from the town of Bear Valley.[34]

Jessie, meanwhile, about a half mile down the road from John's office, set about the task of transforming the family's simple one-story frame house—what local Indians, with an unfortunate touch of unintended irony, soon called the white house—into an oasis of gentility amid the Sierra gold country's wildness. The whitewashed house sat within a fenced-in twelve-acre parcel, handsomely landscaped with gentle paths, flowering shrubs, and pink Castille roses; and, thanks to Jessie's efforts, its appointments soon included fine carpets, a rosewood piano, French wallpapers, and silk curtains. In appearance, the Frémont estate departed from the generally ramshackle style that in those days characterized buildings and settlements in the Sierra's gold country. In the design of their house and grounds, it was as if the couple sought to architecturally underscore John's vision—articulated in his *Geographic Memoir Upon Upper California*—of California as a New World Mediterranean province. To California historian Kevin Starr, writing years later, the couple's Las Mariposas house—soon part of a complex of connected outbuildings—represented a seminal exposition of a Mediterranean approach that would become the state's defining style. It was, he wrote,

> built in a villa-like style, bringing together smaller units in a way which respected the contours of the hills, and used exposed wood and decorative color decades before such a technique became the hallmarks of regional architecture.[35]

But alas, even French wallpaper could not negate the fact that Las Mariposas remained a remote outpost bedeviled by a host of irritants; and Jessie soon wearied of the place. For the summer of 1858, John moved the family back to San Francisco. By the next year, however, the debts at Las Mariposas had grown so daunting, and the work so demanding, that summer in San Francisco was out of the question. As spring gave way to summer, the temperatures in the valley soared so high that the children amused themselves by boiling eggs on the dusty carriage drive leading to their house and made leather shoes for their dogs to keep their paws from blistering.

Seeking refuge, Jessie—recalling a cool, spring-fed grove of oaks atop nearby Mount Bullion, named after her father's sobriquet "Old Bullion Benton"—decided to move the entire family there. For several weeks, living in a tent atop the mountain, the Frémonts, along with the two maids who alternated between the valley house and Mount Bullion, savored their elevated idyll. From "Camp Jessie," Jessie wrote to her friend Francis Preston Blair, "We face an amphitheatre of mountains which rise from the river Merced." And, in the distance, "the cliffs & chasms of the Yosemite Valley are perfectly distinct." Although John occasionally stole a day away from business to go on riding outings with the family, he generally stayed away during the day. Jessie, meanwhile, remained determined to maintain a semblance of normal life. As Lily later recalled, she even made fitful attempts to maintain a regimen of tutoring for the children:

> My mother gave me lessons in history and poetry, as well as reading—a necessary accomplishment of those days—and though I made some progress in those studies, I must confess that I spent more time exploring along the crest of the mountain and into its deep ravines.

The Mount Bullion idyll ended that August after a friendly Indian passing through informed the family that their camp occupied what, in all likelihood, was about to become part of a war ground in an imminent conflict among rival tribes in the area.[36]

❋

Soon after returning to Bear Valley, the family played host to the journalist Horace Greeley, then making his first tour of the West. Though impressed with California's natural wonders, the famous editor, appalled by the state's moral and sanitary conditions, was also struck by what he viewed as California's great need for "virtuous, educated, energetic women"—as many as 100,000, he believed, would be a good start.[37]

According to Jessie, Greeley, while visiting the Frémonts, also had politics on his mind; and, as one of the Republican Party's founders, he sounded out John about another run for the presidency—an idea that the explorer, with Jessie's apparent concurrence, promptly rejected. John was determined to put Las Mariposas on a solid business footing. To her friend Nathaniel Banks, Jessie wrote that, while she had entertained doubts about the land grant in the past, "not as to its capabilities but as to our profiting from them. Now I believe." Even Greeley, that fall, conceded in a letter to the New York *Daily News*, "Col. F is giving his whole time and energies to his own private affairs."[38]

Splendid scenery, occasional visitors, and renewed determination notwithstanding, the Frémonts, particularly Jessie, still felt isolated at Las Mariposas. To Elizabeth Blair Lee, she complained that the "mountains of Bear Valley bounded" her world.[39] The place, she complained, had even changed her hair color—rendering it a "queer tawny color, neither grey nor brown, a kind of feuille morte."[40] Further straining nerves, Frémont and his hired hands that summer became locked in a potentially bloody standoff with the Hornitas League, a band of seventy squatters hired by a rival mining operation. The interlopers departed only after California's governor, Democrat John B. Weller, ordered five hundred state militia troops to Las Mariposas.

❄

In early 1860, acceding to Jessie's request for more civilized surroundings, John purchased, in her name, a handsome house and thirteen acres at the tip of Black Point, an idyllic finger of land—more radiant, Jessie said, than anything conjured by Tennyson—overlooking Alcatraz Island, on San Francisco Bay.[41] At Black Point, the Frémont family settled into, by their standards, a rare interregnum of domestic stability. John, in an increasingly contemplative mood, was thinking about writing his memoirs. He was also, to Jessie's delight, giving himself more time to be a husband and father. To Elizabeth Blair Lee, Jessie wrote:

> Sometimes I think I magnetized Mr. Frémont into home life. He takes part in & likes all the details of our household—the children's plays & witticisms & lessons—he looks after our comforts, & is in fact head of the house. No "wild turkey" left. It's so easy to take care of children when two help. I feel now as if we were a complete & compact family & really Mr. Frémont used to be only a guest—dearly loved & honored but not counted on for worse as well as better.[42]

Beyond that, though Las Mariposas had been, in many ways, a hardship for the family, it had brought a new parity to John and Jessie's relationship, an equality on which the couple continued to build at Black Point. "I am friend and advisor now," she wrote, describing her new relationship with John, to Elizabeth Blair Lee. One acquaintance noted, "Frémont would never transact business without his wife being present, who had a much clearer head than he."[43]

The Frémonts savored San Francisco's teeming social scene and opera life and became the premiere couple of California's growing Anglo society. They hosted a constant stream of influential and interesting visitors—including the soon famous Unitarian minister Thomas Starr King and the writers Richard Henry Dana, Herman Melville, and Bret Harte. Indeed, impressed by the work of the then relatively unknown Harte, Jessie arranged in 1861, through Edward Beale and ultimately President Lincoln, a job for the writer in the San Francisco surveyor general's office, which Beale managed.[44]

In January 1861, however, as his financial troubles deepened, John again left for Europe, to raise new capital for Las Mariposas. Accompanying him were his mining-business associates George W. Wright and Frederick Billings. And although he tried to be discreet—even suggesting that Billings travel aboard another ship—John was also accompanied by his paramour, San Franciscan Margaret Corbett, who traveled in her own stateroom paid for by Frémont. While Wright sought to conceal the affair, Billings, upon learning of it, considered the relationship "disgusting."[45]

As Frémont's dalliance with Corbett and other women over the coming years would make clear, the explorer's restlessness extended beyond geographical wanderlust. Indeed, glancing references to extra-marital dalliances run through the paper trail of Frémont's life like some sotto voce leitmotif. In most cases, the references are unspecific and confined to the letters of third-party correspondents. Only a hand-ful of John's letters hint of inappropriate intimacies, and none confirm them absolutely. And though it's difficult to believe that Jessie did not, at the least, have her suspicions, none of her extant correspondence al-ludes to such matters. Even so, in the absence of conclusive evidence, one may reasonably conjecture that, despite the couple's ongoing closeness in what was, by all accounts, a complicated relationship, by the 1860s a chill had extinguished the careless joy the two once took in each other's company. But though the distance between them would grow over the coming decades, residual affection and practical considerations—including the difficulties of obtaining a divorce in that era—kept the couple within the bonds of marital union.

GENERAL FRÉMONT

THOUGH, by the winter of 1861, John Frémont had ostensibly sworn off politics, national events were prodding his return to public life. Months earlier, after Abraham Lincoln's election to the presidency, Oregon's U.S. Senator, Edward D. Baker, a Lincoln supporter, had visited Frémont with news that the President-elect was considering Frémont for some sort of cabinet position. As it turned out, while Lincoln's soon-to-be Secretary of State William H. Seward thought Frémont would make an able Secretary of War, the President-elect was considering him for U.S. Minister to France. To Senator Baker, however, Frémont, upon hearing of the new administration's interest in him, pleaded that, for now, he wanted to concentrate on resolving his business problems at Las Mariposas. But, he added, if war with the South did come, he would welcome a commission to command an army in the field.[1]

After leaving California in January 1861, Frémont, en route to Europe, made a stop the following month in New York, where he had a brief but cordial meeting with President-elect Lincoln. During their exchange, Frémont joined Lincoln in hoping that war might be avoided. But convinced that conflict was imminent, he also reiterated his desire to lead an army in the field. As it turned out, the first news of war reached Frémont shortly after he reached England in early 1861—a development which, he learned over the next few weeks, made it virtually impossible to raise capital for an American business in either England or France. For Frémont, the news of war was quickly followed by a message telling him that he would soon receive, as he had requested, a commission to lead an army in the field.

✸

Before leaving Europe, Frémont, in a characteristically impulsive gesture, embarked on a self-appointed mission to arrange weapon purchases for the U.S. government: in France, he arranged for the purchase, at a cost of $125,000, of ten thousand rifles. In England, he contracted for $75,000 worth of cannons and shells. And when bureaucratic snags among U.S. officials seemed to threaten the purchases, he ordered that the weapons be shipped, if necessary, at his own personal expense. Finally, after the U.S. Minister to France balked at defraying the costs incurred by Frémont, U.S. Minister to England Charles Adams boldly stepped in, drawing on U.S. funds to pay for both the arms and their transatlantic shipment.[2] Upon sailing into Boston harbor on June 27, Frémont left immediately for Washington, where, for several days, he met with President Lincoln and Montgomery Blair, the new administration's postmaster general. He also found time to visit the Blair family's Silver Spring estate, always a good place to harvest the latest Washington gossip.

Having decided to name Frémont to one of the four new major generalships created that spring, Lincoln had initially considered giving the former explorer an appointment somewhere in the East. The Blairs, however, had other ideas. Francis Preston Blair, Jr.—Frank Blair—in addition to representing St. Louis in the U.S. Congress, had since February 1861 been working in Missouri to quash the growing Confederate insurgency in his home state. The Union effort was going badly in the West, in large part, they believed, because Lincoln's chief general, George B. McClellan, whose command stretched from the Atlantic Seaboard to Missouri, had little understanding of, nor interest in, Western matters. To remedy that situation, the Blairs wanted Lincoln to create a Department of the West, commanded by Frémont.

The President eventually granted the Blairs' request: Frémont's Department of the West would be headquartered in St. Louis and include Illinois and all the states from Missouri to the Rockies plus New Mexico. Once Frémont and his army had the chance to shore up Union support in those places, the Department of the West would also include then-wavering Kentucky.[3]

Like many other men who rose to become generals during the

Civil War, Frémont had never commanded large numbers of men in the field. But while many of those newly minted officers soon established reputations as gifted commanders, Frémont's inexperience would soon prove a glaring liability.

Lincoln tendered Frémont's commission in early July. That same month, meanwhile, Federal forces suffered their first defeat of the war, just outside Washington, at Manassas, Virginia. And the situation in the West was hardly more encouraging, as Missouri—teeming with both Union and Confederate partisans, like some microcosm of the nation as a whole—lapsed into its own intrastate civil war.

Those developments notwithstanding, Frémont, after receiving his commission in early July, went not to Missouri but to New York, where he remained for three weeks. He did not reach St. Louis until the end of the month—a delay that Lincoln partisans later, unfairly, attributed to the new general's preoccupation with personal business. In fact, Frémont's delay arose from the necessity of arranging for the purchase of arms and munitions for a woefully underarmed army.

❖

Missouri's guerrilla war had originated in the border skirmishes of the mid-1850s between slaveholders and antislavery partisans vying to settle the new state of Kansas. More recently, tensions had issued from the pro-Confederate sympathies of Claiborne Fox Jackson, the state's newly elected governor, who, during his inaugural address in January 1861, had vowed common cause with sister states of the South. On the heels of Jackson's pledge came similar vows from the state's new lieutenant governor and two U.S. senators, as well as the majority of its Democrat-controlled legislature. But when, soon thereafter, a state convention called to consider secession voted for Missouri to remain in the Union, the stage was set for a spiraling series of confrontations between pro- and anti-Union forces. Most Missourians were sympathetic to the Southern cause but reluctant to support the state's secession from the Union.

Moving quickly, Governor Jackson seized control of St. Louis's police and mustered the state's pro-Southern militia, which—under the command of former governor and Mexican War General Sterling

Price—promptly seized a small U.S. arsenal at Liberty, near Kansas City, Missouri. On April 17, the same day that Governor Jackson rejected a call from President Lincoln for troops to support the Union war effort, Jackson also sent a secret message to Confederate President Jefferson Davis, requesting artillery to assist in the capture of the federal government's much larger arsenal at St. Louis.

Countering Governor Jackson's every move, Frank Blair—as a congressman and, as of that April, as the colonel of one of the four regiments of Missouri's newly mustered pro-Union Missouri Volunteers—worked on both political and military fronts in his antisecession campaign. With U.S. Army Captain—soon General—Nathaniel Lyon, he worked tirelessly to prevent Missouri from slipping into the Confederacy.

Lyon stayed busy mustering into federal service troops raised by St. Louis's large and largely pro-Union German community, the heart of the city's antisecession constituency. Simultaneously, he also worked to forge the Republican Wide-Awakes, a collection of what had been paramilitary pro-Lincoln campaign organizations, into what soon became known as the Union Home Guards. Though Lincoln had carried only 17 percent of Missouri's popular vote the previous November, in St. Louis he had defeated his Democratic opponent, Stephen Douglas.

Building on that Republican foundation, Lyon and Blair's recruitment efforts soon counterbalanced Governor Jackson's pro-Confederacy militia. In April, they thwarted Jackson's efforts to capture St. Louis's federal arsenal, and on May 10, Lyon, commanding four regiments of German-Americans and two regular companies, surprised and—without firing a shot—captured seven hundred Confederate militia soldiers at Camp Jackson, an ad hoc training field on the edge of St. Louis. And that July, the month that Frémont assumed command in St. Louis, Lyon successfully drove Sterling Price's Confederate militia out of the state's capital, Jefferson City, all the way to Missouri's southwest corner, where Lyon and his forces settled into an occupation of the town of Springfield.

In the wake of Lyon's triumphs, however, came setbacks. Of particular concern to Union strategists, his occupation of Springfield left him and his army stranded with dwindling supplies in the remote southwest corner of the state, with 120 miles lying between them and the nearest railhead. Making matters worse, about half of Lyon's army consisted of three-month volunteers whose terms, that July, were nearing their end. While many of the soldiers would choose to re-enlist, the uncertainty and confusion arising from that circumstance blunted their morale.

Compounding Union woes, much of Missouri had become a violent, balkanized land of bushwhackers, saboteurs, and freelance raiding parties.

And so, on July 25, when General Frémont reached St. Louis, he found a city in relative peace, but much of the rest of the state awhirl in chaos. It was clear that he would have to fight two wars: one against pro-Confederate Missourians engaged in guerrilla actions against Union forces within the state; another against regular Confederate troops determined to invade and secure Missouri as a Rebel state.

Most immediately, Frémont worried about Rebel forces gaining a beachhead at Cairo, Illinois. Strategically situated at the confluence of the Mississippi and Ohio rivers—the gateway to any military incursion into Kentucky—Cairo, in addition to threats posed by Rebel forces within Missouri, also faced possible attack by Confederate General Leonidas Polk. The Rebel general had already seized the tiny river town of New Madrid and was by then planning an assault on Cairo, just upstream. If the Confederates could seize Cairo, Union strategists feared, they could control the entire southern half of Missouri. Should that happen, they believed, it would be easy for the Confederates to extend their control over the southern halves of Illinois and Indiana, and to bring wavering Kentucky into the Confederacy.

✸

Confronting such baleful circumstances, Frémont, upon reaching St. Louis, wasted no time in getting down to work. Ensconcing himself in his new headquarters—a three-story Chouteau Street mansion rented from Jessie Frémont's recently widowed cousin Sarah Benton Brant—he quickly settled into a regimen of eighteen-hour workdays. As his chief of staff, Frémont had appointed General Alexander S. Asboth, a Hungarian who had fought with valor under his nation's famed repub-

lican patriot Louis Kossuth. For his chief topographical engineer, Frémont named yet another Hungarian, Colonel John Fiala; and, as judge
advocate, he appointed Richard M. Corwine, a highly regarded lawyer
from Cincinnati.

Doing nothing to diminish his reputation for imperiousness, Frémont surrounded himself with layers of befeathered and gold-braided
assistants and guards. That so many of his aides were foreigners and
veterans of the 1848 republican nationalist uprisings across Europe
was, if nothing else, a measure of Frémont's distrust of the West Point
graduates who might otherwise have surrounded him. Adding to the
resentments that the foreign aides' presence provoked among U.S.-
born soldiers, many of the aides bore foreign or simply pompous-
sounding titles, such as "adletus to the chief of staff," "military
registrator and expeditor," and "commander of the bodyguard."

Though St. Louis was in relative peace, John and Jessie nonetheless found a city very different from the busily cheerful riverside place
they had both known for so long. "Everything was changed," she later
recalled. Riverboats—their fires out and whistles silent—lay tied up
along the wharves; and "as we drove through the deserted streets we
saw only closed shutters to warehouses and business places." Frémont's headquarters, by contrast, bustled with activity. The Chouteau
Street house, surrounded by a handsome walled garden, made a splendid headquarters, with enough room to allow the Frémonts to work
and live in the same building. But the arrangement also caused local
tongues to wag—many considered the six-thousand-dollar yearly rent,
drawn from Army coffers, excessive. They also questioned the propri-
ety of such a payment to a relative of the general.

While the house's basement quickly became a veritable arsenal, its
first floor soon bustled with staff offices and telegraph and printing
equipment. Frémont established his family residence and his own offices on the second floor, which soon grew cluttered with desks for
himself and various assistants, and with large tables on which he
placed the maps and charts that he constantly pored over. As Ulysses
S. Grant, recently promoted to the rank of general, recalled the scene:

He sat in a room in full uniform with his maps before him.
When you went in he would point out one line or another in a

mysterious manner, never asking you to take a seat. You left without the least idea of what he meant or what he wanted you to do.[4]

Among Frémont's many tasks upon reaching St. Louis was the formulation of a grand Western strategy. For, as he later recalled, Lincoln, when the two men had last spoken at the White House, had given him few directions as to how to proceed:

When I took leave of him, he accompanied me down the stairs, coming out to the steps of the portico at the White House; I asked him then, if there was anything further in the way of instruction that he wished to say to me. "No," he replied, "I have given you carte blanche; you must use your own judgment and do the best you can. I doubt if the States will ever come back."

As Frémont shaped his overall strategy, two key objectives emerged: the end of all rebel activity in Missouri, and a movement of Union troops down the Mississippi to Memphis—and, if things went well, from there all the way to New Orleans. According to Frémont's thinking, should Union forces win control of the Mississippi River— the trunk of the tree—then it would be easy to shake its branches, to launch other actions against Confederate strongholds along the Tennessee, the Ohio, and the great river's other tributaries. To safeguard St. Louis, Frémont ordered a series of entrenchments built around the city. He also occupied and built fortifications at Cape Girardeau, as well as critical railheads at Ironton, Rolla, and Jefferson City, the state capital.

Beyond geostrategic considerations, Frémont also had to devise a way to overcome a chronic shortage of men and matériel. President Lincoln's personal secretaries and, later, biographers John Nicolay and John Hay would later take Frémont to task for squandering, in the Department of the West, what was, by any standard, a wealth of martial talents:

What magnificent capabilities in those early Western volunteers; what illustrious talent in those first regiments found by

Frémont and coming at his call!—Lyon, Grant, Blair, McCler-
nand, Pope, Logan, Schofield, Curtis, Sturgis, Palmer, Hurlbut,
and a hundred others whose names shine on the records of war,
to say nothing of the thousands who, unheralded, went gloriously to manful duty and patriotic death.[5]

Such detractors, however, failed to note that, despite that array of talent, the total force under Frémont's command came to a paltry sixteen
thousand, largely ill-trained, underequipped, poorly organized men
scattered among nine points throughout Missouri. Jessie Frémont—
responding that July to her friend Elizabeth Blair Lee's invocation of
the squandering-of-talents charge—put the case succinctly:

Your letter reached me last night and but for the genuine interest you have in the cause I should have taken it for a sarcasm.
You say all we need is "Generals." That is simply and literally
the whole provision made for this Dept. An arsenal without
arms or ammunition—troops on paper and a thoroughly prepared and united enemy thick and unremitting as mosquitoes.
. . . It's making bricks without straw out here & mere human
power can't draw order of chaos by force of will alone.[6]

By August, with no reinforcements expected, Frémont's situation
showed no signs of improving. From General Benjamin M. Prentiss,
increasingly nervous as he sought to hold Cairo for the Union, Frémont learned that General Polk's six-thousand-man army at New
Madrid had been supplemented by another eleven thousand well-
trained soldiers under the command of General Gideon Pillow. With
the long-feared Confederate assault on Cairo imminent, Frémont now
faced a three-front war: in the southwest, Captain Nathaniel Lyon and
his forces were pinned down at Springfield; in the southeast, General
Prentiss was pleading for reinforcements to shore up the Union line at
Cairo; and, throughout Missouri, Frémont faced growing sabotage by
Confederate irregulars.

By then Frémont had no choice but to warn Lyon, in southwest
Missouri, that no reinforcements were forthcoming. He advised Lyon
to make a tactical retreat north, back to the town of Rolla, the nearest
railhead, but also gave him authority to act on his own discretion in

deciding what to do. In the end, Lyon—urged on by General Franz Sigel, whose own Third U.S. Volunteers were by then at Springfield—decided he could not yield southwest Missouri to Confederate forces. On August 10, Lyon's and Sigel's forces attacked the superior Confederate forces of Generals Sterling Price and Ben McCulloch, which were gathered to their immediate south. In the resulting Battle of Wilson's Creek, fought ten miles south of Springfield, each side lost about thirteen hundred men. But the engagement proved a tactical victory for the Confederates. General Lyon died in the fighting, and the remaining men of his and Sigel's armies—now forced by circumstances to comply with Frémont's original advice—retreated a hundred miles north to Rolla, leaving Price's Rebels in control of southwestern Missouri.

Flushed with victory, Price's army quickly consolidated its control of southwestern Missouri and pushed northward, all the way to the Missouri River and Lexington, Missouri, the most populous town between St. Louis and Kansas City. His force's numbers swelled by new recruits gathered along his march, Price now commanded an army of eighteen thousand troops, who easily surrounded the thirty-five hundred man Union garrison at Lexington. On September 20, culminating a three-day siege, Lexington surrendered to Price's Rebel army.

Frémont, meanwhile, had decided by early August to concentrate on using the resources under his immediate command to reinforce General Prentiss's beleaguered troops at the town of Cairo on the Mississippi River. Boarding his flagship *City of Alton*, he took personal command of the reinforcement operation—a flotilla consisting of thirty-eight hundred soldiers and eight large river steamboats. Faced with such an impressive show of Union force, the Confederate troops threatening Cairo quickly fell back, and the river town remained under Union control for the war's duration. But though Frémont had secured Cairo, he had also, in a little over two months, presided over the loss of about half the state of Missouri to Rebel forces.

❦

Determined to wrest control over affairs in Missouri, General Frémont, on August 30, took a bold step. After conferring with Jessie and his aide Edward M. Davis, a Quaker abolitionist, Frémont that day issued a startling proclamation by which he instituted martial law and stipulated summary execution for all Confederate guerrillas captured behind Union lines. Further encroaching upon President Lincoln's policy prerogatives, Frémont called for the immediate confiscation of the property of, and the freeing of all slaves owned by, Confederate sympathizers in Missouri.[7]

By ordering the manumission of all slaves in Missouri, Frémont had gone far beyond his own past opposition to slavery. Even in the 1856 presidential race, he had balked at calling for slavery's outright abolition. Reflecting that era's standard Free Soil position, Frémont, in a campaign-year letter to Ohio Lieutenant Governor Thomas Ford, had noted, "I am hostile to slavery upon principle & feeling" and "inflexibly opposed to its extension on this continent beyond its present limits." But he was also of "the belief that it ought not to be interfered with where it exists under the shield of state sovereignty."[8]

Frémont's proclamation—particularly his emancipation order—enhanced his popularity within the Republican Party's more vigorously antislavery Radical wing. But it vexed President Lincoln. By downplaying slavery as a cause of the Civil War, Lincoln had hoped to woo wavering border states firmly into the Union. Hoping to resolve the controversy without dismissing Frémont, and thereby antagonizing Republican Radicals, the President, on September 2, penned a letter worth quoting in full:

MY DEAR SIR: Two points in your proclamation of August 30 give me some anxiety:

First. Should you shoot a man, according to the proclamation, the Confederates would very certainly shoot our best men in their hands in retaliation; and so, man for man, indefinitely. It is, therefore, my order that you allow no man to be shot under the proclamation without first having my approbation or consent.

Second. I think there is great danger that the closing paragraph, in relation to the confiscation of property and the liberating [of] slaves of traitorous owners, will alarm our Southern Union friends and turn them against us; perhaps ruin our rather fair prospect for Kentucky. Allow me, therefore, to ask that you

will, as of your own motion, modify that paragraph so as to conform to the first and fourth sections of the act of Congress entitled, "An act to confiscate property used for insurrectionary
purposes," approved August 6, 1861, and a copy of which act I
herewith send you.

This letter is written in a spirit of caution, and not of cen-
sure. I send it by special messenger, in order that it may certainly and speedily reach you.

Yours very truly,

A. Lincoln[9]

A more prudent officer would have taken the President's letter
as an order—a generously worded cautionary order, but an order
nonetheless. But not Frémont: to Lincoln's missive, he responded, on
September 8, with arrogant defiance: "I acted with full deliberation,
and upon the certain conviction that it was a measure right and necessary, and I think so still."[10] Amazingly, even after receiving Frémont's
swaggering reply, Lincoln's hopes persisted of finding a diplomatic
way out of the impasse. On September 11, he issued yet another directive—albeit, this one a public letter:

Your answer, just received, expresses the preference on your
part that I should make an open order for the modification,
which I very cheerfully do. It is therefore ordered that the said
clause of said proclamation be so modified, held, and construed
as to conform to, and not to transcend, the provisions on the
same subject contained in the act of Congress entitled, "An act
to confiscate property used for insurrectionary purposes," approved August 6, 1861, and that said act be published at length,
with this order.[11]

That same month, Lincoln dispatched Postmaster General Montgomery Blair along with Blair's brother-in-law, the Army's Quartermaster General M. C. Meigs, to St. Louis to conduct an inquiry into the
situation, and to offer Frémont some friendly advice from the President. For years, Frémont had enjoyed cordial relations with the Blair
family. Through the family of Senator Benton's late wife, Elizabeth,
Jessie Frémont was related to the Blairs. Reinforcing familial ties, two

Blair brothers, Montgomery and Frank, had both gone to Missouri to establish legal and political careers under the tutelage of Senator Benton.

By late 1861, however, the two clans were approaching a complete break. It hardly helped matters when Frank Blair, after Congress adjourned, returned to St. Louis. Though polite, Frémont failed to confide in him about military matters or welcome his suggestions. Tensions were further exacerbated by Frémont's refusal, in the granting of wartime contracts, to give special consideration to political allies of the Blairs. Moreover, the Blair brothers had also come to genuinely believe him ill-suited for his command.

To them and other observers, Frémont seemed ineffective in suppressing the state's Confederate insurgency. Growing allegations of corruption on Frémont's part in the awarding of military contracts also inflamed resentments. Furthermore, what appeared to be a growing imperiousness on Frémont's part also stirred antipathies. In truth, his behavior in St. Louis approached the bizarre. Visitors seeking an audience with the general in his mansion headquarters complained that it took days to get beyond his ostentatiously bedecked guards. One general, visiting from the East, complained that it took three full days to win a meeting with the reclusive Frémont—and such reports inevitably found their way back to Washington and President Lincoln.

When Postmaster General Montgomery Blair and Army Quartermaster General M. C. Meigs reached St. Louis on September 12, they carried, as guidance, a copy of a letter from the President to General David Hunter of Chicago, whom Lincoln was transferring to St. Louis to assist—and, if necessary, to replace—Frémont:

General Frémont needs assistance which it is difficult to give him. He is losing the confidence of men near him, whose support any man in his position must have to be successful. His cardinal mistake is that he isolates himself, and allows nobody to see him; and by which he does not know what is going on in the very matter he is dealing with.[12]

But as the two talked with Frémont and others in St. Louis, whatever amicable spirit the President hoped to stir there gave way to

harsher sentiments. Talking with Frank Blair and other Frémont detractors, Meigs and Montgomery Blair heard much to confirm their already negative impressions of Frémont's management of affairs in
Missouri. Moreover, by then, Frémont had become embroiled in a bitter feud with Hamilton R. Gamble, recently appointed by a special
state convention of Unionists as the state's provisional governor. Gamble, attempting in a series of meetings with Frémont to convey the
President's wishes, also formed a negative opinion of the general,
which he soon reported to Lincoln.

By fall 1861, as the Frémont-Blair-Lincoln disputes became fodder
for newspapers around the country, it seemed clear to most observers
that Lincoln, weary of dealing with Frémont, planned to terminate his
command. Hoping to thwart that eventuality, Jessie, that September,
rushed from Missouri to Washington. Arriving on the evening of September 9 and checking into the Willard Hotel, she immediately sent a
note to the White House, asking if and when she might see the President. He replied, that same evening, with his own note—"Now, at
once, A. Lincoln." Accompanied by a family friend, Judge Edward
Coles of New York, a fervent abolitionist, Jessie went promptly to the
White House. But by both her and Lincoln's accounts of the exchange, the President remained unmoved by her pleading. According
to Jessie Frémont, Lincoln adamantly insisted that John, rather than
suspecting Frank Blair of venal intentions, should have consulted with
him. Furthermore, Lincoln stressed, had the general consulted with
Blair, he would have learned that his emancipation proclamation for
Missouri had grossly misrepresented the President's intentions. "It
was a war for a great national idea, the Union, and . . . General Frémont should not have dragged the Negro into it," she recalled the
President as saying. Lincoln, for his part, recalled the exchange as primarily a test of his presidential decorum. "She sought an audience
with me," he recalled, "and tasked me so violently with so many
things, that I had to exercise all the awkward tact I have to avoid quarreling with her."[13]

The next day, when the elder Francis Blair visited Jessie Frémont,
the two old friends quarreled bitterly. "Well," said Blair, several
decades her senior, "Who would have expected you to do such a thing
as this, to come here and find fault with the President[?] . . . Look

what Frémont has done; made the President his enemy!"[14] During their two-hour exchange, the senior Blair foolishly let it drop that, five days earlier, Lincoln had received a letter from Frank Blair, Jr., castigating General Frémont, and that it had been that letter which had led the President to dispatch Montgomery Blair and Meigs to St. Louis. In the wake of the exchange, Jessie, in a letter to Lincoln, repeating the elder Blair's account of events, demanded to see all correspondence about the incident. Lincoln, in a letter back to Jessie declining the request, sought to assure her that he bore no hostility toward her husband.

To Jessie, it now seemed abundantly clear that the Blairs were orchestrating a conspiracy to sabotage her husband's reputation with the President. Upon her returning to St. Louis and sharing that conviction with John, the two grew so enraged that John ordered Frank Blair's arrest on charges of insubordination. Though Frémont soon complied with a friendly telegram from Montgomery Blair requesting his brother's release in the interest of war morale, the imprisoned Blair initially—demanding a trial—refused to leave his cell.

✦

The war, meanwhile, raged on. Just south of Cairo, Ulysses S. Grant, the new brigadier general appointed by Frémont, had taken the town of Paducah, Kentucky, at the confluence of the Mississippi and Tennessee Rivers. Ignoring advice from others that he appoint General John Pope to the post, Frémont had placed Grant in charge of southeastern Missouri and southern Illinois, with orders to seize all riverfront positions in Kentucky and Missouri threatened by the Confederates. Frémont's general strategy and Grant's skillful subsequent successful execution of it would pave the way for Grant's later triumphs in the Civil War's Western theater.

While Grant's efforts bolstered Union confidence, reports from northwestern Missouri were less encouraging. At Confederate-occupied Lexington, Missouri, 160 miles up the Missouri River, an army under the command of Colonel James Mulligan, attempting to retake the town, had settled into a grueling duel with troops under Confederate General Price. As Mulligan, soon surrounded by Price's forces, made frantic calls for reinforcements, critics again accused Frémont of having cruelly sacrificed a talented officer on what turned out to be a fool's errand.

Blair and others claimed—falsely—that Frémont had forty thousand soldiers in St. Louis who could have been sent to reinforce Mulligan. In truth, Frémont had but 6,880 ill-trained men in reserve—far too few to rescue Mulligan. Beyond that, even as Frank Blair and others called for him to dispatch troops to Lexington, Frémont, unbeknownst to the public, was receiving telegrams from War Secretary Simon Cameron and the Union's commanding general, Winfield Scott, demanding that he immediately send 5,000 troops east, to protect Washington from an anticipated Confederate assault. Asked by a colleague if he might consider arguing with his superiors that the troops must stay in Missouri, Frémont answered that he had no more stomach for such exchanges. "No," he said, "that would be insubordination, with which I have already been unjustly charged. The capital must be again in danger, and must be saved, even if Missouri fall and I sacrifice myself."[15]

Though Frémont, complying with instructions from Scott and Cameron, asked generals in neighboring states to transfer soldiers to Lexington, none were forthcoming. On September 21, Mulligan's army, accepting the inevitable, formally surrendered. Afterward, Rebel General Price crowed that, while losing only twenty-five of his own men, he had captured thirty-five hundred Union soldiers, a vast array of arms and munitions, and $100,000 worth of commissary goods. The Rebel victory deep behind Union lines proved yet another boon to Confederate propaganda and another blow to Frémont's prestige. Predictably, Frank Blair and other critics trumpeted Mulligan's loss as the latest evidence of what they charged was Frémont's cavalier attitude toward his soldiers' lives.

❋

Five days after Mulligan's defeat, Frank Blair—by then, having accepted his release from jail—lodged formal charges, accusing Frémont of failure to follow orders, conduct unbecoming an officer, waste and corruption, and neglect of duty. As those and other charges reached

Washington, Frémont, aware of his sinking prestige, decided that the time had come for him personally to take the field. The Union cause in the war effort was going badly. But, Frémont resolved, if he could secure just one important victory, perhaps he could turn the war's tide toward Old Glory.

By early October, General Price and his Rebel army, transporting arms and other materials confiscated at Lexington, were working their way toward southwestern Missouri, where they planned to unite with the forces of Confederate General Ben McCulloch. Reorganizing his forces into five new divisions, Frémont set off to vanquish Price and his army. Upon reaching Jefferson City and the outpost he had erected there—"Camp Lily," named for his daughter—Frémont discovered to his disappointment that a thousand wagons shipped to him from the East had been constructed from rotten wood and were broken down along roads leading into the camp. As Frémont's army pushed southwest on the heels of Price's retreating army, chronic shortages of everything from food to horses bedeviled his army's passage, forcing them to embark upon wide-ranging foraging parties.

Even so, Frémont felt reinvigorated to once again be in the field. From his days with the California Battalion, after all, he knew how to conduct field operations far from lines of supply. Writing to Jessie from an encampment near Tipton, Missouri, he exulted, "The army is in the best kind of spirits, and before we get through I will show you a little California practice, that is, if we are not interrupted." Two days later, in another letter to his wife, with visions of capturing Price's army, then moving on to Memphis and points beyond, Frémont had become positively rapturous: "My plan is New Orleans straight; . . . I think it can be done gloriously, especially if secrecy can be kept. . . . It would precipitate the war forward and end it soon and victoriously."[16]

Soon enough, Major Charles Zagonyi and the 150 hand-picked cavalrymen of the so-called Frémont's Bodyguard were attacking Price's remaining troops at Springfield while Frémont's larger force advanced upon the Confederates' larger column. But even as those actions were lifting his hopes, an emissary from President Lincoln was hunting for him with news that he had been relieved of his post.

The President had signed the order dismissing Frémont a week earlier, after hearing a report from War Secretary Cameron and Lorenzo Thomas—both of whom, weeks earlier, had been dispatched to Missouri to produce yet another firsthand report on conditions there. While Cameron held no particular grudge against Frémont, Thomas, a close friend of the Blairs, had been disposed against the general from the very start.

It was past midnight on November 2–3 when the President's official courier caught up with and, through trickery, gained admittance to, the general's camp. Once inside, as the messenger later recalled, he found his way to Frémont's headquarters:

> The general was sitting at the end of quite a long table facing the door by which I entered. I never can forget the appearance of the man as he sat there, with his piercing eye and his hair parted in the middle. I ripped from my coat lining the document, which had been sewn in there, and handed the same to him, which he nervously took and opened. He glanced at the superscription, and then at the signature at the bottom, not looking at the contents. A frown came over his brow, and he slammed the paper down on the table, and said, "Sir, how did you get admission into my lines."[17]

By morning, the news of Frémont's dismissal had thrown a dark cloak of despair over the camp. "It would be impossible to exaggerate the gloom which pervaded our camps," wrote a New York *Herald* correspondent, observing the scene, "and nothing but General Frémont's urgent endeavors prevented it from ripening into general mutiny."[18]

The next evening, when his announced replacement, General David Hunter, had still not arrived, Frémont found a way to revive the men's spirits: gathering his officers in his quarters, he told them that if Hunter failed to appear, he would lead the attack against General Price's army already planned for the next morning. The officers and soon the entire camp greeted Frémont's vow with wild elation. Cheers rose, hats were tossed, a dozen bands were soon serenading their stalwart commander. "I never saw anything at all approaching the excitement this announcement created," observed the *Herald*'s correspondent. "It caused immense cheering, around the headquarters, which spread in all directions, from camp to camp, and there was almost uninterrupted cheering."[19]

But Hunter arrived at 10:00 that evening. He and Frémont repaired to Frémont's headquarters, where Frémont formally relinquished his command and shared his battle plans with the new commander. However, Hunter carried strict orders from Lincoln not to pursue General Price. That, Lincoln had concluded, would pose too many risks. The sun had finally set on what soon became known— after a sympathetic article in *The Atlantic Monthly* likening Frémont's turn in Missouri to Napoleon's vainglorious Elba Island–to–Waterloo saga—as "Frémont's Hundred Days."

❋

Frémont had made mistakes, but his detractors exaggerated his errors and failed to give him credit for his successes: he had, after all, sustained Union control of St. Louis. Beyond that, by having built an armada of Mississippi River warships and by putting Ulysses S. Grant in command of operations on the river, he had helped to create the matériel and leadership infrastructure by which Grant, in a stunning series of victories culminating in the July 1863 Union capture of Vicksburg, secured Union control over the river, thus fatally dividing the Confederacy into two isolated eastern and western sections.

As for Frémont's emancipation order for Missouri—quickly revoked by President Lincoln—it freed, in the end, only two slaves. But the directive did manage to demonstrate the popular appeal among northern voters of elevating the war's objective from mere reunion of the states to the abolition of slavery—and thus laid the groundwork for Lincoln's more wide-ranging Emancipation Proclamation almost one year later. Indeed, years later, Jessie, recounting the episode, made a point of quoting the "Deed of Manumission," signed by her husband, by which Hiram Reed, a slave in St. Louis, was declared "to be free, and forever discharged from the bonds of servitude." The Missouri bondsmen, she wrote, "were the first slaves ever freed in the United States under the authority of the [federal] government, and it will be noticed that in revoking this Emancipation, President Lincoln did not question the authority or power of General Frémont to issue it, but doubted its expediency."[20] Or as John Greenleaf Whittier—ever the Pathfinder's admirer—put it in a poem that season, entitled simply, "To John C. Frémont":

> Thy error, Frémont, simply was to act
> A brave man's part, without the statesman's tact,
> And, taking counsel but of common sense,
> To strike at cause as well as consequence.[21]

❋

After John's dismissal, the Frémonts remained in St. Louis for two weeks as he collected documents to use in vindicating his actions in Missouri. They then traveled to New York and took an apartment on Fourth Avenue. There John played genial host to a steady stream of admiring Radical Republican congressmen and senators. The attention continued into early 1862, when, as John prepared for a congressional investigation into his actions in Missouri, the couple moved back to Washington. That winter, John and Jessie—by then sensing a revival of John's political stock—even found themselves invited guests of President and Mrs. Lincoln at their famous White House party of February 5. There, Jessie later claimed, the admiration among the guests for her husband became so evident that, fearing embarrassment for the President, the couple left early—only to be summoned back by Lincoln. In a telling precursor to Frémont's imminent resurrection as a military commander, the President, upon learning from someone at the party that General George B. McClellan and General Frémont had never met, wanted to introduce the two men.

❋

That spring, Congress's Committee on the Conduct of the War formally exonerated Frémont of most of the charges leveled against him in the Department of the West. With that onus lifted, he was once again formally qualified for military service. To placate Radical Republican critics, Lincoln thus asked him to command the newly created Mountain Department, which included western Virginia, eastern

Kentucky, and parts of Tennessee. Accepting the command, John, along with Jessie and their children Lily and Frank, arrived at his new headquarters, in Wheeling, Virginia, on March 29, 1862. Their other son, Charley, by then had been placed in a school in Litchfield, Connecticut.

As General Frémont settled into his offices in Wheeling's Mc-Clurge Hotel, he resolved to stay clear of local and state politics, but once again, he surrounded himself with a coterie of European aides and guards. To further limit outside interruptions, Jessie soon occupied an anteroom in which she screened all visitors.

Unfortunately, however, John's Mountain Department assignment gave him marching orders, developed by President Lincoln himself, that were entirely unrealistic. The President wanted him to march his army from West Virginia over the mountains into Tennessee, where it was supposed to seize the railroad at Knoxville and rescue that region's Unionist sympathizers. Though, on paper, Frémont commanded an army of twenty-five thousand men, in actuality his troops numbered far fewer; and of those, most were untrained and poorly equipped. But even under the best of circumstances, Lincoln's strategy was flawed. It underestimated the difficulty of the Allegheny wilderness over which Frémont had to march, as well as the talents of his chief adversary, the Confederate military genius General Thomas J. "Stonewall" Jackson.

Frémont entered the field in late March of 1862; and, over the spring and summer, in what came to be known as the Shenandoah Valley Campaign, he was continually outwitted by the crafty Jackson. In June, a frustrated Lincoln consolidated the troops of the Mountain Department into the newly created Army of Virginia, under the command of General John Pope. Frémont, asked to command one of the new army's three divisions, resigned in protest against the diminution of responsibilities.

Once John's resignation became final, Jessie, in the fall of 1862— embarking on what later became a more full-fledged literary career— published her first book, *The Story of the Guard*. Ostensibly an account of Frémont's often maligned "Bodyguard" corps and their victory at Springfield, published to raise funds for fallen members' families, the book also functioned as an apologia for John's command in the Department of the West.

As for John, he spent much of his time during the Civil War's final years indulging his latest obsession, railroad speculation. Even so, he remained a popular figure among Radical Republicans. Dissatisfied with what they regarded as Lincoln's timidity in pressing the war, a Republican splinter party, on May 31, 1864, nominated Frémont as their presidential candidate. But when Democratic nominee General George B. McClellan began showing new strength, the Radicals reconsidered their campaign. More than about Lincoln's alleged timidity, they worried about McClellan's apparent willingness to accept the continued existence of slavery in the South as the price of peace. Fearing that a divided Republican vote might lead to a McClellan victory, Frémont's supporters began seeking a deal with Lincoln and his supporters.

Meanwhile, a host of Republicans—including, most decisively, the poet John Greenleaf Whittier—called on Frémont and convinced him of the moral futility of his projected candidacy. On September 22, Frémont withdrew from the race. The following day, by the terms of a deal brokered by Frémont's camp, Montgomery Blair—once Frémont's close friend, but now among his bitterest enemies—was dismissed from Lincoln's cabinet.

PART VII

THE LIGHT
OF PARTING DAY

1865–87

Backward, amidst the twilight glow,
Some lingering spots yet brightly show,
    On hard roads won;
Where still some grand peaks mark the way
Touched by the light of parting day
    And memory's sun.
    —from "Recrossing the Rocky Mountains,
    After Many Years," by John C. Frémont

MOSES UNREDEEMED 27

YEARS AFTER her father's death, Lily Frémont recalled that
someone had once said that "my father should have been
called Moses, instead of John, for like the biblical character,
he was led up to the hilltop and permitted to view the promised land
below, though he never was permitted to enter."[1] Through the 1850s
and 1860s, John Frémont's efforts to personally prosper from the
forces of Western expansion that his explorations had nourished had,
all too often, ended in frustration—and his star-crossed gambits continued after the Civil War. The family tasted riches during various periods, but Frémont remained constantly in debt, unable to sustain
wealth. As the New York *Times*, years later, put it, "Gen. Frémont
never was a wealthy man, nor did he possess the faculty of money
getting."

In 1865, as the Civil War staggered toward its conclusion, Frémont
purchased from James Watson Webb, editor and owner of the *Morning
Courier and New-York Enquirer*, a two-hundred-acre estate on the Hudson River, just north of Tarrytown, New York. The Frémonts called
the estate Pocaho; and, there, with its gray stone mansion, orchards,
gardens, and forests, the family—now with two sons and a daughter—
cultivated a new life as Gilded Age aristocrats. The Frémont family's
social life now centered on their new neighbors—the Schuylers, As-
pinwalls, Phelpses, and Peabodys—whose palatial estates lined the
river. When not pursuing his new career as a railroad speculator, Frémont spent time hiking and boating with the children or reading in
his extensive library. Upon the death of his idol Alexander von

Humboldt, Frémont had purchased part of the explorer's personal library.[2] The Pathfinder also now had time and money to amass an art collection that included a painting, purchased for four thousand dollars, of the Golden Gate by the Prussian-born painter of the American West Albert Bierstadt. A Frémont admirer, Bierstadt was also a neighbor and friend, whose own Hudson River estate lay just south of Pocaho.

During their flush years at the Pocaho estate, the Frémonts also purchased an island off the Maine coast, where they planned to build a cottage. They also continued to travel—in some cases with the family joining John when he attended to business matters abroad.

In a trip that further bolstered their sense of familial vindication, the Frémonts, in May 1868, traveled to St. Louis, where Jessie, before an enthusiastic audience of forty thousand people in Lafayette Park, unveiled a majestic toga-clad bronze statue of her father—sometimes called "the Old Roman"—by the German-born artist Harriet Hosmer.

❁

Facing mounting debts, Frémont sold his remaining interest in the Las Mariposas estate—which, by then, was awash in debt—in 1863. Entrepreneur and landscape architect Frederick Law Olmsted, hired that year by Las Mariposas' new owners to try to wrest order out of the chaos left behind by Frémont, upon arriving there found a veritable scorched earth of deficit finances. "He seems to have worn out the patience, after draining the purses, of all his friends in California," Olmsted wrote to his father. "I am overrun with visits from his creditors."

By all appearances, however, Frémont remained wealthy, and he continued to invest in commercial ventures, particularly railroads. The outbreak of the Civil War had made it inevitable that the nation's first transcontinental rail line would take a northern route across the continent. But with the return of the southern states to the Union, interest revived in building another, more southerly, line across the continent; and Frémont quickly joined the fray of competing schemers and investors.

During 1863, Frémont had served briefly as a vice-president of the Union Pacific Railroad's eastern division. For a short time, he was also an investor in the Kansas Pacific as well as the Southwest Pacific lines. He served the latter as a vice-president and soon tied it into the proposed Atlantic and Pacific Railroad, which enjoyed a conditional congressional land grant to extend from Springfield, Missouri, to the Pacific. As was typical in such governmental-subsidy arrangements, actual land certificates for parcels along assigned corridors were to be awarded as tracks crossed them.

Those railroad forays all proved unfruitful. But the disappointments they yielded for Frémont paled beside the disaster that would befall him after he became associated, in October 1866, with the incipient Memphis, El Paso, and Pacific line. Although the company had been founded in 1856 and enjoyed a conditional land grant from the state of Texas, construction on the line had been stalled by the Civil War. When Frémont joined the project, agreeing to raise capital to support its construction, only sixty-five miles of rail corridor had been graded, and no tracks laid. Even so, he and his partners had ambitious plans, hoping to transform the line into the Southern Transcontinental Railroad, which would run from Norfolk to San Diego.[3]

Failing to raise adequate funds on U.S. securities markets, Frémont turned toward French capital markets. Through introductions arranged by his brother-in-law, diplomat and Parisian businessman Baron Gauldrée de Boilleau, Frémont arranged, during the fall of 1868, for the Paris brokerage house of Paradis et Cie to sell up to $8,400,000 worth of the company's bonds. Over the next year, close to five million dollars' worth of the rail line's bonds were sold in France. But with those sales came scandal. By the spring of 1869, disclosures about the rail company's finances and business methods filled U.S. and French newspapers. In France, it was revealed, company agents—including Boilleau—had grossly misrepresented the Memphis, El Paso, and Pacific's situation, telling prospective investors that the rail company was already a transcontinental line controlling land stretching from Norfolk to San Diego. They also claimed that the federal government had guaranteed a fixed rate of return on the railroad bonds.

The most damning revelation concerned the very instrument by which the bonds were sold. For foreign offerings to be sold on Paris's Bourse, French law required that such stocks and bonds also be sold on their originating country's main exchange. But because the company's situation had never been listed on the New York Stock Exchange financial standards, the company could not sell its bonds on the Paris exchange. To get around the problem, the company's agents in France created forged certificates, replete with signatures and gold seals, attesting that the offerings were listed on the New York Stock Exchange.[4]

The scandal in Paris broke, as it turned out, as the Frémonts were en route to France for an extended European stay. Upon their arrival in June of 1869, John, by generally refusing to discuss the matters, hardly helped the situation. Though he claimed to have known nothing, early on, about the misrepresentations, he had, at the least, been slow, after learning of them, in acknowledging them to the public. Responding to French outrage, the U.S. Minister in Paris—taking the lead of local newspapers—called for the U.S. Congress to investigate Frémont.

✸

John's attentions that season in Europe were not focused exclusively on railroad business. While Jessie and the children conducted a grand tour of the Continent, he remained in Paris, where, in addition to tending to Memphis, El Paso, and Pacific matters, he also found time to conduct a flirtation with Vinnie Ream, a twenty-two-year-old American sculptor living in Paris. A bright, attractive woman with long brown curls, Ream was sufficiently accomplished to support her family with her artistry. And with the support of some influential congressmen, she had been awarded a federal commission to sculpt a marble statue of the martyred President Lincoln. Even so, some complained at the time that coquetry as much as talent had won her the job. After receiving the commission, she promptly moved to Paris to begin her work.

For much of September of 1869, as John's family toured the Continent, he saw Vinnie almost every day. Later in the month, John joined Jessie and the children for a week of travel in Austria, but once back in Paris, he resumed his calls on Vinnie. Whether or not the two consummated their relationship remains unclear, but John's letters to her strongly suggest a rapport that went beyond mere friendship. On the eve of a visit by Vinnie's parents to Paris, for instance, he wrote her, ostensibly to provide travel suggestions for a trip she and her family planned to make. "This is my little bulletin of business for you this morning my darling," he wrote, concluding the letter. "If I should be happy enough to see you tonight I will make it clearer—otherwise tomorrow. I feel disturbed & disquieted this morning. Frémont." Contacting her again the following day, he made some additional travel suggestions. "What I have been at to you here looks like the letter of a business agent," he then added. "But although, you may not see it, it is a love letter."

When Jessie, Lily, and Frank returned to Paris, John promptly took them to Vinnie's studio. There, Jessie posed for a bust, and the entire family lunched with the artist. A few days later, Vinnie finished the bust, John came for a final visit, and Vinnie left for Munich and Rome with her family. Though it's difficult to believe that Jessie failed to notice the young woman's attraction to John, no evidence has come to light suggesting that she suspected anything more than a friendship. Nor is there any evidence that John continued to see or correspond with Vinnie. As for Vinnie, she hardly lacked for suitors: her address book included a host of admiring male correspondents ranging from Frank Blair to William T. Sherman.[5]

❋

In late November of 1869, the Frémonts returned from Europe to Pocaho. But after a brief stay there, John and Jessie hurried on to Washington, where a congressional investigation into the Memphis, El Paso, and Pacific was getting under way. The probe resulted in more damaging revelations and, afterward, the company's situation continued to deteriorate. By 1871, the line was sliding toward bankruptcy. In France, that March, Frémont and the French promoters of the line were tried on fraud charges resulting from the sale of almost five million dollars of worthless bonds. Frémont, who claimed that insufficient notice precluded his attendance at the trial, was nonetheless convicted in absentia and sentenced to five years in prison.

Gauldrée de Boilleau was convicted and sentenced to three years in prison. Though his brother-in-law Frémont—safely in America—avoided jail, the scandal further muddied his reputation. "Frémont's name stinketh in Paris," his former political aide John Bigelow, then in

Europe, reported. Much of the investors' lost money was never accounted for; and, among the other damaging items, it was revealed that Boilleau, for his "services" to the company, had been paid $150,000. Frémont himself, it was said, may have walked away with more than a million dollars.[6] As the rail line drifted into bankruptcy court, Frémont soon found himself ousted from the company by a clever businessman named John A. C. Gray.

The Memphis, El Paso, and Pacific scandal punctuated what had been a long slide down for John Frémont the entrepreneur. Though talented in navigation, meteorology, and mathematics, John, when navigating the realms of finance had consistently displayed a sloppiness, a lack of attention to details. By the late 1860s, that shortcoming had been joined in his business dealings by a commensurate inattention to ethics—a penchant for duplicity, misrepresentation, and, quite possibly, outright fraud.

❋

Initially, by outward appearances, the Memphis, El Paso, and Pacific's collapse had no effect on the Frémonts' life at Pocaho. Servants still catered to their whims, and pampered guests still passed through the estate's main house. But, soon enough, the family found itself scrambling for cash—trying to call in old claims and hunting for new business ventures. As Jessie lamented, "We had houses and lands and stocks and no money for unpremeditated uses."[7] By the end of 1875, the Frémonts had been forced to sell both Pocaho and a fashionable town house they owned on Manhattan's Nineteenth Street, between Fifth and Sixth Avenues. In a dark irony, Black Point, in San Francisco, had been seized in 1862 by the federal government without compensation so that it could build the U.S. Army's Fort Mason—named after Frémont's old rival from California Conquest days, Lieutenant Colonel Richard Mason.

From their palatial estate on the Hudson, the Frémonts, in 1875—after auctioning most of their prized possessions, including the books John had purchased from von Humboldt's library—moved into what would become, over the next decade, a series of shabby apartments in Manhattan, Staten Island, and New Jersey. As Frémont's fortunes withered, Jessie, to help support the family, began writing freelance magazine and newspaper articles—many of which were recycled into books, and most of which were devoted to celebrating and defending her husband. Frémont, meanwhile, continued his feckless forays into capitalism. At least one business trip that season found him again heading west, but this time on a comfortable passenger rail line. As the train, passing through country that he had explored on foot, horse-, and mule-back three decades earlier, rose into the Rockies, he got out pen and paper and composed a poem. Elegiac in tone, celebratory and bittersweet, it included the stanza

> Backward, amidst the twilight glow,
> Some lingering spots yet brightly show,
>   On hard roads won;
> Where still some grand peaks mark the way
> Touched by the light of parting day
>   And memory's sun.

John sent the poem to Jessie. Touched by what to her seemed a "de profundis cry from him to me," she sent it to *Littell's Living Age*, which published it anonymously. "The General knew nothing of this until I gave him the number with the lines in print," she confided to their friend John Greenleaf Whittier. "He was very pleased. But his is the most reserved and shy nature I ever met."[8]

❋

In 1878, in an apparent reprieve from their travails, Republican President Rutherford B. Hayes appointed Frémont governor of the Arizona Territory. An admirer of the explorer, Hayes had briefly served under Frémont during the Civil War; and as early as 1849, he had tendered the suggestion, adopted by the leading citizens of Lower Sandusky, Ohio, to give the town the name it retains today—Frémont. After John accepted the gubernatorial appointment, he and the family traveled by rail from New York to San Francisco, where John was greeted as a returning hero. From there, they completed the journey to Prescott via rail and mule cart. In the wake of the discovery of rich veins of gold and silver along the Colorado River and in the territory's interior, Arizona, that year, was undergoing a boom—with boomtowns

like Tombstone drawing the money of Eastern capitalists, and entre-
preneurs, prospectors and other optimists, who were soon prowling
about the territory in search of instant fortunes.

Perhaps here in Arizona, Frémont allowed himself to think, he
might recoup what he had lost to squatters, lawyers, and bankers in California. Beyond his mining ventures, Frémont's pursuits in Arizona
came to include railroad, irrigation, and canal proposals. Among his gambits in the latter category, he sought, unsuccessfully, to raise one million
dollars to build a canal that would divert water from the Colorado River
and, if all went as planned, transform a desert basin straddling the
California-Arizona border into an inland sea. It would, he promised, "in-
duce cool and tempering winds to blow over and form clouds to moisten
the parched and arid plains. In short, it would make the whole surrounding country to blossom like a rose." Capturing the quixotic spirit
that animated Frémont's ventures that season, a newspaper, reporting
on the canal plan, headlined its story "Fremont's New Scheme."

Soon after the family, in October 1878, set up their residence in the
territorial capital of Prescott, Frémont—along with Charles Silent, a
territorial supreme court judge—joined the gold- and silver-fever fray.
That fall, the two men inspected potential mine sites around the territory. And, after the legislature adjourned in late winter, they headed
east to find financing for their projects. Typical of the sort of behavior
that soon generated widespread resentments against the governor,
Frémont and Silent's trip was paid for with a two-thousand-dollar appropriation enacted by the territorial legislature to fund a trip to Washington for the purpose of resolving a controversy involving the Salt
River Indian Reservation.

Frémont tended to neglect his gubernatorial duties, spending most
of his time, often in the East, pursuing business ventures. Antagonizing constituents still more, in March 1881, for business reasons, he
moved his family's residence out of the territorial capital of Prescott,
southeast to Tucson. By the following fall, President Chester Arthur
faced growing demands to force Frémont's resignation. Responding to
the pressure, in October 1881 Frémont resigned from office, and the
family returned to New York.

For the next few years, Frémont continued to pursue business ventures. By now, the couple's marriage, by outward appearances, had be-

come more a conceit than the intimate partnership it had once been. Years earlier, more than a few friends and relatives had taken to dismissing John as morally deficient with a penchant for marital infidelity and reckless squandering of the family's money in dubious business schemes. Elizabeth Blair Lee could not comprehend why Jessie allowed her husband to "gamble away his own & her children's bread over & over again . . . and he too faithless even to pretend to live with her." Jessie's own sister Elizabeth referred to John as "Jessie's insanity." Even so, the two Elizabeths conceded that Jessie's loyalty to John remained unshakable. "She belongs to him body & soul," as Elizabeth Blair Lee put it, "& he does with [her] as he pleases as much as he does with his own right hand."[9]

❋

In a break from John's wearying succession of dismal railroad, real estate, and canal schemes, the Frémonts, in 1885, stumbled upon what seemed a genuinely promising commercial venture. That summer, former president Ulysses S. Grant had died of throat cancer. But even as he lay dying, he was in the process of completing a book which, in the end, liberated his family from a long penury to which they had been reduced by his own trail of unsuccessful business ventures. Grant's book was a huge commercial success; and, inspired by it, John and Jessie secured an interested publisher and began work on what became Frémont's *Memoirs of My Life*. Published in 1887 by the Chicago publishing firm of Belford, Clarke & Company, the 655-page book took Frémont's career only up to the conquest of California. It reprinted almost verbatim the earlier government-published expedition reports, glossed over controversies with a patently one-sided perspective—and, in the end, failed to win a large audience. That failure preempted interest by any publishers in what the Frémonts had hoped would be a second volume.[10]

Even more dispiriting for the couple, John, by then, suffered from acute bronchitis—and his doctor was urging him to move to an arid climate. It was that December of 1887 that John and Jessie, carrying rail tickets donated by Collis P. Huntington, left New York for Los Angeles.

THE LEGACIES OF EMPIRE

O N MARCH 5, 1849, within an hour after the new President, General Zachary Taylor, had taken office, the outgoing chief executive James K. Polk was "greatly surprised" by comments his Whig successor made to him. "They were to the effect," Polk recalled, "that California and Oregon were too distant to become members of the Union, and that it would be better for them to be an Independant [*sic*] Gov[ern]ment." Though Taylor believed that Americans would eventually predominate in Oregon and California, he saw the future of both realms ultimately lying outside the American union.

To Polk, these seemed "alarming opinions to be entertained by the President of the U.S." But certainly Polk also knew that his Whig successor's reservations were hardly original.[1] Taylor, after all, was merely giving voice to a long tradition in American political speculation. As far as such things can be known, however, it would be the last time that an American chief executive uttered such reservations. Indeed—showing how quickly and resolutely Americans had accepted the notion of a continental empire—twelve years later, in 1861, when President Lincoln committed the federal government to war against the states of the South, his announced motivation lay not in the abolition of slavery, but rather in the preservation of the Union. Politically and geographically, the nation had traveled a vast distance since Jefferson, half a century earlier, had envisioned the "united States" as a loose confederation of states.

From 1848 onward, hesitations about the dangers of a geographically dispersed United States were rendered increasingly irrelevant by growing American emigration into the Far West—followed by the completion of a transcontinental telegraph line in 1861 and, eight years later, a coast-to-coast rail link and, in short order, other trunk and spur lines that integrated the region into the United States.

For the West's farmers, the nation's growing rail network offered more, better, and cheaper connections to markets. Equally important, railroads brought to Western farmers a growing array of improvements in agricultural technology—including tougher plows, steel rollers, windmills, and barbed wire. And, in the early twentieth century, the federal government began constructing large dams across the West, providing irrigation on a scale inconceivable a generation earlier. Underwriting and encouraging those developments, the United States, during the Civil War and throughout most of the rest of the nineteenth century, stepped up its campaign to wrest traditional lands away from various Indian populations. By 1890, having forced most surviving Indians onto isolated "reservations," the United States could promise Western emigrants, if nothing else, a life free of Indian conflicts. Indeed, in the Midwest, as farmers tapped into the Great Plains' vast Ogallala aquifer, regional boosters managed to persuade much of the public that their realm constituted a boundless "garden"—a proposition as one-dimensional and false as Stephen Long's once-accepted notion of the region as one vast "Great American Desert."

California's gold rush also helped to vanquish lingering doubts that the West could not be fully integrated into the American union. The Sierra gold rush would pass by 1851, but the fever set a pattern that would draw growing numbers of Americans west of the hundredth meridian. In some cases—like the alleged discovery in 1858 of gold in Colorado, which drew possibly 100,000 prospectors to an area near Pike's Peak—the stories turned out to be just that: stories. In other cases—like Nevada's silver Comstock Lode strike of 1859 and the gold and silver strikes at Cripple Creek, Colorado, in 1891—the mines made millions of dollars for those lucky enough to reach them in time. More important, those mines, along with the region's expanding agricultural sector, erected the foundation for the next great epoch in the American West's evolution—the rise of San Francisco, Denver, Los Angeles, and other large cities.

But while those developments bonded the West to the American nation, they proved less effective in realizing Senator Thomas Hart Benton's Road to India. The Panamanian railway survey camps that had sheltered Jessie Frémont on the overland portion of her 1849 isthmus crossing foreshadowed the loss—even before it had been won—of the U.S. monopoly that her father had hoped to win on mechanized Atlantic-to-Pacific travel in the Western Hemisphere. Six years after her crossing, the Panama railroad began regular operations, hastening passengers across the isthmus.

Even more devastating to Senator Benton's vision, in 1869—the same year that the United States completed its transcontinental rail line—the Suez Canal also began operations. By providing Europe with a more direct route to Asia, the Suez Canal obviated Benton's vision of The Road to India. While the various transcontinental routes explored by Frémont and his successors proved, over the years, to be a boon to the U.S. economy, they could not compete with the Suez Canal as a corridor linking Europe and Asia.

Moreover, the glistening pot of gold that lay at the end of Senator Benton's Road to India had been conjured during an era in which the United States lacked—outside the southern Appalachians—any known, substantial deposits of gold and silver. The discovery of gold in California—followed by other strikes of both gold and silver elsewhere in the West—undercut the economic rationale for Benton's Road to India.

Beyond that, Polk's aggressive use of the military to wrest territories from Mexico introduced a new coarseness into U.S. geopolitics that ran afoul of Benton's benign conception of America's role in world history. In his advocacy of a better trade route to the Orient, Benton had sought a peaceable negotiation with Britain of the Oregon question, one that would give the United States secure rights to the Columbia River valley. And, as a veteran proponent of the Santa Fe trade, he wanted no conflicts with Mexico that might jeopardize that commerce. Trade, not more territory, lay at the core of his vision of American empire. Benton accepted U.S. acquisition of Texas, California, and New Mexico only after all three had become political faits accomplis.

✸

America's lust for empire abated after the Civil War. Even so, William H. Seward, Secretary of State for Lincoln and his successor, Andrew Johnson, worked to keep the spirit alive, predicting that destiny foreordained the United States to stretch north to the North Pole and south to the tropics.[2] Seward's efforts to annex such realms as British Columbia and Japan's Bonin Islands failed. In 1867, however, he did succeed in purchasing Alaska from the Russian government.

During the final decades of the nineteenth and the early decades of the twentieth century, however, the old spirit of Yankee empire more robustly revived, reaching a sort of imperial flood tide in 1898, in the Spanish-American War. Much as Frémont had been the heroic paragon of an earlier time, future president Theodore Roosevelt came to personify America's new era of empire building by rushing off to Cuba with a motley band of ex-convicts, Ivy League athletes, Western gunfighters, and assorted other miscreants called the Rough Riders.

As the United States emerged as a world naval power during those years, it gathered a collection of island possessions stretching from Puerto Rico to Hawaii. At first glance, that fin de siècle imperial vision—shaped by earlier figures such as Seward and Commodore Matthew Perry, and later ones such as Alfred Mahan, John Hay, Theodore Roosevelt, Henry Cabot Lodge, and other theorists of maritime empire—bore little resemblance to anything that Benton or Frémont had ever advocated. Its objectives—political, economic, cultural, even spiritual—seemed far broader than Benton's narrowly mercantilist goals.

Then again, Uncle Sam sought the islands collected during those years not for their use as colonies, but as coaling stations and sites for military bases to protect U.S. trade routes to Asia—much as Benton had advocated forts along the overland stretch of his Road to India. Lest Americans overlook the similarities between the two eras, the U.S. postal system, in 1898—the year of the Spanish-American War and Roosevelt's Rough Riders—issued a commemorative stamp depicting John Frémont triumphantly waving the Stars and Stripes atop Fremont Peak. The following year, Roosevelt published his own biography of Thomas Hart Benton.

❈

But even as the United States gathered an empire of sorts in the late nineteenth and early twentieth centuries, the very word *empire* was falling from favor as a national aspiration among many Americans. By then, few Americans realized that, once upon a time, the sprawling lands west of the Mississippi River had been a speculative topic of American empire builders, or that America's leaders, from Washington to Benton, had openly advocated the creation of an American empire.

It was as if, once the continental empire was secured, the complex story of its assemblage was consigned to some forgotten corner of the nation's psychic basement. By the late nineteenth century, when Americans referred to such matters, they tended to invoke not the neutral term *empire* but the newly popular pejorative, *imperialism*—a term, by then, generally ascribed to the policies of other nations.

By the 1880s, when American diplomats talked of projecting their nation's power to other parts of the globe, they talked of extending the blessings of liberty and Protestant conversion. While Mark Twain and other opponents of that era's American empire-building had no reticence about calling what was going on "imperialism" and worse, Roosevelt and his colleagues preferred the blander language of "our new possessions." And the intervening years have only reiterated the American ambivalence toward—and, in many instances, outright opposition to—the doctrines of Benton and his successive theorists of American empire. As the British historian Niall Ferguson put it—anticipating the medium-term consequences of America's stepped-up global activism in the wake of the September 11, 2001, terrorist attacks on New York and Washington—regardless of how much such ambitions persist, "The United States—born in a war against the British Empire—will always be a reluctant ruler of other peoples."[3]

It would be the continental empire nudged toward fruition by John Frémont, inwardly directed, that Americans more readily embraced. In that expansive vision of continental breadth, Americans would find a serviceable view of themselves and their place in history. By turns noble, cruel, realistic, and delusional—in the end, teeming with contradictions—John Frémont's vision of America insinuated itself into the nation's collective psyche. In the Pathfinder's wake, Americans found, to borrow poet John Ashbery's words, that "fine forgetfulness" that "commemorates / Because it does define."

✻

For those whose lives, during the 1840s, had intersected with those of John and Jessie Frémont, the succeeding years yielded a variety of fates. In New Mexico, during the Civil War, Frémont's loyal friend Kit Carson would serve with the Union Army, eventually rising to the rank of brevet brigadier general. Later, he led several U.S. Army campaigns against Southwestern Indian tribes. Mostly, however, Carson spent his remaining years ranching around Taos, New Mexico. He lived long enough to see himself apotheosized into a fictional character in pulp novels and magazines. As early as 1849, in New Mexico, he had the odd experience of fighting his way to the camp of a putative victim of an Indian ambush, only to discover the victim missing and, among her possessions, a book—in all likelihood Charles Averill's *Kit Carson, Prince of the Gold Hunters*, published that year—which she had apparently been reading just before her apparent abduction—"in which I was made a great hero, slaying Indians by the hundreds."[4] Carson died, at age fifty-eight, in 1868.

As for Commodore Robert Stockton—namesake of today's Stockton, California—his dreams of greater military glories in Mexico never came to fruition. Instead, after turning over his responsibilities to Frémont, he departed California, in June of 1847, and led his men on an overland transit back to the East. During the early 1850s, he briefly represented New Jersey in the U.S. Senate (where his fulsome rhetoric won him the epithet "Gassy Bob" Stockton), briefly sought the presidency on an American Party splinter ticket of 1856, then spent his remaining years as a canal and railroad entrepreneur. He died in Princeton in 1861.

Like Stockton, Johann Sutter always dreamed of greater glories. But, in a bitter irony, the gold discovered on his New Helvetia estate led to his ruin. Miners streaming into the region overran and destroyed his properties. By 1852, as the new town of Sacramento crowded out Sutter's remaining operations, he had declared bankruptcy. Though he tried for many years to recover his wealth, he died, in poverty, in 1880. Though the two men had shared a complicated relationship over the years, among the pallbearers at his funeral was John Frémont.

Among Frémont's California adversaries, Mariano Vallejo probably enjoyed the most prosperous life in the years after his clashes with the Pathfinder. Although Frémont, during the Bear Flag uprising, had suspected the Mexican general of anti-American sympathies, Vallejo later became one of the state of California's most prominent citizens—playing an active role in the campaign for statehood, helping to frame the state constitution, and serving in the newly created state senate. He spent his remaining years, until his death in 1890, as a beloved patriarch and rancher in northern California's Sonoma County.

Pío Pico, after fleeing Los Angeles before the American invasion, returned to California in 1848 and spent his remaining years as a prosperous rancher and Los Angeles businessman and civic leader—among his other achievements, he helped to organize the Standard Oil Company of California. He died in 1894. Pico's rival during the final months of Mexico's rule over California, José Castro, also fled before the Americans' arrival, but he too, in 1848, returned to California. After ranching near Monterey for several years, he left, in 1853, for the Mexican state of Baja California, where he took up another government post. He died there, in a brawl, in 1860.

EPILOGUE, 1887–90

WHEN, on Christmas Eve of 1887, the train carrying John and Jessie Frémont from New York pulled into Los Angeles, the couple found a city that bore little resemblance to the tiny pueblo that John had known from his short-lived gubernatorial term four decades earlier. With the arrival, in 1876, of a Southern Pacific Railroad link tying Los Angeles to San Francisco, a real-estate boom had begun to rapidly reconfigure the city.

Between 1880 and 1890, the city's population would swell from eleven thousand to fifty thousand. Eager to join the boom, Frémont immediately began searching for opportunities, eventually becoming involved in the development of Inglewood, a small borough on Los Angeles's southwestern edge. Because, however, the Frémonts had no capital to invest, his involvement in the project was limited: in exchange for the use of his name in promotions, the developers gave to the couple a small Eastlake-style house in the subdivision.[1]

Sadly, however, for the Frémonts, the Los Angeles boom collapsed only months after the couple's return. So severe was the bust that Inglewood's promoters even tried, unsuccessfully, to take back the Frémonts' house. Even so, the couple—deciding that the new town was too "remote and lonesome"—soon moved to a small cottage, closer to downtown Los Angeles, and kept their Inglewood house as a rental property.

Increasingly anxious about the family's finances, Frémont, by the fall of 1888, had left Los Angeles for the East, where he remained through the following summer, pursuing various business ventures and continuing a long-standing campaign to persuade Congress to provide him a military pension. Unsuccessful, he returned to California. In the fall of 1889, his hopes of a pension buoyed by a new Congress, he left once again for New York and Washington.

That spring, in March 1890, Frémont, then seventy-seven years old, telegraphed Jessie with some good news—the U.S. Congress had finally granted him status as a retired general with an annual pension of nearly six thousand dollars. Despite that triumph, however, Frémont remained in the East: he was writing a recollection of the conquest of California for *Century Illustrated* magazine and was otherwise continuing his perpetual hunt for the main chance—this time, hoping to win a large commission through the sale of some California property to a group of English investors.

By July, however, Frémont had grown doubtful that his California property transaction would ever reach fruition. "If the Giuseppi fails," he wrote to Jessie, on the eleventh, referring to the prospective sale, "I have no confidence in anybody here. My love to home. Frémont." Apparently not wanting to alarm Jessie, Frémont made no reference to his failing physical condition. He was very ill.

Sandy Morton, the family's longtime New York doctor, upon visiting the old man that day, became so concerned that, over Frémont's protests, he notified the couple's son Charley—then living, just north of the city, in Ossining, New York. According to Dr. Morton, John was suffering from peritonitis—an inflammation of the bowels, very likely induced by the consumption of contaminated food. When, the next day, Charley reached his father's Twenty-fifth Street boardinghouse, he found him in great pain, with a high fever and a feeble pulse. The following Sunday morning, Frémont began to vomit, then lapsed into unconsciousness. By the day's end, he was dead. To his sister, Lily, Charley later wrote that, just before slipping into unconsciousness, their father said something about going home.

"Home?" Dr. Morton repeated. "What do you call home?"

"California, of course."[2]

❀

Earlier that day, Charley, upon realizing his father's failing condition, had sent Jessie a telegram: "Father is seriously ill." Her daughter, Lily, then living with Jessie, left immediately for the telegraph office, to see if she could find more information. By then, the telegraph office had received another dispatch: "Father is dead. Charley." In tears, Lily rushed back to the house, hoping to reach Jessie ahead of the news.

But she was too late. When she returned, the telegram had already been delivered to the house. "Like a bolt from a clear sky the blow fell," Jessie later recalled. "It is the last telegram I ever opened, it seemed to fairly shrivel up my arm." John's death was difficult news to bear, and for the next thirty-six hours Jessie seemed so stunned that a doctor called to the house by Lily feared the onset of a paralysis. Because of the distance and expense, Jessie was unable to attend her husband's funeral and had to settle for asking Charley to place in his casket a note that she had written to him, along with a miniature photograph of her that John always carried. The rites were without ostentation—for, as Charley wrote, his father "was not a man of parade and display." Afterward, the body was deposited in a vault in a Manhattan funeral home—to be left there until Jessie could decide on a permanent resting place in California.

In the months and years afterward, Jessie continued her work as a writer and as a zealous guardian of John Frémont's reputation. The latter task had taken on more urgency in the wake of disparaging writings by the historian Hubert Bancroft and the California-born Harvard philosopher Josiah Royce—all questioning Frémont's actions during the U.S. conquest of California. Jessie wrote for a variety of magazines—including *Century Illustrated* and Los Angeles booster Charles Lummis's *Out West*. In 1890, she published *Far West Sketches*, which, like most of her earlier books, primarily gathered recollections already published in magazines and newspapers.

Jessie's writings generated scant income, and John's pension had ended with his death. To meet her bills, she was often forced to borrow money from friends. Her circumstances even rendered her unable, as she had hoped, to arrange to have her husband's body brought back to California. After Jessie despaired of being able to raise the money to have the body removed from the Manhattan vault and buried in California, the state legislature took up the issue—but, after vociferous opposition, it was forced to drop the idea. In the end, Jessie had no recourse but to accept an offer from a New York group of a site in Rockland Cemetery, just across the Hudson River from the family's former estate of Pocaho.

In the weeks after John's death, as newspapers spread the word of Jessie's indigence, the U.S. Congress stepped in and, that September, granted her a special widow's pension of two thousand dollars a year. Soon thereafter, a group of Los Angeles women raised funds to build her a new home—a two-story redwood house at the corner of Los Angeles's Hoover and Twenty-eighth Streets. It was there that Jessie lived until her own death, in 1902, at the age of seventy-eight.[3]

❋

A century later, in Los Angeles in 1996, a group of archeologists one afternoon were monitoring excavations for the construction of a new subway stop when, along a median of Lankershim Boulevard, they discerned—at first faintly, then more clearly—the ruins of what appeared to be the foundation of an adobe structure. Digging a little deeper, they came upon the floor tiles of the building—slices of terra cotta still so vivid that they retained the footprints of pets that had scampered across them.

In the days ahead, the archeologists confirmed that the foundation belonged to the main house of Rancho Cahuenga—the same building where, more than a century earlier, Mexico—represented by Pío Pico—had formally turned over the province of California to the United States, represented that day by John Frémont.

As word of the find got out, preservationists and history buffs mounted a campaign to preserve the site. But, because it lay along a major thoroughfare scheduled for widening, they also knew that they faced a tough fight. To a columnist for the *Los Angeles Times*, the site offered, if nothing else, a rare opportunity for Angelenos to show visitors something beyond the traces of actors who "only imitate" the actions of the sort of men and women who actually change history. "Let them come," she wrote, "and stand in the virtual boot prints and spur marks of the real thing, Frémont, the victorious adventurer, Pico the vanquished patriot, here, on these very tiles, where history changed."[4]

In the end, the forces of commerce triumphed—though, in a sense, the ruins were preserved—albeit under tons of asphalt. What had been a median along Lankershim Boulevard within months became a left-turn lane onto Universal Terrace Parkway. As a consolation to the preservationists, before burying the site in asphalt once again, the construction workers covered Campo de Cahuenga with a layer of slurry, a mixture of clays, limestone, and other finely ground substances. By spreading out the weight of the thousands of vehicles that would pass over the ruins each day, said a subway-authority official, the material would help protect the site.

❋

Halfway across the continent, two thousand miles to the east, in St. Louis's Lafayette Park, a bronze, toga-clad Thomas Hart Benton with unrolled map in hand looks west toward the Pacific, and to the fabled ports of India, Japan, and China. "There is the East," reads the inscription beneath. "There lies the Road to India."

Though it was Frémont's continental vision of empire that the nation eventually embraced, nowhere in America does any statue commemorate the senator's son-in-law. But perhaps none is required: for from sea to shining sea, amid the plains and valleys now largely empty of the vanquished Indians and buffalo, amid the ceaseless, nervous, odometer-stripping miles of iron-railed and asphalt Buenaventuras that now bind the republic, John Frémont's continental legacy lies too deeply inscribed on the landscape to ever be summed up with statues, or removed with jackhammers and bulldozers. For, in the end, the American empire he envisioned had been realized on a scale—and in forms—beyond his wildest dreams.

ON TEXTUAL SOURCES
AND PLACE-NAMES

NOTES

BIBLIOGRAPHY

INDEX

ON TEXTUAL SOURCES AND PLACE-NAMES

Lamenting the inevitable losses of property that attend the process of moving, the historian John Hope Franklin once told me, quoting a friend of his, that "three moves equals one fire." If that holds true—and from my own experiences, I'm convinced it does—then John and Jessie Frémont—in their shared peripatetic lives, inhabiting myriad addresses throughout the East and West—suffered the equivalent of about a dozen metaphorical fires.

Beyond that, pondering the paper trail of the Frémonts' lives, we know of at least four very real fires that figure in the long saga of John and Jessie. There was the great San Francisco fire of 1851, which consumed the family's residence there. There was the fire that, in 1855, destroyed the Washington, D.C., home of Jessie's father, Thomas Hart Benton—a fire that consumed the only draft of volume two of his memoirs and the papers that the retired senator had spent a lifetime collecting. There was the fire that, in 1881, destroyed Morrell's Warehouse, in New York City, in which the family had placed, in their daughter Lily's words, all the "belongings that we considered too precious to take with us to the west."

And, finally, there was the private little fire, set by Lily in 1907, years after her parents' deaths, in which she methodically burned most of John's and Jessie's surviving papers. "It is not a cheerful task that of going over and destroying old letters and papers," she wrote to a friend, "but it is better than having them get into wrong hands . . . it is very hard to burn up the letters of those we love."* And beyond those fires, Frémont's own exploring narratives abound in incidents—ranging from mishaps on swollen rivers to snowbound-mountain disasters—in which papers were lost or destroyed.

Fortunately, John's and Jessie's words do survive in other published and unpublished writings. John's narratives chronicling the first two of his three federally funded exploring expeditions of the 1840s were all published by the U.S. Senate

*Elizabeth Benton Frémont, *Recollections*, 177; Elizabeth Benton Frémont to Sallie Preston, Aug. 6, 1907, in Preston-Johnston Papers, University of Kentucky.

and remain available. And in 1887, his commercially published *Memoirs* appeared. Though this work was long out of print, a new paperback edition (John C. Frémont, *Memoirs of My Life*, New York: Cooper Square Press, 2001) was published as work on this book was being completed. While Frémont's *Memoirs* borrow heavily from his exploration *Reports*, this work, by taking his life up to 1848, does add to the historical record his accounts of the Third Expedition and the U.S. conquest of California.

John had planned to write a second volume of the *Memoirs*, but after the first volume proved a commercial failure, he abandoned those plans. In 1891, however, a year after John's death, Jessie—with the assistance of the couple's son John Charles II—wrote their own version of the second volume of John's memoirs. The manuscript—entitled "Great Events in the Life of General John C. Frémont . . . and of Jessie Benton Frémont"—offers a tendentious, stridently one-sided, perspective. Even so, the unpublished manuscript—housed today at the University of California's Bancroft Library—serves as an indispensable source of information on the couple's later years. At the Bancroft, scholars will also find Jessie's own "Memoirs," written in 1901–02, which, sadly, also remains unpublished. Her words also survive in the eight books and scores of magazine articles that she published, most of which consist of personal memoirs. There are also two published collections of daughter Lily's writings—a volume of memoirs and her recently published 1887–91 diary.

Government inquiries into matters of controversy concerning Frémont, as well as pleadings of legal actions, furnish still other glimpses into his life. Beyond those are the hundreds of letters, diaries, and other documents associated with the Frémonts, which lie scattered in archives across the United States. For the Frémonts' actual papers, however, the key repositories are the Library of Congress, the National Archives, the Bancroft Library, and the Huntington Library.

Fortunately, John Frémont's most important papers, related to his years as an explorer, published and unpublished, have been collected and superbly annotated in three volumes edited by Donald Jackson and Mary Lee Spence. Yet another published volume—meeting those same high editorial standards—devoted to Jessie Frémont's papers has been edited by Spence and Jessie Frémont's biographer, Pamela Herr.

❋

While conducting research for this book, when using John Frémont's published writings, I developed an axiom: Trust him on the details, take his conclusions concerning controversies with a grain of salt. When, for instance, John describes the flora that he observed on some particular day, you can generally take that to the bank. But when he addresses matters of controversy involving him, John tended to write with one eye on the defense of some already enunciated public position, the other on his reputation for posterity. Such writings are best read as apologia as much as factual accounts. Jessie's published writings are often equally tendentious, but when dealing with personal matters, her letters offer a revealing window on the Frémonts' lives.

❀

In this book, even in cases in which I have examined an original document, if that document appears in any of the Frémonts' collected papers edited by Donald Jackson, Mary Lee Spence, and Pamela Herr, I have generally cited from those published volumes. I do this for the obvious reason that those volumes are more accessible to scholars than the actual papers. If, however, those published volumes contain an abridgment, however slight, of a particular document that I am quoting, I have tended to cite the original document. I hasten to add, however, that, for the overwhelming majority of scholars interested in these materials, the published volumes of Jackson, Spence, and Herr will be more than adequate.

Finally, a word on place-names: Monikers imposed upon geographical features—particularly in the American West—often have ephemeral lives. Places are named and renamed until one name catches on with mapmakers and the public. In many cases, I have, upon first reference to a place, used both the name by which Frémont referred to that locale and its modern name. To avoid confusion, however, in subsequent references to such places I have generally used the names by which they are now known.

NOTES

ABBREVIATIONS
John Charles Frémont: JCF
Jessie Benton Frémont: JBF
California Historical Society Quarterly: CHSQ

PROLOGUE
1. JBF, "Memoirs," n.p.; "material" from J. C. Frémont, Jr., in Nevins, *Pathmarker*, 607–608; JBF to Nelly Haskell Browne [Dec. 1887], in JBF, *Letters of JBF*, 516–17.

1. THE RISING EMPIRE
1. *DeBow's Review*, July 1849, 4.
2. Greely, *Explorers and Travelers*, 230, 231.
3. Stockton to Polk, Aug. 26, 1846, in JCF, *Expeditions*, II:195.
4. New York *Times*, Apr. 9, 2000.
5. JCF, *Memoirs*, 59; *Littell's Living Age*, July–Aug.–Sept. 1850, 208; Van Alstyne, *Rising American Empire*, 1, 2, 2n; Onuf, *Jefferson's Empire*, 2; Lincoln, *Selected Writings*, 111; Thomson, "Britannia, A Poem," 7.
6. Franklin, "Increase of Mankind," in Franklin, *Autobiography and Other Writings*, 259.
7. Anderson, *Crucible of War*, 219–31; Jefferson, *Writings*, 121.
8. Jefferson to Joseph Priestley, Jan. 29, 1804, ibid., 1141–43.
9. See Hamilton, "No. 9" in Hamilton et al. *Federalist Papers*, 71–76.

2. CHARLES FREMON *FILS*
1. Bigelow, *Fremont*, 11–12; Letter by Doyle in *Virginia Patriot*, August 23, 1811. For more on JCF's parentage, see JCF, *Expeditions*, I, xxi–xxiv; historian Andrew Rolle—departing from the traditional account of the origins of the explorer's father—has suggested that "plausible" Canadian sources suggest that

his name was actually Louis-René Frémont, and that he was from Quebec City (see Rolle, *Frémont*, 2).

2. Anne Beverley [Whiting] Pryor to John Lowry, Aug. 28, 1811, attachment to Pryor divorce petition, in JBF, *Letters of JBF*, 117 n6.

3. JBF notes re Mead Burrill statement, Bigelow Papers, New York Public Library; Deposition MS, Dec. 3, 1811, Virginia State Library, in Nevins, *Pathmarker*, 6, 7.

4. [Richmond] *Virginia Patriot*, July 11, 1811; JCF, *Expeditions*, I:xxiii n4.

5. Bigelow, *Fremont*, 17–22.

6. Article by Thomas Gamble, Savannah *Press*, March 20, 1928. See also JCF, *Expeditions*, I:xxiv n5; Nevins, *Pathmarker*, 8, 9.

7. Bigelow, *Fremont*, 22; James, *Andrew Jackson*, 152–54.

8. JCF, *Expeditions*, I:xxiv n5, xxvi.

9. Roberton recollections, in Upham, *Fremont*, 11–15.

10. Bigelow, *Fremont*, 24–27.

11. JCF, *Memoirs*, 21; expulsion statement from college president, the Reverend Jasper Adams, from College's Faculty Journal, Feb. 3, 1831, in Nevins, 14, *Pathmarker*; recent search of college archives, however, failed to turn up the original document.

12. JCF, *Memoirs*, 19–21.

13. Ibid, 21.

14. Rippy, *Poinsett*, 218.

15. JCF, *Memoirs*, 22; Bigelow, *Fremont*, 28–29; Rippy, *Poinsett*, 23, 163.

16. Prucha, *Sword of the Republic*, 339–64.

17. Rippy, *Poinsett*, 163.

18. JCF, *Memoirs*, 22–24; Robert McKay to Richard Yeadon, and article from Greenville *Patriot and Mountaineer*, both quoted in Charleston *Courier*, Oct. 27, 1856.

19. JCF, *Memoirs*, 24–27; JCF, *Report of the Exploring Expedition to the Rocky Mountains in the Year 1842, and to Oregon and North California in the Years 1843–'44*, 276 [this volume, hereafter cited as JCF, *Report*, includes Frémont's *Report*s from both his First and Second Expeditions].

3. BOUNDARIES WHERE NONE ARE MARKED

1. JCF, *Memoirs*, 30, 31.

2. Bray, *Nicollet*, 1–17, 19–23, 25–46.

3. Ibid., 63–65, 67–94, 95–97, 99–132.

4. Nicollet, *Report*, 77; upon Jacob Astor's retirement in 1834, the Western Department of his American Fur Company was purchased by Pratte, Chouteau and Co. In general parlance, however, the new company, produced by the purchase, was often called the American Fur Company; Nicollet to Chouteau, Jan. 6, 1834, original in Minnesota Historical Society, in Bray, *Nicollet*, 134.

5. Ibid., 154–86; Nicollet to Gabriel Paul and Jules de Mun, Nov. 1, 1836, ibid., 186.

6. Taliaferro to Harris, June 19, 1837, in Nicollet, *On the Plains*, 212.

7. Abert to Poinsett, Jan. 17, 1838, ibid., 214–16.

8. Goetzmann, *Army Exploration*, 6–21.

9. Bray, *Nicollet*, 187–99; Abert to Poinsett, Apr. 7, 1838, in Nicollet, *On the Plains*, 219–20.

10. JCF, *Memoirs*, 32; JCF to Poinsett, June 8, 1838, in JCF, *Expeditions*, I:12–13.

11. JCF, *Memoirs*, 31–32.

12. Ibid., 32. Nicollet to Sibley, Feb. 6, 1838, in Nicollet, *On the Plains*, 217.

13. JCF to Ann B. Hale, June 6, 1838, in JCF, *Expeditions*, I:10.

14. Ibid., 32, 33.

15. JCF to Nicollet, June 8, 1838, in JCF, *Expeditions*, I:12.

16. JCF, *Memoirs*, 59; Nicollet, *Report*, 106.

17. Bray, *Nicollet*, 200–206; Nicollet, *Report*, 30; JCF, *Memoirs*, 34, 35; JCF to Poinsett, Sept. 5, 1838, in JCF, *Expeditions*, I:21–24.

18. JCF, *Memoirs*, 34–35; Bray, *Nicollet*, 205–206; JCF to Poinsett, Sept. 5, 1838, in JCF, *Expeditions*, I:21–24.

19. Nicollet to Sibley, Feb. 6, 1838, in Nicollet, *On the Plains*, 217–18.

20. Nicollet to Sibley, Apr. 26, 1840, in Bray, *Nicollet*, ibid., 256; Nicollet, *On the Plains*, 150.

21. Ibid., 150–51; Bray, *Nicollet*, 291; Iowa border in Nicollet, *Report*, 73–74.

22. Nicollet to Poinsett, Dec. 28, 1838, in Nicollet, *On the Plains*, 230–31.

23. Bray, *Nicollet*, 188.

24. Nicollet, *On the Plains* 54, 62–63.

25. Ibid., 72–73, 79–80; JCF, *Memoirs*, 35–36.

26. Bray, *Nicollet*, 213, 214; JCF, *Expeditions*, I:19 n3; Nicollet, *On the Plains*, 106–108.

27. Nicollet to Poinsett, Dec. 28, 1838, Nicollet, *On the Plains*, 230.

28. JCF to Abert, Jan. 1, 1839, in JCF, *Expeditions*, I:44; Nicollet, *On the Plains*, 111–34.

4. THERE'S GEOGRAPHY FOR YOU!

1. Nicollet to Poinsett, Dec. 28, 1838, in Nicollet, *On the Plains*, 227–32.

2. Goetzmann, *Army Exploration*, 6, 11–13.

3. Ibid., 9, 10; "John James Abert," *Dictionary of American Biography*, XXI (suppl. 1):2, 3; Smith, *Pacific Visions*, 12, 13.

4. Abert to JCF, March 2, 1839, in JCF, *Expeditions*, I:45–46.

5. JCF, *Memoirs*, 38; Nicollet, *On the Plains*, 141–43; Nicollet, *Report*, 107; Bray, *Nicollet*, 225–26.

6. JCF, *Memoirs*, 38–39; Nicollet, *On the Plains*, 145, 166.

7. JCF, *Memoirs*, 38, 39.

8. Nicollet, *On the Plains*, 166.

9. Ibid., 66, 67.

10. Allen, *Passage*, 113–14.

11. Ibid., 1–22; Allen, "The Garden-Desert Continuum," 207–214; James, *Account*, II:361; Pike, *Travels*, 230, 231.
12. JCF, *Memoirs*, 39–40.
13. Ibid., 39–43; Nicollet, *On the Plains*, 170.
14. JCF, *Memoirs*, 42–44.
15. Thomas Hart Benton, U.S. Senate speech, Feb. 7, 1849, in Hafen, *Disaster*, 60.
16. Nicollet, *On the Plains*, 168–93, nn65, 66, 69; JCF, *Memoirs*, 44–48; Nicollet, *Report*, 44–45.
17. Ibid., 49–51.
18. The crest on which Nicollet stood lies near the spot where North Dakota's State Highway 15 crosses the Nelson and Grand Fork county lines. Nicollet, *On the Plains*, 107, 198, 198n107; JCF, *Memoirs*, 52.
19. Ibid., 37, 52–53; Nicollet, *On the Plains*, 198–210.
20. JCF, *Memoirs*, 53–54; JCF, *Expeditions*, I:69 n8; Nicollet, *On the Plains*, 210, 211.

5. WASHINGTON AND THE BENTONS

1. JCF to Poinsett, Jan. 3, 1840, in JCF, *Expeditions*, I:83; Bray, *Nicollet*, 247–48.
2. JCF to Poinsett, Jan. 3, 1840, in JCF, *Expeditions*, I:83, 84.
3. Washington *Daily Union*, Aug. 8, 1845; JCF, *Memoirs*, 55–58; Bray, *Nicollet*, 251–52.
4. Chambers, *Benton*, 18–21; Meigs, *Benton*, 37.
5. Chambers, *Benton*, 57, 58, 101, 104.
6. Ibid., 21–38; Meigs, *Benton*, 276–320.
7. Smith, *Benton*, 77. For a thoughtful essay on Benton's theory of empire, see Smith, *Virgin Land*, 20–37.
8. "Asiatic Commerce," in Benton, *Editorial Articles*, 23.
9. March 1, 1825, Senate speech, ibid., 44; Benton, *Thirty Years' View*, I:13, 14; JCF, *Memoirs*, 59.
10. Benton, *Thirty Years' View*, I:50–54; Chambers, *Benton*, 122.
11. Ibid., 105, 106
12. Maria E. Montoya, "Santa Fe and Chihuahua Trail," *New Encyclopedia of the American West*, 1023, 1024.
13. Benton, *Three Speeches*, 28; Polk, *Diary*, I:375.
14. Chambers, *Benton*, 277, 294–301, 306; JBF, "Senator Benton," in JCF, *Memoirs*, [1], 2, 8.
15. Ibid., 65.
16. Ibid., 64–66.
17. Chambers, *Benton*, 238; JCF, *Memoirs*, 64–67.
18. JBF, *Souvenirs*, 135, 139, 143, 157, 158; JBF, "Memoirs," 13, 19, 20, 26–30.
19. Ibid., 19, 20, 23–25.
20. JBF, *Souvenirs*, 36–37; JBF, "Memoirs," 34; Abert to JCF, June 4, 1841, in JCF, *Expeditions*, I:96; JCF, *Memoirs*, 68.

21. JBF, *Souvenirs*, 38–56; Nicollet to JCF, July 11, 1841, in JCF, *Expeditions*, I:98; JCF *Memoirs*, 68–69. For Des Moines River report, see JCF, *Expeditions*, I:115–20, 120n.
22. Herr, *Jessie Benton Frémont*, 62, 63; F. W. Gody to JCF, Nov. 7, 1841, in Nevins, *Pathmarker*, 69–70.
23. This account of the revelation of the Frémonts' marriage to Jessie's parents and the subsequent events comes largely from an account given by Mrs. Henry Hull, a granddaughter of John and Jessie, as related by Nevins, in *Pathmarker*, 68–71. Herr, in *Jessie Benton Frémont*, presents another version, in which Elizabeth Benton learned of the marriage through happenstance, then confronted Jessie with the news, 64–65; wedding notice from Washington *Globe*, Nov. 27, 1841.

6. TO SOUTH PASS

1. JCF, *Memoirs*, 69.
2. Ibid., 69, 70.
3. Ibid., 71.
4. Ibid., 70, 71.
5. Ibid., 71.
6. Goetzmann, *Army Exploration*, 68.
7. Benton, *Thirty Years' View*, II:478; Benton to Abert, n.d.; Abert to Benton, Apr. 28, 1842; Abert to JCF, Apr. 28, 1842, in Frémont Collection, Southwest Museum; JCF, *Memoirs*, 70–73.
8. JCF, *Memoirs*, 70; purchase vouchers in JCF, *Expeditions*, I:136–58; JBF, *Letters of JBF*, 238n.
9. JCF, *Memoirs*, 73–75; Pay vouchers, in JCF, *Expeditions*, I:146–54.
10. Gilbert, Walker, 203; JCF, *Report*, 9, 10; JCF, *Memoirs*, 74; Pierre Chouteau, in Mafitt MS, Missouri Historical Society, in Nevins, *Pathmarker*, 94; JCF, *Memoirs*, 74; Carson, "Memoirs," 81.
11. Utley, *Life Wild and Perilous*, 174–76.
12. Carson, "Memoirs," 81.
13. Vouchers, Oct. 31, 1842, in JCF, *Expeditions*, I:154–55, 55n.; JCF, *Memoirs*, 74.
14. JCF, *Memoirs*, 74, 75; JCF, *Report*, 8–10; JCF, *Expeditions*, I:144n.
15. JCF, *Report*, 10.
16. JCF, *Memoirs*, 74; JCF, *Report*, 10.
17. Ibid.; Preuss, *Exploring*, 4, 5.
18. JFC, *Report*, 11.
19. Ibid., 17, 18.
20. Ibid., 76; Preuss, *Exploring*, 57.
21. JCF, *Report*, 14; Preuss, *Exploring*, 32, 35.
22. JCF, *Report*, 13, 21.
23. Ibid., 19–23.
24. Ibid., 23.

25. Ibid., 27–29.
26. Ibid., 30, 35, 36.
27. Ibid., 40–44.
28. Ibid., 44–46.
29. JCF, *Memoirs*, 46, 47; JCF to Benton, Nov. 17, 1848, in JCF, *Expeditions*, III:73.
30. JCF, *Report*, 46–47.
31. Ibid., 47–48.
32. Ibid., 53.
33. Ibid., 54.
34. Ibid., 22, 54–57.
35. Ibid., 57–60.

7. FREMONT PEAK AND BACK

1. JCF, *Report*, 61–63; Irving, *Bonneville*, 44, 191; Preuss, *Exploring*, 33; Volpe, "Beyond a Literary Adventure," 15–28. For climbing gear, see JCF, *Expeditions*, I:142, 142–43n.
2. JCF, *Report*, 61, 62; JCF, *Expeditions*, I:257 n62.
3. JCF, *Report*, 62, 63.
4. JCF, *Report*, 63–66; JCF, *Memoirs*, 21.
5. JCF, *Report*, 66, 67; JCF, *Expeditions*, I:263 n63.
6. Preuss, *Exploring*, 40; JCF, *Report*, 66, 67.
7. Preuss, *Exploring*, 41.
8. JCF, *Report*, 68.
9. Preuss, *Exploring*, 43, 44. For debate over which peak JCF climbed, see JCF, *Expeditions*, I:270 n70; and Kelsey, *Wind River*, 174.
10. JCF, *Report*, 68.
11. JCF, *Report*, 68–79; Preuss, *Exploring*, 55, 56, 59; for Bellevue expenditures, see vouchers #3 and #4, in JCF, *Expeditions*, I:147, 148.

8. THE FIRST REPORT AND OREGON FEVER

1. JBF, "Memoirs," 38, 41; JBF, *Year of American Travel*, 24; the flag which John raised in the Rockies and brought back to Jessie can now be found in the Southwest Museum, in Los Angeles.
2. JBF, "Memoirs," 39, 40.
3. Benton, *Thirty Years' View*, II:579.
4. Frémont's injunction on the publication of journals, described in the diary of James Mulligan, participant in Frémont's 1853–54 railroad survey, in JCF, *Expeditions*, III:liv.
5. JCF, *Memoirs*, 162, 163; JCF to Torrey, Nov. 16, 1842, and Torrey to Gray, Nov. 18, 1842; JCF, *Expeditions*, I:128–30.
6. JBF, "Memoirs," 41–42.
7. Ibid., 41, 42; JCF, *Memoirs*, 163.
8. Publication history and excerpt from Abert's letter, in JCF, *Expeditions*, I:168–69.

9. Jackson, *Commentary*, 10, 11, in JCF, *Expeditions*, map portfolio.
10. Carver, *Travels*, 118, 542, in Allen, *Passage*, 26; Allen, *Passage*, 23, 23 n38, 24, 31; Jefferson, "Instructions to Captain Lewis," June 20, 1803, in Jefferson, *Writings*, 1126–32.
11. JCF, *Report*, 70.
12. For astute discussion of "dividing waters" theory, see Allen, *Passage*, 18, 19, 23, 26; Allen, "Division of the Water," [357]–370.
13. *U.S. Magazine and Democratic Review*, July 1845, 77.
14. Emerson, *Journals*, IX:431.
15. Morris, *American Heritage Dictionary*, 40.
16. Ms. in DNA-77, National Archives.
17. JCF, *Report*, 69, 70.
18. Bryant, "The Prairies," in *Poetical Works of William Cullen Bryant*, 133; Miller, "Overland," 43; Irving, *Tour of the Prairies*, 31, in Irving, *Astoria*, 62–67; Thacker, *Prairie Fact*, 116–17; Antelyes, *Tales of Adventurous Enterprise*, 125, 126; Preuss, *Exploring*, 49.
19. Miller, "Overland," 42–43; Longfellow, *Life*, II:65, 66; Whitman, *Leaves of Grass*, 322; Arvin, *Longfellow*, 106n.
20. *Niles National Register*, May 6, 1843.
21. Benton, *Thirty Years' View*, II:478.
22. Ibid., 469.
23. Ibid., 477.
24. Ibid., 579.
25. Abert to JCF, March 10, 1843, in JCF, *Expeditions*, I:160–61.
26. JBF, "Memoirs," 42–43; JCF, *Memoirs*, 165–66.
27. JCF to Kearny [ca. May 8, 1843], in JCF, *Expeditions*, I:343.
28. Bell correspondence, ibid., 343n, 344n; Abert to JCF, ibid., 344, 345; Abert to JCF, May 22, 1843, ibid., 345–346; JCF, *Memoirs*, 165–68; JBF, "Memoirs," 42–43.
29. Abert to JCF, May 22, 1843, in JCF, *Expeditions*, I:345, 346.
30. JBF, "Memoirs," 43, 44; JBF, "Origin," 768–69; JCF, *Memoirs*, 167–68.
31. JCF, *Memoirs*, 166–68; JBF, "Origin," 768–69.

9. RETURN TO THE ROCKIES, AND EXPLORATION OF GREAT SALT LAKE

1. Unruh, *Plains Across*, 119; JCF, *Report*, 105–107.
2. Ibid., 105, 107; Talbot, *Journal*, 40.
3. JCF, *Report*, 107, 109.
4. Ibid., 109, 111; Egan, *Frémont*, 136, 137; JCF, *Expeditions*, I:146, 147n.
5. JCF, *Report*, 111–14.
6. Ibid., 114–16.
7. Ibid., 116.
8. Ibid., 117–21; voucher #85, for lodge purchase, in JCF, *Expeditions*, I:381; Egan, *Frémont*, 142, 143.

9. JCF, *Report*, 121–23.
10. Ibid., 123–34.
11. Ibid., 132–39.
12. Ibid., 139–49.
13. Spence, "The Frémonts and Utah," 289; Ward, "Frémont's Explorations."
14. JCF, *Report*, 151–53.
15. Ibid., 153–57.
16. Ibid., 157–62.
17. Ibid., 162; Talbot, *Journals*, 50.
18. JCF, *Report*, 162–64; Talbot, *Journals*, 50–51.

10. OREGON

1. Preuss, *Exploring*, 92; JCF, *Report*, 164–65.
2. Ibid., 165, 166; Gilbert, *Walker*, 194.
3. JCF, *Report*, 167, 168.
4. Ibid., 170–77; Franzwa, *Oregon Trail Revisited*, 340.
5. Ibid., 175–76.
6. JCF, *Report*, 177–79.
7. Ibid., 178–184; Preuss, *Exploring*, 95, 96.
8. JCF, *Report*, 183–84.
9. Goetzmann, *Army Exploration*, 83–95; JCF, *Report*, 183–84.
10. Ibid., 184–87; Preuss, *Exploring*, 97–98; Goetzmann, *Exploration*, 92.
11. JCF, *Report*, 187–94.
12. Ibid., 187–92; Preuss, *Exploring*, 93–94.
13. JCF, *Report*, 193–94; Burnett, "Recollections," 85–87.
14. JCF, *Report*, 194–95; Burnett, "Recollections," 87.
15. JCF, *Report*, 195–97; Karnes, *Gilpin*, 104.

11. TO THE BANKS OF THE BUENAVENTURA

1. JCF, *Report*, 197–204; JCF, *Expeditions*, I:585n.
2. JCF, *Report*, 203, 204.
3. Ibid., 204.
4. Ibid., 204, 205.
5. Crampton and Griffen, "San Buenaventura," 163–71; Weber, *Spanish Frontier*, 256.
6. JCF, *Report*, 205; JCF, *Expeditions*, I:574 n85.
7. Benton, *Thirty Years' View*, II:580.
8. JCF, *Report*, 206, 207; Dellenbaugh, *Frémont and '49*, 190–91; JCF, *Expeditions*, I:590 n92.
9. JCF, *Report*, 207–11.
10. Ibid., 211–12.
11. Ibid., 196.
12. Ibid., 213–14.
13. Ibid., 215, 216.

14. Ibid., 216–18.
15. Ibid., 218–20. While Frémont specifically stated that, on Jan. 18, he had announced his intentions to lead the party over the Sierra into California, his account of that announcement makes no reference to his plan to proceed to Sutter's Fort. Preuss's journal, however, after recounting the party's southbound passage through Nevada's Granite Mountains, noted that on or about January 4, "it was decided to seek refuge with a Captain Sutter on the Sacramento River" (Preuss, *Exploring*, 105). Whatever the precise timing of Frémont's decisions to enter California and to visit Sutter's Fort, it seems obvious he had been pondering both for some time.

12. WINTER SIERRA

1. JCF, *Report*, 220; Nevins, *Pathmarker*, 150–51; Carson, "Memoirs," 89.
2. Nevins, *Pathmarker*, 151; JCF, *Report*, 219.
3. New York *Spectator*, Dec. 30, 1843 (reprinted from St. Louis *Republican*, Dec. 13, 1843).
4. JCF, *Report*, 219–29. For JCF's Sierra route, see Graham, *Crossing*, and Gianella, "Frémont." For search for cannon, see Allen, *High Up*.
5. Ibid., 229–31.
6. Ibid., 231–34; Preuss, *Exploring*, 108–109.
7. JCF, *Report*, 234–35.
8. Ibid., 235–37.
9. Ibid., 235–47.
10. The Mexican province—or, to employ the term then in use, the "department"—of Alta California actually included, in addition to today's U.S. state of California, much of today's state of Nevada. But Alta California east of the Sierra was sparsely settled by Californios, Spanish-speaking descendants of Iberian ancestry; and, in the common usage of that day, California generally referred to the realm west of the Sierra occupied by today's state of California. In this narrative as well, the term refers to that more restrictive usage.
11. Carson, "Memoirs," 90, 91; JCF, *Report*, 245–51; Sutter, "Diary," 9–10; Dillon, *Sutter*, 145–48.

13. CALIFORNIA IDYLL, AND BACK

1. JCF, *Report*, 248–57.
2. Frémont believed he was at Walker Pass, which lay about fifty air miles to the northeast—see JCF, *Expeditions*, I: 668 n149.
3. JCF, *Report*, 254–59; JCF, *Expeditions*, I:674 n154.
4. JCF, *Report*, 529; JCF, *Expeditions*, I:675 n156.
5. JCF, *Report*, 260; Morgan, *Smith*, 200.
6. JCF, *Report*, 261, 262; JCF, *Expeditions*, I:679 n161; Welsh, *Frémont*, vii, 92.
7. JCF, *Report*, 262–63 (Carson was actually born, in 1809, in Richmond, Kentucky); Preuss, *Exploring*, 127.
8. JCF, *Report*, 263–70.

9. Ibid., 270–71; Gilbert, *Walker*, 5, 6, 203.

10. JCF, *Report*, 271–74; Utah Lake, a freshwater body, lies about thirty miles south of the much larger Great Salt Lake; the two bodies are linked by the Jordan River, which drains into Great Salt Lake.

11. JCF, *Report*, 271–75.

12. For discussion of sublime in American life and art, see Chaffin, "Hart Crane and the American Sublime," 157–62.

13. JCF, *Report*, 276–77.

14. Ibid., 277–90.

14. THE PATHFINDER

1. JBF to Adelaide Talbot, Dec. 3, 1843, and Feb. 1, 1844, in JBF, *Letters*, 15–17; JBF, *Souvenirs*, 163–65; Herr, *Jessie Benton Frémont*, 93–97.

2. JCF, *Memoirs*, 411, 412.

3. Ibid., 412; Benton, *Thirty Years' View*, II:580; JCF to Wilkins, Aug. 28, 1844, in JCF, *Expeditions*, I:363, 364.

4. JCF, *Memoirs*, 414; JBF, "Memoirs," 46–48.

5. JCF, *Memoirs*, 413, 414; JBF, "Memoirs," 47, 48.

6. Thoreau, *Writings*, II:247; JCF, *Expeditions*, I:xix.

7. JBF to JCF, June 16, 1846, in JCF, *Expeditions*, II:150.

8. *U.S. Magazine and Democratic Review*, July 1845, 77; Cincinnati *Chronicle*, n.d., in *Niles National Register*, Feb. 1, 1843.

9. JCF, *Report*, 311.

10. For geographical contributions in the Second Expedition *Report*, see Donald Jackson's fine commentary on the map portfolio of *Expeditions of John Charles Frémont*.

11. JCF, *Memoirs*, 415, 416; JCF, *Report*, 172, 175, 275.

12. JCF *Report*, 255, 256, 277.

13. Ibid., 276, 277.

14. Gudde, "Frémont-Preuss," 169–81.

15. JCF, *Memoirs*, 418, 419.

16. Ibid., 421.

17. Talbot, *Journals*, 47.

18. Handlin, *Bancroft*, 210–14; Pletcher, *Diplomacy of Annexation*, 233, 234.

19. Abert to JCF, Feb. 12, 1845, in JCF, *Expeditions*, I:395–97.

15. GREAT SALT LAKE, GREAT BASIN, AND HUMBOLDT RIVER

1. JCF, *Memoirs*, 424; Martin, *With Frémont*, 2.

2. JCF, *Memoirs*, 424–25; Carvalho, *Incidents of Travel*, 18.

3. Talbot to his mother, Aug. 10, 1845, in Talbot, *Soldier in the West*, 28; Goetzmann, *Exploration and Empire*, 250.

4. JCF, *Memoirs*, 426–28; Martin, *With Frémont*, 4.

5. JCF, *Memoirs*, 429.

6. Ibid., 429, 430; Gilbert, *Walker*, 209–12; JCF, *Expeditions*, II:43 n4.
7. JCF, *Memoirs*, 431.
8. Martin, *With Frémont*, 5; JCF, *Memoirs*, 430.
9. JCF, *Memoirs*, 431–35.
10. Ibid., 436–38; Egan, *Frémont*, 302.
11. JCF, *Memoirs*, 438–39.

16. THE OPENING CLEAR BEFORE ME

1. JCF, *Memoirs*, 439.
2. Ibid., 439–40.
3. *Niles National Register*, June 7, 1845; JCF, *Memoirs*, 439–41.
4. Weber, *Mexican Frontier*, 36–37.
5. Population figures from Hart, *California Companion*, 338, except figure on foreign population, from Weber, *Mexican Frontier*, 206.
6. Weber, *Mexican Frontier*, 206.
7. *Niles National Register*, June 7, 1845.
8. Oct. 24, 1845, entry, in Polk, *Diary*, I:71–72.
9. Harlow, *California Conquered*, 56; Parrot to Buchanan, Sept. 2, 1845, in Manning, *Diplomatic Correspondence*, VIII, 748.
10. Bancroft to Sloat, June 24, 1845, in "Documentary," *California Historical Society Quarterly* [hereafter *CHSQ*], 2:164, 165; Bancroft to Sloat, Oct. 17, 1845, ibid., 2:167–70; Buchanan to Larkin, Oct. 17, 1845, in Larkin, *Papers*, IV:44–47.
11. California *Star*, May 15, 1847.
12. Bidwell, "Frémont in the Conquest of California," 518.
13. JCF, *Memoirs*, 442; Dillon, *Sutter*, 213–14.
14. JCF, *Memoirs*, 441–42.
15. Ibid., 442–48.
16. Ibid., 448–51; JCF to JBF, Jan. 24, 1846, in JCF, *Expeditions*, II:46–48.
17. JCF, *Memoirs*, 453, 454, 457; JCF, *Geographical Memoir*, 32n.
18. Larkin to Buchanan, March 27, 1846, in Larkin, *Papers*, IV:270–73; Larkin to William M. Rogers or Joel Giles, March 6, 1846, ibid., IV:233–34.
19. Castro to Larkin, Jan. 29, 1846; Larkin to Castro, Jan. 29, 1846, ibid., IV, 185–87.
20. JCF, *Memoirs*, 454.
21. Ibid., 454.
22. Edward Kern, journal, Feb. 1, 1846, in JCF, *Expeditions*, II:60; Theodore Talbot to Adelaide Talbot, July 24, 1846, in Talbot, *Soldier in the West*, 40.
23. Edward Kern, journal, Jan. 19, 1846, in JCF, *Expeditions*, II:58, 59; JCF, *Memoirs*, 456; JCF, *Expeditions*, II:62 n9; Bancroft, *History of California*, V:5.
24. José Dolores Pacheco to JCF, Feb. 20, 1846, letter unlocated but alluded to in JCF to José Dolores Pacheco, Feb. 21, 1846, in JCF, *Expeditions*, II:68, 70.
25. JCF to José Dolores Pacheco, Feb. 21, 1846, ibid., II: 68, 71.
26. JCF, *Memoirs*, 454.

27. Ibid., 456–59; José Castro proclamation [March 8, 1846], in JCF, *Expeditions*, II:81; Larkin to Castro and Castro, March 6, 1846, ibid., 76.
28. According to park officials at California's Frémont State Park, most park officials and local historians no longer believe that the park's namesake, Fremont Peak (3,171 feet), was the mountain where Frémont camped during his standoff with Castro's army.
29. JCF, *Memoirs*, 459, 460; Larkin to JCF, March 8, 1846, in JCF, *Expeditions*, II:78, 79.
30. JCF to Larkin [March 9, 1846], in JCF, *Expeditions*, II, 81, 82; Larkin to Manuel Díaz, March 10, 1846, ibid., 84.
31. JCF, *Memoirs*, 460; Gilbert, *Walker*, 215.
32. Larkin open letter, March 9, 1846, in Larkin, *Papers*, IV:243–44; Larkin to Buchanan, March 9, 1846, ibid., 242; Larkin to JCF, March 8, 1846, in JCF, *Expeditions*, II:78–79.

17. TO PROMOTE THIS OBJECT OF THE PRESIDENT

1. JCF, *Memoirs*, 470; Talbot, *Soldier in the West*, 42–43.
2. JCF, *Memoirs*, 470–75.
3. The approximate date of this attack upon the Indians remains a subject of debate. At least two participants, Kit Carson and Thomas Martin—echoed by historians Charles L. Camp, Barbara Warner, and Milo Milton Quaife—place it in early April, before Frémont's party left for Oregon. But in his *Memoirs*, Frémont implies that it occured a month or so later; Carson, *Carson in California* (with notes by Camp), 17, 18; Carson, *Autobiography*, 94, 94n; Martin, *With Frémont*, 7; Warner, *Men of Bear Flag Revolt*, 115; Carson, *Autobiography* (edited by Quaife), 94, 95 n82.
4. Martin, *With Frémont*, 7; Carson, *"Autobiography,"* 94, 95; JCF, *Memoirs*, 516, 517; JCF, *Conquest of California*, 924.
5. Ibid., 474–77.
6. Clyman, *Frontiersman*, 198; Clyman letter alluded to in JCF to Clyman, [April?, 1846], in JCF, *Expeditions*, II:131.
7. Hargrave, "California in 1846," 4, Bancroft Library.
8. Ibid., 4–6.
9. Ibid., 6.
10. JCF, *Memoirs*, 478; Dillon, *Sutter*, 234.
11. Martin, *With Frémont*, 7; Sutter, "Personal Reminiscences," 141–44, Bancroft Library ms.; Sutter to Castro, Apr. 1, 1846, alluded to in Sutter to Castro, May 13(?), 1846, in "Documentary," *CHSQ* 6:80–83.
12. JCF, *Memoirs*, 478–84; Chittenden, *American Fur Trade*, 286; JCF, *Report*, 205.
13. JCF, *Memoirs*, 486.
14. JCF, *Memoirs*, 478–88; Polk, *Diary*, I:83–84.
15. Gillespie to Bancroft, Dec. 13, 1845, in Gillespie, "Further Letters," *CHSQ* 18:219–22.
16. Gillespie to Bancroft, Jan. 16, 1846, in Gillespie, ibid., 18, 222–28.

17. Buchanan to Larkin, Oct. 17, 1845, in Larkin, *Papers*, IV:44–47; Gillespie to Bancroft, August 18, 1846, in Gillespie, "Gillespie and the Conquest of California," *CHSQ* 17:135–40.
18. Ibid., 135–40.
19. Larkin to Leidesdorff, Apr. 25, 1846, in Larkin, *Papers*, IV:348; and Sutter to Castro, May 31, 1846, summarized in Bancroft, *History of California*, V:29 n55.
20. Buchanan to JCF, Nov. 3, 1845, in JCF, *Expeditions*, II:127 n16; JCF, *Memoirs*, 488–90, 508.
21. JCF, *Memoirs*, 489, 490.

18. NEUTRAL CONQUEST

1. JCF, *Memoirs*, 490–92.
2. Ibid., 493–98; JCF to Benton, May 24, 1846, ibid., 499–500; JCF to Gillespie, May 25, 1846, ibid., 504.
3. Ibid., 500–503.
4. Ibid., 509.
5. Ibid.
6. JCF, "Geographical Memoir," 58; JCF, *Memoirs*, 510.
7. JCF, *Memoirs*, 509; Gillespie to Bancroft, July 25, 1846, in Ames, "Gillespie and the Conquest of California," 273, 274; Duvall, *Surgeon*, 22.
8. The party included Merritt, Henry L. Ford, Granville P. Swift, and Robert Semple. The Sacramento *Mercury*, June 25, 1858, lists additional members as Samuel Gibson, W. and T. Potter, Anderson Benson, John Sanders, [Thomas] Cockran, Sam Neil [*sic*], [Henry] Booker, and William Knight—from Rogers, *Ide*, 91 n50.
9. Ford, "Bear Flag Revolution," 2–4, Bancroft Library ms., 41–42; Larkin, "A Circular to Several Americans," July 8, 1846, in Larkin, *Papers*, V:119–21.
10. Larkin to Stearns, Apr. 12, 1845, ibid., III:127.
11. Larkin to Castro and Castro, June 14, 1846, ibid., V:20, 21.
12. Ide, William Brown, "History of . . . the 'Bear Flag Party' " [hereafter, Ide, "Memoirs"], in Ide, Simeon, *Who Conquered California*, 28–30. Although Ide recalled he reached Frémont's Sutter Buttes camp on June 10, other evidence suggests an earlier meeting. According to Frémont, the party left that camp on June 8 (JCF, *Memoirs*, 518).
13. Ide, "Memoirs," 34, 35.
14. According to Ide ("Memoirs," 32–37), Merritt's party returned to Frémont's camp on the evening of June 10 and that same night, around midnight, departed for Sonoma. The departure date for Sonoma, however, has been reliably established as June 12.
15. Martin, *With Frémont*, 12–13.

19. BEAR FLAG

1. U.S. Senate, "California Claims," 13, 55; court-martial testimony, in JCF, *Expeditions*, II, Supplement [hereafter IIS], 374; JCF, *Memoirs*, 508, 509.

2. Ibid., 509; Duvall, *Journal*, 22.
3. Ide, "Memoirs," 35.
4. Edward Kern to Richard Kern, July 29, 1846, Fort Sutter Papers, Huntington Library; JCF, *Memoirs*, 520.
5. Polk to Benton, Sept. 1, 1847, Polk Papers, Library of Congress.
6. Hargrave, "California in 1846," 6–7.
7. Vallejo, "History of the Bear Party," n.p.; Rosenus, *Vallejo*, 108–91; Rogers, *Ide*, 35, 41–46; Ide, "Memoirs," 40–58.
8. Duvall, *Journal*, 20.
9. Ibid., 21–22; JCF to Montgomery, June 16, 1846, in JCF, *Expeditions*, II:151–53.
10. Rogers, *Ide*, 47–48; Montgomery to Frémont, June 10, 1846; JCF to Montgomery, June 16, 1846, in JCF, *Expeditions*, II:146–47, 151–53.
11. Duvall, *Journal*, 21.
12. Bidwell, "Frémont in the Conquest of California," 518–20; JCF, *Memoirs*, 520.
13. Ibid., 521–22; Harlow, *California Conquered*, 109; Bancroft, *History of California*, V:170; *California Claims*, 27, 34; Larkin to Buchanan, July 18, 1846, in Larkin, *Papers*, V:139–42.
14. Marshall, in San Jose *Pioneer*, June 7, 1879, in Rogers, *Ide*, 52.
15. Bancroft, *History of California*, V:170–76; ibid., 172 n2; JCF to Benton, July 25, 1846, in JCF, *Expeditions*, II:183, 184; ibid., 186 n6.
16. JCF, *Memoirs*, 525, 526, 530; Harlow, *California Conquered*, 111, 112.
17. JCF, *Memoirs*, 526, 530, 531; Frémont to Benton, July 25, 1846, in JCF, *Expeditions*, II:181–85; Sloat to Frémont, July 9, 1846, ibid., 168–70; Harlow, *California Conquered*, 111–13.

20. A PAWN FOR EMPIRE

1. Jones, "Pacific Squadron," 191–93; Harlow, *California Conquered*, 118, 119; Sloat's July 7, 1846, proclamation, in Manning, *Diplomatic Correspondence*, VIII: 877 n1.
2. Bancroft, *History of California*, V:230–33; Harlow, *California Conquered*, 123–25.
3. Castro to Pico, July 11, 1846, in "Documentary: The Occupation," *CHSQ*, III:185–86; Bancroft, *History of California*, V:262–63.
4. McLane, *Private Journal*, 84; Gillespie to Navy Secretary, July 25, 1846, in Gillespie, "Gillespie and the Conquest," *CHSQ*, XVII, 277–78; Walpole, Fred., *Four Years in the Pacific*, in JCF, *Memoirs*, 533–34; ibid., 532–53.
5. See Adams, "English Interest," 744–63.
6. JCF, *Expeditions*, II:476 n1.
7. JCF, *Memoirs*, 534–36.
8. Ibid., 544; Stockton to JCF [July 22, 1846], in JCF, *Expeditions*, II:174; Stockton to JCF, July 23, 1846, ibid., 178; Frémont to Benton, July 25, 1846, ibid., 181–85; Harlow, *California Conquered*, 139, 140.
9. Bancroft, *History of California*, V:267; JCF, *Memoirs*, 562–65; Harlow, *California Conquered*, 145, 146.
10. Stockton proclamation, July 29, 1846, in Larkin, *Papers*, V:175–77.

11. Stockton to JCF, Aug. 6, 1846, in JCF, *Expeditions*, II:188, 189; Larkin to Stearns, Aug. [6] 1846, in Larkin, *Papers*, V:184–86.

12. Larkin to Stearns, Aug. 7, 1846, ibid., V:187.

13. Stockton to Castro, Aug. 7, 1846, in Bancroft, *History of California*, 269 n16. For more background on Stockton's naval operations in California, see U.S. Senate, *Report of Secretary of the Navy*, 30th Congress, 2nd Session, Executive, No. 31.

14. Castro to Pico, Aug. 9, 1846, in "Pico's Correspondence," *CHSQ*, XIII:118–19.

15. JCF, *Memoirs*, 566; Talbot to his mother, Aug. 29, 1846, in Theodore Talbot Papers, Library of Congress.

16. Stockton Proclamation, Aug. 17, 1846, in Polk, *Occupation of Mexican Territory*, 29:2, *House Executive Document*, 19, 107–108; Harlow, *California Conquered*, 147–50; JCF, *Memoirs*, 566, 567.

17. Stockton to Polk, Aug. 26, 1846, in JCF, *Expeditions*, II:193–95.

18. Stockton to JCF, Aug. 24, 27, 31 (three letters), 1846, ibid., 192, 193, 196, 198–200.

21. COMMANDANT OF THE TERRITORY

1. JCF, *Memoirs*, 570–73; Gillespie to Bancroft, Feb. 16, 1847, in Gillespie, "Gillespie and the Conquest of California," *CHSQ* 17:283, 284.

2. McLane, *Private Journal*, 86.

3. JCF, *Memoirs*, 572–77.

4. Bancroft, *History of California*, V:322–25; JCF, *Memoirs*, 573–82; Harlow, *California Conquered*, 168–73.

5. JCF to Stockton [Oct. 27, 1846], in JCF, *Expeditions*, II:211–12.

6. Montgomery to Kern, Oct. 15, 1846, Ft. Sutter Papers, Huntington Library; Bancroft, *History of California*, V, 358–59; Herr, *Jessie Benton Frémont*, 171, 172.

7. JCF to Mervine, Nov. 16, 1846, in JCF, *Expeditions*, II:227.

8. JCF, *Memoirs*, 595.

9. Harlow, *California Conquered*, 220–21.

10. Ibid., 222–23; Ames, "Horse Marines," 72–84; McLane, *Private Journal*.

11. Bryant, *What I Saw*, 366–67.

12. JCF to Mervine, Nov. 27, 1846, in JCF, *Expeditions*, II:233–34.

13. Frémont to Mervine, Nov. 27, 1846, ibid.

14. JCF, *Memoirs*, 594–99; Kemble, *Reader*, 99.

15. JCF, *Memoirs*, 599–601; JCF to Stockton, Jan. 3, 1847, ibid., 601; JCF to Stockton, Jan. 2, 1847, in JCF, *Expeditions*, II:249.

16. Harlow, *California Conquered*, 174–92.

17. JCF, *Memoirs*, 601; McLane, *Private Journal*, 102.

18. JCF, *Memoirs*, 601, 602; Bancroft, *History of California*, V:404, 405 n26; for Treaty of Cahuenga, see JCF, *Expeditions*, II:253–54.

22. GOVERNOR FRÉMONT

1. Bryant, "What I Saw," 393, 394; Stockton proclamation [Jan. 16, 1847], in JCF, *Expeditions*, II:267; Kearny to Stockton, Jan. 16, 1847, in JCF, *Expeditions*, II:263.

2. Stockton to Kearny, Jan. 16, 1847, ibid., II:264.

3. Emory to JCF, Jan. 16, 1847; Marcy to Kearny, June 18, 1846, ibid., II:265, 266.

4. Kearny to JCF, Jan. 17 [1847], in JCF, *Expeditions*, II:268; JCF to Kearny, Jan. 17, 1847, ibid., 268–69; Kearny testimony in JCF, *Expeditions*, IIS:238–39.

5. Kearny testimony, in JCF *Expeditions*, IIS:39; Stockton's proclamation [Jan. 16, 1847], ibid., II:267; JCF's proclamation [Jan. 22, 1847], ibid., 275; JCF to Wilson, Jan. 25, 1847, ibid., 280; Harlow, *California Conquered*, 241; JCF testimony, in JCF, *Expeditions*, IIS:422.

6. Griffin, "Diary," n.p., California Historical Society ms.

7. Mason's orders to Kearny were stated in a letter from the Navy Secretary to outgoing Commodore Stockton, a copy of which was sent to Kearny. See John Mason to Stockton, Nov. 5, 1846, in JCF, *Expeditions*, IIS:51–53; Kearny testimony, ibid., IIS:102

8. Shubrick-Kearny proclamation [March 1, 1847], in JCF, *Expeditions*, II:313; Kearny proclamation [March 1, 1847], ibid., 314–15; Kearny to JCF, March 1, 1847, ibid., 310.

9. Kearny to JCF, March 1, 1847, ibid., 310; "Orders No. 2"—Turner to JCF, March 1, 1847, ibid., II:311, 312.

10. Cooke to JCF, March 14, 1847, ibid., II:320; Russell to JCF, March 16, 1847, ibid., II:323.

11. JCF, *California Claims*, 14, 15.

12. Bancroft, *History of California*, V:435; JCF testimony in JCF, *Expeditions* IIS:422.

13. Harlow, *California Conquered*, 256–58; Dellenbaugh, *Frémont*, 374–76.

14. Kearny testimony and Frémont testimony in JCF, *Expeditions*, IIS:104–106, 422, 423; Bancroft, *History of California*, V:443, 444.

15. Harlow, *California Conquered*, 262, 263; Kearny to JCF, May 4, 1847, in JCF, *Expeditions*, II:350–51, 103.

16. Bancroft, *History of California*, V:445–52; Frémont testimony in JCF, *Expeditions*, IIS:274–76, 282. For burial of Donner party corpses, see JCF, *Expeditions*, II:xxxix, xxxix n36.

17. Bigelow, *Frémont*, 214–17; JBF, "Memoirs," 60; Upham, *Frémont*, 270.

18. Polk, June 7, 1847, *Diary*, III:52–53; see also Benton, "Benton Lays his Plans," *CHSQ* 8 (1934), 150–54.

19. Polk, Aug. 17, 1847, ibid., III:120–22.

20. JCF, testimony in JCF, *Expeditions*, IIS:446.

21. JBF, "Memoirs," 53.

23. MEASURING THE EMPIRE

1. Chaffin, *Fatal Glory*, 18–21, 41–43; Webster, *Writings and Speeches*, XVI:423.

2. JBF, "Memoirs," 60; Easterby, *College of Charleston*, 82; "Trustees Minutes," March 10, 1836 [typescript copy], 143, at College of Charleston.

3. Bigelow, *Fremont*, 379–80; JBF, "Great Events," 78.

4. Benton, in Elizabeth Blair Lee to S. P. Lee, Aug. 8, 1848, Blair-Lee Papers, Princeton University; Herr, *Jessie Benton Frémont*, 175.

5. JBF, "Memoirs," 52, 60; JCF, *Expeditions*, III:495–96.

6. Rhoads, in JCF, ibid., III:495.

7. JCF, *Geographical Memoir*, 10.

8. Ibid., 43.

9. Ibid., 14.

10. Ibid., 15, 16.

11. Ibid., 43; for discussion of Mediterranean parallels in California life, see 294–98 and Chapter 12, "An American Mediterranean," 365–414, in Starr, *Americans and the California Dream*; JCF, *Expeditions*, commentary for map portfolio, 15, 16.

12. For Benton-JCF-Wilkes exchanges in *National Intelligencer*, see JCF, *Expeditions*, III:5–6, 16–34; JCF, *Expeditions*, III:xx–xxi.

13. *De Bow's Review*, July 1849, 32.

14. Hafen, *Disaster*, 16–19; Benton speech, ibid., 18.

15. Benton speech, ibid., 18–19.

16. JCF, *Expeditions*, III:xxii.

17. JBF to Carson [May 1863], in JBF, *Letters of JBF*, 352, 353; New York *Herald*, Oct. 13, 1848.

18. JCF, *Expeditions*, III:xxii; Martin, *With Frémont*, 23.

19. JCF to Benton, Nov. 17, 1848, in JCF, *Expeditions*, III:72.

20. Cathcart to C.J. Colville, Oct. 30, 1848, ibid., III:65–66.

21. Richard Kern, "Diary," and Edward Kern, "Diary," in Hafen, *Disaster*, 115, 294.

22. Richard Kern, "Diary," in Hafen, *Disaster*, 115, 116; Cathcart to Colville, Nov. 17, 1848, in JCF, *Expeditions*, III:68; Edward Kern, "Diary," in Hafen, *Disaster*, 294.

23. JCF to Benton, Nov. 17, 1848, in JCF, *Expeditions*, III:73.

24. Edward Kern to "Mary," Feb. 10, 1849, in Hafen, *Disaster*, 217; McGehee, "Narrative," ibid., 146.

25. McGehee, "Narrative," in ibid., 143–46; Utley, *Life Wild and Perilous*, 105; Lamar, *New Encyclopedia of the American West*, 1219.

26. Lupton to Benton, Nov. 28, 1848, in Hafen, *Disaster*, 284.

27. This cursory account of the 1848–49 railway survey's intentions and various locations relies on conclusions reached by Colorado historian Patricia Richmond in her prodigious reconstruction of the expedition—drawn from eighteen years of research in documents and firsthand examination of the mountains through which the expedition passed—published in her 1989 book, *Trail to Disaster*.

28. JCF to JBF, Jan. 27, 1849, JCF, *Expeditions*, III:76.

29. McGehee, "Narrative," in Hafen, *Disaster*, 152.

30. JCF to JBF, Jan. 27, 1849, in JCF, *Expeditions*, III:77.

31. Breckenridge, "Reminiscence," in Hafen, *Disaster*, 184.
32. McGehee, "Narrative," ibid., 159.
33. JCF to JBF, Jan. 27, 1849, JCF, *Expeditions*, III:79.
34. JBF, "Great Events," 84; Preuss, *Exploring*, 149.
35. JCF to JBF, Jan. 27, 1849, in JCF, *Expeditions*, III:79.
36. JCF to JBF, Jan. 27, 1849, ibid., III:84.
37. Preuss, *Exploring*, 144; JCF to JBF, Jan. 27, 1849, in JCF, *Expeditions*, III:76, 80.
38. JBF, "Great Events," 94, 97–99; JBF, *Year of American Travel*, 80, 81; JCF, "Notes," in JCF, *Expeditions*, III:51.
39. Ibid., xxxiii; Breckenridge, "Famous Expedition," 400–408.
40. JBF, "Memoirs," 59.
41. JBF, *Year of American Travel*, 12–13.
42. JBF, "Great Events," 77.
43. The Account of Jessie and company's Isthmus transit is drawn from, JBF, *Year of American Travel*, [chapter four] "Twixt Two Unbounded Seas," 55–63; Elizabeth Benton Frémont, *Recollections*, Chapter 2, "Across the Isthmus of Panama in Forty-Nine," 11–24; JBF, "Memoirs," 61–63; JBF, "Great Events," 102–108.
44. JCF to JBF, Jan. 27, 1849, in JCF, *Expeditions*, III:75.
45. JBF, "Great Events," 108, 109.
46. JBF, *Year of American Travel*, 66–68.
47. Ibid., 67, 68; Talbot H. Green to Thomas Larkin, June 19, 1849, Larkin, *Papers*, VIII:245, 246.
48. JBF, "Great Events," 119.
49. For a summary of Las Mariposas operations, see JCF, *Expeditions*, III:xxxix–lii.
50. Taylor, *Adventures*, 53.
51. Elizabeth Benton Frémont, *Recollections*, 25, 26.
52. David Alan Johnson, *Founding the Far West*, 39. While it's clear that the Frémonts worked on behalf of an antislavery state constitution, there is some doubt as to whether they were in Monterey for the constitutional convention—see ibid., 396 n97.
53. JCF, *Expeditions*, III:xxxv; JBF, *Year of American Travel*, 96–98, 103, 104; Johnson, *Founding the Far West*, 242–43.

24. THE WAGES OF EMPIRE, AND THE FINAL EXPEDITION

1. Benton speech, Feb. 7, 1849, in Hafen, *Disaster*, 49–73.
2. JCF to Thomas Hart Benton, Nov. 17, 1848, in Bigelow, *Fremont*, 360.
3. JBF, "Great Events," 153, 154; Herr, *Jessie Benton Frémont*, 219, 220.
4. JBF to Francis Preston Blair, Aug. 14, 1851, in JBF, *Letters of JBF*, 45–48.
5. JFB, "Great Events," 165–79; Herr, *Jessie Benton Frémont*, 228–31; JBF, *Letters of JBF*, 52n; for more on Frémont's European sojourn, see JBF, *Souvenirs*, 209–314.
6. JBF, *Letters of JBF*, 33n.

7. Richmond, *Trail to Disaster*, 10, 11; Goetzmann, *Exploration and Empire*, 286–88.

8. Carvalho, *Incidents*, 29–33; for identification of William Palmer, see JCF, *Expeditions*, III:404 n7; JBF to Elizabeth Blair Lee, Oct. 14, 1853, in *Letters of JBF*, 53, 54.

9. JBF to Elizabeth Blair Lee, Oct. 14 [1853], ibid., 53, 54.

10. Carvalho, *Incidents*, 34; JBF to Elizabeth Blair Lee, Oct. 14, 1853, in JBF, *Letters of JBF*, 53, 54.

11. Carvalho, *Incidents*, 34–59.

12. Ibid., 59–79; JCF, *Expeditions*, III:lvi.

13. Carvalho, *Incidents*, 80–95.

14. Ibid., 96–97.

15. Ibid., 97, 98.

16. Ibid., 98.

17. Ibid., 133, 134.

18. Ibid., 99–127.

19. Ibid., 128–36.

20. Ibid., 135–45; Babbitt letter, San Francisco *Daily Herald*, March 15, 1854, in JCF, *Expeditions*, III:469 n1; Nevins, *Pathmarker*, 418.

21. JCF to Benton, Feb. 9 and Feb. 9, 1854, both in JCF, *Expeditions*, III:468–71.

22. Schlaer's images appear in Shlaer, *Sights Once Seen*.

23. For these final details and other geographical background in this chapter, see JCF to *National Intelligencer*, June 13, 1854, in JCF, *Expeditions*, III:480–83; for help in reconstructing the exploring party's route during this expedition, the author is grateful to Colorado historian Patricia Richmond, with whom he had extensive conversations.

25. FREE SOIL, FREE MEN, FRÉMONT

1. JBF, *Letters of JBF*, 59 n1.

2. Chambers, *Benton*, 404–408; JCF, *Memoirs*, xvii.

3. JBF to Francis Blair, Nov. 3 [1855], in JBF, *Letters of JBF*, 73, 74; ibid., 74 n2; Herr, *Jessie Benton Frémont*, 239; JBF to Elizabeth Blair Lee, "sat morning July 1855" and n.d. [after May 17], Blair-Lee Papers, Princeton University.

4. JBF, "Great Events," 192; JBF, "Memoirs," 92, 93; Gienapp, *Origins of the Republican Party*, 318.

5. JBF, "Great Events," 193, 194; Gienapp, *Origins of the Republican Party*, 318, 321.

6. Bigelow, *Retrospections*, I:141–43.

7. Greeley to Charles Dana, March 20, 1856, in Greeley, *Greeley on Lincoln*, 133.

8. Greeley, *Autobiography*, 354.

9. Gienapp, *Origins of the Republican Party*, 307–16; JBF, "Great Events," 192, 193.

10. JBF, "Great Events," 192, 193; JCF to Thomas Ford, June 15 [1856], John Bigelow Papers, New York Public Library.

11. Gienapp, *Origins of the Republican Party*, 330.

12. Morgan to Gideon Welles, Sept. 1, 1856, Gideon Welles Papers, Library of Congress; for detailed account of Johnston's withdrawal from race, see Gienapp, *Origins of the Republican Party*, 383–86.

13. Upham, *Fremont*, 359, 363.

14. Sears, *Slidell*, 135, 136; Brooks, in New York *Evening Post*, Oct. 9, 1856.

15. *National Intelligencer*, Oct. 21, 1856.

16. Chambers, *Benton*, 419–20.

17. JBF to Elizabeth Blair Lee, Apr. 25 [1856], in JBF, *Letters of JBF*, 99–100.

18. St. Louis *Leader*, Nov. 4, 1856; Nevins, *Ordeal of the Union*, I:500, 501.

19. JBF to Elizabeth Blair Lee, Aug. 12 [1856], in JBF, *Letters of JBF*, 124–27.

20. Bennett, *Whittier*, 240, 241; JCF, *Expeditions*, III:lxxvii.

21. Gienapp, *Origins of the Republican Party*, 376; Nevins, *Pathmarker*, 442.

22. JBF to Elizabeth Blair Lee [Apr. 18 (1856)], in JBF, *Letters of JBF*, 97–98.

23. Nevins, *Ordeal of the Union*, II:503; published letter from S. G. Goodrich, a former U.S. consul in Paris, in undated (c. early 1850s) clip from unidentified newspaper, in John Bigelow Papers, New York Public Library.

24. William Cullen Bryant to John Howard Bryant, Oct. 14, 1856, in Bryant, *Letters of William Cullen Bryant*, III:395, 396; ibid. 394n; Douglass, *Life and Writings of Frederick Douglass*, II:401.

25. Bigelow, *Fremont*, 20, 21; for good general background on the 1856 Frémont campaign, see Clapp, *Bigelow*, Chapter 26, "A New Party, Campaigning for Frémont," 94–107. For background on Pryor's unsuccessful divorce petition, see JCF, *Expeditions*, I:xxiii n4.

26. Richmond, *Dispatch*, n.d. [1856], quoted in clip from unidentified newspaper, n.d. [1856], in John Bigelow Papers, New York Public Library. Notes from JBF's genealogical research into Frémont's family are found in "Mrs. Fremont's Memorials of the Family of Col. Fremont [*sic*]," in John Bigelow Papers, New York Public Library.

27. Henry M. Field to Bigelow, Sept. 15, 1856, ibid.

28. Preston King to Gideon Welles, March 3, Apr. 9, 21, 1860, Welles Papers, Library of Congress; and Welles to Francis Preston Blair, Apr. 9, 1860, Blair Papers, Library of Congress; Clapp, *Bigelow*, 107; JBF, *Letters of JBF*, 181 n5; JBF, "Great-Events," 202.

29. JBF to Elizabeth Blair Lee, Nov. 18 [1856], in JBF, *Letters of JBF*, 143–45; JBF to Elizabeth Blair Lee, Jan. 11, 1858, ibid., 182–84.

30. JBF to Elizabeth Blair Lee, Nov. 18 [1856], ibid., 143–45.

31. JBF to Elizabeth Blair Lee, July 19, 1857, ibid., 160–63.

32. Chambers, *Benton*, 434; JBF, "Great Events," 207; JBF to Elizabeth Blair Lee, Nov. 4, 1857, JBF, *Letters of JBF*, 174, 174 n1, 175; Elizabeth Benton Frémont, *Recollections*, 81.

33. Chambers, *Benton*, 434, 439; JBF, *Letters of JBF*, 193 n1.

34. JBF to Elizabeth Blair Lee, Apr. 24 [1858], ibid., 194–96; ibid., 196 n3. Las Mariposas described in JBF, ibid., 187–90.

35. Ibid., 187; Starr, *Americans and the California Dream*, 369.
36. JBF to Francis Preston Blair, July 2, 1859, in JBF, *Letters of JBF*, 214–17; Elizabeth Benton Frémont, *Recollections*, 110–14.
37. Isely, *Greeley*, 207–208; JBF, "Great Events," 214.
38. JBF to Banks, Aug. 20, 1859, in JBF, *Letters of JBF*, 219–21; Greeley to New York *Daily News*, Oct. 7, 1859, ibid., 226 n2.
39. JBF to Elizabeth Blair Lee, Sept. 4, 1859, ibid., 189.
40. JBF to Elizabeth Blair Lee, Nov. 15, 1859, ibid., 221–25.
41. Indeed, for several decades, Frémont claimed, during his earliest years in California, to have purchased Alcatraz Island and, as late as the 1880s, sought, to no avail, to press that claim upon the U.S. government (JCF, *Expeditions*, III:lxxi, 117n). For an account of other Frémont land claims in and around San Francisco, see ibid., lxx–lxxiv.
42. JBF to Elizabeth Blair Lee, June 2, 1860, in JBF, *Letters of JBF*, 227–29.
43. JBF to Elizabeth Blair Lee, Aug. 17, 1858, ibid., 211; Clark, Galen, MS: "Reminiscences, 1880," 6, Bancroft Library.
44. JBF to Beale [May 21, 1861], in JBF, *Letters of JBF*, 239, 239 n1; Herr, *Jessie Benton Frémont*, 314, 315.
45. Billings to Trenor W. Park, Jan. 14, Feb. 22, 1861, in Park-McCullough Papers, University of Vermont.

26. GENERAL FRÉMONT

1. Nicolay and Hay, *Lincoln*, IV:401, 402.
2. JBF, "Great Events," n.p.; McMaster, *United States During Lincoln's Administration*, 190, 191.
3. Parrish, *Frank Blair*, 112–13.
4. Nevins, *Pathmarker*, 494; Foote, *Civil War*, I:90; JBF, *Souvenirs*, 166; Herr, *Jessie Benton Frémont*, 326–27.
5. JBF, "Great Events," 222; Nicolay and Hay, *Lincoln*, IV:403, 404.
6. JBF to Elizabeth Blair Lee, July 27 [1861], in JBF, *Letters of JBF*, 255–56.
7. Scott, *War of the Rebellion . . . Official Records*, III:466–67.
8. JCF to Thomas Ford, June 15 [1856], John Bigelow Papers, New York Public Library.
9. Lincoln to JCF, Sept. 2, 1861, in Nicolay and Hay, *Lincoln*, IV:418.
10. JCF to Lincoln, Sept. 8, 1861, ibid., IV:418, 419.
11. Lincoln to JCF, Sept. 11, 1861, ibid., IV:420.
12. Lincoln to Hunter, Sept. 9, 1861, ibid., IV:413.
13. JBF, "Great Events," 270, 271; Tarbell, *Lincoln*, III:65.
14. JBF, "Great Events," 272.
15. Testimony of Schuyler Colfax, March 7, 1862, in *Congressional Globe*, 1128.
16. JBF, *Story of the Guard*, 73, 85.
17. Tarbell, *Lincoln*, II:67, 68. For a detailed account of Lincoln-Frémont tensions over the Department of the West, see ibid., Chapter 24, "The Failure of Frémont."

18. New York *Herald*, Nov. 8, 1861.
19. Ibid.
20. Gerteis, *Civil War St. Louis*, 153; for an astute account of Frémont's generalship in Missouri, see ibid., chapter 5, "A Passion for Seeming," 126–61. See also "Frémont's Hundred Days in Missouri," *Atlantic Monthly* (1862), ix:115–125, 247–58, 372–84; JBF, "Great Events," 267.
21. Bennett, *Whittier*, 275.
22. JBF, "Great Events," 325–29.

27. MOSES UNREDEEMED
1. Elizabeth Benton Frémont, *Recollections*, 76.
2. New York *Times*, Sept. 18, 1890; Ritter, "Richest Colony," 565; JBF to George W. Childs, Jan. 24, 1875, in JBF, *Letters of JBF*, 425, 426; see also ibid., 387, 426n.
3. Ibid., 387–39; JCF to Bierstadt, April 8 [circa 1865], in Joseph Downs Manuscript Collection, Winterthur Museum; Anderson and Ferber, *Bierstadt*, 34, 35, 181; Olmsted to John Olmsted, Oct. 20, 1865, in Roper, *Olmsted*, 245.
4. JBF, *Letters of JBF*, 389, 390.
5. JCF to Ream, Saturday morning [Oct. 2, 1869] and n.d. [Oct. 3, 1869], Vinnie Ream Hoxie Papers, Library of Congress; Herr, *Jessie Benton Frémont*, 388, 389.
6. Bigelow to W. H. Huntington, Aug. 20, 1870, in Bigelow, *Retrospections*, IV:398, 399; JBF, *Letters of JBF*, 390, 391; Herr, *Jessie Benton Frémont*, 390.
7. JBF to Alexander K. McLure, June 25, 1877, in JBF, *Letters of JBF*, 431–33. For more, see Miner, *Transcontinental Railroad*, 43–59; Taylor, *Franco-Texan Land Company*, [3]-62; and JBF, *Letters of JBF*, 388–89.
8. Poem in JBF, "Great Events," n.p.; an account of the poem's publication in JBF to Whittier, Jan. 21–22 [1880], in JBF, *Letters of JBF*, 479–82.
9. Canal plan from New York *Herald*, as reprinted in unidentified newspaper, Frémont Collection, Southwest Museum; Elizabeth Blair Lee to Samuel Phillips Lee, July 21 [1883], in Blair-Lee Papers, Princeton University; JBF's sister Elizabeth quoted in same letters.
10. JBF, *Letters of JBF*, 440–44.

28. THE LEGACIES OF EMPIRE
1. Polk, *Diary*, IV:375–76.
2. Bancroft, *Seward*, II:486.
3. Ferguson, "2011," 79.
4. Carson, "Memoirs," 125, 126, 126 n256.

EPILOGUE, 1887–90
1. Hart, *California Companion*, 242.
2. JBF, "Additions to the Memoirs," n.p.
3. Herr, *Jessie Benton Frémont*, 436, 437, 441.
4. Morrison, Patt, "Ghost of a Chance," Los Angeles *Times*, Apr. 23, 1999.

BIBLIOGRAPHY

MANUSCRIPT COLLECTIONS

California Historical Society: John Strother Griffin Diary.

California State Library, Sacramento: Pierson Barton Reading Collection, Pioneer Manuscript Collection, miscellaneous manuscripts, United States Army, California Battalion of Mounted Riflemen muster rolls, 1846–47.

Society of California Pioneers, San Francisco: Archives.

College of Charleston, College Archives: Board of Trustees Minutes, Academic Affairs-Registrar-Grades files.

Copley Library, La Jolla, California: John Frémont Papers, Jessie Benton Frémont Papers.

Duke University: John Charles Frémont Papers.

Huntington Library: S. L. M. Barlow Papers, Henry Dalton Collection, Harbeck Collection, Fort Sutter Papers, William Alexander Leidesdorff Collection, Josiah Royce Letters, Abel Stearns Papers, and various letters and other materials in the Huntington Manuscripts Collection.

Library of Congress: Blair Papers, Edward William Bok Papers, Horace Greeley Papers, Vinnie Ream Hoxie Papers, Miscellaneous Manuscripts Collection, Joseph Nicollet Papers, Joel Poinsett Papers, James K. Polk Papers, Horace Sawyer Papers, Theodore Talbot Papers, Gideon Welles Papers.

Missouri Botanical Garden Library, St. Louis: John Frémont Collection.

Missouri Historical Society: Abert Papers, Thomas Hart Benton Papers, Chouteau Collections, Andrew Drips Papers, Marius Duvall Papers, Rufus Easton Papers.

National Archives: DNA-77, Records of the Office of the Chief of Engineers, DNA-107, Records of the Office of the Secretary of War.

New York Botanical Garden: John Torrey Papers.

New-York Historical Society: John Frémont, Jessie Benton Frémont, and Thomas Hart Benton files, in Miscellaneous Manuscripts, James Wright Brown Collection.

New York Public Library: John Bigelow Papers, "U.S.S. Congress" Log, John

Charles and Jessie (Benton) Frémont file in Personal Miscellaneous Manuscripts, Horace Greeley Papers, Ferdinand R. Hassler Papers, David Hoffman Papers, Lee Kohns Collection, Thomas F. Madigan Collection.
Princeton University: Blair-Lee Papers.
South Carolina Historical Society: "Annual Report of the President and Directors of the Louisville, Cincinnati and Charleston Rail Road [1837]" in Miscellaneous manuscripts.
Southwest Museum, Los Angeles: Frémont Collection.
University of California, Berkeley, Bancroft Library: Galen Clark "Reminiscences," Hubert Howe Bancroft Miscellaneous Manuscripts, Alfred Baldwin Recollections, James Alexander Forbes Papers, Henry L. Ford: "The Bear Flag Revolution," John Charles Frémont Papers, Frémont Family Papers, Jessie Frémont: "Memoirs" and "Additions to the Memoirs." Jessie Frémont and John Charles Frémont II: MS. "Great Events during the life of General John C. Frémont . . . and of Jessie Benton Frémont." William Gilpin Dictation and Biographical Material, John Grigsby Papers, William H. Hargrave Statements: "Recollections" and "California in 1846," John Hittell Papers, Simeon Ide Papers, Thomas Oliver Larkin Papers, Joseph William McKay Recollections, Jacques Antoine Moerenhout Papers, Henry Lebbeus Oak Correspondence and Papers, Isaac Pettijohn Diary, José de Jesús Pico Papers, Charles Preuss Diaries and Related Materials, Johann Sutter: "Personal Reminiscences." Rosalía Vallejo: "History of the Bear Party."
University of California, Los Angeles: University Library, Department of Special Collections: Archibald Gillespie Papers.
University of Kentucky, Special Collections: Preston-Johnston Papers.
University of Vermont, Special Collections: Park-McCollough Archives.
Henry Francis du Pont Winterthur Museum, Winterthur, Delaware: Joseph Downs Manuscript Collection.

U.S. GOVERNMENT DOCUMENTS AND PUBLICATIONS

Frémont, John Charles. *Northern Boundary of Missouri*. 27th Congress, 3rd Session. H. R. Doc. 38 [Serial 420].
Frémont, John Charles, et al. *California Claims*. 30th Congress, 1st Session, U.S. Senate, Report No. 75. February 23, 1848 [Serial 416].
Frémont, John Charles, et al. *Geographical Memoir Upon Upper California* . . . 30th Congress, 1st Session. Senate Misc. Document 148. Washington, D.C.: Wendell and Van Benthuysen, 1848 [Serial 511].
Frémont, Lieut. J. C. *Report on an Exploration of the Country Lying Between the Missouri River and the Rocky Mountains on the line of the Kansas and Great Platte Rivers*. 27th Congress, 3rd Session. Senate Doc. 243. Washington, D.C., 1843 [Serial 416].
Frémont, Brevet Captain J. C. *Report of the Exploring Expedition to the Rocky Moun-

tains in the Year 1842, and to Oregon and North California in the Years 1843–'44. Washington, D.C.: Gales and Seaton, Printers, 1845. [This volume, quoted extensively in narrative—and cited as JCF, *Report*—includes both the First and Second Expedition *Reports*.]

Nicollet, I. N. [J. N.] *Report Intended to Illustrate a Map of the Hydrographic Basin of the Upper Mississippi River.* 26th Congress, 2nd Session [1841]. Senate Report 237. Washington, D.C., 1843 [Serial 380].

Polk, James K. *Occupation of Mexican Territory. Message from the President . . . to the two houses of Congress.* 29th Congress, 2d Session, Dec. 22, 1846. House Executive Document, 19 [Serial 499].

Scott, Robert N. *The War of the Rebellion, a compilation of the official records of the Union and Confederate Armies.* 130 vol. Washington, 1880–1901.

Stockton, Robert F. *Report of the Secretary of the Navy, communicating copies of Commodore Stockton's Despatches, relating to the military and naval operations in California.* February 16, 1849. 30th Congress, 2d Session, Feb. 16, 1849. Senate Executive Document, 31 [Serial 531].

PUBLISHED ACCOUNTS, LETTERS, AND OTHERS

Benton, Joel, ed. *Greeley on Lincoln.* New York: Baker & Taylor Co., 1893.

Benton, Thomas Hart. *Selections of Editorial Articles from the St. Louis Enquirer on the Subject of Oregon and Texas . . . by the Hon. Thomas Hart Benton.* St. Louis: Missourian Office, 1844.

———. *Three Speeches . . . on the subject of the Annexation of Texas to the United States.* New York [no publisher designated], 1844.

———. *Thirty Years' View; or, A History of the Working of the American Government for Thirty Years, 1820 to 1850.* 2 vol. New York: D. Appleton and Co., 1854, 1856.

———. "Senator Benton Lays His Plans: Some Newly Discovered Material on the Frémont Court-Martial." *California Historical Society Quarterly* 8: 150–54 (June 1934).

Bidwell, John. "Frémont in the Conquest of California." *Century Illustrated Monthly Magazine* 41 (n.s. 69): 518–25 (Feb. 1891).

———. "Life in California Before the Gold Discovery." *Century Illustrated Monthly Magazine* 41 (n.s.): 163–83 (Dec. 1890).

Bigelow, John. *Memoir of the Life and Public Services of John Charles Fremont. . . .* New York: Derby & Jackson, 1856.

———. *Retrospections of an Active Life.* 5 vol. New York: Baker and Taylor Co., 1909–13.

Breckenridge, Thomas E. "Story of a Famous Expedition." *The Cosmopolitan* 21: 400–408 (Aug. 1896).

Bryant, Edwin. *What I Saw in California.* Philadelphia: Appleton and Co., 1848.

Bryant, William Cullen. *Poetical Works of William Cullen Bryant.* New York: AMS Press, 1969. (Reprint of 1903 edition.)

————. *Letters of William Cullen Bryant.* 6 vol. William Cullen Bryant, Jr., and Thomas G. Voss, eds. New York: Fordham University Press, 1975.

Buchanan, James. "The Official Policy for the Acquisition of California." *Century Illustrated Monthly Magazine* 41: 928–29 (April 1891).

Burnett, Peter H. "Recollections and Opinions of an Old Pioneer." *Oregon History Quarterly* 5: 64–99, 139–98, 272–305, 370–402 (1904).

California Historical Society Quarterly. "Documentary" (documents concerning Bear Flag Revolt and U.S. Conquest of California) 1: 72–95 (July 1922); 178–91 (Oct. 1922); 286–95 (Jan. 1923); 2: 69–74 (April 1923); 161–72 (July 1923); 246–51 (Oct. 1923); 350–62 (Jan. 1924); 3: 84–88 (Apr. 1924); 178–90 (July 1924); 270–89 (Oct. 1924); 4: 81–87 (March 1925); 374–91 (Dec. 1925); 5: 184–195 (March 1926); 296–310 (Sept. 1926); 6: 77–90 (March 1927); 181–91 (June 1927); 265–80 (Sept. 1927); 364–74 (Dec. 1927); 7: 79–85 (March 1928); 8: 71–77; 9: 81–86 (March 1930).

Carson, Kit. *Kit Carson in California.* Ed. with notes Charles L. Camp. San Francisco: California Historical Society, 1922.

————. *Kit Carson's Autobiography.* Ed. by Milton Quaife. Chicago: Lakeside Press, 1935.

————. *Kit Carson's Own Story of His Life, as Dictated to Col. and Mrs. D. C. Peters About 1856–1857, and Never Before Published.* Ed. by Blanche C. Grant. Taos: Santa Fe New Mexican Publishing Corp., 1926.

————. "The Kit Carson Memoirs, 1809–1856," in Harvey Lewis Carter, *"Dear Old Kit": The Historical Kit Carson.* Norman: University of Oklahoma Press, 1968, pp. 37–150.

Carvalho, S[olomon] N. *Incidents of Travel and Adventure in the Far West.* New York: Arno Press, 1973. (Reprint of 1857 edition.)

Clyman, James. *James Clyman, Frontiersman; The Adventures of a Trapper and Covered-Wagon Emigrant as told in his own Reminiscences and Diaries.* Edited by Charles L. Camp. Portland, Ore., Champoeg Press [1960].

Douglass, Frederick. *Life and Writings of Frederick Douglass.* Ed. by Philip S. Foner. 4 vol. New York: International Publishers, 1950–55.

Downey, Joseph T. *The Cruise of the Portsmouth, 1845–1847.* Ed. by Howard Lamar. New Haven: Yale University Library, 1958.

————. [Pseudonym: "Filings"]. *Filings from an Old Saw: Reminiscences of San Francisco and California's Conquest by "Filings"—Joseph T. Downey.* Ed. by Fred Blackburn Rogers. San Francisco: John Howell, 1956.

Duvall, Marius. *A Navy Surgeon in California, 1846–1847: The Journal of Marius Duvall.* Ed. by Fred Black Rogers. San Francisco: John Howell, 1957.

Emerson, Ralph Waldo. *Journals and Miscellaneous Notebooks of Ralph Waldo Emerson.* Ed. by Ralph H. Orth and Alfred Ferguson. 16 vol. Cambridge: Harvard University Press, 1960–82.

Franklin, Benjamin. *Autobiography and Other Writings.* Ed. by Ormond Seavey. New York: Oxford University Press, 1993.

Frémont, Elizabeth Benton. *The Arizona Diary of Lily Frémont*. Ed. by Mary Lee Spence. Tucson: University of Arizona Press, 1997.

———. *Recollections of Elizabeth Benton Frémont*. Compiled by I. T. Martin. New York: Frederick H. Hitchcock, 1912.

Frémont, Jessie Benton. *Souvenirs of My Time*. Boston: D. Lothrop Co., 1887.

———. *Far West Sketches*. Boston: D. Lothrop, 1890.

———. "The Origin of the Frémont Explorations." *Century Illustrated Monthly Magazine* 41: 766–71 (March 1891).

———. *The Story of the Guard: A Chronicle of the War*. Boston: Ticknor and Fields, 1863.

———. *A Year of American Travel*. San Francisco: Book Club of California, 1960. (Reprint of 1878 edition.)

———. *Mother Lode Narratives*. Ed. and annotated by Shirley Sargent. Ashland, Ore.: Lewis Osborne, 1970.

———. *Letters of Jessie Benton Frémont*. Ed. by Pamela Herr and Mary Lee Spence. Urbana: University of Illinois Press, 1993.

Frémont, John Charles. "The Conquest of California." *Century Illustrated Monthly Magazine* 41: 917–28 (April 1891).

———. *Memoirs of My Life*. Chicago: Belford, Clarke & Co., 1887.

Frémont, John Charles, et al. *The Expeditions of John Charles Frémont*. Ed. by Mary Lee Spence and Donald Jackson. 3 vol.—with *Volume 2 Supplement* [IIS in endnotes], containing proceedings of Frémont's 1847–48 court-martial; and *Map Portfolio*; and *Commentary* booklet on maps.

Gillespie, Archibald. "Gillespie and the Conquest of California: From Letters Dated February 11, 1846 to July 8, 1848 to the Secretary of the Navy." Ed. and with an introduction by George Walcott Ames, Jr. *California Historical Society Quarterly* 17: 123–40 (June 1938), 271–284 (Sept. 1938).

———. "Further Letters of Archibald H. Gillespie." Edited and with an introduction by Richard R. Stenberg. *California Historical Society Quarterly* 18: 217–28 (Sept. 1939).

Grant, Ulysses S. *Memoirs and Selected Letters*. New York: Library of America, 1990.

Greeley, Horace. *The Autobiography of Horace Greeley, or Recollections of a Busy Life*. New York: E. B. Treat, 1872.

———. *Greeley on Lincoln*. Edited by Joel Benton. New York: Baker & Taylor Co. [c. 1893]

Greely, Adolphus. *Explorers and Travellers*. New York: Charles Scribner's Sons, 1893.

Hafen, LeRoy R., ed. *Frémont's Fourth Expedition: A Documentary Account of the Disaster of 1848–1849, with Diaries, Letters, and Reports by Participants in the Tragedy*. Glendale, Calif.: Arthur H. Clark Co., 1960.

Hamilton, Alexander, James Madison et al. *The Federalist Papers*. New York: Mentor, 1961 [orig. pub. 1788].

Hastings, Lanford W. *Emigrants' Guide to Oregon and California*. Bedford, Mass.: Applewood Books, n.d. (Reprint of 1845 edition.)

Ide, William Brown, "History of . . . the 'Bear Flag Party' " [cited within as Ide, "Memoirs"], in Ide, Simeon, *Who Conquered California*. Glorieta, N.M.: Rio Grande Press, 1967.

Irving, Washington. *Adventures of Captain Bonneville, U.S.A. in the Rocky Mountains and the Far West*. [orig. pub. 1837]. Norman: University of Oklahoma Press, 1961.

———. *Astoria or Anecdotes of an Enterprise Beyond the Rocky Mountains; and A Tour of the Prairies*. New York: John B. Alden, 1887.

James, Edwin, *Account of an Expedition from Pittsburgh to the Rocky Mountains . . . Under the Command of Major Stephen H. Long*. 2 vol. Ann Arbor, Mich.: University Microfilms Inc. 1966. [Reprint of original 1823 edition.]

Jefferson, Thomas. *Writings*. New York: Library of America, 1984.

Kemble, Edward Cleveland. *A Kemble Reader: Stories of California, 1846–1848*. Ed. by Fred Blackburn Rogers. San Francisco: California Historical Society, 1963.

Larkin, Thomas Oliver. *The Larkin Papers, Personal, Business, and Official Correspondence*. 10 vol. Ed. by George P. Hammond. Berkeley: University of California Press, 1951–68.

Lincoln, Abraham. *Selected Speeches and Writings*. New York: Vintage/Library of America, 1992.

Longfellow, Henry Wadsworth. *Life of Henry Wadsworth Longfellow*. Ed. by Samuel Longfellow. Boston: Ticknor and Co., 1886.

Manning, William Ray, ed. *Diplomatic correspondence of the United States*. 12 vol. Washington, Carnegie Endowment for International Peace, 1932–39.

Martin, Thomas S. *With Frémont to California and the Southwest, 1845–1849*. Ed. by Ferol Egan. Ashland, Ore.: Lewis Osborne, 1978. (Dictated in the 1870s.)

McGehee, Micajah. "Rough Times in Rough Places: A Personal Narrative of the Terrible Experiences of Frémont's Fourth Expedition." *Century Illustrated Monthly Magazine* 41: 771–80 (March 1891).

McLane, Louis. *The Private Journal of Louis McLane, U.S.N., 1844–1848*. Ed. by Jay Monaghan. Los Angeles: Dawson's Book Shop, 1971.

Miller, Joaquin. *Overland in a Covered Wagon*. New York: D. Appleton, 1930.

Montaignes, François des [Isaac Cooper]. *The Plains. . . .* Ed. and Intro. by Nancy Albert Mower and Don Russell. Norman: University of Oklahoma Press, 1972. (Journal of JCF's Third Expedition's Canadian River Survey.)

Morrison, Patt. "Does Historic Site Have a Ghost of a Chance?" Los Angeles *Times*, April 23, 1999.

Nicolay, John G. and John Hay. *Abraham Lincoln: A History*. 10 vol. New York: The Century Co., 1890.

Nicollet, Joseph N. *The Journals of Joseph N. Nicollet: A Scientist on the Mississippi Headwaters with Notes on Indian Life, 1836–37*. Trans. by André Fertey and ed. by Martha Coleman Bray. St. Paul, Minn.: Minnesota Historical Society Press, 1970.

———. *Joseph N. Nicollet on the Plains and Prairies: The Expeditions of 1838–39, with Journals, Letters, and Notes on the Dakota Indians*. Trans. and ed. by Edmund

C. Bray and Martha Coleman Bray. St. Paul, Minn: Minnesota Historical Society Press, 1976.

Pico, Pío. "Pío Pico's Correspondence with the Mexican Government, 1846–1848." Ed. and with introduction by George Tays. *California Historical Society Quarterly* 13: 99–149 (June 1934).

———. *Don Pío Pico's Historical Narrative.* Trans. by Arthur P. Botello and ed. by Martin Cole and Henry Welcome. Glendale, Calif.: Arthur H. Clark Co., 1973.

Pike, Zebulon Montgomery. *Exploratory Travels through the Western Territories of North America.* Denver: W. H. Lawrence & Co., 1889 [orig. pub. 1811].

Polk, James K. *The Diary of James K. Polk During his Presidency, 1845 to 1849.* 4 vol. Ed. by Milo Milton Quaife. Chicago: A. C. McClurg & Co., 1910.

Preuss, Charles. *Exploring with Frémont: The Private Diairies of Charles Preuss.* Trans. and ed. by Erwin G. and Elisabeth K. Gudde. Norman: University of Oklahoma Press, 1958.

Revere, Joseph Warren. *A Tour of Duty in California.* Ed. by Joseph N Balestier. New York: C. S. Francis & Co., 1849.

Royce, Josiah. "Light on the Seizure of California." *Century Illustrated Monthly Magazine* 40: 792–94 (Sept. 1890).

———. "Montgomery and Frémont: New Documents on the Bear Flag Affair." *Century Illustrated Monthly Magazine* 41: 780–83 (March 1891).

Smucker, Samuel M. *The Life of John Charles Fremont and His Narrative of Explorations and Adventures in Kansas, Nebraska, Oregon and California.* New York: Miller, Orton & Mulligan, 1856.

Sutter, Johann. "General Sutter's Diary," in *John Sutter and a Wider West.* Ed. by Kenneth N. Owens. Lincoln: Univ. of Nebraska Press, 1994.

Talbot, Theodore. *The Journals of Theodore Talbot, 1843 and 1849–1852: With the Fremont Expedition of 1843 and with the First Military Company in Oregon Territory, 1849–1852.* Portland, Ore.: Metropolitan Press, Publishers, 1931.

———. *Soldier in the West: Letters of Theodore Talbot During His Services in California, Mexico, and Oregon, 1843–53.* Ed. by Robert V. Hine and Savoie Lottinville. Norman: University of Oklahoma Press, 1972.

Taylor, Bayard. *Eldorado, or Adventures in the Path of Empire . . .* New York: Alfred A. Knopf, 1949. (Reprint of 1850 edition.)

Thomson, James. *Works of Mr. James Thomson, with his Last Corrections and Improvements.* 3 vol. London: R. Baldwin et al., 1802.

Thoreau, Henry. *Writings of Henry D. Thoreau: Journal.* 2 vol. Princeton, N.J.: Princeton University Press, 1981, 1984.

Upham, Charles. *Life, Explorations and Public Services of John Charles Fremont* [sic]. Boston: Ticknor and Fields, 1856.

Webster, Daniel. *Writings and Speeches of Daniel Webster.* 18 vol. Boston: Little Brown & Co., 1903.

Whitman, Walt. *Leaves of Grass.* New York: Signet, 1955. [Originally published 1855.]

NEWSPAPERS AND MAGAZINES

Atlantic Monthly
California *Chronicle*
California *Star*
Charleston *Courier*
Cincinatti *Chronicle*
Congressional Globe
Cosmopolitan, The
De Bow's Review
Deseret News
Littell's Living Age
Los Angeles *Times*
National Intelligencer
New York *Evening Post*
New York *Herald*
New York *Spectator*
New York *Times*
New York *Tribune*
Niles National Register
St. Louis *Leader*
Salt Lake City *Tribune*
San Francisco *Daily Herald*
Savannah *Press*
Southern Literary Messenger
United States Magazine and Democratic Review
Virginia Patriot
Washington *Globe*

SECONDARY SOURCES

Adams, Ephraim D. "English Interest in the Annexation of California." *American Historical Review* 14 (1908): 744–763.

Allen, J. L. [John Logan]. "Division of the Waters: Changing Concepts of the Continental Divide, 1804–44." *Journal of Historical Geography* 4: 357–70 (1978).

———. *Passage Through the Garden: Lewis and Clark and the Image of the American Northwest.* Urbana: University of Illinois Press, 1975.

———. "The Garden-Desert Continuum." *Great Plains Quarterly* 5: 207–20 (1985).

Allen, John Logan, ed. *North American Exploration, Vol. 3, A Continent Comprehended.* Lincoln: University of Nebraska Press, 1997.

Ambrose, Stephen E. *Undaunted Courage: Merriwether Lewis, Thomas Jefferson, and the Opening of the American West.* New York: Simon and Schuster, 1996.

Ames, George Walcott, Jr. "Horse Marines in California, 1846." *California Historical Society Quarterly* 18: 72–84 (March 1939).

Anderson, Fred. *Crucible of War: The Seven Years' War and the Fate of Empire in British North America, 1754–1766*. New York: Alfred A. Knopf, 2000.

Anderson, Nancy K. and Linda S. Ferber. *Albert Bierstadt: Art and Enterprise*. Hudson Hills Press, N.Y. and Brooklyn Museum, N.Y., 1990.

Andrews, Thomas F. "Lansford W. Hastings and the Promotion of the Salt Lake Desert Cutoff: A Reappraisal." *Western History Quarterly* 4: 133–50 (April 1973).

Antelyes, Peter. *Tales of Adventurous Enterprise: Washington Irving and the Poetics of Western Expansion*. New York: Columbia University Press, 1990.

Arvin, Newton. *Longfellow: His Life and Work*. Boston: Little, Brown and Co., 1962.

Bancroft, Frederic. *Life of William Seward*. 2 vol. New York: Harper & Brothers, 1900.

Bancroft, Hurbert Howe. *History of California*. 7 vol. San Francisco: The History Co., 1886–90.

[Bayard, Samuel John] *A Sketch of the Life of Robert F. Stockton* . . . New York: Derby and Jackson, 1856.

Bennett, Whitman. *Whittier: Bard of Freedom*. Chapel Hill: University of North Carolina Press, 1941.

Billington, Ray Allen. *Westward Expansion: A History of the American Frontier* (2nd ed.). New York: Macmillan Co., 1960.

Bonney, Orin H. and Lorraine. *Guide to the Wyoming Mountains and Wilderness Areas*. Denver, Colo.: Sage Books, 1960.

Bray, Martha Coleman. *Joseph Nicollet and His Map*. Philadelphia: American Philosophical Society, 1980.

Brown, Lloyd A. *The Story of Maps*. Boston: Little, Brown and Co., 1949.

Brown, Ralph H. *Historical Geography of the United States*. New York: Harcourt, Brace and Co., 1948.

Bruce, Robert V. *The Launching of Modern American Science, 1846–1876*. New York: Alfred A. Knopf, 1987.

Chaffin, Tom. *Fatal Glory: Narciso López and the First Clandestine U.S. War Against Cuba*. Charlottesville: University Press of Virginia, 1996.

———. "Toward a Poetics of Technology: Hart Crane and the American Sublime." *Twentieth-Century Literary Criticism* v. 80: 68–18. Detroit: Gale, 1999.

———. "How the West Was Lost: A Road Trip in Search of the Oregon Trail." *Harper's* 300: 137–40 (June 2000).

Chambers, William Nesbit. *Old Bullion Benton: Senator from the New West*. Boston: Little, Brown and Co., 1956.

Chittenden, Hiram M. *History of American Fur Trade of the Far West*. Stanford, Calif.: Academic Reprints, 1954.

Clapp, Margaret. *Forgotten First Citizen: John Bigelow*. Boston: Little, Brown, and Co., 1947.

Crampton, C. Gregory and Gloria G. Griffen. "The San Buenaventura, Mythical River of the West." *Pacific Historical Quarterly* 25: 163–71 (May 1956).

Dakin, Susanna Bryant. *The Lives of William Hartnell*. Stanford, Calif.: Stanford University Press, 1949.

Dellenbaugh, Frederick S. *Frémont and '49*. New York: G. P. Putnam's Sons, 1914.

DeVoto, Bernard. *The Year of Decision, 1846*. Boston: Little, Brown and Co., 1943.

——. *Across the Wide Missouri*. New York: Houghton Mifflin Co., 1947.

——. *The Course of Empire*. New York: Houghton Mifflin Co., 1952.

Dillon, Richard. *Captain John Sutter: Sacramento Valley's Sainted Sinner*. Santa Cruz, Calif.: Western Tanager, 1981. (Originally published as *Fool's Gold*, 1967.)

Dunlay, Tom. *Kit Carson and the Indians*. Lincoln: University of Nebraska Press, 2000.

Dupree, A. Hunter. *Science in the Federal Government: A History of Policies and Activities*. Baltimore: Johns Hopkins University Press, 1986.

Easterby, J. H., *A History of the College of Charleston, Founded 1770*. Charleston [no publisher indicated], 1935.

Egan, Ferol. *Frémont: Explorer for a Restless Nation*. Garden City, N.Y.: Doubleday & Co., 1977.

Ellison, Joseph. "The Struggle for Civil Government in California, 1846–1850." *California Historical Society Quarterly* 10: 3–26 (March 1931).

Ellison, William H. "San Juan to Cahuenga: The Experiences of Frémont's Battalion." *Pacific Historical Review* 27: 245–61 (August 1958).

Engelson. Lester G. "Proposals for the Colonization of California by England." *California Historical Society Quarterly* 18: 136–48 (June 1939).

Faragher, John Mack. *Women and Men on the Overland Trail*. New Haven: Yale University Press, 1979.

Ferguson, Niall. "2011." New York *Times Magazine*, 150: 76, 78, 79, (Dec. 2, 2001).

Foote, Shelby. *The Civil War: A Narrative, from Fort Sumter to Perryville*. New York: Vintage, 1986. (Originally published in 1958.)

Franzwa, Gregory M. *The Oregon Trail Revisited* (5th ed.). Tucson, Ariz: Patrice Press, 1997.

Gerteis, Louis S. *Civil War St. Louis*. Lawrence: University Press of Kansas, 2001.

Gianella, Vincent P. "Where Frémont Crossed the Sierra Nevada in 1844." *Sierra Club Bulletin* 44 (no. 7): 54–63 (1959).

Gienapp, William E. *Origins of the Republican Party*. New York: Oxford University Press, 1987.

Giffen, Helen S. "The California Battalion's Route to Los Angeles." *Journal of the West* 5: 207–24 (Apr. 1966).

Gilbert, Bill. *Westering Man: The Life of Joseph Walker*. Norman: University of Oklahoma Press, 1985.

Goetzmann, William H. *Army Exploration in the American West, 1803–1863*. New Haven: Yale University Press, 1959.

——. *Exploration and Empire: The Explorer and the Scientist in the Winning of the American West*. New York: Alfred A. Knopf, 1966.

Goodwin, Cardinal. *John Charles Frémont: An Explanation of His Career*. Stanford, Calif.: Stanford University Press, 1930.

Graebner, Norman A. "American Interest in California, 1845." *Pacific Historical Review* 22:13–27 (Feb. 1953).

———. *Empire on the Pacific: A Study in American Continental Expansion.* New York: Ronald Press, 1955.

Graham, Bob. *The Crossing of the Sierra Nevada in the Winter of 1843–44.* Sacramento: Bob Graham, 2000.

Gudde, Erwin G. *Sutter's Own Story: The Life of General John Augustus Sutter and the History of New Helvetia in the Sacramento Valley.* New York: G. P. Putnam's Sons, 1936.

———. "Frémont-Preuss and Western Names." *Names* 5: 169–81 (Sept. 1957).

Guild, Thelma S. and Harvey L. Carter. *Kit Carson: A Pattern for Heroes.* Lincoln: University of Nebraska Press, 1984.

Hafen, Leroy R. *Broken Hand: The Life of Thomas Fitzpatrick, Mountain Man, Guide and Indian Agent* (rev. ed.). Denver: Old West Publishing Co., 1972. (Originally published in 1931.)

Hagan, William T. *American Indians.* Chicago: University of Chicago Press, 1993.

Hague, Harlan and David J. Langum. *Thomas O. Larkin. A Life of Patriotism and Profit in Old California.* Norman: University of Oklahoma Press, 1990.

Handlin, Lilian. *George Bancroft, The Intellectual as Democrat.* New York: Harper & Row, 1984.

Harlow, Neal. *California Conquered: The Annexation of a Mexican Province, 1846–1850.* Berkeley: University of California Press, 1982.

Harrington, M. R. "Our Frémont Flag." *The Masterkey* 26: 132–33 (1952).

Hawgood, John A. "John C. Frémont and the Bear Flag Revolution: A Reappraisal." *Historical Society of Southern California Quarterly* 44: 67–96 (March 1962).

Heffernan, William Joseph. *Edward M. Kern: The Travels of an Artist Explorer.* Bakersfield, Calif.: Kern County Historical Society, 1953.

Herr, Pamela. *Jessie Benton Frémont.* New York: Franklin Watts, 1987.

Hine, Robert V. *Edward Kern and American Expansion.* New Haven: Yale University Press, 1962. (Second edition published as *In the Shadow of Frémont: Edward Kern and the Art of Exploration.* Norman: University of Oklahoma Press, 1982.)

Howard, Thomas Frederick. *Sierra Crossing: First Roads to California.* Berkeley: University of California Press, 1998.

Hubbard, Harry D. *Vallejo.* Ed. by Pauline C. Santoro. Boston: Meador Publishing Co., 1941.

Ide, Simeon. *The Conquest of California: A Biography of William B. Ide.* Oakland, Calif.: Biobooks, 1944. (Reprint of 1880 edition.)

Isely, Jeter Allen. *Horace Greeley and the Republican Party, 1853–1861.* Princeton, N.J.: Princeton University Press, 1947.

James, George Wharton. *Fremont in California.* [Los Angeles: Out West Co.] c.1903.

James, Marquis. *Life of Andrew Jackson.* New York: Bobbs-Merrill Co., 1937.

Johnson, David Alan. *Founding the Far West, California, Oregon, and Nevada, 1840–1890.* Berkeley: University of California Press, 1992.

Johnson, Kenneth M. *The Frémont Court Martial.* Los Angeles: Dawson's Book Shop, 1968.

Jones, Oakah L., Jr. "The Pacific Squadron and the Conquest of California, 1846–1847." *Journal of the West* 5: 187–202 (Apr. 1966).

Karnes, Thomas L. *William Gilpin, Western Nationalist.* Austin: University of Texas Press, 1970.

Kelsey, Joe. *Climbing and Hiking in the Wind River Mountains.* Evergreen, Colo.: Chockstone Press, 1994.

Koebner, Richard. *Empire.* Cambridge: Cambridge University Press, 1961.

Koepp, Donna P., ed. *Exploration and Mapping of the American West: Selected Essays.* Chicago: Speculum Orbis Press, 1986.

LaFeber, Walter. *The New Empire: An Interpretation of American Expansion, 1860–1898* (rev. ed.). Ithaca, N.Y.: Cornell University Press, 1998. (Originally published in 1963.)

LaLande, Jeff. *First Over the Siskiyous: Peter Skeene Ogden's 1826–1827 Journey Through the Oregon–California Borderlands.* Portland, Ore.: Oregon Historical Society Press, 1987.

Lavender, David. *Bent's Fort.* New York: Doubleday & Co., 1954.

Leach, Douglas Edward. *Arms for Empire: A Military History of the British Colonies in North America, 1607–1763.* New York: Macmillan Co., 1973.

Lewis, Ernest Allen. *The Fremont Cannon: High Up and Far Back* (rev. ed.) Penn Valley, Calif.: Western Trails Press, 1981.

Linn, E. A., and Sargent Linn. *The Life and Public Services of Dr. Lewis F. Linn.* New York: D. Appleton and Co., 1857.

Luebke, Frederick C. et al., eds. *Mapping the North American Plains: Essays in the History of Cartography.* Norman: University of Oklahoma Press, 1987.

Lyman, George D. *John Marsh, Pioneer.* New York: Charles Scribner's Sons, 1930.

Marti, Werner H. *Messenger of Destiny: The California Adventures of Archibald H. Gillespie, U.S. Marine Corps.* San Francisco: John Howell, 1960.

McCoy, Drew R. *The Elusive Republic: Political Economy in Jeffersonian America.* Chapel Hill: University of North Carolina, 1980.

McKittrick, Myrtle M. *Vallejo: Son of California.* Portland, Ore.: Binford & Mort, 1944.

McMaster, John Bach. *A History of the People of the United States During Lincoln's Administration.* New York: D. Appleton and Co., 1927.

McPherson, James M. *Battle Cry of Freedom: The Civil War Era.* New York: Oxford University Press, 1988.

Meigs, William M. *The Life of Thomas Hart Benton.* Philadelphia: J.B. Lippincott Co., 1904.

Meinig, D. W. *The Shaping of America, Vol. 1, Atlantic America, 1492–1800.* New Haven: Yale University Press, 1986.

———. *The Shaping of America, Vol. 2, Continental America, 1800–1867.* New Haven: Yale University Press, 1993.

Merk, Frederick. *Manifest Destiny and Mission in American History: A Reinterpretation.* New York: Alfred A. Knopf, 1963.

———. *History of the Westward Movement.* New York: Alfred A. Knopf, 1978.

Miner, H. Craig. *The St. Louis–San Francisco Transcontinental Railroad: The Thirty-fifth Parallel Project.* Lawrence: University Press of Kansas, 1972.

Morgan, Dale L. *Jedediah Smith and the Opening of the West.* New York: Bobbs-Merrill Co., 1953.

"N.M.O.," "Resumé of Frémont's Expeditions." *Century Illustrated Monthly Magazine* 41: 759–66 (March 1891).

Nevins, Allan. *Frémont: Pathmarker of the West.* Lincoln: University of Nebraska Press, 1992. (Originally published as *The World's Greatest Adventurer,* 1928. Revised editions in 1939 and 1955.)

———. *Ordeal of the Union.* Vol. 2, *A House Dividing, 1852–1856.* New York: Charles Scribner's Sons, 1947.

———. *The War for the Union.* Vol. 1, *The Improvised War, 1861–1862.* New York: Charles Scribner's Sons, 1959.

Niven, John. *Martin Van Buren and the Romantic Age of American Politics.* New York: Oxford University Press, 1983.

Nobles, Gregory H. *American Frontiers: Cultural Encounters and Continental Conquest.* New York: Hill and Wang, 1997.

Onuf, Peter S. *Jefferson's Empire: The Language of American Nationhood.* Charlottesville: University Press of Virginia, 2000.

Parrish, William E. *Frank Blair, Lincoln's Conservative.* Columbia: University of Missouri Press, 1998.

Parton, Dorothy M. *The Diplomatic Career of Joel Roberts Poinsett.* Washington, D.C.: Catholic University of America, 1934.

Perkins, Bradford. *Creation of a Republican Empire, 1776–1865.* Cambridge: Cambridge University Press, 1993. (Vol. 1 of *The Cambridge History of American Foreign Relations,* ed. by Warren I. Cohen.)

Peterson, Merrill D. *Thomas Jefferson and the New Nation.* New York: Oxford University Press, 1970.

Pitt, Leonard. *The Decline of the Californios: A Social History of the Spanish-Speaking Californians, 1846–1890.* Berkeley: University of California Press, 1966.

Pletcher, David M. *The Diplomacy of Annexation: Texas, Oregon, and the Mexican War.* Columbia: University of Missouri Press, 1973.

Prucha, Francis Paul. *Sword of the Republic: The United States Army on the Frontier, 1783–1846.* Toronto: Macmillan Co., 1969.

———. *The Great Father: The United States Government and the American Indians.* Lincoln: University of Nebraska Press, 1984.

Putnam, Herbert Everett. *Joel Roberts Poinsett: A Political Biography.* Washington, D.C.: Mimeoform Press, 1935.

Reingold, Nathan, *Science in Nineteenth-Century America.* New York: University of Chicago Press, 1964.

Reingold, Nathan, ed. *Science in America Since 1820*. New York: Science History Publications, 1976.

Richmond, Patricia. *Trail to Disaster*. Denver: Colorado Historical Society, 1989.

Rippy, J. Fred. *Joel R. Poinsett, Versatile American*. Durham, N.C.: Duke University Press, 1935.

Ritter, John A. "The Richest Colony in the World," *Peterson Magazine*: 558–568 (June 1897).

Roberts, David. *A Newer World: Kit Carson, John C. Frémont, and the Claiming of the American West*. New York: Simon & Schuster, 2000.

Rochlin, Phillip. "Fremont on Rocky Mountains." *Historical Society of Southern California Quarterly* 35: 325–34 (Dec. 1933).

Rogers, Fred Blackburn. *Bear Flag Lieutenant: The Life Story of Henry L. Ford*. San Francisco: California Historical Society, 1951.

———. *William Brown Ide, Bear Flagger*. San Francisco: John Howell. 1962.

Rohrbough, Malcolm J. *Days of Gold: The California Gold Rush and the American Nation*. Berkeley: University of California Press, 1997.

Rolle, Andrew. "Exploring an Explorer: Psychohistory and John Charles Frémont." *Pacific Historical Review* 51: 135–63 (May 1982).

———. *John Charles Frémont: Character as Destiny*. Norman: University of Oklahoma Press, 1991.

Roosevelt, Theodore. *Thomas H. Benton*. Boston: Houghton, Mifflin and Co. 1889.

Roper, Laura Wood. *FLO, A Biography of Frederick Law Olmsted*. Baltimore: Johns Hopkins University Press, 1973.

Rosenus, Alan. *General M. J. Vallejo*. Albuquerque: University of New Mexico Press, 1995.

Sabin, Edwin L. *Kit Carson Days*. Chicago: A. C. McClurg & Co., 1914.

Schnell, J. Christopher. "William Gilpin and the Destruction of the Desert Myth." *Colorado Magazine* 64: 131–44 (Spring 1969).

Sears, Louis Martin. *John Slidell*. Durham, N.C.: Duke University Press, 1925.

Sherwood, Glenn V., *Labor of Love: The Life and Art of Vinnie Ream*. Hygiene, Colo.: SunShine Press Publications, 1997.

Shlaer, Robert. *Sights Once Seen: Daguerreotyping Frémont's Last Expedition Through the Rockies*. Albuquerque: Museum of New Mexico Press, 2000.

Shubert, Helen V. "The Men Who Met the Yankees in 1846." *California Historical Society Quarterly* 13: 43–55 (March 1934).

Slotkin, Richard. *The Fatal Environment: The Myth of the Frontier in the Age of Industrialization, 1800–1890*. New York: Atheneum, 1985.

Smith, Elbert B. *Francis Preston Blair*. New York: Free Press, 1980.

———. *Magnificent Missourian: The Life of Thomas Hart Benton*. Philadelphia: J. B. Lippincott Co., 1958.

Smith, Henry Nash. *Virgin Land: The American West as Symbol and Myth*. New York: Vintage, 1950.

Smith, Michael L. *Pacific Visions: California Scientists and the Environment 1850–1915*. New Haven: Yale University Press, 1987.

Smith, William Ernest. *The Francis Preston Blair Family in Politics*. 2 vol. New York: Macmillan Co., 1933.

Spence, Mary Lee. "The Fremonts and Utah." *Utah Historical Quarterly* 44: 286–302 (Summer 1976).

Spindt, H. A. *Notes on [the] Life of Edward Kern*. Bakersfield, Calif.: Kern County Historical Society, 1939.

Stanton, William. *The Great United States Exploring Expedition of 1838–1842*. Berkeley: University of California Press, 1975.

Starr, Kevin. *Americans and the California Dream: 1850–1915*. New York: Oxford University Press, 1973.

Swartzlow, Ruby Johnson. "Peter Lassen, Northern California's Trail Blazer." *California Historical Society Quarterly* 18: 291–314 (Dec. 1939).

Tarbell, Ida M. *Life of Lincoln*. 4 vol. New York: Lincoln History Society, 1900.

Taylor, Virginia H. *The Franco-Texan Land Company*. Austin: University of Texas Press, 1969.

Tays, George. "Mariano Guadalupe Vallejo and Sonoma." *California Historical Society Quarterly* 17: 141–67 (June 1938).

———. "Frémont Had No Secret Instructions." *Pacific Historical Review* 9: 157–71 (June 1940).

Thacker, Robert. *The Great Prairie: Fact and Literary Imagination*. Albuquerque: University of New Mexico Press, 1989.

Thompson, R. A. *Conquest of California*. Santa Rosa, Calif.: Sonoma Democrat Publishing Co., 1896.

Thrower, Norman J. W. *Maps and Civilization: Cartography in Culture and Society*. Chicago: University of Chicago Press, 1996. (Originally published as *Maps and Man* by Prentice-Hall, 1972).

Underhill, Reuben L. *From Cowhides to Golden Fleece: A Narrative of California, 1832–1858, Based upon Unpublished Correspondence of Thomas Oliver Larkin of Monterey*. Stanford, Calif.: Stanford University Press, 1939.

Unruh, John David. *The Plains Across: The Overland Emigrants and the Trans-Mississippi West, 1840–1860*. Urbana: University of Illinois Press, 1993.

Utley, Robert M. *Frontiersmen in Blue: The United States Army and the Indian, 1848–1865*. New York: Macmillan Co., 1967.

———. *A Life Wild and Perilous: Mountain Men and the Paths to the Pacific*. New York: Henry Holt and Co., 1997.

Van Alstyne, Richard W. *The Rising American Empire*. New York: Norton, 1974. (Originally published in 1960).

Van Deusen, Glyndon G. *Horace Greeley: Nineteenth-Century Crusader*. Philadelphia: University of Pennsylvania Press, 1953.

Viola, Herman J. *Exploring the West*. Washington, D.C.: Smithsonian Books, 1987.

Volpe, Vernon. "Viewing the Ground: John C. Frémont in the Snake Country, 1843." *Journal of the West* 29(1):3–15 (1990).

———. "The Frémonts and Emancipation in Missouri." *Historian* 56(2): 339–54 (1994).

————. "Beyond a Literary Adventure: Bonneville's and Frémont's Conquests of the Wind Rivers." *Annals of Wyoming* 71(4): 15–28 (1999).

————. "The Origins of the Frémont Expeditions: John J. Abert and the Scientific Exploration of the Trans-Mississippi West." *Historian* 62(2): 244–63 (2000).

Ward, Bob. "Frémont's Explorations," Salt Lake City *Tribune*, July 3, 2000.

Warner, Barbara R. *The Men of the California Bear Flag Revolt and their Heritage.* Spokane, Wash: Arthur H. Clark Co., 1996.

Weber, David J. *The Mexican Frontier, 1821–1846.* Albuquerque: University of New Mexico Press, 1982.

————. *Richard H. Kern, Expeditionary Artist in the Far Southwest, 1848–1853.* Albuquerque: University of New Mexico Press, 1985.

————. *The Spanish Frontier in North America.* New Haven: Yale University Press, 1992.

Weinberg, Albert K. *Manifest Destiny: A Study of Nationalist Expansionism in American History.* Baltimore: Johns Hopkins Press, 1935.

Welsh, Stanley L. *John Charles Frémont, Botanical Explorer.* St. Louis: Missouri Botanical Garden Press, 1998.

Wheat, Carl I. *Mapping the Transmississippi West.* 5 vol. San Francisco: Institute of Historical Cartography, 1957–63.

Wilford, John Noble. *The Mapmakers.* New York: Alfred A. Knopf, 1982.

Wiltsee, Ernest A. "The British Vice Consul in California and the Events of 1846." *CHSQ* 10: 99–128 (June 1931).

————. *The Truth About Frémont: An Inquiry.* San Francisco: John Henry Nash, 1936.

REFERENCE AND BIBLIOGRAPHIC AIDS

Gudde, Erwin G. *California Place Names* (4th ed. rev., enlarged by William Bright). Berkeley: University of California Press, 1998.

Hart, James D., ed. *A California Companion.* New York: Oxford University Press, 1978.

Lamar, Howard R., ed. *New Encyclopedia of the American West.* New Haven: Yale University Press, 1998.

Malone, Dumas, ed. *Dictionary of American Biography.* 22 vol. New York: Charles Scribner's Sons, 1928–58; revision, in 10 volumes, 1958.

Morris, Richard B., ed. *Encyclopedia of American History* (rev. and enlarged ed.). New York: Harper & Row, 1961.

INDEX